FIRST EDITION

Criminal Law, Criminal Procedure, and the Constitution

Stephanie A. Jirard, J.D.

Shippensburg University

Prentice Hall

Upper Saddle River, New Jersey
Columbus, Ohio

Library of Congress Cataloging-in-Publication Data

Jirard, Stephanie A.
    Criminal law, criminal procedure, and the constitution / Stephanie A. Jirard.
      p. cm.
    Includes bibliographical references.
    ISBN-13: 978-0-13-175631-1
    ISBN-10: 0-13-175631-1
      1. Criminal law--United States.   2. Criminal procedure--United States.
      3. Constitutional law--United States.   I. Title.
    KF9219.J57 2009
    345.73--dc22

                                    2008021789

Executive Editor: Vern Anthony
Acquisitions Editor: Tim Peyton
Editorial Assistant: Alicia Kelly
Director of Marketing: David Gesell
Marketing Manager: Adam Kloza
Marketing Assistant: Alicia Dysert
Production Manager: Wanda Rockwell
Creative Director: Jayne Conte
Cover Design: Bruce Kenselaar
Cover Illustration/Photo: Getty Images, Inc.
Printer/Binder: Hamilton Printing Co.

This book was set in Times Ten Roman 10/12 by Aptara®, Inc. It was printed and bound by Hamilton Printing Co. The cover was printed by Phoenix Color Corp.

Pearson Education Ltd.
Pearson Education Singapore, Pte. Ltd
Pearson Education, Canada, Ltd
Pearson Education–Japan

Pearson Education Australia PTY, Limited
Pearson Education North Asia Ltd
Pearson Educación de Mexico, S.A. de C.V.
Pearson Education Malaysia, Pte. Ltd

Prentice Hall
is an imprint of

www.pearsonhighered.com

10 9 8 7 6 5 4 3 2 1
ISBN 13: 978-0-13-175631-1
ISBN 10:   0-13-175631-1

Dedication

For the source of life's riches, my mother Lillian R. Jirard.

Acknowledgments

Many thanks to my family: my father, Douglas C. Fairhurst; my children, Jackson X., Kennedy Lil, and Gianna Morgan; my friends who I have loved for a lifetime, Monica Palmer, Maria Rivera, Christopher Rodriguez, Wendy Miller, Sandy Tarrant, James Poe, Jr. and Jean Burke; my friends at Shippensburg University; and students Tiffany Jones, Elizabeth McClure, and the late Douglas C. Sluyter for their valuable assistance. Thanks to all at Prentice Hall, Heather Sisan and Brian Baker, of Write With, Inc., for their great editing work, Sarvesh Mehrotra from Aptara for his unfailing patience, and the following reviewers: Kevin Daugherty, *Albuquerque TVI Community College;* Jim Frank, *University of Cincinnati;* and Dr. Lore Rutz-Burri, *Southern Oregon University.*

Preface

This text is designed to introduce undergraduate criminal justice, sociology, paralegal, government, and civic students to the interplay of law enforcement, criminal investigation and interrogation, statutory and common law, criminal procedure, and the overarching principles of the United States Constitution that guides and informs the entire criminal justice process. There are three primary features of the book to facilitate student learning and understanding of the law. My text is designed to give students the skills they need to be competent professionals. First, to understand the law students need to be able to read the law. Judge Learned Hand wrote, "The language of the law must not be foreign to the ears of those who are to obey it." The text contains edited case opinions that illustrate key points of law, but that retain much of the original language and analysis. I have provided in brackets explanations for the legalese. It is important to note that the cases often pit the interests of the government on one side and the liberty interests of the individual on the other side. When the term "government" is used in the text, it is meant to describe a village, town, city, state, or federal body that makes and passes ordinances, rules, regulations, and laws that affect the daily lives of the people.

Students are encouraged to read the cases provided in the text not simply as ancillary material to the explanations provided in the test, but to learn how to engage in legal analysis and interpretation, skills critical for a full appreciation of how the law works. The selection of cases is drawn from leading and current decisions from appellate courts of last resort on the federal and state level, except where an unreported decision can best illustrate the concept. Reading cases will allow students to gain respect for the real language of the court decisions that they not only live under, but may be called upon to enforce. Reading case law also illuminates for the student how society viewed different legal issues over time, which may engender a sense of continuity for the student and instill a sense of predictability in how certain present-day legal issues may be resolved. In short, reading the cases presented in the text is invaluable for a complete understanding of the law and should not be ignored. I have also chosen cases in which the same legal issues and precedents present themselves for students to connect the recurring legal concepts in a variety of different contexts, but I have edited them and eliminated many internal citations, pin cites, and footnotes often without indication. Students should refer to the official case citation and retrieve and consult the complete case. Where specific statutes or regulations are at issue or a pertinent section of the Model Penal Code may be illustrative of the legal concept under discussion, these are included within the body of the text to emphasize the importance of reading the law before turning to the case interpretation of it.

The second feature is a section called "Applying the Rule of Law to the Facts," which explains, from both my litigation perspective and court decisions, how legal rules and doctrines operate in the real world of criminal justice.

The third feature is the key terms, discussion questions, and problem-solving questions provided throughout the text that call upon the students to apply their new legal knowledge in a challenging manner. The chapters end with a summary, web links, a number of suggested additional readings, and endnotes that can serve as an avenue for further independent research. There is a general and a case index, as well as the United States Constitution included in Appendix A and selected excerpts of the Model Penal Code contained in Appendix B.

About the Author

A Massachusetts native, Stephanie A. Jirard is an Associate Professor of Criminal Justice at Shippensburg University in Pennsylvania. She received her B.A. in history from Cornell University and her J.D. from Boston College Law School. She is a former Lieutenant in the United States Navy's Judge Advocate General ("JAG") Corps, where she defended sailors and Marines at courts-martial and administrative discharge boards in Louisiana. At the Navy's personnel headquarters in Washington, D.C., Jirard advised senior command officers in the area of sexual harassment, provided training on processing child sexual abuse and other family abuse cases, and was responsible for the timely processing of all Privacy Act and Freedom of Information Act requests forwarded to the headquarters command. Jirard was a Trial Attorney at the United States Department of Justice in the Civil Division, Torts Branch defending the United States in environmental tort and human radiation experiment lawsuits across the country. She also served as an Assistant United States Attorney and an Assistant Federal Public Defender both in the District of Massachusetts. Her last public service was as an Assistant State Public Defender in the capital litigation unit in Columbia, Missouri, representing indigent men in death-penalty cases.

Table of Contents

CHAPTER

1

The Constitution and Criminal Law

"Over time, from one generation to the next, the Constitution has come to earn the high respect and even, as Madison dared to hope, the veneration of the American people. The document sets forth, and rests upon, innovative principles original to the American experience, such as federalism; a proven balance in political mechanisms through separation of powers; specific guarantees for the accused in criminal cases; and broad provisions to secure individual freedom and preserve human dignity. These doctrines and guarantees are central to the American experience and remain essential to our present-day self-definition and national identity. Not the least of the reasons we honor the Constitution, then, is because we know it to be our own."

— ROPER V. SIMMONS, 543 U.S. 551 (2005)

CHAPTER OBJECTIVES

Primary Concepts Discussed in This Chapter:

1. The role of federalism in the field of criminal law
2. How criminal law fits within the balance of power between the three branches of government
3. The significance of federal jurisdiction to prosecute crimes
4. The nondelegation doctrine
5. The operation of the Supremacy, Necessary and Proper, Equal Protection, and Full Faith and Credit Clauses of the Constitution

CHAPTER OUTLINE

Feature: Government Control of Physician-Assisted Suicide

I. FEDERALISM

1. The Federal Government is a Limited Government
2. Separation of Powers
3. How to Read Case Law and Sources of Law

II. JURISDICTION

1. Federal Jurisdiction and the Commerce Clause
   Box 1.1 *Gonzales* v. *Raich,* 125 S.Ct. 2195 (2005)

III. EXECUTIVE BRANCH POWER

1. Nondelegation Doctrine
   a. The Reach of the Executive Branch over State Powers
   Box 1.2 *Gonzales* v. *Oregon,* 126 S.Ct. 904 (2006)

IV. DUE PROCESS

1. Procedural Due Process
2. Substantive Due Process
   a. Privacy Rights and Abortion
   Box 1.3 *Roe* v. *Wade,* 410 U.S. 959 (1973)
   b. The Return of Abortion to the Criminal Codes

1

Feature: *Chapter-Opening Case Study: Government Control of Physician-Assisted Suicide*

In early 2003, Sam was suffering from pancreatic cancer, a particularly lethal and painful cancer for which there is no known cure. Sam wanted to end his suffering. Fortunately Sam lived in Oregon where state law allows doctors to help their patients commit suicide. The physician-assisted suicide law is called the "Death with Dignity Act."[1] Sam went to Doctor John, and said, "I'm suffering. Could you please prescribe for me a lethal dose of barbiturates so that I may bring about my own death?" Doctor John replied, "Well, I am afraid that in 2001 the federal government through the Department of Justice issued the "Ashcroft Directive"[2] ("Directive") which allows the federal government to prosecute me under federal drug laws for prescribing drugs to assist suicide, even though such activity is legal here in Oregon." Not one to take no for an answer, Sam went to his own lawyer, Suzy, and asked her about the consequences of the Ashcroft Directive in relation to Sam's state-given right to control his own death with a doctor's help. Suzy visited the Department of Justice's web page and found a copy of the Directive, which reads, in part:

November 6, 2001

Memorandum

To: Asa Hutchinson, Administrator, The Drug Enforcement Administration

From: John Ashcroft, Attorney General

Subject: Dispensing of Controlled Substances to Assist Suicide

As you are aware, the Supreme Court reaffirmed last term that the application of federal law regulating controlled substances is uniform throughout the United States and may not be nullified by the legislative decisions of individual states . . . I have concluded that controlled substances may not be dispensed to assist suicide. I hereby determine that assisting suicide is not a "legitimate medical purpose" within the meaning of [federal law] and that prescribing, dispensing, or administering federally controlled substances to assist suicide violates the CSA (Controlled Substances Act, 21 U.S.C. §§801–971 (1994 & Supp. II 1996)). This conclusion applies regardless of whether state law authorizes or permits such conduct by practitioners or others and regardless of the condition of the person whose suicide is assisted.

---

[1]The Oregon Death with Dignity Act, Or. Rev. Stat. §§127.800–127.897.

[2]Ashcroft Directive, published at 66 Fed. Reg. 56607.

Based on the text of the Directive Suzy told Sam, "The Ashcroft Directive says that regardless of state law, federal government policy is supreme. I'm not so sure that the Ashcroft Directive is legal, even though it was written by the United States Attorney General who is the nation's chief law enforcement officer. Based on my legal research, I found that the U.S. Supreme Court held in *Washington* v. *Glucksberg,* 521 U.S. 702 (1997), and *Vacco* v. *Quill,* 521 U.S. 793 (1997), that there was no constitutional right to commit suicide. But the Court did say that states could pass laws making physician-assisted suicide legal. The Oregon lawmakers then passed the Death with Dignity Act, making it legal for a doctor following strict requirements and safeguards to prescribe lethal doses of drugs for patients to end their own lives. Since 1997 when the law came into effect, over 200 Oregonians have ended their lives under the state law. Of course, federal laws regulate all controlled substances—hence the Ashcroft Directive."

Suzy went on to tell Sam that a federal appellate court, the Ninth Circuit Court of Appeals located in California, decided that the Ashcroft Directive was invalid because the states, not the federal government, regulate the medical practices of physicians practicing in their state.[3] Sam asked anxiously, "Does that mean Doctor John can prescribe for me the drugs to kill myself because the Supreme Court said it's legal for the state to make such a law and the federal government cannot interfere with a Supreme Court ruling?"

"Well," Suzy said, "to answer that question the Supreme Court granted a *writ of certiorari* [agree to hear and decide the final outcome of the case] and heard oral argument in October 2005 in the case *Gonzales* v. *Oregon.* The state of Oregon challenged the federal government's authority to interfere with state rules for prescribing medicine regardless of their ultimate use. But to guess at how the U.S. Supreme Court will decide whether Doctor John can help you, I first have to tell you about how the federal government obtains jurisdiction over state matters, the separation of powers between the legislative, executive, and judicial branches, the Supreme Court's role in determining the law of the land, the history of the law and . . ."

INTRODUCTION

This chapter introduces through the lens of criminal law the separation of power and the distribution of prosecutorial authority between the federal and state governments. By exploring the issue of physician-assisted suicide and the language of the Commerce, Supremacy, and Necessary and Proper clauses and the Tenth Amendment, students will learn the difference between federal and state jurisdiction power to prosecute people for a federal and state crime. There is also a discussion of the nondelegation doctrine and the legal limits on power sharing by the three branches of the federal government. The chapter ends with an examination of the history of criminal abortion which illuminates the tension between federal authority to make law, a state's authority to control the health and welfare of its own citizens through its general police power, and the consequences of the U.S. Supreme Court's decisions when it interprets the U.S. Constitution and other state and federal laws.

I. FEDERALISM

1. The Federal Government is a Limited Government

Rule of Law: The U.S. Constitution is the only source of power for the federal government.

---

[3]*Oregon* v. *Ashcroft*, 368 F.3d 1118 (9th Cir. 2004).

After winning the Revolutionary War and gaining independence from Britain, the colonies adopted state constitutions establishing basic rules of governance for their citizens. But the new America needed more government structure and power. In 1781, every state had finally agreed to the Articles of Confederation ("Articles"), which held the original 13 colonies together much as individual treaties might loosely bind a group of small countries. The government format under the Articles was of a Congress composed of representatives from each state that would make decisions about America's foreign affairs. It was soon apparent that the Articles lacked the basic mechanisms to collect and spend money for the general welfare, to defend against enemies, and to regulate trade and commerce with foreign countries.[4] To fix these and other problems, Congress convened in Philadelphia during the summer of 1787 and drafted a Constitution. Many state delegates at the Constitutional Convention were leery of forming a government with a consolidated base of power because of the potential of a central government to abuse the civil liberties of citizens as the colonists had suffered under the British Crown. But the proposed form of a tripartite [3-pronged] system of government dividing power between the legislative, executive and judicial branches consolidated the power in a federal government by dividing it. To ensure the national federal government would not abuse its power, the Constitution made clear that the Constitution itself, the document conceived, written and eventually adopted by the states, would be the only source of power for the federal government. Under the new Constitution the Articles of Confederation yielded to **federalism,** a system in which power is shared between one national government and the many states. Federalism ensures that the federal government has authority over matters within its jurisdiction [area of control] and the states have authority over matters within their respective jurisdictions. The first three words of the Constitution, "We the people," guarantee that the national federal government is one for the people, by the people. As the first Chief Justice of the U.S. Supreme Court John Marshall said, "The people made the Constitution and they can unmake it. It is the creature of their will and lives only by their will." Put another way, if the powers granted to Congress are not specifically listed in the Constitution, Article I, sec. 8, the government cannot do it.

Rule of Law: **The Bill of Rights protects citizens from the awesome power of the government.**

After nine states ratified the Constitution in 1788, one of the first actions of the new Congress was to amend it. The first ten amendments, the **Bill of Rights,** form a cornerstone of criminal law and criminal procedure. They originally only protected people from abuses by the federal government, but beginning in the 1930s and especially in the 1960s, they were applied to the states to give protection in the areas of search and seizures and the taking of confessions. The Court reasoned that the protections of the Bill of Rights were incorporated to apply to the states and protect defendants in the area of criminal procedure. The language of the Bill of Rights is largely negative, mandating that the government "shall not" take certain actions that infringe on people's liberty; for example, the First Amendment says "Congress shall make no law," and the Fourth Amendment says that the law of search and seizure "shall not be violated." The negative language of the Bill of Rights counterbalances the broad grant of authority that the Constitution gives to the federal government.

Rule of Law: **Most criminal law is state law.**

In the realm of federalism, the **Tenth Amendment** says "The powers not delegated to the United States by the Constitution, nor prohibited by it to the states, are reserved to the States respectively, or to the people"; the federal government is constrained to act

---

[4]The Formation of the Union (National Archives Pub. No. 70-13).

by the limits placed upon it by the Constitution and the rest of the power to create laws is left to the states. Each state has a constitution that can grant more power to its citizens than the federal government, but never less. As Alexander Hamilton wrote in the *Federalist Papers* (written and published in New York to enlist support for the 13 colonies to ratify the Constitution), "The Constitution leaves in the possession of each State 'certain exclusive and very important portions of sovereign power.' Foremost among the prerogatives of sovereignty is the power to create and enforce a criminal code."[5] Each state government is largely responsible for passing laws that affect the direct welfare of its citizens, such as laws regulating marriage, divorce, and child custody, and for making decisions such as whether or not to spend tax money on shelters for homeless people or battered women. Ninety percent of criminal law in America is state law, and states have the police power to protect their citizens.

Rule of Law: The Supremacy Clause means that federal law trumps state law, and when the U.S. Supreme Court speaks it is the final word.

Federalism gives states the power to enact laws that represent local morals, for example, legalizing prostitution in Las Vegas, Nevada, legalizing same-sex marriage in Massachusetts, and legalizing physician-assisted suicide in Oregon. Each state has the right to enact laws that reflect its values, but all states must yield to the supremacy of federal authority. By operation of the **Supremacy Clause,** found in Article VI of the Constitution, federal law, including that law as interpreted by the Supreme Court, is "the law of the land." The Supremacy Clause states,

> This Constitution, and the Laws of the United States which shall be made in Pursuance thereof; and all Treaties made, or which shall be made, under the Authority of the United States, shall be the supreme Law of the Land; and the Judges in every State shall be bound thereby, any Thing in the Constitution or Laws of any state to the contrary notwithstanding.

The Supremacy Clause makes state law subordinate to federal law and the decisions of the U.S. Supreme Court the final word when it interprets the Constitution. When the U.S. Supreme Court speaks on an issue, no government, state or federal, can overrule the Supreme Court's interpretation of what the Constitution says.

2. Separation of Powers

Rule of Law: The three branches of government operate under a system of checks and balances. The legislative branch makes law, the executive branch enforces law, and the judicial branch interprets law.

The Constitution limited the federal government's power and dispersed it among the legislative, executive, and judicial branches so that each branch could operate as a system of checks and balances on each of the others. For example, one branch cannot accumulate more power at the expense of the other two. James Madison explained that the division of power in the government served to protect the people as each branch provides a balance: "The power surrendered by the people is first divided between two distinct governments, and then the portion allotted to each, subdivided among distinct and separate departments. Hence a double security arises to the rights of the people. The different governments will control each other at the same time that each will be controlled by itself."[6] The separation of powers that operates in the federal government and that is embodied by Madison's words is illustrated in Figure 1.1.

---

[5]J. E. Cooke, ed. The Federalist No. 9, at 55 (Alexander Hamilton) (1961).

[6]Federalist (No. 51).

FIGURE 1.1 Separation of powers.

Branch	Duties	Checks and Balances
Legislative **Makes Laws**	**Art. I, Sec. 8,** "The Congress shall have the power to . . . make all laws which shall be necessary and proper . . ."	**Art II,** The President may veto a federal law, which then needs 2/3 of Congress to override veto **Art III,** The U.S. Supreme Court can declare federal laws enacted by Congress unconstitutional and invalid
Executive **Enforces Laws**	**Art. II, Sec. 1,** "The executive power shall be vested in a President of the United States of America" President enforces laws passed by Congress	**Art I,** Congress makes the laws that limit or expand President's power **Art III,** The U.S. Supreme Court can declare presidential acts unconstitutional and invalid
Judicial **Interprets Laws**	**Art III, Sec. 1,** "The judicial power of the United States, shall be vested in one supreme court, and in such inferior Courts as the Congress may . . . establish"	**Art I,** Congress can establish other courts **Art II,** President appoints federal judges with advice and consent of Senate

The specific powers granted to the federal government by the Constitution are as follows.

Article I granted to Congress (which is composed of a House of Representatives whose members are determined by a state's population and a Senate whose members include two from every state) the specific rights to ratify treaties, set the budget, determine what laws exist, and "make all laws necessary and proper" to carry out its responsibilities. The Constitution's **necessary and proper** clause is the fulcrum upon which Congress can leverage its power to make law in areas for which there is no specific grant of constitutional authority. For instance, the Constitution is silent on creating a military draft, but Congress has the "implied power" to "make all laws necessary and proper" to fix the problems of the country and, hence, draft men and women to war.

Article II granted to the President duly elected by the people the power to be commander of the armed forces, execute the laws of the United States and appoint cabinet members with the "advice and consent" of the Senate, among other duties. The **advice and consent** of Senate clause is a legislative check on the executive branch to prevent the president from appointing a mere figurehead to a position of federal power. All presidents appoint to high-ranking federal jobs friends, political supporters, and financial contributors to their election campaigns. To ensure that the Executive Branch is not overrun with political cronies, the Senate must confirm these presidential appointments. The Senate Judiciary Committee holds hearings designed to ascertain the qualifications of the nominees—for example, of people who may become justices on the U.S. Supreme Court.

In the criminal law context, the traditional bounds of the advice and consent of the Senate Clause were stretched by operation of the federal law, Uniting and Strengthening America by Providing Appropriate Tools Required to Intercept and Obstruct Terrorism Act (USA "PATRIOT Act")[7] enacted after hijacked planes barreled into the

---

[7]Public Law 107-56.

World Trade Center in New York City, the Pentagon in Washington, D.C., and a field in Shanksville, Pennsylvania, on September 11, 2001. The PATRIOT Act allowed President George W. Bush to appoint U.S. Attorneys who are the chief federal prosecutors in each state for short periods of time without Senate confirmation or approval. Article II gives the President the right to make such federal appointments. U.S. Attorneys uphold federal law and prosecute federal crimes; they do not necessarily wage political battles. But in November 2006, U.S. Attorney General Alberto Gonzales summarily fired eight U.S. Attorneys for "poor performance." These prosecutors were replaced under the PATRIOT Act with attorneys described as "loyal Bushies" by Gonzales' chief of staff Kyle D. Sampson. Congressional hearings ensued to investigate whether the eight prosecutors were purged because of their failure to pursue voting fraud cases against Democratic rivals during the close elections of 2006 where Democrats regained control of the House and Senate. While the President has the prerogative to replace all 93 U.S. Attorneys because they serve at his pleasure as the chief executive, charges were made that Gonzales was turning the enforcement of federal law into a political game, thereby tarnishing the integrity of the Department of Justice. As Edward Gibbon said about Ancient Rome in the 1700s, "The principles of a free constitution are irrevocably lost, when the legislative power is nominated by the executive." Alberto Gonzales resigned as U.S. Attorney General in August 2007.

Article III created one Supreme Court and "such inferior Courts as the Congress may from time to time ordain and establish," which are the lower federal district and courts of appeal, but the Constitution was silent about the scope of judicial power. In 1789, Congress passed the Judiciary Act, which defined the power of the U.S. Supreme Court. One power was the authority of the high Court to issue ***writs of mandamus*** [Latin for "we command," orders forcing a government official to act]. President John Adams was a federalist who was defeated in his reelection bid by Democratic-Republican Thomas Jefferson. Before he left office, Adams worked with his congressional allies to create over 200 administrative posts and a number of judgeships to dilute Jefferson's executive power. Adams made appointments until midnight on his last day of office, but not all commissions to appoint new Justices of the Peace in the District of Columbia were delivered on time. Jefferson was furious at the partisan politics going on behind the scenes and, upon taking the presidential oath, ordered his Secretary of State James Madison not to deliver the remaining commissions. John Marbury and other hopefuls who were expecting Justice of the Peace commissions sued Madison in an effort to get the Supreme Court to issue *writs of mandamus* forcing Jefferson to deliver the commissions. When the Court decided Marbury's case in 1803, Chief Justice John Marshall circumvented a political showdown by declaring invalid Congress's passing of the Judiciary Act granting to the high Court the authority to issue the *writs of mandamus*. Therefore, Jefferson did not have to deliver the commissions.

By deciding Marbury's case, Marshall not only avoided the political struggle between the parties, but also defined the Supreme Court's power under Article III.[8] The *Marbury* decision established the doctrine of **judicial review** in which only the Supreme Court has the right to interpret the Constitution and decide whether the laws made by Congress [the legislative branch], and the acts of the President and the federal agencies he controls and directs [the executive branch], are legal pursuant to the Constitution.[9] The import of the *Marbury* decision cannot be underestimated: "Marshall gave to succeeding judges a national judiciary able to stand equal alongside the other

---

[8]*Marbury* v. *Madison*, 5 U.S. (1 Cranch) 137 (1803).

[9]Mark V. Tushnet. "*Marbury* v. *Madison* and the Theory of Judicial Supremacy." In Robert P. George, ed., *Greatest Cases in Constitutional Law* (Princeton, NJ: Princeton University, 2000), pp. 17–54.

two branches of government."[10] The high Court then went on to interpret the Supremacy Clause to make its word final when the Court interpreted the Constitution or laws passed by federal or state legislatures.

3. How to Read Case Law and Sources of Criminal Law

Rule of Law: You must understand how to read case law in order to understand criminal law and procedure.

The main components of a judicial opinion that you are reading as case excerpts in this text are a synopsis of the facts that form the basis of the case, the legal issues the losing party is asking the court to resolve, and the rules of law and policy that the court applies in resolving the dispute. There are many different sources of criminal law. Once the appellate court makes its decision, in many cases the court writes a decision explaining its ruling. This is called **case law**—law made by judges deciding the cases before them. The American colonists brought with them not only the customs and traditions of England, but also its common law. When disputes arose in England, a judge would bring the parties together and decide the case based on social traditions and customs of the day; thus common law developed. Called judge-made law, one can find **common law** by reading prior cases to determine how similar disputes were resolved. Common law still informs the law today as a reference for how certain legal principles and doctrines have been interpreted throughout history, interpretation that could be applied to present-day cases.

Most criminal laws today are statutes, laws enacted by legislators and codified in state or federal criminal codes, called **statutory law.** Statutes define crimes by elements, or pieces of the whole, which the prosecutor must prove beyond a reasonable doubt before the defendant can be convicted, discussed more fully in chapter 4. Elected officials enact statutes during legislative sessions. Another source of criminal law is the **Model Penal Code** ("MPC"), a document created in the 1960s by the American Law Institute, an organization of law-related professionals. A concise statement of criminal law, the MPC is used in this text as a guide for many states that have adopted MPC language in whole or in part in defining the elements of their respective state crimes, defenses, and sentencing structure. Selected excerpts of the MPC are located in Appendix B, and the student should use the MPC as a reference for the basic elements of statutory crimes. Administrative agencies enact **administrative regulations** to "fill in the gaps" created by the broad grant of authority that was created by statute, but that could not possibly foresee every situation of governmental regulation of human behavior. As illustrated in the *Gonzales* v. *Oregon* case discussed in this chapter, the federal Drug Enforcement Agency ("DEA") was charged with creating guidelines for the distribution of controlled substances to fulfill Congressional intent to punish drug offenders. Another source of criminal law used to control the public's behavior is an **ordinance,** a local regulation enacted to protect the health and safety of the community. Common ordinances dictate everything from how often people can put trash on the street curb to how loud they can play their music past a certain hour in the night. City councils or town hall supervisors are often in charge of issuing ordinances for the good of the public order. All regulations imposed on the public by the government, even local government, must comply with state and federal laws.

In this text, almost all case excerpts are appeals from defendants convicted at trial. A **precedent** is a "rule of law established by the first time by a court for a particular type of case and thereafter referred to in deciding similar cases."[11] Courts look to

---

[10]G. Edward White. *The American Judicial Tradition: Profiles of Leading American Judges.* (New York: Oxford University, 1976).

[11]*Black's Law Dictionary*, 5th ed. (St. Paul, MN: West Publishing, 1979).

precedent to decide cases before them; precedent is the rule of law established when a previous case with similar facts has already been decided by a court of law. The judicial system is established on a hierarchy of power among different courts depending on the court's power to hear and decide certain types of cases. A lower court is bound to follow the precedent established by a higher court. The practice of other judges following previous precedents is called ***stare decisis*** [Latin for "let the decision stand"]. When courts follow previously established law on an issue, such as kidnapping or assault and battery, society can expect that people will be treated consistently and uniformly when they come before the court accused of kidnapping or of assault and battery.

When reading a case, courts often cite to precedent when stating a legal proposition that has already been decided. An example of citing to precedent is provided in the following example. In a case where the legality of an interrogation is at issue, a court might write "custodial interrogations require the suspect [to] be warned of her constitutional rights against self-incrimination and to have an attorney present during questioning. *Miranda* v. *Arizona,* 384 U.S. 436 (1966)." The court will always strive to cite a case, precedent, that establishes the legal authority for the proposition the court just stated. To interpret where to find the case in our *Miranda* example, the first numbers after the case name mean that you can find the case in volume 384 of the United States Reports on page 436, and the year the case was decided was 1966. If one were to go look up the *Miranda* case, it would stand for the legal proposition that the Fifth and Sixth Amendments protect criminal suspects. All lower or inferior courts must follow a higher court's precedent and no court is higher than the U.S. Supreme Court.

The way appellate courts make their decisions, case law, is a very formalized process called following *stare decisis* and precedent.

Rule of Law: The concepts of *stare decisis* and precedent engender society satisfaction with the justice system with the relative predictability of court decisions.

Since America was a colony, our legal system was based on England's tradition of following custom and practice of how cases had been resolved before. If a boundary dispute had been settled by dividing the property in half, then the judge was likely to decide all following cases of boundary disputes in the same manner, by splitting the property down the middle. Following precedent serves society in three ways: it gives the public some comfort to know ahead of time the likely outcome of their cases (no death penalty for a simple assault, for example); it created uniformity in the court structure, which made it easier for judges and others to make decisions; and it gave the public a sense of confidence that criminal laws were to be applied uniformly. If the public can trust its legal system, then it is believed that most people will follow the law rather than break it, because they know they will get a fair day in court.

Understanding case law requires a mastery of the **case brief,** a synopsis that summarizes the major components of a case. Understanding the key components of a case is important because the significance of the court's conclusion—called a holding—and the reasons the court came to a specific conclusion suggest how to apply the law to similar situations that may arise in the future. The components of a case brief are

FACTS: The action people took that brought them to court.

ISSUE: The legal question the court is being asked to answer.

HOLDING: The majority opinion. A majority of the justices who sit on the appellate court agree on a specific outcome for the case. The holding is also the court's answer to the **issue,** which establishes precedent for future cases that present similar issues.

REASONING: The reasons why and how the court arrived at its holding.

CONCURRENCE: The judges who agree and vote with the majority decision, but write a separate opinion to clarify or distinguish their reasoning from the majority decision.

DISSENT: The judges who disagree with the majority decision and write a formal rebuke to the majority opinion. Dissents often refer to the court as if it is a foreign body. It is not uncommon to see language in a dissent such as, "I disagree with the court's holding today . . ." even though the judge writing the dissent is a member of the court.

In reading case law, the notation for the judge delivering the opinion might be "J. Branch." This stands for "Judge" or "Justice" Branch; the "J" is not the judge's first initial. A capitalized "Court" refers mostly to the U.S. Supreme Court, unless an appeals court is referring to itself within the opinion. The U.S. Supreme Court is also referred to as the "high Court." Many court opinions will state "the defendant asserts" or "the defendant contends" to reflect the arguments made on behalf of a defendant. The defendant is not advancing arguments in his own name. His attorney is advancing the arguments on his behalf, and the court simply states that it is the "defendant's" argument.

II. JURISDICTION

Jurisdiction is the authority to hear a certain type of case. For example, through federal prosecutors who bring charges against defendants in federal courts, the federal government has jurisdiction over cases such as counterfeiting that involve the national treasury, crimes on the high seas, crimes against national security or treason, and other crimes that cross state lines. Jurisdiction also refers to the geographic boundaries of a court's authority. A murderer who kills in a state without the death penalty cannot face the death penalty because that state's jurisdiction does not recognize such punishment. But even if the state does not have the death penalty and the killing occurs on federal property, then the federal government, which does have the death penalty, can seek the punishment of death in that state. Such was the case of Kristen Gilbert, a nurse accused of killing patients at a Veteran's Administration hospital in Springfield, Massachusetts. If Gilbert were prosecuted and convicted for the murders by the state of Massachusetts, the maximum penalty allowable under state law would be life in prison, as the state has no death penalty. But Gilbert was prosecuted in U.S. District Court, the federal trial court in Springfield, and federal prosecutors did seek death. However, the jury rebuffed the federal government's request and sentenced Gilbert to life imprisonment.

Concurrent jurisdiction is simultaneous jurisdiction where both the federal and state governments could prosecute for the same crime. In 1995, Timothy McVeigh planted a bomb made out of fertilizer outside the Murrah Federal Building in Oklahoma City, Oklahoma. The bomb was in a rented truck and when it exploded in front of the building, 168 people died. Because the bombing site was federal property, the federal government had jurisdiction to prosecute McVeigh for murder; but the state of Oklahoma could have prosecuted McVeigh on state murder charges as well. A federal jury convicted McVeigh of murder and sentenced him to death, and he was executed in 2001.

Rule of Law: As a general rule, the Commerce Clause is the required nexus for federal jurisdiction over crime. No such nexus is required for a uniquely federal crime such as treason or counterfeiting.

1. Federal Jurisdiction and the Commerce Clause

As discussed previously, congressional power to create and define criminal law is restricted by the specific language of the Constitution. The Constitution in Article 1, sec. 8, grants Congress the power to, among other things, "regulate commerce with foreign nations and among the several states, and with the Indian Tribes" and "make all laws which shall be necessary and proper for carrying into execution the foregoing powers." These clauses, known as the **Commerce Clause** and the **Necessary and Proper Clause,** work together to grant federal jurisdiction over a range of matters that are purely within one state based on their effect on commerce between the states. Commerce is generally defined as commercial intercourse, the buying and selling of goods and services. The Supreme Court has held that if a certain interstate (between states) activity or intrastate (within the state) activity affects interstate commerce, Congress can criminalize it and give the federal government jurisdiction to prosecute the perpetrators. To determine whether federal jurisdiction exists via the Commerce Clause, federal courts examine whether the criminal activity

1. uses channels of interstate commerce (planes, trains, and automobiles);
2. uses the instrumentalities of interstate commerce (wire transfer, telephones); and
3. is an activity that "substantially affect[s] interstate commerce"[12]

The significance of a federal prosecution is that, upon conviction, federal sentences tend to be much harsher than state sentences and federal offenders have no real opportunity for early release through the granting of parole.

Once a decision has been issued, the case name is either underlined or italicized to distinguish the case decision from the parties involved. For example, in the *Gonzales* v. *Raich* case in Box 1.1, Raich was the defendant in a federal criminal prosecution and the Court refers to her on appeal as Raich or the appellant. The appellant is the one seeking the appeal and the appellee is the one trying to maintain the conviction, here U.S. Attorney Gonzales as a representative of the federal government. Once the Court decides the case, the case name is often referred to by the defendant's last name and is italicized, for example the *Raich* case, or the *Miranda* case (*Miranda* v. *Arizona* (1964)).

The cases in this text retain most of the original language, but have been edited to omit internal quotation marks and citations and to include in brackets summaries of omitted material and definitions of technical legal language.

How does the Commerce Clause interact with states' rights protected by the Tenth Amendment? Let's imagine Sam in our opening case study went to visit his friend Betty in California. Betty has been diagnosed with glaucoma, a condition for which marijuana has powerful ameliorative effects; it lessens pressure in the eye cavity which reduces pain for the sufferer. Luckily for Betty, people in California are aware of the many medicinal effects of marijuana and have passed a law permitting its use for certain medical conditions. During Sam's visit, federal drug agents raid Betty's house, confiscate her marijuana, and charge her with violating federal drug laws. On what authority does the federal government act? Unless the Constitution specifically grants the federal government the power to do something, the government has no authority. Under the Tenth Amendment, those powers not delegated expressly to the federal government are left to the states. In Betty's case, California state law allows marijuana use. The primary mechanism for the federal government to obtain jurisdiction over Betty to prosecute her is through the operation of the Commerce Clause. But Betty's marijuana never crossed state lines and has no effect on commerce because it is not bought or sold, simply grown and used. Angel Raich and Diane Monson in California suffered the same fate as Betty. Federal drug agents seized their marijuana plants even after making a determination that their possession was legal. The women sued the federal government and won in the Ninth Circuit Court of Appeals, widely regarded as a liberal circuit that includes the states of California and Oregon, which upheld California's power to be free from federal interference in medical matters. The Supreme Court granted *certiorari* to resolve the question of federal government authority to prosecute drug crimes and decided in favor of the federal government. Pay close attention to the Court's reasoning in the case excerpt in Box 1.1 of why drug activity that occurs intrastate (within one state) is still within the reach of federal jurisdiction.

---

[12]*United States* v. *Morrison*, 529 U.S. 598 (2000).

BOX 1.1

Gonzales v. *Raich,* 125 S.Ct. 2195 (2005)
United States Supreme Court

Justice Stevens delivered the opinion of the Court.

FACTS

California has been a pioneer in the regulation of marijuana. In 1996, California voters passed Proposition 215, now codified as the Compassionate Use Act of 1996 [the Act]. The proposition was designed to ensure that "seriously ill" residents of the State have access to marijuana for medicinal purposes and to encourage Federal and State Governments to take steps towards ensuring the safe and affordable distribution of the drug to patients in need. The Act creates an exemption from criminal prosecution for physicians, as well as for patients and primary caregivers who possess or cultivate marijuana for medicinal purposes with the recommendation or approval of a physician. Respondents Angel Raich and Diane Monson are California residents who suffer from a variety of serious medical conditions and have sought to avail themselves of medical marijuana pursuant to the Act.

[Raich and Monson] have been using marijuana as a medication for several years pursuant to their doctors' recommendation, and both rely heavily on cannabis to function on a daily basis. Indeed, Raich's physician believes that forgoing cannabis treatments would certainly cause Raich excruciating pain and could very well prove fatal.

On August 15, 2002, county deputy sheriffs and agents from the federal Drug Enforcement Administration (DEA) came to Monson's home. After a thorough investigation, the county officials concluded that her use of marijuana was entirely lawful as a matter of California law. Nevertheless, after a 3-hour standoff, the federal agents seized and destroyed all six of her cannabis plants. Respondents thereafter brought this action against the Attorney General of the United States and the head of the DEA seeking injunctive and declaratory relief prohibiting the enforcement of the federal Controlled Substances Act to the extent it prevents them from possessing, obtaining, or manufacturing cannabis for their personal medical use.

ISSUE

The question before us is whether Congress' power to regulate interstate markets for medicinal substances encompasses the portions of those markets that are supplied with drugs produced and consumed locally?

HOLDING

Congress' Commerce Clause authority includes the power to prohibit the local cultivation and use of marijuana in compliance with California law.

REASONING

Shortly after taking office in 1969, President Nixon declared a national "war on drugs." As the first campaign of that war, Congress set out to enact legislation that would consolidate various drug laws on the books into a comprehensive statute, provide meaningful regulation over legitimate sources of drugs to prevent diversion into illegal channels, and strengthen law enforcement tools against the traffic in illicit drugs. That effort culminated in the passage of the Comprehensive Drug Abuse Prevention and Control Act of 1970 ["CSA"]. The main objectives of the CSA were to conquer drug abuse and to control the legitimate and illegitimate traffic in controlled substances. In particular, Congress made the following findings:

3. A majority of the traffic in controlled substances flows through interstate and foreign commerce. Incidents of the traffic which are not an integral part of the interstate or foreign flow, such as manufacture, local distribution, and possession, nonetheless have a substantial and direct effect upon interstate commerce because–
   a. after manufacture, many controlled substances are transported in interstate commerce,
   b. controlled substances distributed locally usually have been transported in interstate commerce immediately before their distribution, and
   c. controlled substances distributed locally commonly flow through interstate commerce immediately prior to such possession . . .

To effectuate these goals, Congress devised a closed regulatory system making it unlawful to manufacture, distribute, dispense, or possess any controlled substance except in a manner authorized by the CSA. In enacting the CSA, Congress classified marijuana as a Schedule I drug. By classifying marijuana as a Schedule I drug, as opposed to listing it on a lesser schedule, the manufacture, distribution, or possession of marijuana became a criminal offense, with the sole exception being use of the drug as part of a Food and Drug Administration pre-approved research study. [Raich and Monson] argue that the CSA's categorical prohibition of the manufacture and possession of marijuana as applied to the intrastate manufacture and possession of marijuana for medical purposes pursuant to California law exceeds Congress' authority under the Commerce Clause. Our decision in [*Wickard* v. *Filburn,* 317 U.S. 111 (1942)] is of particular relevance.

In *Wickard,* we upheld the application of regulations promulgated under the Agriculture Adjustment Act of 1938 which were designed to control the volume of wheat moving in interstate and foreign commerce in order to avoid surpluses and consequent abnormally low prices. Filburn [sowed 23 acres of wheat rather than the federal limit of 11 acres] intending to use the excess by consuming it on his own farm. Filburn argued that [Congress had no authority to regulate crop production not intended for any commerce. In rejecting Filburn's argument, the Court wrote] the effect of the statute before us is to restrict the amount which may be produced for market. That [Filburn's] own contribution to the demand for wheat may be trivial by itself is not enough to remove him from the scope of federal regulation . . .

Wickard thus establishes that Congress can regulate purely intrastate activity that is not itself "commercial" if it concludes that failure to regulate that class of activity would undercut the regulation of the interstate market in that commodity. The similarities between this case and *Wickard* are striking. Like the farmer in *Wickard,* respondents are cultivating, for home consumption, a fungible commodity [goods such as grain or oil where each particle is identical] for which there is an established, albeit illegal, interstate market. More concretely, one concern prompting inclu-

sion of wheat grown for home consumption in the 1938 Act was that rising market prices could draw such wheat into the interstate market, resulting in lower market prices. The parallel concern making it appropriate to include marijuana grown for home consumption in the CSA is the likelihood that the high demand in the interstate market will draw such marijuana into that market. While the diversion of homegrown wheat tended to frustrate the federal interest in stabilizing prices by regulating the volume of commercial transactions in the interstate market, the diversion of homegrown marijuana tends to frustrate the federal interest in eliminating commercial transactions in the interstate market in their entirety. In both cases, the regulation is squarely within Congress' commerce power because production of the commodity meant for home consumption, be it wheat or marijuana, has a substantial effect on supply and demand in the national market for that commodity.

CONCLUSION

[By operation of the Commerce Clause, the federal government can regulate intrastate cultivation and use of the controlled substance marijuana. Raich and Monson] also raise a substantive due process claim and seek to avail themselves of the medical necessity defense. These theories of relief were set forth in their complaint but were not reached by the Court of Appeals. We therefore do not address the question whether judicial relief is available to respondents on these alternative bases. We do note, however, the presence of another avenue of relief. As the Solicitor General [Chief lawyer who represents the United States in front of the Supreme Court] confirmed during oral argument, the statute authorizes procedures for the reclassification of Schedule I drugs. But perhaps even more important than these legal avenues is the democratic process, in which the voices of voters allied with these respondents may one day be heard in the halls of Congress. Under the present state of the law, however, the judgment of the Court of Appeals must be vacated. The case is remanded for further proceedings consistent with this opinion. It is so ordered.

At the conclusion of the *Raich* decision, the Supreme Court reiterated the judiciary's role in the separation of powers that the Court interprets, not makes, law. The Court stated the proper course of action for people dissatisfied with the law was convincing their elected representatives in the federal legislature to change the federal drug laws to decriminalize marijuana. The Court's rationale in *Raich* accepted the proposition that locally grown marijuana does not involve any interstate commerce. That is, if all of the dirt, water, and sunlight used to grow the marijuana seed into the plant was local to California, assuming the seed is a few plants removed from the original plant imported from Mexico, there's no effect on interstate commerce. By relying on the Supreme Court precedent in *Wickard,* however, the court reasoned that illegal drugs grown and consumed locally, albeit for legal medicinal purposes, may affect the supply and demand of illegal drugs in other states, which affects interstate commerce. The very same Commerce Clause issue was presented in *Wickard,* where farmer Filburn's wheat grown and kept for personal consumption could affect the national supply, demand, and price for wheat that the government was trying to stabilize in the Depression's aftermath.

In both the *Raich* and *Wickard* cases, the Court found congressional authority to regulate and criminalize activity that occurs purely within one state's jurisdiction. The Commerce Clause is not without its limits and courts have declined to extend federal jurisdiction for every crime that might have some relation to interstate commerce.

Applying the Rule of Law to the Facts: Is the law legal?

- Nancy was raped while she was a student at Virginia Tech University and sued the University under the federal law, "Violence Against Women Act of 1994." The defendant challenged the legality of the federal law on the basis that there was no nexus between sexual violence and interstate commerce. Is defendant correct?

Yes, in the case *United States* v. *Morrison*, 529 U.S. 598 (2000), the high Court found no such nexus and held the law unconstitutional. The Court reasoned:

> We accordingly reject the argument that Congress may regulate noneconomic, violent criminal conduct based solely on that conduct's aggregate effect on interstate commerce. The Constitution requires a distinction between what is truly national and what is truly local. In recognizing this fact we preserve one of the few principles that has been consistent since the [Commerce] Clause was adopted. The regulation and punishment of intrastate violence that is not directed at instrumentalities, channels, or goods involved in interstate commerce has always been the province of the States.

III. EXECUTIVE BRANCH POWER

1. Nondelegation Doctrine

Rule of Law: Congress can legislate broadly to share its power with its co-branches subject to an "intelligible principle."

Pursuant to Article I of the Constitution, "All legislative Powers herein granted shall be vested in a Congress of the United States." Only a government composed of representatives elected by the people has the power to make laws that govern the people. The U.S. Supreme Court has interpreted Article I to prohibit Congress from sharing its lawmaking power. Philosopher John Locke said, "The power of the legislative, being derived from the people by a positive voluntary grant and institution . . . can have no power to transfer their authority of making laws and place it in other hands."[13] Congress cannot delegate [give] its law-making power to another governmental branch. This is known as the **nondelegation doctrine.**

---

[13]J. Locke. *Second Treatise of Government*. (Wheeling, IL: Harlan Davidson, 1982), p. 87.

But clearly, federal agencies that exist and operate under Article II (the Executive Branch) make rules and regulations that have the force of law. How is this allowed? The U.S. Supreme Court has recognized that Congress cannot possibly know all of the details of the subject matter that is controlled by federal agencies. Congress cannot know the minutiae of nuclear power, of the ebb and flow of the ecology of national forests or wetlands, or of all the details that go into city planning and that drive federal housing policy. Therefore the high Court has said it is legal for Congress to give its power to the executive branch, subject to limitations. These limitations are called an **"intelligible principle."**

If Congress has the power to control federal drug policy, it can delegate that power to the U.S. Department of Justice's Drug Enforcement Agency to make rules and regulations that define what drugs are criminal. But the power Congress delegates to the DEA must be constrained by Congress. In short, the nondelegation doctrine provides no sharing or power between the branches of government, except when necessary for Congress to delegate power to the other branches of government to carry out the congressional duty to run the country. If Congress has the power to legislate and delegates the power it has to an executive agency constrained by an intelligible principle from which an agency can issue rules and regulations, the Court will find that such sharing of power will not violate the Constitution's separation of powers doctrine.

In *Touby* v. *United States,* 500 U.S. 160 (1991), a couple was convicted of conspiring to manufacture Euphoria, a designer drug that the DEA had temporarily classified as a Schedule I controlled substance, a substance that is highly addictive and illegal. The Toubys appealed their convictions, claiming that Congress' authority to enact portions of the federal drug law, the Controlled Substances Act, could not be delegated to the U.S. Attorney General who is in charge of the Department of Justice, which oversees the DEA. The Supreme Court upheld the Toubys' convictions stating that the CSA limited the Attorney General's power and discretion to define criminal conduct and such restraint was the intelligible principle that satisfied "the constitutional requirements of the nondelegation doctrine." Of the intelligible principle, the high Court said in *Mistretta* v. *United States,* 488 U.S. 361 (1989):

> Applying this "intelligible principle" test to congressional delegations, our jurisprudence has been driven by a practical understanding that in our increasingly complex society, replete with ever changing and more technical problems, Congress simply cannot do its job absent an ability to delegate power under broad general directives. Accordingly, this Court has deemed it "constitutionally sufficient if Congress clearly delineates the general policy, the public agency which is to apply it, and the boundaries of this delegated authority."

Applying the Rule of Law to the Facts: Violation of the nondelegation doctrine?

- Amy and Frank lived next to a forest preserve in and around Lake Tahoe, California. They had a few animals, including some goats. Occasionally, the goats would eat grass on federal lands. Amy and Frank were charged with violating federal agriculture regulations specifying where and when animals could eat on federal lands. They challenged the regulations as an unlawful exercise of authority by a federal agency, the U.S. Department of Agriculture, because the executive branch cannot make penal laws.[14]

The goat grazers lose—Congress could not possibly know all the details of how best to control federal land and gave the Executive Branch (in this case, the Agriculture Department) the authority to make rules and regulations, within proper limits.

---

[14]Facts adapted from *United States* v. *Grimaud*, 220 U.S. 506 (1911).

a. The Reach of the Executive Branch over State Powers

In 2000, President Bush appointed former Missouri Senator John Ashcroft as the U.S. Attorney General. The federal attorney general is in charge of the Justice Department under which most federal law enforcement agencies fall, such as the FBI and DEA. As the top chief law enforcement officer in the country, Attorney General Ashcroft revisited the DEA's policy regarding Oregon's use of controlled substances to facilitate its physician-assisted suicide law. When he was a senator, Ashcroft had publicly denounced Oregon's law and took steps to prevent its enactment. As Attorney General he issued a directive, reprinted in part in the opening feature of this chapter, making criminal Oregon's use of controlled substances. Oregon challenged the "Ashcroft Directive" and the case made its way to the U.S. Supreme Court. The *Gonzales* v. *Oregon* case, reprinted in part in Box 1.2, illustrates the tension of federalism in modern-day society.[15]

BOX 1.2

Gonzales v. *Oregon,* 126 S.Ct. 904 (2006)
United States Supreme Court

Justice Kennedy delivered the opinion of the Court.

PROCEDURAL HISTORY

The Controlled Substances Act (CSA or Act), which was enacted in 1970 with the main objectives of combating drug abuse and controlling legitimate and illegitimate traffic in controlled substances, criminalizes, *inter alia* [among other things], the unauthorized distribution and dispensation of substances classified in any of its five schedules. The Attorney General may add, remove, or reschedule substances only after making particular findings, and on scientific and medical matters, he must accept the findings of the Secretary of Health and Human Services (Secretary). The dispute here involves controlled substances listed in Schedule II, which are generally available only by written prescription, 21 U.S.C. §829(a).

A 1971 regulation promulgated by the Attorney General requires that such prescriptions be used "for a legitimate medical purpose by an individual practitioner acting in the usual course of his professional practice." 21 CFR §1306.04. To prevent diversion of controlled substances, the CSA regulates the activity of physicians, who must register in accordance with rules and regulations promulgated by the Attorney General . . . [who] may deny, suspend, or revoke a registration that, as relevant here,

would be "inconsistent with the public interest." 21 U.S.C. §§824(a)(4), 822(a)(2). In determining consistency with the public interest, [the Attorney General] must consider five factors, including the State's recommendation, compliance with state, federal, and local law regarding controlled substances, and "public health and safety." §823(f). The CSA explicitly contemplates a role for the States in regulating controlled substances. The Oregon Death With Dignity Act (ODWDA) exempts from civil or criminal liability state-licensed physicians who, in compliance with ODWDA's specific safeguards, dispense or prescribe a lethal dose of drugs upon the request of a terminally ill patient.

In 2001, the Attorney General issued an Interpretive Rule [the Ashcroft Directive] to address the implementation and enforcement of the CSA with respect to ODWDA, declaring that using controlled substances to assist suicide is not a legitimate medical practice and that dispensing or prescribing them for this purpose is unlawful under the CSA. The State, a physician, a pharmacist, and some terminally ill state residents challenged the Rule.

ISSUE

Whether the Controlled Substances Act allows the United States Attorney General to prohibit doctors from prescribing regulated drugs for use in

---

[15]In both the *Gonzales* v. *Oregon* and the *Gonzales* v. *Raich* cases, Attorney General John Ashcroft was the original party representing the federal government. When Ashcroft resigned upon President Bush's reelection in 2004, new U.S. Attorney General Alberto Gonzales was substituted for Ashcroft in the litigation. Prior case history in both cases remains in Ashcroft's name.

physician-assisted suicide, notwithstanding a state law permitting the procedure?

HOLDING

[No. The Attorney General has exceeded his powers here].

REASONING

"Americans are engaged in an earnest and profound debate about the morality, legality, and practicality of physician-assisted suicide." *Washington* v. *Glucksberg*, 521 U.S. 702 (1997). Oregon voters enacted ODWDA in 1994. For Oregon residents to be eligible to request a prescription under ODWDA, they must receive a diagnosis from their attending physician that they have an incurable and irreversible disease that, within reasonable medical judgment, will cause death within six months. Attending physicians must also determine whether a patient has made a voluntary request, ensure a patient's choice is informed, and refer patients to counseling if they might be suffering from a psychological disorder or depression causing impaired judgment. A second "consulting" physician must examine the patient and the medical record and confirm the attending physician's conclusions. Oregon physicians may dispense or issue a prescription for the requested drug, but may not administer it. The reviewing physicians must keep detailed medical records of the process leading to the final prescription, records that Oregon's Department of Human Services reviews. Physicians who dispense medication pursuant to ODWDA must also be registered with both the State's Board of Medical Examiners and the federal Drug Enforcement Administration.

In 2004, 37 patients ended their lives by ingesting lethal doses of medication prescribed under ODWDA. In 1997, Members of Congress concerned about ODWDA invited the DEA to prosecute or revoke the CSA registration of Oregon physicians who assist suicide. They contended that hastening a patient's death is not legitimate medical practice, so prescribing controlled substances for that purpose violates the CSA. In 2001, John Ashcroft was appointed Attorney General. Perhaps because Mr. Ashcroft had supported efforts

to curtail assisted suicide while serving as a [Missouri] Senator, Oregon Attorney General Hardy Myers wrote him to request a meeting with Department of Justice officials should the Department decide to revisit the application of the CSA to assisted suicide. [Oregon's] Attorney General Myers received a reply letter from one of Attorney General Ashcroft's advisers writing on his behalf, which stated "I am aware of no pending legislation in Congress that would prompt a review of the Department's interpretation of the CSA as it relates to physician-assisted suicide. Should such a review be commenced in the future, we would be happy to include your views in that review." Letter from Lori Sharpe (Apr. 17, 2001), id., at 58a.

On November 9, 2001, without consulting Oregon or apparently anyone outside his Department, the Attorney General issued an Interpretive Rule announcing his intent to restrict the use of controlled substances for physician-assisted suicide. Incorporating the legal analysis of a memorandum he had solicited from his Office of Legal Counsel, the Attorney General ruled "assisting suicide is not a 'legitimate medical purpose' within the meaning of 21 CFR 1306.04 (2001), and that prescribing, dispensing, or administering federally controlled substances to assist suicide violates the Controlled Substances Act." There is little dispute that the Interpretive Rule would substantially disrupt the ODWDA regime. In response the State of Oregon, joined by a physician, a pharmacist, and some terminally ill patients, all from Oregon, challenged the Interpretive Rule in federal court.

Executive actors often must interpret the enactments Congress has charged them with enforcing and implementing. The parties before us are in sharp disagreement both as to the degree of deference we must accord the Interpretive Rule's substantive conclusions and whether the Rule is authorized by the statutory text at all. The Attorney General has rulemaking power to fulfill his duties under the CSA. The specific respects in which he is authorized to make rules, however, instruct us that he is not authorized to make a rule declaring illegitimate a medical standard for care and treatment of patients that is specifically authorized under state law. The starting point for this inquiry is, of course, the language of the delegation

(continued)

BOX 1.2

(continued)

provision itself. In many cases authority is clear because the statute gives an agency broad power to enforce all provisions of the statute.[16] The CSA does not grant the Attorney General this broad authority to promulgate rules. He must instead share it with, and in some respects defer to, the Secretary [of Health and Human Services], whose functions are likewise delineated and confined by the statute. The CSA allocates decisionmaking powers among statutory actors so that medical judgments, if they are to be decided at the federal level and for the limited objects of the statute, are placed in the hands of the Secretary. All decisions of a medical nature are to be made by the Secretary. Law enforcement decisions respecting the security of stocks of narcotics drugs and the maintenance of records on such drugs are to be made by the Attorney General. The structure of the

CSA, then, conveys unwillingness to cede [give] medical judgments to an Executive official who lacks medical expertise. . . .

CONCLUSION

The Government, in the end, maintains that the prescription requirement delegates to a single Executive officer the power to effect a radical shift of authority from the States to the Federal Government to define general standards of medical practice in every locality. The text and structure of the CSA show that Congress did not have this far-reaching intent to alter the federal–state balance and the congressional role in maintaining it. The judgment [preventing the implementation of the Ashcroft directive is affirmed].

The *Oregon* decision was a surprise to legal pundits after the high Court's opinion in *Gonzales* v. *Raich*. Legal scholars believed that the Court would find in favor of the federal government regulating Oregon drugs using similar Commerce Clause reasoning to regulate medical marijuana in California, because controlled substances used for suicide travel in interstate commerce to get to Oregon. The Court's primary focus in *Oregon* v. *Gonzales* was the deference [respect, in the sense of allowing another to take the lead] the legislative and judicial branches give the executive as established by its prior precedents. The Ashcroft Directive, the Court concluded, was an illegitimate exercise of executive power because Congress's enactment of federal drug laws never gave the U.S. Attorney General the "extraordinary authority" to criminalize doctors' actions whenever the physicians "engage in conduct he [Ashcroft] deems illegitimate . . . The text and structure of the [Controlled Substances Act] show that Congress did not have this far-reaching intent to alter the federal-state balance." Therefore, the Court concluded Oregon owed no deference to the Ashcroft Directive's presumptive federal supremacy: Controlling and criminalizing medical practice including the dispensation of Schedule II drugs controlled by the federal government is an issue within the exclusive control of the state.

---

[16]"*See, for example, National Cable & Telecommunications Assn.* v. *Brand X Internet Services*, 545 U.S. — —, (2005) (slip op., at 8) (explaining that a Federal Communications Commission regulation received [executive branch] deference because "Congress has delegated to the Commission the authority to . . . 'prescribe such rules and regulations as may be necessary in the public interest to carry out the provisions' of the Act" (quoting 47 U.S.C. §201(b)); *Household Credit Services, Inc.* v. *Pfennig*, 541 U.S. 232 (2004) (giving [executive branch] deference to a Federal Reserve Board regulation where "Congress has expressly delegated to the Board the authority to prescribe regulations as, in the judgment of the Board, 'are necessary or proper to effectuate the purposes of'" the statute (quoting 15 U.S.C. §1604(a))."

IV. DUE PROCESS

Rule of Law: **The Due Process and Equal Protection Clauses protect citizens in the criminal law arena.**

Both the Fifth and the Fourteenth Amendments contain Due Process Clauses that are identical in language. The primary difference is that the 14th Amendment was ratified after the Civil War and deemed to give newly freed slaves the same rights as citizens. **Due Process** protects citizens from the government depriving them "of life, liberty, or property, without due process of law." The law generally recognizes two types of due process: procedural and substantive.

1. Procedural Due Process

Procedural due process protects life and property by giving citizens advance warning that it intends to interrupt life in some way, called notice, and gives citizens their day in court to protest the government's actions, called an opportunity to be heard. Such protection is granted by the Fifth Amendment's Due Process Clause. An example is if the government plans to charge you with a crime, officials prepare a document that charges you with the crime (notice) and give you a fair trial to present your defense (opportunity to be heard).[17] Procedural due process protections also extend to the following criminal procedure issues: executing search warrants; challenging the legality of an arrest; and challenging the imposition of a death sentence. One of the primary areas of potential government abuse that procedural due process is designed to prevent is in asset forfeiture. **Asset forfeiture** is the taking of property, money, cars, stocks, and bonds that can be traced to criminal activity. The Executive Branch runs the country's asset forfeiture program through the Departments of Justice and Treasury. Criminal forfeiture can be brought as an ancillary action during a criminal prosecution of the defendant or can be brought against the property itself in a civil action, called an *in rem* action, where the case caption would read the United States directly against the property involved, such as *United States* v. *$136,000*.

The extent of the Government's financial stake in drug forfeiture is apparent from a 1990 memo, in which the Attorney General urged United States Attorneys, federal prosecutors at the trial level, to increase the volume of forfeitures in order to meet the Department of Justice's annual budget target: "We must significantly increase production to reach our budget target. . . . Failure to achieve the $470 million projection would expose the Department's forfeiture program to criticism and undermine confidence in our budget projections. Every effort must be made to increase forfeiture income during the remaining three months of [fiscal year] 1990."[18] Many state and local law enforcement agencies benefit from forfeiture actions as well. They have a vested interest in seizing people's property and turning it over the federal government for processing because many state criminal proceedings do not allow for the broad sweep of authority enjoyed by the federal government. By operation of 28 U.S.C. §524(c), the law allows money gained through federal forfeiture actions to be shared based on the local agency's degree of participation in the seizure that resulted in a successful forfeiture. Monies from the forfeiture fund can be used for related training, supplies, travel, investigative expenses, computer equipment, and a general catchall expense fund for "joint law enforcement operations." Many small police agencies can buy new computers, the latest in law enforcement technology; travel across the country to attend forfeiture trainings; and pay informants, all based on their slice of the forfeiture pie that they bring to the federal government.

---

[17]*In re Nelson,* 437 P.2d 1008 (1968).

[18]Executive Office for United States Attorneys, U.S. Department of Justice, 38 United States Attorney's Bulletin 180 (1990).

There is also administrative forfeiture for which no court involvement is needed to seize contraband [anything obviously illegal to possess], any conveyance used to import or transport controlled substances, any monetary instrument, and property that does not exceed $500,000 in value. Once property is seized and sold, and third-party interests are settled, paying off a loan from a car dealership on a car used in drug transactions for instance, the remaining proceeds are deposited into the United States general treasury fund.[19] Forfeiture is big business for the federal government. The case *United States* v. *James Daniel Good Real Property,* 510 U.S. 43 (1993) established the principle that procedural due process demands that the owner of seized property be given notice and an opportunity to be heard to litigate his property interests before the government seizes and sells personal property in a forfeiture action. There, the high Court said the following about a defendant's procedural due process rights to private property that the government takes as a result of the defendant's criminal activity:

> Our cases establish that government action of this consequence must comply with the Due Process Clauses of the Fifth and Fourteenth Amendments. The right to prior notice and a hearing is central to the Constitution's command of due process. "The purpose of this requirement is not only to ensure abstract fair play to the individual. Its purpose, more particularly, is to protect his use and possession of property from arbitrary encroachment—to minimize substantively unfair or mistaken deprivations of property. . . ."

2. Substantive Due Process

Substantive due process protects from government interference the fundamental rights and liberties we enjoy in deciding how to live our lives. Let's say, for example, a young married couple wants to wait to start a family. The couple visits a doctor's office to receive a prescription for birth control pills. The doctor regrets to inform the couple that because the state has an interest in a robust and heavily populated state because more taxpayers equals more revenue, state law prohibits the sale of contraceptives. Can the government interfere in the decisions that affect the couple's personal decisions relating to marriage, procreation, contraception, family relationships, child rearing, and choices in child education, and, if so, does the couple have any protection from such government interference?

The Supreme Court has stated that "matters, involving the most intimate and personal choices a person may make in a lifetime, choices central to personal dignity and autonomy, are central to the liberty protected by the Fourteenth Amendment. At the heart of liberty is the right to define one's own concept of existence, of meaning, of the universe, and of the mystery of human life. Beliefs about these matters could not define the attributes of personhood were they formed under compulsion of the State." *Planned Parenthood of Southeastern Pa.* v. *Casey*, 505 U.S. 833 (1992). If the right is deemed an individual's fundamental right, that right then enjoys protection from interference by the government under substantive due process protections.

The Court uses a two-part test to determine if a personal right at stake is worthy of protection by substantive due process. First, the interest must be considered fundamental and "deeply rooted in this Nation's history and tradition" and "implicit in the concept of ordered liberty, such that neither liberty nor justice would exist if [it] were sacrificed." Second, the Court requires a "careful description" of the asserted liberty interest. Such a description found, for instance, that there is no right to commit suicide and, therefore, no Fourteenth Amendment due process protection to engage a physician to help commit suicide. *Washington* v. *Glucksberg,* 521 U.S. 702 (1997).

---

[19]Authority to start an administrative forfeiture action is found in the Tariff Act of 1930, 19 U.S.C. §1607.

FIGURE 1.2   Venn diagram of competing interests.

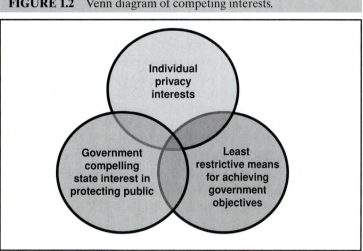

It helps to conceptualize the significance of the liberty interest involved with the rights of the individual on one side of the legal equation overlapping with the "demands of an organized society" on the other side. The government is required to use the least intrusive means on people's liberty to effectuate the state's interest, as represented by Figure 1.2.

The Court will examine whether there is a **rational relationship** between the government's stated purpose in enacting the law and its concomitant intrusion on individual liberty. If the individual rights have traditional roots in our jurisprudence and are fundamental to the intimate personal decisions we make, then the Fourteenth Amendment's Due Process Clause protects those rights from laws that restrict or criminalize such behavior. For example, as late as the 1960s many states had antimiscegenation statutes that made it a crime for whites and African-Americans to marry each other. The first antimiscegenation statute was passed in Maryland in 1661 and at one time or another 41 states had similar laws. In 1958, Richard Loving, who is white, and his wife Mildred who is African-American, were arrested in Virginia for getting married. The state judge agreed to suspend their jail sentence if they agreed to move out of the state. The judge told the Loving couple that God "created the races white, black, yellow and red, and he placed them on separate continents. And but for the interference with his arrangement there would be no cause for such marriages. The fact that he separated the races shows that he did not intend for the races to mix." The judge failed to mention that the only ones punished for "race mixing" through marriage were African-American and white Virginians, not Asian and white or Asian and African-American citizens.

When the U.S. Supreme Court decided the Lovings' case in 1967, they flatly rejected Virginia's argument that the law preventing interracial marriage had a rational relationship to maintaining the "integrity of the white race." *Loving* v. *Virginia,* 388 U.S. 1 (1967). In holding the law unconstitutional, the Court declared

> Marriage is one of the 'basic civil rights of man,' fundamental to our very existence and survival. To deny this fundamental freedom on so unsupportable a basis as racial classifications embodied in these statutes, classifications so directly subversive to the principle of equality at the heart of the Fourteenth Amendment, is surely to deprive all the State's citizens of liberty without due process of law.

The high Court found the right to marry a partner of choice to be a liberty interest protected by substantive due process. By operation of the Supremacy Clause, the *Loving* decision that marriage is a fundamental liberty interest protected by substantive due process, became the law of the land. Even though the *Loving* case dealt with the marriage between an African-American woman and a white man, the Court's decision affects all marriages. Once the Supreme Court interprets the Constitution, it is the final word. If, after the *Loving* decision, the state of Illinois wanted to outlaw marriage between people in wheelchairs and those who can walk, or outlaw the marriage of two mentally retarded individuals, the law would be illegal because the Supreme Court has already interpreted the Constitution's Fourteenth Amendment to allow consenting adults the freedom to marry.

The *Loving* decision was cited prominently by the Commonwealth of Massachusetts in recognizing the right of marriage for the state's same-sex couples in *Goodrich* v. *Department of Public Health,* 440 Mass. 309 (2003). In its opinion, the Massachusetts Supreme Court declared that "barring an individual from the protections, benefits, and obligations of civil marriage solely because that person would marry a person of the same sex violates the Massachusetts Constitution." Marriage is a civil contract, not a religious one. Massachusetts chose to grant all of its citizens the civil benefits of marriage. Because the Massachusetts decision deals solely with a state matter, there is no federal issue that would allow the U.S. Supreme Court to hear any appeal on the state's right to recognize gay marriage.

What about state laws that criminalize sexual conduct between consenting adults? Does the Supreme Court recognize the right to engage in certain sexual practices as the same fundamental liberty interests as marriage? In 2003, the Supreme Court declared unconstitutional a Texas law that made sexual conduct between same-sex couples a crime. The decision in *Lawrence* v. *Texas,* 123 S.Ct. 2472 (2003) represented a reversal of prior Supreme Court precedent. In 1986, the Court upheld a Georgia sodomy statute criminalizing homosexual conduct.[20] Nearly twenty years later, the Court found any rational relationship between the law banning homosexual sodomy and maintaining a moral code was outweighed by the individual liberty interests at stake. The Court began its analysis in *Lawrence* that the protection of liberty under due process was broad. "When homosexual conduct is made criminal by the law of the State, that declaration in and of itself is an invitation to subject homosexual persons to discrimination both in the public and in the private spheres," and such stigma was ruled to be immense and unjust for consenting adults engaging in sexual relations. Justice Kennedy concluded that same-sex couples' "right to liberty under the Due Process Clause gives them the full right to engage in their conduct without intervention of the government. It is a promise of the Constitution that there is a realm of personal liberty which the government may not enter." The Court deemed the individual autonomy rights of consenting adults to engage in the sexual practices of their choice was a fundamental liberty interest deserving of constitutional protection.

Rule of Law: There is no explicit right to privacy in the Constitution; the U.S. Supreme Court has interpreted the Constitution to presume one exists.

a. Privacy Rights and Abortion

Prior to 1973, the only jurisdictions in which a woman could obtain an abortion legally were Washington, D.C., Hawaii, Alaska, and New York. In 1973, the Supreme Court legalized abortion everywhere in the landmark decision *Roe* v. *Wade.* Abortion remains a contentious political issue and many people either hope or fear that the Supreme Court will overturn *Roe* and recriminalize abortion. The recognition of a woman's right

---

[20]*Bowers* v. *Hardwick,* 478 U.S. 186 (1986).

to terminate her pregnancy in its early stages was based, in part, in the Court recognition that

> The mother who carries a child to full term is subject to anxieties, to physical constraints, to pain that only she must bear. . . . Her suffering is too intimate and personal for the State to insist, without more, upon its own vision of the woman's role, however dominant that vision has been in the course of our history. . . .

The basic tenets of the *Roe* decision are as follows:

1. until the fetus is viable, a woman has an unrestricted right to terminate her pregnancy
2. once the fetus is viable, the state (government) has an interest in the life of the fetus and may impose certain restrictions on abortion, but may not outlaw it; and
3. under no circumstances can a state law prevent an abortion when the health and welfare of the mother is at stake.

BOX 1.3

Roe v. *Wade,* 93 S.Ct. 705 (1973)
United States Supreme Court

Justice Blackmun delivered the opinion of the Court.

FACTS

Jane Roe (the name is a pseudonym), a single woman who was residing in Dallas County, Texas, instituted this federal action in March 1970 against the District Attorney of the county [Henry Wade]. She sought a declaratory judgment that the Texas criminal abortion statutes were unconstitutional on their face, and an injunction restraining the defendant from enforcing the statutes.

Roe alleged that she was unmarried and pregnant; that she wished to terminate her pregnancy by an abortion "performed by a competent, licensed physician, under safe, clinical conditions"; that she was unable to get a "legal" abortion in Texas because her life did not appear to be threatened by the continuation of her pregnancy; and that she could not afford to travel to another jurisdiction in order to secure a legal abortion under safe conditions. She claimed that the Texas statutes were unconstitutionally vague and that they abridged her right of personal privacy, protected by the First, Fourth, Fifth, Ninth, and Fourteenth Amendments. By an amendment to her complaint Roe purported to sue "on behalf of herself and all other women" similarly situated.

ISSUE

Are Texas's criminal abortion laws unconstitutional?

HOLDING

Yes. The Texas abortion statutes prohibiting abortions at any stage of pregnancy except to save the life of the mother are unconstitutional; that prior to approximately the end of the first trimester the abortion decision and its effectuation must be left to the medical judgment of the pregnant woman's attending physician, subsequent to approximately the end of the first trimester the state may regulate abortion procedure in ways reasonably related to maternal health, and at the stage subsequent to viability the state may regulate and even proscribe abortion except where necessary in appropriate medical judgment for preservation of life or health of mother.

RATIONALE

We forthwith acknowledge our awareness of the sensitive and emotional nature of the abortion controversy, of the vigorous opposing views, even among physicians, and of the deep and seemingly absolute convictions that the subject inspires. One's philosophy, one's experiences, one's exposure to the raw edges of human existence, one's religious training, one's attitudes toward life and family and their values, and the moral standards one establishes and seeks to observe, are all likely to influence and to color one's thinking and conclusions about abortion.

(continued)

BOX 1.3

(continued)

In addition, population growth, pollution, poverty, and racial overtones tend to complicate and not to simplify the problem. Our task, of course, is to resolve the issue by constitutional measurement, free of emotion and of predilection. "[The Constitution] is made for people of fundamentally differing views, and the accident of our finding certain opinions natural and familiar, or novel, and even shocking, ought not to conclude our judgment upon the question whether statutes embodying them conflict with the Constitution of the United States."

The principal thrust of appellant's attack on the Texas statutes is that they improperly invade a right, said to be possessed by the pregnant woman, to choose to terminate her pregnancy. Appellant would discover this right in the concept of personal "liberty" embodied in the Fourteenth Amendment's Due Process Clause; or in personal, marital, familial, and sexual privacy said to be protected by the Bill of Rights or its penumbras, or among those rights reserved to the people by the Ninth Amendment.

The Constitution does not explicitly mention any right of privacy. In a line of decisions, however, going back as far as *Union Pacific R. Co.* v. *Botsford*, 141 U.S. 250 (1891), the Court has recognized that a right of personal privacy, or a guarantee of certain areas or zones of privacy, does exist under our Constitution. In varying contexts, the Court or individual Justices have, indeed, found at least the roots of that right in the First Amendment . . . in the Fourth and Fifth Amendments . . . in the penumbras of the Bill of Rights . . . in the Ninth Amendment or in the concept of liberty guaranteed by the first section of the Fourteenth Amendment. These decisions make it clear that only personal rights that can be deemed "fundamental" or "implicit in the concept of ordered liberty" are included in this guarantee of personal privacy. They also make it clear that the right has some extension to activities relating to marriage, procreation, contraception, family relationships, and child rearing and education. [citations omitted]

This right of privacy, whether it be founded in the Fourteenth Amendment's concept of personal liberty and restrictions upon state action, as we feel it is, or, as the District Court determined, in the Ninth Amendment's reservation of rights to the people, is broad enough to encompass a woman's decision whether or not to terminate her pregnancy. The detriment that the State would impose upon the pregnant woman by denying this choice altogether is apparent. Specific and direct harm medically diagnosable even in early pregnancy may be involved. Maternity, or additional offspring, may force upon the woman a distressful life and future. Psychological harm may be imminent. Mental and physical health may be taxed by child care. There is also the distress, for all concerned, associated with the unwanted child, and there is the problem of bringing a child into a family already unable, psychologically and otherwise, to care for it. In other cases, as in this one, the additional difficulties and continuing stigma of unwed motherhood may be involved. All these are factors the woman and her responsible physician necessarily will consider in consultation. . . .

With respect to the State's important and legitimate interest in potential life, the "compelling" point is at viability. This is so because the fetus then presumably has the capacity of meaningful life outside the mother's womb. State regulation protective of fetal life after viability thus both has logical and biological justifications. If the State is interested in protecting fetal viability, it may go so far as to proscribe abortion during that period, except when it is necessary to preserve the life or health of the mother. Measured against these standards, [the law] in restricting legal abortions to those "procured or attempted by medical advice for the purpose of saving the life of the mother," sweeps too broadly. The statute limits to a single reason, "saving" the mother's life, the legal justification for the procedure. The statute, therefore, cannot survive the constitutional attack made upon it here. . . .

CONCLUSION

We, therefore, conclude that the right of personal privacy includes the abortion decision, but that this right is not unqualified and must be considered against important state interests in regulation.

b. The Return of Abortion to the Criminal Codes

In *Roe* v. *Wade* the U.S. Supreme Court interpreted various provisions in the Bill of Rights and created a penumbra under which a zone of privacy existed for individuals. If an individual has certain rights, federal or state law cannot make such behavior falling under those rights criminal. In November 2003, President George W. Bush signed into law the Partial-Birth Abortion Ban Act, making it a crime to procure or give one.[21] The Supreme Court previously ruled that a similar ban on the so-called partial-birth abortion was illegal in *Stenberg* v. *Carhart,* 530 U.S. 914 (2000). The primary difference between 90% of the abortions performed across the country, which take place on an outpatient basis during the first trimester of pregnancy, and partial-birth abortion was the advanced development of the fetus in the latter case and the need to partially extract the fetal body before the pregnancy could be terminated. Under the holding of *Roe* v. *Wade,* all abortion laws must have an exception allowing abortion if carrying the baby to term would endanger the mother's life, called the "health-of-the-mother-exception" and the primary flaw in the federal partial-birth abortion ban was that it had no such exception. But in *Gonzales* v. *Carhart,* 127 S.Ct. 1610 (2007), the U.S. Supreme Court upheld the federal law as legal despite its lack of the exception that *Roe* v. *Wade* said was required. In overturning its previous decisions regarding abortion, the high Court shifted its focus from the health of the mother due to an unwanted pregnancy to the risks and consequences to her and her fetus if after consultation with her doctor she decided to terminate her pregnancy. Hours after the U.S. Supreme Court issued the 2007 *Carhart* decision, Alabama legislators introduced House Bill 1 making all abortions in the state illegal.[22] The language of the proposed Alabama law states:

> (c) The practice of abortion is contrary to the health and well-being of the citizens of this state and to the state itself and is illegal in this state in all instances.
> (d) Any person performing an abortion in this state shall be guilty of a felony and, upon conviction, shall be punished as provided in subsection (d) of Code Section 16-5-1. The license of any physician indicted for an alleged violation of this Code section shall be suspended until resolution of the matter. The license of any physician convicted of a violation of this Code section shall be permanently revoked. The provisions of this Code section shall be in addition to any other provisions relating to the killing of a fetus or any other person.

The following table summarizes relevant U.S. Supreme Court rulings on abortion:

Case	Citation	Vote	Holding
Roe v. *Wade*	93 S.Ct. 705 (1973)	7-2	The Constitution has a penumbra of privacy and a woman can legally terminate her pregnancy.
Planned Parenthood v. *Casey*	505 U.S. 833 (1992)	5-4	Laws designed to limit abortion rights may not pose an undue burden on a woman's right to terminate her pregnancy.
Stenberg v. *Carhart*	530 U.S. 914 (2000)	5-4	Nebraska law had no "health and safety of the mother" exception that might make illegal late-term abortion procedures; therefore, the law was unconstitutional.
Ayotte v. *Planned Parenthood*	546 U.S. 320 (2006)	9-0	New Hampshire law requiring the state to notify the parents of minors seeking abortions without "health of the mother" exception was unconstitutional.
Gonzales v. *Carhart*	127 S.Ct. 1610 (2007)	5-4	Congress can make late-term abortion procedures illegal even without a "health and welfare of the mother" exception.

---

[21]Bill No. HR760 (2003, Nov. 5).

[22]Kirk Johnson. "New Push Likely for Restrictions over Abortions." *The New York Times,* April 20, 2007, p. A1.

3. Equal Protection

Equal protection stands for equal treatment under the law. In the interracial marriage context, African-Americans and whites who chose to marry one another were being treated differently under the law than white couples or African-American couples, a practice deemed to violate equal protection and unconstitutional in *Loving* v. *Virginia* (1967). To burden a citizen with criminal penalties for an action, such as marriage, that other same-color couples were doing freely was fundamentally unfair under an equal protection analysis.

Another example of an equal protection analysis is the Supreme Court's decision on the fate of the 2000 presidential election in the case *Bush* v. *Gore*, 531 U.S. 98 (2000), on the legal grounds that the state Supreme Court of Florida violated then-Governor George W. Bush's equal protection rights when it ordered a manual recount of the state's votes. The 2000 election between Republican Texas Governor George W. Bush and Democrat Vice President Albert Gore, Jr., was hotly contested. Although it appeared that Vice President Gore had won the popular vote, the outcome of the election depended on the electoral college votes from Florida. The contest in Florida was very close (Bush's tally was 2,909,135 to Gore's 2,907,351), and Florida law requires a machine recount of ballots when the margin of victory is less than "one-half of a percent . . . of the votes cast." Bush's margin of victory was then 1,784 votes and after the machine recount, it shrunk to 328. Gore petitioned Florida's Supreme Court to recount ballots in some counties by hand because of reports that some votes for Gore were not counted properly. The Florida high court agreed and as the manual recount was underway, Bush appealed to the U.S. Supreme Court to stop the recount. Bush argued that Florida's lack of guidelines for a manual recount meant that Florida officials were treating him differently from Gore, in violation of the Fourteenth Amendment's Due Process and Equal Protection Clauses. In a 5-4 vote, the Supreme Court agreed with Governor Bush and stopped the recount. Mr. Bush was declared the winner of election 2000 and was sworn in as America's 43rd President in January 2001.

4. Full Faith and Credit

Article Four, Section 1, of the Constitution states that "full faith and credit shall be given in each state to the public acts, records, and judicial proceedings of every other state," and complements the Equal Protection Clause. To give **full faith and credit** to a sister state's laws signifies if people are legally married in Kentucky and they move to Iowa, Iowa should recognize the state law of Kentucky and treat the couple as if they had been married in Iowa. If the wife dies in Iowa, she should be entitled as a widow to all of the legal protections and inheritances, just as she would in Kentucky. Recognizing the validity of sister states' laws ensures that citizens will be treated fairly wherever they are in the country. Such reciprocity does not necessarily extend to criminal laws. If a state does not have the death penalty, Iowa for example, and a defendant from Iowa commits a murder in a death-penalty state such as Arizona, the defendant cannot claim immunity from the death penalty because his home state has no such law. Similarly, if a state has amended its constitution to define marriage as between one man and one woman, it does not have to recognise a same-sex marriage legally performed in Massachusetts.

V. Key Terms and Phrases

- commerce clause
- concurrent jurisdiction
- equal protection
- federalism
- forfeiture
- Fourteenth Amendment

- full faith and credit
- intelligible principle
- judicial review
- necessary and proper clause
- nondelegation doctrine
- rational relationship

- procedural due process
- separation of powers
- substantive due process
- Supremacy Clause
- Tenth Amendment

VI. Summary

1. **The role of federalism in the field of criminal law: Federalism** is the dual sharing of power between the federal and state governments. The **Bill of Rights** is a set of amendments to the Constitution in response to the Anti-Federalists' fears and is designed to protect citizens from government abuses. **Article I** of the Constitution established the Legislative Branch which makes laws, **Article II** established the Executive Branch and entrusts to the President and his cabinet the responsibility for enforcing the laws, and **Article III** established the Supreme Court which granted for itself through the case *Marbury* v. *Madison* the authority of judicial review to invalidate the acts and laws of the other two branches. The three branches of government ensure a **separation of powers** within the government and each branch can check the unrestrained power of the coordinate branches.

2. **How criminal law fits within the balance of power between the three branches of government:** The federal government derives its power only from the Constitution and those powers not delegated to the federal government are left to the states and the people pursuant to the **Tenth Amendment**. Most criminal law is state law but for some crimes, both the federal and state governments have **concurrent** [simultaneous] **jurisdiction**.

3. **The significance of federal jurisdiction to prosecute crimes:** The federal government obtains jurisdiction over state criminal matters by operation of the **Commerce Clause** (Article I, sec. 8, cl. 3). If an illegal activity (1) uses channels of interstate commerce (planes, trains, and automobiles); (2) uses the instrumentalities of interstate commerce (wire transfer, telephones); and (3) "substantially affect[s] interstate commerce," the federal government can criminalize the act. The **Executive Branch's** power over state matters is not absolute, as evidenced by *Gonzales* v. *Oregon*, in which the Supreme Court held that the U.S. Attorney General overstepped his legal authority in deciding the federal government could regulate the drugs used by physicians in the state of Oregon to help their terminally ill patients end their lives.

4. **The nondelegation doctrine:** The **nondelegation doctrine** is a product of the Supreme Court interpreting the Constitution allowing Congress to delegate and give its power to federal agencies in the Executive Branch (the Department of Agriculture, for example), as long as Congress provides the agency with an **intelligible principle** to limit the agency's discretion. Although the Constitution is silent on sharing power, the Supreme Court recognized that Congress cannot be expected to run the country without the Executive Branch filling in the details of its laws with relevant rules and regulations.

5. **The operation of the Supremacy, Necessary and Proper, Equal Protection, and Full Faith and Credit Clauses of the Constitution:** By virtue of the **Supremacy Clause**, Article VI of the Constitution, when the Supreme Court interprets the Constitution it is the final word. **Substantive due process** protects rights that are deemed fundamental to the exercise of life, liberty, and the pursuit of happiness while **procedural due process** refers to the mechanisms by which the government deprives those rights, such as forfeiting property, executing a search warrant, effectuating an arrest, depriving a defendant of liberty via a trial, or even imposing a death sentence through the process of execution. **Abortion** is an area of law that illustrates the tension between the federal and state governments. The Court interpreted the Constitution to grant the right of privacy to a woman deciding to terminate a pregnancy in the case *Roe* v. *Wade*. The 2007 decision in *Gonzales* v. *Carhart* may prompt state legislators to return abortion to the criminal codes where it existed prior to 1973. **Equal protection** is the concept of treating everyone equally under the law and the **Full Faith and Credit Clause** guarantees sister state reciprocity for other states' laws that do not run afoul of the host state's own moral code.

VII. Discussion Questions

1. Who are the members of the Executive Branch, what are their qualifications for the job, and how were they selected? What are the duties and responsibilities of the respective federal agencies, such as the Department of the Interior or the Department of Commerce? How do independent agencies such as the United States Agency for International Development advance American interests at home and abroad?

2. What roles do the Tenth Amendment and concurrent jurisdiction play in the state of Oregon enacting its own Death with Dignity Act regulating the conduct of its physicians with respect to prescribing medicine to the terminally ill to end their lives and the U.S. Constitution's silence on the federal government's power to control state medical practice?

3. Based on the Supreme Court's holding in *Gonzales* v. *Oregon*, may Sam from our opening paragraph rest easy that Doctor John can assist him when the time is ready for Sam to end his life? Or do you see other arguments or legal strategies that the federal government could implement to try to stop Oregon citizens from enjoying the benefit of their own laws? Could

Congress enact a federal law banning all physician-assisted suicide nationwide? Should the personal beliefs of an executive branch agency head dictate national policy over the states?

4. Should the U.S. Supreme Court have intervened in the election of 2000? Explain your answer in terms of the separation of powers doctrine. What type of due process claims were raised in the dispute and how can equal protection protect political candidates?

5. Describe the concept of federalism and whether or not the concept is over- or under-utilized in society today.

6. What is the problem with the federal government criminalizing, by operation of the Commerce Clause, most crimes that were traditionally within the realm of the state police power?

7. Explain the difference between substantive and procedural due process and give an example of each.

8. Describe whether the right-to-die movement, which advocates the widespread practice of physician-assisted suicide, relies on liberty or equal protection arguments to advance the personal interest of a competent adult to choose when to die.

9. Discuss the nondelegation doctrine and how it works within the framework of the separation of powers established by the U.S. Constitution.

10. Do forfeiture actions give law enforcement, including informants, a vested interest in connecting personal or real property (real estate) to criminal activity because of the financial benefits and rewards bestowed upon them?

VIII. Problem-Solving Exercises

Problems 1–7 are based on the following sample case:

Bob and Bill were legally married in Massachusetts in 2005. They moved to Louisiana which had amended its state constitution to define marriage as between "one man and one woman." The Louisiana State Supreme Court upheld this state constitutional amendment as legal. Bob and Bill were both employed by the state's Department of Health and when they tried to list each other as "spouse" for health insurance benefits, they were denied because they were not "legally married." Bob and Bill sued the state in the District Court for the Middle District of Louisiana claiming that, under federal precedent and the Equal Protection Clause that required each state to give "Full Faith and Credit" to its sister jurisdictions' rulings, Louisiana should recognize their Massachusetts marriage as valid. In defense, the U.S. Attorneys office under the U.S. Department of Justice answered that federal law only recognized marriage between "one man and one woman" when Congress enacted the Defense of Marriage Act ("DOMA") in 1996.

You are a clerk to U.S. Supreme Court Clerk Clarence Thomas, who asks you to read this text and brief him on how the Court should decide Bob and Bill's case. Justice Thomas specifically asks you to address the following questions:

1. Does the federal government have jurisdiction?

2. How does the Court's precedent of *Loving* v. *Virginia* affect Bob and Bill's case?

3. How does full faith and credit and the Equal Protection Clauses affect the case?

4. Does the Supremacy Clause mandate the Court's enforcement of DOMA?

5. Can the U.S. Supreme Court overturn the Louisiana Supreme Court's ruling?

6. Can the U.S. Supreme Court define marriage, or is that a right reserved to the states by the Tenth Amendment?

7. Can the Louisiana Supreme Court make illegal the act of homosexual sodomy and put Bob and Bill in jail?

IX. World Wide Web Resources

Internet Legal Research

http://www.lib.uchicago.edu/~llou/mpoctalk.html
http://www.findlaw.com
http://www.firstgov.gov/Topics/Reference_Shelf.shtml#Laws
http://www.law.com
http://www.nolo.com/index.cfm

Washburn University School of Law site with many law-related links

http://www.washlaw.edu

U.S. Supreme Court

http://www.supremecourtus.gov

X. Additional Readings and Notes

Federalism

Akhil Reed Amar. "*In the beginning.*" *America's Constitution: A Biography* (New York: Random House, 2005).

Raoul Berger. *Federalism: The Founder's Design.* Norman, OK: University of Oklahoma (1987).

Herbert J. Storing. *What the Anti-Federalists Were for: The Political Thought of the Opponents of the Constitution* (Chicago: University of Chicago, 1981).

Separation of Powers

Steven M. Pyser. "Recess Appointments to the Federal Judiciary: An Unconstitutional Transformation of Senate Advice and Consent." *University of Pennsylvania Journal of Constitutional Law,* Vol. 8 (2006), pp. 61–114.

Criminal Law and the Supreme Court

Bernard Schwartz. *A History of the Supreme Court* (New York: Oxford University, 1993).

Laurence H. Tribe. *God Save this Honorable Court: How the Choice of Supreme Court Justices Shapes Our History.* (New York: Random House, 1985).

Equal Protection

James Trosino. "American Wedding: Same-Sex Marriage and the Miscegenation Analogy." *Boston University Law Review* Vol. 73 (1993), pp. 93–120.

Abortion

Barbara H. Craig and David M. O'Brien. *Abortion and American Politics* (Chatham, N.J.: Chatham House, 1993).

Rosalind P. Petchesky. *Abortion and Woman's Choice: The State, Sexuality, and Reproductive Freedom* (Boston: Northeastern University, 1990).

Leslie J. Reagan. *When Abortion Was a Crime: Women, Medicine, and Law in the United States, 1867–1973* (Berkeley: University of California, 1998).

CHAPTER
How A Criminal Case Works Through the Courts

2

"I can't imagine anyone being stupid enough to say they went fishing in the Berkeley Bay after having committed a crime there. I mean, not even you Scott."

Jackie Peterson's comment to her son, Scott Peterson, was audio taped on January 26, 2003. In April 2003, the bodies of Peterson's wife Laci and a male fetus, his unborn son Conner, washed up on the shore at Berkeley Bay a few miles from where Scott told police he had been fishing the day his pregnant wife disappeared, December 24, 2002.

CHAPTER OBJECTIVES

Primary Concepts Discussed in This Chapter:

1. Meeting society's goals through criminal law
2. How a case travels through the judicial system
3. The paths to the U.S. Supreme Court

CHAPTER OUTLINE

Feature: The People of the State of California v. Scott Lee Peterson, SC55500A, 2003

I. FROM ARREST TO TRIAL

1. The Purpose of Criminal Law
2. The Role of the Prosecutor
   a. Reliance on the Police Investigation
   b. Prosecutorial Discretion
      i. Prosecutorial Discretion and the Death-Penalty Decision
      Box 2.1 California Penal Code 190.2
   c. Prosecutorial Ethics
3. The Role of the Defense Counsel
   a. Zealous Advocate
4. The Role of the Trial Judge
   a. Neutral and Detached

II. THE ADVERSARY SYSTEM

1. The Arrest and Charging Process
2. Bringing Criminal Charges Against a Suspect
   a. The Grand Jury
   b. Booking
   c. Initial Appearance
   d. Bail Determination
   e. Preliminary Hearing
3. Pretrial Motions
4. Plea Bargaining
   a. Types of Pleas
   b. The Plea Colloquy

III. TRIAL

1. The Presumption of Innocence and the Burden of Proof
2. Opening Statements
3. The Presentation of Evidence
   a. Direct and Circumstantial Evidence
   b. Physical Evidence
      i. Evidence Collection
   c. Testimonial Evidence
      i. Lay Witnesses
      ii. Expert Witnesses
      iii. Scientific Evidence
   d. Demonstrative/Documentary Evidence
   e. Hearsay
4. Closing Arguments
5. Jury Instructions
   a. Charge Conference
   b. Jury Instructions
6. Deliberations
7. Verdict
   a. Verdict Form
8. After Conviction

IV. HOW A CASE GETS TO THE U.S. SUPREME COURT

1. Federal Issue Required

V. Key Terms and Phrases

VI. Summary

VII. Discussion Questions

VIII. Problem-Solving Exercises

IX. World Wide Web Resources

X. Additional Readings and Notes

Feature: *Chapter-Opening Case Study: The People of the State of California* **v.** *Scott Lee Peterson, SC55500A, 2003*

On December 24, 2002, at 5:48 p.m., the Modesto, California, Police Department received a 9-1-1 call from Ron Grantski who reported that his step-daughter Laci Peterson was "missing." Patrol officer Jon Evers was dispatched to Peterson's house at 523 Covena Avenue. Officer Evers met Laci's husband, Scott, who explained that he had returned to the house at 4:30 that afternoon from a day of fishing at the Berkeley Bay located just outside San Francisco, 90 miles away from Modesto. Scott told Evers that when he arrived home, Laci was not there but her car was in the driveway, her purse was hanging inside a closet, and their dog McKenzie was in the back yard with a leash attached. Laci was eight months pregnant. Since Scott and Laci were expected for dinner at Laci's mother's house at 8:00, Scott showered, ate cold pizza, and then called mutual friends to see if anyone had seen Laci. Scott then called

Laci's mother, Sharon Rocha, and reported that Laci was "missing."[1] Ron Grantski next called the police.

Officer Evers asked Scott for permission to search the house. As the first officer on the scene, Evers had to "make sure that no family, no friends, no neighbors would come in and out. We basically froze the residence and called out, you know, investigations."[2] Investigations is the detective branch of the Modesto Police Department. Detective Steve Brocchini received the call and when he arrived at the Petersons' house, he began to ask Scott questions. Scott retold his "gone fishing" story and when Brocchini asked what type of fish Scott was trying to catch, Scott had no answer. Scott took the officers to his business warehouse where he stored his fishing boat. In early December 2002 Scott had bought the boat secondhand and had used it for the first time this Christmas Eve. Scott was then invited to the police station for an interview. He was given his so-called *Miranda* warnings and the interview began at 12:01 on Christmas Day. Shortly after the bodies of Laci and a male fetus identified as her unborn son, whom she and Scott had planned to name Conner, washed up on the shore of Berkeley Bay in April 2003—but before their identities could be confirmed by genetic analysis—Scott was arrested 30 miles from the Mexico border. Scott had dyed his naturally brunette hair blonde, had grown a full beard and moustache, and had in his possession $15000 cash, a number of pieces of identification, including his brother's driver's license, and a bag full of clothes.

In the four months since Laci had disappeared, investigators had learned a lot about Scott: that he had been having an affair with a massage therapist from Fresno, California, named Amber Frey; told Amber he would be free to pursue their relationship more fully in January 2003; paid cash for the boat that he used to fish in the Berkeley Bay, but never registered it or mentioned its purchase to other family members; left two messages on Laci's cell phone while he was fishing on Christmas Eve, even though those close to Laci knew her battery had been dead for a week; traded in Laci's car to buy himself a bigger truck; and made inquiries to a friend in real estate about selling his house fully furnished. The investigation focused quickly on Scott as the one responsible for his wife's disappearance. By the time he was arrested, officers and the Stanislaus County Prosecutor's office had enough evidence to charge and prosecute Scott for murder. In November 2004 Scott was convicted and sentenced to death for the first-degree murder of Laci and the second-degree murder of Conner. He sits in San Quentin prison while appealing his case.

INTRODUCTION

The criminal justice system is dependent upon the ethical and professional behavior of its participants—law enforcement officers who investigate crime, prosecutors who decide what, if any, charges to bring against the accused, the defense counsel who must become a zealous advocate for his or her client despite any personal beliefs or knowledge that the client may be guilty, the judge who must remain neutral and detached from the facts of the case and apply the law in an even-handed manner, the jury that must fairly and impartially decide the facts of a case based only on the evidence presented at trial, the corrections officers who may be entrusted with the care of the convicted person in

---

[1]Preliminary Hearing Testimony of Sharon Rocha (2003, October 31) [Transcript] Stanislaus County Superior Court, California, http://www.scottisinnocent.com/Bibliography/Prelim (accessed on November 26, 2004).

[2]Preliminary Hearing Testimony of Jon Evers (2003, October 31) [Transcript] Stanislaus County Superior Court, California, http://www.scottisinnocent.com/Bibliography/Prelim (accessed on November 26, 2004).

prison for years, and the probation or parole officer who must help the offender reintegrate into society and prevent him from reoffending.

Using Peterson's death-penalty case as a guide, this chapter is designed to familiarize students with the terminology often used in the criminal trial process and will introduce a criminal case and describe the criminal trial process. The student should use the chapter to get a feel for how a criminal case works its way through the court process, which party in the criminal justice system is responsible for each phase of bringing a case to trial, and how the duties of the various participants overlap. The chapter has no excerpted cases; to the extent that the Constitution is implicated in the issues presented here, the cases are presented in chapter 13.

I. FROM ARREST TO TRIAL

1. The Purpose of Criminal Law

Rule of Law: The purpose of criminal law is for an offender to pay back what his crime has taken from society.

As society became more industrialized, public shaming, flogging in the town square, and the death penalty as the sole methods of legal punishment gave way to other penological [punishment] goals, such as incapacitation, deterrence, rehabilitation, and restitution. Prisons were viewed as a more humane solution to corporal punishment and random executions, and they were considered equal-opportunity institutions: all convicted would serve a prison sentence regardless of economic or social class.[3] Incapacitation through **incarceration** by removing the offender from society has been a method of punishment from the public stocks of the early colonial days to the more formalized and rigid structure of modern-day prisons which began in the late 1800s with the building of Eastern State Penitentiary ("Eastern State") in Philadelphia, Pennsylvania. Eastern State was once the largest and most expensive building in America. Designed in 1821 by architect John Haviland, Eastern State was built around the Quaker philosophy that inmates would acquire the discipline they so obviously lacked through solitary confinement, called "separation from other damned souls." Eastern State had seven cellblocks that radiated like spokes of a tire from the central hub of an observatory. Guards could not easily observe inside the cells but constant surveillance was unnecessary. The 250 cells were models of efficiency; each had a toilet, running water and a walled yard outside the cell to permit exercise—all activities conducted without other human contact. A report in 1831 noted that "[n]o prisoner is seen by another, after he enters the wall. When the years of his confinement have passed, his old associates in crime will be scattered over the earth, or in the grave . . . and the prisoner can go forth into a new and industrious life, where his previous deeds are unknown."[4] The practice of solitary incarceration was known as the "Pennsylvania silent system" and became known not for its success at rehabilitating offenders, but for slowly driving the prisoners insane. The last inmate left in 1970 and Eastern State is open today as a tourist attraction.

Incarceration as society's punishment of choice has shaped most modern penal policy. Early prisons that were not modeled after Eastern State were overcrowded, dirty, and dangerous places. Prisoners were poorly supervised and not segregated according to sex, age, or type of offense committed. Guards personally profited by selling liquor and providing prostitutes to inmates.

---

[3]Adam J. Hirsch *The Rise of the Penitentiary* (New Haven, CT: Yale University, 1992).

[4]Mark Perrott. *Hope Abandoned: Eastern State Penitentiary* (The Pennsylvania Prison Society, 1999), p. 11; Harry E. Barnes. *The Evolution of Penology in Pennsylvania: A Study in American Social History.* (Montclair, NJ: Patterson Smith, 1968).

Deterrence is preventing others from committing a crime by imposing a severe sanction on one offender as a warning. Watching an offender receive harsh punishment was meant to deter [prevent] others from committing a crime lest the same pain and public humiliation befall them. **Rehabilitation** means to restore and offer the offender programs in employment, substance abuse treatment, and social skills to reduce the probability that the offender will commit additional crimes and return to prison.[5] Rehabilitation was once a very popular corrections model to work with offenders to help their eventual reintegration back into society. But by the late 1970s and early 1980s with the rise in drug crime and the increase in the number of repeat offenders in what appeared to be the revolving door of justice, society began to view rehabilitation as a waste of resources. Politicians claimed their opponents who were "soft on crime" were responsible for the revolving door, an image that played prominently in the 1988 defeat of Democratic presidential nominee, Massachusetts Governor Michael S. Dukakis. Republican candidate George H. W. Bush's campaign manager Lee Atwater ran a very successful television advertisement titled "weekend passes" showing African-American murderer and rapist Willie Horton and a revolving door. Horton was a Massachusetts prisoner and the state's corrections policy had a weekend furlough program. Horton was on a weekend pass in June 1986 and did not return. In Maryland in April 1987, Horton viciously beat a woman and her boyfriend, then raped the woman. The advertisement linking Dukakis as a chief state executive who favored a revolving door prison policy that encouraged an offender's rehabilitation and reintegration into society dogged Dukakis throughout the campaign. The public was becoming tired of treating criminals well at the expense of good and decent citizens.

Restitution is making the offender pay the victim and/or society back for the harm he caused. Similar to, but different from, the concept of rehabilitation, which focuses on the offender's behavior, restitution focuses on the victim's loss and what the offender can do to make the victim whole again. The theory behind restitution is that the victim and community work together to ensure that the offender addresses the damage done as he rejoins society. Restitution through a court order of paying fines is a typical restorative action.

2. The Role of the Prosecutor

Rule of Law: Law enforcement does not decide what charges to bring; only the prosecutor makes that decision.

a. Reliance on the Police Investigation

The purpose of a **criminal investigation** is to determine who is responsible for committing crime and involves "measuring, photographing, videotaping and sketching the scene, searching for evidence; identifying, collecting, examining and processing physical evidence; questioning victims, witnesses and suspects; and recording all statements and observations in notes."[6] The first officer on the scene, called the **first responder,** must obtain medical attention for any injured victims, then secure the crime scene to preserve evidence that may be introduced to convict an offender at a later trial, and, finally, interview all witnesses to learn what they saw or heard. Preserving evidence in the state in which it was originally found is of paramount importance to ensure its integrity for the state to use in an effort to convict the offender.

An investigator should always ask questions and strategize with colleagues to facilitate and direct the investigation. Crime investigations often involve extraordinary

---

[5]Edward W. Seih. *Community Corrections and Human Dignity*. (Boston, MA: Jones and Bartlett, 2006).

[6]Wayne W. Bennett and Kären M. Hess. *Criminal Investigation*. (Belmont, CA: Wadsworth Thompson, 2001).

manpower resources, especially in high-profile cases. In Scott Peterson's case, 300 officers from 92 jurisdictions worked 10,000 tips that generated 50 hours of audio taped interviews, 1,500 pages of reports and 42,000 pages of documents. Investigators worked for over two years and the county spent millions of dollars bringing Peterson to justice. Investigators realized on the very night of Laci's disappearance that Scott Peterson's fishing story was inconsistent with the crime scene evidence.

One way to ensure that officers perform their duties properly is to restrain their arrest power. Because the arrest power that police officers have over the general public is all encompassing, officers are bound by a strict Code of Ethics in the performance of their duties. As you read an excerpt of the Law Enforcement Code of Ethics, determine what you believe to be the most important job of a law enforcement officer.

LAW ENFORCEMENT CODE OF ETHICS

As a law enforcement Officer my fundamental duty is to serve mankind; to safeguard lives and property; to protect the innocent against deception, the weak against oppression or intimidation, and the peaceful against violence or disorder; and to respect the Constitutional rights of all men to liberty, equality, and justice.

I will keep my private life unsullied as an example to all; maintain courageous calm in the face of danger, scorn or ridicule; develop self-restraint; and be constantly mindful of the welfare of others. In thought and deed in both my personal and professional life, I will be exemplary in obeying the laws of the land and the regulations of my department. Whatever I see or hear of a confidential nature or that is confided to me in my official capacity will be kept ever secret unless revelation is necessary in the performance of my duty.

I will never act officiously or permit personal feelings, prejudice, animosities, or friendships to influence my decisions. With no compromise for crime and with relentless prosecution of criminals, I will enforce the law courteously without fear or favor, malice or ill will, never employing unnecessary force or violence and never accepting gratuities.

I recognize the badge of my office as a symbol of public faith, and I accept it as a public trust to be held so long as I am true to the ethics of the police service. I will constantly strive to achieve those objectives and ideals, dedicating myself before God to my chosen profession . . . law enforcement. (Reprinted with permission)

b. Prosecutorial Discretion

Once law enforcement officers start an investigation and identify possible offenders, they forward their reports to the prosecutor's office for the initiation of formal charges against suspects who may become criminal defendants. A prosecutor represents "the people": the citizens' and society's interests that have been injured by the criminal. In some jurisdictions state prosecutors may be called District Attorneys. They are usually elected officials, except in Connecticut and New Jersey, where they are appointed. Different from district attorneys who prosecute criminal crimes, Attorneys General generally prosecute civil matters on behalf of a state. In Wyoming, the state Attorney General investigates and prosecutes consumer complaints and environmental crimes while law enforcement matters are controlled by local jurisdictions.

The U.S. Attorney General is the chief law enforcement officer for the country in charge of the U.S. Department of Justice ("DOJ"). The DOJ is an executive branch agency responsible for a wide range of programs including national drug interdiction efforts to running the federal prison system. The head federal prosecutor in a federal district is called the United States Attorney, and his or her subordinates, Assistant United States Attorneys, are under the U.S. Attorney General. Federal prosecutors prosecute federal crimes on behalf of the United States. The way that the federal government obtains jurisdiction to prosecute crime was covered in chapter 1.

The prosecutor makes the **charging decision** and decides what, if any, charges to bring against an offender. She also decides whether to drop charges—a process called *nolle prosequi*—and decides whether to accept a defendant's guilty plea and, in first-degree murder cases in death-penalty jurisdictions, decides whether or not to seek death as a sentence. These activities are called **prosecutorial discretion.**[7] The reasons prosecutors make certain decisions are as unique and varied as each individual person. Prosecutors are human and are not immune from the influences of societal expectations, their constituents' passions and prejudices, and the counsel of their professional colleagues in making decisions about how to treat defendants. Some of the factors that a prosecutor weighs in determining what charges to bring against a suspect are

- The nature and seriousness of the crime
- The specific or general deterrent effect of prosecution
- The suspect's relative responsibility with respect to the crime
- The suspect's criminal history
- The suspect's willingness to cooperate in the investigation or prosecution of others
- If convicted, the consequences to the suspect[8]

Since the prosecutor alone determines which charges to bring and which defendants may offer a guilty plea that can be accepted, the prosecutor has been described "as the single most powerful figure in the administration of criminal justice."[9]

i. Prosecutorial Discretion and the Death-Penalty Decision   In death-penalty states the prosecution decides whether or not to make a first-degree murder case a capital case. Every first-degree murder case could, ostensibly, be a death-penalty case. Death cases are first-degree murder "plus" a special, or aggravating, circumstance. In Scott Peterson's case, the prosecutor decided to seek death because of the special circumstance that Peterson had "committed more than one murder in the first or second degree in this proceeding," "a special circumstance within the meaning of Penal Code Section 190.2(a) (3)." As you read the California death penalty statute reprinted in Box 2.1, ask yourself how easy it would be to seek death as a sentence for any intentional killing. Special circumstance #14, for example, refers to any killing that was "heinous, atrocious or cruel," defined as a "conscienceless or pitiless crime that is unnecessarily torturous to the victim" while special circumstance #18 includes a killing that is torturous to the victim.

c. Prosecutorial Ethics

No one in the criminal justice system reviews the prosecutor's decision whether or not to pursue or drop charges against a suspect, or whether or not to seek the death penalty–except at the federal level where the local federal prosecutors must seek and obtain the U.S. Attorney General's approval to seek the death penalty.[10] The prosecutor is bound to act ethically in all criminal prosecutions to ensure that the defendant receives due process in the form of a fair trial. In order to ensure that the defendant receives a fair trial, the prosecutor must give the defendant any and all evidence in state possession

---

[7]Roscoe Pound. "Discretion, Dispensation and Mitigation: The Problem of the Individual Special Case," *New York University Law Review,* Vol. 35 (1960); Wayne R. LaFave. *Arrest: The Decision to Take a Suspect into Custody.* (Boston: Little, Brown, 1964).

[8]Adapted from the *United States Attorneys' Manual* (Washington, DC: Government Printing Office, April 2004).

[9]Kenneth J. Melilli. "Prosecutorial Discretion in an Adversary System." *B.Y.U. Law Review* (1992), pp. 669–704.

[10]Susan L. Caulfield. "Life or Death Decision: Prosecutorial Power vs. Equality of Justice." *Journal of Contemporary Criminal Justice,* Vol. 5, No. 4 (1994), pp. 233–247.

BOX 2.1

According to California Penal Code 190.2

a. The penalty for a defendant who is found guilty of murder in the first degree is death or imprisonment in the state prison for life without the possibility of parole if one or more of the following **special circumstances** has been found under Section 190.4 to be true:

1. The murder was intentional and carried out for financial gain.

2. The defendant was convicted previously of murder in the first or second degree. For the purpose of this paragraph, an offense committed in another jurisdiction, which if committed in California would be punishable as first or second degree murder, shall be deemed murder in the first or second degree.

3. The defendant, in this proceeding, has been convicted of more than one offense of murder in the first or second degree [Scott Peterson's case.]

4. The murder was committed by means of a destructive device, bomb, or explosive planted, hidden, or concealed in any place, area, dwelling, building, or structure, and the defendant knew, or reasonably should have known, that his or her act or acts would create a great risk of death to one or more human beings.

5. The murder was committed for the purpose of avoiding or preventing a lawful arrest, or perfecting or attempting to perfect, an escape from lawful custody.

6. The murder was committed by means of a destructive device, bomb, or explosive that the defendant mailed or delivered, attempted to mail or deliver, or caused to be mailed or delivered, and the defendant knew, or reasonably should have known, that his or her act or acts would create a great risk of death to one or more human beings.

7. The victim was a peace officer, as defined in [California law] who, while engaged in the course of the performance of his or her duties, was intentionally killed, and the defendant knew, or reasonably should have known, that the victim was a peace officer engaged in the performance of his or her duties; or the victim was a peace officer, as defined in the above-enumerated sections, or a former peace officer under any of those sections, and was intentionally killed in retaliation for the performance of his or her official duties.

8. The victim was a federal law enforcement officer or agent who, while engaged in the course of the performance of his or her duties, was intentionally killed, and the defendant knew, or reasonably should have known, that the victim was a federal law enforcement officer or agent engaged in the performance of his or her duties; or the victim was a federal law enforcement officer or agent, and was intentionally killed in retaliation for the performance of his or her official duties.

9. The victim was a firefighter, as defined [by California law] who, while engaged in the course of the performance of his or her duties, was intentionally killed, and the defendant knew, or reasonably should have known, that the victim was a firefighter engaged in the performance of his or her duties.

10. The victim was a witness to a crime who was intentionally killed for the purpose of preventing his or her testimony in any criminal or juvenile proceeding, and the killing was not committed during the commission or attempted commission, of the crime to which he or she was a witness; or the victim was a witness to a crime and was intentionally killed in retaliation for his or her testimony in any criminal or juvenile proceeding. As used in this paragraph, "juvenile proceeding" means a proceeding brought pursuant to Section 602 or 707 of the Welfare and Institutions Code.

11. The victim was a prosecutor or assistant prosecutor or a former prosecutor or assistant prosecutor of any local or state prosecutor's office in this or any other state or of a federal prosecutor's office, and the murder was intentionally carried out in retaliation for, or to prevent the performance of, the victim's official duties.

12. The victim was a judge or former judge of any court of record in the local, state, or federal system in this or any other state, and the murder was intentionally carried out in retaliation for, or to prevent the performance of, the victim's official duties.

13. The victim was an elected or appointed official or former official of the federal government, or of any local or state government of this or any other state, and the killing was intentionally carried out in retaliation for, or to prevent the performance of, the victim's official duties.

(continued)

BOX 2.1

(continued)

14. The murder was especially heinous, atrocious, or cruel, manifesting exceptional depravity. As used in this section, the phrase "especially heinous, atrocious, or cruel, manifesting exceptional depravity" means a conscienceless or pitiless crime that is unnecessarily torturous to the victim.
15. The defendant intentionally killed the victim by means of lying in wait.
16. The victim was intentionally killed because of his or her race, color, religion, nationality, or country of origin.
17. The murder was committed while the defendant was engaged in, or was an accomplice in, the commission of, attempted commission of, or the immediate flight after committing, or attempting to commit, the following felonies:
    A. Robbery in violation of Section 211 or 212.5.
    B. Kidnapping in violation of Section 207, 209, or 209.5.
    C. Rape in violation of Section 261.
    D. Sodomy in violation of Section 286.
    E. The performance of a lewd or lascivious act upon the person of a child under the age of 14 years in violation of Section 288.
    F. Oral copulation in violation of Section 288a.
    G. Burglary in the first or second degree in violation of Section 460.
    H. Arson in violation of subdivision (b) of Section 451.
    I. Train wrecking in violation of Section 219.
    J. Mayhem in violation of Section 203.
    K. Rape by instrument in violation of Section 289.
    L. Carjacking, as defined in Section 215.
    M. To prove the special circumstances of kidnapping in subparagraph (B), or arson in subparagraph (H), if there is specific intent to kill, it is only required that there be proof of the elements of those felonies. If so established, those two special circumstances are proven even if the felony of kidnapping or arson is committed primarily or solely for the purpose of facilitating the murder.
18. The murder was intentional and involved the infliction of torture.
19. The defendant intentionally killed the victim by the administration of poison.
20. The victim was a juror in any court of record in the local, state, or federal system in this or any other state, and the murder was intentionally carried out in retaliation for, or to prevent the performance of, the victim's official duties.
21. The murder was intentional and perpetrated by means of discharging a firearm from a motor vehicle, intentionally at another person or persons outside the vehicle with the intent to inflict death. For purposes of this paragraph, "motor vehicle" means any vehicle as defined in Section 415 of the Vehicle Code.

---

which the defendant can use to defend himself. The process whereby the state turns over its evidence is called discovery and the evidence that tends to prove a defendant's innocence is called exculpatory evidence, discussed more fully in chapter 13.

In a well-publicized 2007 case, Durham, North Carolina prosecutor Michael B. Nifong was disbarred [no longer allowed to practice law] from the state bar association because of "egregious" misconduct in bringing rape charges against three lacrosse players from Duke University. Nifong brought the charges against the players even after receiving exculpatory evidence that semen samples collected from the alleged victim matched none of the students. Nifong then made public statements implying that the students were guilty—statements that were in violation of state professional standards prohibiting pretrial comments on the guilt or innocence of the accused.[11] The State Ethics Committee which oversees the professional responsibility for all attorneys licensed in the state found that Nifong had exploited the rape case to further his own political agenda as he was running for reelection during the highly publicized charging process. He was sentenced and served one day in jail.

---

[11]*See generally,* Duff Wilson. "At Ethics Hearing, Duke Prosecutor is Called Unprofessional." *The New York Times,* June 15, 2007, p. A.19

3. The Role of the Defense Counsel

Rule of Law: In order for the advocacy system to work smoothly, all communications between the defense lawyer and client are privileged and confidential.

a. Zealous Advocate

The defense counsel occupies a unique position in the criminal justice system. Despite any beliefs or knowledge that the client might be guilty, the defense lawyer must be a **zealous advocate** and represent his or her client's interests vigorously at all stages of the criminal trial process. The major professional association for all attorneys, the American Bar Association ("ABA"), has promulgated ethical rules found in the Model Rules of Professional Conduct ("Rules") and the Model Code of Professional Responsibility ("Code"). The Rules mandate that a lawyer act "with zeal in advocacy upon the client's behalf,"[12] which means that the attorney "should pursue a matter on behalf of a client ... and may take whatever lawful and ethical measures are required to vindicate a client's cause or endeavor."[13] Anything less than using every legitimate effort to advance the client's interests betrays the legal system.[14] All attorneys are bound by these Rules and Codes, which are often codified by state bar associations as well. Violations of ethical obligations can lead to censure, sanctions, or in severe cases, criminal prosecution. For attorneys to perform their job properly, communication between the attorney and client is confidential. The attorney–client privilege allows the justice system to function at its best when a client has no fear that what he says to his lawyer will be used against him. In addition, client confidentiality ensures that the attorney is truly the client's advocate and not just a tool of the court system.[15] Criminal defense attorneys need not disclose information that will subject their clients to further prosecution.

4. The Role of the Trial Judge

Rule of Law: The judge at trial acts as a referee and is not supposed to take sides or have preconceived conclusions about the guilt or innocence of the criminal defendant.

a. Neutral and Detached

A judge wears many hats within the criminal justice system: He signs search and arrest warrants, makes bail determinations, makes sure that the defendant understands the charges against him, takes the defendant's plea to the charge, appoints counsel if the defendant cannot afford to hire one, hears pretrial motions, usually **motions to suppress** evidence against a defendant at trial, and makes evidentiary rulings during the trial—for example, whether or not certain scientific evidence is admissible. A judge also instructs the jury on the law that applies to the facts of the case. Pretrial motions—those made before trial—are heard in front of the judge only. The reason the judge alone makes decisions on pretrial matters such as what evidence will be admitted or excluded at trial is that those decisions could affect the outcome of the jury's verdict. Sometimes judges can make decisions on pretrial motion matters on the legal briefs alone. Motions and legal briefs are written requests for a judge to make a decision in one party's favor with supporting legal research

---

[12]Megan M. Wallace. "The Ethical Considerations of Defense Strategies When Confronted with Victim-Impact Statement: Give Us Dirty Laundry?!", *T. M. Cooley Law Review,* Vol. 13 (1996), pp. 991–1012, citing Model Rules of Professional Conduct, Rule 1.3 cmt. (1983).

[13]*Ibid*.

[14]*Ibid*. Citing Model Code of Professional Responsibility EC 7-1 n.3 (1980) (citing William J. Rochelle and Harvey O. Payne. "The Struggle for Public Understanding." *Texas Bar Journal,* Vol. 25 (1962), pp. 109–159).

[15]Other similar privileges recognized by state law extend to priest/penitent; doctor/patient; psychotherapist/patient and husband/wife.

that supports the lawyer's position. If one party files a motion, the other usually files a brief in opposition to the motion. If the defense files a motion to suppress certain evidence, the prosecution will file a motion arguing against the judge granting the motion. Sometimes, when a defendant is, for example, claiming that police conducted an illegal search or made an illegal arrest, the judge holds a hearing and takes testimony from witnesses, such as the police officers involved in the search or seizure, and even the defendant himself. The judge then renders a decision on the motion after the evidentiary hearing. If the defendant does testify on his own behalf at a pretrial hearing, his testimony can only be used against him at a later trial if he testifies at his trial.

Another very important job for the judge is to instruct the jury on the law of the case before they retire to decide the case. Jury instructions are different in every case. For instance, in a bar fight where self-defense was an issue in the case and someone died, the judge would read to the jury the legal definition of murder, manslaughter, and self-defense. Before and throughout the trial, the judge is to remain **neutral and detached,** which means the judge is not to take sides during or before trial, nor is the judge to have any personal stake in the outcome of the case, as represented by the statue of justice—a woman wearing a blindfold, with a scale in one hand and a sword in the other.[16] The judge should be "blind" to the issues in the case before hearing the facts and evidence, to avoid favoring one party over the other.

State trial judges are selected by five different methods: governor's appointment, legislative selection, merit selection, nonpartisan election, and partisan election. Some states use a combination of methods. In Pennsylvania, for example, a judge is elected by partisan election, but at the end of his or her term, there is a nonpartisan question on the ballot that asks whether the judge should be retained. In 2005, for the first time in Pennsylvania history, voters failed to retain a judge on the Pennsylvania Supreme Court due to voter outrage over pay raises that state officials passed for themselves and that the judges approved.

II. THE ADVERSARY SYSTEM

Rule of Law: The American judicial system is an adversary system—two sides against each other as the best model to extract the truth.

America's adversary system of justice is designed to get to the truth. Other than the constitutional provisions that protect defendants at trial, there exists no national criminal procedure. Some jurisdictions may bring all serious charges by felony indictment in those states that require it, while other states do not. Some states may require a unanimous verdict for conviction of a criminal offense, while others find a 10-2 verdict sufficient to convict. Preferred methods to conduct a trial may vary from judge to judge within one court system too. Lawyers who regularly practice in front of certain judges are the greatest source of information about how cases are tried in a certain judge's courtroom. There are inherent advantages to the government prosecuting citizens for crimes and corresponding protections for defendants from abuses by the government. The following chart summarizes these powers and protections.[17]

---

[16]Sometimes, judges cross the line of remaining neutral and unbiased. In a domestic violence case, a judge reportedly remarked about the husband's violence, "What's wrong with that? You've got to keep them in line once in a while." The judicial oversight board initiated proceedings to remove the judge because the judge could not be impartial in listening to the victim's testimony if he believed it was okay for a man to slap his wife. ("Court Upholds Removal of Rockland Judge." *The New York Times,* March 31, 1999.)

[17]Adapted from Edith Greene, Kirk Heilbrun, William H. Fortune, and Michael T. Nietzel. *Wrightsman's Psychology and the Legal System* (6th ed.). (Belmont, CA: Thomson Wadsworth, 2007).

Prosecution	Defense
Can create testimony through the offering of plea bargains to codefendants	Can compel the testimony of witnesses through the court's subpoena power
In a death-penalty case, can exclude all jurors who are opposed to the death penalty	Is protected against the state removing jurors based on race or gender
Gets the first and last bite of the apple at trial with opening and closing statements	Defendants need do nothing at trial as the burden of proving guilt rests solely with the government
Can decide who to charge and what charges to bring	Cannot be tried for the same crime twice by the same sovereign [governmental body]

Students should research the state practice and procedure in their respective jurisdictions. The following information details the most common practices in courts across the country.

1. The Arrest and Charging Process

Charges leading to a suspect's arrest or detention are initiated in a number of ways. Officers can arrest suspects on the spot based on probable cause (discussed more fully in chapter 12) that the suspect committed a crime. Sometimes complaints are filed at the station and a bench warrant—signed by a judge—orders the suspect to appear in court at a specific time and place. If the suspect fails to appear and fails to make alternative arrangements to appear, he or she may be subject to arrest when spotted on the street.

2. Bringing Criminal Charges Against a Suspect

There are two types of "charging documents" that transform a suspect into a defendant, an indictment or an information. Unlike a trial jury that determines the defendant's innocence or guilt, a grand jury decides only whether there is enough evidence to bring felony charges by way of returning an **indictment,** a formal charge. An **information,** on the other hand, is a written accusation by a prosecutor. Both charging documents contain the basic facts and allegations sufficient to notify the suspect of the charges. If there is sufficient evidence to hold a defendant in custody awaiting disposition of the charges, the defendant is said to be "bound over" for trial.

a. The Grand Jury

A **grand jury** is a collection of citizens called to hear evidence presented by prosecutors to determine whether there is sufficient evidence to charge someone or a corporate entity with a crime. A federal grand jury hears about possible federal crimes and state grand juries hear about state crimes, but there is no requirement for states to use grand juries to bring criminal charges against suspects.[18] A federal grand jury has anywhere from 16 to 23 members, while the size of the state grand jury depends on the jurisdiction. Pennsylvania Criminal Procedure Rule 222 states, "during its term, the investigating grand jury shall consist of not less than 15 nor more than 23 legally qualified jurors, and the remaining alternates." In Connecticut, the number of grand jurors is from one to three. The potential grand jurors' names are retrieved from lists of voting rolls and driver's licenses. Grand jurors are chosen and sworn by a judge to serve for an

---

[18]*Hurtado* v. *California,* 110 U.S. 516 (1884).

extended period of time to hear evidence and decide whether or not there is sufficient evidence to bring felony charges against a person or a corporation. Federal law[19] and many states require prosecutors to seek an indictment for all crimes punishable by imprisonment for a term exceeding one year or at hard labor. If the prosecutor does not have to bring charges by an indictment, he or she may charge by an "information."

Grand jury proceedings are conducted in secret and only the prosecutor, investigators, grand jurors, and witnesses are allowed inside the grand jury room. Unlike a criminal trial, there is no defense counsel present to ask witnesses questions or otherwise defend the target of the investigation in a grand jury proceeding; there is no judge, either. If a witness brings a lawyer with him to the grand jury, the lawyer must wait outside the room while the witness testifies. The length of time a grand jury convenes may be from one month to one year. A federal grand jury may serve for 18 months, a time limit that can be extended in 6-month increments. A grand jury has subpoena power to force witnesses to come before it and testify, and to bring with them certain evidence the grand jury wants to see and examine. If a majority of the grand jurors believe there is probable cause that a crime has been committed, which means that it is more likely than not that a crime has been committed and a specific person or corporation has committed it, they vote to "return" the indictment. An indictment is returned in open court with no one else present to preserve the anonymity of the grand jurors' identity and the secrecy of their proceedings and the foreperson swears to the judge that the "True Bill" (indictment) is correct.[20] If a majority of grand jurors is not convinced that probable cause exists that a crime has been committed, they return a "No Bill" and no criminal charges are filed.

Witnesses, regardless of whether or not they are targets of the investigation, can invoke their right not to answer questions on the grounds that the answers may lead to criminal charges against them. This practice is commonly known as "pleading the Fifth" by taking the Fifth Amendment's protection not to incriminate oneself. The end result of "pleading the Fifth" is that the grand jurors cannot use any evidence the witness would have provided to make their probable cause determination in deciding whether or not to return an indictment.

b. Booking

After arrest, which is the initiation of the suspect's deprivation of liberty, the suspect is booked. At booking, details of the suspect's name, time of arrest, and charge are entered into the police log. If the suspect is going to be detained in lockup for a period of time, he is searched and his personal belongings inventoried and stored. If the person is detained, he usually has to be brought before a magistrate (who is a judge but who has considerably less power than a judge selected or elected to the bench) for the next step in the process.

c. Initial Appearance

The length of time a suspect may be detained before being brought before a magistrate or judicial officer with the power to adjudicate the legality of the initial detention varies from jurisdiction to jurisdiction, but most states require that the person be brought before a judge at the next available business day or within 72 hours. If the suspect is arrested on Friday night at 10:00 P.M. and held in jail, the first business day will be Monday morning. The U.S. Supreme Court has said it is reasonable to hold someone for 48 hours before determining whether there is sufficient evidence to warrant a probable cause hearing, but any longer than that shifts the burden to the state to explain the

---

[19]Fed. R. Crim. P. 7(a)(1).

[20]Fed. R. Crim. P. 6(f).

reason for the delay.[21] At some initial appearances, the judge must determine whether there is enough probable cause to believe that the suspect is more likely than not the one who committed the crime. Once in front of the magistrate, the suspect is informed of the charges against him, of his rights to remain silent and have counsel appointed if he cannot afford one, and, if the charge is serious, of his right to a jury trial.

∂. Bail Determination

The determination of bail is enunciated in the Eighth Amendment that it not be excessive, but there are certain situations in which the option of bail need not be offered to a suspect. Technically, **bail** is an amount of money or collateral—that is, a house, boat, or something of value, that the court keeps in case the defendant, once released, fails to show up at the next court hearing. The options for the court are to release the defendant on his own recognizance, which means that the court trusts the defendant to show up to court again on his own volition; set certain pretrial release conditions that must be met while the defendant remains outside custody awaiting disposition of the charges by plea or trial (such as drug testing or seeking gainful employment); detain the defendant and permit other judicial procedures to take place such as probation revocation; or detain the defendant until trial. In federal court, federal law[22] lists a series of factors for the judge to consider before making the decision to let the person out on bail—factors that are common in state courts as well:

1. the nature and circumstances of the offense charged
2. the weight of the evidence
3. the history and characteristics of the person, including
   - the defendant's character
   - physical and mental condition
   - family ties
   - employment
   - financial resources
   - length of residence in the community
   - community ties
   - past conduct
   - history of drug or alcohol abuse
   - criminal history
   - record of appearance at prior court appearances
   - whether at the time of the current offense, the defendant was already on some sort of judicial release, and
   - the nature and seriousness of the danger to any person or the community that would be posed by the defendant's release.

If the crime is serious, such as murder, another crime of violence, or a large drug distribution conspiracy, the government may simply move to detain the defendant based on the danger posed to the public by his release or his serious risk of flight. If he's facing a possible death sentence, for example, he may have no incentive to return for a trial. If he's in the country illegally, he may simply return to his country of origin rather than face jail time and certain deportation afterward.

---

[21]In *County of Riverside* v. *McLaughlin*, 500 U.S. 44 (1991), the U.S. Supreme Court held a 48-hour time period between arrest and the first appearance before the magistrate legal in situations where the probable cause determination was held simultaneously with the arraignment.

[22]The Bail Reform Act of 1984, 18 U.S.C. §3142.

A bail bondsman or bonding agent collects a percentage of the bail, which he keeps even if the defendant shows up for court. If the defendant fails to show up—sometimes called "jumping bail"—the bondsman is responsible for the entire amount to the court. One famous bail bondsman, Duane Chapman, whose reality television show "Dog the Bounty Hunter" made him famous, goes after people to catch them for court to get his money back. He caught convicted rapist Andrew Luster, heir to makeup mogul Max Factor, who fled to Mexico in 2003 rather than face charges of drugging women before he raped them and videotaped his crimes. Luster was tried in absentia [without his presence] and sentenced to 124 years in prison. Chapman found Luster in Mexico where bounty hunting is considered a crime and the Mexican government considered Chapman's actions an affront to their national laws. The government charged Chapman with illegal detention, and Chapman was arrested at his home in Hawaii and returned to Mexico, where he posted $300,000 bail, then "jumped bail" himself and returned to the United States.[23] Chapman failed to show up for court in Mexico, and eventually, in 2008, a Mexican court ruled that Chapman could not be extradited [returned] from the United States to face the kidnapping charges, whereupon the case was dropped.

e. Preliminary Hearing

In most cases the preliminary hearing is a rubber stamp validation of the prosecutor's charges. The purpose of the **preliminary hearing** is to test the sufficiency of the charges by introducing evidence that tends to show there is enough probable cause to bind the defendant over for trial. There is no jury present, and it is the judge who determines if there is sufficient probable cause—not proof beyond a reasonable doubt that the defendant is guilty, but merely that there is enough evidence to let the jury determine the truth of the matter. Because witnesses are called forward and sworn to tell the truth, the defense often gets a firsthand glimpse of the strength and quality of the prosecution's case. On the other hand, if the defense counsel has an opportunity to cross-examine these witnesses, which he does, and he chooses not to or is ill-prepared to because the state has not yet complied with its discovery obligations discussed in chapter 13, the defense counsel is ill prepared to conduct a sufficient cross examination. If the witness disappears before trial, the witness's statement may come in as substantive evidence against the accused. It is for this particular purpose that a defendant may waive [give up] the right to a preliminary hearing given that the outcome will usually be that the defendant is bound over for trial anyway. Usually the rules of evidence are relaxed, and hearsay [an out-of-court statement offered for its truth] is admissible. Likewise, the defendant typically does not testify at the hearing because if she chooses to testify at trial, then her previous sworn testimony given at the preliminary hearing can be used against her if her story changes.

3. Pretrial Motions

A **motion** is an application or a petition for a court order to do something to benefit the movant [the one seeking to gain something from the court]. In the law, motions are referred to as "pleadings," "prayers for relief," or requests for a particular "remedy." If a defendant believes that his confession was taken in violation of his constitutional rights, he can file a motion with the court for the "relief," or "remedy," of suppressing, or keeping out, his confession at trial. While there is a list of standard motions lawyers file before, during, and after trial, the type of motion is constrained only by the lawyer's creativity and initiative. Sometimes, counsel can seek a motion suppress—that is, to

---

[23]Lawrence Van Gelder. "Legislators Rally Behind Bounty Hunter." *The New York Times,* October 12, 2006, p. B2.

prevent some specific evidence from being introduced at trial, such as testimony on a drug courier profile or certain privileged statements. All motions contain (1) statements of fact upon which the motion is based and (2) the applicable law that supports the movant's arguments.

Typically a defendant files a **motion to dismiss** all or some of the charges against him because of legal defects in the investigation or charging process. As the case progresses, motions to dismiss can be made because the prosecutor lacks evidence to prove the charges against the defendant. If the defendant has one or more codefendants, he can file a **motions to sever** to ask for separate trials from the codefendants or a motion to sever certain charges on the grounds that consolidating all the charges would prejudice the defendant and prevent him from obtaining a fair trial.

A **motion *in limine*** is a motion made before or during the trial to keep certain evidence from the jury, or to keep the prosecutor from asking a witness certain questions, or to keep the lawyers from arguing certain matters. In a **motion to change venue,** the defendant asks to have his case tried in a place that is outside the district or county where the crime occurred because he fears that he will not get a fair trial due to extensive pretrial publicity about notorious crimes.

4. Plea Bargaining

Rule of Law: Plea bargains occur in 90% of criminal cases and are a necessary and vital tool to keep court dockets [schedules] flowing smoothly.

A **plea bargain** is a mutual exchange between the prosecutor and the defendant for mutual benefit and gain. The state obtains a sure guilty plea from the defendant (which is always in doubt if the defendant elects to go to trial), and the defendant gets a sure sentence, usually for less time because he agreed to plead guilty to lesser charges. In most jurisdictions, the plea bargain is not binding on the court and even though there is an agreed-upon sentence, the court can choose to ignore the agreed-upon sentence and the defendant cannot withdraw his guilty plea if the court refuses to abide by the plea agreement. The plea bargaining process often involves **charge bargaining,** in which the state will reduce charges it could bring against the defendant in exchange for a guilty plea.

a. Types of Pleas

There are many types of **guilty pleas,** pleas in which the defendant admits to all elements of the offense, agrees to waive all constitutional rights that protect him, and agrees to submit to the state's authority to sentence him for the crime. In *North Carolina* v. *Alford,* 400 U.S. 25 (1970), the U.S. Supreme Court upheld the constitutionality of a plea, called an **Alford plea,** before the court. In this type of plea, the defendant pleads guilty and yet denies committing the crime. The legal justification for allowing such a practice, according to the Court in *Alford,* is that "reasons other than the fact that he is guilty may induce a defendant to so plead . . . [and] he must be permitted to judge for himself in this respect." The Court seems to recognize, and many state jurisdictions agree, that defendants sometimes do plead guilty to minimize the chance of receiving a stiffer penalty if they proceed to trial.

A **conditional plea** is taken when the defendant wishes to challenge a judge's ruling on the admissibility of evidence despite her guilty plea. Often, defendants file motions to suppress certain evidence before trial. If the judge rules against them and admits the evidence against the accused, the defendant may plead guilty on the condition that she still be allowed to appeal the judge's ruling on the admissibility of the incriminating evidence. Of course, there is a risk that the defendant will plead guilty and be sentenced to prison, and then the appellate court will rule in the defendant's favor.

The defendant has already been incarcerated and it is small solace that the trial judge was mistaken in admitting the incriminating evidence against her. If the court agrees, the defendant can plead "no contest" or "*nolo contendere,*" called a "*nolo* plea" whereby the defendant admits that the government has enough evidence to convict the defendant at trial, but the defendant does not admit guilt to the charge or the elements of the offense. In most guilty pleas, the judge must establish that the defendant is guilty of the offense, but in a *nolo* plea "the law is clear that the factual basis requirement of [Federal] Rule 11 does not apply to a *nolo* plea," even though the very purpose of that requirement is "to ensure the accuracy of the plea through some evidence that a defendant actually committed the offense."

In a **plea pursuant to a negotiated plea** agreement, the judge does not have to accept either the guilty plea or a negotiated plea agreement, but the government must honor its promises made pursuant to a plea agreement. In the majority of cases, the judge does abide by the plea agreement because not to honor such agreements may encourage other defendants not to bother entering into plea agreements with the government. But legally, even if there is a plea agreement, the judge does not have to honor it and the defendant, legally, cannot withdraw his guilty plea on the basis that the judge did not honor the agreed-to provisions. The judge informs the defendant of all of these items before taking the plea in which for a brief period of time, the defendant is hopelessly naked in terms of what sentence might be imposed. If there is a plea agreement with the government, the government and defendant must honor its terms, but not the court.

Applying the Rule of Law to the Facts: Is it legal to vacate [make void] a plea bargain?

- A juvenile charged with murder agreed to plead guilty and testify against his adult codefendant in exchange for a dismissal of the murder charge and a sentence to a juvenile facility for being an accessory, conditions that were granted. When the state believed the juvenile lied at the trial of his adult codefendant, they moved to vacate [void] the bargained-for sentence and brought back the murder charge.[24] Is this legal?

Yes, when the defendant chose to violate the terms of the agreement, the bargain no longer existed.

b. The Plea Colloquy

In order to take a guilty plea from a defendant, the judge must be satisfied that the defendant, indeed, is guilty of all the elements of the offense as charged and that a jury might find him guilty if he proceeded to trial. This is called a **plea colloquy.** The judge must also ask the defendant in open court if he understands all of the constitutional rights he is waiving [giving up] by pleading guilty. That is, he is giving up his right to remain silent, his right to be represented at trial by a lawyer, a right to have a lawyer help him choose a jury of his peers who would hear and decide his case and who would have to be instructed that he is innocent until proven guilty, and the right to have the prosecution prove him guilty beyond a reasonable doubt. The judge must then ask certain questions, again in open court and on the record with the court reporter taking everything down for transcript purposes, to determine whether the defendant is competent to waive those rights and is willingly, knowingly, and intelligently giving up all of his rights and pleading guilty. The judge will ask the defendant about his educational background, if he is under the influence of any drugs, if anyone is promising him anything in exchange for pleading guilty, and if anyone is forcing him to plead guilty. Of course, the defendant would not be pleading guilty if, in most cases, he were *not* being offered some inducement in the form of a plea bargain to plead guilty in exchange for a reduction of charges or an agreed-upon sentence. The judge must then inform the defendant

---

[24]Adapted facts from *People* v. *Collins*, 53 Cal. Rptr. 2d 367 (1996).

that if there is a plea agreement with the government for a certain specified sentence, the judge is not bound to honor it.

Applying the Rule of Law to the Facts: Can a defendant withdraw a guilty plea?

- In June 2007, a U.S. Senator was arrested in a sex sting in a men's room in a Minneapolis, Minnesota, airport. In August, he pled guilty to disorderly conduct. In September, he filed a motion to withdraw his guilty plea on the grounds that he was confused and did not have sufficient legal counsel. Should the court grant his motion?

No, the guilty plea may not be withdrawn. Given the nature of the plea colloquy and Senator Larry Craig's access to counsel, he voluntarily and knowingly pled guilty.

III. TRIAL

Rule of Law: In criminal law, the trial process is the search for the truth in which the prosecutor represents the people (victim); the defense lawyer represents the defendant; the judge does not take sides, rules on the admissibility of evidence, and imposes sentence; and the jury decides guilt, innocence, and sometimes make a sentence recommendation.

The defendant usually has a choice to go in front of a bench trial with just a judge deciding the case or in front of a jury. The defendant must decide whether to go before a judge who is experienced in criminal matters and may be less horrified by hearing, for example, a child-rape case, or to go before a jury where, in a death-penalty case, for example, it may be difficult for the state to persuade 12 strangers to agree unanimously to sentence the defendant to death.

1. The Presumption of Innocence and the Burden of Proof

At trial, the prosecution maintains the **burden of proof** to convince a jury **beyond a reasonable doubt** that the defendant is guilty of the crime charged. In the case *In re Winship,* 397 U.S. 358 (1970), U.S. Supreme Court Justice Harlan wrote, "I view the requirement of proof beyond reasonable doubt in a criminal case as bottomed on a fundamental value determination of our society that it is far worse to convict an innocent man than to let a guilty man go free." The Court explained that the reasonable doubt standard:

> [P]lays a vital role in the American scheme of criminal procedure. It is a prime instrument for reducing the risk of convictions resulting from factual error. Accordingly, a society that values the good name and freedom of every individual should not condemn a man for commission of a crime when there is reasonable doubt about his guilt . . . It is also important in our free society that every individual going about his ordinary affairs have confidence that his government cannot adjudge him guilty of a criminal offense without convincing a proper fact finder [jury or judge] of his guilt with utmost certainty.

Conversely, a defendant need not prove anything at trial. He may, if he chooses, provide a defense, cross-examine witnesses, or testify on his own behalf, but he need not do anything. At trial, the defendant enjoys a **presumption of innocence**—a presumption that he is innocent until the government proves him guilty. A presumption is an assumption; the law requires that the jury assume that the defendant is innocent until the prosecution overcomes that presumption with evidence that the defendant committed the crime.

2. Opening Statements

Opening statements are brief summaries of what the attorneys expect the evidence to show during the trial. Such statements are not arguments and what the attorneys say during opening statements is actually not evidence. Opening statements give the attorneys an opportunity to tell a story of why the jury should find in their favor and the evidence that will be introduced at trial that will convince the jury that their ultimate conclusion is correct. The prosecutor makes her opening statement first because the government has the burden of proof at trial. The defense counsel can present an opening statement immediately after the government does or wait until the government rests and make an opening statement at that time.

3. The Presentation of Evidence

After opening statements the prosecution calls its witnesses. Witnesses may be the officers who first responded to the crime scene, the family members who last spoke to the victim, or witnesses who came into contact with the defendant and could relate what his demeanor or statements were. When a lawyer calls a witness to the stand, the examination is called direct examination. The questions are open-ended, meaning that there is no suggested answer and the questions are designed to allow the witness to do all of the talking. Most direct examination questions begin with *who, what, where, how, why, when,* and *where?* In direct examination the goal is to let the witness tell the story. After direct examination, the opposing counsel gets an opportunity to conduct cross-examination.

The goal of cross-examination is very different from direct examination and often involves attacking a witness's credibility as one way to reach the truth.[25] In cross-examination, lawyers try to highlight any inconsistencies in the witness' testimony, and to expose any bias the witness may have in testifying. The cross-examination question is a close-ended question, one that suggests the answer and invites the witness to simply answer yes or no. Hypothetically, if Scott Peterson took the witness stand, the following close-ended questions would suggest the answer:

PROSECUTOR: You went fishing?

PETERSON: (Yes).

PROSECUTOR: On Christmas Eve?

PETERSON: (Yes).

PROSECUTOR: In San Francisco Bay?

PETERSON: (Yes).

PROSECUTOR: You launched your boat?

PETERSON: (Yes).

PROSECUTOR: From the pier?

PETERSON: (Yes).

PROSECUTOR: On the beach?

PETERSON: (Yes).

PROSECUTOR: The same beach where your wife and son's bodies were found?

PETERSON: (Yes).

During the trial, each side—the prosecution and the defense—tries to establish the strength of its own case while tearing down the other's case by exposing the other side's weaknesses. The party with the burden of proof—the prosecution—presents its

---

[25]John H. Wigmore. *A Treatise on the System of Evidence in Trials at Common Law 1367, at 1697* (Boston: Little, Brown, 1904).

"case in chief" first, and when it "rests," the defendant presents his case. In short, the order of a trial proceeds as follows:

1. Opening statements, first by prosecutor, then defense
2. Prosecutor presents case in chief by introducing evidence tending to prove defendant guilty
    a. Prosecutor conducts direct examination of witnesses
    b. Defense conducts cross-examination of prosecution's witnesses
    c. Prosecution may conduct additional direct or defense cross-examination as permitted by judge
3. Prosecutor rests
4. Defense presents its case in chief by introducing evidence tending to show that the government has failed to meet its burden of proof
    a. Defense conducts direct examination of witnesses
    b. Prosecution conducts cross-examination of defense witnesses
    c. Defense may conduct additional direct or prosecution cross-examination as permitted by judge
5. Defense rests
6. Prosecutor may offer case in rebuttal, to counter any evidence offered by defense
7. If allowed, defense may answer in surrebuttal
8. Closing arguments, first by prosecutor, then defense, and prosecutor gets final word
9. Charging conference out of presence of jury
10. Jury instructions
11. Jury deliberations
12. Jury renders a verdict

a. Direct and Circumstantial Evidence

Typical jury instructions distinguish between direct and circumstantial evidence as follows: "**Direct evidence** is evidence that directly proves a fact. It is evidence which by itself, if found to be true, establishes that fact. **Circumstantial evidence** is evidence that, if found to be true, proves a fact from which an inference of the existence of another fact may be drawn. A factual inference is a deduction that may logically and reasonably be drawn from one or more facts established by the evidence. It is not necessary that facts be proved by direct evidence. They may be proved also by circumstantial evidence or by a combination of direct and circumstantial evidence. Both direct and circumstantial evidence are acceptable as a means of proof. Neither is entitled to any greater weight than the other."[26]

Direct evidence can come from an eyewitness who was there in the room when the victim was shot, while circumstantial evidence is what convicted Scott Peterson. No one actually saw Peterson kill his wife and place her body in the San Francisco Bay, but all of the other facts—his statement that he was fishing there, a dog that found his wife's scent leading away from Peterson's warehouse in the direction of the Bay, Peterson's unusual behavior in the search for his "missing" wife (for example, not wanting to be seen on camera or seen laughing and smiling at candlelight vigils held in the hopes of her safe return)—led the jury to infer that Peterson had committed murder.

b. Physical Evidence

i. Evidence Collection   Evidence technicians are called to the crime scene to collect and catalogue where evidence was found. A **chain of custody** is a tracking device that "links" the evidence, similar to chain links, from initial discovery to the defendant's trial. To ensure that evidence has not been altered, substituted, or tampered with, the

---

[26]Peter M. Tiersma. "Communicating with Juries: How to Draft More Understandable Instructions." The *Scribes Journal of Legal Writing*, Vol. 10 (2005/2006), pp. 1–52.

chain of custody records every person who has touched the evidence from initial retrieval to trial. A weak link in the chain of custody caused by officer neglect in filling out the form correctly may allow the defense counsel to successfully challenge the authenticity of the evidence at trial. Authenticity means that a piece of evidence is what it purports to be. For example, all cocaine looks alike. How can a prosecutor state with certainty that the bag of cocaine the prosecutor seeks to be introduced against the defendant at trial is the same cocaine that was seized from him? As the Supreme Court of Alabama said, "The chain of custody is composed of 'links.' A 'link' is anyone who handled the item. . . . In order to show a proper chain of custody, the record must show each link and also the following with regard to each link's possession of the item: '(1) the receipt of the item; (2) the ultimate disposition of the item, i.e., transfer, destruction, or retention; and (3) the safeguarding and handling of the item between receipt and disposition.'"[27] A typical chain of custody form is attached to the bag or envelope that contains the actual evidence and includes the following information:

1. Identity of item.
2. Time, date, location, and condition of seized evidence.
3. Signature of officer who seized item.
4. Signature of every other individual who handled the item—for example, the officer at the evidence locker, the officer who retrieved the item for testing at the lab, the technician who tested the item at the crime lab, and the officer who brought the item to trial.
5. Whether any changes were made to the item during testing.

Most evidence bags are secured with tape and initialed by the officer every time the bag is opened. An evidence tag is attached to large items which arc stored at police headquarters. Before trial, a defendant's lawyer will have an opportunity to view all of the evidence, take photographs of the evidence, and in some cases, conduct independent laboratory testing of the item. The chain of custody protocol must be followed, and the custody form must indicate that the bag was opened at the defendant's request. At trial, an officer usually identifies the evidence and the custody chain which may then satisfy the admissibility requirements.

c. Testimonial Evidence

Witnesses at trial testify and give testimonial evidence. There are two types of witnesses at trial: the lay witness, who is a regular person describing the facts and events relating to the trial; and the expert witness, usually one who is hired by either side to give technical or specialized testimony about the matters involved at trial.

i. Lay Witnesses   Federal and state governments have their own rules of evidence that are statutory. The federal government has codified its rules of evidence into the Federal Rules of Evidence ("FRE") passed by Congress, and many states have patterned their rules of evidence after the federal rules, including adopting the federal system's numbering of the rules. For example, FRE 701 defines a "lay witness" and so, too, do most states' rules numbered 701. A **lay witness** is an average person who can testify in court about things he or she knows, such as the speed a car was traveling, whether or not someone was intoxicated, and whether or not someone the lay witness knew very well was mentally competent. Before a witness can testify at trial, the witness must be personally familiar with the subject he or she is talking about. A fisherman may know something about the steak he eats, but would probably be poorly qualified to testify to what a butcher does on a daily basis. Likewise, a person who was not an eyewitness to the crime or who was not present during the crime would be a

---

[27] *Ex Parte Holton,* 590 So.2d 918 (Ala. 1991).

poor witness to testify about what happened during the crime. Before evidence can be considered by the jury, lawyers must follow formalized procedures to get evidence admitted, while the opposing counsel may object to its introduction and try to keep the evidence from the jury. Only the judge decides which evidence is admissible or inadmissible. The jury can decide the case only on the evidence admitted during trial.

ii. Expert Witnesses   In certain trials, the jury needs detailed scientific or technical knowledge to make their decision about guilt or innocence, and the prosecution or defense hires an **expert witness** who is paid to evaluate the case and render an opinion in favor of the side that hires him or her. For example, many lay people may not know or understand the sophisticated accounting procedures of Enron Energy Corporation, procedures that a jury would have to understand before the jury could decide whether corporate officers willfully and knowingly defrauded the company's shareholders by the accounting practices they used. There are two legal standards governing the admissibility of expert testimony. One, still viable in states such as Pennsylvania, is the standard enunciated in *Frye* v. *United States,* 293 F. 1013 (D.C. Cir. 1923), where the admissibility of lie detector results as scientific evidence was too unreliable. The court stated:

> Just when a scientific principle or discovery crosses the line between the experimental and demonstrable stages is difficult to define. Somewhere in this twilight zone the evidential force of the principle must be recognized, and while courts will go a long way in admitting expert testimony deduced from a well-recognized scientific principle or discovery, the thing from which the deduction is made must be sufficiently established to have gained *general acceptance* in the particular field in which it belongs [emphasis added].

The *Frye* standard became known as the "general acceptance" standard: if the science or technique had achieved general acceptance in the relevant scientific community that used it, it would be admissible in court. Federal courts announced a new standard in the case *Daubert* v. *Merrill Dow Pharmaceuticals,* 509 U.S. 579 (1993). In *Daubert,* petitioners were minor children born with serious birth defects who brought a lawsuit alleging that the defects had been caused by the mothers' ingestion of Bendectin, a prescription drug to combat nausea. At trial, the judge excluded the petitioners' scientific evidence because it failed the general acceptance test. On appeal, the U.S. Supreme Court held that the acceptance test was too narrow and enunciated five factors a judge should look at in determining whether expert testimony would be admissible at trial:

1. Has the theory the expert will testify about been tested?
2. Has it been subject to peer review?
3. What is the known rate of error?
4. Do standards and controls to test the theory or instrument exist?
5. Is the theory/instrument generally accepted within the relevant scientific community?

The trial judge, deemed the "gatekeeper," determines whether the expert's proposed testimony sufficiently meets the *Daubert* criteria. In a subsequent case, *Kuhmo Tire Co., Ltd.* v. *Carmichael,* 119 S.Ct. 1167 (1999), the high Court held that the *Daubert* admissibility standard applied to all expert testimony introduced in federal courts, not just "scientific" knowledge.

iii. Scientific Evidence   In Scott Peterson's case, DNA (Deoxyribonucleic acid) analysis was used to identify Laci and Conner Peterson after their bodies washed up from the Berkeley Bay. Officers had retrieved DNA samples from Laci's mother, Sharon Rocha, who shared a common genetic pattern with both Laci and Conner. DNA testing was also an issue when investigators discovered one hair lodged in a pair of pliers found in Peterson's boat. An expert cannot know that a hair found at a crime scene belongs to a specific individual. Experts can testify that the hair found is "similar to" or "consistent with" a suspect's hair, but cannot conclude with 100% scientific accuracy that a hair came from a specific person's body. The prosecution in Peterson's case sought to introduce expert testimony that the hair from the pliers could belong to Laci. The defense objected on the grounds that since the hair had no root, the DNA needed for testing, mitochondrial DNA (mtDNA), was insufficient for analysis. Mitochondria are the parts of the cell that generate energy, and they have DNA that is different from the DNA found in the cell's nucleus. The DNA from the mitochondria is passed only from the mother and is a powerful tool to track one's maternal lineage. Peterson's prosecutors offered expert opinion that although the hair sample lacked nuclear DNA, test results on the hair's mtDNA revealed that 1 in 112 people in the area of Modesto, California, shared a common genetic profile and Laci Peterson (as determined by her mother's DNA samples) was one of those 112 people. The judge allowed the hair to be introduced into evidence on the grounds expressed in *Frye* and followed in California state courts that the new and novel methods of mtDNA testing were generally accepted within the scientific community and were therefore reliable.

d. Demonstrative/Documentary Evidence

Demonstrative/documentary evidence is anything that can help a jury, or a judge in a case where the defendant chooses a bench trial, understand the issues in the case. Where oral testimony may describe a crime scene, a photograph of the crime scene will be much more helpful to the jury and is something they can take back into the deliberation room as they consider the evidence in the case. Common types of demonstrative/documentary evidence introduced at trial are photographs, maps, illustrations, and models that show a particular place or scene.

e. Hearsay

The technical definition of **hearsay** is a written or spoken statement made outside of court and offered in court to prove the truth of the matter in issue. Hearsay is generally excluded from trial because the individual making the out-of-court statement or providing the written document cannot be challenged, which deprives the defendant of his right to confrontation. Allowing hearsay evidence at trial also prevents the jury from examining the demeanor and credibility of the person making the statement because that person is typically not in court. The U.S. Supreme Court has said about hearsay:

> The hearsay rule, which has long been recognized and respected by virtually every State, is based on experience and grounded in the notion that untrustworthy evidence should not be presented to [the court]. Out-of-court statements are traditionally excluded because they lack the conventional indicia of reliability: they are usually not made under oath or other circumstances that impress the speaker with the solemnity of his statements; the declarant's word is not subject to cross examination; and he is not available in order that his demeanor and credibility may be assessed by the jury. *Chambers* v. *Mississippi*, 410 U.S. 284 (1973).

In criminal trials, even if the defendant does not testify, his out-of-court statements may be introduced against him at trial because such admissions are not included in the prohibition against admitting hearsay in court.

Applying the Rule of Law to the Facts: Is hearsay admissible testimony at trial?

- A police officer testified at a defendant's trial that he had received information that there was "a black male, wearing all black clothing, carrying a gun on the 2500 block of North Franklin Street" in Philadelphia. The officer testified that after receiving that information he proceeded to North Franklin Street and arrested the defendant, an African-American male in all black clothing who turned and ran when he saw the police officer. Is the description hearsay?

Yes, the description of the defendant was made out of court and offered for the truth of the matter in issue: that the defendant was dressed in black and had a gun. The testimony should not have been allowed at trial, and the defendant's conviction was overturned.[28]

4. Closing Arguments

After each side has presented its case, the prosecutor and defense counsel each get to make closing arguments to the jury. In a closing argument, the lawyers are summing up the evidence for the jury and arguing that if the evidence is viewed most favorably to their side, the jury should find in their favor. Since the prosecution has the burden of proof, this side is allowed to make its closing argument first, then the defense counsel makes an argument, and then the prosecution gets to address the jury again to rebut any argument made by the defense counsel.

5. Jury Instructions

a. Charge Conference

Before closing arguments, the judge often meets with the lawyers, who submit proposed jury instructions that each side would like the judge to give to the jury. This meeting is called a **charge conference.** If the judge does not give an instruction, the jury cannot consider the charge. For example, in the 1997 case of Louise Woodward, a British nanny tried in Cambridge, Massachusetts, with killing eight-month-old Matthew Eappen by shaking him and causing brain damage, after which his parents ended his life support, defense lawyers refused to submit a manslaughter instruction. Therefore, the only verdict the jury could return was murder or acquittal, and they chose murder. The judge lowered the charge to manslaughter after the verdict based on the evidence at trial (there was no evidence that Woodward intentionally killed the baby) and Woodward returned to England after 289 days in jail.

b. Jury Instructions

After both counsel make closing arguments, the judge instructs the jury on the law to apply to the facts. **Jury instructions** are technical definitions that define the elements of the crimes charged, that give the applicable defenses, if any, and that define burdens of proof and presumptions. A standard jury instruction, for instance in a criminal case where the defendant did not take the stand in his defense, is that the jury can draw no adverse inference from the defendant's invocation of his right to remain silent. Some instructions inform the jury how it can consider certain evidence, perhaps for a limited purpose. Or the instructions tell the jury that its members are allowed to make certain conclusions about evidence—for example, if a witness was testifying because of a promise by the prosecutor for reduced jail time.

The judge in Scott Peterson's case, Judge Alfred Delucchi, had to rule on the admissibility of all evidence during the trial and, at the close of the case, had to give the jury instructions to follow during their **deliberations**—private discussions among jury members with the aim of reaching a verdict. On November 3, 2004, Judge Delucchi instructed the jury that

> If you find the defendant in this case guilty of murder in the first degree, then you must determine if the following special circumstances is true or untrue: That the defendant Scott Peterson committed more than one murder in the first or the second degree in this proceeding. The people have the burden of proving the truth of a special circumstance.

---

[28]*United States* v. *Sallins*, 993 F.3d 344 (3rd Cir. 1993).

If you have a reasonable doubt as to whether a special circumstance is true, you must find it to be not true.

Unless an intent to kill is an element of a special circumstance, if you are satisfied beyond a reasonable doubt that the defendant actually killed a human being, you need not find the defendant intended to kill in order to find a special circumstance to be true. In order to find a special circumstance alleged in this case to be true or untrue, you must agree unanimously. . . . Murder is classified into two degrees. If you should find the defendant guilty of murder, you must determine and state in your verdict whether you find the murder to be of the first or second degree. If you are convinced beyond a reasonable doubt and unanimously agree that the crime of murder has been committed by a defendant, but you unanimously agree that you have a reasonable doubt whether the murder was of the first or second degree, you must give the defendant the benefit of that doubt and return a verdict fixing the murder as of the second degree.

Based on these instructions, the jury found Peterson guilty.

6. Deliberations

After the end of the presentation of evidence and closing arguments by counsel, the jury retires to the deliberation room to render a verdict. During deliberations, all of the jurors, excluding the alternates chosen at the beginning of trial, assess the credibility of witnesses and weigh the evidence admitted at trial to render a verdict. It is the jury's first opportunity to discuss the case. Even if the trial lasted for weeks and the jury was together taking breaks and eating lunch together and, in the case of a sequestered jury, sleeping in the same hotel together, the judge has admonished them not to talk about the facts of the case because all of the evidence has yet to be introduced. The start of deliberations is the first opportunity the jurors have to talk about the evidence, what they thought of the witnesses, and their credibility, digesting the judge's instructions in applying the law to the facts of the case. Deliberations are secret, because society wants to encourage jurors to speak freely and openly. Sometimes jurors have questions and send them out in written form to the bailiff, who passes them on to the judge, who then calls the lawyers in to decide how to answer the jury's questions. Often, the judge will not answer the jury's questions about the law; rather, the judge will ask the jury to reflect on the instructions that he or she read to it. Juries do not receive the often confusing jury instructions in writing and cannot take notes on what the instructions say or mean and are often left to squabble among themselves about what the law means. If deliberations come to a standstill and the jury seems deadlocked—unable to make a decision—then the judge will often give an *Allen*-charge that says keep going until a decision is made.

7. Verdict

In federal and most state jurisdictions, the verdict in a criminal case must be unanimous; that is, all jurors must agree. Some states allow a verdict to be 10-2 in favor of conviction and the U.S. Supreme Court has held that allowing split verdicts is constitutional.

a. Verdict Form

Before the jury retires for deliberations, the Clerk of Court will hand the bailiff the verdict forms which are to be filled out and signed by the jury foreperson. The **verdict form** will reflect the charges and defenses that were the substance of the jury instructions given by the judge. Once the jury begins its deliberations, they typically elect a jury foreperson who will then be tasked with tallying votes on the charges and, when a verdict is reached, fills out the verdict form and signs it as a true conclusion of the jury. A mistake made on the presentation of the charges on the verdict form may be a mistake that results in the defendant being granted a new trial on appeal.

8. After Conviction

Once a defendant has been convicted at trial, the defendant's case moves to appellate courts. There are two types of appellate courts: the intermediate and the court of last resort. This concept is important to remember because the outcome of criminal cases may hinge on whether or not a defendant has "exhausted his remedies" at the appropriate level of appeal. Appellate courts do not relitigate the case. There is not another mini-trial on appeal. The appeals court will receive the court transcript made by the court reporter who took down every word of what happened from jury selection to side-bars—those conversations the counsel has with the judge out of earshot of the jury. The exhibits and evidence that were admitted at trial will also be preserved for review.

A sports analogy works best in describing what an appeals court does. Let's imagine a football game where the quarterback throws a touchdown pass to his receiver in the end zone. There is a rule that both of the receiver's feet have to be inbounds for the catch to count as a touchdown, unless he is pushed out by an opposing player. Let's also imagine that the referee signaled the catch a touchdown and the opposing team decided to challenge the call. If this were a court case, the team that scored the touchdown would be the prosecution and the party challenging the call would be the defense. The referee allowing the touchdown to count—making the ruling on the field—would be the trial judge.

To take our sports analogy one step further, instead of the trial judge reviewing instant replay to see if the receiver's feet were inbounds, there would be an appeal to a higher authority in a booth high in the stadium who would review the call. If the higher-authority reviewing officials were an appeals court, they would not be looking at instant replay to see if the player's feet were inbounds but rather at whether or not the referee made the right call according to the rules book. That is, when a case is appealed, the appeals court is not in a position to totally second-guess the facts introduced at trial—feet inbounds or not; rather, the court is reviewing the situation to see if the judge followed the rules of law concerning the trial procedure. That being said, there are times when appellate courts do look at the sufficiency of the evidence to sustain the charges—the instant replay—but their primary job is reviewing a case to ensure all the rules of law were followed.

IV. HOW A CASE GETS TO THE U.S. SUPREME COURT

Rule of Law: The U.S. Supreme Court chooses what cases it will hear and decide, and all such cases must involve a federal or constitutional issue.

1. Federal Issue Required

The United States has a two-tiered court system called a dual court system. The two courts run parallel to each other like two sets of train tracks that may eventually meet at the same big train station: the U.S. Supreme Court. On one track are the state systems that may vary how a case works through the trial and appellate courts, and on the other train track is the federal system. As shown in Figure 2.1, both state and federal court systems have trial courts where cases are initially heard and appellate courts where the losing party at trial often complains about the outcome at trial. In criminal law, typically the losing party is a convicted criminal defendant.

One thing to note about the dual court system is that both the state and federal courts have some separation between minor and felony cases. For example, many states have trial courts of limited jurisdiction that handle misdemeanor offenses criminally or small claims offenses civilly. In some states, courts of limited jurisdiction are not presided over by a judge or even a trained lawyer. There may be no uniform protocol

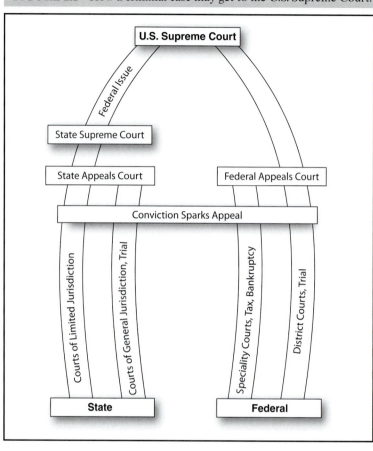

FIGURE 2.1 How a criminal case may get to the U.S. Supreme Court.

or rules of law followed and no court reporter to transcribe the proceedings, and the entire activity may be no more than an opportunity for the community to rake in some extra cash. Local courts are a reflection of the community members that staff them and run off a budget fixed by the local commissions.

Most of the cases discussed in this text are felony cases that were heard by courts of general jurisdiction, or trial courts with more authority than a court of limited jurisdiction. Courts of general jurisdiction can hear all types of cases. Depending on the state, courts may have different titles, and it may be confusing to determine from a court's title what type of authority the court has to hear specific cases. New York State, by way of illustration, refers to its courts of limited jurisdiction as its trial courts of general jurisdiction and refers to its appellate court as the state supreme court.

The appeal travels through the state court system depending on the state's court structure. An example of a two-tiered system is Maryland's: appeals are heard first by the Court of Special Appeals and then the Court of Appeals, commonly known in other jurisdictions as the State Supreme Court. An illustration of a three-tiered system is an appeal from a conviction in New York that travels from the lower appellate courts, to the intermediate appellate division to the highest appeals court, the Court of Appeals.

Appellate courts are typically composed of three to six judges and the U.S. Supreme Court has nine. In the federal circuit, after the initial denial of the motion for a new trial, the appeal travels to the Circuit Court of Appeals for the federal circuit in which the federal trial court sits. Cases appealed from both Nebraska and Arkansas go

FIGURE 2.2   Geographic boundaries of United States Courts of Appeals and United States District Courts.

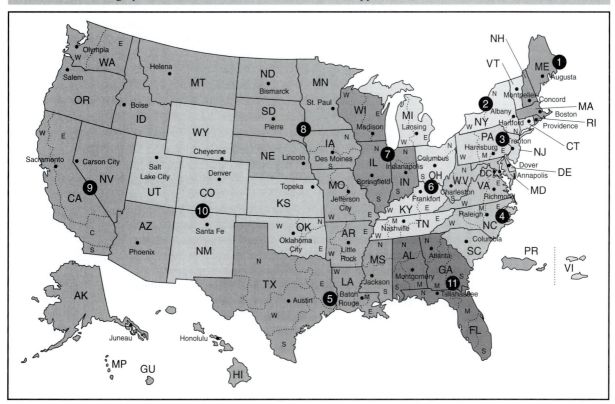

to the Circuit Court of Appeals for the Eighth Circuit. See Figure 2.2 for the state juris-
dictional boundaries for each federal court of appeals, there are 11 Federal Circuit
Court of Appeals.

Once the appellate court makes its decision, it can affirm, which means uphold, the
lower court's decision or **reverse** [overturn] the lower court's decision, which means to
nullify the jury's verdict and **remand** the case [send the case back] to the trial court
with the admonishment to take the appellate court's decision into account in retrying
the case. When the case is remanded, the original defendant may be granted a new trial
or an additional evidentiary hearing, or perhaps may be granted a new sentencing
phase, to name a few of the options. When cases are remanded for new court hearings,
sometimes the results are the same.

The U.S. Supreme Court today operates as the country's highest appellate court. The
U.S. Supreme Court receives thousands of petitions to hear cases. For those it wishes to
hear, the court grants a *writ of certiorari,* which roughly translates to a request to bring
the case record forward. One of the factors the court uses to decide which cases to hear
is the national import of the Court's decision. As we learned in chapter 1, by operation of
the Constitution's Supremacy Clause, once the Supreme Court speaks, it is the final
word. So, rather than take one case that may affect a small segment of the population, the
high Court will take a case that affects everyone. The Court will also take cases in which
lower courts have been divided on rulings on the same or similar issues. For example, one
federal court of appeal may have interpreted the Federal Sentencing Guidelines broadly
while another federal court of appeal may have interpreted the Guidelines narrowly. The
U.S. Supreme Court would take that case to resolve the conflict among the lower federal
circuits. Federal courts have jurisdiction over general types of cases involving the United
States as a party; federal laws or the U.S. Constitution; uniquely federal matters such as

patent laws, copyright violations, bankruptcy, and customs matters; disputes between citizens who reside in different states; or disputes involving $75,000 or more. Some cases come before the Supreme Court on direct appeal of federal matters, such as the constitutionality of a death sentence, but most cases come to the Court by way of *writ of certiorari,* by which the Court chooses to hear specific cases if at least five out of the nine justices agree to hear the case.

V. Key Terms and Phrases

- *Alford* plea
- bail
- booking
- burden of proof
- chain of custody
- charge bargaining
- charge conference
- charging decision
- circumstantial evidence
- closing argument
- conditional plea
- criminal investigation
- deliberations
- deterrence
- direct evidence

- dual court system
- evidence collection
- expert witness
- first responder
- grand jury
- guilty plea
- incarceration
- indictment
- information
- initial appearance
- jury instructions
- lay witness
- motion
- motion to suppress
- neutral and detached

- opening statements
- plea bargaining
- plea colloquy
- preliminary hearing
- presumption of innocence
- pretrial motions
- prosecutorial discretion
- remand
- restitution
- reverse
- scientific evidence
- verdict form
- *writ of certiorari*
- *writ of mandamus*
- zealous advocate

VI. Summary

1. **Meeting society's goals through criminal law:** The primary goal of criminal law is to make the offender repay what he has taken from society by committing crime. **Incapacitation** is locking him up in prison, **deterrence** is punishing him harshly as an example to others, **rehabilitation** is giving the offender skills to successfully reintegrate into society, and **restitution** is making the offender pay money to compensate victims financially.

2. **How a case travels through the judicial system:** After a suspect is arrested and police identify what criminal conduct supports a criminal charge, the prosecutor decides what charges to bring. After the **booking process,** in which the suspect's personal information is processed into the system, the suspect must be brought before a judge within a reasonable time, usually 48 hours, for an **initial appearance. A bail determination** is made, and the suspect is released into the community, to await trial if he is not a danger to others or does not pose a flight risk. A defendant may file many **pretrial motions,** or applications for court orders. The defendant may file a **motion to dismiss** the case for a number of reasons—for example, that her right to a speedy trial has been violated or that potentially exculpatory evidence has been destroyed. A **motion *in limine*** asks the court to rule on the admissibility of evidence before trial. A defendant may move to be severed from her codefendants to ensure her

right to a fair trial, and may move to change **venue,** the place where the trial will be held, because of extensive pretrial publicity or other factors that may reduce her chance of receiving a fair hearing. Plea agreements benefit both prosecutors and defendants. In exchange for eliminating some charges or for promising to argue for leniency in sentencing in front of the judge, the prosecutor gets a sure conviction while the defendant gets a known and certain jail time. There are many types of pleas, but all defendants must successfully survive the **plea colloquy** in which the judge ensures that the defendant is making an intelligent, voluntary, and knowing waiver of all of his trial rights by pleading guilty. The prosecution carries the burden of proving the defendant guilty beyond a reasonable doubt and presents evidence first. Both sides make an opening statement that tells the jury what the evidence will show during trial. The primary types of evidence at trial are **direct evidence** such as a gun, witness testimony about who saw the events in question, test results, and **circumstantial evidence** from which the jury can infer that the defendant is guilty by facts, taken together, that are not direct proof of the defendant's guilt but which lead to that logical conclusion. After the prosecution presents its case, the defendant can present his case, although, legally, the defense does not have to put forth a case. Before **closing arguments,** the attorneys meet with the judge for a **charge conference** and discuss what verdict forms to submit to the jury. After closing arguments, in which both counsels summarize the evidence and argue why the jury should find the defendant not guilty or guilty, the jury deliberates and makes a decision. The jury fills out a **verdict form** that announces its verdict.

3. **The way a case gets to the U.S. Supreme Court:** America has a **dual court system** with trial and ap-

pellate courts at both the state and the federal level. Once a defendant loses at trial by getting convicted, he or she often complains about legal errors that were made during trial to an appellate court. If a state case involves a federal issue, the defendant can appeal to a federal appellate court. The highest federal appellate court is the U.S. Supreme Court, which decides what cases it wants to hear when it grants *writs of certiorari*.

VII. Discussion Questions

1. What are the problems with an elected judiciary? Would you want your criminal case to come before a judge who was running for reelection on a "get tough on crime" campaign message? Why or why not?

2. Do you agree with Justice Harlan that it is better to let the guilty go free than to convict an innocent man? Is the execution of an innocent man the price to pay for keeping the death penalty, because no system can be perfect? What price of error are you willing to pay to have the criminal justice system to operate smoothly, even if your closest friends and family were the innocent ones caught in the system?

3. Describe the steps of the criminal justice system a suspect goes through from arrest to the beginning of trial.

4. Why are the protections afforded a criminal defendant by the United States Constitution important to

the criminal justice system? Explain your answer in reference to public confidence in the criminal justice system.

5. The defense counsel must zealously advocate for her client even if she believes or knows that her client is guilty. Why does the American Bar Association's Canon of Ethics prohibit the defense counsel from informing the authorities or the court that her client is guilty?

6. During the criminal trial process, why does the prosecution have the burden of proof? Why don't we force the defendant to prove he's innocent?

7. Do you think the U.S. Supreme Court should hear any and all cases? What would happen to the administration of justice in this country if the Supreme Court were an open court?

VIII. Problem-Solving Exercises

1. During jury deliberations in a trial in which a body was dumped into the water, one of the jurors brought in from home maps of the waterways in question to help the jury reach a decision as to whether the victim's body could have traveled downstream without the defendant's help. What is the proper recourse for the defendant in this situation?

2. In a negotiated plea agreement with the government, the defendant agreed to plead guilty to the reduced charge of false imprisonment for holding his wife hostage during a domestic dispute in return for an agreed-upon sentence to 36 months, even though the statutory maximum penalty for the charge was 56 months. After conducting the plea colloquy and establishing the facts and basis for defendant's guilt, the judge found the defendant guilty and sentenced the defendant to 56 months. Can the defendant now withdraw his guilty plea on the basis that the court did not honor his plea agreement with the state? Why or why not?

3. While awaiting trial in a jail cell, Vern struck up a conversation with his cell mate, George. Vern was

awaiting trial on statutory rape charges and was facing significant jail time and George was accused of killing two people in a drug deal gone bad. After sharing a cell for three months with George, Vern sent a note to his lawyer asking to meet. When Vern met with his attorney, Vern said he had some information about George's case that he wanted to share with the prosecutors. Vern met with prosecutors and told them that he had heard George confess to the murder. Although Vern provided no new details of the crime other than what was available in the news, prosecutors negotiated a plea agreement with Vern whereby in exchange for his testimony against George, Vern could plead guilty to a reduced charge and be sentenced to time served. At George's trial, Vern testified that George admitted to the killings and denied having made a plea agreement in exchange for his testimony. Can the defense object on hearsay grounds to Vern's testimony about his conversation with George and is it misconduct not to notify the defense about Vern's plea bargain?

IX. World Wide Web Resources

National Center for State Courts

http://www.ncsconline.org/

X. Additional Readings and Notes

Plea Bargaining

Brandon J. Lester. "System Failure: The Case for Supplanting Negotiation with Mediation in Plea Bargaining." *Ohio State Journal on Dispute Resolution,* Vol. 20 (2005), pp. 563–595.

Trial

Joseph L. Lester. "Presumed Innocent, Feared Dangerous: The Eighth Amendment's Right to Bail." *Northern Kentucky Law Review,* Vol. 32 (2005), pp. 1–65.

Jury Deliberations

Torrence Lewis. "Toward a Limited Right of Access to Jury Deliberations." *Federal Communications. Law Journal,* Vol. 58 (2006), pp. 195–213.

Cory Spiller. "*People* v. *Harlan*: The Colorado Supreme Court Takes a Step Toward Eliminating Religious Influence on Juries. *Denver University Law Review,* Vol. 83 (2005), pp. 613–638.

CHAPTER

Criminal Law and the First Amendment

"It is poignant but fundamental that the flag protects those who hold it in contempt . . ."

—TEXAS V. JOHNSON, 491 U.S. 397 (1989)

CHAPTER OBJECTIVES

Primary Concepts Discussed in This Chapter:

1. The activities protected by the First Amendment
2. Achieving public order without suppressing speech and expression
3. The legal difference between pornography and obscenity
4. The legal restrictions on students' free speech rights
5. Freedom of religion when certain religious practices may be considered criminal

CHAPTER OUTLINE

Feature: Abby and Her First Amendment Freedoms

I. PROTECTED SPEECH

1. Analytical Framework for First Amendment Issues
   a. Content-Based Regulation of Speech
   b. Time, Manner, and Place Restrictions
   c. Facial Validity
   d. Overbreadth
   Box 3.1 *Bair & Wray* v. *Shippensburg University,* 280 F. Supp.2d 357 (M.D. Pa. 2003)
   e. Vagueness
2. Symbolic Expression
   a. Flag Desecration
   b. Cross Burning
   Box 3.2 *Virginia* v. *Black,* 538 U.S. 343 (2003)

II. UNPROTECTED SPEECH

1. Clear and Present Danger
2. Fighting Words
3. Obscenity
4. Free Speech and the Internet
   Box 3.3 *Ashcroft* v. *Free Speech Coalition,* 535 U.S. 234 (2002)

III. SPECIAL FIRST AMENDMENT ISSUES

1. Schools
2. Prisoners

IV. FREEDOM OF ASSOCIATION

Feature: *Chapter-Opening Case Study: Abby and Her First Amendment Freedoms*

Abby is a white supremacist who has advocated the overthrow of the government. She has made bombs and detonated them in affluent white areas in the hopes that residents would blame the neighboring minority community for the destruction of property, thus starting a race war. In order to further her criminal aims, Abby cruises through the minority neighborhood at night screaming racial epithets [legally, it is okay to hate, but it is not okay to spew fighting words and disturb the peace at 2 A.M.]. Other times, Abby stands on a street corner in the middle of rush-hour traffic holding placards depicting gruesome photographs of aborted fetuses while screaming, "We need to overthrow the government because of their tolerance for abortion. The president and his cabinet are terrorists who should be destroyed. Won't you join me in destroying the evil?" [legally, speech cannot create danger to public safety].

Once, Abby was chased into the white community where she had prearranged a cross burning on an affluent white family's lawn [cross-burning not meant to intimidate is legal]. As she was cackling with glee at the cross burning, her husband called to tell her that their 21-month-old baby was burning with fever. Relying on her religious beliefs that prayer and peyote heal all sickness [it is legal to have this religious belief], Abby ingested the hallucinogenic peyote and prayed over the baby for days instead of taking the baby to the hospital, and the baby died [it is illegal to let children die due to lack of medical care]. An autopsy showed that the baby was suffering from a very common form of pneumonia that is readily treatable with antibiotics. In the aftermath of her baby's death, Abby became depressed and started to collect pornography [a legal activity]. She ordered some hard-core pornography online and did not even open some of the packages, but a few of the magazines contained photographs of underage children in various sexually solicitous poses [in order to convict her for this, the prosecution would have to prove Abby's *scienter* — her knowledge of the content of the publications]. The police have arrested Abby for the racial epithets, the cross burning, the peyote use, the death of her baby, and her possession of pornography. In her defense, she has claimed the protections of the First Amendment. How will Abby's case be resolved?

INTRODUCTION

This chapter explores defenses to criminal charges on the basis of the freedoms guaranteed by the First Amendment with special emphasis on constitutional analysis to establish whether such expression or communication is protected from criminal punishment.

When courts examine free speech issues and whether such speech should be criminalized and suppressed, the term "speech" typically includes expressive conduct, such as nude dancing or giving someone the middle finger, and freedom of association, such as belonging to a hate group such as the Ku Klux Klan whose members have the freedom to "associate" with one another, even though the actual language of the First Amendment does not mention such protection. Speech such as words that incite violence, words that by their very utterance pose a clear and present danger to public safety, and obscene material such as child pornography are not protected by the First Amendment. The forum in which the speech takes place, such as a public park or on the Internet, affects whether the government can restrict the speech that takes place in the forum, and the status of the individual as a student, public employee, or other person affects whether that person's freedom of speech can be restricted. The final section examines the freedom to engage in certain religious practices that remain free from government interference, such as sacrificing live animals as part of a worship service, and practices that are not protected, such as relying on prayer in lieu of seeking life-saving medical care for minor children. Freedom of speech, expression, and religion form the basis for all of our democratic principles.

Rule of Law: The first five words of the First Amendment are "Congress shall make no law . . ."

I. PROTECTED SPEECH

The First Amendment was drafted and enacted as a direct result of abuses by the Crown. In the early colonies, the King licensed all printers, and those who complained of his governance in the press were prosecuted for seditious libel, a crime defined by Black's Law Dictionary (1987) as advocating "the overthrow of the government by force or violence." As a twentieth century Justice Louis Brandeis said about the First Amendment:

> Those who won our independence . . . believed liberty to be the secret of happiness and courage to be the secret of liberty. They believed that freedom to think as you will and to speak as you think are means indispensable to the discovery and spread of political truth; that without free speech and assembly discussion would be futile; that with them, discussion affords ordinary adequate protection against the dissemination of noxious doctrine; that the greatest menace to freedom is an inert people; that public discussion is a political duty; and that this should be a fundamental principle of the American government.[1]

Justice Brandeis gave voice to why the First Amendment is the basis for democracy's strength by promoting the voice of a free America. If people are legally protected when they wish to express unpopular and even offensive ideas, democracy flourishes.

1. Analytical Framework for First Amendment Issues

The First Amendment provides "Congress shall make no law . . . abridging [compromising, infringing] the freedom of speech, or of the press; or of the right of the people peaceably to assemble, and to petition the Government for a redress of grievances." The Constitution allows people to be as hateful as they want and protects racists, homophobes, misogynists, and those who dislike others based on their religious beliefs or practices. To act on those hatreds is legally prohibited as a hate crime, but one can voice them freely as long as the words cannot be construed as "fighting words" described reword.

---

[1]*Whitney v. California,* 274 U.S. 357 (1927).

Rule of Law: The government cannot suppress speech because some people do not like it or find it offensive.

a. Content-Based Regulation of Speech

In general, the government cannot regulate the content of speech or make laws that control speech, which is defined as the words spoken or the message communicated. If the government attempts to regulate the message conveyed by speech it is called **content-based regulation** of speech, and it violates the First Amendment. When a person challenges the government's content-based regulation of speech, a court will use **strict scrutiny**–meaning that they will examine under the most powerful of microscopes the government's motive for regulating such speech and whether the regulation is the **least restrictive means** to carry out the government's objectives without infringing on personal freedoms. If one wanted to criticize the government and say "all those in government should burn in a forest fire," to restrict that speech on the basis of the speaker's message would be impermissible unless such government restriction served a compelling state interest. A **compelling state interest (CSI)** is a government interest of the highest order to protect the health, safety and welfare of its citizens. Content-based restriction of speech must survive the court's strict scrutiny analysis. In order to survive a court's strict scrutiny analysis, the government regulation infringing on speech must:

1. be necessary to achieve a CSI,
2. be narrowly drawn to achieve that interest, and
3. be the least restrictive means to achieving the government's interest.

If the government regulation, law, or statute infringes upon a freedom protected by the First Amendment, the law must be declared invalid if it does not serve a compelling state interest and is not narrowly tailored to advance the government's interest. To determine if the law survives and is valid, courts will use the strict scrutiny analysis. A strict scrutiny analysis can be best illustrated by cases that involve laws that treated the races differently. The high Court eventually found these laws to violate the Fourteenth Amendment's Equal Protection Clause.

A case in the 1960s, *McLaughlin* v. *Florida*, 379 U.S. 184 (1964), challenged a Florida statute that prohibited African-Americans and whites from sleeping together in hotels and motels. The statute §798.05 provided that:

> Any negro man and white woman, or any white man and negro woman, who are not married to each other, who shall habitually live in and occupy in the nighttime the same room shall each be punished by imprisonment not exceeding twelve months, or by fine not exceeding five hundred dollars . . .

Using strict scrutiny, the Court found that the government had no compelling state interest that was properly advanced by keeping people of different races from staying together in hotel rooms (while people of the same race were allowed to stay together). The court said that if the law was designed to prevent promiscuous sex, it was not narrowly tailored to achieve those goals (on nonracial grounds) and must, therefore, fail for violating the Constitution.

Rule of Law: Courts will examine government restrictions on speech under strict scrutiny.

b. Time, Manner, and Place Restrictions

Rarely will the government come right out and admit that it is regulating speech because of the message conveyed by the speaker; such restriction would obviously violate the First Amendment. The government often defends regulation of speech on its prerogative to control the time, manner, and place speech takes place. For instance, people have every right to protest against war, but they cannot at 2 A.M. on a quiet residential street take a bullhorn and advertise their views in an effort to gain the attention of a captive audience.[2] In our chapter opening scenario, Abby has every right to voice her opinion, but not disturb the peace while communicating her views, which may be construed as fighting words, discussed below.

The government can legally regulate speech when it does so for reasons independent of the speech's content or message. It can regulate the time, place, and manner of speech for the benefit of public safety and community. Speech in a **public forum** may not be restricted unless the restriction is narrowly tailored to serve a significant government interest. "The privilege [of access to] the streets and parks for communication of views on national questions may be regulated in the interest of all; [but] it must not, in the guise of regulation, be abridged or denied."[3] The fact that the speaker could convey his message at a different time or place is insufficient alternative to justify the content-neutral restriction on expression, and mere government convenience is not a significant enough government interest to withstand judicial scrutiny. In order to be valid as a **time, manner, and place restriction,** a regulation must meet a three-part test:[4]

1. It must be "justified without reference to the content of the regulated speech"; in other words, it must be content neutral.
2. It must be narrowly tailored to serve a significant governmental interest; the interest cannot be equally well served by a means that is substantially less intrusive of First Amendment interests.
3. It must leave open alternative channels for communication of the information.

The definition of narrowly tailored is that the government must merely avoid choosing means to implement its laws to achieve its objective that are "substantially broader than necessary to achieve the government's interest."[5] For example, to reduce citizen complaints that rock concerts in the city were too loud, the New York City government made musicians use city-provided equipment and speakers. Rock artists challenged the City's regulation, arguing that restriction of their noise infringed on the groups' rights to freedom of expression, but they lost. The court decided the City could regulate noise as a valid time, manner, and place restriction that was not "substantially broader than necessary" to serve the government's interest.

c. Facial Validity

When a law is challenged under the First Amendment, the court will first look at the statute or law to determine whether it's "facially valid," which means it appears legal on its face: a quick read of the law does not show any apparent constitutional infirmity. In one case a statute did not allow peaceful picketing near a school but did allow picketing as part of a teacher's strike. The court said that discriminating between protesters based on what they were picketing about and what they were going to say was prohibited content-based discrimination.[6] Even if the statute looks content neutral on its face and seems to apply to everyone, the court will look to see whether the statute's enactment was motivated to discriminate against one particular practice or viewpoint, an analysis engaged in the case *Church of the Lukumi Babalu Aye, Inc.,* discussed below in Box 3.4.

Rule of Law: An overbroad law punishes both legal and illegal speech.

d. Overbreadth

Invoking the overbreadth doctrine is one of the most effective ways the U.S. Supreme Court can protect freedom of speech. A law is **overbroad** in First Amendment analysis if it

---

[2]*See Grayned* v. *Rockford,* 408 U.S. 104 (1972) (government can regulate time, manner and place of speech that might disrupt school located nearby)

.[3]*Hague* v. *CIO,* 307 U.S. 496 (1939).

[4]*See Clark* v. *Community for Creative Non-Violence,* 468 U.S. 288 (1984); *Metromedia, Inc.* v. *San Diego,* 453 U.S. 490 (1981); *Cox* v. *Louisiana,* 379 U.S. 559 (1965).

[5]*Ward* v. *Rock Against Racism,* 491 U.S. 781 (1989).

[6]*Police Department of Chicago* v. *Mosley,* 408 U.S. 92 (1972).

condemns speech that is both protected and unprotected under the First Amendment. The mother of a fallen soldier who died in an unpopular military invasion can lead peaceful protests outside the President's summer retreat home because of her right to criticize the government. Likewise, a religious sect's protest at military funerals with signs claiming that the dead soldiers died as a direct result of society's tolerance for sexual diversity is protected by the First Amendment, even though most mourners find such a message offensive and patently false. Simply because speech is offensive to the general public is not a legal basis to restrict the speech. In 2006, Kentucky enacted a law to keep protesters at least 300 feet away from a funeral. The law was aimed at stopping people associated with the Westboro Baptist Church of Topeka, Kansas, from holding signs that declared the soldier was dead because of American tolerance for homosexuality. A federal judge prevented the law from being enforced because it violated the First Amendment on the grounds that it restricted" all expression of speech within the buffer zone (the area next to the funeral home), including activities along nearby streets or inside homes."[7] The protesters have a right to free speech protected by the First Amendment. If a state enacts a law to restrict the funeral protesters, and the law states that no one can peaceably assemble in front of a funeral home with the intent to injure or harass others, then the law is illegal because it is overbroad: it punishes protected activity under the First Amendment—assembling in front of a funeral home—along with an activity that is not protected under the First Amendment, namely, making speech to injure or harass others.

In Pennsylvania, college administrators' efforts to promulgate a code of conduct prohibiting harassing people based on race or gender was found to be overbroad and chilled the free speech of students who have every right to express their thoughts even if their speech may bc considered insensitive or offensive by others.

FIGURE 3.1 Venn diagram of overbreadth analysis.

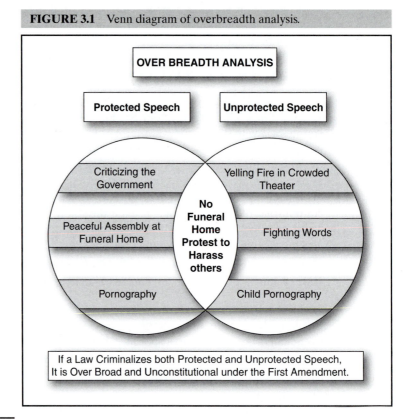

[7]John Stamper. "Protest Law Halted: Free-Speech Issues at Funeral Cited." *Lexington Herald-Leader,* September 27, 2006.

BOX 3.1

Walter A. Bair and Ellen Wray v. *Shippensburg University,* 280 F.Supp.2d 357 (M.D. Pa. 2003) U.S. District Court for the Middle District of Pennsylvania

Judge Jones issued the following Order:

This case presents us with the difficult question whether portions of an obviously well-intentioned student code of conduct enacted by a state university can withstand First Amendment scrutiny . . .

B. THE UNIVERSITY SPEECH CODE

[Bair and Wray] frame their arguments as to the constitutionality of the University's speech policies by initially characterizing two University publications, the University Catalog and the University Student Handbook [the Swataney] [considered together as the "Speech Code"]. The objectionable portions of the University Speech Code as cited within the parties' submissions are set forth below. The University Catalog contains a Code of Conduct which provides the following in its Preamble:

Students, as members of the academic community, are encouraged to engage in a sustained, critical and independent search for knowledge. The University community supports this endeavor by developing policies and procedures that safeguard the freedoms necessary for the pursuit of truth and knowledge. The University will strive to protect these freedoms if they are not inflammatory or harmful toward others. It is therefore expected that students will exercise these freedoms in a manner that does not infringe upon the rights of others in the community. Behavior that interferes with the living conditions, co-curricular activities, working environments, teaching mission, research activities, study conditions, and/or administrative functions of the University is unacceptable. Acts of intolerance directed toward other community members will not be condoned.

The University has propounded the Racism and Cultural Diversity Statement which provides as follows:

As an institution of higher learning, Shippensburg University is committed without qualification to all aspects—moral, legal and administrative—of racial and cultural diversity. It is the unequivocal position of Shippensburg University to prohibit racism/ethnic intimidation and harassment; and to affirm cultural diversity, social justice and equality.

Racism shall be defined as the subordination of any person or group based upon race, color, creed or national origin. It shall be a violation of this policy for any person or group to maliciously intend to engage in any activity (covert or overt) that attempts to injure, harm, malign or harass, that causes the subordination, intimidation and/or harassment of a person or group based upon race, color, creed, national origin, sex, disability or age.

Shippensburg University's commitment to racial tolerance, cultural diversity and social justice will require every member of this community to ensure that the principles of these ideals be mirrored in their attitudes and behaviors.

Plaintiff Walter Bair is entering his senior year at Shippensburg University and is therefore subject to the provisions of the University Speech Code. According to the allegations set forth in the First Amended Complaint, Bair "fears that the discussion of his social, cultural, political and/or religious views . . . may be sanctionable under applicable University [S]peech [C]ode." Plaintiff Ellen Wray is a recent graduate of Shippensburg University and maintains that while in attendance there "she was reluctant to advance certain controversial theories or ideas regarding any number of political or social issues because . . . she feared that discussion of such theories might be sanctionable under applicable University [S]peech [C]ode." Plaintiffs both allege that they were members of student organizations which hold opinions and beliefs that might be sanctionable under the Code. In sum, Plaintiffs assert that the University Speech Code has "had a chilling effect on [their] rights to freely and openly engage in appropriate discussions of their theories, ideas and political and/or religious beliefs."

In this case, Plaintiffs have asserted that the University Speech Code is unconstitutional because it is facially overbroad and vague.

A. OVERBREADTH

The facial challenge to Shippensburg University's Speech Code on overbreadth grounds will only

(continued)

BOX 3.1

(continued)

succeed upon a finding that there is "a likelihood that the [the Code's] very existence will inhibit free expression by inhibiting the speech of third parties who are not before the Court." [*Saxe v. State College Area School District,* 240 F.3d 200, 214 (3rd. Cir. 2001)]. As noted by [then-judge on the Third Circuit Court of Appeals and now Associate Justice on the U.S. Supreme Court] Judge Alito in *Saxe,* the Supreme Court held in *Tinker v. Des Moines Independent Community School District,* 393 U.S. 503 (1969), that because students do not "shed their constitutional rights to freedom of speech or expression at the school house gate," the regulation of student speech in the public schools "is generally permissible only [if] the speech would substantially disrupt or interfere with the work of the school or the rights of other students." *Saxe,* 240 F.3d at 211; *see also Grayned v. City of Rockford,* 408 US. 104 (1972) (reiterating that public schools have a "compelling interest in having an undisrupted school session conducive to the students' learning"). Under *Tinker,* only "if a school can point to a well-founded expectation of disruption—especially one based on past incidents arising out of similar speech"—may the speech regulation pass constitutional muster.

Read collectively, the cited portions of the Speech Code would lead a reasonable person to believe that the University sets a number of restrictions on student conduct. Indeed, the language of the Code instructs students that they must "mirror" the University's ideals as they apply to racial tolerance, cultural diversity and social justice. On its face, it is apparent that the Code of Conduct prohibits speech that is protected by the First Amendment. The amorphous term "acts of intolerance" within the Preamble of the Code can be reasonably interpreted to encompass speech, not just conduct, that intimates intolerance. So construed, the provision of the Code prohibiting acts of intolerance directed at others, which by its terms provides that it is not limited to the examples of prohibited acts cited therein, could certainly be interpreted as prohibiting speech that is protected by the First Amendment. Likewise, the sentence within the Community Regulations of the Code of Conduct that bans students from taking part in "acts of intolerance" which "demonstrate malicious intent towards others" could be understood to prohibit speech that demonstrates malicious intent. While it is true that First Amendment protections do not extend to some forms of speech, these exclusions do not apply to the foregoing. *R.A.V.,* 505 U.S. at 383 (1992) (*citing Roth v. United States,* 354 U.S. 476 (1957) (obscenity); *Beauhamais v. Illinois,* 343 U.S. 250 (1952) (defamation); *Chaplinsky v. New Hampshire,* 315 U.S. 568 (1942) ("fighting words"); *Simon & Schuster, Inc. v. Members of N.Y. State Crime Victims Bd.,* 502 U.S. 105 (1991). As such, we conclude that the cited provisions are overbroad . . .

Now, Therefore It Is Ordered That:

2. The operation of the [overbroad] provisions of Code of Conduct shall be enjoined [prohibited from being enforced] until further order of Court.

s/John E. Jones III

United States District Judge

Rule of Law: A vague law leaves people guessing what conduct or speech is criminal.

e. Vagueness

A law is **vague** and therefore unconstitutional if the conduct it seeks to make criminal "is so unclearly defined that persons of common intelligence must necessarily guess at its meaning and differ as to its application." *Connally v. General Construction Co.,* 269 U.S. 385 (1926). Vagueness may invalidate a criminal law for either of two independent reasons. First, it may fail to provide the kind of notice that will enable ordinary people to understand what conduct it prohibits; second, it may authorize and even encourage arbitrary and discriminatory enforcement. *See Kolender v. Lawson,* 461 U.S. 352 (1983).

"Edward Lawson is an African American man, who at the time of this case, wore his hair on long dreadlocks. After being continually harassed and questioned by police when he appeared in white neighborhoods, he challenged a California law 'that requires persons who loiter or wander on the streets to provide a 'credible and reliable' identification and to account for their presence when requested by a police officer.' The Court found that the law gave too much power to police to stop individuals for vaguely-defined reasons, and could unconstitutionally infringe upon citizens' rights to freedom of movement."

The doctrine of invalidating laws under the doctrine of vagueness stems from the due process requirement of fair notice to the public of what conduct is prohibited and will be punished. If the statute fails to give a person of ordinary intelligence fair notice that their conduct is prohibited by law, it is vague. The problem with vague or over-broad laws with respect to the First Amendment are their "**chilling effect**" on speech, which means that such a law acts like cold water and ice on people's expressive conduct—in other words, the law may make them clam up and not speak. If a person does not know whether or not he will be arrested or imprisoned for what he says, then his instinct to speak freely may be "chilled" and he will restrain himself from speaking freely for fear of criminal punishment.

Applying the Law to the Facts: Which statute is vague or overbroad?

- **Law A** says no one can legally make sounds or gestures that are offensive to others. **Law B** says no one can make sounds that are offensive to others or that may, by their very utterance, incite the public to violence.

Law A is vague and violates the First Amendment because there is no way a reasonably intelligent person can tell what sounds or gestures may be offensive to one person and may not be for another—too difficult to define. Law B is overbroad because it criminalizes protected speech, in this case the right to be offensive, and properly criminalizes unprotected speech, in this case the fighting words that incite violence.

Rule of Law: The First Amendment protects expression, such as nude dancing and flag burning.

2. Symbolic Expression

In *United States* v. *O'Brien,* 391 U.S. 367 (1968), the U.S. Supreme Court upheld the conviction of a man who burned his draft card under the law that made criminal the willful and knowing mutilation or destruction of a draft card. O'Brien appealed his conviction on the claim that burning his draft card was symbolic expression protected by the First Amendment. The high Court said:

> This Court has held that when "speech" and "non-speech" elements are combined in the same course of conduct, a sufficiently important governmental interest in regulating the nonspeech element can justify incidental limitations on First Amendment freedoms. We think it clear that a government regulation is sufficiently justified if it is within the constitutional power of the Government; if it furthers an important or substantial governmental interest; if the government interest is unrelated to the suppression of free expression; and if the incidental restriction on alleged First Amendment freedoms is no greater than is essential to the furtherance of that interest. We find that the [law punishing draft-card burning] [meets] all of these requirements and consequently that O'Brien can be constitutionally convicted for violating it.

Thus, the Court balanced the competing interests of O'Brien's free speech rights and the government's interest in upholding the draft law and found that the infringement upon O'Brien's right to express himself by burning the card was minimal and therefore his "expression" could be made criminal.

In *Frye* v. *Kansas City Missouri Police Department*, 375 F.3d 785 (8th Cir. 2004), abortion protesters convened on a busy intersection at 11:00 A.M. on June 23, 2001, displaying color photographs of aborted fetuses. Responding police officers determined that the colored posters were creating a public safety hazard to motorists driving by and 5 of the protesters were arrested for violating the city's loitering ordinance. In March 2002, 11 protesters brought suit against the city and the police alleging violations of their freedom of speech, freedom of assembly, equal protection, and right to be free from false arrest. In response, the officers asserted a right to qualified immunity. The federal appellate court held in favor of the officers, for even though the protesters had a constitutional right to protest against abortion, the officers' actions in moving the protesters were a minimal imposition when weighed against the potential harm caused by distracted drivers. As in the *O'Brien* analysis, people have a First Amendment right to expressive conduct but the government may place minimal limits on that conduct if it is outweighed by public safety interests. In our opening scenario, Abby can criticize the government and even advocate its demise, but she cannot attract attention for her message by showing gruesome photographs during rush hour and creating a public hazard.

a. Flag Desecration

A very powerful form of symbolic speech is burning the American flag in protest. There have been many attempts to outlaw such activity, but each law fails under a First Amendment analysis because people have a right to protest the government without having such rights suppressed. In *Texas* v. *Johnson*, 491 U.S. 397 (1989), in which the U.S. Supreme Court struck down a Texas statute that outlawed flag burning, Justice Kennedy, in a concurring opinion, expressed the displeasure that many members of the public would have for the Court's opinion that it is a lawful act of expression to burn the flag, especially those "who have had the singular honor of carrying the flag into battle," but he went on to remind America that "[i]t is poignant but fundamental that the flag protects those who hold it in contempt." The flag is where we get the power to burn it. In response to the *Johnson* decision, the federal government enacted the Flag Protection Act of 1989 ("Act") that punished anyone who "knowingly mutilates, defaces, physically defiles, burns, maintains on the floor or ground, or tramples upon any flag of the United States . . .", but the Act was declared illegal because it suppressed speech and expression based on the content of the speech, which is unconstitutional. *United States* v. *Eichman,* 496 U.S. 310 (1990).

Rule of Law: It is legal to burn a cross as expressive speech. It is not legal to burn a cross with the intent to intimidate.

b. Cross Burning

Burning a cross is expressive speech protected by the First Amendment. Statutes that try to punish cross burning as symbolic hate speech typically fail on either vagueness or overbreadth grounds because such a law would punish speech on the basis of its content—racial pride, hatred of others—restrictions on speech that the First Amendment prohibits. An example of a hate speech law that failed on overbreadth grounds is in the case *R.A.V.* v. *City of St. Paul,* 505 U.S. 377 (1992), where the hate crime ordinance provided:

> Whoever placed on public property or private property a symbol, object, appellation, characterization or graffiti, including, but not limited to, a burning cross or Nazi swastika, which one knows or has reasonable grounds to know arouse anger, alarm or resentment in others on the basis of race, color, creed, religion or gender commits disorderly conduct and shall be guilty of a misdemeanor.

Teenage defendants taped broken chair legs together into a cross and burned it inside the fenced yard of an African-American family, acts that are criminal as trespass or arson. But the teenagers were prosecuted under the hate-crimes ordinance instead. Teenager R.A.V. (initials to protect his juvenile identity) was convicted under the ordinance and the U.S. Supreme Court overturned his conviction because the ordinance discriminated on the basis of a person's viewpoint. The law was overbroad because it lawfully prohibited fighting words which arouse "anger alarm or resentment in others," but unlawfully regulated speech made "on the basis of race, color, creed, religion or gender." But after the *R.A.V.* decision, the Court upheld a Virginia statute in *Virginia* v. *Black,* 538 U.S. 343 (2003), that outlawed cross burning on the grounds that the statute specifically made cross burning "fighting words" [discussed below] which enjoy no protection under the First Amendment. The Virginia statute recites:

> It shall be unlawful for any person or persons, with the intent of intimidating any person or group of persons, to burn, or cause to be burned, a cross on the property of another, a highway or other public place. Any person who shall violate any provision of this section shall be guilty of a Class 6 felony. Any such burning of a cross shall be prima facie evidence of an intent to intimidate a person or group of persons.

In the *Black* case, white men drove a truck onto the property of the African-American Jubilee family in the middle of the night and burned a cross in the yard. Read the history of cross burning in America provided in the excerpt of *Virginia* v. *Black* reprinted in part in Box 3.2, a history that allowed the Court to equate the speech expressed by cross burning with fighting words which allows the government to suppress it legally. The court distinguished the two cross-burning cases on the grounds that cross burning is a protected form of expression, but once it crossed the line and was done in an effort to intimidate or harass others, cross burning became fighting words that the government could legally suppress. In our opening scenario, Abby's cross burning may be interpreted as intimidating fighting words, even if burned on a white neighbor's lawn. If Abby burned the cross in her own back yard, it would be legal.

BOX 3.2

Virginia v. *Black,* 538 U.S. 343 (2003)
Supreme Court of the United States

Justice O'Conner delivered the opinion of the Court.

REASONING

Cross burning originated in the 14th century as a means for Scottish tribes to signal each other.[8] Sir Walter Scott used cross burnings for dramatic effect in The Lady of the Lake, where the burning cross signified both a summons and a call to arms.[9] Cross burning in this country, however, long ago became unmoored from its Scottish ancestry. Burning a cross in the United States is inextricably intertwined with the history of the Ku Klux Klan. The first Ku Klux Klan began in Pulaski, Tennessee, in the spring of 1866. Although the Ku Klux Klan started as a social club, it soon changed into something far different. The Klan fought Reconstruction and the corresponding drive to allow freed blacks to participate in the political process. Soon the Klan imposed "a veritable reign of terror" throughout the South.[10] The Klan employed tactics such as whipping, threatening to burn people at the stake, and murder.[11] The Klan's victims included blacks, southern whites who disagreed with the Klan, and "carpetbagger" northern whites.

The activities of the Ku Klux Klan prompted legislative action at the national level. In 1871, "President Grant sent a message to Congress indicating that the Klan's reign of terror in the Southern States had rendered life and property insecure." *Jett* v.

(continued)

---

[8]Citation from case: See M. Newton and J. Newton. *The Ku Klux Klan: An Encyclopedia* (1991), p. 145.

[9]Citation from case: See W. Scott, The Lady of The Lake, canto third.

[10]Citation from case: S. Kennedy, Southern Exposure 31 (1991).

[11]Citation from case: W. Wade. *The Fiery Cross: The Ku Klux Klan in America* (1987), pp. 48–49.

BOX 3.2

(continued)

Dallas Independent School Dist., 491 U.S. 701 (1989). In response, Congress passed what is now known as the Ku Klux Klan Act. *See* "An Act to enforce the Provisions of the Fourteenth Amendment to the Constitution of the United States, and for other Purposes," 17 Stat. 13 (now codified at 42 U.S.C. §§1983, 1985, and 1986). President Grant used these new powers to suppress the Klan in South Carolina, the effect of which severely curtailed the Klan in other States as well. By the end of Reconstruction in 1877, the first Klan no longer existed.

The genesis of the second Klan began in 1905, with the publication of Thomas Dixon's The Clansmen: An Historical Romance of the Ku Klux Klan. Dixon's book was a sympathetic portrait of the first Klan, depicting the Klan as a group of heroes "saving" the South from blacks and the "horrors" of Reconstruction. Although the first Klan never actually practiced cross burning, Dixon's book depicted the Klan burning crosses to celebrate the execution of former slaves. Cross burning thereby became associated with the first Ku Klux Klan. When D.W. Griffith turned Dixon's book into the movie The Birth of a Nation in 1915, the association between cross burning and the Klan became indelible. In addition to the cross burnings in the movie, a poster advertising the film displayed a hooded Klansman riding a hooded horse, with his left hand holding the reins of the horse and his right hand holding a burning cross above his head. Soon thereafter, in November 1915, the second Klan began.

From the inception of the second Klan, cross burnings have been used to communicate both threats of violence and messages of shared ideology. The first initiation ceremony occurred on Stone Mountain near Atlanta, Georgia. While a 40-foot cross burned on the mountain, the Klan members took their oaths of loyalty. This cross burning was the second recorded instance in the United States. The first known cross burning in the country had occurred a little over one month before the Klan initiation, when a Georgia mob celebrated the lynching of Leo Frank by burning a "gigantic cross" on Stone Mountain that was "visible throughout."

The new Klan's ideology did not differ much from that of the first Klan. As one Klan publication emphasized, "We avow the distinction between [the] races, . . . and we shall ever be true to the faithful maintenance of White Supremacy and will strenuously oppose any compromise thereof in any and all things." Violence was also an elemental part of this new Klan. By September 1921, the *New York World* newspaper documented 152 acts of Klan violence, including 4 murders, 41 floggings, and 27 tar-and-featherings.

Often, the Klan used cross burnings as a tool of intimidation and a threat of impending violence. For example, in 1939 and 1940, the Klan burned crosses in front of synagogues and churches. After one cross burning at a synagogue, a Klan member noted that if the cross burning did not "shut the Jews up, we'll cut a few throats and see what happens." In Miami in 1941, the Klan burned four crosses in front of a proposed housing project, declaring, "We are here to keep niggers out of your town . . . When the law fails you, call on us." And in Alabama in 1942, in "a whirlwind climax to weeks of flogging and terror," the Klan burned crosses in front of a union hall and in front of a union leader's home on the eve of a labor election. These cross burnings embodied threats to people whom the Klan deemed antithetical to its goals. And these threats had special force given the long history of Klan violence.

The Klan continued to use cross burnings to intimidate after World War II. In one incident, an African-American "school teacher who recently moved his family into a block formerly occupied only by whites asked the protection of city police . . . after the burning of a cross in his front yard." And after a cross burning in Suffolk, Virginia during the late 1940's, the Virginia Governor stated that he would "not allow any of our people of any race to be subjected to terrorism or intimidation in any form by the Klan or any other organization."[12] These incidents of cross burning, among others, helped prompt Virginia to enact its first version of the cross-burning statute in 1950.

---

[12]Citation from case: D. Chalmers. *Hooded Americanism: The History of the Ku Klux Klan* (1980), p. 333.

Applying the Rule of Law to the Facts: Is it legal to outlaw hateful or violent expression?

- California passed a criminal law outlawing hateful and violent expression in video games. Gamers sued saying that such restriction of their video games violated their First Amendment rights.

The government cannot outlaw random expressions of hate or violence in virtual reality. The California law enacted in October 2005 made criminal the sale of violent video games to minors and required such videos be labeled. An injunction was issued preventing the implementation of the law and on August 6, 2007, U.S. District Court Judge Ronald Whyte held the law invalid on free speech grounds.

Rule of Law: There is a class of speech, including fighting words and child pornography, that the First Amendment does not protect and that the government can suppress and regulate.

II. UNPROTECTED SPEECH

Certain types of speech enjoy no protection under the First Amendment. Although our democracy cherishes and values the marketplace of ideas to advocate change through public discourse and discussion, there are some types of political speech that cross the line.

1. Clear and Present Danger

Political speech that poses a "clear and present danger" to the public by advocating lawless acts that would endanger others can be legally suppressed.[13] The clear and present danger test did not survive and was replaced with a new test which stated that speech could be suppressed if:

1. the speech "is directed to inciting or producing imminent lawless action," and
2. the speech is also "likely to incite or produce such action."[14]

The intertwinement of incitement and imminent harm was the focus in *Watts* v. *United States,* 394 U.S. 705 (1969), in which an African-American protesting the Vietnam conflict said to a crowd, "[i]f they ever make me carry a rifle, the first man I want to get in my sights is L.B.J. [President Lyndon Baines Johnson]. They are not going to make me kill my black brothers." Watts was convicted under a statute making threatening the life of the president a crime. The high Court overturned his conviction because Watts' threat was conditional—only if sent to Vietnam would Watts endanger Johnson's life—and because the audience laughed at him when he said it.

2. Fighting Words

What happens when the purported audience finds the proposed speech offensive and hateful? May the government restrict the speech because of the negative effect such speech will have on the listeners? **Fighting words** are those words which "by their very utterance inflict injury" *Chaplinsky* v. *New Hampshire,* 315 U.S. 568 (1942). But most speech cannot be restricted even if it is vulgar and includes four-letter words because "profane, offensive language is nonetheless First Amendment speech." In *Cohen* v. *California,* 403 U.S. 15 (1971), Cohen wore a jacket with the slogan "F*** the draft" in a Los Angeles courthouse where women and children were present. He was charged under the statute that made criminal the intentional "disturbing the peace or quiet of

---

[13]*Schenck* v. *United States,* 249 U.S. 47 (1919).

[14]*Brandenburg* v. *Ohio,* 395 U.S. 444 (1969).

any . . . person [by] offensive conduct," and convicted. In overturning his conviction, the U.S. Supreme Court explained that Cohen's message was not obscene, that the people in the courthouse were not a "captive audience" which could not escape from Cohen's message if they wanted to, and that the state's argument that Cohen was arrested to protect the body politic was insufficient when weighed against government restriction of Cohen's free speech rights. The Court said that the function of the First Amendment was to "remove governmental restraints for the arena of public discussion." It is sometimes difficult to draw the line between free speech and protecting the public.

In the 1970s, American Nazis wanted to protest in the Village of Skokie, Illinois, home to approximately 5,000 Nazi concentration camp survivors. The Village tried to stop the Nazis from marching on the grounds that the predominately Jewish community would suffer great harm. Just before the march was scheduled, the Village enacted several ordinances prohibiting the displaying of "any materials which promote or incite racial or religious hatred". . . including "public display of markings and clothing of symbolic significance," which could be interpreted to include swastikas and military uniforms. The federal courts reviewing Skokie's ordinances held them unconstitutional on the basis that government cannot restrict speech on the inherent evils its content contains. *Collin* v. *Smith,* 578 F.2d 1197 (7th Cir. 1978).

3. Obscenity

Since the advent of photography there has been a market for sexually stimulating photographs of naked men and women. There has been much litigation over the definition of obscene material written or photographic work designed to arouse or excite the viewer sexually. The difficulty in agreeing on one solid definition is best exemplified by U.S. Supreme Court Justice Potter Stewart who said about obscenity, "I know it when I see it."[15] The legal test courts use today to establish whether a book, movie, piece of art, or other expressive conduct is obscene was enunciated by the Supreme Court in *Miller* v. *California,* 413 U.S. 15 (1973). If the item is judged obscene, it is not protected by the Constitution and the government has the right to suppress it and keep it from the public. In this case, Marvin Miller mailed sexually explicit brochures from Los Angeles, California, that advertised books titled "Sex Orgies Illustrated" and "Intercourse" and arrived in people's mailboxes as unsolicited advertisements. Miller was arrested and convicted under California state obscenity law when an elderly woman received one of Miller's mailings, complete with graphic depictions of sexual content on the cover. The high Court overturned Miller's conviction and enunciated a three-part test used to define whether certain material is obscene. All three parts of the *Miller* test must be met for a work to be defined as obscene. The judge or jury at trial must resolve whether:

1. "the average person applying contemporary community standards" would find the work, taken as a whole, appeals to the **prurient interest** [defined as "a shameful or morbid interest in nudity, sex, or excretion."[16]]
2. the work depicts or describes, in a patently offensive way, sexual conduct specifically defined by the applicable state law; and
3. the work, taken as a whole, lacks serious literary, artistic, political or scientific value.

The distinction between obscene material that is illegal and material that an individual may legally possess in his or her home went one step further in *New York* v. *Ferber,* 458 U.S. 747 (1982). In this case, the Court allowed the state of New York to prohibit child pornography even if such pornography was not obscene under the *Miller* test. Congress first tried to protect children from sexual exploitation when it passed the Protection of

---

[15]*Jacobellis* v. *Ohio,* 378 U.S. 184 (1964).

[16]*Attorney General* v. *Book Named "John Cleland's Memoirs of a Woman of Pleasure,"* 349 Mass. 69.

Children Against Sexual Exploitation Act of 1977[17] that punished using minors in visual depictions of sexually explicit conduct with the knowledge it would travel in interstate commerce. As the high Court said in *Ferber* "The prevention of sexual exploitation and abuse of children constitutes a government objective of surpassing importance." This was a major tenet of the Court's decision in *Osborne* v. *Ohio,* 495 U.S. 103 (1990), in which the Court made even mere possession of child pornography illegal. One victim of child pornography described its lasting damaging effects as the photographs are out in circulation, never to be retracted or removed:

> I was born into an insane family where my grandfather physically and sexually abused me from a young age until I was fifteen. Part of what he did was send me to strangers' homes for child prostitution where I was also used for child pornography. My grandfather would take pictures of me, as well as show me haunting pictures of other kids who looked drugged and dazed. I have nightmares, flashbacks and struggle with everyday tasks that most people take for granted. There is a haunting that surrounds me constantly, reminding me that I don't have control over keeping my past a secret. The pictures that were taken when I was so young are still out there. Who knows where they are and how many people have seen them. I wonder if they will show up when I least expect it. I am away from the abuse now, but know that someone could be pleasuring himself while looking at my pictures or showing them to kids.[18]

With the advances in technology from motion pictures, to home videocameras, the World Wide Web, webcams, digital processors, scanners, and home photoshop software, it has been difficult to stop the proliferation of child pornography. One text states that the reason child pornography has spawned widely is "that no one with access to the Internet need ever pay for any type of access to digital images depicting pornography again. Thousands of newsgroups, Web sites, e-groups and file servers offer every conceivable sex act . . . both free and for nominal fees. Home movies of the actual sexual assault of children can easily be made with inexpensive digital video cameras and posted on the Internet within minutes of the event or may even be posted live."[19] In our opening scenario, if Abby discovers child pornography in the materials that she ordered online, she must immediately destroy them or face prosecution for illegal possession.

4. Free Speech and the Internet

The proliferation of pornographic web sites on the Internet and the ready access by everyone, including children, to these sites led Congress to enact the Communications Decency Act ("CDA") of 1996.[20] The CDA made it a crime to post "indecent" or "patently offensive" materials that could be accessible to minors. In 1997, the U.S. Supreme Court held, in *Reno* v. *American Civil Liberties Union,* 117 S.Ct. 2329, that the CDA violated the First Amendment because the law suppressed access to speech that millions of adults had a right to access on the Internet, such as pornography, that could be declared "indecent."

Congress also enacted the Child Pornography Prevention Act ("CPPA"),[21] which sought to add to the definition of child pornography "any visual depiction, including any photograph, film, video, picture, or computer or computer-generated image or picture" that "is or appears to be of a minor engaging in sexually explicit conduct." The law was challenged on the grounds that it abridged the freedom of speech by denying access to computer-generated porn that involved no real children. The U.S. Supreme Court agreed and struck down that provision of the CPPA in *Ashcroft* v. *Free Speech Coalition.*

---

[17]Pub. L. No. 95-225, 92 Stat. 7 (1977).

[18]Monique M. Ferraro and Eoghan Casey. *Investigating Child Exploitation and Pornography: The Internet, the Law and Forensic Science.* (Burlington, MA: Elsevier Academic Press, 2005).

[19]*Ibid.*

[20]Communications Decency Act of 1996, Pub. L. No. 104-104 (1996).

[21]18 U.S.C. §2251 et seq.

BOX 3.3

Ashcroft v. *Free Speech Coalition,* 535 U.S. 234 (2002)
Supreme Court of the United States

Justice Kennedy delivered the opinion of the Court.

ISSUE

We consider in this case whether the Child Pornography Prevention Act of 1996 (CPPA), 18 U.S.C. §2251 et seq. [et seq. = and more], abridges the freedom of speech. The CPPA extends the federal prohibition against child pornography to sexually explicit images that appear to depict minors but were produced without using any real children. The statute prohibits, in specific circumstances, possessing or distributing these images, which may be created by using adults who look like minors or by using computer imaging. The new technology, according to Congress, makes it possible to create realistic images of children who do not exist . . .

HOLDING

The prohibitions of [the CPPA] are overbroad and unconstitutional.

REASONING

By prohibiting child pornography that does not depict an actual child, the statute goes beyond *New York* v. *Ferber,* 458 U.S. 747 (1982), which distinguished child pornography from other sexually explicit speech because of the State's interest in protecting the children exploited by the production process. As a general rule, pornography can be banned only if obscene, but under *Ferber,* pornography showing minors can be proscribed whether or not the images are obscene under the definition set forth in *Miller* v. *California,* 413 U.S. 15 (1973). *Ferber* recognized that "the *Miller* standard, like all general definitions of what may be banned as obscene, does not reflect the State's particular and more compelling interest in prosecuting those who promote the sexual exploitation of children."

Before 1996, Congress defined child pornography as the type of depictions at issue in *Ferber,* images made using actual minors. 18 U.S.C. §2252 (1994 ed.). The CPPA retains that prohibition at 18 U.S.C. §2256(8)(A) and adds three other prohibited categories of speech, of which the first,

§2256(8)(B), and the third, §2256(8)(D), are at issue in this case. Section 2256(8)(B) prohibits "any visual depiction, including any photograph, film, video, picture, or computer or computer-generated image or picture" that "is, or appears to be, of a minor engaging in sexually explicit conduct." The prohibition on "any visual depiction" does not depend at all on how the image is produced. The section captures a range of depictions, sometimes called "virtual child pornography," which include computer-generated images, as well as images produced by more traditional means. For instance, the literal terms of the statute embrace a Renaissance painting depicting a scene from classical mythology, a "picture" that "appears to be, of a minor engaging in sexually explicit conduct." The statute also prohibits Hollywood movies, filmed without any child actors, if a jury believes an actor "appears to be" a minor engaging in "actual or simulated . . . sexual intercourse." §2256(2).

These images do not involve, let alone harm, any children in the production process; but Congress decided the materials threaten children in other, less direct, ways. Pedophiles might use the materials to encourage children to participate in sexual activity. "[A] child who is reluctant to engage in sexual activity with an adult, or to pose for sexually explicit photographs, can sometimes be convinced by viewing depictions of other children 'having fun' participating in such activity." Furthermore, pedophiles might "whet their own sexual appetites" with the pornographic images, "thereby increasing the creation and distribution of child pornography and the sexual abuse and exploitation of actual children." Under these rationales, harm flows from the content of the images, not from the means of their production.

The First Amendment commands, "Congress shall make no law . . . abridging the freedom of speech." The government may violate this mandate in many ways, but a law imposing criminal penalties on protected speech is a stark example of speech suppression. The CPPA's penalties are indeed severe. A first offender may be imprisoned for 15 years. §2252A(b)(1). A repeat offender faces a prison sentence of not less than 5 years and not more than 30 years in prison. While even minor punishments can chill protected speech, *see Wooley* v. *Maynard,* 430 U.S. 705 (1977), this case provides a textbook example of why we permit facial challenges to statutes that burden expression. With these severe penalties in force, few legitimate movie producers or book publishers, or few other speakers in any capacity, would risk distributing images in or near the uncertain reach of this law. The Constitution gives significant protection from overbroad laws that chill speech within the First Amendment's vast and privileged sphere. Under this principle, the CPPA is unconstitutional on its face if it prohibits a substantial amount of protected expression. *See Broadrick* v. *Oklahoma,* 413 U.S. 601 (1973).

The sexual abuse of a child is a most serious crime and an act repugnant to the moral instincts of a decent people. In its legislative findings, Congress recognized that there are subcultures of persons who harbor illicit desires for children and commit criminal acts to gratify the impulses. Congress also found that surrounding the serious offenders are those who flirt with these impulses and trade pictures and written accounts of sexual activity with young children. Congress may pass valid laws to protect children from abuse, and it has, e.g., 18 U.S.C. §§2241, 2251. The prospect of crime, however, by itself does not justify laws suppressing protected speech. *See Kingsley Int'l Pictures Corp.* v. *Regents of Univ. of N.Y.,* 360 U.S. 684 (1959) ("Among free men, the deterrents ordinarily to be applied to prevent crime are education and punishment for violations of the law, not abridgment of the rights of free speech"). It is also well established that speech may not be prohibited because it concerns subjects offending our sensibilities. *See FCC* v. *Pacifica Foundation,* 438 U.S. 726 (1978) ("The fact that society may find speech offensive is not a sufficient reason for suppressing it"); *see also Reno* v. *ACLU,* 521 U.S. 844 (1997) ("In evaluating the free speech rights of adults, we have made it perfectly clear that 'sexual expression which is indecent but not obscene is protected by the First Amendment'");

Carey v. *Population Services Int'l,* 431 U.S. 678 (1977) ("The fact that protected speech may be offensive to some does not justify its suppression").

As a general principle, the First Amendment bars the government from dictating what we see or read or speak or hear. The freedom of speech has its limits; it does not embrace certain categories of speech, including defamation, incitement, obscenity, and pornography produced with real children. While these categories may be prohibited without violating the First Amendment, none of them includes the speech prohibited by the CPPA.

The CPPA prohibits speech despite its serious literary, artistic, political, or scientific value. The statute proscribes the visual depiction of an idea—that of teenagers engaging in sexual activity—that is a fact of modern society and has been a theme in art and literature throughout the ages. Both themes—teenage sexual activity and the sexual abuse of children—have inspired countless literary works. William Shakespeare created the most famous pair of teenage lovers, one of whom is just 13 years of age. *See* Romeo and Juliet, act I, sc. 2, l. 9 ("She hath not seen the change of fourteen years"). In the drama, Shakespeare portrays the relationship as something splendid and innocent, but not juvenile. The work has inspired no less than 40 motion pictures, some of which suggest that the teenagers consummated their relationship, e.g., Romeo and Juliet (B. Luhrmann director, 1996). Shakespeare may not have written sexually explicit scenes for the Elizabethan audience, but were modern directors to adopt a less conventional approach, that fact alone would not compel the conclusion that the work was obscene.

Contemporary movies pursue similar themes. Last year's Academy Awards featured the movie, Traffic, which was nominated for Best Picture.[22] The film portrays a teenager, identified as a 16-year-old, who becomes addicted to drugs. The viewer sees the degradation of her addiction, which in the end leads her to a filthy room to trade sex for drugs. The year before, American Beauty won the Academy Award for Best Picture.[23] In the

(continued)

---

[22]Citation in case: *See* "Predictable and Less So, the Academy Award Contenders," *The New York Times,* February 14, 2001, p. E11.

[23]Citation in case: *See* "'American Beauty' Tops the Oscars," *The New York Times,* March 27, 2000, p. E1.

BOX 3.3

(continued)

course of the movie, a teenage girl engages in sexual relations with her teenage boyfriend, and another yields herself to the gratification of a middle-aged man. The film also contains a scene where, although the movie audience understands the act is not taking place, one character believes he is watching a teenage boy performing a sexual act on an older man.

Our society, like other cultures, has empathy and enduring fascination with the lives and destinies of the young. Art and literature express the vital interest we all have in the formative years we ourselves once knew, when wounds can be so grievous, disappointment so profound, and mistaken choices so tragic, but when moral acts and self-fulfillment are still in reach. Whether or not the films we mention violate the CPPA, they explore themes within the wide sweep of the statute's prohibitions. If these films, or hundreds of others of lesser note that explore those

subjects, contain a single graphic depiction of sexual activity within the statutory definition, the possessor of the film would be subject to severe punishment without inquiry into the work's redeeming value.

CONCLUSION

The Government may not suppress lawful speech as the means to suppress unlawful speech. Protected speech does not become unprotected merely because it resembles the latter. The Constitution requires the reverse. "The possible harm to society in permitting some unprotected speech to go unpunished is outweighed by the possibility that protected speech of others may be muted. . . ." The overbreadth doctrine prohibits the Government from banning unprotected speech if a substantial amount of protected speech is prohibited or chilled in the process.

Applying the Rule of Law to the Facts: Is the law legal?

- In an effort to curb the advanced technology that makes catching child pornographers difficult, the federal government prohibited speech that "reflects the belief, or that is intended to cause another to believe" that materials contain illegal child pornography. Conviction under the prohibition carried a 20-year sentence. The law was challenged as overbroad, as it sweeps under its umbrella a substantial amount of constitutionally protected speech.

The law is legal and not overbroad. On May 19, 2008, the U.S. Supreme Court upheld the defendant's conviction. Even though fake child pornography is protected under the *Ashcroft v. Free Speech* decision, the Court held that marketing fake child pornography is a crime. *United States* v. *Williams*, 553 U.S.__(2008).

In *Reno* v. *American Civil Liberties Union*, 521 U.S. 844 (1997), the U.S. Supreme Court examined the CDA under strict scrutiny because the law could chill the free-speech interests of adults in accessing legal pornography even though the law was trying to protect minors from accessing the same material. The Court held the CDA unconstitutional because the law impermissibly regulated the content of the speech (preventing adults from looking at dirty pictures).

After CDA was struck down, Congress enacted the Child Online Protection Act ("COPA") in 1988[24] to prevent children from gaining access to sexually explicit material on the Internet. The law tried to remedy the defect in CDA by specifically narrowing COPA's criminal reach to commercial for-profit sites while incorporating the *Miller* test

---

[24]Child Online Protection Act, 47 U.S.C. §231 (2005). Information for this section derived from Betsy A. Bernfeld "Free Speech and Sex on the Internet: Court Clips COPA's Wings, but Filtering May Still Fly." *Wyoming Law Review,* Vol. 6 (2006), pp. 223–253.

for obscenity to prevent materials from being accessed by people younger than 17 years old. Many free-speech advocates immediately sued for an injunction to prevent the implementation of COPA. An **injunction** is when one party approaches a court for an order for the offending party to "please stop immediately." In the COPA case, the free-speech advocates argued that the criminal sanctions of fines up to $50,000 per violation and six months in prison had a "chilling" effect on the free speech rights of adults to access pornography on the Internet, an activity protected by the First Amendment. Less restrictive means were available to the government to achieve its compelling state interest of protecting children from harmful material on the Internet, including

1. Placing filters on computers of public access,
2. aggressively enforcing existing laws that protected children from sexually explicit material, and
3. renewing efforts to educate children on how to avoid such material on the Internet.

Thus, the free-speech advocates claimed that COPA was constitutionally defective under the First Amendment, and the U.S. Supreme Court agreed. *Ashcroft* v. *American Civil Liberties Union,* 542 U.S. 656 (2004).

Congress then passed the Children's Internet Protection Act ("CIPA") in 2001. How the law works is that a library cannot receive federal monies unless it adopts a filtering program to keep minors from accessing material that is harmful or obscene. The law does allow librarians to disable the filters for adults or for minors conducting *bona fide* research. The American Library Association brought suit against the government and won at the trial level but the U.S. Supreme Court reversed and found in favor of the government mandating the filters. In response to the argument that withholding federal funding for libraries that are often in desperate need of money on the basis of their refusal to place filters on their public computers is harmful to those institutions, the Supreme Court stated in *United States* v. *American Library Ass'n, Inc.,* 539 U.S. 194 (2003), that "Government entities [libraries] do not have First Amendment rights." The Court continued its analysis and stated when Congress dispenses public monies to government programs, it can also place limits on how those funds are used. The Court made the analogy that filtering Internet access was just like a librarian making decisions about what books to buy for the library shelves. Justice Stevens offered a biting dissent in disagreement with the majority holding when he said that CIPA "operates as a blunt nationwide restraint on adult access to 'an enormous amount of valuable information' that individual librarians could not possibly review. Most of that information is constitutionally protected speech. In my view, this restraint is unconstitutional."

But the high Court also noted that library filtering of computers to prevent minors from accessing harmful material was not foolproof and could block harmless material that minors could legally access. Filtering has a tendency to **overblock** materials people have a right to access on the web, such as information on "breast" cancer which would be blocked via a filter. In addition, it **underblocks** some sexually explicit materials, for example pornography sites found on foreign web sites for which the filter does not recognize the language. A filter may also only be able to screen text, not images. Because many pornography sites scan text as an image file, people would still be able to access sexually explicit sites directly. Some free-speech advocates promote the idea that all adults should ask their librarian to remove the filter when they use a computer in a public library as a matter of course, which the adult has a right to do, to remove any stigma from asking to have the block removed. The librarian has no right to ask the adult why he or she wants the block removed, or what material the user plans to access on the Internet, any more than the librarian can ask why the adult is checking out certain books or stop the adult from taking certain books out on the basis of the books' content.

III. SPECIAL FIRST AMENDMENT ISSUES

Rule of Law: **Students' free speech rights may be limited.**

1. Schools

In *Tinker* v. *Des Moines Independent Community School District,* 393 U.S. 503 (1969), students who wore black armbands to protest the Vietnam Conflict were suspended. The Supreme Court held in favor of the students' free speech rights and said "in the absence of a specific showing of constitutionally valid reasons to regulate their speech, students are entitled to freedom of expression of their views." The Court said student speech and expression should be allowed unless it materially and substantially disrupted the work and discipline of the school. In later cases, however, the Court limited the protections of *Tinker* in *Bethel School District No. 403* v. *Fraser,* 478 U.S. 675 (1986), where the Court upheld the disciplining of a student who gave a speech peppered with sexual innuendo. The court ruled that the school had the power to regulate student speech or conduct that is "vulgar" or "offensively lewd."

The other situation in which schools can regulate speech is when student speech might appear to be sponsored by the school. The Second Circuit Court of Appeals held that a school district violated a seventh-grader's First Amendment rights when it made him cover with tape images that depicted a martini glass, three lines of cocaine, a razor blade, and a straw which suggested that President George W. Bush used illegal drugs. The school argued it had the right under the *Fraser* decision to ban "plainly offensive" speech in a school setting, but the court said while the images "may cause school administrators displeasure and could be construed as insulting and in poor taste," the images were not in the same category as the offensive sexual speech prohibited in *Fraser*.[25] But on the opposite side of the coast in California, the Ninth Circuit Court of Appeals upheld a school's decision to ban a T-shirt with a slogan that denigrated gays and lesbians on the grounds that the T-shirt "collides with the rights of other students in the most fundamental way." As is often the focal point of debate regarding hate speech, in a strongly worded dissent, Justice Alex Kozinski wrote "One man's civic responsibility, is another man's thought control."[26]

In a recent U.S. Supreme Court ruling, the high court voted against a student's expression of free speech if it directly conflicted with the school's educational mission however broadly the school wanted to define it. In *Morse* v. *Frederick,* 127 S.Ct. 2618 (2007), as the 2002 Olympic Torch passed Juneau, Alaska, high school student Joseph Frederick unfurled a banner, "BONG HiTS 4 JESUS," meant as a joke and to retaliate against the school principal Deborah Morse, who had previously disciplined him. Ms. Morse confiscated the banner, destroyed it, and suspended Frederick. The case made its way to the high Court because of the tension between a student's free-speech rights and the school's ability to educate students without undue interference. The U.S. Supreme Court found in favor of the school. The Court viewed the banner as advocating the use of illegal drugs and held: "Because schools may take steps to safeguard those entrusted to their care from speech that can reasonably be regarded as encouraging illegal drug use, the school officials in this case did not violate the First Amendment by confiscating the pro-drug banner and suspending Frederick." The Court said that if the principal had failed to act, the drug message "would [have sent] a powerful message to the students . . . about how serious the school was about the dangers of illegal drug use . . . The First Amendment does not require schools to tolerate at school events student expression that contributes to those dangers." The dissent saw the case as being not about drugs, but about free speech, and questioned whether a banner

---

[25]Daniel Wise. "'Offensive' Speech Gets Narrow Reading." *New York Law Journal,* September 5, 2006.

[26]Henry Weinstein. "Court Lets Schools Ban Inflammatory T-shirts." *LA Times* website, *http://www.latimes.com* (accessed April 21, 2006).

that said "Wine sips 4 Jesus" could be constitutionally banned because it promoted alcohol use which poses similar, if not greater, danger to students.

Applying the Rule of Law to the Facts: Can political speech be censored?

- A seventh-grader wore a T-shirt intimating that President George W. Bush was a drunk driver and snorted cocaine. The school principal told him to either change his shirt or cover its message with duct tape. Legal suppression of speech?

No, the school could not force the student to change the shirt. Just because the school found the shirt's message offensive is not sufficient legal justification to suppress the speech.[27]

- A right-to-life group ran a television advertisement criticizing Democrat Senator Russ Feingold for not voting for President Bush's judicial appointments. The group was sued for violating the McCain–Feingold law, which tries to prevent special interest groups from circumventing the campaign contribution limits to campaigns by running ads as a "political message." Can the ads be suppressed?

No. The high Court held "Discussion of issues cannot be suppressed simply because the issues may also be pertinent in an election. Where the First Amendment is implicated, the tie goes to the speaker, not the censor." *Federal Election Commission* v. *Wisconsin Right to Life, Inc.*, 127 S.Ct. 2652 (2007), held that the right-to-life group had a constitutional right under the First Amendment to make and run the ads. The Court upheld such "issue advocacy"—pro-life messages under the guise of political complaints— even though corporations were funding it, as long as the advertisement did not suggest "to vote for or against a specific candidate."

2. Prisoners

Prisoners traditionally have less freedom than the general public. The public policy supporting the infringement of a prisoner's Fourth Amendment right to be free from unreasonable search and seizure is that a convict forfeits his or her rights as an ordinary citizen and that for the good of the order and security of the prison environment, corrections officers have the right to search and seize at will. In Pennsylvania, one prison disallowed certain reading materials—nonreligious newspapers and magazines— for inmates who were classified as especially disruptive and resistant to other disciplinary measures. The prison deemed these materials to be rewards as an incentive for these particularly "bad" prisoners to show better behavior. The prisoners challenged the policy on the grounds that the prison could not rob them of their First Amendment rights to be free from prison censorship of reading materials. To bolster their point, the inmates pointed out that religious reading material was allowed. The U.S. Supreme Court decided against the prisoners in *Beard* v. *Banks*, 542 U.S. 406 (2006) and held that courts should defer to prison officials to design policy needs that further the legitimate prison objectives of internal security, including using the privileges of reading materials as an incentive for prisoners to exhibit better behavior.

IV. FREEDOM OF ASSOCIATION

Rule of Law: Gangs and hate groups have a First Amendment right to associate with one another.

The First Amendment does not explicitly mention freedom of association, but the U.S. Supreme Court has interpreted such a right as part of freedom of speech, expression,

---

[27]Based on *Guiles* v. *Marineau,* Second Circuit Court of Appeals (August 31, 2006), Docket Nos. 05-0327-vs(L); 05-0517-cv (XAP).

press, assembly, and petition. If the individual can do it legally by himself so, too, he can do it with others. In order for the government to infringe on the right to associate, it must be shown that

1. The government interest is compelling and
2. The government's objective cannot be achieved by less restrictive means.

One area rife with cases trying to prevent people from associating is gang activity. As the drug trade increased in large metropolitan areas so, too, did gang activity. States tried to stem the violence associated with gangs by enacting ordinances that prohibited gang members from gathering and punished those that did. One such ordinance in Illinois was challenged and reached the U.S. Supreme Court. In *City of Chicago* v. *Morales,* 527 U.S. 41 (1999), the high Court examined the ordinance that "prohibits 'criminal street gang members' from loitering in public places. Under the ordinance, if a police officer observes a person whom he reasonably believes to be a gang member loitering in a public place with one or more persons, he shall order them to disperse. Anyone who does not promptly obey such an order has violated the ordinance." The Court concluded that the ordinance's broad sweep violates the requirement that a legislature establish minimal guidelines to govern law enforcement and also violates the principle of legality, discussed in Chapter 4, because the law was too vague to give notice of the prohibted conduct. The ordinance encompasses a great deal of harmless behavior: In any public place in Chicago, persons in the company of a gang member maybe ordered to disperse if their purpose is not apparent to an officer. While the high Court discussed the First Amendment implications of the ordinance, it eventually invalidated the law on the grounds that it violated the due process clause of the Fourteenth Amendment.

Rule of Law: The First Amendment has two religious clauses: the Establishment Clause and the Exercise Clause.

V. FREEDOM OF RELIGION

1. The Establishment Clause

The freedom of religion expressed in the First Amendment is two pronged: it protects the establishment of religion and the practice of religion. The so-called **Establishment Clause** has been interpreted to separate church and state so that neither entity is involved in the other's affairs. The test for whether a law violates the doctrine of separation of church and state is called the *Lemon* test enunciated in *Lemon* v. *Kurtzman,* 403 U.S. 602 (1971):

1. The challenged statute must have a secular (nonreligious) legislative purpose.
2. The statute's principal or primary effect must be one that neither advances nor inhibits religion, and
3. the statute must not foster an excessive government entanglement with religion.

In 2005, the U.S. Supreme Court noted that the *Lemon* test was applied in a piecemeal fashion and was not helpful in deciding the case before it, *Van Orden* v. *Perry,* 125 S.Ct. 2854 (2005). In the *Van Orden* case, the Court was asked to decide whether a display of the religious tenets of the Ten Commandments at the Texas state capitol violated the separation of church and state. The court found that the display was one of several monuments and historical markers representing the people of the state of Texas and that it represented a part of state history, so the monument survived the Establishment Clause challenge. On the same day the *Van Order* decision was announced, the Court reached an opposite result in a similar case in *McCreary County* v. *ACLU of Kentucky,* 545 U.S. 844 (2005), where the high Court was asked to rule on the legality under the Establishment Clause of the placement of gold-framed copies of the Ten Commandments in the hallways of Kentucky courthouses. The Court upheld the removal of the displays on the grounds that the county governments could have a preference and primary purpose of promoting certain religious displays over others, which violated the Constitution.

Other Establishment Clause challenges in criminal justice happen in challenges to faith-based religious programs. In *Moeller* v. *Bradford County,* residents of this Pennsylvania county sued the county for administering a prison program with taxpayer money that featured proselytizing and prayer, thereby violating the Establishment Clause's required separation between church and state.[28] In April 2007, the case settled and the County agreed to

> Forbid county contractors from pressuring or coercing program participants to attend or participate in religious activities; bar publicly funded programs from discriminating based on religion in providing services; prohibit the use of any public funds for the support of any religious activities, including religious instruction, worship and proselytization; prohibit the use of public money to purchase religious materials or for the construction or maintenance of religious buildings; and regularly monitor compliance with these rules by all religiously affiliated contractors.[29]

2. The Exercise Clause

While religious beliefs enjoy absolute protection under the First Amendment, those religious practices which offend societal norms or subvert the social order can be regulated.[30] The government may regulate certain religious practices, outlawing polygamy or drug use in religious ceremonies, for example. But it may not infringe upon other practices; for instance, it would not allow firing a worker because his Sabbath is on Saturday, and it could not deny a solicitation permit to Jehovah's Witnesses on the basis of their religion.[31]

BOX 3.4

Church of the Lukumi Babalu Aye, Inc. v. *City of Hialeah,* 508 U.S. 520 (1993)
Supreme Court of the United States

Justice Kennedy delivered the opinion of the Court.

FACTS

This case involves practices of the Santeria religion, which originated in the 19th century. When hundreds of thousands of members of the Yoruba people were brought as slaves from western Africa to Cuba, their traditional African religion absorbed significant elements of Roman Catholicism. The resulting syncretion, or fusion, is Santeria, "the way of the saints." The Cuban Yoruba express their devotion to spirits, called orishas, through the iconography of Catholic saints, Catholic symbols are often present at Santeria rites, and Santeria devotees attend the Catholic sacraments. The Santeria faith

(continued)

---

[28]444 F.Supp.2d 316 (M.D. Pa. 2006).

[29]http://www.aclupa.org/pressroom/bradfordcountysettleslawsu.htm (accessed August 30, 2007).

[30]*See Reynolds* v. *United States,* 98 U.S. 145 (1878).

[31]*See Dep't of Human Resources* v. *Smith,* 494 U.S. 872 (1990) (allowing the denial of worker's compensation benefits to Native Americans who were fired from a private drug rehabilitation center for ingesting peyote as part of a religious ritual); *Sherbert* v. *Verner,* 374 U.S. 398 (1963) (overturning dismissal of a Seventh-Day Adventist for refusing to work on Saturdays because law benefited Sunday Sabbath observers—outcome would have been different if the Saturday Sabbath observer refused to work at all).

BOX 3.4

(continued)

teaches that every individual has a destiny from God, a destiny fulfilled with the aid and energy of the orishas. The basis of the Santeria religion is the nurture of a personal relation with the orishas, and one of the principal forms of devotion is an animal sacrifice. The sacrifice of animals as part of religious rituals has ancient roots. Animal sacrifice is mentioned throughout the Old Testament, and it played an important role in the practice of Judaism before destruction of the second Temple in Jerusalem. In modern Islam, there is an annual sacrifice commemorating Abraham's sacrifice of a ram in the stead of his son.

According to Santeria teaching, the orishas are powerful but not immortal. They depend for survival on the sacrifice. Sacrifices are performed at birth, marriage, and death rites, for the cure of the sick, for the initiation of new members and priests, and during an annual celebration. Animals sacrificed in Santeria rituals include chickens, pigeons, doves, ducks, guinea pigs, goats, sheep, and turtles. The animals are killed by the cutting of the carotid arteries in the neck. The sacrificed animal is cooked and eaten, except after healing and death rituals.

Petitioner Church of the Lukumi Babalu Aye, Inc. (Church), is a not-for-profit corporation organized under Florida law in 1973. The Church and its congregants practice the Santeria religion. In April 1987, the Church leased land in the city of Hialeah, Florida, and announced plans to establish a house of worship as well as a school, cultural center, and museum [with the goal] to bring the practice of the Santeria faith, including its ritual of animal sacrifice, into the open. The prospect of a Santeria church in their midst was distressing to many members of the Hialeah community, and the announcement of the plans to open a Santeria church in Hialeah prompted the city council to hold an emergency public session on June 9, 1987.

First, the city council adopted Resolution 87-66, which noted the "concern" expressed by residents of the city "that certain religions may propose to engage in practices which are inconsistent with public morals, peace or safety," and declared that "the City reiterates its commitment to a prohibition against any and all acts of any and all religious groups which are inconsistent with public morals, peace or safety." Next, the council approved an emergency ordinance, Ordinance 87-40, which incorporated in full, except as to penalty, Florida's animal cruelty laws. Fla. Stat. ch. 828 (1987). Among other things, the incorporated state law subjected to criminal punishment "whoever . . . unnecessarily or cruelly . . . kills any animal." §828.12. The city council responded at first with a hortatory enactment, Resolution 87-90, that noted its residents' "great concern regarding the possibility of public ritualistic animal sacrifices" and the state law prohibition. The resolution declared the city policy "to oppose the ritual sacrifices of animals" within Hialeah and announced that any person or organization practicing animal sacrifice "will be prosecuted." In September 1987, the city council adopted three substantive ordinances addressing the issue of religious animal sacrifice. Ordinance 87-52 defined "sacrifice" as "to unnecessarily kill, torment, torture, or mutilate an animal in a public or private ritual or ceremony not for the primary purpose of food consumption," and prohibited owning or possessing an animal "intending to use such animal for food purposes." It restricted application of this prohibition, however, to any individual or group that "kills, slaughters or sacrifices animals for any type of ritual, regardless of whether or not the flesh or blood of the animal is to be consumed." The ordinance contained an exemption for slaughtering by "licensed establishment[s]" of animals "specifically raised for food purposes." Declaring, moreover, that the city council "has determined that the sacrificing of animals within the city limits is contrary to the public health, safety, welfare and morals of the community," the city council adopted Ordinance 87-71. That ordinance defined "sacrifice" as had Ordinance 87-52, and then provided that "it shall be unlawful for any person, persons, corporations or associations to sacrifice any animal within the corporate limits of the City of Hialeah, Florida."

The final Ordinance, 87-72, defined "slaughter" as "the killing of animals for food" and prohibited slaughter outside of areas zoned for slaughterhouse use. All ordinances and resolutions passed the city council by unanimous vote. Violations of each of the four ordinances were punishable by fines not exceeding $500 or imprisonment not exceeding 60 days, or both.

ISSUE

[Do] city ordinances regulating animal sacrifice, but effectively prohibiting only sacrifice as practiced by [a particular] religion [violate] the First Amendment's free exercise of religion clause?

HOLDING

[Yes].

REASONING

The Free Exercise Clause of the First Amendment, which has been applied to the States through the Fourteenth Amendment, provides that "Congress shall make no law respecting an establishment of religion, or prohibiting the free exercise thereof. . . ." In addressing the constitutional protection for free exercise of religion, our cases establish the general proposition that a law that is neutral and of general applicability need not be justified by a compelling governmental interest even if the law has the incidental effect of burdening a particular religious practice. *Employment Div., Dept. of Human Resources of Ore.* v. *Smith,* 494 U.S. 872 (1990). Neutrality and general applicability are interrelated, and, as becomes apparent in this case, failure to satisfy one requirement is a likely indication that the other has not been satisfied. A law failing to satisfy these requirements must be justified by a compelling governmental interest and must be narrowly tailored to advance that interest. These ordinances fail to satisfy the *Smith* requirements. We begin by discussing neutrality.

In our Establishment Clause cases we have often stated the principle that the First Amendment forbids an official purpose to disapprove of a particular religion or of religion in general. Indeed, it was "historical instances of religious persecution and intolerance that gave concern to those who drafted the Free Exercise Clause." *Bowen* v. *Roy,* 476 U.S. 693 (1986).[32] These principles, though not

often at issue in our Free Exercise Clause cases, have played a role in some. In *McDaniel* v. *Paty,* 435 U.S. 618 (1978), for example, we invalidated a state law that disqualified members of the clergy from holding certain public offices, because it "impose[d] special disabilities on the basis of . . . religious status." On the same principle, in *Fowler* v. *Rhode Island,* we found that a municipal ordinance was applied in an unconstitutional manner when interpreted to prohibit preaching in a public park by a Jehovah's Witness but to permit preaching during the course of a Catholic mass or Protestant church service. Although a law targeting religious beliefs as such is never permissible, if the object of a law is to infringe upon or restrict practices because of their religious motivation, the law is not neutral, and it is invalid unless it is justified by a compelling interest and is narrowly tailored to advance that interest. There are, of course, many ways of demonstrating that the object or purpose of a law is the suppression of religion or religious conduct. To determine the object of a law, we must begin with its text, for the minimum requirement of neutrality is that a law not discriminate on its face.

A law lacks facial neutrality if it refers to a religious practice without a secular meaning discernible from the language or context. We reject the contention advanced by the city that our inquiry must end with the text of the laws at issue. Facial neutrality is not determinative. The Free Exercise Clause, like the Establishment Clause, extends beyond facial discrimination. The Clause "forbids subtle departures from neutrality," and "covert suppression of particular religious beliefs." The record in this case compels the conclusion that suppression of the central element of the Santeria worship service was the object of the ordinances.

First, though use of the words "sacrifice" and "ritual" does not compel a finding of improper targeting of the Santeria religion, the choice of these words is support for our conclusion. There are further respects in which the text of the city council's enactments discloses the improper attempt to target Santeria. Resolution 87-66, adopted June 9, 1987, recited that "residents and citizens of the City

(continued)

---

[32]Citation in case: *See* J. Story, *Commentaries on the Constitution of the United States §§991–992* (abridged ed. 1833) (reprint 1987).

BOX 3.4

(continued)

of Hialeah have expressed their concern that certain religions may propose to engage in practices which are inconsistent with public morals, peace or safety," and "reiterate[d]" the city's commitment to prohibit "any and all [such] acts of any and all religious groups." No one suggests, and on this record it cannot be maintained, that city officials had in mind a religion other than Santeria.

We begin with Ordinance 87-71. It prohibits the sacrifice of animals, but defines sacrifice as "to unnecessarily kill . . . an animal in a public or private ritual or ceremony not for the primary purpose of food consumption." The definition excludes almost all killings of animals except for religious sacrifice, and the primary purpose requirement narrows the proscribed category even further, in particular by exempting kosher slaughter. It suffices to recite this feature of the law as support for our conclusion that Santeria alone was the exclusive legislative concern. The net result of the gerrymander is that few if any killings of animals are prohibited other than Santeria sacrifice, which is proscribed because it occurs during a ritual or ceremony and its primary purpose is to make an offering to the orishas, not food consumption. Indeed, careful drafting ensured that, although Santeria sacrifice is prohibited, killings that are no more necessary or humane in almost all other circumstances are unpunished.

Ordinance 87-40 incorporates the Florida animal cruelty statute, Fla. Stat. §828.12 (1987). Its prohibition is broad on its face, punishing "whoever . . . unnecessarily . . . kills any animal." The city claims that this ordinance is the epitome of a neutral prohibition. The problem, however, is the interpretation given to the ordinance by respondent [city of Hialeah] and the Florida attorney general. Killings for religious reasons are deemed unnecessary, whereas most other killings fall outside the prohibition. The city, on what seems to be a *per se* basis, deems hunting, slaughter of animals for food, eradication of insects and pests, and euthanasia as necessary. There is no indication in the record that respondent has concluded that hunting or fishing for sport is unnecessary. Indeed, one of the few reported Florida cases decided under §828.12 con-

cludes that the use of live rabbits to train greyhounds is not unnecessary. Further, because it requires an evaluation of the particular justification for the killing, this ordinance represents a system of "individualized governmental assessment of the reasons for the relevant conduct." Respondent's application of the ordinance's test of necessity devalues religious reasons for killing by judging them to be of lesser import than nonreligious reasons. Thus, religious practice is being singled out for discriminatory treatment.

The legitimate governmental interests in protecting the public health and preventing cruelty to animals could be addressed by restrictions stopping far short of a flat prohibition of all Santeria sacrificial practice. If improper disposal [of dead animals], not the sacrifice itself, is the harm to be prevented, the city could have imposed a general regulation on the disposal of organic garbage. It did not do so. Indeed, counsel for the city conceded at oral argument that, under the ordinances, Santeria sacrifices would be illegal even if they occurred in licensed, inspected, and zoned slaughterhouses. Thus, these broad ordinances prohibit Santeria sacrifice even when it does not threaten the city's interest in the public health. The District Court [the lower trial court] accepted the argument that narrower regulation would be unenforceable because of the secrecy in the Santeria rituals and the lack of any central religious authority to require compliance with secular disposal regulations. It is difficult to understand, however, how a prohibition of the sacrifices themselves, which occur in private, is enforceable if a ban on improper disposal, which occurs in public, is not.

The neutrality of a law is suspect if First Amendment freedoms are curtailed to prevent isolated collateral harms not themselves prohibited by direct regulation. That the ordinances were enacted "'because of,' not merely 'in spite of'" their suppression of Santeria religious practice, is revealed by the events preceding their enactment. The minutes and taped excerpts of the June 9 session, both of which are in the record, evidence significant hostility exhibited by residents, members of the city council, and other city officials toward the Santeria religion and its practice of animal sacrifice. The public crowd that attended the June 9 meetings interrupted statements by council members critical of Santeria with cheers and the brief comments of Pichardo with taunts. When Councilman Martinez, a supporter of the ordinances, stated that in prerevolution Cuba "people were put in jail for practicing this religion," the audience applauded. Other statements by members of the city council were in a similar vein. For example, Councilman Martinez, after noting his belief that Santeria was outlawed in Cuba, questioned: "If we could not practice this [religion] in our home-land [Cuba], why bring it to this country?" Councilman Cardoso said that Santeria devotees at the Church "are in violation of everything this country stands for." Councilman Mejides indicated that he was "totally against the sacrificing of animals" and distinguished kosher slaughter because it had a "real purpose." The "Bible says we are allowed to sacrifice an animal for consumption," he continued, "but for any other purposes, I don't believe that the Bible allows that." The president of the city council, Councilman Echevarria, asked: "What can we do to prevent the Church from opening?"

Various Hialeah city officials made comparable comments. The chaplain of the Hialeah Police Department told the city council that Santeria was a sin, "foolishness," "an abomination to the Lord," and the worship of "demons." He advised the city council: "We need to be helping people and sharing with them the truth that is found in Jesus Christ." He con-

cluded: "I would exhort you . . . not to permit this Church to exist." The city attorney commented that Resolution 87-66 indicated: "This community will not tolerate religious practices which are abhorrent to its citizens. . . ." Similar comments were made by the deputy city attorney. This history discloses the object of the ordinances to target animal sacrifice by Santeria worshippers because of its religious motivation.

A law burdening religious practice that is not neutral or not of general application must undergo the most rigorous of scrutiny. To satisfy the commands of the First Amendment, a law restrictive of religious practice must advance "interests of the highest order" and must be narrowly tailored in pursuit of those interests. The compelling interest standard that we apply once a law fails to meet the *Smith* requirements is not "water[ed] . . . down" but "really means what it says." A law that targets religious conduct for distinctive treatment or advances legitimate governmental interests only against conduct with a religious motivation will survive strict scrutiny only in rare cases. It follows from what we have already said that these ordinances cannot withstand this scrutiny.

CONCLUSION

In sum, the neutrality inquiry leads to one conclusion: The ordinances had as their object the suppression of religion. These ordinances are not neutral, and the court below committed clear error in failing to reach this conclusion. Reversed.

Applying the Rule of Law to the Facts: **How far can legal regulation of religious practices go?**

- Members of a church drink hoasca, a tea brewed from plants found in the Amazon rainforest that contains a hallucinogen banned under federal drug laws. The plants were seized by customs officials and church members were threatened with prosecution. Did the government go overboard and violate the members' freedom of religion rights?

Yes. At least preliminarily, the government failed to show that by seizing the plants, the government's compliance with international drug law outweighed the church members' rights under the Religious Freedom Restoration Act of 1993 that prohibits government from burdening religious practice.[33] Abby, in the scenario, can legally believe peyote heals all, but Abby may be charged with manslaughter for failing to provide adequate medical care for her baby. The government's interest in the health and welfare of children outweighs her religious freedom.

---

[33]Adapted from *Gonzales* v. *Centro Espirita Beneficente União Do Vegetal, et alia,* 546 U.S. 418 (2006).

VI. Key Terms and Phrases

- child pornography
- chilling effect
- clear and present danger
- commercial speech
- compelling state interest (CSI)
- content-based regulation
- expressive conduct
- facial review
- fighting words
- First Amendment

- injunction
- least restrictive means
- narrowly tailored
- obscenity
- offensive speech and conduct
- overblock
- overbreadth
- prior restraint
- protected speech

- public forum
- strict scrutiny
- symbolic speech
- time
- manner
- place
- underblock
- unprotected speech
- vague

VII. Summary

1. **The activities protected by the First Amendment:** The **First Amendment** provides that "Congress shall make no law . . . abridging freedom of speech," which includes expressive conduct. If the government regulates speech on the basis of its content—where "content" means "what you are saying" (criticizing the government, for example)—then citizens may feel that their free-speech rights have been "chilled." Such laws would have a **chilling effect** on free speech rights. The law prevents **content-based regulation of speech,** unless there is a **compelling state interest** (CSI) in regulating the speech. The government regulation must be the **least restrictive means** to not burden speech, but the government can place **time, manner, and place restrictions** on speech. People have a right to be free from annoyances in the middle of the night, for example, but speech cannot be censored merely because the speech is offensive to some people. Two doctrines that protect speech are the **overbreadth** doctrine, which invalidates laws that proscribe protected and unprotected speech, and the **void for vagueness** doctrine, which says that if men of reasonable intelligence have to guess at the meaning of the law's words, it is void.

2. **Maintaining public order without suppressing speech and expression: Fighting words** are words that, by their very utterance, are likely to provoke immediate violence and, as such, are not protected by the First Amendment. Other speech that is unprotected is speech that poses a **clear and present danger,** which again is a call to incite immediate lawless activity. Although offensive to some, **expressive conduct** or **symbolic speech** which conveys an idea that is protected is legal. Activities such as nude dancing, wearing a jacket that swears at the military draft, burning the flag, or being a Nazi and holding a public march through a town heavily populated by Holocaust survivors—although all may be considered offensive—are legal. **Cross burning** is legal as long as it is not meant to intimidate. Speech in a **public forum** is given special rights because the First Amendment encourages the free expression of ideas. Simply because the conduct may offend people does not mean it's illegal.

3. **The legal difference between pornography and obscenity: Pornography**, which includes photographs or movies that depict adults engaged in sexual activity or sexually provocative poses, is **protected speech** and is legal under the First Amendment. **Child pornography** which depicts minors engaged in sexual activity with each other or with adults is **unprotected speech** by the First Amendment. The test for **obscenity,** known as the *Miller* test, defines a work as obscene if, by contemporary community standards, it depicts work that appeals to prurient interest, is patently offensive sexually, and taken as a whole has no serious literary, artistic, political, or scientific value. If the photograph, book, movie, or other work meets all three prongs of the *Miller* test, it is obscene and not afforded protection under the First Amendment.

4. **The legal restrictions on student free speech rights: Students** do not give up their free speech rights at the front door of the school, but the government has an interest in regulating behavior that undermines the educational mission. **University Speech Codes** on college campus must be narrowly tailored when colleges seek to promote racial harmony and tolerance for diversity without suppressing the free-speech rights of students to express dislike for people on the basis of their race, gender, or sexual orientation.

5. **Freedom of religion when certain religious practices may be considered criminal:** The **Establishment Clause** and the **Exercise Clause** of the First Amendment give absolute protection to religious beliefs, but the government can restrict certain religious practices that contravene societal duties and are subversive to good order. For example, it outlaws polygamy, illegal drug use in religious ceremonies, and praying over seriously ill children in lieu of obtaining medical care. But prohibiting the establishment of a church in a specific neighborhood because the community does not like the practices of that religion is unconstitutional.

VIII. Discussion Questions

1. The U.S. Supreme Court said in *Free Speech Coalition,* "First Amendment freedoms are most in danger when the government seeks to control thought or justify its laws for that impermissible end." Which do you think are more dangerous, thoughts or actions? Should we punish people for their thoughts alone?

2. There are many religious organizations that may or may not have ties to terrorist activities. Do individuals have a right to associate with other people, some of whom may advocate criminal activity?

3. Do government officials have a legal obligation to uphold the morals of the community? Can those morals be based on majority religious beliefs or preferences? Was it hypocritical for Hialeah's elected and health officials to invoke God and the teachings of the Bible to condemn the Santerians' worship practice? Is not the goal of the First Amendment to protect all who practice, no matter what their religion?

4. Imagine that it is the year 2020. Congress has passed a law that would abolish the First Amendment, and the Supreme Court has interpreted the law as legal. What would society look like, especially American newspapers, television shows, documentary movies and political discourse and dialogue?

5. Would you sign a loyalty oath in order to get a job you really wanted? Why or why not? Would you feel compelled to honor the oath once you took it? Using First Amendment principles, explain why such oaths are constitutional.

6. Why are religious organizations tax-exempt if there is legal separation between church and state? What is the public policy reason for excusing religious organizations from contributing to the economic health of the country? On the basis of the First Amendment, can religious organizations support political issues, causes, and candidates?

7. On what First Amendment grounds did the court determine that blocking Internet use at public libraries is legal?

8. Why did our founding fathers think that freedom of speech, religion, and press, and to peaceably assemble and petition for redress, were so important that they made these freedoms the First Amendment Congress passed?

IX. Problem-Solving Exercises

1. The Delaware Breach of the Peace statute provides that "Whoever placed on public or private property a symbol, object, appellation, including but not limited to, a burning cross, Nazi swastika, a stuffed doll in likeness of the President of the United States, which one knows or has reasonable grounds to know arouses anger, alarm or resentment in others, shall be guilty of a felony."

   John Smith, a devout member of the Santeria church, made a stuffed doll in the likeness of President Bush and in one of the local University's free speech zones, hung the doll in a tree and lit it on fire. At Smith's trial, he appeared in court wearing chicken feathers and the judge told him to take them off. Smith refused and said he was wearing the feathers to honor his god, Icarus. The judge held Smith in contempt. Discuss any defenses to the felony and contempt charges Smith may have.

2. Charlie and Ken agreed to email photographs taken by the late photographer Robert Mapplethorpe to their friend Hank, who lived in Alaska. The photos included images of various genitalia nailed to boards, groups of naked men kissing, assorted nipple piercings, and nude children. As Charlie hit the "send" button, the power failed and the photos never made it to Hank. Charlie and Ken have been charged with attempted distribution of obscene material. In their defense, the men say the photos are art. Who will win, the state or the defendants?

3. Mary opposed the United States' military operations in Iraq. She went to a public park and stood on a grassy knoll and began addressing a group of 12–15 people. Mary said, "Let's demand accountability from the government. If members of the administration won't pull our troops out of the Middle East, let's assemble and detonate bombs and plant them outside of all the military bases until the government has to withdraw from Iraq." No one listening responded to Mary's speech but one listener waved in approval. Mary was arrested under a state statute that prohibited "advocating insurrection against the federal government." Mary claims she has a complete defense in the First Amendment. Is Mary correct? Why or why not?

4. The state of Michigan promulgated a statute that required every publicly employed individual to list every year "every organization to which he has belonged or regularly contributed within the preceding five years." Sally refused and was fired. What is her best constitutional defense?[34]

---

[34]*Shelton v. Tucker,* 364 U.S. 479 (1960).

X. World Wide Web Resources

First Amendment

http://www.law.cornell.edu/wex/index.php/first_amendment

Obscenity

http://www.law.umkc.edu/faculty/projects/ftrials/conlaw/obscenity.htm

XI. Additional Readings and Notes

Obscenity

Andrew Koppelman. "Does Obscenity Cause Moral Harm?" *Columbia Law Review,* Vol. 105 (2005), pp. 1636–1679.

Jacqueline B. Watanabe. "Real Problems, Virtual Solutions: The (Still) Uncertain Future of Virtual Child Pornography Legislation." *Journal of Technology Law & Policy,* Vol. 10 (2005), pp. 196–222.

First Amendment

Brent E. Dye. "*Frye* v. *Kansas City Missouri Police Department:* When Public Safety Issues Clash with the Freedom of Speech." *Northern Kentucky Law Review,* Vol. 32 (2005), pp. 327–348.

Stephen M. Feldman. *Please Don't Wish Me a Merry Christmas: A Critical History of the Separation of Church and State.* (New York: New York University, 1997).

Kenneth Lasson. "Incitement in the Mosques: Testing the Limits of Free Speech and Religious Liberty." *Whittier Law Review,* Vol. 27 (2005), pp. 3–76.

Eric J. Nies. "The Fiery Cross: *Virginia* v. *Black,* History, and the First Amendment." *South Dakota Law Review,* Vol. 50 (2005), pp. 182–217.

Andrew P. Stanner. "Toward an Improved True Threat Doctrine for Student Speakers." *New York University Law Review,* Vol. 81 (2006), pp. 385–417.

CHAPTER 4

The Criminal Law Basics: Intent, Acts, Causation, Parties, and Inchoate Crimes

*"The law presumes that a person intends the necessary and natural consequences
of his act."*

UNITED STATES V. U.S. GYPSUM CO., 438 U.S. 422 (1978)

CHAPTER OBJECTIVES

Primary Concepts Discussed in This Chapter:

1. How criminal liability attaches to an individual wrongdoer
2. The legal duty to help people in peril or prevent crime
3. The end result of setting a crime in motion
4. The definitions of parties to crime
5. The legal principles assigning responsibility for the inchoate crimes of solicitation, conspiracy and attempt

CHAPTER OUTLINE

Feature: Hurricane Katrina, August 2005

I. *MENS REA*

1. *Mens Rea* and the Model Penal Code
Box 4.1 Ohio's Requirements for Criminal Liability
   a. Purposely
   b. Knowingly
   c. Recklessly
   d. Negligently
2. Intent
   a. Specific and General Intent
   Box 4.2 *Linehan* v. *Florida,* 442 So. 2d 244 (Fla. App. 1983)
   b. Transferred Intent
   c. The *Scienter* Requirement
   d. Strict Liability
   e. Principle of Legality
   Box 4.3 *Commonwealth* v. *Twitchell,* 617 N.E.2d 609 (Mass. 1993)
   f. Element Analysis

II. *ACTUS REUS*

1. The Duty to Act
2. Possession as an Act
3. Status as an Act

III. CAUSATION

1. Factual Cause
2. Proximate/Legal Cause

Feature: *Chapter-Opening Case Study: Hurricane Katrina, August 2005*

In New Orleans, Louisiana, on August 27, 2005, a few days before Hurricane Katrina hit land, officials asked the owners of a local nursing home, Steven Smith, 65, and his wife Mary, 62, whether they wanted to move the 71 residents to a safe shelter. The Smiths said no. They had been caring for the elderly at their nursing home for over ten years and had a spotless record. Steve assured officials that they would evacuate if necessary, but he later changed his mind saying, "If I evacuate by putting the sick and infirm on buses to take them to a shelter 100 miles away, some people on feeding tubes might die." On August 29, 2005, Katrina made landfall and the levee close to the nursing home broke. Floodwaters raged inside the nursing home and rose to the roof of the one-story nursing home, trapping the residents inside [was this flood foreseeable?] Neighbors paddled boats to the nursing home roof, smashed holes through the roof, and pulled 27 residents to safety, but 34 others drowned. A prosecutor charged the Smiths with 34 counts of homicide under the statute

> "Whoever purposely, knowingly, recklessly, or negligently causes the death of another, shall be guilty of homicide."

The Smiths were charged with manslaughter but asserted in their defense that they had no duty to save the residents and that they did not cause their deaths [Factual Cause: "but for" the Smiths' refusal to evacuate, the residents would not have died; Proximate Cause: was the residents' deaths foreseeable by the Smiths from their decision to stay put?; Intervening Cause: were there any events that broke the causal chain from the defendant's conduct and the ultimate harm, the deaths of the residents?].

The Smiths weren't the only people in court after Katrina. Once the mandatory evacuation order for New Orleans was issued, people who did not have transportation out of the city crammed into the Louisiana Superdome ("Dome"). Ken, who was pushed to the Superdome in a wheelchair and who was attached to a blood purification system that required electricity to run, was put inside the Dome next to an electrical outlet. Once the power lines went down leaving the city without electricity, Ken's battery-operated back-up generator could keep the purification system pumping for only one hour.

One man, Billy Bob [principal], approached Charles [accessory], and asked if he wanted to make some easy money by robbing all of the old people in the Dome [solicitation]. Charles agreed [conspiracy]. Billy Bob declared, "Once we rob these people, we can get out of here and they'll never find us. I'll hit the people in the heads and take their money, and you come up after me to threaten them that if they report us to the police, you'll kill them." Carrying out their plan, Billy Bob hit Ken over the head to rob him. Unbeknownst to Billy Bob, at the time of the robbery Ken's generator had been without power for two hours and Ken was dying.

Sondra, who had been standing in line to use the women's restroom, witnessed Ken being robbed but did nothing to help [no affirmative duty for bystanders to assist crime victims in peril]. Ken died within the hour. As agreed in their plan, Charles walked up and pointed a gun at Ken after Billy Bob had robbed him. Not realizing that Ken was already dead at this point, Charles said, "If you squeal about the robbery, I'll kill you." When Ken did not reply, Charles shot Ken, intending to kill him [attempted murder, impossibility to commit the crime because of Ken's death no defense]. Charles never noticed Ken was dead.

City officials, desperate to evacuate residents from the Superdome, chartered every available bus, even those that recently had failed safety inspections. At the time there was a city ordinance in effect that stated, "all moving vehicles must have current inspections and fully operational brakes." One bus filled with evacuees got stuck in traffic on the interstate when the back brakes caught fire. Fifteen people trapped at the back of the bus died from smoke inhalation. Their families have sued the City of New Orleans and city officials for causing their deaths [duty by statute].

Billy Bob was charged with solicitation and, along with Charles, was charged with conspiracy and murder for the death of Ken. Sondra was charged for failing to help Ken when she was an innocent bystander and saw him in need. Who will win their cases?

INTRODUCTION

This chapter examines the basics of criminal law concepts that remain the same regardless of jurisdiction, such as *mens rea, actus reus,* intent, criminal causation, parties to crimes as well as how society punishes the crimes of attempt, solicitation, and conspiracy.

I. *MENS REA*

Rule of Law: In order for an individual to be found guilty of a crime, the state must prove beyond a reasonable doubt that the offender had the required mental state to commit the crime.

In criminal law the defendant's state of mind when he committed a crime, or *mens rea,* is critical in order for judges and juries to assign the proper level of responsibility for the crime. A contract killer who murders for money and kills his victim after loading a pistol, pointing it, and shooting at the victim's vital organs is more responsible, blameworthy, and culpable than a man who is obeying the speed limit in a residential neighborhood who kills a child who unexpectedly runs into the street. The *mens rea* is the springboard for the criminal act, called the *actus reus*. Based on the state of mind of the offender, the law defines crimes and grades offenses, such as the difference between murder and manslaughter in the previous example. The reason society wants to define an offender's state of mind is based on society's belief that the punishment should reflect his true criminal intent in committing the crime. In late summer 2006, John Mark Karr made headlines by admitting to the unsolved murder of child beauty queen JonBenet Ramsey, found murdered in her home on Christmas Day 1996. In reported stories of his "confession," Karr stated that he had killed the child "accidentally" and not "intentionally." Karr's statements indicate his awareness that a purposeful, willful, and intentional act is punished much more harshly than a reckless or negligent act that may be characterized as an "accident." Karr was eventually eliminated as a suspect when biological evidence excluded him as the killer.

Some crimes that are regulatory in nature, such as food inspections at restaurants and traffic offenses, require no *mens rea* for the offender to be found guilty. Such crimes are called strict liability crimes, discussed later in this chapter. One is guilty under strict liability by the simple act of committing the prohibited conduct, regardless of intent.

Early church doctrine defined acts that harmed society in terms of moral purity.[1] In early common law, *mens rea* was an "essential element of criminality" where "it was universally accepted" that both an evil intent and the act of felony were both required to find someone guilty.[2] Early definitions of *mens rea* were described as acting "wantonly," "heedlessly," "maliciously," with a "depraved heart," "evil," and with "knowledge aforethought." Today, crimes are defined by legislatures enacting statutes defining the forbidden conduct and the required mental state necessary, since the police power is left to the states and the U.S. Constitution has no criminal code.[3] Students should be aware that each state may define similar crimes differently. Students are advised to research their respective state jurisdictions and criminal codes to learn the proper definition of each crime. A typical law is illustrated in the Ohio statute reprinted in part in Box 4.1 that requires for criminal liability a culpable mental state, a voluntary act, and the absence of a defense, such as intoxication, that might interfere with the formation of the requisite physical state or *actus reus*.

1. *Mens Rea* and the Model Penal Code

In an effort to streamline the various definitions of mental states used to assign criminal responsibility for an offender's actions, the Model Penal Code ("MPC" excerpts in Appendix B) offered four standard definitions of *mens rea* states. The states listed in order of culpability from most to less serious are purposely, knowingly, recklessly, and negligently. The *mens rea* states that define a criminal state of mind are exclusive—that is, one cannot possess more than one mental state at a time even if a law will punish many different *mens rea* states for a specific crime. In fact, one cannot both intentionally and negligently shoot someone even if a statute criminalizes

---

[1] Harold J. Berman. *Law and Revolution: The Formation of the Western Legal Tradition*. (Cambridge, MA: Harvard University, 1983).

[2] Francis B. Sayre. "*Mens Rea*." *Harvard Law Review*, 45 (1932).

[3] *Powell* v. *Texas*, 392 U.S. 514 (1968).

BOX 4.1

Ohio Revised Code Annotated §2901.21 (2008).
Requirements for criminal liability

A. Except as provided in division (B) of this section, a person is not guilty of an offense unless both of the following apply:
   1. The person's liability is based on conduct that includes either a voluntary act, or an omission to perform an act or duty that the person is capable of performing;
   2. The person has the requisite degree of culpability for each element as to which a culpable mental state is specified by the section defining the offense.
B. When the section defining an offense does not specify any degree of culpability, and plainly indicates a purpose to impose strict criminal liability for the conduct described in the section, then culpability is not required for a person to be guilty of the offense. When the section neither specifies culpability nor plainly indicates a purpose to impose strict liability, recklessness is sufficient culpability to commit the offense.
C. Voluntary intoxication may not be taken into consideration in determining the existence of a mental state that is an element of a criminal offense.

Voluntary intoxication does not relieve a person of a duty to act if failure to act constitutes a criminal offense. Evidence that a person was voluntarily intoxicated may be admissible to show whether or not the person was physically capable of performing the act with which the person is charged.

D. As used in this section:
   1. Possession is a voluntary act if the possessor knowingly procured or received the thing possessed, or was aware of the possessor's control of the thing possessed for a sufficient time to have ended possession.
   2. Reflexes, convulsions, body movements during unconsciousness or sleep, and body movements that are not otherwise a product of the actor's volition, are involuntary acts.
   3. "Culpability" means purpose, knowledge, recklessness, or negligence, as defined in section 2901.22 of the Revised Code.
   4. "Intoxication" includes, but is not limited to, intoxication resulting from the ingestion of alcohol, a drug, or alcohol and a drug.

---

the "intentional, reckless, or negligent killing of another." Figure 4.1 illustrates how the *mens rea* states resemble the food chain in the sea, where the biggest fish of purpose eats the lesser fish of knowledge, which eats the smaller fish of recklessness, which eats the smallest fish of negligence. The bigger the fish, the higher the state of moral culpability and the more severe the punishment for the offense committed with the respective state of mind. The public policy reasons behind separating *mens rea* states are similar to the reasons we recognize certain defenses. Society does not hold the person who kills another on purpose to the same level of culpability as the careless smoker who falls asleep with a lit cigarette, setting a house on fire and killing people trapped inside. The average sentences for such crimes differ based on the *mens rea* of bringing about the result where people are harmed.

Rule of Law: Purposely means the offender acted specifically to bring about the desired result.

a. Purposely
The Model Penal Code §2.02 defines <u>Purposely</u> in the following way.

A person acts purposely with respect to a material element of an offense when
   i. if the element involves the nature of his conduct or a result thereof, it is his conscious object to engage in conduct of that nature or to cause such a result; and

FIGURE 4.1   Big fish *mens rea* eats little fish *mens rea*.

ii.   if the element involves the attendant circumstances, he is aware of the existence of such circumstances or he believes or hopes that they exist.

Purposefully is defined as taking an act to bring about a specific result. If a wife puts bullets in a gun, points the gun at her husband, and pulls the trigger with the specific intent to kill him, she has acted purposefully in pulling the trigger to bring about a specific result, her husband's death.

Rule of Law: Knowingly means the offender was substantially certain that his conduct would bring about a specific result.

b. Knowingly
The MPC §2.02 defines <u>Knowingly</u> in the following way.

A person acts knowingly with respect to a material element of an offense when

i.   if the element involves the nature of his conduct or the attendant circumstances, he is aware that his conduct is of that nature or that such circumstances exist; and

ii.   if the element involves a result of his conduct, he is aware that it is practically certain that his conduct will cause such a result.

Knowing is acting not to bring about a specific result but knowing that such a result is substantially likely to occur from one's actions. If a suspect running from the police is caught and flails his arms in an effort to free himself from police clutches, he can be convicted of assault because he knew that his actions of resisting arrest would cause injury to an officer, even though the reason he resisted was to escape. But the knowing requirement does not mean that the defendant knew a specific injury would result from his conduct, and the state need not prove that the defendant knew his acts would cause injury.[4] If Bill rams his car at high speed into Suzy's car, Bill may be charged with

---

[4]*State* v. *Dixon,* 2004 Ohio App. LEXIS 2141.

knowing that his actions would likely cause Suzy injury, even if he did not specifically intend to cause Suzy a specific injury or did not know what specific injury Suzy would suffer.

Rule of Law: Recklessly means the offender was aware of the risk of harm to others that his actions created, and he ignored the risk.

c. Recklessly

The MPC §2.02 defines <u>Recklessly</u> in the following way.

> A person acts recklessly with respect to a material element of an offense when he consciously disregards a substantial and unjustifiable risk that the material element exists or will result from his conduct. The risk must be of such a nature and degree that, considering the nature and purpose of the actor's conduct and the circumstances known to him, its disregard involves a gross deviation from the standard of conduct that a law-abiding person would observe in the actor's situation.

An example of reckless conduct would be drag racing on a crowded street at rush hour. The racers are aware of the risk of injury to others that their behavior—driving too fast—creates, and yet they ignore the risk. Similarly, a lifeguard who allows children to swim at high tide when a hurricane storm surge is approaching is aware of the risk his behavior creates—allowing swimming when a rip tide could cause the children to drown—yet he ignores it and allows them to swim anyway.

Rule of Law: Negligently means the offender is unaware of the risk of harm his behavior creates, but he should be aware.

d. Negligently

The MPC §2.02 defines <u>Negligently</u> in the following way.

> A person acts negligently with respect to a material element of an offense when he should be aware of a substantial and unjustifiable risk that the material element exists or will result from his conduct. The risk must be of such a nature and degree that the actor's failure to perceive it, considering the nature and purpose of his conduct and the circumstances known to him, involves a gross deviation from the standard of care that a reasonable person would observe in the actor's situation.

At times it is difficult to distinguish reckless from negligent conduct. Reckless is being aware that actions create a substantial and unjustifiable risk that someone will be injured, and ignoring that risk. Negligent is taking actions that create a substantial and unjustifiable risk that someone will be injured, and being unaware of that risk. Such ignorance of the risk is criminal when harm results. Negligence is the least culpable mental state often used to hold people criminally responsible for accidents or harm caused by their ignorance. Take by way of illustration a college student who may have an opportunity to engage in consensual sexual conduct. If the student refuses to use a condom, such behavior is reckless. Most students are aware of the risk of contracting sexually transmitted diseases by engaging in unprotected sex. Choosing to ignore the risk of disease transmission is reckless. Negligence is when the student consumes so much alcohol that he or she is unaware that a condom is not being used during consensual relations and is, therefore, unaware of the transmission risk.

If the student engaged in unprotected sexual intercourse and was suffering from an incurable and potentially fatal bloodborne disease, such as the Human Immunodeficiency Virus ("HIV") that causes Acquired Immunodeficiency Disease Syndrome ("AIDS"), their *mens rea* would be knowing, because they knew by their actions that the disease could be sexually transmitted. But infecting their partner with HIV was presumably not the reason they engaged in the sexual act;

nonetheless, they were aware of the substantial likelihood of infecting their unsuspecting partner with HIV.

2. Intent

Rule of Law: Specific intent = purposely; General intent = knowingly.

a. Specific and General Intent

A parallel to *mens rea* is the concept of intent and sometimes scholars use the terms interchangeably. A common understanding of *mens rea,* state of mind, is that the offender intends that his actions bring about a specific result. As discussed above, the law is careful to assign only as much criminal responsibility as warranted by the offender's conduct. Distinctions in the type of crime committed are separated by the level of intent required to commit the act. Some crimes require **specific intent,** such as when the offender uses a lead pipe to crush someone's nose with the specific intent to bring about the desired result—a broken nose. **General intent** crimes occur when the offender wants to take a specific action, but does not necessarily desire a specific result. As one court said, "[g]eneral criminal intent exists when from the circumstances the prohibited result may reasonably be expected to follow from the offender's voluntary act, irrespective of a subjective desire to have accomplished such result."[5] Today the distinctions between specific and general intent are less common but remain viable to determine if the offender can avail himself of certain defenses, for example intoxication for a specific intent crime in jurisdictions that recognize the defense. The difficulty in distinguishing general from specific intent crime is provided in the excerpt from the reasoning provided in *Linehan* v. *Florida* reprinted in part in Box 4.2. The defendant, Linehan, set fire to his girlfriend's apartment, and a squatter who lived in a storage room died as a result. Linehan was drunk at the time, but was convicted of arson and felony: a murder wherein the act of committing a felony—the arson—caused the death. Linehan appealed his conviction and argued that his voluntary intoxication was a defense to the arson. The Florida appellate court disagreed with Linehan. They decided that intoxication can be a defense to forming specific intent, but not a general intent crime such as arson. In the reproduced portion of the case in Box 4.2, the court struggles with the historical development of the distinction between specific and general intent.

BOX 4.2

Linehan v. *Florida,* 442 So. 2d 244 (1983)

"We find that arson . . . is a general intent crime to which voluntary intoxication is not a defense. [The arson statute] Section 806.01 provides, in pertinent part:

1. Any person who willfully and unlawfully by fire or explosion, damages or causes to be damaged:
    a. any dwelling whether occupied or not, or its contents. . . . [will be guilty of arson].

We construe the word "willfully" in the arson statute to mean that the accused need have had only a general criminal intent. The distinction between "specific" and "general" intent crimes is nebulous and extremely difficult to define and apply with consistency. Although the difference between acts done deliberately and accidentally is not difficult to grasp, the "specific" versus "general" intent test requires a close distinction between different types of intent.

---

[5]*Myers v. State,* 422 N.E. 2d 745 (1981).

The difficulty is compounded by a variety of different types of statutory wording to which to apply the distinction. On the surface, particular statutes defining criminal offenses which contain the words "willfully" or "intentionally" might be thought to encompass "specific intent" crimes simply because they contain words denoting intent as a requisite mental state. However, that approach would ignore a fundamental concept of criminal law that there are three broad categories of crimes: (1) "strict liability" crimes . . . which are criminal violations even if done without intent to do the prohibited act; (2) general intent crimes; and (3) specific intent crimes. *See* W. LaFave & A. Scott, *Handbook on Criminal Law* §28 (1972).

The inclusion of words denoting a state of mind as an element of the offense (e.g., "willfully" or "intentionally") serves to distinguish general intent and specific intent crimes from strict liability crimes. But the distinction between general intent and specific intent depends upon how words denoting state of mind are used in a statute . . . A "general intent" statute is one that prohibits either a specific voluntary act or something that is substantially certain to result from the act (e.g., damage to a building is the natural result of the act of setting a building afire). A person's subjective [personal to him] intent to cause the particular result is irrelevant to general intent crimes because the law ascribes to him a presumption that he intended such a result.

> "[A] man is to be taken to intend what he does, or that which is the necessary and natural consequence of his own act." . . .

Thus, in general intent statutes words such as "willfully" or "intentionally," without more, indicate only that the person must have intended to do the act and serve to distinguish that conduct from accidental (noncriminal) behavior or strict liability crimes. In *Love* v. *State,* 107 Fla. 376 (1932), the Florida Supreme Court did not directly refer to "general" or "specific" intent, but in defining the type of intent requisite for statutory arson ap-

peared to construe arson as a general intent crime: "A 'willful' setting fire to or burning would be such an act consciously and intentionally, as distinguished from accidentally or negligently done . . . "

Specific intent statutes, on the other hand, prohibit an act when it is accompanied by some intent other than the intent to do the act itself or the intent (or presumed intent) to cause the natural and necessary consequences of the act. For example, section 817.233, Florida Statutes (1981) [arson with the intent to commit fraud], defines a specific intent crime when it refers to "any person who willfully and with intent to injure or defraud the insuror sets fire to . . . any building." Accordingly, a crime encompassing a requirement of a subjective intent to accomplish a statutorily prohibited result may be a specific intent crime. The existence of a subjective intent to accomplish a particular prohibited result, as an element of a "specific intent" crime, is perhaps most clearly evident in the crime of first degree, premeditated murder. Other examples are burglary, which requires the intent to commit an offense in a structure or conveyance in addition to the intentional act of entering, and kidnapping, which requires the subjective intent, *inter alia* [among other things] to hold for ransom in addition to the intentional act of confining, abducting or imprisoning . . .

Thus, to be a "specific intent" crime, a criminal statute which contains words of mental condition like "willfully" or "intentionally" should include language encompassing a subjective intent, for example, intent to cause a result in addition to that which is substantially certain to result from a statutorily prohibited act. Accordingly, section 806.01(1) of the Florida arson statute, which says that a person who "willfully . . . by fire . . . damages . . . any dwelling" is guilty of arson, defines a general intent crime. Damage to a dwelling is the natural consequence of setting a dwelling afire, and there is no additional wording of the statute which requires a subjective intent to cause the damage.

b. Transferred Intent

Rule of Law: Transferred intent ensures that the offender is held accountable even if he harms an unintended target.

Transferred intent is specific intent in which the offender intends to cause harm, but hurts or damages the wrong target. We see the doctrine of transferred intent most often in homicide cases where the defendant has bad aim and kills an innocent victim. Surely, no one wants to let the offender go free simply because he made a mistake and claims, "But I did not mean to kill Sally, I was aiming at Tommy." If a robber aims and shoots intending to kill hostage who ducks just in time and the bullet hits and kills another customer, the shooter cannot escape liability by claiming the dead victim was not the intended target. The robber is responsible for the specific intent first-degree murder because the intent transferred. Likewise, if an arsonist intentionally burns down a house or causes damage to property and it turns out to be the wrong property, the doctrine of transferred intent applies to hold the offender accountable. An offender has the same defenses under the doctrine of transferred intent as he would have in an ordinary case. For instance, Sam does not mean to kill Amy, only hurt her. When Sam shoots at Amy, but Amy ducks and Sam kills Bill instead, Sam still has a defense that he only meant to cause serious bodily harm to Amy, not death, and his defense to killing Bill transfers as well. Likewise if a police officer were executing a lawful arrest and unintentionally caused injury to a bystander, the officer's defense of making a justified arrest would extend to the bystander.

c. The Scienter Requirement

Rule of Law: Scienter is knowledge.

A common law concept similar to *mens rea* is **scienter,** which is a legal term for knowledge. Some crimes require that the defendant possess sufficient knowledge to attach criminal liability to his or her conduct. For instance, to be charged with assaulting a police officer, an offender would typically have to know that the victim was a police officer. In some states, knowledge of the officer's status is required before the defendant can be found guilty of such an offense. In federal law, there is no such scienter requirement.[6] In *United States* v. *Feola,* 420 U.S. 671 (1975), undercover federal law enforcement agents agreed to purchase heroin from Feola and others. Feola and his confederates planned to deliver fake heroin to their prospective buyers, the undercover officers or, alternatively, to rob them. They were convicted of conspiracy to assault federal officers, convictions that were upheld by the U.S. Supreme Court despite Feola's pleas that he had no knowledge that the buyers were federal agents and that he lacked the scienter required to sustain his conviction. The high Court upheld Feola's conviction because the law required just an intent to assault, not necessarily actually to assault a federal officer, an intent Feola and friends had with their initial unlawful conduct. The Court declared that to hold otherwise—that Feola and friends could go home despite their criminal acts—would give no protection to undercover officers and society could not abide by such a such result.

Applying the Rule of Law to the Facts: Is scienter required for a conviction?

- Sally went to her brother Bob's house and said, "I need to stay here for a few days; can you help me out?" Two days later police arrested Bob for obstructing justice by hiding a fugitive—his sister Sally. Does the law require Bob to have known Sally was wanted by the law in order to be convicted of the charges?

Yes, the required scienter is the knowledge that the fugitive is wanted and that the people looking for her are, indeed, law enforcement officers.

d. Strict Liability

Rule of Law: Under strict liability, an offender is guilty for the act alone; no mental state is required.

---

[6]18 U.S.C.A. §111. Assaulting, resisting, or impeding certain officers or employees.

Under early common law, crimes were often defined or separated based on their perceived evil or damage to society. Crimes were referred to as either *mala in se* or *mala prohibita*. **Mala in se** are crimes that are deemed inherently dangerous to society, such as murder, rape, and arson. The law prohibits such crimes because they always cause great harm. **Mala prohibita** acts are defined as crimes because society wants to punish certain behavior it finds morally repulsive. For example, if a driver blasted her car stereo, such an act is not an inherent crime, but the city or town might have a noise ordinance making loud noises a crime because it disturbs the peace. *Mala prohibita* crimes generally are strict liability crimes that require no *mens rea* or intent to be shown for the offender to be found guilty of the crime. **Strict liability** statutes are typically regulatory to protect the general public. Strict liability crimes generally fall into statutes prohibiting or constraining the sale of liquor, food, or drugs; motor vehicle violations; and safety regulations passed for the general well-being of the general public.[7] The typical punishment is a fine and not jail. The public policy reasons for enacting and upholding strict liability statutes are that they ensure conformity of behavior by a majority of the general public. The Supreme Court described the genesis of strict liability crimes in *Morissette* v. *United States,* 342 U.S. 246 (1952).

> Congestion of cities and crowding of quarters called for health and welfare regulations undreamed of in simpler times. Wide distribution of goods became an instrument of wide distribution of harm when those who dispersed food, drink, drugs, and even securities, did not comply with reasonable standards of quality, integrity, disclosure and care. Such dangers have engendered increasingly numerous and detailed regulations which heighten the duties of those in control of particular industries, trades, properties or activities that affect public health, safety or welfare.

Thus, a manager at a gas station where they sell hot dogs that roll under hot lights for three hours or more might receive a citation from the city health inspector for serving tainted food products, regardless of whether the station manager "intended" or "knew" [had the requisite *mens rea*] that the food sat out for far too long. Punishing the manager solely on the basis of the act of leaving food out to spoil, and not her subjective intent to harm the public with contaminated hot dogs, sends a message to all establishments serving food that they had better pay attention to the quality of the food they sell or suffer the consequences. Traveling above the speed limit is often a strict liability crime. If people know they will receive an expensive fine if caught speeding regardless of their excuse or *mens rea* while driving fast, they will generally obey the speed limit which, in turn, protects the general public from unnecessary car accidents caused by reckless driving.

Understanding how crimes are defined first requires a discussion of the principle of legality and a look at element analysis.

e. Principle of Legality

Society needs to clearly define criminal conduct to inform people which acts are criminal. The **principle of legality** requires that the law notify what conduct will be punished. To give citizens fair warning of what conduct will be punished fosters respect for the law. Many states have written criminal codes based on the Model Penal Code's elements of crimes that establish liability on the part of the offender, discussed below. To criminalize specific conduct, the government must state with specificity what behavior will be punished and what behavior, if engaged in, will not be a crime. If the

---

[7]Francis B. Sayre. "Public Welfare Offenses." *Columbia Law Review,* Vol. 33 (1933).

statute is vague, the law cannot stand under the legality principle. In the case *Commonwealth* v. *Twitchell,* reprinted in part in Box 4.3, David and Ginger Twitchell were practicing Christian Scientists. Followers of this religion rely on prayer for healing sickness, rather than medical intervention. When the Twitchells' son Robyn died from a bowel obstruction that could have been easily repaired by surgery, the couple was prosecuted and convicted of manslaughter for failing to acquire the necessary medical care to save Robyn's life. On appeal, the Massachusetts Supreme Court remanded their case based, in part, on the legality principle. Years before the Twitchells' case, the Christian Scientist headquarters had sought legal guidance from the state Attorney General concerning parents who followed their faith rather than state law with respect to obtaining medical care for minor children. The Twitchells should have been allowed to argue at trial that they relied to their detriment on the Attorney General's opinion that reliance on prayer instead of medicine was legal. Therefore the principle of legality was violated because the law was unclear. Finding both the law governing faith-based healing and the state's legal response to the Church's inquiry nonspecific, the Massachusetts high court reversed the Twitchells' conviction. The state declined to prosecute the Twitchells again, but the couple remained under court order to provide medical care for their other children until they reached adulthood.

BOX 4.3

Commonwealth v. *Twitchell,* 617 N.E.2d 609 (1993)
Supreme Judicial Court of Massachusetts

Judge Wilkins delivered the opinion of the court.

PROCEDURAL HISTORY

David and Ginger Twitchell appeal from their convictions of involuntary manslaughter in connection with the April 8, 1986, death of their two and one-half year old son Robyn. Robyn died of the consequences of peritonitis caused by the perforation of his bowel which had been obstructed as a result of an anomaly known as Meckel's diverticulum. There was evidence that the condition could be corrected by surgery with a high success rate.

FACTS

The defendants are practicing Christian Scientists who grew up in Christian Science families. They believe in healing by spiritual treatment. During Robyn's five-day illness from Friday, April 4, through Tuesday, April 8, they retained a Christian Science practitioner, a Christian Science nurse, and at one time consulted with Nathan Talbot, who held a position in the church known as the "Committee on Publication." [The "Committee on Publication"

for each State is a one-person committee authorized by the church's founder, Mary Baker Eddy, to explain Christian Science to the community and to give advice to practitioners. Talbot was head of all the Committees on Publication in the country]. As a result of that consultation, David Twitchell read a church publication concerning the legal rights and obligations of Christian Scientists in Massachusetts. That publication quoted a portion of G.L.c. 273, §1 [General Law Chapter 273, section 1], as then amended, which, at least in the context of the crimes described in that section, accepted remedial treatment by spiritual means alone as satisfying any parental obligation not to neglect a child or to provide a child with physical care. We shall subsequently discuss this statute in connection with the defendants' claim, rejected by the trial judge, that the spiritual treatment provision in G.L.c. 273, §1, protects them from criminal liability for manslaughter. [The spiritual treatment provision read as follows: "A child shall not be deemed to be neglected or lack proper physical care for the sole reason that he is being provided remedial treatment by spiritual means alone in accordance with the tenets and practice of a recognized church or religious denomination by a duly accredited practitioner thereof."]

We need not recite in detail the circumstances of Robyn's illness. The jury would have been warranted in concluding that Robyn was in considerable distress and that, in the absence of their belief in and reliance on spiritual treatment, the parents of a child in his condition would normally have sought medical treatment in sufficient time to save that child's life. There was also evidence that the intensity of Robyn's distress ebbed and flowed, perhaps causing his parents to believe that prayer would lead to the healing of the illness. On the other hand, the jury would have been warranted in finding that the Twitchells were wanton or reckless in failing to provide medical care for Robyn, if parents have a legal duty to provide a child with medical care in such circumstances and if the spiritual treatment provision of G.L.c. 273, §1, did not protect them from manslaughter liability.

ISSUE

[Did the Twitchells have an affirmative legal duty to obtain medical care despite their reliance on prayer, and could they be prosecuted for manslaughter by breaching that duty, based on the Massachusetts law in effect at the time that they could rely on spiritual treatment without fear of criminal prosecution?]

HOLDING

We shall conclude that . . . the spiritual healing provision in G.L.c. 273, §1, did not bar a prosecution for manslaughter in these circumstances. We further conclude, however, that special circumstances in this case would justify a jury's finding that the Twitchells reasonably believed that they could rely on spiritual treatment without fear of criminal prosecution. This affirmative defense should have been asserted and presented to the jury. Because it was not, there is a substantial risk of a miscarriage of justice in this case, and, therefore, the judgments must be reversed.

REASONING

We shall first consider whether the law generally imposes a parental duty to provide medical services to a child, the breach of which can be the basis of a conviction for involuntary manslaughter. The Common-

wealth presented its case on the theory that each defendant was guilty of involuntary manslaughter because the intentional failure of each to seek medical attention for their son involved such "a high degree of likelihood that substantial harm will result to" him as to be wanton or reckless conduct. Our definition of involuntary manslaughter derives from the common law. A charge of involuntary manslaughter based on an omission to act can be proved only if the defendant had a duty to act and did not do so.

The defendants argue, however, that any common law duty of care does not include a duty to provide medical treatment and that there is no statute imposing such a duty except G.L.c. 273, §1, which, in turn, in their view, provides them with complete protection against any criminal charge based on their failure to seek medical treatment for their son. In their argument that the common law of the Commonwealth does not include a duty to provide medical treatment, the defendants overlook *Commonwealth* v. *Gallison,* 421 N.E.2d 757 (1981). In that case, we upheld a conviction of manslaughter, saying that a parent who "made no effort to obtain medical help, knowing that her child was gravely ill," could be found guilty of wanton or reckless involuntary manslaughter for her child's death caused by her omission to meet her "duty to provide for the care and welfare of her child."

We, therefore, consider the impact, if any, of G.L.c. 273, §1, on this case. The defendants argue that the spiritual treatment provision in §1 bars any involuntary manslaughter charge against a parent who relies, as they did, on spiritual treatment and who does not seek medical attention for his or her child, even if the parent's failure to seek such care would otherwise be wanton or reckless conduct. We disagree.

Section 1 of G.L.c. 273 provides no complete protection to a parent against a charge of involuntary manslaughter that is based on the parent's wanton or reckless failure to provide medical services to a child. The spiritual treatment provision refers to neglect and lack of proper physical care . . . as bases for punishment: (1) neglect to provide support and (2) wilful failure to provide necessary and proper physical care. These concepts do not underlie involuntary manslaughter. Wanton or reckless conduct is not a form of negligence. Wanton or reckless conduct does not involve a wilful

(continued)

BOX 4.3

(continued)

intention to cause the resulting harm. An involuntary manslaughter verdict does not require proof of wilfulness. Thus, by its terms, the spiritual treatment provision in §1 does not apply to involuntary manslaughter.

The defendants argue that the failure to extend the protection of the spiritual treatment provision to them in this case would be a denial of due process of law because they lacked "fair warning" that their use of spiritual treatment could form the basis for a prosecution for manslaughter. Fair warning is part of the due process doctrine of vagueness, which "requires that a penal statute define the criminal offense with sufficient definiteness that ordinary people can understand what conduct is prohibited and in a manner that does not encourage arbitrary and discriminatory enforcement." Many fair warning challenges involve statutes that are unconstitutionally vague on their face, such as vagrancy statutes. *See, e.g., Papachristou* v. *Jacksonville,* 405 U.S. 156 (1972). Even if a statute is clear on its face, there may not be fair warning in the circumstances of particular defendants. The defendants here argue that they have been denied fair warning . . . because they were officially misled by an opinion of the Attorney General. We find some merit in [this] contention . . .

It is obvious that the Christian Science Church's publication on the legal rights and obligations of Christian Scientists in Massachusetts relied on the Attorney General's 1975 opinion [on the issue of criminal prosecution for failing to obtain medical care for children]. That opinion was arguably misleading because of what it did not say

concerning criminal liability for manslaughter. If the Attorney General had issued a caveat concerning manslaughter liability, the publication (which, based on such portions of it as appear in the record, is balanced and fair) would have referred to it in all reasonable likelihood. Nathan Talbot, who served as the Committee on Publication for the church and with whom the Twitchells spoke on the Sunday or Monday before Robyn's death, might well have given the Twitchells different advice. Although it has long been held that "ignorance of the law is no defence" (*Commonwealth* v. *Everson,* 2 N.E. 839 (1885)), there is substantial justification for treating as a defense the belief that conduct is not a violation of law when a defendant has reasonably relied on an official statement of the law, later determined to be wrong, contained in an official interpretation of the public official who is charged by law with the responsibility for the interpretation or enforcement of the law defining the offense. *See* Model Penal Code §2.04(3)(b) (Proposed Official Draft 1962). The defense rests on principles of fairness grounded in Federal criminal cases in the due process clause of the Fifth Amendment to the United States Constitution.

CONCLUSION

For these reasons, the judgments must be reversed, the verdicts must be set aside, and the cases remanded for a new trial, if the district attorney concludes that such a prosecution is necessary in the interests of justice.

Applying the Rule of Law to the Facts: Is the law legal?

- A man punched his wife in her stomach, causing her unborn baby to die. The man was prosecuted under the law which said "murder is the killing of a human being." Legal research indicates "human being" to mean one born alive. Did the man commit murder?

No, in the case *Keeler* v. *Superior Court,* 470 P.2d 617 (1970), the principle of legality mandates the crime of murder can only be charged for one born alive, and this baby was not.

f. Element Analysis

Rule of Law: To find a defendant guilty, the prosecution must prove each and every element [piece] of a crime beyond a reasonable doubt.

Elements are like spokes on a wheel, without which the wheel could not turn; each **element** is an integral part of the crime that the prosecutor must prove beyond a reasonable doubt in order to convict the defendant. The elements of a criminal definition typically include a *mens rea* state [purposefulness, knowingness, recklessness, or negligence], and the prohibited conduct the law seeks to prevent or punish. For example, the basic elements of kidnapping are the intentional [*mens rea*] forcible seizure, confinement, and asportation—the significant movement [the *actus reus*]—of another. If the prosecutor fails to prove one element of the crime, the defendant must be found not guilty of the charge. Learning the elements of crimes is a great aid in understanding what type of proof the state is required to introduce to convince a jury of the defendant's guilt. Sometimes elements of charged crimes overlap. The same elements that might support a charge of assault and battery will also be included in the more serious charge of attempted murder. If and when the defendant is convicted of attempted murder, the **lesser included offense** ("LIO"), such as putting the victim in fear (a type of assault) and unlawful touching (battery), will be merged into the more serious offense. Often prosecutors charge a defendant with many different crimes to ensure that he gets convicted of at least one crime. If the defendant is convicted of the more serious charge, the lesser charges are subsumed into the more serious offense; that is the doctrine of **merger.**

II. *ACTUS REUS*

Rule of Law: To be criminal, a person's acts must be voluntary.

Under the traditional common law, a person could not be charged with a crime for having criminal thoughts alone. Although that may be changing with increased regulatory control of pedophiles, typically individuals are free to think of committing criminal acts, and as long as they do not act on those desires or intentions, they are safe from the law. In the law, the term *actus reus* means "guilty act"—a voluntary act that gives rise to criminal liability. The Model Penal Code has expressly excluded the following acts from those making one criminally responsible:

1.   A reflex or convulsion,
2.   A bodily movement during unconsciousness or sleep,
3.   Conduct during hypnosis or resulting from hypnotic suggestion, and
4.   A bodily movement that otherwise is not a product of the effort or determination of the actor, either conscious or habitual.

There must be **concurrence**—the joining of the *mens rea* and the *actus reus* at the same time—for criminal liability to attach to an offender. If Joe wants his neighbor dead and thinks about it all day and, while at the supermarket, backs out of his parking space without looking and strikes a pedestrian, later discovered to be his hated neighbor Frank, Joe will not be liable for intentional murder. His murderous thoughts about Frank did not form the springboard of the act of running Frank over. The concurrence requirement saves the criminal justice system from pursuing fruitless prosecutions for criminal acts unconnected to any intent, even though those acts may be punished under a theory of negligence.

1. Duty to Act

To determine whether someone has a duty to act under the law, the omission of which would lead to criminal liability, the first question to ask is to whom does the actor owe a duty of reasonable care? In the seminal civil tort [injury] case *Palsgraf* v. *Long Island*

Railroad, 162 N.E. 99 (N.Y. 1928), a woman was waiting on a train platform to go to Rockaway Beach, New York, when an outbound train stopped at the station. As the train was moving away from the station, a man carrying a package of fireworks jumped onto the train while one guard grabbed his arm and another pushed him from behind to get him onto the train. The package of fireworks fell from the man's arms onto the rails, exploded, and knocked over a set of scales next to Mrs. Palsgraf, who was injured. She sued the train company for her injuries, claiming that the employees' actions of pulling and pushing the man caused the fireworks to fall and explode, but her lawsuit failed. The court said "Proof of negligence in the air, so to speak, will not do . . . negligence is the absence of care, according to the circumstances." When the court decided that the railroad owed Mrs. Palsgraf no duty of care from the railroad employees' innocent act of helping a man aboard a train, her lawsuit alleging that the railroad was negligent failed. The employees' actions were not negligent toward Mrs. Palsgraf; rather, the railroad owed a duty of care directly to the man pushed and pulled before he boarded the train. The court concluded that the scope of a duty to act to prevent harm to another is defined by "[t]he risk [of harm] reasonably to be perceived defines the duty to be obeyed." The defendant owes a duty of care only to those who might naturally or probably be injured by his actions.

Society perceives a person's duty to act to prevent harm to others as a paramount duty. For example, Italian poet Dante Alighieri's *The Divine Comedy,* written during medieval times, described a descent into purgatory and hell, with the layers graded in terms of seriousness. The lowest level of hell is inhabited by those who have breached certain positions of trust, as Alighieri deemed such betrayal to be worse than a crime of passion or violence.[8] Under the law today, we still punish those who have a certain duty of care to others and who breach that care by some act of commission or omission [failure to act]. Different types of duty are recognized by the law. There is a **duty by contract:** for example, after a tenant signs a lease with a landlord, the landlord then has a duty by law to provide a habitable apartment (heat, light, no excessive insect infestation) that will be recognized in a court of law, and the tenant has a duty to pay rent. Similarly, there is a **duty created by statute,** such as the law to stay at the scene of an automobile accident and, in some instances, to render aid to known victims. In a **duty by relationship,** a parent, spouse, or other responsible family member has a duty not to harm others to whom they are related and to take affirmative action through reasonable care to provide medical, dental, and educational aid to a dependent family member. The failure to do so could be considered a criminal act. There is also an **assumption of the duty,** which is freely given with no attendant legal obligation. An individual who is an expert swimmer is not required by law to try and rescue a floundering swimmer in distress. But if someone undertakes the duty to rescue, then it is incumbent upon the would-be rescuer to finish the job. That is, if a person on a crowded beach sees a swimmer in distress and says to the crowd of onlookers, "I'll save him; everybody stay here," and then halfway to the drowning victim, the rescuer changes his mind and turns back to shore, his actions prevented others from undertaking a rescue attempt and he may be responsible for thwarting a successful rescue attempt.

How does the law define to whom we owe a duty? Some duties are easy to define, such as those of a parent to a child, a hospital to a patient, or a spouse to a spouse. What happens when, not owing a duty under law, a bystander assumes a duty by pulling an occupant out of a burning vehicle? Is the bystander required to rescue all the other victims in the accident, too? Is everybody who could have been saved, but was not, a victim of the bystander's inaction? **Good Samaritan laws** protect people who rescue

---

[8]*See* Paul G. Chevigny. "From Betrayal to Violence: Dante's Inferno and the Social Construction of Crime." *Law & Social Inquiry,* Vol. 26 (2001), pp. 787–818.

others in peril from lawsuits. Bad Samaritan laws punish people for failing to help victims in need.[9] All U.S. jurisdictions have a Good Samaritan statute whereby people who help others in distress are immune from liability for the help they give. While each state's laws are different—for instance, in some states only those who are certified and trained as first-aid responders are protected from a lawsuit and in other states all helpers are immune—there are some general features common to most Good Samaritan laws:

1. There is no duty to act to help unless a duty by relationship exists.
2. The help provided cannot be in exchange for money or financial reward.
3. The person giving aid need not put himself in any danger by providing services, but if there is no threat of harm and the giving of aid has begun, usually the first one to give aid should stay until help arrives.

Only five American jurisdictions have laws imposing a duty, in certain circumstances, on the bystander to attempt a rescue of a stranger in peril or to contact the authorities: Hawaii, Minnesota, Rhode Island, Wisconsin, and Vermont.[10] Minnesota's duty to rescue law provides the following stipulations:

> ***Duty to assist.*** A person at the scene of an emergency who knows that another person is exposed to or has suffered grave physical harm shall, to the extent that the person can do so without danger or peril to self or others, give reasonable assistance to the exposed person. Reasonable assistance may include obtaining or attempting to obtain aid from law enforcement or medical personnel. A person who violates this subdivision is guilty of a petty misdemeanor.

Typically, there is no affirmative duty to report a crime. Jeremy Strohmeyer followed seven-year-old Sherrice Iverson into the women's restroom at the Primm Valley Hotel's casino and proceeded to put his hand over her mouth as his friend David Cash, Jr., watched. When Cash left, Strohmeyer raped and killed Sherrice. There were no laws on the books in Nevada to make Cash's inaction a crime, and despite public outcry, he continued his studies at the University of California at Berkeley.

Wisconsin's duty to assist law applies only if a crime has occurred, not an accident or other situation that threatens life or limb. The law provides:

> ***Duty to aid victim or report crime.*** Any person who knows that a crime is being committed and that a victim is exposed to bodily harm shall summon law enforcement officers or other assistance or shall provide assistance to the victim. A person need not comply with this subsection if any of the following apply:
> 1. Compliance would place him or her in danger.
> 2. Compliance would interfere with duties the person owes to others.
> 3. Assistance is being summoned or provided by others.

In our chapter-opening scenario, Sondra had no duty either to assist Ken from being robbed or to report that a crime had been committed and she will win her case, but the bus company had a duty created by statute to keep the brakes in good working order and will lose their case.

2. Possession as an Act

In strict legal terms, possession of drugs, possession of contraband, and possession of illegal weapons are not voluntary acts, but under the law, possession of contraband is treated as the necessary *actus reus* to hold the one who possess criminally responsible. There are two types of possession generally recognized in the law, actual and

---

[9]Damien Schiff. "Samaritans: Good, Bad and Ugly: A Comparative Law Analysis." *Roger Williams University Law Review,* Vol. 11 (2005), pp. 77–141.

[10]Haw. Rev. Stat. Ann. 663-1.6; Minn. Stat. Ann. 604A.01(1); R.I. Gen. Laws 11-56-1; Wis. Stat. Ann. 940.34; 12 Vt. Stat. Ann. Tit. 519.

constructive. **Actual possession** is when the person has the prohibited or illegal items in their possession—vials of crack cocaine in a pants pocket, for instance. **Constructive possession** is a legal fiction that arises when certain facts could lead a jury to infer the necessary facts to make an offender criminally responsible, where one is deemed to have possessed the incriminating items simply because those items were in an area over which a person exercised dominion and control even if the offender did not have physical possession at the time he was caught. For example, three roommates share an apartment and share common living areas, the bathroom, kitchen and living room. All roommates are deemed to have control over their common living areas. If the roommates are aware that there are bricks of marijuana hidden in the freezer and do nothing to terminate the possession (that is, throwing the marijuana away), then when the police come to execute a search warrant, all roommates can be arrested for "possession" of narcotics. The burden of proof on the state to prove the elements of possession beyond a reasonable doubt will largely hinge on the state's ability to prove that all the roommates knew or should have known that the drugs were in the freezer. The Model Penal Code, section 2.01, expressly provides that criminal liability may attach for possession if:

1. The possessor knowingly procured or received the thing possessed.
2. The possessor was aware of his control thereof for a sufficient period to have been able to terminate his possession.

3. Status as an Act

Is one's personal status as an alcoholic, drug addict, or pedophile a criminal act? The answer is no. Even though one's personal status as a drug addict may lead to criminal activity, such as stealing to support one's habit, the mere act of being a drug addict is not criminal. In *Robinson* v. *California,* 370 U.S. 660 (1962), the U.S. Supreme Court held unconstitutional a California statute that criminalized status as an addict. The Court invalidated the statute, and any others like it across the country, because "a law which made a criminal offense of such a disease would doubtless be universally thought of to be an infliction of cruel and unusual punishment in violation of the Eighth and Fourteenth Amendments . . ." Lower courts in subsequent cases, such as the New York state case of *People* v. *Tocco,* 525 N.Y.S.2d 137 (N.Y. 1988), discussed whether alcoholism is a disease. If it were, it would make alcoholics exempt from crimes committed while under the influence, because the alcoholic would have no control over his status. Thus, if the court recognized that being an active alcoholic means chronic involuntary intoxication, the alcoholic could never be prosecuted for actions committed while he or she was drunk. The court went on to distinguish the status of being an alcoholic from the physical act of drinking and stated, "Alcoholics should be held responsible for their conduct; they should not be penalized for their condition."

III. CAUSATION

Rule of Law: To be guilty of causing the harm/death of another, the defendant must be both the factual and proximate cause of the harm/death.

The concept of criminal **causation** serves to assign the appropriate level of blame in accordance with the offender's *mens rea* state (purposely, knowingly, recklessly, or negligently) and the actual harm the offender caused by her acts. For a defendant to be held responsible for a victim's harm or death, he must be both the factual and legal cause of the ultimate harm. **Factual cause** is the "but for" causation of the victim's harm. The factual cause is established by asking the question, "but for the defendant's acts, would the ultimate harm have happened?" If the answer is no, then the defendant is the factual cause of the harm. By way of illustration, in our opening scenario, "but for" the Smiths' decision not to move their patients before Hurricane Katrina, would the residents have drowned? If the answer is "no" then the defendants are the factual cause of their deaths. The next question is, "Is the defendant the proximate cause, the naturally foreseeable last event that caused the harm?" If the answer is "yes" then the defendant will be criminally responsible for causing the harm. In order for the defendant to be the **proximate cause,** the harm suffered by the victim must have been foreseeable [predictable] by the defendant at the time of his initial conduct. Even if the ultimate harm suffered by the victim was foreseeable, there may be an **intervening cause** that breaks the causal chain between the original offender and the victim's harm. But the existence of an intervening cause may not totally relieve the defendant from liability, as some jurisdictions find that if the defendant's initial conduct created intervening events they do "not operate to exempt a defendant from liability if the intervening event was put into operation by the defendant's" actions.[11]

For instance, is it foreseeable that not evacuating the old and infirm from a one-story nursing home during a hurricane will lead to drowning deaths? Not necessarily. The breach in the New Orleans levees was an event that had never before occurred in the city and that had not been anticipated, even though the city suffered extensive flooding damage during Hurricane Betsey in 1965. The 2005 levee breech could be an intervening cause, breaking the causal chain from the nursing home operators' negligence in not evacuating the residents to the deaths of the residents.[12]

To find the Smiths responsible for the residents' deaths, the harm that ultimately occurred has to be of the type and nature that naturally flows from the offenders' conduct. If the managers decided not to evacuate the residents, and instead of the levee collapsing, terrorists bombed the nursing home, the harm suffered by the residents from the bombing would not be foreseeable. Such an event would be too remote a possibility from the initial decision not to evacuate the residents, and the managers would not be liable. The law seeks to punish people for the natural consequences of their acts, not freakish random acts, even if their initial conduct started the chain of events that ended in harm. If one friend chases another into a swollen creek where he drowns, the drowning is a natural, foreseeable consequence of the initial chasing act. But if one friend chases another into a swollen creek where she is picked up by a band of pirates and forced to walk the plank to her death, this event is not a foreseeable consequence from the initial act of chasing. The chaser is the factual cause of the death: But for the chase into the creek, no death would have occurred. However, the harm suffered must be reasonably foreseeable as a natural consequence of the defendant's actions, which the pirate abduction is not. If an offender is not both the factual and legal cause of the victim's harm, he may not escape criminal liability completely, but may be charged with a lesser offense, such as manslaughter rather than murder.

Another illustration of the causation doctrine is a man who smokes a cigarette while pumping gas, causing the pump to explode. The subsequent explosion sends metal from the pump hurtling through the air, and two patrons pumping gas at nearby pumps are impaled by flying debris. Is the smoker the factual cause of the patrons' deaths? But for his smoking, would the patrons have died? The answer is no, so the smoker is the factual cause. Is the smoker the proximate cause of the patrons' deaths? Is being killed by flying metal a natural and foreseeable consequence of an explosion

---

[11]*Delawder* v. *Commonwealth,* 196 S.E.2d 913 (Va. 1973); *Baxley* v. *Fischer,* 134 S.E.2d 291 (Va. 1964).

[12]On September 7, 2007, Sal and Mabel Mangano were acquitted of 35 counts of negligent homicide and a number of counts of cruelty to the infirm from the events of Hurricane Katrina and their Louisiana nursing home. http://news.yahoo.com/s/ap/20070908/ap_on_re_us/katrina_nursing_home_deaths (accessed on September 8, 2007.

at a gas station? The answer is yes, so the smoker is the proximate cause and may be liable for the patrons' deaths. The last question to ask is whether there is any intervening causes breaking the causal chain between the offender and the victim? The answer here is no, keeping the smoker liable for the ultimate harm because he is both the factual and legal cause of the deaths.

But what if the gas station explosion rocked an ambulance traveling a mile away just as an emergency worker was inserting an intravenous line into a patient and the explosion caused the needle to penetrate the patient's neck with fatal results? The smoker would not be responsible, because that type of death, a needle in the neck, is not reasonably foreseeable from the act of smoking at the pumps. There can be more than one proximate cause of an ultimate harm and each person whose act contributes to the harm will be held responsible.

In our opening scenario, can the City of New Orleans be held responsible for chartering buses with defective brakes that caught fire in traffic, killing travelers on the bus? The hiring of the bus is the factual cause of the travelers' deaths, and deaths may be foreseeable from the act of hiring defective buses. Even if those in charge were reckless or negligent, causation analysis may still ascribe liability for city officials. In the case *New Jersey* v. *Pelham,* reprinted in part in Box 4.4, the New Jersey high court examines the issue of causation and whether to hold the defendant liable for a car accident that caused the victim such severe injuries that he requested to be taken off life support and subsequently died. Of note, the dissent argues that the defendant should not be held responsible for the victim's intentional and volitional acts. New Jersey is one of the few jurisdictions that bases its causation statute on the MPC §2.03, reprinted in Appendix B, and it amended the language to remove responsibility for unpredictable and unforeseeable acts in the causal chain.

BOX 4.4

New Jersey v. *Pelham,* 824 A.2d 1082 (2003)
Supreme Court of New Jersey

Justice LaVecchia writing for a majority of the Court.

FACTS

The facts of the horrific car accident in which [the] defendant, Sonney Pelham, was involved are summarized from the trial record. On the evening of December 29, 1995, William Patrick, a sixty-six-year-old lawyer, was driving his Chrysler LeBaron . . . At approximately 11:42 p.m., a 1993 Toyota Camry driven by [the] defendant struck the LeBaron from behind. The LeBaron sailed over the curb and slid along the guardrail, crashing into a utility pole before it ultimately came to rest 152 feet from the site of impact. The Camry traveled over a curb and came to rest in a grassy area on the side of the highway. Patrick was making "gurgling" and "wheezing"

sounds, and appeared to have difficulty breathing. His passenger, Jocelyn Bobin, was semiconscious. Emergency crews extricated the two using the "jaws of life" and transported them to Robert Wood Johnson University Hospital (Robert Wood Johnson). Bobin was treated and later released.

At the accident scene, Officer Heistand smelled an odor of alcohol on [the] defendant's breath, and noted that he was swaying from side to side and front to back. Three field sobriety tests were conducted. Defendant failed all three. Two separately administered tests indicated that [the] defendant's blood alcohol content (BAC) at that time was .18 to .19. Experts assessed his BAC between .19 and .22 at the time of the accident.

On March 13, 1996, Patrick was transferred to the Kessler Institute for Rehabilitation (Kessler), because it specialized in the care of patients with spinal cord injuries. When he arrived, Patrick was unable to breathe on his own, and was suffering from multi-organ system failure. Medication was required to stabilize his heart rhythm. He was extremely weak, with blood-protein levels that placed him at high risk of death. He was unable to clear secretions in his airways, and thus his oxygen levels would drop requiring medical personnel repeatedly to clear the secretions. Complications from the ventilator caused pneumonia to recur due to his inability to cough or to protect himself from bacteria. Bowel and urinary tract infections continued.

While at Kessler, Patrick also was monitored by psychiatric staff. He presented as depressed, confused, uncooperative, and not engaged psychologically. At times he was "hallucinating," even "psychotic." The staff determined that he was "significantly" brain injured. Nonetheless, Patrick was aware of his physical and cognitive disabilities. During lucid moments, he expressed his unhappiness with his situation, and, on occasion, tried to remove his ventilator. Patrick improved somewhat during the month of April, but then his condition rapidly regressed. By early May, severe infections returned, as well as pneumonia. It was undisputed at trial that Patrick had expressed to his family a preference not to be kept alive on life support. Because of his brain damage, his lack of improvement, and his severe infections Patrick's family decided to act in accordance with his wishes and remove the ventilator. He was transferred to Saint Barnabas Medical Center and within two hours of the ventilator's removal on May 30, 1996, he was pronounced dead. The Deputy Middlesex County Medical Examiner determined that the cause of death was sepsis and bronchopneumonia resulting from multiple injuries from the motor vehicle accident.

ISSUE

[W]hether a jury may be instructed that, as a matter of law, a victim's determination to be removed from life support is a foreseeable event that does not remove or lessen criminal responsibility for death.

HOLDING

[W]e hold that there was no error in instructing the jury that a victim's decision to invoke his right to terminate life support may not, as a matter of law, be considered an independent intervening cause capable of breaking the chain of causation triggered by defendant's wrongful actions.

REASONING

New Jersey has been in the forefront of recognizing an individual's right to refuse medical treatment. It is now well settled that competent persons have the right to refuse life-sustaining treatment. Even incompetent persons have the right to refuse life-sustaining treatment through a surrogate decision maker. We turn then to examine the effect to be given to a victim's exercise of that right in the context of a homicide trial.

Defendant was charged with aggravated manslaughter, which, according to the New Jersey Code of Criminal Justice (Code), occurs when one "recklessly causes death under circumstances manifesting extreme indifference to human life." The trial court charged the jury on aggravated manslaughter and the lesser-included offense of second-degree vehicular homicide, defined as "[c]riminal homicide ... caused by driving a vehicle or vessel recklessly." Causation is an essential element of those homicide charges.

The Code defines "causation" as follows:

... a. Conduct is the cause of a result when: (1) It is an antecedent but for which the result in question would not have occurred; and (2) The relationship between the conduct and result satisfies any additional causal requirements imposed by the code or by the law defining the offense. ...

c. When the offense requires that the defendant recklessly or criminally negligently cause a particular result, the actual result must be within the risk of which the actor is aware or, in the case of criminal negligence, of which he should be aware, or, if not, the actual result must involve the same kind of injury or harm as the probable result and must not be too remote, accidental in its occurrence, or dependent on another's volitional act to have a just bearing on the actor's liability or on the gravity of his offense.

The causation requirement of our Code contains two parts, a "but-for" test under which the defendant's conduct is "deemed a cause of the event if the event would not have occurred without that

(continued)

BOX 4.4

(continued)

conduct" and, when applicable, a culpability assessment. Under the culpability assessment, [w]hen the actual result is of the same character, but occurred in a different manner from that designed or contemplated [or risked], it is for the jury to determine whether intervening causes or unforeseen conditions lead to the conclusion that it is unjust to find that the defendant's conduct is the cause of the actual result. Although the jury may find that the defendant's conduct was a "but-for" cause of the victim's death, it may nevertheless conclude that the death differed in kind from that designed or contemplated [or risked] or that the death was too remote, accidental in its occurrence, or dependent on another's volitional act to justify a murder conviction.

Our Code, like the Model Penal Code (MPC), does not identify what may be an intervening cause. Instead, the Code "deals only with the ultimate criterion by which the significance of such possibilities ought to be judged." Removal of life support, as it relates to causation, should be judged only by the criteria of the Code, assuming that the law recognizes the possibility that removal can be an intervening cause. While "another's volitional act" undoubtedly would require a jury to consider whether, for example, a doctor's malpractice in treating a crime victim constituted an intervening cause that had broken the chain of causation after a criminal defendant's act, we do not believe, as the dissent suggests, that the Legislature intended the reference to "another's volitional act" to include a crime victim's decision to be removed from life support.

"Intervening cause" is defined as "[a]n event that comes between the initial event in a sequence and the end result, thereby altering the natural course of events that might have connected a wrongful act to an injury." *Black's Law Dictionary* (7th ed. 1999). Generally, to avoid breaking the chain of causation for criminal liability, a variation between the result intended or risked and the actual result of defendant's conduct must not be so

out of the ordinary that it is unfair to hold defendant responsible for that result.[13] A defendant may be relieved of criminal liability for a victim's death if an "independent" intervening cause has occurred, meaning "an act of an independent person or entity that destroys the causal connection between the defendant's act and the victim's injury and, thereby becomes the cause of the victim's injury." *People* v. *Saavedra-Rodriguez,* 971 P.2d 223 (Colo. 1998) (explaining Wharton's rule on intervening cause); see generally Charles E. Torcia, 1 Wharton's Criminal Law §26 (15th ed. 1993) (stating that independent intervening cause that defendant cannot foresee is sufficient to relieve defendant of criminal responsibility for homicide).

The question we address, then, is whether the removal of the victim's life support may constitute, as a matter of law, an "independent intervening cause," the significance of which a jury may evaluate as part of a culpability analysis.

The longstanding, clear policy of this State recognizes the constitutional, common-law, and now statutorily based right of an individual to accept, reject, or discontinue medical treatment in the form of life supporting devices or techniques. We agree with the widely recognized principle that removal of life support, as a matter of law, may not constitute an independent intervening cause for purposes of lessening a criminal defendant's liability. Removal of life support in conformity with a victim's expressed wishes is not a legally cognizable cause of death in New Jersey. Removal of life-sustaining treatment is a victim's right. Because the exercise of the right does not break unexpectedly, or in any extraordinary way, the chain of causation that a defendant initiated and that led to the need for life support, it is not an intervening cause that may be advanced by the defendant.

CONCLUSION

[Conviction upheld].

---

[13]Citation in case: Wayne R. LaFave and Austin W. Scott, Jr., *Handbook on Criminal Law* §35 (1972).

IV. PARTIES TO CRIME

In common law, parties to crimes were defined either as principals who actually committed the crime or as accessories, those who helped the principals commit the crime or escape afterward. The common law distinction between principals and accessories went further and separated such parties by degree, such as a principal in the first or second degree, or an accessory before or after the fact—distinctions based on the level of participation and involvement of each actor. A man who robbed a grocery store would be a principal in the first degree, while his mother who went inside the store to distract the manager and the security guard would be a principal in the second degree based on her aiding and abetting [helping to commit] the crime.[14] Today in many modern statutes, the distinction remains for principals in the first and second degree while accessories retain their common law definitions, but are treated the same as principals for sentencing purposes.

1. Principals and Accessories

Rule of Law: Common law distinguished between principals and accessories to determine grades of punishment; under today's modern statutes, they are typically punished equally.

A **principal** is the primary perpetrator of a crime. Under common law, principals were divided into the first and second degree. A principal in the first degree is one who actually committed the crime and one in the second degree was one who aided, counseled, and assisted the commission of the crime and was present during the crime. An **accessory** is one who was absent during the commission of the crime but who participated as a contriver, instigator, or advisor. If the accessory gives help to the principal before the crime, she is called an **accessory before the fact.** If she helps the principal escape from the crime scene or hide from authorities, she is called an **accessory after the fact.** The common-law distinction between principals and accessories was important for sentencing such offenders; society wanted to punish more harshly those who had actually committed the crime than those who merely helped. Today under many state statutes, the distinctions between principals and accessories are blurred and they are punished equally. The philosophy behind punishing them equally is that the crime could not be committed without both accessories and principals playing primary roles. The Michigan statute which is titled "Abolition of distinction between accessory and principal" is such an example and provides

> Every person concerned in the commission of an offense, whether he directly commits the act constituting the offense or procedures, counsels aids and abets in its commission may hereafter be prosecuted, indicted, tried and on conviction shall be punished as if he had directly committed such offense. Accessories may be convicted even if the principal has not and many current statutes simply specify that an accomplice is accountable legally for the conduct of another, without referring to the historical categories.

In *Raymond Lee Sutton/Virginia Gray Sutton v. Virginia,* 324 S.E.2d 665 (1985), a woman was convicted under the common-law distinction of being a principal in the second degree in helping her husband rape her physically challenged niece. The court reasoned that since the aunt had an active and equal role in forcing her niece to submit to sexual relations, she was deemed a more culpable principal rather than an accessory, which would have resulted in a lesser sentence.

---

[14]*See Sutton* v. *Virginia,* 324 S.E.2d 665 (Va. 1985).

V. INCHOATE CRIMES

In the law, the term **inchoate crimes** refers to crimes that are incomplete, but they are still crimes. In some ways, unsuccessful criminals pose more of a danger to society than successful criminals, because of their repeated attempts to achieve their criminal goals. The inchoate crimes are solicitation, which is asking or inducing someone to help commit a crime; conspiracy, which is typically an agreement between two or more people "to do an unlawful act or a lawful act by unlawful means"; and attempt, which is when one has the *mens rea* to commit the crime, but the *actus reus* is thwarted and the criminal act remains incomplete.

1. Solicitation

Rule of Law: Solicitation is asking someone to commit a crime.

Solicitation is asking someone to commit a crime, defined by the Model Penal Code as "asking, encouraging or demanding another commit a crime or an attempt to commit a crime." The crime is often associated with prostitution, where the sex worker will be charged with "solicitation," asking people to engage in the criminal activity of paying money in exchange for sexual favors. To be convicted of solicitation, an offender must demonstrate specific intent to engage someone else in the commission of the crime: the act of asking is the crime. Early solicitation statutes divided the crime into degrees, but most states have enacted comprehensive statutes which stipulate that once one person invites another to commit a crime, the harm has been done and the asker should have criminal liability. In our opening hypothetical scenario, Billy Bob solicited Charles in the criminal enterprise of robbing people inside the Superdome during Hurricane Katrina.

It is a defense to voluntarily renounce the solicitation; that is, once you have asked someone to commit a crime, you may change your mind and withdraw by telling the person you solicited that you no longer wish to commit the crime, or by notifying the authorities that they should attempt to prevent the crime. Some jurisdictions require active persuasion to prevent the one who solicited from going forward. Pennsylvania's statute is illustrative of this requirement

> It is a defense that the actor, after soliciting another person to commit a crime, persuaded him not to do so or otherwise prevented the commission of the crime, under circumstances manifesting a complete and voluntary renunciation of his criminal intent.

It is not a defense that the person so solicited could not have committed a crime—for example, if a businessman solicits murder by hiring a hit man to kill his partner, and the hitman turns out to be an undercover police officer. The businessman will still be guilty of solicitation because the facts as he believed them to be, if true, would have led to the commission of the crime. Solicitation is not prosecuted as an attempt crime because the solicitous acts are preparatory in nature and attempts require *actus reus* that goes beyond mere preparation.

2. Conspiracy

Rule of Law: Conspiracy is an agreement to commit a crime.

The crime of **conspiracy** consists of two basic elements:

1. A criminal act, which may be an agreement, and
2. A criminal intent.

The first element of conspiracy is that the agreement must involve a criminal act, which is the essence of conspiracy. Some statutes require an overt act taken in furtherance of commission of the crime in addition to the original agreement to commit a crime. The agreement to commit a crime does not have to be written; usually it is oral. Intent may be inferred from the facts and circumstances of the case, but close analysis of the alleged agreement is important to determine:

1. Whether more than one party was involved.
2. Whether the requisite criminal intent was present.
3. Whether there were one or more conspiracies.

Prosecutors charge defendants with conspiracy because the government can obtain a conviction for conspiracy even if the ultimate crime the conspirators tried to achieve was not completed and their criminal objective failed. For example, Tom and Kate get together and agree to rob the bank. If they take an overt act toward the completion of their planned act, they will be guilty of conspiracy even if they never accomplish the robbery. An example of a state statute of conspiracy is Texas's Penal Code that provides in pertinent part:

Tex. Penal Code, Title 4 Inchoate Offenses, Chapter 15 Preparatory Offenses §15.02 (2006).

§15.02. CRIMINAL CONSPIRACY

a. A person commits criminal conspiracy if, with intent that a felony be committed:
1. he agrees with one or more persons that they or one or more of them engage in conduct that would constitute the offense; and
2. he or one or more of them performs an overt act in pursuance of the agreement.
b. An agreement constituting a conspiracy may be inferred from acts of the parties.
c. It is no defense to prosecution for criminal conspiracy that:
1. one or more of the coconspirators is not criminally responsible for the object offense;
2. one or more of the coconspirators has been acquitted, so long as two or more coconspirators have not been acquitted;
3. one or more of the coconspirators has not been prosecuted or convicted, has been convicted of a different offense, or is immune from prosecution;
4. the actor belongs to a class of persons that by definition of the object offense is legally incapable of committing the object offense in an individual capacity; or
5. the object offense was actually committed.
d. An offense under this section is one category lower than the most serious felony that is the object of the conspiracy, and if the most serious felony that is the object of the conspiracy is a state jail felony, the offense is a Class A misdemeanor.

a. Limitations on Parties to Conspiracy

The law establishes some limitations on parties to the crime of conspiracy even though not all jurisdictions recognize these limitations. One limitation on the extent of a conspiracy is the **Wharton Rule,** named after its author, Francis Wharton, that the rule specifies that when individuals engage in crimes that, by definition, require more than one person, they may not be prosecuted for conspiracy to commit those crimes; a third party must be involved for a conspiracy to exist. Crimes that qualify under the Wharton Rule are acts such as adultery, bigamy, and incest. Another limitation on conspiracy liability is the husband-and-wife rule. Under the common law a husband and wife were considered to be one person and because liability under conspiracy doctrine requires two or more persons, the couple could not conspire to commit a crime. This position was accepted in the United States in earlier days, based primarily on the assumption that the husband "owned" his wife who was under his dominion and control at all times. As other laws relating to the relationship between husband and wife have changed (for example, in many states today, a man can be charged with raping his wife, which was not historically possible according to early laws), so has the law of conspiracy. Today a wife may legally act independently of her husband, so the two of them may commit conspiracy and be charged individually.

A third limitation on parties to conspiracy is the two-or-more rule, requiring that for a conspiracy to exist two or more persons must be involved. Although it is obvious that the definition of conspiracy precludes one person from conspiring alone, courts have taken different positions on what happens if, for example, one of two alleged conspirators is acquitted. Technically, if there are only two alleged conspirators and one is acquitted, the other may not be convicted, as there would be only one party to the conspiracy. Some courts have taken this position, while others look to the reason why a second alleged coconspirator was not convicted. For example, if one defendant was granted immunity in exchange for testifying against the second coconspirator, a conspiracy conviction may be upheld on the defendant without immunity. A similar issue arises when the person charged with conspiracy allegedly conspired with a person who had no intention of carrying out the conspiracy, but as long as the intent existed, the conspirator can be convicted of the conspiracy nonetheless.

Defenses to a conspiracy charge include renunciation of the agreement [removing oneself from the agreement] by communicating to other coconspirators that one wants out. Renunciation is difficult to prove but the defense is often provided by law as illustrated by the Pennsylvania statute, which provides:

> It is a defense . . . that the actor, after conspiring to commit a crime, thwarted the success of the conspiracy, under circumstances manifesting a complete and voluntary renunciation of his criminal intent.[15]

If an original conspirator successfully presents a renunciation defense, he may be acquitted on the original conspiracy charges. In our opening chapter scenario, Billy Bob solicited Charles to engage in the robbery scheme in the Superdome, and once Charles agreed, their criminal enterprise became a criminal conspiracy. But if Charles had declined, he could be acquitted of conspiracy.

3. Attempt

Rule of Law: **Convictions for attempt crimes punish unsuccessful criminals.**

Attempt is a crime when one takes steps toward the commission of a crime and has a specific intent to commit that crime but, for some reason, is unable to complete the crime. Although in early English common law the attempt to commit a crime by itself was not a crime, it soon became a separate and distinct crime, and today most states criminalize the conduct of the unsuccessful criminal. Many jurisdictions have one statute that covers all attempt crimes, while some include a separate statute for each crime [attempted rape, attempted robbery]. An illustration of a comprehensive attempt statute can be found in the Texas Criminal Code, which provides in pertinent part:

Tex. Penal Code, Title 4 Inchoate Offenses, Chapter 15 Preparatory Offenses §15.01 (2006).

§15.01. ATTEMPT

a. A person commits an offense if, with specific intent to commit an offense, he does an act amounting to more than mere preparation that tends but fails to effect the commission of the offense intended.

b. If a person attempts an offense that may be aggravated, his conduct constitutes an attempt to commit the aggravated offense if an element that aggravates the offense accompanies the attempt. . . .

---

[15]18 Pa. C.S. sec. 903 (2007).

c. An offense under this section is one category lower than the offense attempted, and if the offense attempted is a state jail felony, the offense is a Class A misdemeanor.

The crime of attempt has two elements:

1. A criminal intent, and
2. A criminal act.

The intent to commit an attempt crime is the intent to commit acrime that, for some reason, the defendant is unable to complete. Generally, there must be a criminal act taken in furtherance of committing the crime which, again, the defendant is unable to complete. Usually courts require that the defendant went beyond merely preparing for the crime and moved toward committing the crime. Preparing to commit a crime may be drawing a map of the bank to rob, while attempting to commit a crime involves taking direct steps to rob the bank, such as conducting surveillance and assembling the burglar tools outside of the bank ready to go inside. If the defendant is apprehended by police outside the bank right before gaining entry, he may be charged with attempted robbery. A nonexhaustive list of steps taken toward the commission of the crime which may lead to criminal liability for attempt may be found in the Model Penal Code's "substantial step" test. If the defendant takes one of these "substantial steps" toward completing the crime, he may be guilty of attempt.

MPC §5.01 CRIMINAL ATTEMPT

2. Conduct Which May Be Held Substantial Step . . .
   a. lying in wait, searching for or following the contemplated victim of the crime;
   b. enticing or seeking to entice the contemplated victim of the crime to go to the place contemplated for its commission;
   c. reconnoitering the place contemplated for the commission of the crime;
   d. unlawful entry of a structure, vehicle or enclosure in which it is contemplated that the crime will be committed;
   e. possession of materials to be employed in the commission of the crime, which are specially designed for such unlawful use or which can serve no lawful purpose of the actor under the circumstances;
   f. possession, collection or fabrication of materials to be employed in the commission, at or near the place contemplated for its commission, where such possession, collection or fabrication serves no lawful purpose of the actor under the circumstances;
   g. soliciting an innocent agent to engage in conduct constituting an element of the crime.

Applying the Rule of Law to the Facts: Is it a joke or a criminal attempt?

• Two middle-school girls were caught giggling as they were about to put rat poison into their teacher's cup of coffee. Did the girls take a "substantial step" to try to kill the teacher, or were they playing a practical joke?

In *State v. Reeves,* 916 S.W.2d 909 (Tenn. 1996), the girls were held accountable for attempted murder.

a. Impossibility

The law punishes attempt crimes, although not as severely as completed crimes, on the theory that the attempter's moral blameworthiness is equal to the successful criminal in culpability. Ralph Damms forgot to put bullets in the gun when he aimed at his wife's head and pulled the trigger more than once. He was convicted of attempted murder. The judges were convinced that the fact the gun was not loaded was a mistake on

Damms's part and, had he done as he intended, Damms would have been successful in his attempt to kill his wife. Damms appealed on the grounds that it was impossible to kill his wife with an unloaded gun, but the court disagreed. If the defendant has the intent and takes steps toward completion of the crime, the defense of impossibility will not be successful. There are two types of impossibility, legal and factual. Does the defense of **impossibility**—that it was physically impossible to commit the crime—relieve the potential perpetrator of criminal responsibility? The answer is no. In present-day law, the defense of impossibility is often raised in cases where men are lured into believing they will meet an underage teenager for sex, an illegal tryst set up on the Internet. But the "teen" is in reality an undercover police officer. When the men are arrested for attempted sex with a minor, they claim that since no real teenager was involved it would be impossible to have sex with this nonexistent teen. Courts have upheld the attempt convictions of men on the grounds that their *mens rea* and *actus reus* concurred to propel the men to take steps to achieve their criminal act—sex with minors—and the fact that no real minors were involved is irrelevant.

In the *Indiana* v. *Haines* case reprinted in part in Box 4.5, the judge granted defendant Haines's motion to vacate [remove, declare null and void] his conviction of attempted murder charges when he thought he could infect rescue workers with HIV—a result the judge found to be an impossibility, which was the basis for his decision to vacate Haines's conviction. In a rare appeal by the state to reinstate the conviction, the appellate court found in favor of the state and overturned the trial judge's decision to let Haines go free. In our opening scenario, Charles committed attempted murder of Ken when he shot him intending to kill him, not realizing that Ken was already dead because his generator had stopped working. Charles had both the specific intent *mens rea* and committed an act, *actus reus*, and he will not escape liability just because his attempt failed and it is impossible to kill a dead man.

BOX 4.5

Indiana v. *Haines*, 545 N.E.2d 834 (1989)
Court of Appeals of Indiana, Second District

Judge Buchanan delivered the opinion of the court.

PROCEDURAL HISTORY

[T]he State of Indiana (the State), appeals from the trial court's grant of . . . Donald J. Haines' (Haines) motion for judgment on the evidence, claiming that the trial judge erred in vacating the jury's verdicts of three counts of attempted murder . . .

FACTS

On August 6, 1987, Lafayette, Indiana, police officers John R. Dennis (Dennis) and Brad Hayworth drove to Haines' apartment in response to a radio call of a possible suicide. Haines was unconscious when they arrived and was lying face down in a pool of blood. Dennis attempted to revive Haines and

noticed that Haines' wrists were slashed and bleeding. When Haines heard the paramedics arriving, he stood up, ran toward Dennis, and screamed that he should be left to die because he had AIDS. Dennis told Haines they were there to help him, but he continued yelling and stated he wanted to f*** Dennis and "give it to him." Haines told Dennis that he would "use his wounds" and began jerking his arms at Dennis, causing blood to spray into Dennis' mouth and eyes. Throughout the incident, as the officers attempted to subdue him, Haines repeatedly yelled that he had AIDS, that he could not deal with it and that he was going to make Dennis deal with it.

Haines also struggled with emergency medical technicians Dan Garvey (Garvey) and Diane Robinson threatening to infect them with AIDS and began spitting at them. When Dennis grabbed

Haines, Haines scratched, bit, and spit at him. At one point, Haines grabbed a blood-soaked wig and struck Dennis in the face with it. This caused blood again to splatter onto Dennis' eyes, mouth, and skin. When Dennis finally handcuffed Haines, Dennis was covered with blood. He also had scrapes and scratches on his arms and a cut on his finger that was bleeding. When Haines arrived at the hospital, he was still kicking, screaming, throwing blood, and spitting at Dennis, Garvey, and another paramedic, Rodney Jewell. Haines again announced that he had AIDS and that he was going to show everyone else what it was like to have the disease and die. At one point, Haines bit Garvey on the upper arm, breaking the skin. Roger Conn, Haines' homosexual lover and former roommate, recalled that Dr. Kenneth Pennington (Pennington) informed Haines that he had the AIDS virus. Haines told Conn that he knew AIDS was a fatal disease.

Haines was charged with three counts of attempted murder. At trial, medical experts testified that the virus could be transmitted through blood, tears, and saliva. They also observed that policemen, firemen, and other emergency personnel are generally at risk when they are exposed to body products. One medical expert observed that Dennis was definitely exposed to the HIV virus and others acknowledged that exposure of infected blood to the eyes and the mouth is dangerous, and that it is easier for the virus to enter the blood stream if there is a cut in the skin. Following a trial by jury, Haines was convicted of three counts of attempted murder on January 14, 1988. On February 18, 1988, Haines moved for judgment on the evidence as to the three counts of attempted murder, which the trial court granted.

ISSUE

[Did Haines commit attempted murder with the HIV virus?]

HOLDING

[Yes.]

REASONING

When the trial judge sentenced Haines on February 2, 1988, he made this statement:

> I believe my decision in this case was made easier by the State's decision to not introduce any medical expert

scientific evidence. The State believed that the disease known as AIDS was irrelevant to its burden of proof; that only the intent or state of mind of the defendant was relevant. I disagree with that. All of us know that the conduct of spitting, throwing blood and biting cannot under normal circumstances constitute a step, substantial or otherwise, in causing the death of another person, regardless of the intent of the defendant. More has to be shown, more has to be proven, in my judgment. And the more in this case was that the conduct had to be coupled with a disease, a disease which by definition is inextricably based in science and medicine.

> There was no medical expert evidence that the person with ARC [AIDS Related Complex] or AIDS can kill another by transmitting bodily fluids as alleged in this case. And there was no medical evidence from any of the evidence that the defendant had reason to believe that he could transmit his condition to others by transmitting bodily fluids as are alleged in this case. The verdicts of the jury as to attempted murder will be set aside and judgment of conviction of battery on a police officer resulting in bodily injury as a Class D felony will be entered on each of the three counts. A sentence of two years will be ordered on each of the three counts. Those sentences will run consecutively because I find aggravating circumstances and I will set those out at this time.

The trial judge's failure to consider all of the evidence and his comment at the February 2, 1988, sentencing hearing that he weighed the evidence in deciding whether to grant judgment on the evidence constituted error. Contrary to Haines' contention that the evidence did not support a reasonable inference that his conduct amounted to a substantial step toward murder, the record reflects otherwise. At trial, it was definitely established that Haines carried the AIDS virus, was aware of the infection, believed it to be fatal, and intended to inflict others with the disease by spitting, biting, scratching, and throwing blood. Haines misconstrues the logic and effect of our attempt statute. While he maintains that the State failed to meet its burden insofar as it did not present sufficient evidence regarding Haines' conduct which constituted a substantial step toward murder, subsection (b) of [Indiana Code, section] 35-41-5-1 provides: "It is no defense that, because of a misapprehension of the circumstances, it would have been impossible for the accused person to commit the crime attempt."

In *Zickefoose* v. *State,* 388 N.E.2d 507 (1979), our supreme court observed: "It is clear that section (b) of our statute rejects the defense of

(continued)

BOX 4.5

(continued)

impossibility. It is not necessary that there be a present ability to complete the crime, nor is it necessary that the crime be factually possible. When the defendant has done all that he believes necessary to cause the particular result, regardless of what is actually possible under existing circumstances, he has committed an attempt. The liability of the defendant turns on his purpose as manifested through his conduct. If the defendant's conduct in light of all the relevant facts involved, constitutes a substantial step toward the commission of the crime and is done with the necessary specific intent, then the defendant has committed an attempt."

In accordance with [Indiana's attempt statute] the State was not required to prove that Haines' conduct could actually have killed. It was only necessary for the State to show that Haines did all that he believed necessary to bring about an intended result, regardless of what was actually possible. While we have found no Indiana case directly on point, the evidence presented at trial renders any defense of inherent impossibility

inapplicable in this case. *See King* v. *State,* 469 N.E.2d 1201 (1984) (a defendant's intent and conduct is a more reliable indication of culpability than the hazy distinction between factual and legal impossibility). In addition to Haines' belief that he could infect others there was testimony by physicians that the virus may be transmitted through the exchange of bodily fluids. It was apparent that the victims were exposed to the AIDS virus as a result of Haines' conduct.

CONCLUSION

From the evidence in the record before us we can only conclude that Haines had knowledge of his disease and that he unrelentingly and unequivocally sought to kill the persons helping him by infecting them with AIDS, and that he took a substantial step towards killing them by his conduct believing that hc could do so, all of which was more than a mere tenuous, theoretical, or speculative "chance" of transmitting the disease. [Conviction for attempted murder reinstated]

In August 1990, Donald Haines was sentenced to 30 years for his attempt crime, but died in prison the following year.

VI. Key Terms and Phrases

- *actus reus*
- assumption of the duty
- causation
- concurrence
- constructive intent
- constructive possession
- duty by contract
- duty by relationship

- elements
- factual cause
- general intent
- Good Samaritan Laws
- intervening cause
- knowingly
- *mala in se*
- *mala prohibita*

- *mens rea*
- negligently
- principle of legality
- proximate cause
- purposely
- recklessly
- scienter
- strict liability

VII. Summary

1. **How criminal liability attaches to an individual wrongdoer:** The law seeks to assign an appropriate level of punishment based on the defendant's *mens rea,* or guilty state of mind, at the time the crime was committed. The most common *mens rea* states are **purposely** which is **specific intent** (the actor desires his

   conduct to cause a specific result); **knowingly,** which is a **general intent** crime (the actor undertakes an action but not necessarily to bring about a specific result); **recklessly,** where the actor ignores the risk of harm his behavior creates, and **negligently,** where the actor is unaware of the risk of harm his behavior creates. To be found responsible for a crime, there must be **concurrence,** a joining of *mens rea* with *actus reus,* a voluntary act that leads to criminal liability. Some crimes that are defined as acts, such as **possession** of drugs, can be proven by surrounding circumstances such as **constructive** (legal fiction) **intent** or **constructive possession.** Other so-called acts, such as personal status such as drug addict, may not be punished, but status as a pedophile may lead to legal restrictions. Crimes that require a *mens rea* state are usually *mala in se* crimes, acts that are inherently evil, such as rape or murder, and also require **scienter,** which is knowledge that the acts engaged in are criminal, such as receiving stolen property known to be stolen. Some crimes are **strict liability** crimes or *mala prohibita* (they are crimes because society includes them among acts it wants to prohibit). They require no *mens rea*, and the actor will be guilty simply by performing the illegal act.

2. **The legal duty to help people in peril or prevent crime:** The law imposes a legal requirement to care for people in certain relationships recognized in law, such as a **duty by relationship,** such as parent/child; **duty by contract,** such as landlord/tenant; and **duty by statute,** such as police officer/citizen. There are also acts of kindness freely given, **assumptions of the duty** which, if undertaken, may impose legal liability if these acts create more danger. Many states have **Good Samaritan laws** that protect certain professions, such as emergency medical technicians, and others who try and help people in emergency situations from criminal and civil liability.

3. **The end result of setting a crime in motion:** A causation analysis of the facts examines whether a person should be held responsible for committing certain acts. First, is the actor the **factual cause** of the harm? That is, "but for" the actor's initial conduct would the harm have happened? Next, is the actor the **proximate cause** of the harm? Was the ultimate harm foreseeable by the actor's initial conduct? Last, were there any **intervening causes** that broke the causal chain from the actor's initial conduct to the ultimate harm? If the actor is both the factual and legal cause and there are no intervening causes, she will be liable for the harm caused.

4. **The definitions of parties to crime:** Under common law, individuals who helped criminals, but did not directly participate in a crime, were punished less severely than those actually participating in the crime. Today the modern trend in state statutes is to treat **principals** to crime—the offenders—the same as **accessories,** those who are there or who are close by when the crime is being committed and who assist the principals. An **accessory before the fact** helps the principal get ready to commit the crime by giving aid, instruction, or materials, while an **accessory after the fact** might give shelter to the fugitive.

5. **The legal principles assigning responsibility for the inchoate crimes of solicitation, conspiracy and attempt:** The law seeks to punish those who try to commit crimes and fail or are otherwise incomplete. **Solicitation** is asking someone else to commit a crime, **conspiracy** is an agreement to commit a crime, and **attempt** is having the *mens rea* and taking a substantial step toward completing the crime, but for some reason not being able to complete it. **Impossibility**—the fact that it would be impossible to complete the crime—is often no defense to attempt crimes, because society seeks to punish the intent and criminal effort to complete the act.

VIII. Discussion Questions

1. Do you believe that the Twitchell couple should have known that Massachusetts state law would punish them for the death of their son? Even if the Twitchells received conflicting legal advice, can such reliance absolve them of their son's death when reliance on prayer alone was an insufficient cure?

2. What goals in society do possession laws help achieve? Are the possession laws construed so loosely that someone could be held criminally liable for being in the wrong place at the wrong time? On what type of evidence, other than proximity to contraband, would you like to see a court base its conviction of a defendant?

3. Do you agree with the concept of criminal causation that the defendant should be responsible for just those acts which were not only natural and probable consequences of his initial acts, but also foreseeable? How many criminal defendants can actually foresee the myriad of events that may or may not intervene to cause a victim's death? Do you think society should focus on the factual cause alone and as long as the defendant started the ball rolling by his initial illegal conduct, the law should hold him ultimately responsible no matter what the ultimate outcome? Why or why not?

4. What is the public rationale for enforcing strict liability laws, and what alternative can you suggest to make all crimes have a *mens rea* requirement?

5. Give the definitions of the *mens rea* states of purposely, knowingly, recklessly and negligently and give a brief example of each sufficient to show your understanding of the differences and similarities among the four mental states.

6. Why is the concept of causation necessary in criminal law, and what do you think the criminal court system

would look like if causation were not a requirement to hold the original offender accountable?

7. Explain the theory behind holding all members of a conspiracy liable, and explain why society punishes attempt crimes even though the offender was an unsuccessful criminal.

8. Explain the significance of the principle of legality both in the development of criminal law and in present-day statutory analysis.

IX. Problem-Solving Exercises

1. Dave is on his way to kill his grandfather when his car breaks down on the highway. In his car, he has a gun, bullets, and a "to-do" list to commit the murder and escape. The police stop to help Dave on the highway, discover his murder plot, and arrest him. The prosecutor charges Dave with attempted murder. Dave raised the defense of impossibility. Dave asserts that because his car broke down, it was impossible for him to kill his grandfather. Therefore, he is not guilty of any attempt crime. Which side will win at trial?

2. Mark suffered from a seizure disorder for which he took medication. One day, Mark forgot to take his medicine. While driving with his wife Wendy, Mark felt a seizure coming on. Mark pulled over and Wendy injected Mark with anti-seizure medicine. The medicine caused Mark to become suicidal. When Mark started to drive again he drove straight toward another car. The other driver swerved to avoid a collision with Mark, but they both crashed,

and Mark and the other driver died at the scene. Wendy has been charged under the following statute:

"Anyone who purposely, knowingly, recklessly or negligently causes the death of another shall be guilty of a felony." Wendy said that she did not intend for anyone to get hurt when she lawfully injected Mark with the medicine. Will Wendy be found guilty under the statute for causing both deaths? Explain your answer fully.

3. A 40-year-old mother of five shakes a crying baby to make the baby stop crying. In the same courtroom is a 12-year-old babysitter who shook her baby sister to stop her from crying. Both infants died, and both defendants are charged with first-degree, specific intent murder. You are a defense attorney appointed to represent both defendants. How would you defend each, based on the prosecution's theory that both caretakers acted purposely?

X. World Wide Web Resources

Law and Society Association

http://www.lawnadsociety.org

XI. Additional Readings and Notes

Mens rea

Elaine Chiu. "The Challenge of Motive in the Criminal Law." *Buffalo Criminal Law Review,* Vol. 8 (2005), pp. 653–729.

Justin D. Levinson. "Mentally Misguided: How State of Mind Inquiries Ignore Psychological Reality and Overlook Cultural Differences." *Howard Law Journal,* Vol. 1 (2005), pp. 1–29.

Jason M. Horst "Imaginary Intent: The California Supreme Court's Search for a Specific Legislative Intent That Does Not Exist." *University of San Francisco Law Review,* Vol. 39 (2005), pp. 1045–1072.

Jeffrey Rowe. "Revisiting *Robinson*: The Eighth Amendment as Constitutional Support of the Theories of

Criminal Responsibility." *University of Maryland Law Journal of Race, Religion, Gender and Class,* Vol. 5 (2005), pp. 95–127.

Peter K. Westen. "Getting the Fly Out of the Bottle: The False Problem of Free Will and Determinism." *Buffalo Criminal Law Review,* Vol. 8 (2005), pp. 599–652.

Actus Reus

M. Varn and Anoop Chandola. "A Cognitive Framework for *Mens Rea* and *Actus Reus*: The Application of Contracts Theory to Criminal Law." *Tulsa Law Review,* Vol. 35 (2000), pp. 383–397.

CHAPTER

Crimes Against the Person

5

"What I've concluded from decades of working with murderers and rapists and every kind of violent criminal is that an underlying factor that is virtually always present to one degree or another is a feeling that one has to prove one's manhood, and that the way to do that, to gain the respect that has been lost, is to commit a violent act."

DR. JAMES GILLIGAN, PROFESSOR, NEW YORK UNIVERSITY[1]

CHAPTER OBJECTIVES

Primary Concepts Discussed in This Chapter:

1. The similarities and differences between the crimes of assault and battery
2. Distinguishing kidnapping from false imprisonment
3. The elements and defining characteristics of sex-related offenses
4. The type of behavior that separates degrees of homicide
5. Stalking and hate crimes

CHAPTER OUTLINE

FEATURE: CRIMES AGAINST THE PERSON

I. CRIMES AGAINST THE PERSON

1. Assault and Battery
   a. Aggravated Assault and Battery
2. Terroristic Threats
3. Kidnapping and False Imprisonment
   Box 5.1 *Colorado* v. *Torres,* 141 P. 3d 931 (2006)
4. Stalking
5. Hate Crimes

II. SEX OFFENSES

1. Rape
   Box 5.2 *Pennsylvania* v. *Berkowitz,* 641 A.2d 1161 (1994)
   a. Rape Shield Laws
   b. Statutory Rape
      i. Mistake of Age as a Defense to a Charge of Statutory Rape
   c. Incest
   d. Deviate Sexual Conduct

III. HOMICIDE

1. First- and Second-Degree Murder
2. Manslaughter
   a. Heat of Passion
   Box 5.3 *Commonwealth* v. *Schnopps,* 417 N.E.2d 1213 (Mass. 1981)

---

[1]Bob Herbert. "A Volatile Young Man, Humiliation and a Gun." *The New York Times* OP-ED, April 19, 2007, p. A27.

Feature: *Chapter-Opening Case Study: Crimes Against the Person*

Ben, Jerry, and Kathy were desperate for money. Kathy said her stepmother, who lived nearby, owned some very expensive diamond jewelry and they should take it tonight. Kathy went to her stepmother's house, and later that night Ben and Jerry knocked on the door. The stepmother answered the door, and Ben and Jerry, posing as insurance salesmen, asked to come inside. Once inside, Jerry said to the stepmother, "Don't scream or I'll punch your lights out!" [threat as assault] They took the stepmother to her bedroom and tied her up [battery, false imprisonment]. When the stepmother got loose, Ben and Jerry blocked the bedroom door so she couldn't get out [false imprisonment]. Ben then punched the stepmother in the face and knocked her out [aggravated battery]. Ben then said to Jerry, "Jeez, she looks like she hasn't had sex in a long time, I'm sure she wants it now." Ben pulled down the stepmother's pants and tried to insert his penis into her vagina, but he was only able to penetrate her a little [rape]. Frustrated by his own impotence, Ben lifted the stepmother, put her in the trunk of their car, and drove off with Kathy and Jerry [kidnapping].

They stopped at a convenience store, and Kathy said that the Korean-American grocer who owned the store gave her a funny look. Ben said, "Welcome to America, macaca," as Ben hit him over the head with a beer bottle causing severe lacerations, cuts and bruises on his face [hate crime]. The trio ran out of the store, and Kathy suggested that they steal a nice new four-door sedan sitting in the store parking lot. Ben and Jerry agreed when they saw a young woman get out of the sedan and left it running. The threesome jumped inside and started to pull away when they heard a baby crying in the back seat. They drove for 20 miles before they pulled over because the baby's crying was hurting their ears, and they left the baby at a well-lit rest area, sure that someone would find the baby. By the time state troopers pulled the sedan over for speeding, the baby had died at the rest area [felony murder] and back at the convenience store, the stepmother was found in the trunk of the first car dead of asphyxiation [felony murder]. What crimes have the three friends committed?

INTRODUCTION

This chapter examines the most common crimes against the person that involve assaults on physical dignity, such as assault and battery; the *mens rea* distinctions that separate one type of homicide from another, first degree murder from manslaughter for example; the myriad of sex offenses and the similarities and differences of each type of sex crime; the relatively recent legislative pronouncements against crimes motivated by hatred of someone because of personal characteristics such as gender, race, ethnicity, or sexual orientation; and the crime of stalking, a crime committed most often by the mentally ill who suffer from a type of obsessive–compulsive disorder and repeatedly harass, threaten, and physically intimidate the object of their attention.

I. CRIMES AGAINST THE PERSON

1. Assault and Battery

Rule of Law: **The threat of harm, assault, and the actual physical harm, battery, are two different crimes, although in modern statutes assault is often called battery.**

Traditionally assault and battery were two distinct crimes. Assault was the crime of placing someone in fear of a hurtful touch, and battery was the actual hurtful or offensive touching. Today, under most penal statutes, the terms are intertwined with each other, and assault often describes conduct that was traditionally battery. Someone might say, "John assaulted Billy when he punched him in the face," describing the punch as the assault when, technically under the common law, the assault happened when Billy was put in fear of John's incoming punch, not when he was actually punched. The Model Penal Code §211.1 definition of assault reflects both the common law definition and the modern statutory approach of defining assault. One commits **assault** when one:

1. Attempts or does cause bodily injury to another.
2. Negligently causes injury to another with a deadly weapon.
3. Puts another in fear of imminent bodily injury.

A common example of traditional assault is the parent who raises a hand to strike a child, causing the child to flinch and recoil in fear of being hit. The parent has technically "assaulted" the child, but since he has lawful authority to discipline the child, such parental action is unlikely to be treated as a crime. The threat of physical injury in an assault must be imminent, and the defendant must have the apparent ability to carry out the threat of harm immediately. A threat to beat someone to a pulp an hour later is not an assault because—even though the offender may have the apparent ability to carry out the threat, the threat of physical harm may never materialize—there may be many intervening events separating the threat from the occurrence of the action. The assault need not be committed with hands. If a person points an unloaded gun at someone who is ignorant that the gun has no bullets, such an act constitutes an assault under the principles above.[2]

Under common law, the **battery** was the touching of another that was harmful or offensive. The elements of battery are the:

1. intentional
2. unconsented to
3. touching of another
4. that is harmful or offensive.

The touching is unlawful if the person being touched has not consented. A female waitress at a bar may get pinched on the buttocks as a matter of routine in the

---

[2]*See Allen* v. *Hannaford,* 138 Wash. 423 (1926).

course of her employment, but it does not mean she has consented to such unwanted touching because she chose to be a waitress. The pinch constitutes battery. The offensiveness of the touching is often defined by the circumstances surrounding the touching; spitting in someone's face could be construed as a battery, as is grabbing a plate out of someone's hand.

a. Aggravated Assault and Battery

The significance of elevating a crime to "aggravated" status means that upon conviction, the defendant's sentence may be harsher, and the prison sentence, if any, may be longer. In aggravated assault cases, the crime is often defined by the status of the victim. If an assault is committed upon a prison guard, police officer, young child, or one who suffers from a mental or physical disability, then the assault may be elevated to "aggravated" status. A simple assault is typically a misdemeanor but an aggravated assault is usually a felony. Similarly, battery is elevated to aggravated status when the amount of force used is excessive or committed with the intent to cause serious bodily harm to the victim, as illustrated in New Mexico's aggravated battery statute reprinted below. Both assault and battery may be aggravated if they are done in the commission of another crime, for instance, assault or battery committed during a rape or assault or battery committed during a robbery with a dangerous weapon would constitute the higher form of the crime. If a man hit, groped, and squeezed a woman in an attempt to rape her, but did not commit the rape, his actions would be considered aggravated battery because of the harmful and offensive nature of the act, which, by its very definition, was unlawful.

NEW MEXICO STATUTE ANNOTATED §30-3-5 (2008) AGGRAVATED BATTERY

A. Aggravated battery consists of the unlawful touching or application of force to the person of another with intent to injure that person or another.

B. Whoever commits aggravated battery, inflicting an injury to the person which is not likely to cause death or great bodily harm, but does cause painful temporary disfigurement or temporary loss or impairment of the functions of any member or organ of the body, is guilty of a misdemeanor.

C. Whoever commits aggravated battery inflicting great bodily harm or does so with a deadly weapon or does so in any manner whereby great bodily harm or death can be inflicted is guilty of a third degree felony.

In the chapter's opening scenario, once Ben and Jerry were inside the stepmother's house, Jerry assaulted the stepmother by placing her in fear of an imminent battery when he told her, "Don't scream or I'll punch your lights out." Jerry had the apparent ability to carry out the battery immediately. Ben then battered the woman when he punched her in the face and knocked her out. Both the assault and the battery were aggravated because the offenders were engaged in the commission of another crime, burglary, when the assault and battery took place.

Another form of aggravated battery is the common law crime of mayhem, which is the malicious and permanent disfigurement of another. The elements of **mayhem** are the:

1. specific intent
2. to commit a battery
3. with the result of permanent disfigurement, such as cutting off a nose, putting out an eye, or rendering an appendage such as an arm, hand, or ear useless.

Under present-day statutes, mayhem has been redefined as aggravated battery.

2. Terroristic Threats

A crime similar to the assault of placing one in fear of imminent physical harm is the making of terroristic threats. **Terroristic threats** are made when the offender

1. threatens to commit violence
2. with the purpose of terrorizing another or
3. with the purpose of causing the evacuation of a public venue, such as making a bomb threat to cause people to flee an airport, school, or other inhabited building.

The *mens rea* for making terroristic threats is a reckless disregard for the risk of harm to the public, which will react in fear to the threat and cause pandemonium in trying to escape. The crime also encompasses repeatedly using the telephone to make threatening calls or otherwise harassing another person by threatening his or her safety.

3. Kidnapping and False Imprisonment

Rule of Law: The primary difference between kidnapping and false imprisonment is the degree of asportation – the movement of the victim.

Under common law, false imprisonment was interfering with a person's physical liberty by unlawful confinement, while kidnapping was the forcible taking of a person from one place to another. Such a distinction in the amount of movement—called asportation—is the focal point in defining the crimes in modern statutes today. Common statutory elements define **kidnapping** as the:

1. unlawful
2. asportation [transportation]
3. of another
4. by force or threat of force.

In contrast to kidnapping, the crime of **false imprisonment** is the restraint of another's liberty against that person's will without significant asportation. If the movement of the victim is incidental to another crime, for example moving a rape victim from a park bench to behind a nearby bush to conceal the act of rape from public view, such movement of the victim is incidental to the rape and will not be considered the separate crime of kidnapping. But, if in order to effectuate the rape, the offender places the victim in a car and drives her two or three miles away from the park in order to commit the rape, he may be charged with the additional crime of kidnapping. The analysis is not necessarily on the distance the offender moves the victim, but whether the *mens rea* for the movement is just to effectuate the initial crime or is, indeed, a separate crime for which the prosecution can meet all elements and sustain the burden of proof. Most jurisdictions today classify kidnapping as a serious felony and describe a series of conditions that define kidnapping. These conditions, which include holding an individual for ransom money or to perpetrate another crime, are illustrated by Hawaii's kidnapping statute:

> **HAWAII REVISED STATUTES §707-720 (2008) KIDNAPPING**
> 1. A person commits the offense of kidnapping if the person intentionally or knowingly restrains another person with intent to:
>   a. Hold that person for ransom or reward;
>   b. Use that person as a shield or hostage;
>   c. Facilitate the commission of a felony or flight thereafter;
>   d. Inflict bodily injury upon that person to a sexual offense;
>   e. Terrorize that person or a third person; or
>   f. Interfere with the performance of any governmental or political function.
> 2. Except as provided in subsection (3), kidnapping is a class A felony.
> 3. In a prosecution for kidnapping, it is a defense which reduces the offense to a class B felony that the defendant voluntarily released the victim, alive and not suffering from serious or substantial bodily injury, in a safe place prior to trial.

Hawaii's kidnapping statute includes the caveat that if the victim is released prior to trial, the seriousness of the grading of the offense will be reduced. The primary difference between kidnapping and false imprisonment is the amount of time an offender can receive as a prison sentence upon conviction. A kidnapping sentence is generally substantially longer than one for false imprisonment.[3]

In the opening-case scenario, when Ben and Jerry blocked the door of the stepmother's bedroom preventing her from leaving, they committed the crime of false imprisonment. When Ben, Jerry, and Kathy placed the stepmother in the trunk of the car and drove away for miles, they kidnapped her. In analyzing the amount of asportation to distinguish between kidnapping and false imprisonment, read the following case, *Colorado* v. *Torres,* in which the defendant was convicted of second-degree kidnapping because the court found that he had specific intent *mens rea* to confine the victim above and beyond the incidental movement in the commission of another offense.

As the ease with which couples could obtain a divorce increased over the past decades, so, too, did the number of custody disputes involving minor children with attendant custody decrees issued by courts. Some custody disputes end with one parent kidnapping his or her own children to prevent the other parent from having a relationship with the children. If a parent kidnaps his or her own child and crosses state lines, the federal Parental Kidnapping Prevention Act[4] becomes relevant. This law was enacted to "deter interstate abductions and other unilateral removal of children undertaken to obtain custody and visitation awards." The *mens rea* of parental kidnapping is the specific intent to keep the child or children away from one parent, and the *actus reus* is the actual asportation of the child or children away from the other parent's dominion and control. The America's Missing Broadcast Emergency Response ("AMBER") alert system is a nationwide electronic notification system that distributes important information about abducted children and the offender, such as vehicle description, license plate numbers, direction traveling, and last location seen. The information appears on electronic billboards and television stations in hopes that the kidnapping victim will be found, and it is responsible for finding many victims in the critical first few hours after abduction. The information distribution system was named after 9-year-old Amber Hagerman, a kidnap victim from Texas.[5] As with any kidnapping, studies show that time is of the essence in trying to recover the victim.

4. Stalking

Rule of Law: The *mens rea* for stalking is that the offender should have known his or her repetitive harassment caused distress for the victim.

Stalking is a compulsive act usually performed by an offender who most likely suffers from a mental illness and who continually harasses and threatens the object/victim of his or her obsession. Of course, having a mental illness is not a crime. Stalkers usually exhibit the same type of behavior that revolves around the delusion [false fixed belief]

---

[3]For example, section 97-3-53 of the Mississippi statute that defines the punishment for kidnapping any child under the age of 16 states, "if the jury fails to agree on fixing the penalty at imprisonment for life, the court shall fix the penalty at not less than one (1) year nor more than thirty (30) years in the custody of the Department of Corrections."

[4]P.L. 96-611 §7(1)(7), 28 U.S.C. §1738A (2002).

[5]The U.S. Department of Justice has published recommended criteria for states to follow for the issuing of an AMBER alert:

1. Law enforcement has a reasonable belief that an abduction has occurred.
2. The child is under 17 years old.
3. Law enforcement believes the child is in imminent danger of serious bodily injury or death.
4. There is enough descriptive information about the abduction and the child to assist in the recovery of the child.

BOX 5.1

Colorado v. Torres, 141 P. 3d 931 (2006)
Court of Appeals of Colorado

Judge Nieto delivered the opinion of the court.

FACTS

In May 2003, Torres and his girlfriend, G.W., ended their two-month relationship. On the day Torres moved out of G.W.'s home, he called her several times to ask whether he could come over and do his laundry, but she refused. Later that night, Torres appeared at G.W.'s back door and demanded that he be let in. When G.W. refused, Torres became agitated; he pounded on the window, demanded to know to whom she was talking on her cell phone, and swore at her and her seven-year-old son, A.C. A.C. then ran to a telephone and called 911. Torres eventually broke the window on the back door, reached in, unlocked the door, and went into the house. G.W. told the 911 operator that Torres had come inside her home, but once inside, he hung up the 911 call, grabbed G.W. by the hair, and dragged her into the living room while he screamed that he wanted to know where the cell phone was. A.C. tried to help G.W. by grabbing and hitting Torres's arms, but Torres pushed A.C. out of the way and into a wall.

Meanwhile, the police arrived, and G.W. attempted to signal to them by banging on a window and screaming. Torres responded by covering her mouth and forcing her from the first floor living room into the basement of the home. Once there, Torres forced G.W. into a bedroom, tried to close the door, and blocked her exit; then he demanded that G.W. stop screaming and apologized for hurting her. While in the basement, Torres smashed G.W.'s cell phone. A jury convicted him of second degree kidnapping, third degree assault, and criminal mischief. This appeal followed [on several issues, kidnapping only discussed here].

ISSUE

Torres contends that the evidence was insufficient to support a conviction for second degree kidnapping because his movement of G.W. was insubstantial and did not substantially increase her risk of harm.

HOLDING

We disagree [with Torres and conclude that he did kidnap G.W.].

REASONING

Whether a defendant's conduct substantially increased the risk of harm to a victim is not a material element of second degree kidnapping. The asportation element of this crime is simply that the defendant seized and carried another person from one place to another. *People* v. *Harlan,* 8 P.3d 448 (Colo. 2000). However, where the prosecution relies on insubstantial movement to prove second degree kidnapping, a showing that the insubstantial movement substantially increased the risk of harm to a victim will suffice to support the conviction. *People* v. *Owens,* 97 P.3d 227 (Colo. App. 2004). Here, it is undisputed that after the police arrived and G.W. tried to signal to them, Torres forced her from the ground level of her house into the basement. This movement of G.W. from the first floor of her home to the basement, where she could not be seen from outside the building, was not insubstantial. However, even if this movement could be considered insubstantial, it is clear that the asportation greatly increased G.W.'s risk of harm.

The record shows that Torres moved G.W. to the basement only after she began to pound on a window and scream to gain the attention of arriving police officers. Moreover, before Torres moved G.W. to the basement, he had already broken into her house, dragged her by her hair, punched her in the face, shoved her minor son, and thrown her into a sliding glass door. Once in the basement, Torres moved G.W. into a room, attempted to close the door, blocked her exit, and demanded that she stop screaming. G.W. testified that she continued to scream because she feared that the police would not find her if she remained silent.

This evidence, taken as a whole and in the light most favorable to the prosecution, is clearly sufficient to support a finding beyond a reasonable doubt that Torres increased G.W.'s risk of harm by forcing her into the basement.

CONCLUSION

Accordingly, the evidence was sufficient to convict Torres of second degree kidnapping.

that they must be in contact with their target, either for a love reason or in an attempt to hurt, harm, or kill the object of their attentions. Actress Rebecca Schaeffer from the 1990s television show "My Sister Sam" was 21-years-old when she was shot and killed by an obsessive fan who had stalked her for two years. The killer had paid a private detective to retrieve Schaeffer's home address from driver's license records. Her murder led to legislative changes to create the crime of stalking, but to also protect people's personal information contained in public records. Other notable cases of celebrity stalking have been Uma Thurman, whose male stalker ended up outside her home in New York City, and the pop star Madonna, who received bizarre letters and was repeatedly physically harassed by a stalker who was finally arrested on her property. Madonna was a reluctant witness at his trial because, as she said, he got exactly what he wanted, which was to share her physical presence and have her attention fixated on him. Some psychological findings about stalkers reveal the following information:[6]

1. The most common form of stalking involves single males who are obsessed with women with whom they have had prior intimate relations.

2. Axis I mental disorders are evidence in the majority of stalkers and likely include drug and alcohol addictions, mood disorders, or schizophrenia.

3. Axis II personality disorders are also evidence in a majority of stalkers, particularly Cluster B, although both Cluster A (paranoid personality disorder) and Cluster C (dependent personality disorder) are evidence in some cases.

4. Empirical research is beginning to support the theoretical hypothesis that stalking is a pathology of attachment, evident in the subject's early childhood attachment disruptions and a recent, major loss in adulthood prior to the advent of the stalking.

5. At least half of stalkers explicitly threaten their victims, and even though most threats are not carried out, the risk of violence likely increases when there is an articulated threat.

6. Most stalkers are not violent around their objects, but if they are, it is usually directed toward the object of their stalking rather than toward property or a third party.

The federal government makes stalking that crosses state lines a crime, and some states have enacted laws designed to prevent "cyberstalking"—continuous unlawful harassment by means of electronic communication devices such as computers and telephones.

In Illinois, stalking is a serious felony, and the state's antistalking statute provides: Illinois Statute 720.

ILLINOIS CONSOLIDATED STATUTES 5/12-7.3

a. A person commits stalking when he or she, knowingly and without lawful justification, on at least two separate occasions follows another person or places the person under surveillance or any combination thereof and:

1. at any time transmits a threat of immediate or future bodily harm, sexual assault, confinement or restraint and the threat is directed towards that person or a family member of that person; or

2. places that person in reasonable apprehension of immediate or future bodily harm, sexual assault, confinement or restraint; or

3. places that person in reasonable apprehension that a family member will receive immediate or future bodily harm, sexual assault, confinement, or restraint.

Subsection (d) of the statute states that a defendant "places a person under surveillance" by remaining present outside the person's school, place of employment, vehicle, other place occupied by the person, or any residence other than the residence of the defendant. Subsection (e) stipulates that the words "follows another person" mean

---

[6]J. R. Meloy, ed. *The Psychology of Stalking*. (San Diego, CA: Academic Press, 1998).

"(i) to move in relative proximity to a person as that person moves from place to place or (ii) to remain in relative proximity to a person who is stationary or whose movements are confined to a small area." However, subsection (e) points out that to follow another person does not include following the person within the residence of the defendant. Subsection (g) defines "transmit a threat" as a "verbal or written threat or a threat implied by a pattern of conduct or a combination of verbal or written statements or conduct." Finally, subsection (h) broadly defines "family member."

The essence of stalking is the repetitive attempts to contact someone who has repeatedly made the offender aware that his or her advances and attention are unwelcome and unwanted.

5. Hate Crimes

Rule of Law: It is legal in America to hate others, but it is illegal to hurt others based on that hate.

The First Amendment protects freedom of speech, which includes hateful and hurtful expression. This country has many freedoms, and the freedom to dislike someone because of the person's background, religious beliefs, race, gender, or sexual orientation is one of them. But once those permissible thoughts go beyond speech into actions, then the individual who took action may be punished or have his or her punishment enhanced because of targeting someone because of who they are, which is a **hate crime.** The New York Hate Crimes Statute, Penal Code section 485.05 (2006) provides that a person commits a hate crime when he "commits a specified offense [such as assault, kidnapping, sex abuse, or degrees of homicide] and either . . .

(a) intentionally selects the person against whom the offense is committed or intended to be committed in whole or in substantial part because of a belief or perception regarding the race, color, national origin, ancestry, gender, religion, religious practice, age, disability or sexual orientation of a person, regardless of whether the belief or perception is correct . . ." The legal import of being convicted of a specified offense that was motivated by hate because of the victim's personal characteristics is usually an enhanced sentence subject to the legal constraints of sentencing law as discussed in chapter 14.

It is sometimes difficult to prove that a crime was committed for the sole purpose that the offender was motivated by hate. In August 2006, four Chinese-Americans were beaten in Queens, New York, it was believed, because of their ethnicity. The two teenage white assailants were charged with assault and hate crimes based largely on the testimony from one of the victims who said, "They did it because I was Asian." The newspaper account of the beating relates the existence of racial tensions in the working-class section of Queens that had been aggravated by an influx of Korean restaurants, salons, and markets that have seemingly squeezed out earlier immigrant groups of Germans and Italians.[7] Many of the Chinese and Korean immigrants are economically successful, which may have led to the choice of victims.

In the chapter's opening scenario, Ben's statement "Welcome to America, macaca" to the storekeeper may enhance his sentence under the state's hate law if he is convicted of the battery. Such sentence enhancements have withstood challenges by convicted defendants on the grounds that such enhancements violate their freedom to hate under the First Amendment. In *Wisconsin* v. *Mitchell,* 113 S.Ct. 2194 (1993), the defendant's sentence for aggravated battery was enhanced because he selected his victim because he was white. On appeal, Mitchell argued that to enhance his sentence, the state would have to impermissibly introduce evidence that he selected his victim based

---

[7]Michelle O'Donnell. "Accusations of a Hate Crime Expose Tensions." *The New York Times,* August 15, 2006, p. B3.

on protected speech—that he hated white people—and it would chill his free speech rights to punish him for such expression. The high Court rejected his argument because it is permissible to use speech as evidence as proof of motive, such as in a treason prosecution, so such use did not violate Mitchell's First Amendment's rights.

II. SEX OFFENSES

There are a variety of crimes defined under the rubric of sex offenses: rape, sexual assault, sodomy, incest, and statutory rape. Typically in sex offenses, sex is used as a means to dominate and control the victim whether or not such acts are sexually gratifying. A penis or object is used to defile a bodily orifice such as the mouth, vagina, or anus of another, and such penis/object is a weapon used to commit the offense much like a handgun is a weapon used to commit armed robbery. Sex-related offenses are crimes of violence, not sex. Traditional beliefs that people engage in sexual activity with people to whom they are attracted make it impossible to understand how a handsome high school football star could rape his elderly aunt or retarded neighbor. In fact, as explored by the U.S. Department of Justice's March 2007 literature review male prison rape does not occur because of a lack of female companionship; prison rape occurs as an act of dominance in a confined corrections setting with a defined hierarchy of power. Such an awareness of the power dynamic in sex offenses is critical to understanding the *mens rea* of such crimes.

1. Rape

Rule of Law: Sex crimes are crimes of violence. Sex is the tool used to commit the crime.

Under common law, rape was defined as "carnal knowledge of a woman against her will." Rather than focus on the offender's actions during a rape, the law turned its attention to the victim's state of mind regarding consent to decide whether or not the sexual intercourse constituted rape. Early development of rape law was a disastrous mine field for female victims. A woman's claim of rape was not to be believed if she could not show physical injury proving that she resisted "to the utmost." Wives could not refuse their husband's demands for sex because "the husband cannot be guilty of a rape committed by himself upon his lawful wife, for by their mutual matrimonial consent and contract, the wife hath given up herself in this kind unto her husband, which she cannot retract."[8] Judges instructed juries that an alleged victim's testimony about rape was inherently untrustworthy because "women lie about their lack of consent [to engage in sexual relations] for various reasons: to blackmail men, to explain the discovery of a consensual affair, or because of psychological illness."[9]

Rape law changed rapidly in the late 1960s and early 1970s when birth control for unmarried women was legalized, a woman's right to decide in consultation with her physician to terminate an unplanned pregnancy was legalized, and leading feminist scholars changed the legal discourse on rape by defining it as an extension of patriarchal dominance. As Susan Brownmiller wrote in *Against Our Will* (1975), her seminal work on rape, "Man's discovery that his genitalia could serve as a weapon to generate fear must rank as one of the most important discoveries of prehistoric times, along with his use of fire and the first crude stone axe. From prehistoric times to the present, I believe, rape has played a critical function. It is nothing more or less than a conscious process of intimidation by which *all* men keep *all* women in a state of fear." (emphasis in original).[10]

---

[8]Matthew Hale. *History of the Pleas of the Crown* (1847), p. 629, 633.

[9]George E. Dix and Michael M. Sharlot. *Criminal Law,* 4th ed. (Belmont, CA: Wadsworth Publishing, 1999).

[10]*See* Susan Brownmiller. *Against Our Will.* (New York: Simon & Schuster, 1975).

By defining rape as a tool to oppress female victims, the law began to change to give female victims more legal protections in rape cases. The most dramatic legal development of this era was the passage of rape-shield laws to prevent victim character assassination through cross-examination which implied that the victim was, at best, of loose moral character and, at worst, "asking" to be raped by the way she moved, dressed, or behaved.

Today, most rape statutes are different depending upon jurisdiction but many are gender-neutral and do not define a rape victim solely as female. Furthermore, in many areas men can be charged with raping their wives, and the requirement that the woman physically resist the attack has been eliminated. The common definition of rape is an act of sexual intercourse committed without consent and that is accomplished by forcible compulsion—making the victim submit to the sex act.

The traditional, common law elements of **rape** were:

1. penile penetration, however slight (emission not required)
2. by force or threat
3. against a victim's will and without that person's consent.

In the chapter opening scenario, Ben raped the stepmother when he placed his penis inside her vagina only a little while she was unconscious and, therefore, unable to consent. It is enough to prove rape to show that the victim did not consent and was threatened to the extent that she believed resistance would be futile. Most rape statutes do not include a required *mens rea* state, because, to be guilty of rape, one must necessarily engage in forcible conduct. "Although the *actus reus* of rape has two critical components—force and absence of consent—issues of *mens rea* have revolved almost exclusively around the element of nonconsent, that is, the defendant's state of mind with respect to the victim's consent. Very little attention has been paid to the *mens rea* applicable to the element of force, that is, the defendant's state of mind with respect to the presence of force. For example, in discussing the types of *mens rea* issues that arise in rape cases, one commentary noted that 'the mistake-of-fact defense in a rape prosecution is almost always that the actor thought the victim had consented' and then dropped a footnote to make the point that 'it is highly unlikely that a defendant would be mistaken about whether he is having intercourse'—thus completely ignoring the question of *mens rea* as applied to the element of force."[11]

What happens when a victim initially consents to engage in sexual activity and then changes her mind and withdraws her consent once the act has started? Can she still be raped under the law? The answer is that it depends on the jurisdiction. In Illinois, it is still rape if the victim initially consents, then says no, and the sexual act continues. Illinois law states that a woman who changes her mind after saying yes to sexual intercourse "is not deemed to have consented to any sexual penetration or conduct that occurs after he or she withdraws consent during the course of that sexual penetration or sexual conduct."[12] Illinois law is in clear contrast to other states' laws, such as Maryland and North Carolina, where a woman's initial consent deprives a prosecutor from bringing a rape charge; in those states the victim cannot be legally raped because she agreed to the initial penetration.[13]

In *Pennsylvania* v. *Berkowitz,* two undergraduate students at East Stroudsburg State University in Pennsylvania were acquaintances. The defendant, Berkowitz, was the roommate of the victim's boyfriend. Berkowitz and the victim had a sexual

---

[11]Douglas N. Husak and George C. Thomas III. "Date Rape, Social Convention, and Reasonable Mistakes." *Law & Philosophy,* Vol. 11 (1992), pp. 95–126.

[12]720 Ill. Compiled Stat. Ann. 5/12- 17 (2008).

[13]*Battle* v. *State*, 414 A.2d 1266 (Md. 1980); *State* v. *Way*, 254 S.E.2d 760 (N.C. 1979); *People* v. *Vela*, 172 Cal. App.3d 237 (Cal. Ct. App. 1985).

encounter that she described as rape and he described as consensual. Berkowitz was convicted, but his rape conviction was overturned because the victim did not allege that Berkowitz had used "forcible compulsion" to commit the rape. If the victim merely says no to sex, but the offender does not force the victim to submit to sex, in Pennsylvania there is no rape.[14] In the excerpt of the appeal reprinted here, the Pennsylvania Supreme Court confirmed the dismissal of the conviction. Students are urged to check their respective state definitions for acts of sexual violence and abuse.

BOX 5.2

Pennsylvania v. Berkowitz, 641 A.2d 1161 (1994)
Supreme Court of Pennsylvania

Judge Cappy delivered the opinion of the court.

FACTS

The complainant, a female college student, left her class, went to her dormitory room where she drank a martini, and then went to a lounge to await her boyfriend. When her boyfriend failed to appear, she went to another dormitory to find a friend, Earl Hassel. She knocked on the door, but received no answer. She tried the doorknob and, finding it unlocked, entered the room and discovered a man sleeping on the bed. The complainant originally believed the man to be Hassel, but it turned out to be Hassel's roommate [Berkowitz]. [Berkowitz] asked her to stay for a while and she agreed. He requested a back rub and she declined. He suggested that she sit on the bed, but she declined and sat on the floor.

[Berkowitz] then moved to the floor beside her, lifted up her shirt and bra and massaged her breasts. He then unfastened his pants and unsuccessfully attempted to put his penis in her mouth. They both stood up, and he locked the door. He returned to push her onto the bed, and removed her undergarments from one leg. He then penetrated her vagina with his penis. After withdrawing and ejaculating on her stomach, he stated, "Wow, I guess we just got carried away," to which she responded, "No, we didn't get carried away, you got carried away."

ISSUE

[If the sexual assault victim does not consent to the sexual contact but is nevertheless never threatened with physical force, is it rape?]

HOLDING

[No. Under the law of the Commonwealth, forcible compulsion to make the victim submit to the sexual intercourse is a necessary element of rape].

REASONING

In reviewing the sufficiency of the evidence, this Court must view the evidence in the light most favorable to the Commonwealth as verdict winner, and accept as true all evidence and reasonable inferences that may be reasonably drawn therefrom, upon which, if believed, the jury could have relied in reaching its verdict. If, upon such review, the Court concludes that the jury could not have determined from the evidence adduced that all of the necessary elements of the crime were established, then the evidence will be deemed insufficient to support the verdict.

The crime of rape [in Pennsylvania] is defined as follows:

> **[18 PA.C.S.A.] §3121. RAPE**
> A person commits a felony of the first degree when he engages in sexual intercourse with another person not his spouse:
> 1. by forcible compulsion;
> 2. by threat of forcible compulsion that would prevent resistance by a person of reasonable resolution;
> 3. who is unconscious; or
> 4. who is so mentally deranged or deficient that such person is incapable of consent.

The victim of a rape need not resist. "The force necessary to support a conviction of rape need only

---

[14]Pennsylvania v. Berkowitz, 609 A.2d 1338 (1992) (first appeal discussing sufficiency of evidence).

be such as to establish lack of consent and to induce the [victim] to submit without additional resistance. The degree of force required to constitute rape is relative and depends on the facts and particular circumstance of the case." In regard to the critical issue of forcible compulsion, the complainant's testimony is devoid of any statement which clearly or adequately describes the use of force or the threat of force against her. In response to defense counsel's question, "Is it possible that [when Berkowitz lifted your bra and shirt] you took no physical action to discourage him?" the complainant replied, "It's possible." When asked, "Is it possible that [Berkowitz] was not making any physical contact with you . . . aside from attempting to untie the knot [in the drawstrings of complainant's sweatpants]?" she answered, "It's possible." She testified that "He put me down on the bed. It was kind of like–he didn't throw me on the bed. It's hard to explain. It was kind of like a push but not—I can't explain what I'm trying to say." She concluded that "it wasn't much" in reference to whether she bounced on the bed, and further detailed that their movement to the bed "wasn't slow like a romantic kind of thing, but it wasn't a fast shove either. It was kind of in the middle."

She agreed that [Berkowitz's] hands were not restraining her in any manner during the actual penetration, and that the weight of his body on top of her was the only force applied. She testified that at no time did [Berkowitz] verbally threaten her. The complainant did testify that she sought to leave the room, and said "no" throughout the encounter. As to the complainant's desire to leave the room, the record clearly demonstrates that the door could be unlocked easily from the inside, that she was aware of this fact, but that she never attempted to go to the door or unlock it.

As to the complainant's testimony that she stated "no" throughout the encounter with [Berkowitz], we point out that, while such an allega-

tion of fact would be relevant to the issue of consent, it is <u>not</u> relevant to the issue of force. In *Commonwealth* v. *Mlinarich*, 542 A.2d 1335 (1988), this Court sustained the reversal of a defendant's conviction of rape where the alleged victim, a minor, repeatedly stated that she did not want to engage in sexual intercourse, but offered no physical resistance and was compelled to engage in sexual intercourse under threat of being recommitted to a juvenile detention center. The [o]pinion . . . acknowledged that physical force, a threat of force, or psychological coercion may be sufficient to support the element of "forcible compulsion," if found to be enough to "prevent resistance by a person of reasonable resolution." However, under the facts of *Mlinarich*, neither physical force, the threat of physical force, nor psychological coercion were found to have been proven, and this Court held that the conviction was properly reversed by the Superior Court.

Accordingly, the ruling in *Mlinarich* implicitly dictates that where there is a lack of consent, but no showing of either physical force, a threat of physical force, or psychological coercion, the "forcible compulsion" requirement under 18 Pa.C.S. §3121 is not met. Moreover, we note that penal statutes must be strictly construed to provide fair warning to the defendant of the nature of the proscribed conduct [to meet principle of legality requirements].

Reviewed in light of the above described standard, the complainant's testimony simply fails to establish that [Berkowitz] forcibly compelled her to engage in sexual intercourse as required under [the law]. Thus, even if all of the complainant's testimony was believed, the jury, as a matter of law, could not have found [Berkowitz] guilty of rape.

CONCLUSION

We hold that the Superior Court did not err in reversing [Berkowitz's] conviction of rape.

Applying the Rule of Law to the Facts: Is it rape?

- Max invited Lucy over for drinks and slipped her a sleeping pill in her soda. When Lucy was sleeping, Max had sexual intercourse with Lucy. At his rape trial, Max's defense was that Lucy was unconscious and therefore never said no to his sexual advances or resisted, so he should be found not guilty. Is it rape?

Yes, if the victim due to a medical condition, a physical infirmity or a tender age is incapable of giving consent, it is still rape.

a. Rape Shield Laws

Rule of Law: Rape Shield Laws were enacted to prevent revictimization of sexual assault victims during the defendant's trial.

To encourage rape victims to come forward and report the crime and to prevent character assassination at trial of those victims who did come forward, the federal government and many states enacted **rape shield laws,** which limit the type of questions defense counsel representing the offender on trial for rape can ask the victim, while at the same time preserving the defendant's constitutional right to confront witnesses against him by showing that the victim could be lying. Federal Rule of Evidence ("FRE") Rule 412 is similar to many state statutes that control the type of questioning that is permissible of a sex victim about his or her sexual past.

FRE 412 SEX OFFENSE CASES; RELEVANCE OF ALLEGED VICTIM'S PAST SEXUAL BEHAVIOR OR ALLEGED SEXUAL PREDISPOSITION

a. <u>Evidence generally inadmissible.</u> The following evidence is not admissible in any civil or criminal proceeding involving alleged sexual misconduct except as provided in subdivisions (b) and (c):

    1. Evidence offered to prove that any alleged victim engaged in other sexual behavior.

    2. Evidence offered to prove any alleged victim's sexual predisposition,

b. <u>Exceptions:</u>

    1. In a criminal case, the following evidence is admissible, if otherwise admissible under these rules:

        A. Evidence of specific instances of sexual behavior of the alleged victim offered to prove that a person other than the accused was the source of semen, injury or other physical evidence;

        B. Evidence of specific instances of sexual behavior by the alleged victim with respect to the person accused of the sexual misconduct offered by the accused to prove consent or by the prosecution; and

        C. Evidence the exclusion of which would violate the constitutional rights of the defendant.

The significance of the rape shield laws is that a defendant cannot introduce as evidence the alleged victim's reputation of loose sexual morality or promiscuity because such factors are irrelevant to whether or not on this occasion with this particular defendant she consented and was forced to submit to an unwanted act of sexual intercourse. But, the defendant does have a right to introduce evidence of a victim's past sexual behavior with him, because the victim's willingness to consent to sex with the defendant in the past may have affected his *mens rea* about whether or not she was consenting on the night of the alleged rape. Also allowable under rape shield laws is evidence of a victim's past sexual conduct to prove that some other person is the source of injury or semen. The defense in criminal law circles is that "Some Other Dude Did It" (S.O.D.D.I.), and the defendant has a constitutional right under the Sixth Amendment's confrontation clause to cross-examine the victim to prove that another man may have been the perpetrator. This is the exception in FRE 412 rape shield law that allows "Evidence the exclusion of which would violate the constitutional rights of the defendant."

b. Statutory Rape

Rule of Law: Statutory rape is often defined by the age of the parties involved in sexual intercourse.

Different from forcible rape is **statutory rape** where criminal liability attaches because of the age of the victim even though the victim may have "consented" to the sexual activity.

The early public policy supporting the enactment of statutory rape laws was that a woman below a certain age was incapable of consenting to sexual acts even if she were naked on a bed and shouting "Come get me!" The crime developed in early common law to protect the chastity "of vulnerable, virtuous young women, treating them as 'special property in need of special protection'" and to prevent teenage pregnancy—a legitimate government interest recognized by the U.S. Supreme Court in *Michael M.* v. *Superior Court of Sonoma County,* 450 U.S. 464 (1981), because children born to teenagers most often need state welfare benefits for food and shelter and other government financial support until they reach adulthood.

To punish offenders for committing statutory rape presupposes that minors cannot consent to sexual activity when, clearly, some teenagers can. Author Rigel Oliveri writes that the changes in statutory rape laws in the 1970s paralleled the changes around female control of reproductive freedom and more protection for rape victims. Due to the feminist movement, women began to demand power to define their own sexual experiences. "The atmosphere of sexual liberation and women's empowerment may have caused some feminists, if anything, to want to expand girls' sexual freedom and options and to abandon outdated expectations of chastity for teen girls," Oliveri writes. If controlling one's body was an important goal for women, some state laws still viewed a woman's right to willingly engage in sexual activity as negative. It was a legally recognized defense in a statutory rape case that the victim was "promiscuous" and was, therefore, incapable of being raped.[15]   Today most statutory rape laws define the crime as sex between teenagers and people who are at least 4 years older. For example, it qualifies as statutory rape for a 20-year-old to have sex with a 15-year-old, but not for a 17-year-old to have sex with a 15-year-old. In most jurisdictions, if the older person has sex with a child and not a teenager, or a person who is disabled, the crime becomes aggravated and the penalties increase accordingly.

i. Mistake of Age as a Defense to a Charge of Statutory Rape   What happens when the defendant claims "an honest and reasonable mistake of fact regarding the victim's age?" Can a defendant's mistake of fact that the child was the age of consent be a defense? Early statutory rape statutes were strict liability—if the sex act was committed, regardless of *mens rea* or intent, the defendant was guilty. But as the penalty for rape increased to long prison sentences, legislatures amended their statutory rape laws to require *mens rea* and, on the flip side, to allow certain defenses, most often that the offender thought the victim was of age. The age of consent to engage in sex acts varies based on jurisdiction from 14 to 18 years old. But states are still free under their general police power to recognize the defense of mistake. North Dakota recognizes such a defense: "When criminality depends on the victim being a minor, it is an affirmative defense, that the actor reasonably believed the victim to be an adult."[16] But New Jersey does not: "It shall be no defense to a [statutory rape] prosecution that the actor believed the victim to be above the age stated for the offense, even if such a mistaken belief was reasonable." N. J. Stat. sec. 2C: 14-5 (2008).

In *State* v. *Guest,* 583 P.2d 836 (Alaska 1978), two defendants were charged with the statutory rape of a 15-year-old girl, and the issue in the case was whether the statute was strict liability, for it failed to list an applicable *mens rea* state. The Supreme Court of Alaska held that when a statute was not of the regulatory, health, and welfare type commonly associated with strict liability crimes, such as speeding

---

[15]Rigel Oliveri. "Statutory Rape Law and Enforcement in the Wake of Welfare Reform." *Stanford Law Review,* Vol. 52 (2000), pp. 463–508.

[16]N.D. Cent. Code 12.1-20-01(2) (2008).

and health inspection, then "either a requirement of criminal intent must be read into the statute or it must be found unconstitutional." Thus, the Alaska high court held with respect to its statutory rape law, if the statute required an intent/*mens rea* element, then the law would also permit the affirmative defense of mistake, which the defendants in *Guest* were allowed to raise.

c. Incest

Rule of Law: Incest is sexual relations among nonspousal family members.

Incest is sexual relations between family members, regardless of how they are related by blood, adoption, or marriage. An example of popular culture transforming an incestuous relationship into a "consensual affair" is the case of Susan Smith who in October 1994 drowned her two young sons at the John D. Long Lake in Union, South Carolina. Smith initially blamed "a black man" for kidnapping her children, but after a week of denials she finally confessed to Sheriff Howard Wells. As details of Susan's life emerged during her death-penalty trial for killing the boys, the jury learned that Susan's biological father had committed suicide when she was 6-years-old and that her mother had remarried a man named Beverly Russell who was a prominent community civic and religious leader. When Susan tried to commit suicide at age 13, school officials and others learned that Susan was an incest victim and that Beverly had been sexually molesting her for years. The family's response to Beverly's incest was family counseling rather than criminal prosecution. As a result of that decision, the abuse continued up until a few weeks before Susan drowned her boys; by then Susan was a 23-year-old married mother of two. As the media learned of Susan's past, the news reports characterized the adult relationship between Beverly and Susan as a "consensual affair" because, under the law, Susan had reached the age of consent and essentially had "aged out of" the incest prohibition.

It is an important legal distinction to ask whether childhood victims of sexual abuse can, once they reach adulthood, eventually "consent" to sexual relations with their abusers. Under the Maine statute outlawing incestuous relationships, marriage between family members can render the incest void. The Maine statute defining incest is illustrative of the crime's elements:

17-MAINE REVISED STATUTES ANNOTATED §556 (2005) INCEST

1. A person is guilty of incest if the person is at least 18 years of age and:
   A. Engages in sexual intercourse with another person who the actor knows is related to the actor within the 2nd degree of consanguinity; or
   B. Violates paragraph A and, at the time of the incest, the person has 2 or more prior Maine convictions for violations of this section.
      1-A. It is a defense to a prosecution under this section that, at the time the actor engaged in sexual intercourse with the other person, the actor was legally married to the other person (emphasis added).
      1-B. As used in this section "sexual intercourse" means any penetration of the female sex organ by the male sex organ. Emission is not required.
      1-C. As used in this section, "related to the actor within the 2nd degree of consanguinity" has the following meanings.
   A. When the actor is a woman, it means the other person is her father, grandfather, son, grandson, brother, brother's son, sister's son, father's brother or mother's brother.
   B. When this actor is a man, it means the other person is his mother, grandmother, daughter, granddaughter, sister, brother's daughter, sister's daughter, father's sister or mother's sister.

Note that marriage to the relative is a defense to Maine's incest statute. The marriage exception for incest crimes illustrates the often-competing family interests at stake in sex abuse prosecutions. On the one hand, society has a viable interest in maintaining an intact family unit. On the other hand, individuals do not have free license to sexually abuse others by virtue of the accident of family relations. Louisiana, Indiana, Michigan, Ohio, and South Dakota have marriage provisions similar to Maine's.

∂. Deviate Sexual Conduct

The history of sexual crimes includes acts called deviate sexual intercourse, such as **sodomy,** which consists of penile and oral or penile and anal contact. The U.S. Supreme Court struck down laws criminalizing sodomy between consenting heterosexual and homosexual adults in *Lawrence* v. *Texas* (2003), but many state statutes still outlaw certain types of sodomy, especially those acts involving unwilling partners, children, and other vulnerable victims. As an illustration, Michigan defines sodomy as a "detestable crime against nature either with mankind or with any animal," while in California, sodomy is defined primarily as penile–anal contact.

III. HOMICIDE

Homicide is the killing of one human being by another. In seventeenth century England the traditional definition of homicide was "When a man of sound memory and of the age of discretion unlawfully kills any reasonable creature in being, and under the King's peace, with malice aforethought, either express or implied by the law, the death taking place within a year and a day." Sir James Stephen in his *Digest of the Criminal Law*[17] defined **malice aforethought** as the predetermination (premeditation) to commit an unlawful act, especially murder:

> "One or more of the following states of mind preceding or co-existing with the act or omission by which death is caused, and it may exist where that act is premeditated.
> a. An intention to cause the death of, or grevious [sic] bodily harm to, any person, whether such person is the person actually killed or not;
> b. knowledge that the act which causes death will not probably cause the death of, or grevious (sic) bodily harm to, some person, whether such person is the person actually killed or not, although such knowledge is accompanied by indifference whether death or grevious (sic) bodily harm is caused or not, or by a wish that it may not be caused;
> c. an intent to commit any felony whatever;
> d. an intent to oppose by force any officer of justice on his way to, in, or returning from the execution of the duty of arresting, keeping in custody, or imprison, or the duty of keeping the peace or dispensing an unlawful assembly, provided that the offender has notice that the person killed is such an officer so employed . . ."

Many modern day statutes are comprehensive and provide for all types of homicide under one legal rubric, as illustrated by the Pennsylvania statute.

1. First- and Second-Degree Murder

In general the elements of **first-degree murder** are

1. the willful, deliberate, and premeditated
2. killing
3. of another.

---

[17]*Report of the Royal Commission on Capital* Punishment, 1949–1953 (1953), pp. 25–28.

The term <u>willful</u> means specific intent to bring about the victim's death; <u>deliberate</u> means the offender had a cool mind able to think rationally and was not acting under any rage, fear, or prejudice; and <u>premeditated</u> means that the offender at least planned the killing in some way, either by lying in wait or by bringing a weapon to the place of the crime. In many state jury instructions, deliberate and premeditated can mean as little as picking up a loaded gun, pointing it, and pulling the trigger, but historically the terms meant to punish those who clearly gave the killing some thought in cool reflection before they intentionally killed their victim. Usually the jury has to infer the offender's intent to kill from the circumstances surrounding the killing. The **deadly weapon doctrine** allows the jury to infer specific intent to kill by the use of any object used in a manner designed to cause serious bodily injury or death. For instance, a pencil may be intended for writing, but when it is used to poke out someone's eyeballs or is sharpened to a fine point and plunged in a victim's jugular vein, that pencil is a deadly weapon, and if the person dies, the jury can infer that the defendant meant to kill, not merely to injure.

Under the law of most state jurisdictions, if the offender uses a deadly weapon to commit murder, the specific intent to bring about the victim's death can be inferred from the use of the weapon. A deadly weapon is anything used in a manner to cause serious bodily harm or death (see the preceding example of a pencil used as a deadly weapon). If the victim of an attack with an unconventional weapon dies as a result of the injuries, a jury is free to infer that the offender meant to cause the victim's death, which may be sufficient for a first-degree murder conviction.

The elements of **second-degree murder** are

1. the willful and intentional intent to commit serious bodily harm
2. that results in the death
3. of another.

Second-degree murder is defined typically as missing one of the elements of first-degree murder (the willfulness, the premeditation, or the deliberateness). A murder that results from an offender's desire to commit serious bodily harm (but not necessarily death) is considered to be in the second degree. For example, if Tommy strikes Joey's nose with a book intending to cause serious bodily harm in breaking his nose, but instead the cartilage in his nose pierces his brain causing death, the murder will be in the second degree.

When is someone dead for purposes of a homicide prosecution? If a victim suffers serious harm and is put on life support, is he still alive? Many state jurisdictions define brain death as "dead" for murder statutes, and if the family cuts off life support, the offender may still be prosecuted for murder even though he is not the immediate cause of death. Another outdated concept is the year-and-a-day-rule which still retains vitality in federal courts. Essentially, if the victim died within one year and one day after suffering harm at the offender's hands, the offender would legally be responsible for the death. With the advances of medical technology and more awareness as to causes of death, the rule has limited applicability, but in most situations where there might be present-day confusion about the interpretation of statues, the common law fills in the gaps.

Applying the Rule of Law to the Facts: What degree of murder is it?

- One night in a trailer park, Ted struck his wife Debbie and she went running to her ex-husband, Steve's, trailer. Ted followed Debbie in and Steve threw Ted out. Ted went to his trailer and retrieved an 8-inch kitchen knife, but left it near his front door. As Ted went outside, he saw Steve coming toward him. Ted went back to his trailer and grabbed the knife. When Steve saw Ted with the knife, he kicked at Ted, and Ted swiped the knife at Steve just as Steve moved closer. The knife entered Steve's side and he died shortly thereafter. Ted said he only meant to scare Steve and had no intent to kill him. What degree of murder is it?

Second-degree murder. Ted had the intent to commit serious bodily harm upon Steve when he swung the knife at him.[18]

2. Manslaughter

Rule of Law: Manslaughter is an intentional killing done in the heat of passion or an unintended killing that is an accident.

Manslaughter may be voluntary or involuntary, the difference being that in **voluntary manslaughter** the person takes the act that results in death willingly. Voluntary manslaughter is an intentional killing done in the heat of passion, in which the offender was provoked by acts that would make a reasonable man in the offender's shoes react violently. The provoking act must be so severe that other people would react violently as well. A mother sitting in court who is listening to her 6-year-old daughter recount the abuse suffered at the hands of the mother's live-in-boyfriend may commit manslaughter when she reaches for a deputy's gun and shoots her boyfriend in the face as he turns to give her the middle finger during the daughter's testimony. Should we judge the provoking act on the basis of how any mother sitting in the court would react or how a reasonable man would react? The elements of voluntary manslaughter are:

1. unlawful killing
2. of another
3. committed under the heat of passion or sufficient provocation.

The classic example of **involuntary manslaughter** is a drunk-driving car accident that results in death. The person drinking at dinner has no intention of killing someone and, when he gets into his car, is intending to drive home, not to kill someone. The fact that he causes an accident due to his drunken state is unintentional, and the killing is treated as manslaughter. The elements of involuntary manslaughter are the:

1. unlawful killing
2. of another

a. Heat of Passion

Typically in a manslaughter situation, one of the elements that defines murder is missing. In a manslaughter that arises out of the "heat of passion," the element of cool deliberation is missing from the first-degree formula of willful, premeditated, and deliberate action. It is thought in the law that if one has a hot, enraged mind, one cannot "think straight" and properly reflect on the consequences of one's actions. Of course, such rationale presupposes that the offender is unconscious of the consequences in putting bullets in a gun, cocking the hammer, and pulling the trigger, but such is the reasoning. It should be noted that for heat of passion provocation, words are never sufficient provocation to justify killing someone and reducing the charge from murder to manslaughter. That is, if someone says, "Jeez, you are the nastiest person I have ever known," the response to kill will not be justified or excused merely because such words made the offender's blood boil. But in certain situations, words that convey an act that would cause a reasonable person in the offender's shoes to kill, then the act is deemed adequate provocation.

---

[18]Facts adapted from *Hallowell* v. *Delaware*, 298 A.2d 330 (1972).

As illustrated in the *Commonwealth* v. *Schnopps* case reprinted in part in Box 5.3, does the claim of infidelity suffice as sufficient provocation to justify a manslaughter instruction to reduce the partner's murder charge?

Commonwealth v. Schnopps, 417 N.E.2d 1213 (1981)
Supreme Judicial Court of Massachusetts

Justice Abrams delivered the opinion of the court.

FACTS

Schnopps testified that his wife had left him three weeks prior to the slaying. He claims that he first became aware of the problems in his fourteen-year marriage at a point about six months before the slaying. According to the defendant, on that occasion he took his wife to a club to dance, and she spent the evening dancing with a coworker. On arriving home, the defendant and his wife argued over her conduct. She told him that she no longer loved him and that she wanted a divorce. Schnopps became very upset. He admitted that he took out his shotgun during the course of this argument, but he denied that he intended to use it. One day in September, 1979, the defendant became aware that the suspected boyfriend used a "signal" in telephoning Schnopps' wife. Schnopps used the signal, and his wife answered the phone with "Hi, Lover." She hung up immediately when she recognized Schnopps' voice. That afternoon she did not return home. Later that evening, she informed Schnopps by telephone that she had moved to her mother's house and that she had the children with her. She told Schnopps she would not return to their home. Thereafter she "froze [him] out," and would not talk to him. During this period, the defendant spoke with a lawyer about a divorce and was told that he had a good chance of getting custody of the children, due to his wife's "desertion and adultery." On the day of the killing, Schnopps had asked his wife to come to their home and talk over their marital difficulties. Schnopps told his wife that he wanted his children at home, and that he wanted the family to remain intact. Schnopps cried during the conversation, and begged his wife to let the children live with him and to keep their family together. His wife replied, "No, I am going to court, you are going to give me all the furniture, you are going to have to

get the Hell out of here, you won't have nothing." Then, pointing to her crotch, she said, "You will never touch this again, because I have got something bigger and better for it."

On hearing those words, Schnopps claims that his mind went blank, and that he went "berserk." He went to a cabinet and got out a pistol he had bought and loaded the day before, and he shot his wife and himself. When he "started coming to" as a result of the pain of his self-inflicted wound, he called his neighbor to come over and asked him to summon help. The victim [Schnopps's wife] was pronounced dead at the scene, and the defendant was arrested and taken to the hospital for treatment of his wound.

ISSUE

[In these circumstances, [was] the judge required to instruct the jury on voluntary manslaughter?

HOLDING

[Yes, conviction reversed, new trial ordered].

REASONING

[Jury] [i]nstructions on voluntary manslaughter must be given if there is evidence of provocation deemed adequate in law to cause the accused to lose his self-control in the heat of passion, and if the killing followed the provocation before sufficient time had elapsed for the accused's temper to cool. *See Commonwealth* v. *Stokes*, 374 Mass. 583 (1978); *Commonwealth* v. *Coleman*, 366 Mass. 705 (1975). A verdict of voluntary manslaughter requires the trier of fact to conclude that there is a causal connection between the provocation, the heat of passion, and the killing. *See Commonwealth* v. *Soaris*, 275 Mass. 291 (1931); R. Perkins, Criminal Law 69 (2d ed. 1969).

Schnopps argues that "[t]he existence of sufficient provocation is not foreclosed absolutely because a defendant learns of a fact from oral statements rather than from personal observation," and that a sudden admission of adultery is equivalent to a discovery of the act itself, and is sufficient evidence of provocation. Schnopps asserts that his wife's statements constituted a "peculiarly immediate and intense offense to a spouse's sensitivities." He concedes that the words at issue are indicative of past as well as present adultery. Schnopps claims, however, that his wife's admission of adultery was made for the first time on the day of the killing, and hence the evidence of provocation was sufficient to trigger jury consideration of voluntary manslaughter as a possible verdict.

The Commonwealth quarrels with the defendant's claim, asserting that the defendant knew of his wife's infidelity for some months, and hence the killing did not follow immediately upon the provocation. Therefore, the Commonwealth concludes, a manslaughter instruction would have been improper. The flaw in the Commonwealth's argument is that conflicting testimony and inferences from the evidence are to be resolved by the trier of fact, not the judge. Withdrawal of the issue of voluntary manslaughter in this case denied the jury the opportunity to pass on the defendant's credibility in the critical aspects of his testimony. The portion of Schnopps' testimony concerning provocation created a factual dispute between Schnopps and the Commonwealth. It was for the jury, not the judge, to resolve the factual issues raised by Schnopps' claim of provocation. We do not question the propriety of the verdict returned by the jury. However, based on the defendant's testimony, voluntary manslaughter was a possible verdict. Therefore, it was error to withhold "from the consideration of the jury another verdict which, although they might not have reached it, was nevertheless open to them upon the evidence." *Commonwealth* v. *McCauley*, 355 Mass. 554 (1969).

CONCLUSION

For the reasons stated, the judgment of the Superior Court is reversed, the verdict of murder in the first degree is set aside, and the case remanded for a new trial. So ordered.

3. Felony Murder

Rule of Law: If a death occurs in the commission of a felony, all cofelons are responsible for the death.

Felony murder is a widely criticized method of attaching accomplice liability for murder. Many jurisdictions have repudiated the doctrine, but it is still a valid basis for the death penalty in some states and under the federal jurisdiction. The felony murder doctrine provides that if one is engaged in the commission of a felony (burglary, rape, arson, felonious escape, mayhem, robbery, kidnapping) and someone dies, everyone involved in the felony is responsible for the death. The theory behind the felony murder doctrine is that certain enumerated felonies are so inherently dangerous to human life that everyone who commits one is liable for any death that ensues. Critics of the doctrine find fault with holding people responsible for the death even if they had no intent to kill and even if they did not kill. Felony murder is a legal fiction in which we transfer the intent to commit the felony to the intent to kill if a death results from the commission of the felony. The elements of **felony murder** are:

1.   in the commission or attempted commission of a felony
2.   a death occurs, and
3.   there is a nexus (connection) between the felony and the death.

The causation analysis establishes the nexus between the felony and the death:

a.   But for the commission or attempted commission of the felony, the death would not have occurred (factual cause).

b. The death was a foreseeable consequence of the perpetration of the felony (legal cause).

c. There are no intervening causes breaking the causal chain between the felony and the death.

The analysis focuses on the point at which the liability of the accomplice stops. If a cofelon is fleeing the scene of the felony and strikes a motorist dead in the attempted escape from the felony, most people would have no problem holding that offender liable under the theory that flight from the felony is still part of the felony, and people should be held responsible under a simple "but for" causation analysis. That is, "but for" the felony, would the victim have died? If the answer is no, then the felony is the cause of death.

But what happens after arrest? In *Auman* v. *People*, 109 P.3d 647 (Colo. 2005), the Colorado Supreme Court held Lisl Auman, who had been arrested and placed in the back of a police cruiser, liable for the death of a police officer who was killed by her accomplice Mattaeus Jaehnig after Auman had been arrested. On November 12, 1997, Auman and a group of friends that included Jaehnig broke into Auman's ex-boyfriend's apartment to retrieve her belongings, but they also stole some items that did not belong to her. The police pursued Auman and Jaehnig in a stolen Trans-Am in a high speed chase that included Auman holding the steering wheel while Jaehnig shot at officers. The two parked at Jaehnig's apartment complex and ran into the woods. Auman turned herself in and was arrested. Minutes later, Jaehnig shot and killed Officer VanderJagt and then killed himself with VanderJagt's weapon. The jury was instructed that Auman could be found guilty if they "found beyond a reasonable doubt that . . . [the] death was caused by anyone 'in the course of or in the furtherance of [a felony], or in the immediate flight therefrom.'" Auman argued that not only was she not in immediate flight from the burglary, but that Jaehnig's drug use (he was allegedly high on methamphetamines) was an intervening cause severing the causal chain from Auman's initial actions in participating in the burglary and the officer's ultimate death. Auman was convicted of second-degree burglary and first-degree felony murder and sentenced to life without parole. On appeal, the state high court held that Auman's arrest did not terminate flight from the felony for Auman to escape liability for the officer's death. The problem with Auman's case is that the theory of proximate causation should hold true in any murder case—that is, "you are guilty for the logical consequences of your actions."[19] The consequences of one's actions must be reasonably foreseeable to satisfy the proximate cause requirement that there be no intervening act in which the felon did not participate and which the felon could not predict.

As author Tomerlin writes:

> . . . Michigan requires an accomplice to have intent to kill and therefore, entirely abolished the common law felony murder rule through case law. Similarly, Hawaii and Kentucky have abolished their felony murder statutes. Ohio eliminated the felony murder statute and changed it to involuntary manslaughter. Minnesota and Wisconsin have likewise reduced the degree of felony murder and the punishment that couples it. Moreover, the state supreme court in New Mexico determined that there must be a *mens rea* requirement for felony murder. Other states have reduced the punishment that accompanies felony murder. Alaska, Louisiana, New York, Pennsylvania, and Utah all have reduced felony murder to second degree murder instead of first degree murder.

The Model Penal Code §210 attempted to eliminate felony murder, but the amendment was not embraced by many jurisdictions. Even in those death-penalty states that have reduced felony murder to second-degree murder, certain felonies are

---

[19]Beth Tomerlin. "Stretching Liability Too Far: Colorado's Felony Murder Statute in Light of *Auman*." *Denver University Law Review,* Vol. 83 (2005), pp. 639–664, *citing* Joshua Dressler. *Understanding Criminal Law,* 3d. ed. (2001).

aggravating circumstances that make the offender eligible for the death penalty. For instance, California Penal Code 190.2 lists aggravating factors of the state's death penalty statute reprinted in chapter 2, such as the killing during the felonies of robbery, rape, arson, and burglary. In *Enmund* v. *Florida,* 458 U.S. 782 (1982), the getaway driver of the car who did not kill, but who still received the death penalty, was considered to have received excessive punishment in violation of the Eighth Amendment's ban on cruel and unusual punishment. See how the high Court incorporates its reasoning in *Enmund* to the *Tison* felony—murder case in Box 5.4.

BOX 5.4

Tison v. Arizona, 481 U.S. 137 (1987)
Supreme Court of the United States

Justice O'Conner delivered the opinion of the Court.

FACTS

Gary Tison was sentenced to life imprisonment as the result of a prison escape during the course of which he had killed a guard. After he had been in prison a number of years, Gary Tison's wife, their three sons Donald, Ricky, and Raymond, Gary's brother Joseph, and other relatives made plans to help Gary Tison escape again. The Tison family assembled a large arsenal of weapons for this purpose. Plans for escape were discussed with Gary Tison, who insisted that his cellmate, Randy Greenawalt, also a convicted murderer, be included in the prison break. The following facts are largely evidenced by petitioners' detailed confessions given as part of a plea bargain according to the terms of which the State agreed not to seek the death sentence. The Arizona courts interpreted the plea agreement to require that petitioners testify to the planning stages of the breakout. When they refused to do so, the bargain was rescinded and they were tried, convicted, and sentenced to death.

On July 30, 1978, the three Tison brothers entered the Arizona State Prison at Florence carrying a large ice chest filled with guns. The Tisons armed Greenawalt and their father, and the group, brandishing their weapons, locked the prison guards and visitors present in a storage closet. The five men fled the prison grounds in the Tisons' Ford Galaxy automobile. No shots were fired at the prison. After leaving the prison, the men abandoned the Ford automobile and proceeded on to an isolated house in a white Lincoln automobile that the brothers had

parked at a hospital near the prison. At the house, the Lincoln automobile had a flat tire; the only spare tire was pressed into service. After two nights at the house, the group drove toward Flagstaff. As the group traveled on back roads and secondary highways through the desert, another tire blew out. The group decided to flag down a passing motorist and steal a car. Raymond stood out in front of the Lincoln; the other four armed themselves and lay in wait by the side of the road. One car passed by without stopping, but a second car, a Mazda occupied by John Lyons, his wife Donnelda, his 2-year-old son Christopher, and his 15-year-old niece, Theresa Tyson, pulled over to render aid.

As Raymond showed John Lyons the flat tire on the Lincoln, the other Tisons and Greenawalt emerged. The Lyons family was forced into the backseat of the Lincoln. Raymond and Donald drove the Lincoln down a dirt road off the highway and then down a gas line service road farther into the desert; Gary Tison, Ricky Tison, and Randy Greenawalt followed in the Lyons' Mazda. The two cars were parked trunk to trunk and the Lyons family was ordered to stand in front of the Lincoln's headlights. The Tisons transferred their belongings from the Lincoln into the Mazda. They discovered guns and money in the Mazda which they kept, and they put the rest of the Lyons' possessions in the Lincoln.

Gary Tison then told Raymond to drive the Lincoln still farther into the desert. Raymond did so, and, while the others guarded the Lyons and Theresa Tyson, Gary fired his shotgun into the radiator, presumably to completely disable the vehicle. The Lyons and Theresa Tyson were then escorted to the Lincoln

(continued)

BOX 5.4

(continued)

and again ordered to stand in its headlights. Ricky Tison reported that John Lyons begged, in comments "more or less directed at everybody," "Jesus, don't kill me." Gary Tison said he was "thinking about it." John Lyons asked the Tisons and Greenawalt to "give us some water . . . just leave us out here, and you all go home." Gary Tison then told his sons to go back to the Mazda and get some water. Raymond later explained that his father "was like in conflict with himself. . . . What it was, I think it was the baby being there and all this, and he wasn't sure about what to do."

The petitioners' statements diverge to some extent, but it appears that both of them went back towards the Mazda, along with Donald, while Randy Greenawalt and Gary Tison stayed at the Lincoln guarding the victims. Raymond recalled being at the Mazda filling the water jug "when we started hearing the shots." Ricky said that the brothers gave the water jug to Gary Tison who then, with Randy Greenawalt went behind the Lincoln, where they spoke briefly, then raised the shotguns and started firing. In any event, petitioners agree they saw Greenawalt and their father brutally murder their four captives with repeated blasts from their shotguns. Neither made an effort to help the victims, though both later stated they were surprised by the shooting. The Tisons got into the Mazda and drove away, continuing their flight. Physical evidence suggested that Theresa Tyson managed to crawl away from the bloodbath, severely injured. She died in the desert after the Tisons left.

Several days later the Tisons and Greenawalt were apprehended after a shootout at a police roadblock. Donald Tison was killed. Gary Tison escaped into the desert where he subsequently died of exposure. Raymond and Ricky Tison and Randy Greenawalt were captured and tried jointly for the crimes associated with the prison break itself and the shootout at the roadblock; each was convicted and sentenced. The State then individually tried each of the petitioners for capital murder of the four victims as well as for the associated crimes of armed robbery, kidnapping, and car theft. The capital murder charges were based on Arizona felony—murder law providing that a killing occurring during the

perpetration of robbery or kidnapping is capital murder, Ariz. Rev. Stat. Ann. §13-452 (1956) (repealed 1978), and that each participant in the kidnapping or robbery is legally responsible for the acts of his accomplices, Ariz. Rev. Stat. Ann. §13-139 (1956) (repealed 1978). Each of the petitioners was convicted of the four murders under these accomplice liability and felony—murder statutes. Arizona law provided for a capital sentencing proceeding, to be conducted without a jury, to determine whether the crime was sufficiently aggravated to warrant the death sentence. The judge found three aggravating factors:

1. The Tisons had created a grave risk of death to others (not the victims).
2. The murders had been committed for pecuniary gain.
3. The murders were especially heinous.

The judge found no statutory mitigating factors. (Ricky was 20 and Raymond was 19 and neither had prior felony records.) Importantly, the judge specifically found that the crime was not mitigated by the fact that each of the petitioners' "participation was relatively minor." Rather, he found that the "participation of each petitioner in the crimes giving rise to the application of the felony murder rule in this case was very substantial." The trial judge also specifically found that each "could reasonably have foreseen that his conduct would cause or create a grave risk of death." The judge sentenced both petitioners to death.

ISSUE

[W]hether the [Tison brothers'] participation in the events leading up to and following the murder of four members of a family makes the sentences of death imposed by the Arizona courts constitutionally permissible although neither petitioner specifically intended to kill the victims and neither inflicted the fatal gunshot wounds.

HOLDING

Although [the Tison brothers] neither intended to kill the victims nor inflicted the fatal wounds, the record might support a finding that they had the culpable mental state of reckless indifference to human life. The Eighth Amendment does not prohibit the death penalty as disproportionate in the case of a defendant whose participation in a felony that results in murder is major and whose mental state is one of reckless indifference.

REASONING

In *Enmund* v. *Florida* [458 U.S. 782 (1982)], this Court reversed the death sentence of a defendant convicted under Florida's felony—murder rule. Enmund was the driver of the "getaway" car in an armed robbery of a dwelling. The occupants of the house, an elderly couple, resisted and Enmund's accomplices killed them. The Florida Supreme Court found the inference that Enmund was the person in the car by the side of the road waiting to help his accomplices escape sufficient to support his sentence of death:

> "'The only evidence of the degree of [Enmund's] participation is the jury's likely inference that he was the person in the car by the side of the road near the scene of the crimes. The jury could have concluded that he was there, a few hundred feet away, waiting to help the robbers escape with the Kerseys' money. The evidence, therefore, was sufficient to find that the appellant was a principal of the second degree, constructively present aiding and abetting the commission of the crime of robbery. This conclusion supports the verdicts of murder in the first degree on the basis of the felony murder portion of section 782.04(1)(a).'" *Enmund* v. *Florida,* 458 U.S. at 786.

[The Tison brothers] argue strenuously that they did not "intend to kill" as that concept has been generally understood in the common law. We accept this as true. Traditionally, "one intends certain consequences when he desires that his acts cause those consequences or knows that those consequences are substantially certain to result from his acts." W. LaFave & A. Scott, Criminal Law §28, p. 196 (1972); *see Lockett* v. *Ohio,* (equating intent with purposeful conduct); *see also* Perkins, A Rationale of Mens Rea, 52 Harv. L. Rev. 905, 911 (1939). As petitioners point out, there is no evidence that either Ricky or Raymond Tison took any act which he desired to, or was substantially certain would, cause death. [T]he Arizona Supreme Court attempted to reformulate

"intent to kill" as a species of foreseeability. The Arizona Supreme Court wrote:

> "Intend [sic] to kill includes the situation in which the defendant intended, contemplated, or anticipated that lethal force would or might be used or that life would or might be taken in accomplishing the underlying felony." . . . Participants in violent felonies like armed robberies can frequently "anticipat[e] that lethal force . . . might be used . . . in accomplishing the underlying felony."

On the other hand, it is equally clear that petitioners also fall outside the category of felony murderers for whom *Enmund* explicitly held the death penalty disproportional: their degree of participation in the crimes was major rather than minor, and the record would support a finding of the culpable mental state of reckless indifference to human life. We take the facts as the Arizona Supreme Court has given them to us.

A critical facet of the individualized determination of culpability required in capital cases is the mental state with which the defendant commits the crime. Deeply ingrained in our legal tradition is the idea that the more purposeful is the criminal conduct, the more serious is the offense, and, therefore, the more severely it ought to be punished. The ancient concept of malice aforethought was an early attempt to focus on mental state in order to distinguish those who deserved death from those who through "Benefit of . . . Clergy" would be spared. 23 Hen. 8, ch.1, §§3, 4 (1531); 1 Edw. 6, ch.12, §10 (1547). Over time, malice aforethought came to be inferred from the mere act of killing in a variety of circumstances; in reaction, Pennsylvania became the first American jurisdiction to distinguish between degrees of murder, reserving capital punishment to "wilful, deliberate and premeditated" killings and felony murders. 3 Pa. Laws 1794, ch. 1766, pp. 186–187 (1810). More recently, in *Lockett* v. *Ohio*, 438 U.S. 586 (1978), the plurality opinion made clear that the defendant's mental state was critical to weighing a defendant's culpability under a system of guided discretion, vacating a death sentence imposed under an Ohio statute that did not permit the sentencing authority to take into account "the absence of direct proof that the defendant intended to cause the death of the victim." *Id.*, at 608 (opinion of

(continued)

BOX 5.4

(continued)

Burger, C. J.); *see also Eddings* v. *Oklahoma,* 455 U.S. 104 (1982). Similarly, we hold that the reckless disregard for human life implicit in knowingly engaging in criminal activities known to carry a grave risk of death represents a highly culpable mental state, a mental state that may be taken into account in making a capital sentencing judgment when that conduct causes its natural, though also not inevitable, lethal result.

CONCLUSION

[M]ajor participation in the felony committed, combined with reckless indifference to human life, is sufficient to satisfy the *Enmund* culpability requirement. The Arizona courts have clearly found that the former exists [for the Tison brothers]; we now vacate the judgments below and remand for determination of the latter in further proceedings not inconsistent with this opinion.

The Supreme Court held that the death penalty can be awarded to a cofelon in a felony murder who does not intend to kill and who does not participate in the killing, but who, nevertheless, has the *mens rea* of reckless indifference to life. On remand, the Arizona Supreme Court found that the Tison brothers did not manifest a reckless indifference to life by their actions, and they were sentenced to life in prison. Because Randy Greenawalt was found to be a major participant in the killings, his death sentence withstood challenge and he was executed on January 23, 1997. In the chapter's opening scenario, Ben, Jerry, and Kathy would all be responsible for the death of the stepmother and the baby under the felony murder rule because they were all involved in the burglary and kidnapping that led to the stepmother's death in the trunk of the vehicle, and even though they did not intend to kidnap the baby, the connection to stealing the car and the baby's death would make them all liable under this doctrine.

IV. Key Terms and Phrases

- AMBER (America's Missing Broadcast Emergency Response) alert
- assault
- battery
- deadly weapon doctrine
- false imprisonment
- felony murder
- first-degree murder
- hate crime

- heat of passion
- homicide
- incest
- justifiable homicide
- kidnapping
- malice aforethought
- manslaughter
- mayhem
- premeditation
- provocation

- rape
- rape shield laws
- second-degree murder
- sex offense
- sodomy
- stalking
- statutory rape
- year-and-a-day-rule

V. Summary

1. **The similarities and differences between the crimes of assault and battery:** Under common law, assault and battery were two distinct crimes. **Assault** is placing someone in fear of an imminent **battery** which is defined as the intentional, unconsented to touching of another that is harmful or offensive. Today, most state statutes refer to crimes that combine traditional battery elements as assault. Both assault and battery can be **aggravated,** which will result in stiffer sentences upon conviction. Such a determination often is based on whether the victim was a child, police officer, or prison guard.

2. **Distinguishing kidnapping from false imprisonment: Kidnapping** is the unlawful confinement and taking (asportation) of a person by force or threat of force, while **false imprisonment** is restraining a person's liberty of movement without the asportation. Analysis to distinguish between the crimes focuses on whether the movement of the victim is incidental to the commission of another crime, for example moving someone down the stairs to effectuate a rape, versus a separate and distinct crime with the *mens rea* to remove the person as a separate crime.

3. **The elements and defining characteristics of sex-related offenses:** Typically, **sex offenses** are abuses of power and are committed by inserting a penis or other object into a body orifice (mouth, vagina, or anus) of another. The elements of **rape** are sexual intercourse against a woman's will and without her consent. Some type of forcible compulsion is required in addition to the victim's nonconsent to the act. If the victim is mentally retarded or under the influence of drugs or alcohol or if the consent is procured by fraud, trickery, and deceit, it is rape. **Statutory rape** occurs when a partner is legally below the age of consent, even if the victim consents. The history of statutory rape is from a strict liability to a *mens rea*–based defense, which allows mistake of age as a valid defense. **Incest** defines sexual relations between non-spousal family members regardless of whether they are related by blood, marriage, or adoption. **Deviate sexual intercourse** often defines crimes against children or **sodomy,** which is defined as oral–genital contact or anal penetration. Sodomy is legal between consenting adults.

4. **The type of behavior that separates degrees of homicide: First-degree murder** is willful, premeditated, and deliberate, which means that the offender carried out the act with specific intent and with a cool mind, and planned or thought about it prior to the act of the killing. **Homicide** is the killing of another. Some homicides are justified, such as those which occur in self-defense or in an accident. **Second-degree murder** occurs when the offender intends to commit serious bodily harm and a death results. **Manslaughter** is an unintentional killing and can happen with sufficient provocation, as in a **heat of passion** killing or a vehicular homicide situation, where a killing happens on the basis of reckless and negligent conduct, such as when **drinking and driving.** The **deadly weapon doctrine** allows the jury to infer specific intent to kill by the offender's use of any object in a manner designed to cause serious bodily injury or death. The anachronistic **year-and-a-day-rule** is the common law causation requirement that if the victim died more than one year and one day after the offender caused harm, the offender would not be considered the legal cause of death. The concept of brain death is often used to determine death of those victims on life support. **Felony murder** is when a death results from the attempted commission or the actual commission of a felony.

5. **Stalking and hate crimes: Stalking** is a type of obsessive–compulsive behavior usually exhibited by mentally ill defendants who simply cannot divert their attention from the victim. Such acts that constitute stalking include surveillance, monitoring, letter writing, believing that the victim will reciprocate love to the offender, and the constant sending of electronic mail and telephone messages. A **hate crime** is an act against a victim based on the victim's race, ethnicity, gender, or sexual orientation. While everyone has the freedom to hate in this country, no one is free to hurt people on the basis of that hate, and offenders may receive enhanced penalties in sentencing if it is determined by the jury that the defendant's actions were motivated by a person's racial, ethnic, gender, or sexual orientation.

VI. Discussion Questions

1. In the *Schnopps* case, why did the appellate court believe that the wife's words indicating she was having an affair or may have been unfaithful was the equivalent to her husband walking in on his wife in the arms of another lover, the classic "heat of passion" case? Why also did they believe the husband when he was the only one to testify as to the "provoking" act, given that the only other witness to that act, the wife, was dead? On retrial, Schnopps was again convicted even with the jury receiving the heat of passion instruction that made Schnopps' defense viable.

2. Grassroots organizations such as Mothers Against Drunk Driving ("MADD") have successfully made the dangers of drunk driving widely known, and public education efforts have been linked to reducing the number of highway fatalities. Do you think that prosecuting drunk drivers for intentional murder might have the same deterrent effect on drunk driving fatalities as the MADD public awareness campaign? Why or why not?

3. If the public policy justification for the felony murder rule is to deter and punish people who engage in inherently dangerous felonies, what is the reason for punishing people for deaths that may be unrelated to the initial felony, such as in Lisl Auman's case?

4. What is your opinion on giving the death penalty to a felon who did not intend to kill during a felony that nonetheless resulted in a murder? Do you agree that the felony murder rule is an antiquated exception to the fundamental principles of criminal law?

5. What is the public policy rationale in the law to make marriage a defense to the crime of incest?

6. How long do you think premeditation should be to qualify and satisfy the element for first-degree murder?

7. Has stalking as a crime increased over time, or is it just society's new awareness of disorders such as obsessive–compulsive disorder?

8. Do you agree with the limitations placed on defense counsel by rape shield laws, or do such restrictions interfere with the defendant's Sixth Amendment's right to confront witness against him? Explain the competing societal interests fully.

VII. Problem-Solving Exercises

1. Billy is drunk at a college fraternity party. He invites Marian up to his room. After kissing fervently and taking off her clothes just before penetration, Marian says, "No. Stop!" Incensed, Billy inserts his penis only slightly between Marian's labia. The next day Billy is charged with rape. Does Billy have any defenses?

2. One morning, Jake and Sally set out to burglarize a jewelry store. The plan was to take as much jewelry as possible—no one was supposed to get hurt. The first store they went to burglarize was closed, so Jake and Sally abandoned their criminal plan and went for breakfast. As they were shopping for napkins later that day at Super Discount, Sally looked at the diamonds in the jewelry case and motioned to Jake. "Get a load of these," she said and gave a wink and nod to Jake as she patted her concealed weapon. Jake took out his pistol and ordered the clerk to step aside as Jake collected all the diamonds and put them in a bag. The Discount Greeter, the one who says, "Hi and welcome" when customers enter the store, who happened to be a 78-year-old ex-cop, rushed to the jewelry clerk's aid. Just as police arrived, Jake grabbed the Greeter and took him hostage in a desperate act of escape. Jake, the greeter, and Sally got to their car and led police on a high-speed chase for many miles which resulted in the greeter's being accidentally killed by police gunfire. Jake was captured immediately, but Sally escaped. What crimes have Jake and Sally committed? Discuss whether the prosecution can prove all of the elements of the charges, and discuss any defenses Jake and Sally may have.

3. Max and Lucy were having an affair that ended badly. Shortly after the affair ended, Lucy saw Max in the grocery store parking lot and took a bottle of champagne and snuck up behind Max, hoping to crush his skull. Just as Lucy swung the bottle at Max's head, he bent down to pick up a quarter he had just dropped. Lucy's aim was perfect, but Max ducked down in the nick of time and Lucy ended up just swinging the bottle in the air. Lucy crept away before Max noticed her. What crimes have been committed?

4. Ken and Fred hated each other. They were next-door neighbors who always had an unkind word to say to one another after Ken called the animal control board to complain that Fred's dog was left out all night and barked incessantly. As a result of the complaint, Fred had to get rid of his dog. One day the two were cutting the hedges that spread out along the boundary of their property. As Ken was at one end of the hedges, Fred began to taunt Ken. Fred said to Ken, "I hear your wife was at the local tavern looking to score some real action. Word around town is that you're too small to fulfill her needs," at which point Ken took his hedge trimmers, which looked like large scissors, and stuck them in Fred's torso. Fred later died. When police came to arrest Ken, he confessed that he only meant to hurt Fred, not to kill him. What crimes against Ken can be charged?

5. Bobby and Vickie had suffered through 10 years of a tumultuous marriage. Finally, Vickie had enough and decided to leave Bobby. Upon coming home one day and seeing Vickie's belongings gone from their marital home, Bobby began to call Vickie's friends to find her. When they would not give Bobby information about Vickie's whereabouts, Bobby began to leave messages on their answering machines that said, "If you don't tell me where Vickie is, I'm going to come over there and burn your house down." Bobby left hundreds of similar messages on Vickie's cell phone, on her friends' answering machines, and on Vickie's e-mail account stored on her computer. Bobby began to call the burger joint where Vickie worked, and when her manager refused to put Vickie on the telephone, Bobby called an anonymous tip to the police station that there was a bomb planted underneath the french-fry fryer. When the threat was relayed to the burger joint, everybody ran out of the joint screaming. Bobby was sitting nearby, and when he saw Vickie run out of the joint, he shot and killed her. What crimes, if any, can Bobby be charged with?

VIII. World Wide Web Resources

National Sexual Assault Resource Center

http://www.nsvrc.org

National Institute of Justice, Sexual Victimization of College Women (2000)

http://www.ojp.usdoj.gov/nij/pubs-sum/182369.htm

National AMBER Alert

http://www.ojp.usdoj.gov/amberalert/

IX. Additional Readings and Notes

Murder

Carolyn B. Ramsey. "Intimate Homicide: Gender and Crime Control 1880–1920." *University of Colorado Law Review,* Vol. 77 (2006), pp. 101–190.

Manslaughter

Bradford Bigler. "Sexually Provoked: Recognizing Sexual Misrepresentation as Adequate Provocation." *UCLA Law Review,* Vol. 53 (2006), pp. 784–831.

CHAPTER 6

Crimes Against Property

Ownership is the right to enjoy and dispose of things in the most absolute manner [and] the word property is used . . . to denote legal relations between persons with respect to a thing.[1]

CHAPTER OBJECTIVES

Primary Concepts Discussed in This Chapter:

1. The legal foundation for possessory rights in property
2. The legal basis for differentiation in property crimes
3. Definitions of computer-related crimes
4. White-collar crimes
5. Burglary, robbery, and arson crimes

CHAPTER OUTLINE

Feature: Theft Crimes

I. THEFT CRIMES

1. Larceny
   Box 6.1 *Regina* v. *Feely,* 2 W.L.R. 201 (1973)
2. False Pretenses
3. Embezzlement
4. Forgery and Passing Bad Checks
   a. Counterfeiting
5. Receiving Stolen Property
6. Extortion
7. Identity Theft
   a. Phishing
8. Computer Crimes
   Box 6.2 *Fugarino* v. *State,* 531 S.E.2d 187 (Ga. 2000)
9. Consolidated Theft Statutes

II. WHITE-COLLAR CRIME

1. Mail and Wire Fraud
   Box 6.3 *United States* v. *Walters,* 997 F.2d 1219 (7th Cir. 1993)
2. RICO
   a. The Statute

III. BURGLARY

---

[1]*French Civil Code,* Article 544 (1804) and *Restatement of Property,* Chap. 1, Introductory Note (1936).

Feature: *Chapter-Opening Case Study: Theft Crimes*

When the first government check came into "The Family Toy Company" to pay as part of a government contract to make toys for underprivileged kids, Kelly, an employee, deposited the check in the corporate bank account. However, she kept $40,000 to satisfy a personal gambling debt, with every intention of paying the company back when she hit the lottery [embezzlement]. While Kelly was at the bank depositing the check, two men, Sal and Dom, with what looked like pistols but were really fake guns, walked in and demanded that the teller put all the money from the cash drawer into bags [robbery]. They escaped, and later that night Sal followed the bank teller home, intending to burn her house down. The teller took her dog out for a walk, leaving her back window open. To get inside, Sal had to remove the screen [burglary = breaking and entering with the intent to commit a felony once inside]. He then climbed in carrying a gas can and poured gasoline all over. Before he lit a match, he noticed that the teller's home computer was on. Sal went over and saw the teller's wallet with her identification and credit cards next to her computer screen. Sal logged on to the Internet auction site E-Bay™ and, putting in the teller's name, address, and credit card information, purchased the entire DVD set of the original Star Trek series and had it delivered to a post office box that he controlled [identity theft]. As Sal sat at the teller's computer and accessed her personal information, he discovered e-mails that clearly indicated the teller was having an illicit love affair. Sal created a fictitious e-mail account on the teller's computer and then sent her an e-mail from the account threatening the teller with exposing the love affair if she did not send a money order for $500 to his post office box [computer crime, extortion]. Sal then downloaded and printed all of the teller's and lover's e-mails to keep for himself. He also downloaded the latest copy of Windows 2007 installed on the computer's hard drive and took it away on a portable disk [computer theft]. Sal then lit a match before he ran out, but only a small part of the carpet burned [arson].

The next day, Sal went to sell his old car. Before he did so, he turned back the odometer from 100,000 to 10,000 miles. When an elderly couple came to purchase his car, Sal lied and told them that the car had only 10,000 miles on it [false pretenses]. Delighted to buy such a good car for $500, the old man said, "Great, I've been looking for a car with such low miles, and this car is just what I'm looking for." Sal told the couple, "Wonderful, I'm sure the car will last you a lifetime" [noncriminal puffery, exaggeration]. Sal then left to check his post office box for his Star Trek DVDs, and on his way back home, he saw the elderly couple, stranded on the side of the road in his old car with the hood up and the engine steaming. What crimes can Kelly, Sal, and Dom be charged with, and what will be the outcome of their cases?

INTRODUCTION

Historically, there have been many different and artificial distinctions between theft crimes. Professor George Fletcher has defined these distinctions as arbitrary, adding that "[v]irtually all the academic writing in the field expresses impatience with the distinctions among larceny, embezzlement, larceny by trick, and obtaining property by false pretenses. The thrust of the law for the last two centuries has been toward the creation of a unified law of theft offenses . . ."[2] This chapter examines the development of the legal recognition of property rights, the various methods an offender can use to deprive the owner of his possessory interest in his property, the traditional common law distinctions, and the current trend toward consolidation of theft crimes into one comprehensive statute. We also look at the abundance of computer-based crimes and the efforts to prevent it at the local, state, and federal levels.

I. THEFT CRIMES

Rule of Law: To be a thief, one must have the specific intent to steal.

1. Larceny

Larceny is the wrongful taking and carrying away [asportation] of the personal property of another without the owner's consent [trespass]. **Personal property** is defined as things that are moveable—for example, Ipods and books—as distinguished from **real property,** which is land and other fixtures attached to the property. The *mens rea* of larceny is the intent to steal and permanently deprive the owner of the property. The intent to permanently deprive the owner of the property or its value must be present at the time of the taking of the property. The trespassory [without the owner's consent] taking may be actual trespass—the real taking and carrying away of the property—or constructive, if committed by trick or fraud. As the law of theft crimes developed so, too, the definitions of certain types of behavior that qualified as theft.

Larceny as defined in early English law was *trespass de bonis asportatis* [trespass for goods carried away], but not all interference with an owner's possessory rights in his property qualified as larceny. To be guilty of larceny, the person taking the property need not have damaged, converted, or disposed of the property—he only needed to take it without the owner's consent. **Conversion** is the legal term for acquiring someone's property and transforming it for personal use and benefit. Therefore, if the owner gave the property willingly, there was no larceny. If a would-be thief only borrowed an item with the intent to return it, there was no larceny. If people acquired property lawfully and then converted it to their own use, there was no larceny. Essentially there was no adequate legal definition for the above situations. So the common law responded by defining various theft situations as larceny by trick, embezzlement, and false pretenses, distinctions that are confusing and arbitrary. Today modern statutes give one comprehensive definition of larceny as illustrated by the Massachusetts statute, Chapter 266, Section 30.

---

[2]George Fletcher. "The Metamorphosis of Larceny." *Harvard Law Review,* Vol. 89 (1976).

MASS. GENERAL LAW—CHAPTER 266: SECTION 30. LARCENY; GENERAL PROVISIONS AND PENALTIES

Section 30.

1. Whoever steals, or with intent to defraud obtains by a false pretense, or whoever unlawfully, and with intent to steal or embezzle, converts, or secretes with intent to convert, the property of another as defined in this section, whether such property is or is not in his possession at the time of such conversion or secreting, shall be guilty of larceny.

2. The term "property", as used in the section, shall include money, personal chattels, a bank note, bond, promissory note, bill of exchange or other bill, order or certificate, a book of accounts for or concerning money or goods due or to become due or to be delivered, a deed or writing containing a conveyance of land, any valuable contract in force, a receipt, release or defeasance, a writ, process, certificate of title, a public record, anything which is of the realty or is annexed thereto, a security deposit, electronically processed or stored data, either tangible or intangible, data while in transit, telecommunications services, and any domesticated animal, including dogs, or a beast or bird which is ordinarily kept in confinement.

As seen in the Massachusetts law, the basic elements of larceny are:

1. trespassory taking
2. of another's property
3. by carrying away or secreting
4. with the intent to permanently deprive the owner of possession.

Today, grading of the offense of larceny as either a misdemeanor or felony depends on the value of the property stolen. The crimes are simple larceny when the property's value is less than $250 or grand larceny for more valuable property. In examining the *mens rea* of larceny crimes, what happens when the intent to deprive the owner of possession is temporary and not permanent? It is common in business transactions for the one who owns the property, called a **bailor,** to give legal possession by the operation of a contract, but not ownership, to a **bailee** who is entrusted to care for the property until sale or other legal disposition. For example, a bailor may own boatloads of cigarettes, but it is the bailee who signs for them at the dock and is responsible for loading them onto the truck for delivery for sale at retail outlets. It would be a crime if the bailee violated his fiduciary duty [duty to care for and protect something with monetary value] with respect to the cigarettes and sold them for a reduced rate for personal profit. What happens if the bailee's intent is to merely borrow the money from the bailor and pay it back soon? In the English case, *Regina* v. *Feely,* 2 W.L.R. 201 (1973), the court examined whether someone who plans to "pay back" money could be found guilty of larceny and held that the question of intent to steal was one for the jury, not the judge.

Rule of Law: **False pretenses is the crime of lying to obtain property, a title to property, or another thing of value.**

2. False Pretenses

The common law definition of false pretenses, lying to induce another to turn over his or her property, is still salient today. For the prosecutor to prove false pretenses, she has to "prove that the defendant obtained title or possession of money or personal property of another by means of an intentional false statement concerning a material fact upon which the victim relied in parting with the property."[3] The elements of **false pretenses** are[4]:

1. obtaining property
2. by a false representation (a lie)

---

[3]*People* v. *Drake,* 462 N.E. 2d 376 (1984).

[4]*See* Wayne R. LaFave. *Criminal Law,* 4th ed. (St. Paul, MN: Thomson/West, 2003).

BOX 6.1

Regina v. *Feely*, 2 W.L.R. 201 (1973)
Court of Appeal

Judge Lawton delivered the opinion of the court.

FACTS

Defendant was a branch manager for a firm of bookmakers. In September 1971 the firm sent a circular to all branch managers that the practice of borrowing from tills was to stop. Defendant nevertheless took about £30 from a branch safe on October 4. On October 8 he was transferred to another branch. His successor discovered a cash shortage of about £40, and defendant gave him an IOU [paper stating debt owed] for that amount. Though his successor did not report the deficiency, a member of the firm's security staff did and asked defendant for an explanation. Defendant accounted for about £10 by reference to some bets he had paid out, but as to the balance he said that he had taken it because he was "stuck for cash." Defendant stated he borrowed the £30 intending to pay it back and that his employers owed him about £70 from which he wanted them to deduct the money. Trial testimony showed that the firm did owe him that amount. He was convicted of theft of the £30. [The judge instructed the jury] that if the defendant had taken the money from either the safe or the till . . . it was no defence for him to say that he had intended to repay it and that his employers owed him more than enough to cover what he had taken. The trial judge put his direction in stark terms: "As a matter of law, members of the jury, I am bound to direct you, even if he were prepared to pay back the following day and even if he were a millionaire, it makes no defence in law to this offence. If he took the money, that is the essential matter for you to decide."

At no stage of his summing up did he leave the jury to decide whether the prosecution had proved that the defendant had taken the money dishonestly. This was because he seems to have thought that he had to decide as a matter of law what amounted to dishonesty and he expressed his concept of dishonesty as follows: "if someone does something deliberately knowing that his employers are not prepared to tolerate it, is that not dishonest?"

ISSUE

[C]an it be a defence in law for a man charged with theft and proved to have taken money to say that when he took the money he intended to repay it and had reasonable grounds for believing and did believe that he would be able to do so?

HOLDING

[Yes, it's a defense—but the jury should decide only whether or not the defendant was guilty of the theft].

REASONING

[T]he Theft Act 1968 ("Act") . . . is clear; nearly all the old legal terms to describe offences of dishonesty have been left behind; larceny, embezzlement, and fraudulent conversion have become theft; receiving stolen goods has become handling stolen goods; obtaining by false pretences has become obtaining pecuniary advantage by deception. Words in everyday use have replaced legal jargon in many parts of the Act. "Theft" itself is a word known and used by all and is defined as follows:

> "A person is guilty of theft if he dishonestly appropriates property belonging to another with the intention of permanently depriving the other of it. . . ."

In section 1(1) of the Act . . . the word "dishonestly" can only relate to the state of mind of the person who does the act which amounts to appropriation [to take exclusive possession of]. The Crown [prosecution] did not dispute this proposition, but it was submitted that in some cases (and this, it was said, was such a one) it was necessary for the trial judge to define "dishonestly." We do not agree that judges should define what "dishonestly" means. People who take money from tills and the like without permission are usually thieves; but if they do not admit that they are by pleading guilty, it is for the jury, not the judge, to decide whether they have acted dishonestly.

CONCLUSION

For these reasons we allowed the appeal.

3. of a material past or present fact
4. that the defendant knew to be false
5. in order to induce the owner to transfer title to his property to the liar.

The false representation made to persuade the property owner to give it to the thief may be written or oral. The thief must know that the misrepresentation is untrue at the time of the making, and the lie must directly convince the owner to confer title to the property, or possession of the property if it is money. In the normal business exchange, there is no law that requires total disclosure of all information during a transaction. The concept of *caveat emptor*—buyer beware—still applies in certain transactions. At government auctions of seized property, such items are sold "as is," with no warranty or guarantee to their condition—buyer beware. There is an opportunity before the sale to inspect the goods, but the buyer is put on notice that if he or she buys something and it does not work, it is not the seller's responsibility.

A seller must not intentionally lie about the material condition of the item to be sold in an effort to get the buyer to part with his money. In order to qualify as a false representation, the statement must be about a material present or past fact, not an expectation, hope, or promise of things to come true in the future. The statement, "Buy my car and I'm sure you are going to get at least another 100,000 miles out of it," is not actionable when the car engine explodes five miles down the road even though the representation of expectation of how long the car would last is what enticed you to buy the car in the first place. The person must know it is a lie for the intentional *mens rea* to steal to apply.

If the seller states that the car has 20,000 miles on it and it actually has 200,000 miles on it, the discrepancy in mileage is a material fact. If the seller says that the car was recently cleaned and, in fact, it has not been, this discrepancy is not a material fact; old cheerios stuffed in the back seat have less bearing on the decision to buy a car than excessive mileage does. A good rule of thumb to determine whether a fact is material is to ask if it would change the outcome of the transaction. In our chapter opening scenario, Sal is guilty of false pretenses in turning back the car's odometer which induced the elderly couple to buy his car, but his mere puffery and expectation, expressed as a hope that the car would last them a lifetime, is not actionable under false pretenses.

It is a defense to a charge of false pretenses that the buyer knew of the lie, but bought anyway. If the buyer inspects under the hood and knows full well that the engine has 200,000 miles on it and buys it despite the claim of 20,000 miles, he cannot successfully press a claim that he was deceived because the lie did not induce the purchase. It is important to note that the crime of false pretenses requires that title to the property pass to the offender as a result of the lie. Under common law, if mere possession passed to the offender as a result of a lie, that crime was **larceny by trick.**

Applying the Law to the Facts: What type of theft is it?

- Aaron was caring for an elderly lady when he convinced her that, in order for him to properly protect her assets should she have to move to a nursing home, she should transfer the title to her home to his name. Believing that Aaron knew what he was talking about, the woman transferred the deed to Aaron. State law at the time did not require the woman to put her home in Aaron's name.

Aaron has committed false pretenses; he lied about a material fact which induced the woman to turn over title to her property.

3. Embezzlement

Rule of Law: Embezzlement is stealing property one acquired lawfully.

Sometimes the temptation of having access to money is too much to resist for certain people, and they resort to stealing when they have a fiduciary duty to protect the assets. **Embezzlement** is the conversion of property belonging to another that was acquired lawfully. The one factor that distinguishes embezzlement from other theft crimes is that the thief acquires the property lawfully before converting it to his own use. The typical people who embezzle are those who have lawful access to money, such as bailors, trustees, attorneys, accountants, and those who act in a relationship of trust over money within an organization. The elements of embezzlement are the

1. lawful acquisition and conversion of
2. personal property
3. of another
4. with the intent to permanently deprive the owner of possession.

The concept of "personal property of another" is a legal fiction for embezzlement purposes. For example, a bank employee might embezzle money from the bank, which is not a person. The property does not "technically" belong the bank—it belongs to depositors, and the bank uses it in various ways for the depositors' benefit, such as giving the money out as loans and paying the depositors interest. But the teller does have a fiduciary duty to safeguard the money. A fiduciary duty is a protective status to safeguard the interests of another. In our opening scenario, Kelly embezzled her employer's money when she kept a portion of the Toy Company's money, even if she intended only to "borrow" the money.

Interviews with convicted embezzlers led criminalist Donald Cressy to compile a sociological profile of those who abused positions of financial trust. Cressy discovered that certain events triggered typically honest people to steal from their employers. Many embezzlers whom Cressy interviewed in jail said, "I had no idea I was going to do this until the day it happened," or "For two years I have been trying to understand why I did this after being honest all my life," or "I thought this looked like a pretty good score so I took it."[5] While the typical embezzler seemingly took an opportunity that presented itself unexpectedly, Cressy discovered a common set of life situations among embezzlers at the time they started to steal. A typical scenario is the following:

1. A personal problem arises that the thief feels he cannot share with others.
2. The problem appears solvable by money.
3. The embezzler develops technical skills that allow him or her to steal the money without detection.
4. The embezzler adopts a mind-set that deceives him or her into thinking that the theft is temporary. The thief has every intention of returning the money, but never does.

Other research indicates that embezzlers are people who have high levels of debt, change jobs frequently, and have lower incomes than employees in similar positions with other companies. People who embezzle the most often are contractors working on commission—where salary is determined by how much product they sell. A way to detect an embezzler is to watch for an employee's rising spike in disposable income. Studies show that as a rule "persons who embezzle do not hide the money in a secret account; they tend to spend the money as soon as they embezzle it."[6] Embezzlers sometimes steal other items of value over which the company has loose oversight, such as the company's stock of products and supplies, including electronics, jewelry, or other small items. They also may pad expense accounts and submit false reimbursement claims for money never spent. Behavior that might appear benign when examined

---

[5]Donald Cressy. *Other People's Money: A Study in the Social Psychology of Embezzlement.* (Belmont, CA: Wadsworth, 1953).

[6]*See generally* Cliff Roberson. *Preventing Employee Misconduct: A Self-Defense Manual for Businesses.* (Lexington, MA: D.C. Heath, 1986).

from a law enforcement perspective may indicate the embezzlers in the company. They tend to be people who:

1. do not take vacations, turn down promotions, and regularly work overtime
2. prevent others from having access to records
3. work on company records excessively because, in their words, the records have to be "checked" or rewritten for neatness
4. are defensive regarding questions about their routine work activities
5. have creditors calling at work
6. explain a rapid increase in income as an inheritance or winning the lottery
7. have a new and improved standard of living[7]

There are certain defenses to embezzlement, as there are for most specific intent crimes. If one converted property by negligence, there's no embezzlement. Mistake of both law and fact are other defenses. For example, if Trudy the lawyer was under the mistaken impression that she could keep a client's money as payment, there's no embezzlement. Similarly, if Trudy made a mistake of law and believed that she was entitled to keep a portion of a dead client's estate as payment, then, again, in the absence of intent to steal, there is no embezzlement.

4. Forgery and Passing Bad Checks

Rule of Law: Forgery and uttering is stealing by trickery with paper.

A common theft crime committed by an act of fraud is writing checks for goods and services without sufficient funds to cover the check, called uttering fraudulent checks. **Uttering** is the passing of counterfeit or forged documents in the stream of commerce. The *mens rea* is the intent to defraud the owner who may believe the document is real. The clerk at the office supply store believes the person signing the check is the legal owner of the funds in the bank. He turns over the office supplies based on that belief. To successfully prosecute the crime, the prosecution must prove that the defendant knew at the time of uttering the check that there was not enough money in the bank account to pay the vendor. If, for example, the person had an automatic debit card in a joint account and wrote a check at the grocery store while his partner was buying a plasma screen television depleting the account, there would be insufficient *mens rea* to defraud the grocery store passing the "bad paper."

A similar crime of fraud is **forgery,** which is altering a written instrument with the intent to obtain property as a result of such deceit. For the crime of forgery, the instrument, if genuine and real, must create some right or legal obligation of significance. If someone forges Justin Timberlake's signature on a poster to impress a date, there is no forgery because the fraudulent signature induced no transfer of property. If someone forged Timberlake's signature and sold it as an authentic autograph, then the crime would be forgery. Forgery can also occur by interposing or adding numbers to checks, making 10,000 into 100,000, for instance. Forgery is a crime because it creates legal obligations for the victim without his or her knowledge and consent.

The elements of **forgery** are:

1. a material alteration of
2. an existing document
3. with the intent to deprive the owner of a thing of value permanently.

---

[7]*Ibid.*

Applying the Rule of Law to the Facts: Is it forgery?

- Tom signed the victim's name on the victim's credit card receipt and then argued that the receipt was not a "writing" under the forgery statute.[8]

Yes, it is forgery. A credit card receipt is a signed sales receipt that evidences a contract for the sale of goods between the buyer and seller, and Tom altered that legal relationship and is guilty.

a. Counterfeiting

Forgery is different from, but similar to, the federal crime of **counterfeiting,** which is making fake stuff or fake money and passing it off as real. Article I, Section 8, of the Constitution grants exclusive power to Congress to "coin money, regulate the value thereof, and to foreign coin, and to fix the Standard of weights and measures," which makes counterfeiting American money a uniquely federal crime. A high school boy who made fake $20 bills on his color copier at home, purchased fast food items for a nominal fee, and received real money back in change was convicted under the federal counterfeiting statute 18 U.S.C. §471: "Whoever, with intent to defraud, falsely makes, forges, counterfeits, or alters any obligation or other security of the United States, shall be fined or imprisoned not more than 20 years, or both."

Counterfeiting money is not the only counterfeiting crime. The Senate Committee on the Judiciary convened hearings in March 2004 on counterfeiting and theft of tangible intellectual property. Many of those who testified spoke of the immeasurable harm done to American businesses by the lack of a comprehensive and effective law enforcement mechanism.[9] Delaware Senator Joseph Biden said "American intellectual property is an immensely valuable resource. Failing to protect it is equivalent to letting coal be stolen from our mines or water taken from our rivers. The U.S. Customs Service estimates that counterfeiting costs the U.S. more than $200 billion every year and has resulted in the loss of 750,000 American jobs."

5. Receiving Stolen Property

Rule of Law: To be convicted of receiving stolen property, the defendant has to know that it is stolen.

For many theft crimes to be profitable, the thief not only has to steal another's property, but in some cases needs someone else to buy it. The people who routinely give money for stolen goods they later turn around and sell to others are called the slang term "fences," as a fence is between two parties. The crime of receiving stolen property is the *actus reus* of obtaining another's property with the scienter of knowing that it is stolen with the *mens rea* intent to permanently deprive the rightful owner of the property. The elements of the crime of **receiving stolen property** are:

1. receipt of property
2. knowing that the property was stolen
3. with the intent to deprive the owner of possession permanently.

The *mens rea* can be proved through actual knowledge, as when the original thief informs the recipient of its stolen nature, or by constructive knowledge that receiving property at such a reduced rate indicates that the item must have been stolen. For instance, if Sam were approached by a thief who wanted to sell for $200 an authentic Rolex watch that retails for approximately $1,500, the prosecutor could argue that Sam's willful ignorance about the origin of the watch was constructive knowledge that

---

[8]Facts adapted from *Pennsylvania* v. *Sargent,* 823 A.2d 174 (2003).

[9]108th Congress, Second Session, March 23, 2004. U.S. Government Printing Office. Washington: 2005.

he knew it was stolen. No one can legitimately buy a genuine Rolex watch for $200. The last element of the crime is that the defendant must intend to keep the property from the owner, whether by keeping it, selling it to another, giving it away, or destroying it. It is a federal crime to receive stolen property that travels in interstate commerce.

6. Extortion

Rule of Law: Extortion is blackmail—threatening someone into performing certain acts or paying money to keep the defendant from ruining the victim's business, reputation, or relationship.

Often called blackmail, **extortion** is the acquisition of the property of another by threatening to injure the victim's person, relationships, reputation, or financial status to force the victim to turn over the property. If a judge learns that an attorney has embezzled money from a client and threatens to expose the lawyer to the authorities, then the judge's threat is legal. But if the judge offers to stay silent if the lawyer pays him $10,000, the judge has committed extortion by threatening to harm the lawyer's reputation and personal integrity (in the form of a threatened deprivation of liberty in a possible jail sentence) in satisfaction of all elements. The Model Penal Code defines extortion as

> **§223.4 THEFT BY EXTORTION**
> A person is guilty of theft if he purposely obtains property of another by threatening to:
> 1. inflict bodily injury on anyone or commit any other criminal offense; or
> 2. accuse anyone of a criminal offense; or
> 3. expose any secret tending to subject any person to hatred, contempt or ridicule, or to impair his credit or business repute; or
> 4. take or withhold action as an official, or cause an official to take or withhold action; or
> 5. bring about or continue a strike, boycott or other collective unofficial action, if the property is not demanded or received for the benefit of the group in whose interest the actor purports to act; or
> 6. testify or provide information or withhold testimony or information with respect to another's legal claim or defense; or
> 7. inflict any other harm which would not benefit the actor.

It is an affirmative defense to prosecution based on paragraphs (2), (3) or (4) that the property obtained by threat of accusation, exposure, lawsuit, or other invocation of official action was honestly claimed as restitution or indemnification for harm done in the circumstances to which such accusation, exposure, lawsuit, or other official action relates, or as compensation for property or lawful services.

Applying the Rule of Law to the Facts: Is it extortion?

- Jake and Marianne were having an affair. Marianne was married to another man. She ended the affair and argued with Jake over money she had lent him. Jake threatened to reveal their affair unless Marianne continued to have sexual relations with him, which she did. Jake also planned to reveal their affair to Marianne's husband if she pestered him about the money he owed to her.[10]

Yes, extortion statutes generally condemn forcing people to perform certain acts or to transfer things of value under compulsion and intimidation based upon an "embarrassing truth." In our opening scenario, Sal committed extortion when he threatened to expose the teller's illicit affair unless she paid him $500.

---

[10]*Illinois* v. *Downey,* 458 N.E.2d 160 (1983).

7. Identity Theft

Rule of Law: Identity theft is posing as someone else to obtain something of value.

Given the advent of technology and Internet accessibility of access to the World Wide Web in people's homes, posing as someone else by taking their online identity is one of the fastest growing crimes in the country today. **Identity theft** is stealing unique identifying characteristics of someone such as a name, address, e-mail address, date of birth, social security number, bank account number, or credit card numbers to acquire something of value. The Connecticut identity theft statute defines personal information as "a motor vehicle operator's license number, Social Security number, employee identification number, mother's maiden name, demand deposit number, savings account number or credit card number." Some methods of committing identity theft are:

1. opening a new credit card account in the victim's name
2. forging checks from the victim's bank accounts
3. opening a bank account in the victim's name and writing checks
4. using the victim's birth date or social security number for personal gain.

A 2003 survey sponsored by the Federal Trade Commission ("FTC"), the federal agency responsible for watching the goods and services in the marketplace, estimated that approximately 27.3 million people had their identities stolen in the previous five years, resulting in nearly $50 billion dollars lost to businesses and consumers and $5 billion dollar lost in out-of-pocket expenses. Identity theft is not a new crime. Long before computers could be used as instruments to commit theft, as author Jennifer Lynch writes in the Berkeley Technology Law Journal, people were pickpockets, dove into dumpsters for discarded financial records, stole preapproved credit card applications from mailboxes, completed change-of-address forms to divert victims' mail, and accepted low-level employment to gain and steal consumers' social security numbers to parlay into financial gain. These types of crime account for the majority of identity theft cases, but the Internet and the increased use of databases for storing consumer information has allowed thieves easier access to greater quantities of individual information at one time." Many laws criminalize identity theft and offer protection for consumers. At the federal level, laws against credit card fraud, wire fraud, bank fraud, and identity theft can be used against identity thieves. Almost every state has its own criminal and consumer protection laws that deal with identity theft. In our opening scenario, Sal committed identity theft by using the teller's personal information to purchase Star Trek DVDs online.

13 VIRGINIA STATUTES ANNOTATED §2030 (2006) IDENTITY THEFT

a. No person shall obtain, produce, possess, use, sell, give, or transfer personal identifying information belonging or pertaining to another person with intent to use the information to commit a misdemeanor or a felony.

b. No person shall knowingly or recklessly obtain, produce, possess, use, sell, give, or transfer personal identifying information belonging or pertaining to another person without the consent of the other person and knowingly or recklessly facilitating the use of the information by a third person to commit a misdemeanor or a felony.

c. For the purposes of this section, "personal identifying information" includes name, address, birth date, Social Security number, motor vehicle personal identification number, telephone number, financial services account number, savings account number, checking account number, credit card number, debit card number, picture, identification document or false identification document, electronic identification number, educational record, health care record, financial record, credit record, employment record, e-mail address, computer system password, or mother's maiden name, or similar personal number, record, or information.

d. This section shall not apply when a person obtains the personal identifying information belonging or pertaining to another person to misrepresent the person's age for the sole purpose of obtaining alcoholic beverages, tobacco, or another privilege denied based on age.

e.   It shall be an affirmative defense to an action brought pursuant to this section, to be proven by a preponderance of the evidence, that the person had the consent of the person to whom the personal identifying information relates or pertains.

f.   A person who violates this section shall be imprisoned for not more than three years or fined not more $5,000.00, or both. A person who is convicted of a second or subsequent violation of this section involving a separate scheme shall be imprisoned for not more than ten years or fined not more than $10,000.00, or both.

Applying the Rule of Law to the Facts: Is it identity theft?

• A school principal was informed of a derogatory web page on myspace.com that was purportedly created by the principal, but was actually created by the student. On the site were profanity-laced tirades attributable to the principal. Since the myspace account was created with a private profile and only persons accepted as friends by the creator of the web page were allowed full access to the page and its comments, the principal had no access to the page.[11]

No identity theft of the principal's personal information and the student's delinquency finding overturned.

• A woman owned a used clothing store and signed a yearlong lease for $1,500 a month. She made several timely payments then abruptly stopped. The keys were returned to the landlord with a note that she was abandoning the lease. She was sued for breach of contract and, in her defense, claimed that she was in another state conducting business and she was a victim of identity theft committed by her son who wrote the letter and returned the keys.[12] The evidence she submitted were response letters from the state attorney general's office when she complained about her identity being stolen. Sufficient evidence to sustain a defense?

No, proprietor was guilty of falsifying records with a forged identity for financial gain.

a. Phishing

"Dear Paypal valued member, it has come to our attention that your account information needs to be updated due to inactive members, frauds and spoof reports. If you could please take 5–10 minutes out of your online experience and renew your records you will not run into any future problems. However failure to update your records will result in account suspension. Please follow the link below to login to your account and renew your account information . . ."[13]

Phishing is the fraudulent use of spoofed e-mail and spoofed websites. The fabricated materials often use company trademarks and logos to appear to represent a legitimate financial institution or Internet Service Provider ("ISP") with which the consumer has an account, linked to banks and online shopping sites like eBay, PayPal, US Bank, or Citibank. The real danger of being a victim of a phishing attack is that victims may not find out about the theft until long after it has occurred. Phishing e-mails elude fraud and spam filters. The Anti-Phishing Working Group estimates that there were over 500 unique phishing attacks per week in July 2004 alone.[14] Like most Internet criminals, phishers are hard to catch.

[11]Adapted from facts of *A. B.* v. *Indiana*, 863 N.E.2d 1212 (2007).

[12]Facts adapted from unpublished opinion *Donati* v. *Demello-Daves*, A108594 (2006 Cal. App. Unpub. LEXIS 786).

[13]Information for this section derived from Jennifer Lynch. "Identity Theft in Cyberspace: Crime Control Methods and Their Effectiveness in Combating Phishing Attacks." *Berkeley Technical Law Journal*, Vol. 20 (2005), pp. 259–281.

[14]Anti-Phishing Working Group, http://www.antiphishing.org (accessed on February 3, 2005). The Anti-Phishing Working Group ("APWG") is an industry association that teams software makers, banks, ISPs, and law enforcement to study and combat phishing.

Their spoof sites are generally online for no more than 54 hours and disappear before law enforcement officials have working information on how to shut them down.

Recent phishing activity has targeted the country's largest corporate executives. During the week of April 14, 2008, many chief executives received e-mail messages that appeared to be official subpoenas issued from federal courts in California. Computer experts call phishing attacks on the rich and powerful "whaling" and those attacks directed at one particular individual "spear phishing." Clicking on a link in the fake subpoena downloaded software that surreptitiously recorded keystrokes and transmitted the data to a remote server. Thus, criminals at the remote site (most likely in China, say authorities) could capture personal passwords and other sensitive corporate financial data. The administrative office of the federal courts alerted the public to the scam, but the notice may have arrived too late for some.[15] All industry experts agree that phishing on such a grand scale is hard to detect and ensnares thousands of victims. The culprits use multiple ISPs and redirect services. In the 2004 "Operation Firewall," the Federal Bureau of Investigation and the Secret Service, two federal law enforcement agencies, focused on three Internet websites that provided a forum for selling and buying personal identification information and identity theft tutorials online. The Secret Service arrested 28 suspects from eight states and six foreign countries who were involved in stealing more than 1.7 million credit card numbers and other financial information causing more than $4.3 million in financial losses.[16]

8. Computer Crimes

Rule of Law: Computer crimes either use the computer to commit the crime or violate the computer's integrity.

The federal government gives computer crime a broad definition. **Computer crimes** are generally defined as any violations of criminal law that involve a knowledge of computer technology for their perpetration, investigation, or prosecution.[17] Computer crimes cover a wide variety of activities, the nature and sophistication of which make them difficult to prosecute. "[P]eople may encrypt data so that even if law enforcement seizes or intercepts the data, they will be unable to understand its contents or use it as evidence. The nature of the Internet allows people to engage in criminal conduct online with virtual anonymity."[18] While there is no concrete definition of computer crime, there are three general areas of computer protection that criminal law statutes are designed to combat or protect:

1. Protection of privacy
2. Prosecution of economic crimes
3. Protection of intellectual property

Similar to federal statutes, many state statutes divide computer crimes into three categories: crimes where a computer is the target, crimes where a computer is a tool of the crime, and crimes where a computer is incidental. First, a computer may be the object of a crime when computer hardware or software is stolen. Second, a computer may be the subject of the crime when it is the target of attack—for example, when spam, worms, viruses, and Trojan horses infect computer hard drives and software rendering the computer inoperable. Such subject-type crimes are often committed by disgruntled business employees who want to cause maximum damage to their employer's ability to conduct

---

[15]John Markoff. "Larger Prey are Targets of Phishing." *The New York Times,* April 16, 2008, p. C1.

[16]Robert Lemos. "Secret Service Busts Suspected ID Fraud Ring", CNET News.com, October 28, 2004. http://news.com.com/Secret+Service+busts+suspected+ID+fraud+ring/2100-7348_3-5431419.html.

[17]*See generally* DOJ Computer Crime Manual.

[18]Dana L. Bazelon, Yun Jung Choi, and Jason F. Conaty. "Computer Crimes." *American Criminal Law Review,* Vol. 43 (2006), pp. 259–310.

business. Professional hackers and juveniles who may want to prove their intellectual superiority are the types of offenders likely to commit subject-type computer offenses. Third, computers may be an <u>instrument</u> used to commit traditional crimes such as identity theft, child pornography, copyright infringement, and mail and wire fraud. Computers enable criminals to commit the same types of property, theft, or pornography crimes, but in the different forum of the World Wide Web. A typical state statute identifying and punishing computer crimes is illustrated by the Georgia statute reprinted below.

OFFICIAL CODE OF GEORGIA ANNOTATED §16-9-93 (2006)
COMPUTER CRIMES DEFINED; EXCLUSIVITY OF ARTICLE;
CIVIL REMEDIES; CRIMINAL PENALTIES

a. <u>Computer theft.</u> Any person who uses a computer or computer network with knowledge that such use is without authority and with the intention of:

　1. Taking or appropriating any property of another, whether or not with the intention of depriving the owner of possession;

　2. Obtaining property by any deceitful means or artful practice; or

　3. Converting property to such person's use in violation of an agreement or other known legal obligation to make a specified application or disposition of such property shall be guilty of the crime of computer theft.

b. <u>Computer Trespass.</u> Any person who uses a computer or computer network with knowledge that such use is without authority and with the intention of:

　1. Deleting or in any way removing, either temporarily or permanently, any computer program or data from a computer or computer network;

　2. Obstructing, interrupting, or in any way interfering with the use of a computer program or data; or

　3. Altering, damaging, or in any way causing the malfunction of a computer, computer network, or computer program, regardless of how long the alteration, damage, or malfunction persists shall be guilty of the crime of computer trespass.

c. <u>Computer Invasion of Privacy.</u> Any person who uses a computer or computer network with the intention of examining any employment, medical, salary, credit, or any other financial or personal data relating to any other person with knowledge that such examination is without authority shall be guilty of the crime of computer invasion of privacy.

d. <u>Computer Forgery.</u> Any person who creates, alters, or deletes any data contained in any computer or computer network, who, if such person had created, altered, or deleted a tangible document or instrument would have committed forgery under Article 1 of this chapter, shall be guilty of the crime of computer forgery. The absence of a tangible writing directly created or altered by the offender shall not be a defense to the crime of computer forgery if a creation, alteration, or deletion of data was involved in lieu of a tangible document or instrument.

e. <u>Computer Password Disclosure.</u> Any person who discloses a number, code, password, or other means of access to a computer or computer network knowing that such disclosure is without authority and which results in damages (including the fair market value of any services used and victim expenditure) to the owner of the computer or computer network in excess of $500.00 shall be guilty of the crime of computer password disclosure.

　. . .

h. <u>Criminal Penalties.</u>

　1. Any person convicted of the crime of computer theft, computer trespass, computer invasion of privacy, or computer forgery shall be fined not more than $50,000.00 or imprisoned not more than 15 years, or both.

　2. Any person convicted of computer password disclosure shall be fined not more than $5,000.00 or incarcerated for a period not to exceed one year, or both.

BOX 6.2

Fugarino v. *State*, 531 S.E.2d 187 (2000)
Court of Appeals of Georgia

Judge Ellington delivered the opinion of the court.

FACTS

Fugarino worked as a computer programmer for a company that designed software for land surveyors. During his employment with the company Fugarino became a difficult employee. Fugarino's employer was concerned about his unusual behavior. On the day of the trespass, Fugarino was informed that another employee had been hired by the company in an unrelated technical support position, and Fugarino began to go "berserk." Fugarino became very angry and told another employee that he was upset that someone was being hired to take his place, that the code was his product, that no one else was going to work on his code, that nobody was going to take his place and that he was "going to take his code with him." This employee then observed Fugarino deleting massive amounts of files. "Pages were being highlighted and a whole system appeared to be being erased."

Fugarino himself admitted that "he was going to delete it [the code] from the machine. . . ." When this employee told the owner of the company what he had seen, the owner confronted Fugarino. Fugarino told him that the code was his, that "the blood of his dead son" was in the code and that the owner "would never get to make any money from that code." The owner managed to get Fugarino to leave the office and secured the company's computer. He then discovered that Fugarino had added additional layers of password protection to the computer's system, and he was unable to access the program code. Fugarino returned to the office later that evening and again confronted the owner stating that he "would never be able to sell that code, that he would fix it so [the owner] never sold the code." The owner was forced to have Fugarino removed by police. At trial a police investigator trained in the recovery of computer evidence testified that he examined the computer and confirmed that large amounts of data had been deleted from the system. Based on this evidence, the jury convicted Fugarino of one count of computer trespass.

ISSUE

[Did] the State produce sufficient evidence to prove beyond a reasonable doubt that Fugarino deleted materials from his employer's computer in violation of (Official Code of Georgia Annotated) O.C.G.A. §16-9-93 (b)?

HOLDING

[Yes]. Testimony showed that Fugarino used a computer owned by the company with the intention of deleting or removing data from that computer.

REASONING

The burden on the State was not to show that Fugarino had completed the act of deleting or removing data from his computer but to show that he had used a computer, knowing that he did not have the authority to do so, with the intention of deleting data. There is sufficient evidence in this case to allow a reasonable trier of fact to find that a computer trespass had occurred. Fugarino further contends . . . that the State failed to produce any evidence to prove beyond a reasonable doubt that Fugarino's use of the computer at issue was knowingly "without authority". . . . The term "without authority" is defined by the legislature in O.C.G.A. §16-9-92 (11) as "the use of a computer or computer network in a manner that exceeds any right or permission granted by the owner of the computer or computer network."

The owner of the company testified that he did not give Fugarino authority or permission to delete portions of the company's program. Moreover, the vindictive and retaliatory manner in which Fugarino deleted large amounts of computer code indicates that he knew he lacked authority to do so. Therefore, there was sufficient evidence to allow a rational trier of fact to conclude beyond a reasonable doubt that Fugarino used a computer, owned by his employer, with knowledge that such use was without authority and with the intention of removing programs or data from that computer.

CONCLUSION

[Conviction] affirmed.

Georgia's statute criminalizes accessing computer files without authorization and knowingly transmitting a program that causes damage to a computer with or without the intention to cause the ultimate harm. In our opening scenario, Sal committed a computer crime by accessing the teller's personal computer without authorization and then downloading without authority the latest version of Windows 2007 to carry away with him.

Recent computer-crime criminal statutes define online threats as computer crime and have amended harassment statutes to include computers and electronic communication devices. Congress has enacted or is trying to enact a number of laws to criminalize the use of computers to produce false identification documents and to enhance penalties when personal information is misused via computer.[19] On May 15, 2008, 50-year-old Lori Drew was charged under a federal anti-fraud statute for creating a fake identity on MySpace to harass a 13-year-old girl, who then committed suicide. The federal government has jurisdiction because the social web site's server is in California and Ms. Drew and the victim are from Missouri. The indictment alleges Drew violated MySpace's user agreement by posing as a teenage boy "to further a torturous act, namely, intentional infliction of emotional distress" when the "boy" told the young victim "the world would be a better place" without her.

9. Consolidated Theft Statutes

Because of the confusion created by many different theft statutes, legislators have moved to consolidate all theft crimes into one statute. The primary change in law enforcement of theft crimes under a consolidated theft statute is that prosecutors no longer need to charge the specific crime that has occurred. At trial, if the jury decides that a defendant has committed a larceny and not an embezzlement, they can still convict under the consolidated statute. Under common law, if the defendant was charged with embezzlement, not larceny, the jury would be forced to acquit if they determined that the defendant committed larceny rather than embezzlement.

Consolidation usually includes only misappropriations of property that do not pose serious risks to life. Robbery is usually not included in consolidated theft statutes because it carries a significant threat of harm or personal injury to the victim. The crimes that are included in consolidation statutes are not always punished equally. It is common to grade such offenses on the basis of the amount of property appropriated, the nature of the theft, and the type of property stolen.

The Model Penal Code contains a comprehensive consolidation of theft offenses. Provided that a defendant is not prejudiced by doing so, the specification of one theft crime by the prosecution does not prohibit a conviction for another. So if the defendant is specifically charged with larceny, he or she may be convicted of false pretenses or embezzlement. The Code recognizes the following forms of theft:

1. Theft by taking
2. Theft by deception
3. Theft by extortion
4. Theft of property known to be mislaid, misdelivered, or lost by one who does not make any reasonable attempt to find the rightful owner
5. Receipt of stolen property
6. Theft of professional services by deception or threat
7. Conversion of entrusted funds
8. Unauthorized use of another's automobile

The Code declares that thefts are felonies of the third degree if the amount stolen exceeds $500 or if the property stolen is a firearm, automobile, airplane, motorcycle, motorboat, or other vehicle. In cases of receipt of stolen property, if the receiver of the

---

[19]For example, Internet False Identification Act of 2000, Pub. L. 105-277.

property is a fence or middleman, then it is a felony of the third degree regardless of the value of the property.

If during the commission of a theft the defendant inflicts serious bodily injury upon another, threatens serious bodily injury, or threatens to commit a felony of the first or second degree, the crime is robbery and it counts as a felony of the second degree. If the defendant attempts to kill or cause serious bodily injury, it is a felony of the first degree. Forgery is treated as a separate offense. Forgery of money, securities, postage stamps, stock, or other documents issued by the government is a felony of the second degree. If the forged document affects legal relationships, such as wills and contracts, it is a felony of the third degree. All other forgeries are misdemeanors.

II. WHITE-COLLAR CRIME

There are many definitions used to describe **white-collar crime,** but all definitions revolve around the basic concept of a person in a position of trust using his or her influence and power to steal from the public. Corporations and businesses are typically owned by shareholders, or people who invest their money in the company by buying stock. Let us assume that to start the Microsoft Corporation, cofounder Bill Gates asked people to invest money in his company. If an investor gave Bill $1000, she would receive in return stock that represented part ownership of Microsoft. If the company did well and prospered, the investor could sell her stock and get her money back—and also receive any profit from the increased value of the company, called the rate of return. People usually invest their money in corporations on a promised rate of return on their initial investment. Corporate executives answer to the shareholders to act in the best interests of the company; in essence, they protect the shareholders' initial investments, take actions that benefit the corporation, and take actions that do not harm the company.

One of the largest corporate frauds in recent history was the collapse of Enron, once the seventh-largest company in the country. Initially Enron provided energy, gas, and electricity; later, it branched out into broadband Internet and other ventures designed to infiltrate the global economy. When regulators gave Enron permission to use mark-to-market accounting, a practice that allows companies to count ideas as profits, Enron began "cooking" the books and recording anticipated earnings as real profit. When the company could no longer service its debt because the anticipated earnings never materialized, it had to file for bankruptcy and collapsed entirely within seven months. The chief executives, Kenneth Lay, Jeffery Skilling, and Andrew Fastow, were charged with knowingly projecting false information that kept the stock prices high, which all three men and many more senior executives cashed in on, when in fact the shares were nearly valueless. Fastow became a government informant and testified against Skilling and Lay, who were both convicted on a number of fraud counts in May 2006. Lay died unexpectedly on July 5, 2006, of heart disease, and his death rendered his conviction null and void. Skilling was sentenced to 24 years and 4 months in prison. Fastow faced over 20 years in prison, entered into a plea agreement with the government for no more than 10 years, and was eventually sentenced to 6 years because the judge found his help in prosecuting the cases invaluable to the government.

The majority of white-collar crimes are prosecuted federally because such crimes usually involve many activities that cross state lines. In addition, because of the size and scope of the investigations, many state and local law enforcement agencies do not have the specialized training in securities and other types of fraud to prosecute the cases.

Since their jurisdiction extends only to their respective state borders, they cannot execute many of the necessary warrants and investigative tools in other states. Moreover, given the complexities of extensive financial transactions, many of which have been carefully and cleverly designed to hide fraudulent practices, such investigations and prosecutions are expensive and lengthy. The Securities and Exchange Commission ("SEC") is the federal administrative agency tasked with investigating fraud in business and corporations that issue stock (securities). The SEC is an investigative body that turns to the Department of Justice or the Economic Crime Division of the local United States Attorney's office for criminal prosecution. Those who suffer economic losses due to securities fraud can also seek remedy in civil court, as can the SEC on behalf of defrauded shareholders.

1. Mail and Wire Fraud

Rule of Law: If the method of stealing uses a mail delivery system or wire communication, such crimes are properly prosecuted under the mail and wire fraud statutes.

Mail and wire fraud are very similar crimes, and the statutes preventing such crimes are often used in conjunction with one another. The **mail fraud** statute punishes the use of the mails and private delivery carriers to commit fraud, while **wire fraud** punishes the use of wire-based systems like telephones, fax machines, modems, and the Internet to commit fraud. The statutes are used today to prosecute a variety of schemes designed to defraud the public and cheat institutions such as banks, insurance companies, and businesses by counterfeiting, blackmail, and bribery. As described by former U.S. Supreme Court Chief Justice Warren Burger, the mail fraud statute was the traditional first line of defense to catch new fraudulent schemes that take legislators time to define and criminalize. *United States* v. *Maze,* 414 U.S. 395 (1974). For example, in 1994, Congress amended the statutes to specifically punish telemarketing fraud and increased the punishment for schemes targeted at senior citizens, a vulnerable population. Such schemes often involve a telephone call promising prizes and other things of value if only the senior first sends a check or money order to claim his or her "prize." As one federal prosecutor explained about the flexible use of these statutes,

> [T]he mail fraud statute, together with its lineal descendant, the wire fraud statute, has been characterized as the "first line of defense" against virtually every new area of fraud to develop in the United States in the past century. Its applications, too numerous to catalog, cover not only the full range of consumer frauds, stock frauds, land frauds, bank frauds, insurance frauds, and commodity frauds, but have extended even to such areas as blackmail, counterfeiting, election fraud, and bribery. In many of these and other areas, where legislatures have sometimes been slow to enact specific prohibitory legislation, the mail fraud statute has frequently represented the sole instrument of justice that could be wielded against the ever-innovative practitioners of deceit.[20]

The elements of the mail/wire fraud crimes are very similar, although both crimes can be charged independent of one another and often are. The mail fraud statute[21] and the

---

[20]Ryan Y. Blumel. "Mail and Wire Fraud." *American Criminal Law Review,* Vol. 42 (2005), pp. 677–698 *citing* Jed S. Rakoff. "The Federal Mail Fraud Statute (Part I)." *Duquesne Law Review,* Vol. 18 (2005).

[21]The mail fraud statute, 18 U.S.C. §1341, reads "Whoever, having devised or intending to devise any scheme or artifice to defraud, ... for the purpose of executing such scheme or artifice or attempting so to do, places in any post office or authorized depository for mail matter, any matter or thing whatever to be sent or delivered by the Postal Service, ... shall be fined under this title or imprisoned not more than 20 years, or both."

wire fraud statute[22] have the following elements in common that the prosecution must prove:[23]

1. a scheme to defraud that includes a material deception
2. with the intent to defraud, and
3. use of the mail (United States Postal Service), private commercial carriers (such as United Parcel Service ("UPS"), or Federal Express) or wires in furtherance of that scheme
4. that did result in the loss of something of value, money, or honest public services.

The first common element in both mail and wire fraud statutes is a **scheme to defraud,** which is trying to take something of value from another by a trick, lie, or deceitful practice. Similar to the crime of false pretenses, the deceit in a mail or wire fraud scheme must be about something material to the transaction—something important and not merely collateral or ancillary.[24] Unlike the crime of false pretenses, mail or wire fraud crime need not cause the victim of the deception to turn over anything of value—the scheme to defraud need not be successful in order for liability to attach. The defendant merely has to instigate the scheme to be liable.

The second element common to both the mail and wire fraud statutes is that the defendant must have possessed the **intent to defraud** the victim. Sometimes advertisers puff up their descriptions of their product's effectiveness in order to induce a buyer to try the product. Again, as in a false pretenses type of crime, one who merely expresses an opinion about something cannot be charged with intent to defraud. For instance, the statement, "If you buy my car, I think it will last another year," is not actionable if the car dies one mile down the road. In an intent-to-defraud situation, the seller knows the information is false and represents the fact as true with the intent to obtain something of value (usually money) from the victim. The seller may make specific claims like "This weight loss supplement is totally safe and guaranteed to help you lose 10 pounds in 48 hours" (when no supplement can safely do this) or "This land has clear title" (when a lien indicating that the property was used as security for payment was attached to the property many years ago).

The third common element is **using the mails or the wires** or knowing that the mails and wires would be used even if the defendant himself did not use them. In *Pereira* v. *United States,* 347 U.S. 1 (1954), the high Court said that when someone acts "with knowledge that the use of mails will follow in the ordinary course of business, or where such use can reasonably be foreseen, even though not actually intended, then he 'causes' the mails to be used". The same criteria apply to wire transmissions. If a person went to the bank to effectuate a wire transfer or knew that checks deposited would cause funds to be electronically transferred from one account to another, the element has been met. Note that the intent element in mail/wire fraud is for the fraud itself, not necessarily the use of the mails or wires. That is, the *mens rea* applies to the trick or deceit to get something of value, and it becomes mail or wire fraud because of the manner in which the fraud is carried out—by using the mails or wires.

The last common element is causing the **loss of money or property, or the theft of honest services.** Causing the loss of something valuable is fairly easy to define—using fraud to get people's money or things that represent money, for example, checks, loans,

---

[22]The wire fraud statute, 18 U.S.C. §1343, provides that "Whoever, having devised or intending to devise any scheme or artifice to defraud, . . . by means of wire, radio, or television communication in interstate or foreign commerce, any writings, signs, signals, pictures, or sounds for the purpose of executing such scheme or artifice, shall be fined under this title or imprisoned not more than 20 years, or both."

[23]Information for this section derived from Skye L. Perryman. "Mail and Wire Fraud." *American Criminal Law Review,* Vol. 43 (2006), pp. 715–738.

[24]*See Neder* v. *United States,* 527 U.S. 1 (1999).

BOX 6.3

United States v. *Walters,* 997 F.2d 1219 (1993)
United States Court of Appeals for the Seventh Circuit

Judge Easterbrook delivered the opinion of the court.

OPINION

Norby Walters, who represents entertainers, tried to move into the sports business. He signed 58 college football players to contracts while they were still playing. Walters offered cars and money to those who would agree to use him as their representative in dealing with professional teams. Sports agents receive a percentage of the players' income, so Walters would profit only to the extent he could negotiate contracts for his clients. The athletes' pro prospects depended on successful completion of their collegiate careers. To the NCAA [National Collegiate Athletic Association], however, a student who signs a contract with an agent is a professional, ineligible to play on collegiate teams. To avoid jeopardizing his clients' careers, Walters dated the contracts after the end of their eligibility and locked them in a safe. He promised to lie to the universities in response to any inquiries. Walters inquired of sports lawyers at Shea & Gould whether this plan of operation would be lawful. The firm rendered an opinion that it would violate the NCAA's rules but not any [criminal] statute.

Having recruited players willing to fool their universities and the NCAA, Walters discovered that they were equally willing to play false with him. Only 2 of the 58 players fulfilled their end of the bargain; the other 56 kept the cars and money, then signed with other agents. They relied on the fact that the contracts were locked away and dated in the future, and that Walters' business depended on continued secrecy, so he could not very well sue to enforce their promises. When the 56 would neither accept him as their representative nor return the payments, Walters resorted to threats. One player, Maurice Douglass, was told that his legs would be broken before the pro draft unless he repaid Walters' firm. A

75-page indictment charged Walters and his partner Lloyd Bloom with conspiracy, RICO violations (the predicate felony was extortion), and mail fraud.

The fraud: causing the universities to pay scholarship funds to athletes who had become ineligible as a result of the agency contracts. The mail: each university required its athletes to verify their eligibility to play, then sent copies by mail to conferences such as the Big Ten. After a month-long trial and a week of deliberations, the jury convicted Walters and Bloom.

... "Whoever, having devised ... any scheme or artifice to defraud, or for obtaining money or property by means of false or fraudulent pretenses, representations, or promises ... places in any post office or authorized depository for mail matter, any matter or thing whatever to be sent or delivered by the Postal Service ... or knowingly causes [such matter or thing] to be delivered by mail" commits the crime of mail fraud. 18 U.S.C. §1341. Norby Walters did not mail anything or cause anyone else to do so (the universities were going to collect and mail the forms no matter what Walters did), but the Supreme Court has expanded the statute beyond its literal terms, holding that a mailing by a third party suffices if it is "incident to an essential part of the scheme," *Pereira* v. *United States,* 347 U.S. 1 (1954). While stating that such mailings can turn ordinary fraud into mail fraud, the Court has cautioned that the statute "does not purport to reach all frauds, but only those limited instances in which the use of the mails is a part of the execution of the fraud." *Kann* v. *United States,* 323 U.S. 88 (1944). Everything thus turns on matters of degree. Did the schemers foresee that the mails would be used? Did the mailing advance the success of the scheme? Which parts of a scheme are "essential"? Such questions lack obviously right answers, so it is no surprise that each side to this case can cite several of our decisions in support.[25]

(continued)

---

[25]"Compare *United States* v. *McClain,* 934 F.2d 822 (7th Cir. 1991), and *United States* v. *Kwiat,* 817 F.2d 440 (7th Cir. 1987), among cases reversing convictions because use of the mails was too remote or unforeseeable, with *Messinger* v. *United States,* 872 F.2d 217 (7th Cir. 1989), among many cases holding that particular uses of the mails were vital to the scheme and foreseeable."

BOX 6.3

(continued)

"The relevant question...is whether the mailing is part of the execution of the scheme as conceived by the perpetrator at the time." *Schmuck* v. *United States,* 489 U.S. 705 (1989). Did the evidence establish that Walters conceived a scheme in which mailings played a role? We think not—indeed, that no reasonable juror could give an affirmative answer to this question. Walters hatched a scheme to make money by taking a percentage of athletes' pro contracts. To get clients he signed students while college eligibility remained, thus avoiding competition from ethical agents. To obtain big pro contracts for these clients he needed to keep the deals secret, so the athletes could finish their collegiate careers. Thus deceit was an ingredient of the plan. We may assume that Walters knew that the universities would ask athletes to verify that they were eligible to compete as amateurs. But what role do the mails play? The plan succeeds so long as the athletes conceal their contracts from their schools (and remain loyal to Walters). Forms verifying eligibility do not help the plan succeed; instead they create a risk that it will be discovered if a student should tell the truth. *Cf. United States* v. *Maze,* 414 U.S. 395 (1974). And it is the forms, not their mailing to the Big Ten, that pose the risk. For all Walters cared, the forms could sit forever in cartons. Movement to someplace else was irrelevant. The question remains whether Walters caused the universities to use the mails. A person "knowingly causes" the use of the mails when he "acts with the knowledge that the use of the mails will follow in the ordinary course of business, or where such use can reasonably be foreseen." *United States* v. *Kuzniar,* 881 F.2d 466 (7th Cir. 1989). The paradigm is insurance fraud. Perkins tells his auto insurer that his car has been stolen, when in fact it has been sold. The local employee mails the claim to the home office, which mails a check to Perkins. Such mailings in the ordinary course of business are foreseeable. Similarly, a judge who takes a bribe derived from the litigant's bail money causes the use of the mails when the ordinary course is to refund the bond by mail. The prosecutor contends that the same approach covers Walters [but we disagree and do not find Walters guilty of mail fraud].

or titles to cars. The more difficult analysis involves the theft of honest services. The question must be asked who owes a duty to give honest services, such that a scheme to defraud those services through graft, bribery, and illegal gratuities, discussed above, can be criminally prosecuted.

In 2002, Congress passed the Sarbanes–Oxley Act[26] that increased punishment for white-collar crimes from 5 to 20 years in prison.

2. Rico

a. The Statute

The Racketeer Influenced and Corrupt Organizations ("RICO") statute was enacted by Congress in the 1970s to increase federal prosecutorial power to combat organized crime. **RICO** was conceived as a weapon for prosecution of organized crime, but it has become the basis of prosecution against white-collar criminals as well. Given broad and liberal interpretation by courts, RICO has been successfully used to prosecute many organizations, legal and illegal, that engage in a pattern of racketeering activity that harms the public. RICO has both a criminal and civil arm and government entities as well as individuals can sue under RICO for economic relief caused by an organization's criminal activities.

---

[26]Pub. L. No. 107-204, 16 Stat. 745.

**RACKETEER INFLUENCED AND CORRUPT ORGANIZATIONS (RICO);
STATEMENT OF FINDINGS AND PURPOSE; ORGANIZED CRIME CONTROL
ACT OF 1970, 84 STAT. 922-923**

The Congress finds that:

1. organized crime in the United States is a highly sophisticated, diversified, and wide-spread activity that annually drains billions of dollars from America's economy by unlawful conduct and the illegal use of force, fraud, and corruption;

2. organized crime derives a major portion of its power through money obtained from such illegal endeavors as syndicated gambling, loan sharking, the theft and fencing of property, the importation and distribution of narcotics and other dangerous drugs, and other forms of social exploitation;

3. this money and power are increasingly used to infiltrate and corrupt our democratic processes;

4. organized crime activities in the United States weaken the stability of the nation's economic system, harm innocent investors and competing organizations, interfere with free competition, seriously burden interstate and foreign commerce, threaten domestic security, and undermine the general welfare of the Nation and its citizens . . .

    18 U.S.C. §§1961–1962 RICO

The elements the government has to prove for a RICO offense are:

1. The defendant committed two or more predicate acts.
2. The commission of the predicate acts formed a pattern of racketeering activity.
3. The money gained was reinvested in an enterprise.
4. The enterprise affected interstate commerce.

To be charged with a RICO offense, the defendant must first commit two or more predicate acts. The **predicate acts** include a variety of state and federal crimes, but the most notable ones are under state jurisdiction include extortion, kidnapping, murder, arson, robbery bribery, dealing in obscene matter, and drug dealing. The predicate acts under federal jurisdiction are most white-collar crimes such as bankruptcy, securities fraud, welfare fraud, murder for hire, sexual exploitation of children, illegal gambling, and drug dealing, as well as uniquely federal crimes such as counterfeiting and immigration offenses, to name just a few examples.[27]

Critics of RICO prosecutions decry the expansiveness of the federal government's reach to prosecute offenders under the wide variety of predicate crimes. For example, federal agents were prosecuted under RICO for accepting bribes that were deposited in offshore accounts; the predicate act was bribery, and the interstate commerce aspect was money laundering offshore. In another RICO case, the Outlaw Motorcycle Club's illegal drug distribution and prostitution ring were the predicate acts that formed a pattern of racketeering activity; the income derived from such acts was invested and had an effect on interstate commerce. A third successful RICO prosecution was the case of local thugs who offered protection to businesses operating in the gang's territory. The thugs committed extortion (pay the protection money or suffer economic harm); kidnapped, robbed, and killed rival thugs to keep them from profiting on the protection services; and then invested the money gained, affecting interstate commerce.[28]

---

[27]Michelle Sacks, Thomas Coale, and Lara Goldberg. "Racketeer Influenced and Corrupt Organizations." *American Criminal Law Review,* Vol. 42 (2005), pp. 825–874.

[28]Examples taken from the following cases: *United States* v. *Vogt,* 910 F.2d 1184 (4th Cir. 1990); *United States* v. *Watchmaker,* 761 F.2d 1459 (11th Cir. 1985); *United States* v. *Wong,* 40 F.3d 1347 (2d Cir. 1994).

III. BURGLARY

Rule of Law: **Burglary is not stealing: It is breaking and entering a structure with the intent to commit a felony once inside.**

Under common law, burglary was a crime against habitation, the place where one lives, and the elements were that the offender broke into and entered a dwelling during the nighttime. In popular culture, a burglar is a cartoon figure wearing a striped shirt carrying a bag of contraband. Such a portrayal has led the public to conclude that burglary is stealing, but it is so much more. Modern statutes have eliminated the nighttime requirement, and a dwelling can be any type of building, not necessarily a residence. The elements of **burglary** as represented in modern statutes today are:

1.   the unlawful breaking and entering
2.   into any structure
3.   with the intent to commit a felony or felonious theft
4.   once inside.

Burglary's breaking and entering requirement means the changing or altering of a structure to enter with the intent, formed before one does the breaking, to commit a felony, such as rape, arson, or felonious larceny, once inside. The breaking and entering typically means that the structure has to be physically altered to get inside. Walking into an open door is trespass, not breaking. But slipping a credit card to open a lock on a dorm room satisfies the breaking element; and if, at the door, one formed the intent to commit a felony, such as rape, once inside, then the crime is burglary. The breaking element of burglary can be accomplished through fraud and deceipt. One can also burglarize one's own home. For instance, if a husband who has received a court order to stay away from his home to prevent abuse comes to the door of his own home with the intent to harm his wife but tells her that he just "wants to talk" so that she will let him inside, he has committed a burglary.

If an art thief realizes that a socialite has a Renoir painting on her wall and poses as a vacuum salesperson to get inside the house to steal the Renoir, it is burglary. But if the thief did not know that the Renoir or anything of value was inside the house until after he entered the socialite's home, it is not burglary because the intent to commit felonious theft was not formed until after the offender was inside the home. In our opening scenario, Sal committed burglary when he had the intent to commit arson at the teller's house and had to remove a screen to gain entry through the back window. His crime was breaking and entering by altering the structure of the back window with the intent to commit an arson, which is a felony, an intent clearly formed before the breaking. To be guilty of burglary, the offender need not complete the intended felony once inside; an attempt of the intended felony is sufficient.

In Oklahoma, Burglary in the Second Degree is defined by 21 O.S. [Oklahoma Statute] 1971, §1435:

> "Every person who breaks and enters any building or any part of any building, room, booth, tent, railroad car, automobile, truck, trailer, vessel or other structure or erection, in which any property is kept, or breaks into or forcibly opens, any coin operated or vending machine or device with intent to steal any property therein or to commit any felony, is guilty of burglary in the second degree."

Applying the Rule of Law to the Facts: Is it burglary?

- One night, Kyle was visiting his brother at a warehouse where the brother was a security guard. Kyle looked around the warehouse and broke open a door where he thought stereos were stored. He was charged with burglary and raised the defense that he did not steal anything.

Yes, Kyle has committed burglary. Actual stealing is not an element of burglary. "When it is shown that one accused of burglary broke and entered . . . it is presumed he did so with the intent to steal."[29]

IV. ROBBERY

Rule of Law: Robbery is larceny plus assault/battery.

Robbery is the taking of personal property of another by force or threat of force. The distinguishing feature of robbery is that there is an immediate threat of bodily harm to, or the actual use of force on, the victim. So a victim of pickpocketing who never feels his wallet disappearing from his back pocket is not a victim of robbery. But a woman walking down the street whose purse is snatched from her shoulder is the victim of a robbery because of the use of force. The common law elements of **robbery** which are largely retained in statutes today are

1. a trespassory taking
2. and asportation
3. of personal property
4. with force or threat of force
5. from the person or in the presence of another.

How are the elements of robbery used to support a conviction of bank robbery or robbery of a jewelry store, for example? As discussed in talking about constructive possession, a bank teller is presumed to have constructive possession over the money and is therefore deemed under the legal fiction the "owner" of the property for robbery purposes. The same analysis holds true, too, for the jewelry counter cashier. This element distinguishes robbery from larceny in that it involves the aggravating factor of risk of harm to another by forcibly taking property from the person or in the person's presence. If a robber must struggle with the victim to be successful in taking the property, it is robbery, not larceny. But the threat of force will do as well. If the robber passes a note to the bank teller, as Sal and Dom did in the opening chapter scenario, and the note says, "Put all the money in the bag or I'll shoot you," it is robbery by virtue of the threat of force. Similar to the crime of assault, in which threats of a battery are made, this crime must involve a threat that is imminent and capable of being carried out immediately. If the threat of harm is in the future, the crime is extortion, not robbery.

As in most theft crimes, the *mens rea* of the defendant is to take from the owner what rightfully belongs to the owner. In *Arizona* v. *Felix* reprinted in part in Box 6.4, the issue before the court is whether the defendant's conviction for armed robbery can stand given that he used an inhaler rather than a real gun. These cases often arise when the robber does not have a weapon but simulates having one—putting his hand in his jacket, for instance, to make the victim believe he is armed—or when the robber uses a toy gun, for example. In many jurisdictions, the defendant can still be charged with armed robbery.

---

[29] *Lyons* v. *Oklahoma*, 516 P.2d 283 (Okl. Cr. 1973).

BOX 6.4

Arizona v. *Felix*, 737 P.2d 393 (1986)
Court of Appeals of Arizona, Division Two, Department A

Judge Fernandez delivered the opinion of the court.

FACTS

On December 6, 1985, the victim stopped at a self-service Texaco gas station in Casa Grande, Arizona, to purchase gasoline. As the victim left the cashier's booth, [Felix] stepped behind him, poked him in the ribs with something and said either, "I have a light trigger finger" or "I have an itchy trigger finger." The victim asked [Felix] if he had a gun, and [Felix] replied, "Yes, I have a gun. Give me your money." The cashier noticed something was wrong and called the police. As the victim turned away to get his wallet, the cashier yelled at [Felix] to leave. The victim then saw a nasal inhaler in [Felix's] hand. The police arrived soon after and arrested [Felix], who was standing behind the service station. A nasal inhaler was found in [Felix's] right front pants pocket during the booking procedure.

ISSUE

[Was the evidence sufficient to support Felix's conviction for attempted armed robbery, since Felix] argues that a nasal inhaler cannot constitute a simulated weapon?

HOLDING

On appeal a reviewing court does not engage in reweighing the evidence. We find sufficient evidence was produced to support [Felix's] conviction.

REASONING

In 1983 the armed robbery statute was amended to include a simulated deadly weapon. A.R.S. [Arizona Revised Statutes] §13-1904(A) now reads as follows:

A. A person commits armed robbery if, in the course of committing robbery as defined in §13-1902, such person or an accomplice:
   1. Is armed with a deadly weapon or a simulated deadly weapon; or
   2. Uses or threatens to use a deadly weapon or dangerous instrument or a simulated deadly weapon.

Although there are no Arizona cases interpreting the phrase "simulated deadly weapon," it is not a difficult phrase to understand and interpret. A.R.S. §13-105(10) defines "deadly weapon" as "anything designed for lethal use. The term includes a firearm." "Simulate" is a word with a common, easily understood meaning which is defined as follows: "1. To have or take on the appearance, form, or sound of; imitate. 2. To make a pretense of; feign. . . ." *The American Heritage Dictionary* 1142 (2d college ed. 1982). Appellant's use of a nasal inhaler to simulate the barrel of a gun pressed against the victim's body thus falls within the meaning of the term "simulated deadly weapon."

CONCLUSION

[Conviction] Affirmed.

V. ARSON

Under common law, arson was the malicious burning of another's home. As with the other theft crimes, the initial definition did not include much behavior that was definitely criminal, but not covered by the law. For example, it did not count as arson if a homeowner burned his or her own house, or burned his or her business contained in a warehouse, because the definition was restricted to dwellings where people live. Today, **arson** is defined by statute, and the elements are:

1. the intentional and unlawful
2. burning
3. of any structure.

Arson is often separated by degrees, so a burning committed recklessly or negligently is often punished less harshly that a first-degree arson. Such separation of arson into degrees is best illustrated by the Iowa arson statute, reprinted below.

IOWA CODE §712.1 (2008)
Arson defined.

1. Causing a fire or explosion, or placing any burning or combustible material, or any incendiary or explosive device or material, in or near any property with the intent to destroy or damage such property, or with the knowledge that such property will probably be destroyed or damaged, is arson, whether or not any such property is actually destroyed or damaged. Provided, that where a person who owns said property which the defendant intends to destroy or damage, or which the defendant knowingly endangers, consented to the defendant's acts, and where no insurer has been exposed fraudulently to any risk, and where the act was done in such a way as not to unreasonably endanger the life or property of any other person the act shall not be arson.

2. Causing a fire or explosion that damages or destroys property while manufacturing or attempting to manufacture a controlled substance in violation of section 124.401 is arson. Even if a person who owns property which the defendant intends to destroy or damage, or which the defendant knowingly endangers, consents to the defendant's act, and even if an insurer has not been exposed fraudulently to any risk, and even if the act was done in such a way as not to unreasonably endanger the life or property of any person, the act constitutes arson.

Arson is typically a general intent crime. That is, the offender needs only to start the fire to burn a structure, and does not not need to undertake the burning, for the specific result of the structure burning to the ground. In the opening scenario, Sal committed arson when he burned the teller's carpet in her house, even though just a little of the carpet was damaged. Sal will most likely be charged with **criminal mischief,** which is the damaging of property, even if the damage destroys only the property's surface, as when a tombstone or statue is defaced.

VI. Key Terms and Phrases

- arson
- bailee
- bailor
- burglary
- computer crimes
- conversion
- criminal mischief
- embezzlement
- extortion
- false pretenses
- forgery
- identity theft
- larceny
- larceny by trick
- phishing
- real property
- receiving stolen property
- robbery
- uttering

VII. Summary

1. **The legal foundation for possessory rights in property:** Ownership of property, particularly **real property,** which is land, granted many legal privileges that were not available to non–land owners, such as the right to vote or to be elected to office. Early common law theft crimes, called **larceny,** were punishable by death. The early definitions of larceny did not punish many theft situations in which the thief first acquired someone else's property lawfully and then kept it for himself when he was under a legal obligation to return it, or the owner mistakenly trusted the thief with possession of the property and the thief then disposed of it for his or her own personal use. One or example is **larceny by trick,** today called **false pretenses,** which means making a false statement to another (lying) to induce another to turn over title or possession of property (if money). **Conversion** is the legal term whereby the thief transforms (converts) another's property for his own use. A **bailor** owns the property and often trusts a **bailee** who controls and possesses the property for disposition.

2. **The legal basis for the differentiation in property crimes:** Scholars condemn many of the technical distinctions of common law crimes, and the modern trend has been to consolidate theft crimes in one statute. This statute keeps the basic elements of **larceny**—the taking of property without the owner's consent with the intent to permanently deprive the owner—and then defines the distinctions on the basis of how another's property is acquired, lawfully in **embezzlement,** by deceit in **false pretenses,** or by threat in **extortion**. To be found guilty of **receiving stolen property,** the defendant must have knowledge that the property is stolen when he takes possession of it. **Uttering** is passing checks, and **forgery** is signing someone else's signature, which may constitute legal tender, for example on a credit card receipt or at the bottom of a check, in order to steal something of value. **Counterfeit** violations are defined as crimes against the property value of the thing illegally copied and sold as if genuine. The true value of the property is the public's perception that the item is genuine.

3. **Definitions of computer-related crimes:** The advent of technology has created a new way to commit crimes that are, in essence, not necessarily new. Computer crimes are commonly called **cybercrimes** and are defined as thefts and fraud committed by using computers or as theft of a computer itself or of its hardware or software. The Federal Trade Commission has listed simple preventive measures to reduce, if not completely eliminate, the risk that a thief will commit **identity theft** by stealing one's personal identifying information in order to obtain things of value.

Phishing is setting up a realistic-looking fake and fraudulent website that appears to accept legitimate payment for goods and services on the Internet, such as buying items at Internet auction or performing online banking functions.

4. **Definitions of white-collar crime:** White-collar crime is usually business-related crime committed by a variety of fraudulent schemes by people in positions of power. **Mail fraud** is using the mail service and private carriers such as United Parcel Service or Federal Express to commit a scheme to defraud, while **wire fraud** uses telephones, fax machines, and wire transfers for the same purpose. Mail and wire fraud are predicate offenses for Racketeer Influenced and Corrupt Organizations Act ("RICO") offenses. **RICO** was enacted by Congress in 1970 to combat organized crime by enacting a comprehensive criminal statute under which defendants can be convicted if they commit two or more predicate acts, be they state and/or federal crimes, to form a pattern of racketeering and if money obtained from such enterprise affects interstate commerce.

5. **Definitions of burglary, robbery, and arson crimes:** Taking property by force or threat of force is **robbery,** while **burglary** is breaking into and entering a structure with the intent to commit a felony once inside. The intent to commit the felony must be formed before the offender enters to constitute burglary. **Arson** is the malicious burning of a structure, and **criminal mischief** is the damaging of property, either through acts of vandalism or through the specific intent to deface the property. The property need not be destroyed, it is enough if the integrity of the structure is defaced, such as painting a public statue.

VIII. Discussion Questions

1. Do you agree that the *mens rea* of larceny is an issue for the jury to decide? Do you think that it is fair for someone to be convicted of larceny when they intended only to borrow the item? If you lent a car to a friend with the expectation that he or she would return it in good working order, and your friend returned it as a smoking, hulking heap on the back of a flatbed tow truck and made no effort to repair or replace the car, would you feel comfortable saying that your friend did not "steal" the car because he or she had no intent to permanently deprive you of your car, even though you no longer have a car?

2. If you were a company's loss prevention specialist, what procedures would you design or implement to detect or prevent employee embezzlement?

3. In New York City, merchants whose wares are in black plastic bags hand passersby laminated cards with photos of knock-off Gucci, Louis Vuitton, and Donny Brook handbags, all of which look genuine but are, in fact, not. What harm, if any, to the American economy do these illegal vendors represent, and with what crimes, if any, can these vendors be charged?

4. The owner of Toby, billed as "the cutest little bunny on the planet," threatened in www.savetoby.com that on June 30, 2005, "Toby will die. I am going to eat him. I am going to take Toby to a butcher to have him slaughter this cute bunny," if visitors to his website did not send money totaling $50,000 to save Toby's life.[30] Do you think that the elements of extortion are

---

[30]Stephen E. Sachs. "Saving Toby: Extortion, Blackmail, and the Right to Destroy." *Yale Law and Policy Review,* Vol. 24 (2006), pp. 251–261 *citing* http://www.savetoby.com."

met by the bunny's owner promising NOT to destroy his own property in exchange for payment? Most laws are designed to punish those who threaten the property of others, not their own property. If Toby's owner killed and ate him live on webcam, could he be prosecuted under the Model Penal Code definition of extortion that defines a threat as an expression of intent "to inflict any other harm which would not benefit the actor"?

5. Do you think there should be some leniency in the law for those who commit armed robberies without using real weapons? Does using a toy gun pose the same danger to the public as an authentic weapon? What is the public policy supporting the equal punishment of using a nasal inhaler as a weapon?

6. The Drake Hair Braiding Company sold plastic braiding tools that made it appear easy to arrange long hair into complicated French braids. The company sold the braiding tools through sales agents and direct mailings that showed consumers how the sophisticated braids could be made in three easy steps. In reality, the Drake Company knew that the average consumer could not operate the tools correctly and easily. Can the Drake Company be prosecuted under the mail fraud statute for making faulty claims, or is Drake involved in mere puffery about the braiding tools, which is not criminally actionable?

IX. Problem-Solving Exercises

1. SAFECO was a road construction firm whose employees belonged to the Teamsters' Local Union. Mike, the union treasurer, collected members' dues money and deposited it in the Union's bank account. Mike's wife needed an urgent liver transplant, and Mike had to come up with the $10,000 insurance deductible immediately. Mike told the doctor, "I know where I can borrow the money," and he went to the bank and withdrew $10,000 of the Union's money. Mike also told his mother that she needed to put the title of her house in Mike's name because the hospital wanted to make sure that Mike "had enough money." Mike's mother transferred the title to her house to Mike. On the way into the hospital to visit his wife after her surgery, Mike saw a woman carrying beautiful flowers and wrenched the flowers from the woman's hands as he ran past. A police officer caught up to Mike and arrested him. What theft crimes, if any, has Mike committed?

2. An employee was about to be fired from his job as a computer data processor at a large company. Before he left, he changed the passwords on his hard drive to prevent his employer from accessing the encrypted data. The company had no way of retrieving the data without the password, which the employee would not disclose. The employee left the company and was charged under the statute which provides that unauthorized access of a computer is unlawful. Access is defined as "to instruct, communicate with, store data in, retrieve data from, or otherwise make use of the computer." At the time that he changed the passwords, the former employee had authorization to access the computer. Does he have a valid defense? Explain your answer fully.

3. Sam is thinking of having sexual intercourse with Betty in her dorm room. He knows that she is sleeping, but wants to surprise her with a bouquet of roses. So instead of waking her, he jimmies the lock to her dorm room by sliding a plastic credit card by the lock. Once inside, he wakes Betty with the flowers and asks if she'd like to have sex with him. When she refuses, Sam decides to rape Betty. What crimes, if any, has Sam committed?

4. An employment agency that specializes in the hiring of temporary workers in the southeastern states had a steady stream of clients in the wake of the rebuilding efforts after Hurricanes Katrina and Rita wrought mass destruction along the Gulf Coast. A small construction company, Cliffy Enterprises, hired many temporary employees. When the cost of living in parts of Louisiana rose, Cliffy Enterprises began to fire its full-time staff and replace them with the cheaper day laborers supplied by the employment agency. The workers were likely illegal workers who crossed over the Texas border from Mexico and willingly accepted less pay and no employment benefits from Cliffy. In return for finding the workers, Cliffy paid a percentage of the money it saved on employees' salaries to the agency to ensure a steady supply of the cheaper labor. Two of the remaining full-time employees at Cliffy went to the U.S. Attorney's office in New Orleans and reported what they believed to be criminal conduct committed by Cliffy and the employment agency. What would the federal prosecutors have to show to bring a criminal RICO action against Cliffy and the employment agency?

X. World Wide Web Resources

Department of Justice Asset Forfeiture/Money Laundering Section

http://www.usdoj.gov/criminal/afmls.html

U.S. Attorney's Manual on RICO Prosecutions

http://www.usdoj.gov/usao/eousa/foia_reading_room/ usam/title9/110mcrm.htm

Federal Trade Commission, Identity Theft Homepage

http://www.consumer.gov/idtheft

The Internet Crime Complaint Center (IC3) is a partnership between the Federal Bureau of

Investigation (FBI) and the National White Collar Crime Center (NW3C)

http://www.ic3.gov/

XI. Additional Readings and Notes

Burglary

Joshua Getzler. "Use of Force in Protecting Property." *In Memoriam J.W.H. Theoretical Inquiries in Law,* Vol. 7 (2006), pp. 132–166.

Forgery

Jeffrey Malkan. "What is a Copy?" *Cardozo Arts & Entertainment Law Journal,* Vol. 23 (2005), pp. 420–463.

James S. Rogers. "The New Old Law of Electronic Money." *Southern Methodist University Law Review,* Vol. 58 (2005), pp. 1253–1322.

Sara K. Stadler. "Forging a Truly Utilitarian Copyright." *Iowa Law Review,* Vol. 91 (2006), pp. 610–671.

Receiving Stolen Property

Mark Feldstein. "The Jailing of a Journalist: Prosecuting the Press for Receiving Stolen Documents." *Communication Law and Policy,* Vol. 10 (2005), pp. 137–177.

Extortion

Matthew T. Grady. "Extortion May No Longer Mean Extortion After *Scheidler* v. *National Organization for Women, Inc.*" *North Dakota Law Review,* Vol. 81 (2005), pp. 33–73.

Stephen E. Sachs. "Saving Toby: Extortion, Blackmail, and the Right to Destroy." *Yale Law and Policy Review,* Vol. 24 (2005), pp. 251–261.

Identity Theft

Penelope N. Lazarou. "Small Businesses and Identity Theft: Reallocating the Risk of Loss." *North Carolina Banking Institute,* Vol. 10 (2006), pp. 305–327.

Jennifer Lynch. "Identity Theft in Cyberspace: Crime Control Methods and Their Effectiveness in Combating Phishing Attacks." *Berkeley Technology Law Journal,* Vol. 20 (2005), pp. 259–300.

Computer Hacking

Richard W. Downing. "Shoring Up the Weakest Link: What Lawmakers Around the World Need to Consider in Developing Comprehensive Laws to Combat Cybercrime." *Columbia Journal of Transnational Law,* Vol. 43 (2005), pp. 707–762.

David J. Icove, Karl A. Seger, and William VonStorch. *Computer Crime: A Crimefighter's Handbook* (Cambridge, MA: O'Reilly & Associates, 1995).

Orin S. Kerr. "Digital Evidence and the New Criminal Procedure." *Columbia Law Review,* Vol. 105 (2005), pp. 279–318.

CHAPTER

Crimes that Harm the Public

7

The function of wisdom is to discriminate between good and evil

CICERO

CHAPTER OBJECTIVES

Primary Concepts Discussed in This Chapter:

1. Crimes against the public; the criminal justice system's response to addictive crimes such as gambling and drug and alcohol offenses; the definition of public corruption
2. The prosecution of terrorism under criminal law
3. The relevant statutes to prosecute environmental crimes
4. Legal redress when the government causes harm in tort

CHAPTER OUTLINE

Feature: Crimes that harm the public

I. CRIMES AGAINST THE PUBLIC

1. Gambling
2. Prostitution
3. Drug and Alcohol Offenses
   a. Illegal Drugs
   b. Alcohol Offenses
   c. Drinking and Driving
4. Firearm Offenses
5. Breach of the Peace
   a. Riot and Unlawful Assembly
   b. Vagrancy and Panhandling
   Box 7.1 *Loper* v. *New York City Police Department,* 999 F.2d 699 (2d. Cir. 1993)

II. PUBLIC CORRUPTION

1. Bribery
2. Perjury, False Statements, and Obstruction of Justice

III. TERRORISM

1. The USA PATRIOT Act
   a. The Patriot Act at Work
   b. Detention of Terror Suspects
2. Treason
   a. Sedition

IV. ENVIRONMENTAL CRIMES

1. The Statutes
   a. Clean Air Act
   b. Clean Water Act
   c. Resource Conservation and Recovery Act
   d. Comprehensive Environmental Response, Compensation and Liability Act

---

Feature: *Chapter-Opening Case Study: Crimes that Harm the Public*

Richard grew up in a strict religious household where scripture was taken literally. When Richard became an adult and ran for political office, he ran on a platform that the laws of society should reflect religious morality. When he won the election, Richard introduced legislation to make illegal all sexual activity not undertaken for procreation purposes within the confines of a legal marriage.

Before running for office, he had worked in a group home for troubled young adults. One of the residents was Nancy, an 18-year-old who had been kicked out of her house years before. She was working to obtain her General Educational Development diploma. On the weekends, she would perform sexual favors in exchange for cash outside the Empire Bar downtown. The bartender, Charlie, gave Nancy protection from uncooperative or belligerent customers, but soon his fees for such services escalated to $100 a night, and Nancy had to work just to pay Charlie's fees [living off the earnings of a prostitute]. Charlie had to charge Nancy so much money because he was addicted to gambling online. Every night he would log on to an Internet gambling site, enter his credit card number, and lose about $250. To frustrate the federal government's ban on Internet gambling by shutting down U.S. bank transfers, Charlie opened an account in Aruba [illegal gambling on U.S. soil].

After a while, the weekend life took a toll on Nancy, and she began to shoot methamphetamine—"crank"—which reduced her need for sleep so she could keep working [consumption of illegal drugs]. Nancy was caught buying drugs and was arrested and placed in jail.

Little did Richard know that on one occasion when he was away at the state house, his teenage son Mike was hosting a party at his house. An adult supplied a keg of beer for the underage party-goers. One of the teenagers, Sam, got drunk at Richard's house and drove away, killing an innocent pedestrian [adults liable for underage drinking of their guests]. When the pedestrian's family sued Richard, he had to put his house up for sale for money to pay lawyers' fees in his defense.

A presale inspection revealed that the water supply into Richard's house was contaminated. Further inspection revealed that chemicals released by a nearby Army installation that had been closed down since the 1980s had leached into Richard's water supply [Clean Water Act]. A review of the government contracts awarded for proper hazardous waste disposal indicated that Congressman John Sweat had awarded the no-bid contract to a company called "We Clean It." The company's chief operating officer was Sweat's wife Mary, and she had a controlling interest of stock in the clean-up company [public corruption].

When federal agents asked Sweat about the details of awarding the contract to his wife's company, he lied and said that he had no recollection of something so long ago [obstruction of justice].

Upon learning of Congressman Sweat's corruption, 300 protesters gathered outside the U.S. Capitol to demand his removal from office. One protester, Rick, asked passers-by for money [panhandling]. Jan and Theresa not only began chanting for Sweat's impeachment from office, but also started to openly criticize U.S. foreign policy. Some of their statements seemed to support terrorist activities. Undercover police officers followed Jan and Theresa to their car, took down their license plate number, found out where they lived, and, upon learning sufficient identifying information, obtained a warrant under the Foreign Intelligence Surveillance Act. The warrant allowed officers to enter the women's home and plant listening devices without notifying them of the government's surveillance ["sneak and peek" warrants]. On one telephone conversation overheard by the officers, Jan made a donation to a charity based in Afghanistan. When Jan and Theresa were charged under the federal statute making it a crime to provide financial support to terrorist organizations, the women challenged the surveillance as a violation of the Fourth Amendment right against unreasonable search and seizure. The government responded that the PATRIOT Act allows "sneak and peek" warrants when an investigation has national security implications.

How should the above legal situations be resolved?

INTRODUCTION

Crimes against morality and **public corruption** crimes are defined in relation to the religious moralism that has formed the backbone of American law since the country's infancy and on the moral precept that one should not steal, lie, or otherwise take advantage of a public trust. Moral crimes are typically *mala prohibitia,* behavior made criminal by statute for which there is little criminal sanction. They are typified by regulatory crimes such as speeding, food preparation transgressions, and underage drinking, and are distinct from *mala in se* crimes—inherently evil acts such as rape, murder, or incest. Some crimes against morality (and hence against the public) are called victimless crimes because the people who engage in them ostensibly do so consensually.[1] These crimes include gambling, prostitution, and the use of illicit drugs. "Those who favor criminalization of such behaviors insist most fundamentally that all societies need to enforce a common morality and that such behavior fall inside the limits of what should be permitted by law. They further maintain that these behaviors inflict harm on those who engage in them, and that a decent society has the obligation to protect its less careful members from their own self-destructive impulses."[2] The common expression "you can't legislate morality" means that if people are generally predisposed to behave in a morally repulsive manner, no law enacted by a legislative body will instill an inner moral compass into them.

I. CRIMES AGAINST THE PUBLIC

1. Gambling

Rule of Law: Gambling not sponsored by the state is illegal.

---

[1]Steven Vago. *Law and Society,* 8th ed. (Upper Saddle River, NJ: Pearson Education, Inc., 2006).

[2]Robert F. Meier and Gilbert Geis. *Victimless Crime? Prostitution, Drugs, Homosexuality, Abortion* (Los Angeles: Roxbury Publishing, 1997).

Gambling is placing money, bets, and wagers that a certain outcome in a game of chance or sporting event will occur. In the past, bookmaking operations and sports betting were neighborhood affairs, but "[n]owadays more than 90 percent of Americans live within 200 miles of a legal casino, where people legally bet some $640 billion a year and lose about $51 billion of that amount."[3] States have legalized certain types of gambling, such as participating in multistate lotteries and betting on animal races. State governments garner public support for their gambling business by linking gambling proceeds to the public benefit, such as education (in Missouri) or programs for senior citizens (in Pennsylvania). Native Americans control their own tribal lands and have opened casinos and entertainment resorts on their land, in Connecticut, Arizona, and other states.

Enforcement efforts aimed at curtailing illegal gambling have been generally ineffective because most people who engage in the act do not complain to the police. Federal law prohibiting illegal gambling is related to interstate commerce laws because payments or wagers may be transmitted across state lines. Federal law enforcement efforts against gambling tend to focus on organized crime; all such statutes must have an interstate commerce nexus for Commerce Clause jurisdiction. Because of the nature of most illegal small-time gambling operations, most prosecution efforts fall on local law enforcement.

While many people may be arrested for illegal gambling, few are convicted. Society considers catching rapists, murderers, and child molesters to be a more worthy goal of police law enforcement efforts. But gambling, legal or illegal, may lead to problems in society. Studies show that the people who spend money on gambling are the ones who are least able to afford it. Moreover, gambling can be an addictive activity. People may remain committed to engaging in inherently destructive behavior because they are waiting to hit it big. A visit to a casino will find generally older Americans playing one slot machine repeatedly, fearful of getting up because the odds are that the machine has to hit sometime and they fear it will be once they leave that chair. "Elder adults remain a prime target for the [gambling] industry. Casinos, in particular, court those over 65 and older with cheap buffets, free drinks, free transportation, money-back coupons, and other discounts"[4] to entice seniors with lots of free time on their hands into the casinos to spend their money.

Gambling on the Internet is very lucrative, and like most Internet-based activities, it is very difficult to control through law enforcement activities. On October 14, 2006, President George W. Bush signed the Unlawful Internet Gambling Enforcement Act, 31 U.S.C. §§5361–5367 which made it illegal for American banks to transfer money to online gambling sites. Many online gambling sites operate internationally and skirt the law by having American banks transfer funds to foreign banks, which then distribute the money to the gambling sites.[5] According to the Congressional Budget Office, which conducted a study of the costs associated with the implementation of the new law, the law prohibits "businesses from accepting credit cards, checks, or other bank instruments from gamblers who illegally bet over the Internet." Within 270 days of the law's enactment, federal regulatory agencies were required to draft policies "that could be used by financial institutions to identify and block gambling-related transactions that are transmitted through their payment systems. Compliance with those prohibitions and regulations would be enforced by various federal agencies as well as state governments, and violations would be subject to new civil remedies and criminal penalties."[6] But America's gambling laws are inconsistent; the 1978 Interstate Horseracing Act allows for off-track betting on horses, including over the Internet, but not other offshore betting

---

[3]Steven Vago. *Law and Society,* 8th ed. (Upper Saddle River, NJ: Pearson Education, Inc., 2006).

[4]*Ibid.*

[5]Charles Murray. "The G.O.P.'s Bad Bet." *The New York Times,* October 19, 2006, p. A29.

[6]Peter H. Fontaine. Congressional Budget Office, May 26, 2006. http://www.cbo.gov/doc.cfm?index=7230.

that the country deems a threat to "public order and public morals."[7] In our chapter's opening scenario, Charlie's Aruba account to gamble online would violate U.S. law.

In March 2007, the founder of BetOnSports, Gary Kaplan, was arrested in the Dominican Republic for extradition to Missouri. There, he and the cofounder of the company, David Carruthers, were named in a 22-count indictment related to conspiracy, fraud, and racketeering on taking Internet gambling bets from patrons in the United States. The racketeering conspiracy charge alleges that the defendants agreed to conduct an enterprise through a pattern of racketeering acts, including repeated mail fraud, wire fraud, operation of an illegal gambling business, and money laundering.

Applying the Rule of Law to the Facts: Is it illegal gambling?

- For six years, a noted professional athlete transferred pit bulls across state lines to breed in his kennel. On some occasions, other dog owners would bring their dogs to the athlete's estate to fight the athlete's dogs. The athlete gave money to his friends to establish a purse, the value of which was estimated at hundreds to thousands of dollars, to be won by the owner of the victorious dogs. Only close associates were able to attend the fights, and some made side bets on their own about the outcome of the dog fight. The athlete never made side bets on the dog fights. Is this activity, setting aside the cruelty-to-animals issue, illegal gambling?

Yes, supplying the necessary funds for the purse to be won by the owner of the winning dog is illegal gambling.

2. Prostitution

Rule of Law: Prostitution is exchanging sexual services for a thing of value.

Often called "the world's oldest profession," prostitution is typically defined as "the market exchange of sex for money." Feminist scholars write "We use the term "money" for simplicity but intend it to encompass both money and money's worth so as not to exclude bartering situations in which sex is exchanged for shelter, drugs, or other goods or services."[8] The term "john" was invented by women in the business to convey the notion that men who purchase sex are indistinguishable from one another. As a practice, for generations prostitution has defied efforts to eliminate it. It continues to survive "because it offers a commodity that cannot be readily found in other sexual arenas. That commodity involves the marketplace exchange of money for the unemotional provision of sexual gratification with no strings attached."[9] Prostitution is called a victimless crime because it appears that the two parties are engaging in consensual sexual conduct, but in reality, sex workers are a vulnerable population. Most prostitutes have a history of childhood physical and sexual abuse, many were recruited into the trade at age 12 or 13 years old, and they have an extraordinarily high rate of homelessness, drug use, and victimization by physical and sexual assaults.[10] New York Governor Eliot Spitzer resigned on March 12, 2008, when he was exposed as a regular customer of a prostitution ring; it was reported that at least one woman he had paid for sex was formerly homeless and turned to prostitution to pay her rent. In 1988, 130 sex workers were interviewed in San Francisco, California, to study how violent their lives were. The respondents reported that since entering prostitution, 82% of them had been assaulted, 68% had being raped, and 48% had been raped more than five times.[11] It is a crime to be a prostitute or to live off the income

---

[7]"Authorities Arrest Founder of Internet Gambling Site." *The New York Times,* March 31, 2007. p. B9.

[8]Beverly Balos and Mary Louise Fellows. "A matter of Prostitution: Becoming Respectable." *New York University Law Review,* Vol. 74 (1999), pp. 1220–1303.

[9]Robert F. Meier and Gilbert Geis. *Victimless Crime? Prostitution, Drugs, Homosexuality, Abortion* (Los Angeles: Roxbury Publishing, 1997).

[10]Ine Vanwesenbeeck. *Prostitutes' Well Being and Risk* (Amsterdam: VU Uitguerij, 1994).

[11]Melissa Farley and Howard Barkan. "Prostitution, Violence and Posttraumatic Stress Disorder." *Women & Health,* Vol. 27, No. 3 (1993), pp. 37–49.

of a prostitute. In our opening scenario, Nancy is guilty of being a prostitute and Charlie is guilty of living off of her earnings. Prostitutes can be either male or female, but their customers are overwhelmingly male.

The Model Penal Code §251.2 defined prostitution and related sex offenses as follows.

MPC §251.1 OPEN LEWDNESS
1. <u>Prostitution.</u> A person is guilty of prostitution, a petty misdemeanor, if he or she:
    a. is an inmate of a house of prostitution or otherwise engages in sexual activity as a business; or
    b. loiters in or within view of any public place for the purpose of being hired to engage in sexual activity . . .
2. <u>Promoting Prostitution.</u> . . . The following acts shall, without limitation of the foregoing, constitute promoting prostitution:
    a. owning, controlling, managing, supervising or otherwise keeping, alone or in association with others, a house of prostitution or a prostitution business; or
    b. procuring an inmate for a house of prostitution or a place in a house of prostitution for one who would be an inmate; or
    c. encouraging, inducing, or otherwise purposely causing another to become or remain a prostitute . . .

Because prostitution is viewed as a public nuisance, most people arrested for such crimes spend little to no time in jail and are often released with minimal bail. If convicted, they usually serve light sentences. In Las Vegas, Nevada, prostitution is legal. There are certain regulatory activities associated with the places that allow prostitution; women must have physical examinations and condom use is required.

One common crime associated with prostitution is the solicitation [asking] of another for sexual favors. In 2007, two elected officials were arrested for soliciting sex in men's rooms from undercover officers. One was Idaho Senator Larry Craig, who eventually pled guilty to disorderly conduct and then tried, unsuccessfully, to withdraw his guilty plea and another was Florida State Representative Robert W. Allen, a legislative aide for presidential hopeful John McCain.

3. Drug and Alcohol Offenses

a. Illegal Drugs

The history of criminalizing illegal drug possession and use has been a hodgepodge effort of legal reform. In the early twentieth century, opiates and cocaine were legal medicine. In order to limit opiate ingestion and the addiction often associated with opium use, Congress passed the Pure Food and Drug Act of 1906,[12] which was:

> . . . a direct effort to place some federal controls on patent medicines that contained opiates, cocaine, and other drugs. By requiring manufacturers of over-the-counter patent medicines to label their products and to disclose the amount of drugs contained in them, the government hoped to greatly reduce the use of such medicines.[13]

The next federal effort at drug control was The Harrison Act (1914), which allowed certain opiates to be used as medicine while also criminalizing their sale and possession. The Marijuana Tax Act passed in 1937 criminalized the sale of marijuana, a drug associated with criminal activity. There was little, if any, scientific data or research to support any definitive conclusions about the effects of recreational drug use, other than the addictive nature of such use, but illegal drug use was soon commonplace in American society. During the 1940s and 1950s, avant-garde artists such as writers Jack Kerouac,

---

[12]Public Law 59-384, 59th Congress, Session I, June 30, 1906.

[13]Steven R. Belenko, ed. *Drugs and Drug Policy in America: A Documentary History* (Westport, CT: Greenwood Press, 2000).

author of *On The Road* (1957); William S. Burroughs, author of *The Naked Lunch* (1959); and poet Allen Ginsburg, author of "Howl" (1956), began to explore and advertise through literature the liberating effects of drugs. At the same time, some of the most influential jazz musicians of the day succumbed to the ravages of their addictions. These included Charlie "Bird" Parker, Billie Holiday, and Miles Davis. In the 1960s and 1970s, many young American servicemembers brought back from Vietnam and Laos heroin addictions, while college students not only smoked marijuana freely but also experimented with lysergic acid diethylamide ("LSD") and other mind-altering substances.

When it was clear that the American middle class was infected with drug use and addiction—problems formerly believed to be the exclusive province of the inner-city poor—President Nixon advanced an aggressive law enforcement and drug treatment approach as a way to reduce drug-related crime. In 1970, Congress passed the Comprehensive Drug Abuse Prevention and Control Act ("Controlled Substances Act"), which consolidated the numerous federal drug laws then in existence. President Nixon also created the Drug Enforcement Administration ("DEA") to oversee federal enforcement of federal drug laws. The new effort to combat illegal drugs was a multipronged approach that attacked the importation of drugs from foreign countries, incapacitated the distribution chain from supplier to street dealer, and provided prevention and treatment programs for the buyers and addicts. At the behest of Nixon, Congress also funded money for research and training on substance abuse issues, and funded the establishment of treatment centers across the country. From 1970 to 1974, Nixon also spent an additional $400 million dollars on drug prevention education. He named Dr. Jerome H. Jaffe, who pioneered the use of methadone to treat heroin addiction, as the first director of the newly created Special Action office for Drug Abuse Prevention, thereby elevating drug prevention to the forefront of the national consciousness and presenting it as a preventive measure to reduce drug-associated crime.[14] "[T]he positive effects of this approach resulted in fewer arrestees with addiction, a dramatic decline in the national crime rate, and a drop in the number of heroin-related deaths. As Nixon left office, he could claim delivery on his promise to reduce drug-related crime, the first reduction in seventeen years."[15]

Experts agree that drug prevention education in schools has the biggest and most dramatic effect on whether drug use becomes prevalent in adulthood. At a congressional hearing in 2005, Representative Souder of Indiana remarked that national drug use prevention programs were "a vital component of any drug control strategy" and that prevention was "the most important component since it is a demand for drugs that attracts supply. Prevention aimed at reducing drug use by young people is, in turn, the most important kind of demand reduction."[16]

But federal drug policy shifted dramatically in the 1980s and 1990s. That era's "war on drugs" established many of the drug laws we live with today, such as those that established mandatory minimum prison sentences for offenders who dealt with specific quantities of "any mixture or substance" of specific drugs. Mandatory sentencing had the most impact on the cocaine/crack trade. Crack is cocaine that is boiled down, diluted with additives such as baking soda, and crystallized into a "rock" form, which the user typically smokes for an automatic stimulating effect on the brain. The crack scourge took hold in the inner cities because crack cocaine was relatively inexpensive compared with other illegal drugs. During the 1980s, pure powder cocaine sold for

---

[14]David F. Musto. *The American Disease: Origins of Narcotic Control* (New York: Oxford University, 1987).

[15]E. Michelle Tupper. "Children Lost in the Drug War: A Call for Drug Policy Reform to Address the Comprehensive Needs of Family." *Georgetown Journal on Poverty Law & Policy,* Vol. 12 (2005), pp. 325–354.

[16]Committee on Government Reform. *Drug Prevention Programs and the Fiscal Year 2006 Drug Control Budget: Is the Federal Government Neglecting Illegal Drug Use Prevention?* (Serial No. 109 71) (Washington, DC: Government Printing Office, 2005).

hundreds of dollars for an ounce while one rock of diluted crack sold for $5–10. The shift away from a comprehensive approach to education and drug prevention programs to harsher sentences and punitive sanctions led to an explosion in the prison population, especially among the poor. Legal scholar Steven Vago writes about the changes in the criminal justice system as a result of the drug war:

> In 1996, more than 1.5 million people were arrested for drug offenses; the nation's prisons, which in 1980 housed fewer than 30,000 drug offenders, harbored nearly 300,000 less [than 20 years] later. Drug offenders comprised a third of all persons convicted of a felony in State courts and . . . [i]n 2004, the United States had the highest substance abuse rate in any industrialized nation. The American market absorbs well over 60 percent of the world's production of illegal drugs.[17]

Drug education and prevention efforts have seen much less success in the face of the extraordinary addictive qualities of crack cocaine and methamphetamine. For many people in society, lawmakers and lawbreakers alike, marijuana has come to be viewed as a drug that is in a category different from cocaine, heroin, or the other opiate-based stimulants and depressants. There are initiatives across the country to decriminalize the possession and use of marijuana, and, as discussed in chapter 1, some states have allowed the legal use of marijuana for medicinal purposes.

b. Alcohol Offenses

Alcohol offenses cover a wide range of behaviors from being intoxicated in public to supplying minors with alcohol. The early efforts to control alcohol consumption surrounded temperance movements typically led by distraught wives who wanted to prevent alcohol from destroying their husbands, who not only were frequently drunk, but spent money on alcohol rather than on family obligations. The movement's high point of success was 1919, when the Eighteenth Amendment to the Constitution was passed. This amendment outlawed the sale, manufacture, and distribution of alcohol in the United States. The period during which it was in effect was known as Prohibition. The Eighteenth Amendment was repealed in 1933 by the Twenty-First Amendment; most historians now consider the prohibition experiment to have been unsuccessful and costly. Some social scientists credit prohibition with the rise in power of organized crime, which was willing to supply bootleg liquor to Americans who were unwilling to forego alcohol.

But not all government efforts to control alcohol consumption have been so disastrous. In the mid-1980s, the federal government responded to the great number of drunk-driving fatalities by enacting the National Minimum Drinking Age Act ("NMDA"),[18] which tied federal funding for state transportation needs to the state's minimum drinking age of 21 years old.

To prevent their teenage children from endangering themselves or others by drinking and driving, some parents host parties at which teens can drink as long as they do not drive. Parents supply the alcohol to the underage teenagers, itself a crime. All states have laws that punish adults who corrupt minors by providing drugs or alcohol or by introducing underage individuals to sexual activity. Can a parent who hosts a party for teenagers with alcohol be held responsible if one of the guests leaves and hurts an innocent victim?

Massachusetts law provides that "whoever furnishes . . . alcohol for a person under 21 years of age shall be punished by a fine of not more than $2,000 or by imprisonment for not more than one year or both."[19] In 2004, Mr. and Mrs. Moulton of Danvers, Massachusetts, allowed their teenage daughter and her friends to drink Jack Daniels

---

[17]Steven Vago. *Law and Society,* 8th ed. (Upper Saddle River, NJ: Pearson Education, Inc., 2006).

[18]Pub. L. No. 98-363, 6(a), 98 Stat. 435, 437 (1984) (codified as amended at 23 U.S.C. §158 (2000).

[19]Mass. Gen. Laws Ch. 138, 34 (2004).

whiskey, beer, rum, and other intoxicants at a party at their house to celebrate after their high school prom.[20] The Moultons took all of the kids' car keys, and Mr. Moulton even joined the kids' celebration. For their efforts in trying, in their view, to protect the kids from drinking and driving, the parents received probation for 18 months, were fined $500, and were ordered to complete 40 hours of community service. Many states have laws that make it a crime for an adult to furnish liquor to individuals who are not yet 21 years old. Such laws can be difficult to enforce, considering that 18-year-olds are legal adults. Can and should people who supply an underage drinker with alcohol be responsible if that person is later involved in a car accident or otherwise hurts someone?

c. Drinking and Driving

Driving under the influence ("DUI") laws generally punish people for operating a motor vehicle such as a car, truck, or boat while under the influence of alcohol. If a person kills someone while operating a motor vehicle while under the influence, the crime is generally manslaughter. Often, to be convicted of being legally impaired, the driver's blood alcohol content ("BAC") must be at least 0.08, as determined by a breathalyzer test administered on the scene or by a blood test taken at a hospital. California's vehicle Code provides, in part, that

§23152

a. It is unlawful for any person who is under the influence of any alcoholic beverage or drug, or under the combined influence of any alcoholic beverage and drug to drive a vehicle.

b. It is unlawful for any person who has a 0.08 percent or more, by weight, of alcohol in his or her blood to drive a vehicle.

c. It is unlawful for any person who is addicted to the use of any drug to drive a vehicle. (It is unlawful for any person who has 0.04 percent or more, by weight, of alcohol in his or her blood to drive a commercial motor vehicle, as defined in section 15210).

Some state statutes, such as Arizona's DUI law, which follows, use the concept of "controlling" the vehicle as opposed to "driving" the vehicle. Do you think it makes a difference for finding someone guilty?

§28-1381. DRIVING OR ACTUAL PHYSICAL CONTROL WHILE UNDER THE INFLUENCE

It is unlawful for a person to drive or be in actual physical control of a vehicle in this state under any of the following circumstances:

1. While under the influence of intoxicating liquor, any drug, a vapor-releasing substance containing a toxic substance or any combination of liquor, drugs or vapor-releasing substances if the person is impaired to the slightest degree.

2. If the person has an alcohol concentration of 0.10 or more within two hours of driving or being in actual physical control of the vehicle and the alcohol concentration results from alcohol consumed either before or while driving or being in actual physical control of the vehicle.

3. While there is any drug defined in section 13-3401 or its metabolite in the person's body.

If the vehicle is a commercial motor vehicle that requires a person to obtain a commercial driver's license as defined in section 28-3001 and the person has an alcohol concentration of 0.04 or more.

---

[20]*See* William J. Bernat. Party on? The excellent adventures of social host liability in Massachusetts. *Suffolk University Law Review,* Vol. 39 (2006) pp. 981–1000.

What does the Arizona statute mean by having physical control? Could a driver who is asleep at the wheel while drunk and parked in a parking lot be charged with DUI? If a driver leaves a bar, gives his friend the keys, and decides to sleep it off in the car and tells his friend to return in the morning, can the driver be arrested for DUI because he is "in control" of the vehicle, even if he cannot drive it? The problem with drinking and driving is, of course, the crimes people commit when in the car and intoxicated.

People who drink and drive and kill innocent people are almost never charged with murder because they lack the specific intent to kill. But in October 2006, Martin R. Heidgen was convicted of murder in New York for driving the wrong way on a highway when he smashed head-on into a limousine with returning wedding guests, killing the chauffeur, Stanley Rabinowitz, and 7-year-old Katie Flynn. It took the jury five days to reach a decision, and twice the jurors reported that they were deadlocked, but the judge admonished the jury to keep deliberating. Analysts say the jury was most likely struggling with reconciling an activity that some adults engage in—drinking and driving—and equating that behavior with the actions of a murderer who may shoot to kill another.[21]

4. Firearm Offenses

Rule of Law: The U.S. Supreme Court has not interpreted the Second Amendment to allow citizens to possess firearms.

The Second Amendment states, "A well regulated Militia, being necessary to the security of a free State, the right of the people to keep and bear Arms, shall not be infringed." Popular culture has interpreted the Second Amendment as a right to bear arms, but courts have not recognized a federal constitutional right to own firearms. It is a privilege to own guns, and such a privilege can be regulated or removed by a governmental body. Gun ownership is a highly regulated and licensed activity, and some people are categorically prohibited from legally owning firearms, such as convicted felons, people addicted to drugs or any controlled substance, servicemembers who received dishonorable discharges, fugitives from justice, and mentally disabled people. The Gun Control Act of 1968[22] is the federal law that regulates gun ownership, and like every federal law, is dependent upon an interstate commerce nexus. The federal gun law prohibits the interstate transfer of firearms and limits the transfer and sale of weapons to licensed firearm dealers. The Brady Handgun Violence Prevention Act[23] was named after President Reagan's Press Secretary James Brady, who was critically wounded by a handgun during John W. Hinckley, Jr.'s assassination attempt on Reagan's life in 1981. "The Brady Bill" mandated a waiting period before people could purchase a handgun in any state, a requirement no longer in effect now that states can run National Instant Criminal Background Checks to get background information quickly.

The U.S. Supreme Court held, in *Printz* v. *United States,* 521 U.S. 898 (1997), that the federal government could not impose the financial burden upon the states to run background checks. Such a burden would run afoul of the Tenth Amendment, which says, "The powers not delegated to the United States by the Constitution, nor prohibited by it to the States, are reserved to the States respectively, or to the people." In 1994, the federal government enacted a ban on possessing assault weapons in the Violent Crime and Law Enforcement Act, but that Act expired in 2004, although many laws remain on the books to restrict the sale and possession of certain weapons such as machine guns. Despite the many federal laws that regulate weapons, state and local law enforcement are responsible for the majority of firearm licensing and registration requirements.

---

[21]Paul Vitello. "Alcohol, a Car and a Fatality. Is it Murder?" *The New York Times,* October 22, 2006, p. 1.

[22]Pub. L. No. 90-618, 82 Stat. 1213, now codified in Chapter 44 of Title 18, United States Code.

[23]Pub. L. No. 103-159, 107 Stat. 1536 (Nov. 30, 1993).

In a recent challenge to the local prohibition on possessing firearms in one's home, the case *Parker* v. *District of Columbia,* 478 F.3d 370 (2d. Cir. 2007), held in favor of the D.C. residents in holding that the Second Amendment did protect an individual's right to have handguns in the home. The District is our seat of government and has long prohibited its residents from legally being armed in their homes. In 2007, the U.S. Supreme Court granted *certiorari* to hear the appeal, and it will decide whether the Second Amendment grants individuals a right to bear arms.

In stark contrast to the District of Columbia's former law banning handguns in the home, in 1982 the city of Kennesaw, Georgia, enacted city ordinance 34-1a under the Civil Emergencies provision that required heads of households to maintain firearms. After Hurricane Katrina hit the Gulf Coast in 2005, the town of Greenleaf, Idaho, adopted a similar measure out of concern that it would get an influx of people displaced from Louisiana and Mississippi. Ordinance 208, sponsored by Steven Jett, who said, "We could get refugees,"[24] was passed on November 14, 2006:

"HEADS OF HOUSEHOLDS TO MAINTAIN FIREARMS"
In order to provide for the emergency management of the city, and further in order to provide for and protect the safety, security and general welfare of the city, and its inhabitants, it is recommended that every household residing in the city limits maintain a firearm, together with ammunition therefore, and obtain appropriate training relating to proper, safe and lawful handling of firearms." Section 2, Chapter 6, Subsection 2 of the Greenleaf, Idaho City Code.[25]

Applying the Rule of Law to the Facts: Do people have a right to bear arms?

- Freddy was a police officer who was convicted of misdemeanor domestic violence for beating his wife. State and federal law prevented convicted batterers from possessing firearms. Freddy said his right to earn a living trumped licensing laws on gun possession. Which side is correct?

The government. Freddy can be legally disqualified from possessing a firearm even though his job requires it as a condition of employment, so he must find a different profession.[26]

5. Breach of the Peace

Rule of Law: The First Amendment grants the right to peaceably assemble, but no such gathering may advance criminal objectives.

a. Riot and Unlawful Assembly

As discussed in chapter 3, people have a First Amendment right to get together in a peaceful manner. There are times when crowds become unruly, and there are various laws to punish people for their behavior when they are in a group. **Unlawful assembly** as a crime occurs when police officers ask a group of five or more people to disperse and they refuse. They can be charged with unlawful assembly, which is typically a misdemeanor. Similar crimes are **disorderly conduct,** in which people get together and disturb

---

[24]Jesse Harlan Alderman. "Idaho Town Asks Residents to Own Guns." *The Associated Press,* November 16, 2005. http://news.yahoo.com/s/ap/20061116/ap_on_re_us/gun_law&printer=1.
It is worth noting that the town of Greenleaf was founded by pacifist Quakers who are nonviolent and oppose gun ownership, and the law provides for exemptions based on religious reasons. Also, note that contrary to Jett's assertion and fear, Americans cannot be refugees within their own country.

[25]William Yardley. "Proposal Urges Citizens to Arm for City Growth." *The New York Times,* October 12, 2006, p. A16.

[26]*Gillespie* v. *City of Indianapolis,* 185 F.3d 693 (7th Cir. 1999).

the peace but do not intend to incite violence, and **disturbing the peace,** in which a party or some other gathering produces noise late at night when people are trying to sleep. **Riots** are criminal because people who participate in riots are often intent on mass destruction of public and private property, and people may be harmed or killed. The state of California is well-known for riots in its major cities that are sparked by perceived injustice at the hands of the criminal justice system. What separates a riot from an unlawful assembly is the intent and actions to cause damage. The elements of a riot are:

1. at least three people
2. sharing a common purpose
3. to commit, or facilitate the commission of, a felony or misdemeanor,
4. with intent to prevent or coerce official action or the use of a firearm.[27]

The test to determine whether a speaker's words are a call to others to engage in lawless conduct was developed by the U.S. Supreme Court in *Brandenburg* v. *Ohio,* 395 U.S. 444 (1969). The case revolved around an incident in which the leader of the Ku Klux Klan extorted his followers that "if our President, our Congress, our Supreme Court, continues to suppress the white, Caucasian race, it's possible that there might have to be some revengeance [sic] taken." Brandenburg was convicted under the Ohio statute that made it criminal to encourage "the duty, necessity, or propriety of crime, sabotage, violence, or unlawful methods of terrorism as a means of accomplishing . . . political reform . . ." On appeal, the high Court overturned his conviction, stating that in order for Brandenburg's speech to present a "clear and present" danger to others, it had to both incite or produce "imminent lawless action" and be "likely to incite or produce such action." Since Brandenburg's speech did not meet both prongs of the clear and present danger test, his speech was legal.

Police officers must determine whether speakers are peaceful demonstrators whom they must protect from hecklers—for example, anti-war protesters heckled by people who pass by. The police must generally protect the peaceful protesters and arrest the hecklers. Or, if the officers determine that the antiwar speech is threatening and is promoting immediate lawless action, they must arrest the protesters.

Applying the Rule of Law to the Facts: When is a crowd guilty of riot?

- A large, noisy crowd had gathered around an intersection in the city. Police arrived and were dispersing the crowd when a man began shouting from the doorway of a nearby bar. The man refused to obey police requests to go inside the bar, and when he refused, they tried to arrest him. Once inside, police and bar patrons engaged in a "tug of war" over the man. One bar maid began to scream obscene remarks at the police—remarks that were intended to excite patrons, to cause the patrons to prevent the man's arrest, and to encourage them to harm the police. She was later arrested on a charge of riot "by participating with two or more persons in a course of disorderly conduct, to wit: making an unreasonable noise and offensively coarse utterance and addressing abusive language to Police Officers, with intent to prevent official action, to wit: dispersal by members of the Police Department of a crowd of more than 10 persons."[28]

This incident is not a riot. The bar maid was trying to help the man elude what she perceived to be an unlawful arrest. The elements of riot did not exist, since she did not have, as her intent with two others, the sole purpose of preventing the police from doing their job as they tried to disperse the crowd, because the crowd they were trying to disperse was outside the bar.

---

[27]*Feinstein* v. *City of New York,* 283 N.Y.S. 335 (1935).

[28]Facts adapted from *Squires* v. *State,* 277 A.2d 686 (Del. 1971).

An example of a state statute that defines riot, unlawful assembly, disorderly conduct, and breach of the peace is Mississippi's law:

MISSISSIPPI BREACH OF THE PEACE DEFINITION OF RIOT AND UNLAWFUL ASSEMBLY; DISORDERLY CONDUCT; CERTAIN ACTS PERFORMED WITH INTENT TO PROVOKE BREACH OF PEACE; PENALTIES.[29]

1. Whoever with intent to provoke a breach of the peace, or under circumstances such that a breach of the peace may be occasioned thereby:

   a. crowds or congregates with others in or upon shore protecting structure or structures, or a public street or public highway, or upon a public sidewalk, or any other public place, or in any hotel, motel, store, restaurant, lunch counter, cafeteria, sandwich shop, motion picture theatre, drive-in, beauty parlor, swimming pool area, or any sports or recreational area or place, or any other place of business engaged in selling or serving members of the public, or in or around any free entrance to any such place of business or public building, or to any building owned by another individual, or a corporation, or a partnership or an association, and who fails or refuses to disperse and move on when ordered so to do by any law enforcement officer of any municipality, or county, in which such act or acts are committed, or by any law enforcement officer of the State of Mississippi, or any other authorized person, or

   b. insults or makes rude or obscene remarks or gestures, or uses profane language, or physical acts, or indecent proposals to or toward another or others, or disturbs or obstructs or interferes with another or others, or

   c. while in or on any public bus, taxicab, or other vehicle engaged in transporting members of the public for a fare or charge, causes a disturbance or does or says, respectively, any of the matters or things mentioned in paragraph (b) to, toward, or in the presence of any other passenger on said vehicle, or any person outside of said vehicle or in the process of boarding or departing from said vehicle, or any employee engaged in and about the operation of such vehicle, or

   d. refuses to leave the premises of another when requested so to do by any owner, lessee, or any employee thereof, shall be guilty of disorderly conduct, which is made a misdemeanor, and, upon conviction thereof, shall be punished by a fine of not more than two hundred dollars ($200.00), or imprisonment in the county jail for not more than four (4) months, or by both such fine and imprisonment . . .

b. Vagrancy and Panhandling

Rule of Law: It is not a crime to depend on the generosity and kindness of strangers.

Is it a crime for a **panhandler** to ask strangers on the street for money? What if the panhandler stalks people at automated teller machines ("ATMs"), bus stops, or bank doors and follows people until they make a generous donation to his cup: is his behavior then criminal? In times past, a **vagrant** or "hobo" was a person who had no home, who drifted from place to place, and who worked odd jobs for food and a little money before moving on to the next town. Most state laws outlawing vagrancy were broad and intended to punish a wide variety of undesirable behaviors. More recently, in an effort to curb gang activity, states have passed antiloitering statutes that prohibit young people from congregating on street corners. These laws have survived challenges on the basis of the First Amendment right to peaceably assemble, because states have a legitimate law enforcement need to prevent crime and can do so by enforcing curfews and other crime prevention measures.

---

[29]Mississippi Code Ann. §97-35-3 (2008).

However, at least one federal appellate court has held that a law designed to protect the public from people asking for money went too far and violated the panhandler's constitutional rights, as reprinted in part in Box 7.1.

BOX 7.1

Loper v. *New York City Police Department*, 999 F.2d 699 (1993)
United States Court of Appeals for the Second Circuit

Judge Miner delivers the opinion of the court.

FACTS

The district court in this case has certified a plaintiff class consisting of all "needy persons who live in the State of New York, who beg on the public streets or in the public parks of New York City." The court defined a "needy person" as "someone who, because of poverty, is unable to pay for the necessities of life, such as food, shelter, clothing, medical care, and transportation." The judgment declared unconstitutional on First Amendment grounds the following provision of the New York Penal Law:

A person is guilty of loitering when he:

1. Loiters, remains or wanders about in a public place for the purpose of begging. . . .

REASONING

The City Police regard the challenged statute as an essential tool to address the evils associated with begging on the streets of New York City. They assert that beggars tend to congregate in certain areas and become more aggressive as they do so. Residents are intimidated and local businesses suffer accordingly. Panhandlers are said to station themselves in front of banks, bus stops, automated teller machines and parking lots and frequently engage in conduct described as "intimidating" and "coercive." Panhandlers have been known to block the sidewalk, follow people down the street and threaten those who do not give them money. It is said that they often make false and fraudulent representations to induce passers-by to part with their money. The City Police have begun to focus more attention on order maintenance activities in a program known as "community policing." They contend that it is vital to the program to have the statute available for the officers on the "beat" to deal with those who threaten and harass the citizenry through begging.

It is ludicrous, of course, to say that a statute that prohibits only loitering for the purpose of begging provides the only authority that is available to prevent and punish all the socially undesirable conduct incident to begging described by the City Police. There are, in fact, a number of New York statutes that proscribe conduct of the type that may accompany individual solicitations for money in the city streets. For example, the crime of harassment in the first degree is committed by one who follows another person in or about a public place or places or repeatedly commits acts that place the other person in reasonable fear of physical injury. If a panhandler, with intent to cause public inconvenience, annoyance or alarm, uses obscene or abusive language or obstructs pedestrian or vehicular traffic, he or she is guilty of disorderly conduct. A beggar who accosts a person in a public place with intent to defraud that person of money is guilty of fraudulent accosting. The crime of menacing in the third degree is committed by a panhandler who, by physical menace, intentionally places or attempts to place another person in fear of physical injury.

The sidewalks of the City of New York fall into the category of public property traditionally held open to the public for expressive activity. Conduct of a communicative nature cannot be regulated in "these quintessential public forums" in the same manner as it can be regulated on the streets of a military reservation. Having established that begging constitutes communicative activity of some sort and that, as far as this case is concerned, it is conducted in a traditional public forum, we next examine whether the statute at issue: (1) is necessary to serve a compelling state interest and is narrowly tailored to achieve that end; or (2) can be characterized as a regulation of the time, place and manner of expression that is content neutral, is narrowly tailored to serve significant government interests and leaves open alternate channels of communication.

First, it does not seem to us that any compelling state interest is served by excluding those who beg in a peaceful manner from communicating with their fellow citizens. Even if the state were considered to have a compelling interest in preventing the evils sometimes associated with begging, a statute that totally prohibits begging in all public places cannot be considered "narrowly tailored" to achieve that end. The plaintiffs have demonstrated that they are entitled to the relief they seek. *See Clark* v. *Community for Creative Non-Violence,* 468 U.S. 288 (1984).

CONCLUSION

The [statute violates the First Amendment. Panhandlers have the right to station themselves in public places and request money from passers-by.].

II. PUBLIC CORRUPTION

Public corruption is a broad term under which many crimes are committed, all of which have as their essence the taking or robbing from the public the basic right to honest government services by those elected or appointed as fiduciaries [caretakers] of the public trust. An example of public corruption is the 2006 case of Ohio Representative Bob Ney. Ney admitted that he entered into a conspiracy and made false statements in taking money, gifts, and favors in return for his official acts in Congress on behalf of convicted lobbyist Jack Abramoff and the clients Abramoff represented. While the specific crimes to which Ney pleaded guilty could be committed by anyone, Ney's position as a public servant sworn to uphold the law and to preserve the integrity of the legislative process by representing the interest of the public in general and, more specifically, his constituents back in Ohio who had elected Ney to office, elevates his crimes from garden-variety white-collar crime to public corruption. History is replete with examples of people in positions of public trust abusing that power for personal gain. This section examines three of the most common forms of public corruption that may be committed by public officials or by others: bribery, perjury [making false statements], and obstructing justice. These crimes dilute the integrity of the institutions of justice upon which we all depend to be free from undue or unlawful influence.

Such language has been successfully used to prosecute public corruption cases such as that of former Governor of Connecticut, John G. Rowland. Rowland pleaded guilty in 2004 to "conspiracy to deprive the State of Connecticut and its citizens of the intangible right to the honest services of its Governor." He violated the mail fraud statute, 18 U.S.C. §1346 when he received gifts from businesses that were seeking lucrative contracts with the state, and he caused the mails to be used in the illegal gratuity scheme, which ended up defrauding the people of Connecticut from the honest services of their elected official.[30] The crime of influencing a public official to benefit one particular person or business entity is fraud upon the public because the official is a fiduciary of public good, and it is a crime to abuse that trust by not being honest or faithful to the oath of office. In addition to the intangible rights of honest service owed to the public by public officials, intellectual rights are also protected from theft by the use of mails and wires.

---

[30]Joshua A. Kobrin. "Betraying Honest Services: Theories of Trust and Betrayal Applied to the Mail Fraud Statute, §§1346." *New York University Annual Survey of American Law,* Vol. 61 (2006), pp. 779–822.

1. Bribery

Rule of Law: Bribery is exchanging something of public value for personal gain.

One of the most common ways to corrupt a government official is to bribe him or her. Title 18 U.S.C. §201 provides the elements of **bribery**:

1. A public official must be involved: the definition of official, as defined by *Dixson v. United States,* 465 U.S. 482 (1984), is "whether the person occupies a position of public trust with official federal responsibilities;"

2. The defendant must have offered to give or receive a "thing of value": interpreted by the defendant's subjective view of what is valuable. What one crook deems valuable, another might not think so. If public official behavior is influenced by the thing of value, it satisfies this element.

3. The act must involve something official: if the official acted in a way that was legally permissible within her scope of employment, even if the act she took was not part of her defined duties, she could be held criminally responsible if the government proves she took the official act in exchange for a thing of value.

To determine whether a crime of bribery has been committed, courts examine the party's *mens rea* and intent in giving the thing of value to the official, which distinguishes the act from merely presenting a gift.[31] Bribery requires the specific intent to influence a public official's actions and is different from an illegal gratuity, which is payment for a public act that may or may not happen. The difference between a bribery conviction and an illegal gratuity conviction is that bribery carries a term of imprisonment up to 15 years, while the gratuity charge carries a maximum sentence of 2 years.

Applying the Rule of Law to the Facts: When is it bribery?

- A Congressman's wife was paid $35,000 in consulting fees from a company the same year, the company was awarded a no-bid [no other competition] defense contract worth $2 million dollars that her husband had pushed while he was in Congress.[32] Is hiring the wife it bribery of the Congressman?

Disgraced and convicted lobbyist Jack Abramoff often hired wives, sons, and daughters of lawmakers to do administrative work as a form of bribery for the lawmaker to exert his influence on behalf of Abramoff's clients. In our opening scenario, Congressman Sweat's no-bid contract to the cleaning company his wife controlled is a form of public corruption.

- A Southern congressman had his own company, LifeLine, which had many investors. One technology company, WebWorld, contacted LifeLine to solicit the congressman's help in influencing domestic federal agencies to adopt WebWorld products. When a search warrant was executed at the congressman's home in Washington, D.C., federal agents discovered $90,000 in cash in the freezer. What evidence does the government need to prove bribery and obstruction of justice charges?

The government needs evidence that the lawmaker sought and received money in exchange for using his congressional office to promote the individual business interests of WebWorld.[33]

The federal bribery statutes go hand in hand with the federal extortion statute to fight government corruption. Recent guilty pleas in Washington show how thin the line may seem between seeking influence in Washington as a lobbyist and engaging

---

[31]*See generally* P. J. Meitl, Peter I. Minton, and Beth Dyer. "*Public corruption.*" *American Criminal Law Review,* Vol. 42 (2005), pp. 781–824.

[32]"Former Congressman's Wife Worked for Contract Winner: No Bid Deal Was Awarded Same Year." *The New York Times,* March 31, 2007, p. A11.

[33]Facts based on the 2007 indictment of Louisiana Representative William J. Jefferson.

in bribery. California Representative Randy "Duke" Cunningham took $2.4 million in bribes, including cash, checks, antiques, and yachts, to benefit defense contractors who also bought his home above market value, paid off his mortgages, and allowed Cunningham to live a lavish lifestyle. Cunningham was bold enough to make a recipe list of how much money he expected in return for his legislative favors. Similarly, Kansas congressional candidate Adam Taff used campaign funds to buy a house. Lobbyist Jack A. Abramoff bribed Texas Representative Tom DeLay, who was indicted for wielding congressional influence on behalf of Abramoff's clients. Abramoff had stolen from and defrauded some of his clients, including Native American tribes seeking gaming benefits.[34] Representative DeLay had to step down as Speaker of the House when his corruption was exposed. Government corruption has always been a problem, but after the 2000 presidential election, the selling of government favors was widespread and rampant. "In 2004 and 2005, more than 1,060 government employees were convicted of corrupt activities, including 177 federal officials, 158 state officials, 360 local officials and 365 police officers, according to F.B.I. statistics. The number of convictions rose 27 percent from 2004 to 2005."[35]

2. Perjury, False Statements, and Obstruction of Justice

Rule of Law: Lying under oath or derailing a government investigation falls under the rubric of public corruption.

Perjury is willfully lying under oath in a judicial, administrative, or legislative proceeding. False statement and obstruction of justice statutes seek to protect the integrity of judicial, administrative, and legislative proceedings. **Obstruction of justice** is any act that interferes with those proceedings by, for instance, destroying or altering physical evidence, procuring false testimony, and threatening witnesses, jurors, and others involved in official proceedings. One definition of **false statements** can be found in the federal statute 18 U.S.C. §1001, which makes it a crime to knowingly and willfully make a false statement to the United States or to any department thereof.

Despite the impression given by press accounts of the verdict, homemaking maven Martha Stewart served five months in a federal prison not for insider trading [benefiting from nonpublic information that might affect the price of stock], but for lying to federal investigators. *United States* v. *Martha Stewart,* 323 F.Supp.2d 606 (S.D.N.Y. 2004). Specifically, Stewart purposely misled investigators questioning the beneficial timing of the sale of her stock in the ImClone company and was found guilty of, among other things, making the following false statements:

1. She told federal investigators that she instructed her stockbroker, Peter Bacanovic, to sell her ImClone shares only after he said the shares were trading below $60 per share.
2. She told investigators that during the same telephone call with Bacanovic she discussed the stock of her own company, Martha Stewart Living Omnimedia (MSLO).
3. She told investigators that she sold her stock on that specific day because she did not want to be bothered during her vacation.

Stewart was convicted of both asserting false statements and obstructing justice. The statutes empower prosecutors to go after not only criminals attempting to obstruct justice, but anyone who interferes with a federal investigation, regardless of their motivation. In our opening scenario, Sweat's lie that he did not remember the details of the illegal contract derailed the investigation and obstructed justice.

---

[34]Janet Novack and Matthew Swibel. "Inside Washington's Green Zone." *Forbes,* December 26, 2006, p. 50.
[35]David Johnston. "F.B.I.'s Focus on Public Corruption Includes 2,000 Investigations." *The New York Times,* May 11, 2006, p. A32.

III. TERRORISM

Rule of Law: **Terrorism is using illegal means to achieve illegitimate political objectives.**

1. The USA PATRIOT Act

The September 11, 2001 (9/11), airline hijackings led to the death of nearly 3,000 people, injured scores of others, destroyed the World Trade Center Towers in New York City, damaged the Pentagon in Washington, D.C., and caused the crash of flight United 93 in Shanksville, Pennsylvania. On October 26, 2001, Congress responded by enacting the Uniting and Strengthening America by Providing Appropriate Tools Required to Intercept and Obstruct Terrorism Act of 2001, otherwise known as the USA PATRIOT Act.[36] The Act contains ten Titles and consolidates law enforcement resources to investigate threats to national security with the aim of preventing another such terrorist attack on the United States.

Terrorism is generally understood as people committing acts involving threats, murder, and mayhem to achieve illegitimate political goals. Supporters of the USA PATRIOT Act praise its authority to gather and share investigative information between law enforcement agencies, while its critics point to the dismantling of citizens' civil liberties, especially in the search and seizure context, to fight an amorphous "war on terror."

a. The PATRIOT Act at Work

Prior to 9/11, there were laws on the books that allowed for the investigation and prosecution of certain crimes. The PATRIOT Act expanded these laws. In 1968, Congress passed the Omnibus Crime Control and Safe Streets Act.[37] Title III of the Safe Streets Act (commonly called Title III) established procedures for the government to obtain wiretaps as an investigative tool. In 1978, Congress enacted the Foreign Intelligence Surveillance Act ("FISA"),[38] to allow eavesdropping on foreign agents when such activity was "the purpose" of the investigation; that is, if the purpose of conducting electronic surveillance was to obtain foreign intelligence, the government could obtain a FISA warrant to conduct "sneak and peek" searches, and no notice of the search had to be given to the investigative target. When FISA was enacted, the traditional Fourth Amendment requirement of probable cause, as discussed in chapter 9, was required to obtain a search warrant. The PATRIOT Act amended FISA to eliminate the probable cause requirement for warrants so long as gathering foreign intelligence was a "significant purpose" of the investigation. The PATRIOT Act also expanded Title III authority for the government to use "trap and trace" devices that record telephone devices dialing into a particular location. Under the PATRIOT Act, the devices may be used "to obtain foreign intelligence information not concerning a United States person or to protect against international terrorism or clandestine intelligence activities."[39] On March 2, 2006, Congress reauthorized the PATRIOT Act and made certain provisions permanent that were temporary measures when the law was first enacted:

1. Allowed broad sharing of criminal investigation information between federal law agencies, whether their primary focus was foreign or domestic intelligence
2. The crimes for which wiretaps could be sought under Title III were expanded to include offenses involving chemical weapons, threats involving weapons of mass destruction or nuclear arms, and computer espionage

---

[36]USA PATRIOT Act of 2001, Pub. L. No. 107-56, 115 Stat. 272.

[37]Pub.L. 90-351, 42 U.S.C. §3711.

[38]50 U.S.C. §1802.·

[39]PATRIOT Act, Section 214, amending FISA, 50 U.S.C. §1842.

3. Internet service providers (ISPs) may reveal customer records in emergencies in order to save lives and will be immune from civil liability for such actions

4. Victims of computer trespass [hacking] are permitted to request law enforcement assistance to apprehend offenders[40]

Many legal scholars claim that the government's investigatory authority under the PATRIOT Act has been misused. One man who was the target of a federal terrorism investigation eventually sued the government over the scope of those provisions of the Act used to monitor and record his activities. Brandon Mayfield was a lawyer who converted to Islam and who was arrested in 2004 as a material witness in the terror bombing of trains in Madrid, Spain. Mayfield became an international terror suspect when the Federal Bureau of Investigation ("FBI") misread his fingerprint. The government eventually apologized and paid Mayfield $2 million dollars in a settlement, but not before, under PATRIOT Act authority, the FBI had obtained a FISA warrant and conducted secret searches of Mayfield's home, downloaded information from his computer, and planted electronic listening devices in his home. In our opening scenario, Jan and Theresa's best legal challenge to the "sneak and peek" warrant will be based on their First Amendment right to protest thereby depriving the government the authority to investigate their "suspected" terrorism.

The PATRIOT Act is designed to help law enforcement investigate crimes, but the bulk of prosecution of terrorism-related offenses falls under four primary federal statutes titled "Terrorism," "Material Support to Terrorists," "Material Support to a Foreign Terrorist Organization," and "Financial Support to a Foreign Terrorist Organization."[42] Prosecutions under these statutes for committing terrorist acts, helping terrorists, or helping to fund terrorist activities have not always been successful for the government. According to New York University's Center on Law and Security, the government wins a conviction in terror-related cases only 29% of the time. Some notable cases include the 2007 prosecution of the Holy Land Foundation, a charity dedicated to Palestinian and other Muslim causes, on the grounds that the Foundation gave "material support" to terrorist groups. The Texas jury either acquitted or deadlocked on the charges, and did not return any guilty verdicts. Also in 2007, José Padilla, who gained notoriety as a United States citizen held and detained as an "enemy combatant," a classification that allowed Padilla to be detained for close to four years before trial, was convicted on terror-related conspiracy charges and sentenced in 2008 to 17 years in prison. In April 2008, the government failed for a second time to convince a jury to convict six Florida men accused of conspiring to blow up the Sears Tower in Chicago as part of an al Qaeda terrorism plot. As in the first trial of the men, the second jury was deadlocked and a mistrial declared. The federal government vowed to take the men to trial for a third time.

b. Detention of Terror Suspects

A component of the government's effort to investigate crime is the ability to detain and interrogate witnesses or suspects who may or may not have information that relates to a criminal investigation. Beginning in 2002, American forces seized suspects who are believed to be linked to terrorist organizations such as al-Qaeda and the Taliban and have held approximately 500 of them at the Naval Base in Guantánamo Bay, Cuba, labeling the suspects "enemy combatants." Calling the detainees enemy combatants allows the Executive Branch to hold and treat them differently from prisoners of war or other criminal suspects.

---

[40] USA PATRIOT Improvement and Reauthorization Act of 2005, Pub. Law 109–177-Mar. 9, 2006.

[41] David Sarasohn. "A Charge Against the Patriot Act." *The Oregonian*, September 12, 2007, p.C4.

[42] The statutes are, respectively, 18 U.S.C. §2332; 18 U.S.C. §§2339A & B, and 50 U.S.C. §1705.

But detainees' rights and access to the American justice system have been vigorously litigated on American soil. The primary cases heard by the U.S. Supreme Court are *Rasul* v. *Bush*, 542 U.S. 466 (2004) and *Hamdi* v. *Rumsfeld*, 542 U.S. 507 (2004). In *Rasul*, the Court held that American courts do have jurisdiction over foreign nationals held at Guantánamo Bay, but did not address the issue of the legality of the detainees' imprisonment. In *Hamdi*, decided the same day as *Rasul*, the Court considered whether an American citizen (Hamdi),—an American who fought for the Taliban— could be classified as an enemy combatant and denied due process through the normal criminal trial process.[43] The high Court held that Hamdi's detention was lawful under the express Congressional authority to the President under the Authorization for Use of Military Force statute that allowed captured U.S. citizens to be classified as enemy combatants who could be tried before military tribunals rather than U.S. criminal courts. In response to the Court's decisions, Congress passed the Detainee Treatment Act of 2005,[44] which specifically denied the right to file *habeas corpus* petitions [writs/motions filed to challenge the legality of a prisoner's detention] for noncitizens held as enemy combatants at Guantánamo Bay, effectively overruling the high Court's decision in *Rasul*.

The next case to address detainee court access via the military tribunal system that the Executive Branch established to bring the detainees to trial was *Hamdan* v. *Rumsfeld*, 126 S.Ct. 2749 (2006). In this case, the Supreme Court held that using the procedural safeguards afforded by the Uniform Code of Military Justice ("UCMJ") could be a proper avenue for trying the suspects, rather than the illegal military commissions proposed by the President.

Largely in response to the U.S. Supreme Court's ruling in *Hamdan*, Congress hammered out the Military Commissions Act of 2006 ("MCA"). President George W. Bush signed this act into law on October 17, 2006, calling it "a way to deliver justice to the terrorists we have captured." The enactment of the MCA illustrates how the three branches of government work as explored in chapter 1. The MCA gave the Legislative Branch endorsement to the Executive Branch's exercise of power concerning detainees that the Judicial Branch found excessive in its *Hamdan* decision.[45] The MCA authorizes the President to issue an executive order clarifying the rules for questioning high-level detainees. Such questioning previously included techniques such as sleep deprivation and water-boarding (which makes the suspect feel as if he is drowning). The MCA also sets up a separate system of justice for anyone the administration classifies as an "unlawful enemy combatant," defined as those who fight against the United States and also those who have "purposefully and materially supported hostilities against the United States," thereby including in the prosecutorial net those who provide financial or material support to terrorists.

The first person to go through a war tribunal at Guantánamo was David Hicks, a 31-year-old Australian who had waited five years and four months for a trial. Hicks pled guilty to training with al-Qaeda, guarding a Taliban tank, and scouting a closed American embassy in Afghanistan. International human rights critics contended that Hicks was forced to plead guilty in order to go home, and they point to the coercive nature of his plea agreement, which required him to declare in open court that he had "never been illegally treated" by American forces during his captivity, including "the entire period of

---

[43]*See generally* Jay Alan Bauer. "Detainees Under Review: Striking the Right Constitutional Balance Between the Executive's War Powers and Judicial Review." *Alabama Law Review*, Vol. 57 (2006), pp. 1081–1103.

[44]Pub. L. No. 109-148 §1005(e), 119 Stat. 2680, 2742-44.

[45]Sheryl Gay Stolberg. "President Signs New Rules to Prosecute Terror Suspects." *The New York Times*, October 18, 2006, p. A14.

your detention by the United States at Guantánamo Bay, Cuba."[46] Hicks was released on May 20, 2007, and sent to Australia to finish serving his sentence. In April 2008, as the government was preparing to bring Hamdan (from the Supreme Court case) to trial, the former chief prosecutor at Guantánamo Colonel Morris Davis testified that, although he believed Hamdan to be guilty, in contravention of the notion of fair and blind justice in military trials, he was pressured to bring charges against high-profile detainees before elections for "strategic political value."

2. Treason

The only crime mentioned in the Constitution is treason. Article III, section 3 states:

> ***CLAUSE 1:***   Treason against the United States shall consist only in levying War against them, or in adhering to their Enemies, giving them Aid and Comfort. No person shall be convicted of Treason unless on the testimony of Two Witnesses to the same overt Act, or on Confession in open Court.

> ***CLAUSE 2:***   The Congress shall have Power to declare the Punishment of Treason, but no Attainder of Treason shall work Corruption of Blood, or Forfeiture except during the Life of the Person attained.

Treason is levying war against the United States from within the country. To sustain a treason charge requires the testimony of two witnesses to the alleged treasonous acts. The last treason conviction to withstand U.S. Supreme Court review was the case of Tomoya Kawakita, convicted in 1952 of helping the Japanese war effort. Two other convictions that were overturned on appeal were the 1943 conviction of Hans Haupt, the father of a German saboteur, and Anthony Cramer, convicted of aiding a German saboteur in 1945. The *mens rea* is the intent to betray the United States with two witnesses to the treasonous act. The elements of **treason** are:

1. a person who owes allegiance to the United States
2. levies war or adheres to an enemy of the United States and
3. commits an overt act and
4. possesses treasonable intent
5. with two attesting witnesses.

Treason prosecutions are rare, but on October 11, 2006, the U.S. Justice Department charged an American with treason for the first time in fifty years. The DOJ accused Adam Yahiye Gadahn, a convert to Islam, of giving "aid and comfort" to al-Qaeda by appearing in a series of highly publicized videotapes urging violence against the United States.[47] According to the government, Gadahn has appeared in five videos, most recently one released on September 11, 2006, that praised the hijackers who died on that date in 2001 while declaring the United States "enemy soil." In a videotape in 2004, he declared that "the streets of America shall run red with blood." Gadahn is not in American custody. He's believed to be in Pakistan, and the State Department has posted a $1 million reward for information leading to his capture. According to an interview with *The New York Times,* Professor Peter S. Margulies, an expert on national security issues, questioned whether the government had met the requirement that two witnesses would speak to Gadahn's alleged acts of treason. Margulies said, "You need witnesses who are actually familiar with the terms of cooperation of the person charged—whether they were coerced, whether they were paid—and that seems to be lacking here in this case."

---

[46]William Glaberson. "Some Bumps at Start of War Tribunals at Guantánamo." *The New York Times,* April 1, 2007, p. 20.

[47]Eric Lichtblau. "American in Qaeda Tapes Accused of Treason." *The New York Times,* October 12, 2006, p. A20.

a. Sedition

Sedition has been recognized as a crime since the first days of the Constitution. The Alien and Sedition Acts of the late eighteenth century defined **sedition** as the crime of writing false, scandalous, or malicious stories about the government; lengthened the residency period to become a citizen; and amplified the President's authority to deport dangerous aliens. The sedition laws were controversial because of their effect on the free speech right to criticize the government, and many prominent Americans opposed the laws, including Thomas Jefferson and James Madison. **Espionage** is spying and giving away government secrets to benefit a foreign power. Today the Logan Act prohibits individuals from corresponding with foreign governments in relation to disputes such governments may have with the United States, and prohibits the recruitment of United States servicemembers to act against the United States.[48] Many forms of espionage and subversive activities are federal crimes and share the common *mens rea* element of the intent to harm the security interests of the United States and the performance of overt acts in furtherance of that objective.

IV. ENVIRONMENTAL CRIMES

1. The Statutes

Criminal law students must have some familiarity with environmental laws, the crimes associated with hazardous waste, and the corporations that can be criminally or civilly liable, as well as their Chief Executive Officers ("CEOs"). It also behooves law enforcement to know when they must clean up drug labs how to properly dispose of such waste. The **Environmental Protection Agency** ("EPA") is the Executive Branch agency responsible for criminal and civil enforcement of environmental laws, but often criminal prosecutions are handled by the Department of Justice's Environmental Resource and Natural Division. What follows is a summary of the best-known laws designed to protect both the environment and public health from unscrupulous actors who might pollute with impunity. In a recent U.S. Supreme Court ruling that surprised many legal scholars, the high Court decided that the federal government has the authority to regulate carbon dioxide and other greenhouse gasses produced by motor vehicles. The ruling in *Massachusetts* v. *EPA*, 127 S.Ct 1438 (2007), instructs the EPA to reconsider its refusal to regulate greenhouse gasses and eliminate its "laundry list" of excuses for not doing so. The ruling does not require the federal government to regulate such gasses.

a. Clean Air Act

The **Clean Air Act** (1970), 42 U.S.C. 7401 et. seq. requires at a minimum that "for a discrete set of pollutants and based on published air quality criteria that reflect the latest scientific knowledge, the EPA must establish uniform national standards at a level that is requisite to protect public health from the adverse effects of the pollutant in the ambient air."[49] By law, the Clean Air Act penalizes those who knowingly violate federal or state regulations designed to achieve EPA ambient air quality. "The Act directs the EPA to prescribe national air quality standards at a level sufficient to protect the public health and welfare. Each state is required to adopt an implementation plan of its own for that state. If a state implementation plan is approved by the EPA, its requirements become federal law and are fully enforceable in federal court."[50]

---

[48]18 U.S.C. §2384.

[49]*Whitman* v. *American Trucking Assn's, Inc.,* 531 U.S. 457 (2001).

[50]*Her Majesty, The Queen* v. *City of Detroit,* 874 F.2d 332 (6th Cir. 1989).

b. Clean Water Act

As the name implies, the **Clean Water Act** (1972), 33 U.S.C. 1251 et. seq. is designed to protect people's welfare, health, and the environment by controlling how much pollution can legally be discharged in different waterways and navigable systems in the United States. The criminal provisions are "public welfare legislation" because the Clean Water Act "is designed to protect the public from potentially harmful or injurious items," and it criminalizes "a type of conduct that a reasonable person should know is subject to stringent public regulation and may seriously threaten the community's health and safety." The provisions of the Clean Water Act allow for private parties to be held criminally responsible even if they are not personally responsible. Mr. Hanousek was a roadmaster employed by the Pacific & Arctic Railway and Navigation Company when an independent contractor struck an oil line, spilling thousands of gallons of oil into the river. He was indicted and convicted for negligently discharging oil into a navigable water of the United States. He was fined $5,000 and sentenced to six months in jail, then to some period of time in a halfway house, then to a term of supervised release. The U.S. Supreme Court refused to hear his appeal, thereby preserving his conviction. In a dissent from the order denying his *writ of certiorari,* Justice Thomas said that the Court should review his case for an opportunity to distinguish criminal environmental statutes from "public welfare offenses" which are often strict liability.[51]

c. Resource Conservation and Recovery Act

The **Resource Conservation and Recovery Act** (1976), 42 U.S.C. 6901 et seq. sets standards for the management of hazardous waste and contains clean-up provisions for existing contaminated sites. The objectives of RCRA are to protect the health of citizens by assessing criminal liability if companies and private parties fail to dispose of hazardous waste properly.

d. Comprehensive Environmental Response, Compensation and Liability Act

Commonly called Superfund, the Comprehensive Environmental Response, Compensation and Liability Act (1980), 42 U.S.C. §9601 et seq. was enacted to fund the clean-up of toxic waste sites, many of which were polluted by companies no longer in business. To get money for Superfund, companies that generate such waste are taxed directly. The most controversial provision of the law is that property owners are strictly liable for any hazardous waste on their property, even if they were unaware that previous owner dumped the waste, and the owner must clean up their property if it is contaminated. The EPA and state environmental agencies both oversee the Superfund. In our chapter's opening scenario, Richard would be responsible for the clean-up costs associated with his property even though he was not the one responsible for the contamination.

The difference between Resource Conservation and Recovery Act and Superfund is that RCRA manages the day-to-day regulation of handling hazardous waste and CERCLA manages post-contamination clean-up. The statute assigns liability for costs for the clean-up between polluting parties and landowners. Superfund's reach is also retroactive, which means parties may be liable for cleaning up waste that was dumped prior to the law's enactment in the 1980s.

V. SUING THE GOVERNMENT FOR HARM

1. Federal Tort Claims Act

Rule of Law: A victim of a government tort [harm] must bring suit under the FTCA within two years of discovering the injury, or the lawsuit will be forever barred.

---

[51] *United States* v. *Hanousek,* 176 F.3d 1116 (9th cir. 1999), cert. denied, 582 U.S. 1102 (2000).

Because the federal government is the sovereign, it alone can consent to how and where it may be sued by citizens, foreign governments, and business entities. The **Federal Tort Claims Act** ("FTCA") was passed in 1946 after being under consideration for nearly 30 years[52] as a way to allow people to sue the government for injuries caused by government employees. 28 U.S.C. §1346(b) Prior to the enactment of the FTCA, the only recourse for people harmed by government employees was a direct appeal to Congress for a private relief measure to award some money from the federal treasury. The government is typically immune from civil lawsuits; for example. a military service-member is prohibited from bringing a medical malpractice suit against the government for harm suffered at a military hospital. The government chooses not to waive its immunity in medical malpractice lawsuits so the servicemember has no viable avenue to sue. The FTCA specifies the specific circumstances under which the federal government will allow itself to be a defendant in civil court. The FTCA conferred jurisdiction on federal courts only to hear claims for monetary damages for

> "injury or loss of property, person injury or death caused by the negligent or wrongful act or omission of any employee of the Government while acting within the scope of his office or employment, under circumstances where the United States, if a private person, would be liable to the claimant in accordance with the law of the place where the act or omission occurred."

The statute of limitations [period] during which the lawsuit may be brought is "within two years after such claim accrues or unless action is begun within six months after the date of mailing, by certified or registered mail, of notice of final denial of the claim by the agency to which it was presented."[53] The two-year period in which to bring a suit is absolute and may not be waived. The administrative agency must be given a chance to resolve the claim before adjudicating the claim through litigation in federal court. This requirement is due to the recognition that the vast number of claims involve a small number of federal agencies, such as the Department of Veterans Affairs or the United States Postal Service. The Postal Service, for example. has over 80,000 vehicles that may be involved in accidents in which people are hurt, so it is important for the agency to have the opportunity to settle claims without resorting to a court of law. The basic parameters of the FTCA set out in §1346(b), §§2674, and 2675 detail the timing requirements, the waiver of sovereign immunity, and the types of claims that can be brought.

The United States is liable in tort

1. for personal injury, death, or property damage
2. caused by negligent or wrongful acts or omissions
3. by a government employee acting within the scope of his office or employment
4. in the same manner, and to the same extent, as a private person under like circumstances
5. in accordance with the law of the place (state) where the act or omission occurred, and
6. for money damages, but not for interest before judgment or for punitive damages.

The government decides whether or not it wants to waive its immunity. It also decides how the FTCA lawsuits are heard: only in federal court and only in front of a federal judge without a jury present. Like other legal doctrines, the FTCA contains exceptions to the rule. The **Discretionary Function Exception** ("DFE") allows the government to escape liability for acts that government employees committed in the administration of their government functions and decisions. That is, if the harm that the plaintiff alleges is the result of a decision that was made as part of the government

---

[52]*See generally* Gregory C. Sisk. *Litigation with the Federal Government* (New York: Foundation Press, 2000).
[53]28 U.S.C. §2401(b).

functionary's carrying out his or her administrative duties, then the government can escape liability. The language of the FTCA specifies that if the harmful acts were "based upon [a government employee's] exercise or performance or the failure to exercise or perform a discretionary function or duty . . ." then no claim against the government can be successful "whether or not the discretion involved be abused." The reasoning behind the DFE is that the government wants its workers to be free from the fear of frivolous lawsuits for the decisions they make. The law presumes that government workers make the best decisions that they can with all available information at hand at the time and that the government should not be sued if those decisions turn out to cause some people harm, because the decisions were made on behalf of the public good.

Applying the Rule of Law to the Facts: When does the Discretionary Function Exception apply?

- In the 1940s and 1950s, the United States Air Force disposed in clay sewer systems industrial solvents that were used as airplane degreasers. Clay disposal systems were common at that time, and scientists did not know then that the degreaser was a possible human carcinogen [causes cancer in humans]. Sally's daughter was born with a birth defect, and Sally claims that it's because her groundwater is contaminated from waste disposed by the nearby Air Force base 40 years earlier. Will Sally's FTCA suit survive?

No, the government's decision was part of the discretionary decision-making that all government employees must engage in when fulfilling their duties. Thus, the Air Force is protected and immune from lawsuits.

VI. Key Terms and Phrases

- bribery
- contempt
- crimes against morality
- discretionary function exception (DFE)
- disturbing the peace
- drug and alcohol offenses
- environmental statutes
- espionage
- false statements
- firearm offenses
- gambling
- illegal gratuity
- obstruction of justice
- panhandling
- perjury
- prostitution
- public corruption
- riot
- sedition
- terrorism
- unlawful assembly
- USA PATRIOT Act
- vagrancy

VII. Summary

1. **How and why do we define crimes against the public: Crimes against morality** are largely defined by behavior deemed "immoral" or against the grain of mainstream society. Society punishes behaviors that disturb or interfere with the order found in a peaceful society. Among such behaviors are **disturbing the peace,** which is typically loud behavior that disrupts others; **unlawful assembly,** where at least five people are threatening violence or actually committing violence; **riot,** which is five or more people committing violence, **vagrancy,** which is being homeless and loitering in public areas; and **panhandling,** which is begging from passers-by in the street. Other offenses that not only are annoyances, but have the potential to cause great bodily harm and even death, are **firearm offenses.** There is no constitutional right to own a gun, and there are

many federal and state laws that regulate gun possession and many conditions under which someone can suffer a firearm "disability." People with these conditions, such as a conviction for domestic violence, cannot lawfully possess a gun.

2. **The criminal justice system response to addictive crimes such as gambling, drugs, and alcohol offenses: Gambling** is wagering on events such as sports or card games for money and is considered a victimless crime, as is **prostitution,** which is receiving payment or other things of value in exchange for sexual favors. Even though prostitution involves consenting people, the nature of the prostitute relationship is usually exploitive, and the profession is filled with violence and drugs. Illegal **drugs and alcohol** can lead to addiction for which the proper remedy is rehabilitation and treatment, but because those who

use illegal substances often are involved in crime, sometimes violent, the criminal justice system must respond appropriately with punishment as well as rehabilitation.

3. **The definition of public corruption: Public corruption** describes the breach of fiduciary duty by people in positions of public trust, such as those elected or appointed as public servants. Many crimes constitute public corruption, but the most common are **bribery,** in which the public official accepts something of value to affect his or her official action; **perjury,** which is lying under oath, usually to cover up and conceal an initial illegal action; and making **false statements** to federal officials with the intent to deceive. All of those acts can constitute **obstruction of justice,** which is deliberately interfering with the administration of justice in a judicial, legislative, or administrative proceeding.

4. **The prosecution of terrorism under criminal law:** Terrorism is understood as acts of threats, murder, and mayhem perpetrated to achieve illegitimate political goals. Crimes against the national security of the United States have traditionally been punished under laws that deal with **espionage** (spying), **sedition** (plotting to harm the interests of the United States), and **treason** (waging war against the United States). The Executive Branch has held hundreds of suspects with alleged ties to al-Qaeda and the Taliban in Afghanistan at the U.S. Naval Base in Guantánamo Bay, Cuba. Legal wrangling over the continued detention of the so-called terror suspects and their access to American courts has been the subject of much litigation and congressional action. The U.S. Supreme Court held that detainees do have limited access to American justice and that the President's proposal to bring the suspects to trial in front of military commis-

sions was unconstitutional. Thus, the high Court rejected the Executive Branch's argument in *Hamdan* v. *Rumsfeld* (2006) that using the Uniform Code of Military Justice to try the suspects was too cumbersome. Instead, Congress passed the Military Commissions Act stripping federal courts of jurisdiction to hear detainee cases.

5. **The relevant statutes to prosecute environmental crimes:** Environmental crimes are those that hurt the nation's air, water, and land. Congress' reaction to concerns about pollution was to enact a series of laws that both restricted what companies could do with their waste and forced the offenders to pay for the clean-up of sites previously contaminated. The **Comprehensive Environmental Response, Compensation and Liability Act,** also known as Superfund because it collects and distributes payment for massive clean-up efforts, forces polluters to clean up, and may apply retroactively from before its enactment in 1980. The **Resource Conservation and Recovery Act** enacted in 1974 sought to prevent the creation of hazardous waste sites. Among the very first laws enacted by President Nixon in the early 1970s were the **Clean Air Act,** enacted in 1970 to set standards for how much pollution could be emitted into the country's air, and the **Clean Water Act,** enacted in 1972 to regulate and control the pollution in America's waterways.

6. **Legal redress when the government causes harm in tort:** The federal government decides under which circumstances people can sue. Under the **Federal Tort Claims Act** enacted by Congress, people harmed by the government must bring suit within two years after such claim accrues. An exception to the FTCA is the **Discretionary Function Exception,** which protects government actors for the decisions they make on behalf of the public good.

VIII. Discussion Questions

1. Should states have the final say in setting drug policy or in making certain drugs criminal while allowing for the personal use of so-called recreational drugs free from the crash of federal drug policy?

2. What is the identifiable harm to society that laws prohibiting illegal gambling are designed to protect when so much gambling is legal? Does the support of state-sponsored lotteries or horse and dog racetracks detract from the argument that illegal gambling hurts society? If the government could tax all illegal activity to generate revenue for the state or federal treasury, would your analysis change?

3. Do you agree with the majority in the *Cleveland* v. *United States,* 329 U.S. 14 (1946), case where the law against white slavery was used to punish polygamy

that crossed state lines, that "Whether an act is immoral within the meaning of the statute is not to be determined by the accused's concepts of morality. Congress has provided the standard"? Which segment of society has the power to define morality?

4. Research the issue of whether permissive gun ownership laws such as in Idaho and Georgia lead to lower crime rates or whether tough restrictions on gun ownership have any effect on the crime rate, either increasing it or decreasing it, in communities with these restrictions.

5. In the fight against global terrorism, should we compromise our civil liberties if it will prevent future terrorist attacks? Is there a difference between being inconvenienced by having to take shoes off at an

airport security checkpoint and the government monitoring, without a warrant, telephone calls originating in or ending in a foreign county even when those phone calls are made by American citizens?

6. What harm, if any, to the United States' interests can come by giving those suspected of aiding al-Qaeda or the Taliban the full rights and protections that American citizens, or even illegal immigrants on American soil, enjoy? How do you think the U.S. Supreme Court will decide if it has power to continue to hear detainee petitions that they are being held illegally, despite the Military Commissions Act that deprives the high Court of the power to hear those claims?

IX. Problem-Solving Exercises

1. The chairman of the House Ways and Means Committee, the congressional committee that oversees the distribution of lucrative federal contracts, had a hard time securing seats to the last public taping of the popular reality television series "Gimme Some Love," starring Flavor Pop, a former rap group member. Stu, who was a lobbyist (someone who gets paid to bring his client's business to the lawmaker's attention), had tickets to the taping and asked the chairman whether, in exchange for complimentary (free) tickets that had no monetary value, he could meet with the chairman to discuss his client, Company Tallman, which made airplane windshields. The chairman took the tickets from Stu with glee and said "Sure!" The chairman later had lunch with Stu and, two months later, spoke before the defense appropriations committee in favor of awarding Company Tallman a defense contract worth $10 million dollars. The chairman was later charged under the federal bribery statute. Should he be convicted?

2. At the end of a racially tense criminal case in which a white man was charged with raping an African-American teenager, several people gathered on the street corner outside and began to chant, "No justice, no peace." When the verdict of acquittal was announced to the public, the chant changed to "Let's burn this courthouse down!" Several protesters were arrested and charged with inciting a riot; the protesters say they were merely exercising their First Amendment freedom of speech rights to criticize the verdict. Who will win, the government or the protesters?

3. The police swarmed into a church and shut down the weekly bingo game, citing state law prohibiting betting on games of chance. Is the police action legal?

4. Six suspects in the War on Terror were taken from their homeland in Afghanistan and placed in the American prison in Guantánamo Bay, Cuba. After 24 months, they still had not met with a lawyer, had not been advised of the charges against them, and had no idea when or whether they would be brought before a judge or tribunal to clear their names. All proclaimed their innocence and filed *habeas corpus* petitions in federal court for the District of Columbia naming the Secretary of Defense as the defendant. Given the rulings in *Hamdi* and *Hamdan* and the Military Commissions Act of 2006, what is the likely outcome of the detainees' challenges to their alleged unlawful confinement?

X. World Wide Web Resources

Terrorism Research Center

http://www.terrorism.com

FBI Homepage on Public Corruption

http://www.fbi.gov/hq/cid/pubcorrupt/pubcorrupt.htm

Environmental Justice

http://www.epa.gov/compliance/environmentaljustice/

Prostitution in the Middle Ages

http://www.brown.edu/Departments/Italian_Studies/
dweb/society/sex/prostitution.shtml

XI. Additional Readings and Notes

Panhandling

Jordana Schreiber. "Begging Underground? The Constitutionality of Regulations Banning Panhandling in the New York City Subway System." *Cardozo Law Review,* Vol. 27 (2006), pp. 1517–1548.

Prostitution

Ariela R. Dubler. "Immoral Purposes: Marriage and the Genus of Illicit Sex." *Yale Law Journal,* Vol. 115 (2006), pp. 758–812.

Daria Snadowsky. "The Best Little Whorehouse Is Not in Texas: How Nevada's Prostitution Laws Serve Public Policy, and How Those Laws May Be Improved." *Nevada Law Journal,* Vol. 6 (2005), pp. 217–247.

Gambling

Anisha S. Dasgupta. "Public Finance and the Fortunes of the Early American Lottery." *Bridgeport Law Review/Quinnipiac Law Review,* Vol. 24 (2006), pp. 227–264.

Joseph L. Lester. "B-I-N-G-O! The Legal Abuse of an Innocent Game." *St. Thomas Law Review,* Vol. 18 (2005), pp. 21–52.

Disturbing the Peace

Jessica Conaway. "Reversion Back to a State of Nature in the United States Southern Borderlands: A Look at Potential Causes of Action to Curb Vigilante Activity on the United States/Mexico Border." *Mercer Law Review,* Vol. 56 (2005), pp. 1419–1455.

Thomas W. Korver. "*State* v. *Robinson*: Free Speech, or Itchin' for a Fight?" *Montana Law Review,* Vol. 65 (2004), pp. 385–409.

Drugs and Alcohol

Christopher Haas. "Owner and Promoter Liability in "Club Drug" Initiatives." *Ohio State Law Journal,* Vol. 66 (2005), pp. 511–568.

Erin N. Linder. "Punishing Prenatal Alcohol Abuse: The Problems Inherent in Utilizing Civil Commitment to Address Addiction." *University of Illinois Law Review* (2005), pp. 873–901.

Drinking and Driving

Victor E. Flango. "DWI Courts: The Newest Problem-Solving Courts." *American Judges Association Court Review,* Vol. 42 (2005), pp. 22–24.

Martin W. Judnich. "DUI Prosecution: An Analysis of the Portable Breath Test." *The Montana Lawyer,* Vol. 31 (2005), pp. 18–28.

Public Corruption

Sandra Caron George. "Prosecutorial Discretion: What's Politics Got to Do with It?" *Georgetown Journal of Legal Ethics,* Vol. 18 (2005), pp. 739–758.

Vincent R. Johnson. "Ethics in Government at the Local Level." *Seton Hall Law Review,* Vol. 36 (2006), pp. 716–779.

USA PATRIOT Act of 2001

Christopher P. Raab. "Fighting Terrorism in an Electronic Age: Does the Patriot Act Unduly Compromise Our Civil Liberties?" *Duke Law & Technology Review* (2006), pp. 3–21.

CHAPTER

8

Defenses

"I saw the best minds of my generation destroyed by madness, starving hysterical
   naked . . .

who demanded sanity trials accusing the radio of hypnotism & were left with their insanity & their hands & a hung jury . . .

with the absolute heart of the poem of life butchered out of their own bodies good to
   eat a thousand years."

ALLEN GINSBERG, "HOWL" (1956)

CHAPTER OBJECTIVES

Primary Concepts Discussed in This Chapter:

1. The public policy reasons for recognizing defenses to crime
2. The different variations of the *mens rea*–based defenses, such as infancy, intoxication, and
   insanity
3. The various defenses based on justification and excuse, such as self defense, necessity, duress,
   and justification
4. The consequences of making a mistake of law or a mistake of fact
5. Battered woman syndrome, the defense of entrapment, and the statute of limitations

CHAPTER OUTLINE

Feature: *Chapter-Opening Case Study: How the Mind Works*

Billy had a rough childhood. In tenth grade, Billy dropped out of school, but he was smart and had an entrepreneurial spirit. He started his own candy-making business, but was soon seduced by the easy money of selling drugs in the neighborhood. Billy was a successful drug dealer and soon began to fear physical retaliation from rival drug gangs. At age 19, Billy's best friend was shot to death, and no one was ever caught or arrested for the murder. Billy started the unusual practice of barricading himself in his house each night, to make sure he was safe inside. He also placed pieces of paper inside the doorjamb when he left, so that when he returned he would see immediately whether anyone had entered or left since he had been there. He began sleeping with a loaded gun under his pillow and became so worried that he might be assassinated, that he would hide when he saw a car of a certain color. He also believed that he was under surveillance by some higher authority. One night, Billy was pacing at the front door watching through a slit in the shades. His friends, who had come to his house for dinner, were used to Billy's paranoia by now and ignored him. He began to scream at the group and asked why they were trying to kill him. Some of Billy's friends became nervous and started to move toward the door. Billy would not let anybody leave the house and called 9-1-1 for help because he believed that his friends were surrounding him to kill him. When one friend opened the door to get outside, Billy started shooting and killed three people. He was arrested shortly afterward. In his confession to the police, Billy said he had to shoot because "it was them, or me."

INTRODUCTION

As discussed previously in this text, criminal liability attaches with the concurrence of *mens rea* and *actus reus*. Society wants to hold offenders accountable for the crimes they intend to commit, or in fact commit, by acts of recklessness or negligence. If the offender's state of mind is compromised, either by a mental disorder, a mistake of fact, or drug or alcohol intoxication, or if the offender is under duress and is being forced to commit a crime by threats of bodily harm or death, the law may reduce his or her culpability by recognizing certain affirmative defenses. The common **affirmative defenses** in criminal law are alibi, mistake, infancy, intoxication, duress, and insanity.

Affirmative defenses are separated into two categories: defenses of criminal acts that were completely justified, such as acts of self-defense, and defenses of criminal acts that are excused under the law. One example of the latter would be a situation in which the *mens rea* that produced the act was defective due to mental disability on the part of the offender. The distinction between defenses that are justified and those which are excused has been defined in the following way:

> Claims of justification conceded that the definition of the offense is satisfied, but challenge whether the act is wrongful; claims of excuse concede that the act is wrongful, but seek to avoid the attribution of the act to the actor. A justification speaks to the rightness of the act; an excuse, to whether the actor is accountable for a concededly wrongful act.[1]

This chapter examines the basic defenses in criminal law and how they operate to relieve a criminal actor from certain specific punishment under the law. Some defenses have already been discussed previously in conjunction with the specific crime to which they apply. For example, the defense of impossibility was raised in the discussion of attempt crimes in Chapter 4, and some of the constitutional issues raised in the context of criminal procedure as it relates to defenses are explored in Chapter 13.

I. HOW DEFENSES ARE RAISED

In a criminal trial, the state or federal government represented by the prosecution carries the burden of proof to prove every element of an offense beyond a reasonable doubt. Under common law, the burden of proving "affirmative defenses—indeed, 'all circumstances . . . of justification, excuse or alleviation'—rested on the defendant."[2] The term **burden of proof** encompasses two intertwined and similar concepts: the burden of production and the burden of persuasion. The burden of proof proving beyond a reasonable doubt that the crime was committed and that the defendant committed it remains with the prosecution at all times. The **burden of persuasion** means the responsibility at trial to introduce enough evidence to convince the jury. The defendant enjoys a Fifth Amendment right not to incriminate herself, and this means that if she chooses, she need not raise any defense to the crime. That is, she is under no legal obligation to produce evidence to show that she did not commit the crime as charged—the burden of proving her guilty remains with the state and never shifts to her to prove her innocence. But in modern society, people—especially defendants and jurors—expect that if she claims she's innocent, she will defend herself and at least try to prove her innocence. But most defense counsel request the judge to instruct the jury before deliberations that the burden of proof remains with the state and that the jury can draw no adverse or negative inference from the defendant's invoking her right to remain silent. Many people believe that a defendant who has "nothing to hide" would willingly take an oath and get up on the witness stand to tell her side of the story. But many factors weigh upon a defendant's ability to testify, such as mental status, educational background, and past criminal history. These factors may counsel against putting a nervous

---

[1]George P. Fletcher. *Rethinking Criminal Law*. (Baltimore: Johns Hopkins University, 1978).

[2]*Patterson* v. *New York*, 432 U.S. 197 (1977) (quoting 4 W. Blackstone, Commentaries 201).

defendant up on the witness stand to withstand verbal sparring with the prosecutor, a trained lawyer who may have much courtroom experience.

But if the defense chooses to raise a defense, she has what is called the **burden of production** during trial. The burden of production is the minimal amount of evidence that would be legally sufficient under the law for the issue of the defense to be considered by the jury. For instance, if Nancy wanted to assert the defense that she was too intoxicated to form the specific intent for first-degree murder [willful, premeditated, and deliberate], she would have to introduce sufficient evidence that she was drunk. Evidence might be testimony by the bartender and friends; observations by the police officers who witnessed her slurred speech, stumbling gait, and the alcohol smell on her breath; or testimony by the physician who noted her blood alcohol level when he drew a sample. Introducing such evidence would allow the judge to give the jury an intoxication instruction that would read "if you find the defendant was intoxicated to negate *mens rea* . . . ." If Nancy just sat quietly at trial, confident that everyone knew she was drunk when she committed the crime, but introduced no evidence to raise the issue, the judge would be legally bound not to instruct the jury on the law of intoxication because there had not been a minimum quantity of evidence introduced. Nancy would not have met her burden of production.

For some defenses, the defendant has to notify the prosecution that he or she intends to raise those defenses at trial—for example, a defense based on the impaired mental status of the defendant at the time of the crime or on alibi. The law wants to give the prosecution an opportunity to rebut the defense—for example, have the defendant evaluated by his or her own mental health expert or, if the alibi is true, not waste the court's time and society's judicial resources in taking an innocent defendant to trial. State jurisdictions differ over the amount of evidence required to sustain the burden of production. Some courts call raising an affirmative defense a burden of proof and require that the defendant prove the defense beyond a reasonable doubt, such as the state of Oregon and the insanity defense. Other jurisdictions allow the defendant to introduce evidence by a preponderance of evidence standard, which typically means 51% on a scale from 1 to 100, or on a clear and convincing standard that is more than a preponderance but less than beyond a reasonable doubt. To be clear, the prosecution always retains the burden of proof to introduce enough evidence of all necessary elements of the crime beyond a reasonable doubt, and any evidentiary obligation placed on the defense to shift that burden is a violation of the defendant's due process rights to a fair trial.[3]

If the defense successfully meets its burden of production with respect to the existence of a defense, the judge will instruct the jury on the law that governs the defense. The jury is free to disregard the defense raised or to give it great weight as they do with every other piece of evidence. If the jury does recognize the defense, it typically means a reduced sentence for the defendant.

II. Competency

Rule of Law: Due process requires that a defendant understand the trial proceedings and be able to assist in her defense.

The balancing of an individual's liberty interest against the state's interest in executing a lawful sentence becomes more difficult when the defendant is mentally ill. As stated earlier, having a mental illness is not a crime. What happens when the wheels of justice begin to churn and the person caught in the system is mentally ill? The first layer of analysis begins with the point at which the mental illness becomes apparent. If a defendant is or becomes mentally ill before trial, the state cannot forcibly medicate him to

---

[3]*See In re Winship*, 397 U.S. 358 (1970); *Mullaney* v. *Wilbur*, 421 U.S. 684 (1975).

stand trial. That is, the defendant's due process rights outweigh the state's interest in bringing the case to trial. The issue then becomes how long the state can keep the defendant locked up awaiting his or her recovery from mental illness.

a. Competency to Stand Trial

Competency means that the defendant possesses the mental faculties required to be a meaningful participant in all stages of the criminal trial process, from initial arrest, through sentencing, to execution via the death penalty if applicable. To be competent to stand trial, a defendant must

1. understand the nature of the court proceedings against him and
2. be able to assist his counsel in his defense.

He must know what role the prosecutor, judge, and defense counsel play, he must understand the consequences of exercising his rights to remain silent or to testify at trial, and he must be aware of the consequences of a conviction. He must also be able to competently assist his counsel to prepare his defense. If one of those prongs is missing, the defendant is not able to stand trial.[4] In *Riggins* v. *Nevada*, 504 U.S. 127 (1992), Riggins was charged with murder and, while awaiting trial, had experienced **psychotic** [break from reality] episodes. He was treated with Mellaril, a strong drug that can produce noticeable zombie-like side effects. Riggins wanted to go off the medication prior to trial but the court refused. He defended against the murder charges on the basis of insanity, but was convicted and sentenced to death. The Supreme Court overturned his conviction and vacated his death sentence on the basis that once Riggins asked to be taken off the medication, the state had to establish the medical necessity for forcing him to continue the medication.

The analysis for medicating defendants is different once the defendant has been convicted. In *Washington* v. *Harper*, 494 U.S. 210 (1990), a prisoner became psychotic and was entitled to a hearing before being forcibly medicated—that is, medicated against his will. The U.S. Supreme Court held that the state could force medication against a prisoner's will as long as an independent body determined that such medication was necessary. The requirement for forcible medication was that the defendant had to be a danger to himself or others and that the forced medical treatment had to be in the defendant's best interest. If the danger test is not met, the state cannot forcibly medicate the defendant. *Sell* v. *United States*, 539 U.S. 166 (2003).

III. THE DEFENSES BASED ON EXCUSE

1. Alibi and Consent

Rule of Law: Alibi and consent are complete defenses.

Alibi and consent are examples of complete defenses, which means that if the judge or jury accepts the defense as true, the defendant will be acquitted and go home. An **alibi** defense means that, at the time the crime occurred, the defendant was somewhere else and can prove it. For example, if the crime happened in Phoenix, Arizona, while the defendant was on the Great Wall of China, and the defendant can prove his or her whereabouts with plane tickets, photographs, and eyewitnesses, then the defendant will be acquitted. If successfully raised, an alibi defense disproves the government's contention that the defendant is the perpetrator of the crime. Prior to trial, as in the case of insanity, the defendant has an affirmative obligation to notify the government that he intends to raise such a defense at trial to give the government an opportunity to disprove it. If the state confirms the defendant's alibi, there may be no need for a trial.

---

[4]*Drope* v. *Missouri*, 420 U.S. 162 (1975).

Consent is the willing participation of the actor. For some crimes, the consent of the alleged victim may influence the *mens rea* of the defendant. There are crimes in which the consent, or willingness of the victim to participate in the crime, is a defense to the offender's liability, most notably for the crime of rape where the victim's consent is an essential element of the crime. Typically, whether or not the victim consented to the act giving rise to criminal liability is no defense; for example, it is not a valid defense in a murder case that the victim begged to be killed. Likewise, agreeing to become a fraternity or sorority pledge does not mean that one consents to alcohol poisoning or other initiation rites that may lead to serious bodily injury or death.

2. Mistake

Rule of Law: Mistakes of fact or law can be defenses in limited-fact situations.

Everybody makes mistakes. In criminal law, the question becomes, when do those mistakes excuse criminal liability? There are two types of mistakes: mistakes in fact and mistakes in law. A **mistake in fact** is when the offender takes certain action, believing certain facts to be true that, upon later discovery, are found not to be true, thus saving the offender from liability. For example, there are two similar-looking raincoats hanging on a coatrack at a restaurant. A man who retrieves a raincoat believing that he is the owner will not be charged with theft when he gets home and discovers that the raincoat actually belongs to someone else. The mistake in fact negates the man's *mens rea* for theft. As an example of a situation in which a mistake in fact does not necessarily save the offender from liability, consider the case of a high school student uninitiated in drug use who buys what he believes to be marijuana, but what is in reality common oregano. Buying oregano is not a crime, but such a mistake may not completely alleviate the student from an attempt charge. Another such example—one in which a mistake in fact definitely will not save the offender from liability—is that of a man who shoots another man in the head to kill him, not recognizing that his victim is already dead from a heart attack. The fact that you cannot kill the dead will not relieve the attacker of an attempted murder charge.

Ignorance of the law is no defense, but a defendant may claim **mistake in law** if he believes that certain legal principles do or do not apply to him and he is mistaken. A professor claiming that books bought at a bookstore qualify as a business expense deduction on his federal tax return may claim mistake of law if, indeed, it turns out that such purchases are not covered. He will probably have to pay the tax, but may avoid criminal prosecution for making the deduction in the first place. The Model Penal Code §2.04 in Appendix B provides the basic outline of mistake as a defense.

In *United States* v. *Anthony*, 24 F.Cas. 829 (1873), the famous suffragist [advocate for women's right to vote] Susan B. Anthony was indicted for voting for a candidate for Congress, which was a crime because at the time federal law allowed only men to vote. Could Anthony raise the defense that she believed, as an American citizen, that she had the right to vote and voted in accordance with her belief? The answer was no. Anthony knew that it was illegal for her as a woman to cast a vote and had to suffer the consequences of a criminal conviction for her illegal act.

Applying the Rule of Law to the Facts: When is mistake a legal defense?

- Cheek, an airline pilot, was a plaintiff in a civil suit that challenged the legality of the American government to collect income taxes. He was indicted and charged under the federal law that made it a crime to "willfully" not pay taxes. Representing himself and testifying on his own behalf at trial, Cheek asserted that he was mistaken about what the law required concerning his obligation to pay taxes and that such a mistake negated the willfulness *mens rea* requirement that was the basis of his conviction. Is Cheek's mistake defense legal?

Whether or not Cheek's mistake defense is legal is for the jury, not the judge, to decide. Because mistake is a *mens rea* defense and the government has to prove each and every element of the crime, including the *mens rea* element, if the jurors believe that Cheek's mistake was reasonable, they may vote for acquittal.[5]

3. Infancy

Each state has different laws addressing the proper treatment of children in the legal system. **Infancy** as a defense means that, due to his or her young age, the defendant could not possess the requisite state of *mens rea* to commit certain crimes. Despite the differences among the jurisdictions, there are general rules of applicability to keep in mind when examining an infancy defense. One general rule is the rule of presumptions. A presumption is a device in the law that suggests conclusions about certain facts. Under common law, there was a legal presumption that children under the age of seven had no capacity to form *mens rea*, a guilty mind. The presumption that children seven and under cannot form *mens rea* is irrebuttable. An **irrebuttable** presumption is irrefutable and cannot be overcome by additional evidence. For example, in 2001 first-grader Kayla Rollins was shot and killed by a six-year-old classmate. Under the law, the child who shot her could not be prosecuted, because the law believes that a child of that age is incapable of forming the requisite *mens rea* (purposeful, knowing, reckless, or negligent) to be held responsible, despite the community's outrage over the killing and desire to hold a criminal prosecution.

A **rebuttable presumption** means that other facts can overcome the presumption. It is a rebuttable presumption that children between the ages of 8 and 14 do not have the capacity to form *mens rea*, but that presumption can be overcome if the state shows that the child had the capacity to appreciate the criminality of his or her conduct.[6] For example, on March 24, 1998, two boys—Andrew Golden, 11, and Mitchell Johnson, 13—broke a window to reach in and release two locks at Golden's grandparents' house, where they stole four pistols, three rifles, and one Remington .30-06 deer hunting rifle with a high-powered telescope on top. The boys went to Westside Middle School in Jonesboro, Arkansas, and perched behind a grassy knoll outside the school. Golden crept down to the school and pulled a fire alarm, then ran back to the knoll and a waiting Johnson. When the schoolyard filled with children, Golden and Mitchell fired into the crowd. They killed four children and a teacher, shooting the teacher, Shannon Wright, twice. Nine other children and another teacher were wounded. Under the common law, there is a rebuttable presumption that the boys could not form *mens rea*, but the prosecution could overcome that presumption by showing that the boys planned the killings, took steps to achieve their criminal aims, and were aware of the criminality of their conduct when they drove off in a stolen van in an effort to flee. The boys were found "delinquent," the Arkansas equivalent to guilty after the judge rejected the boys' insanity and incompetency pleas. State law only provided for the boys to be held until they reached the age of 18 years, but additional federal gun charges allowed the boys to be kept confined until they reached 21 years of age. Mitchell Johnson was released from a federal detention facility in August 2005, and Golden was released in May 2007.[7]

The defense of infancy should not be confused with juvenile delinquency and juvenile court matters. Children over the age of 14 can form *mens rea*, and are typically brought before juvenile courts designed to handle cases involving children. However, according to some state jurisdictions, juveniles charged with serious crimes such as

---

[5]*Cheek* v. *United States*, 498 U.S. 192 (1991).

[6]*In re Gault*, 387 U.S. 1 (1967).

[7]"Arkansas School Shooter Turns 21, Freed." *United Press International*, August 10, 2005.

murder or rape may be transferred to adult court. Even if juveniles are transferred to adult court, they are not eligible for the death penalty. If they commit murder before the age of 18, they cannot be sentenced to death, even if they would be adults at the time of the execution. *Roper v. Simmons*, 543 U.S. 551 (2005).

4. Intoxication

Rule of Law: Intoxication can result from the use of alcohol or drugs and may be voluntary or involuntary (a person could be unaware that someone put an intoxicating agent in a drink or food).

Dependent on the jurisdiction, a state may or may not recognize intoxication as a defense to committing a crime. **Intoxication** means that one's central nervous system is affected by the ingestion of toxic substances, most commonly alcohol or drugs, both illegal and prescription. The state must recognize the defense for it to be valid. For example, Missouri does not recognize voluntary intoxication due to drugs or alcohol as a defense, and the state statute provides that "A person who is in an intoxicated or drugged condition, whether from alcohol, drugs or other substance, is criminally responsible for conduct." RS Mo 562.076.1. In contrast, Pennsylvania does allow the intoxication defense to reduce the specific intent of first-degree murder to the general intent of third-degree murder. Pennsylvania's statute provides that "neither voluntary intoxication nor voluntary drugged condition is a defense to a criminal charge, nor may evidence of such conditions be introduced to negative the element of intent of the offense, except that evidence of such intoxication or drugged condition of the defendant may be offered by the defendant whenever it is relevant to reduce murder from a higher degree to a lower degree of murder." 18 Pa.C.S. §308. Federal law also allows the defendant to introduce evidence that she was impaired by intoxicants if it negates specific intent to commit the crime. Virtually all jurisdictions recognize the defense of involuntary intoxication, in which the defendant was unknowingly drugged and committed a crime.

5. Duress

Rule of Law: Duress is being forced to commit a crime by threat of bodily harm or death; duress is rarely a defense to murder.

Although duress and necessity are both defenses in which people are forced to act in a certain way, the defenses are prompted by dissimilar factual situations. **Duress** in the common law excused the actions of a criminal when those actions were compelled by threats from another human being. In contrast, traditionally, the necessity defense "is available when a person is faced with the choice of two evils and must then decide whether to commit a crime or an alternative act that constitutes a greater evil."[8] Under duress, the actor is acting without free will; under the defense of necessity, the actor is actively choosing one lesser evil. The duress defense excuses the criminal actor from liability if it can be shown that she acted out of fear of imminent serious bodily injury to herself or others close to her. Duress is rarely a defense to murder. So if the defendant was approached by a man who said, "Go kill a high-ranking executive at the bank or I'll kidnap and torture your children," the defense of duress may be unavailable to her at her murder trial. The elements of the duress defense are:

1. imminent threat of serious bodily injury or death
2. apparent ability to carry out the threat
3. no reasonable opportunity to escape the harm other than to commit the crime.

---

[8]*United States v. Dorrell*, 758 F.2d 427 (9th Cir. 1985).

Courts hold that the threat has to be immediate, not in the distant or even near future. The avenue of escape must be foreclosed to the defendant for the defense to be valid. Often an opportunity to go to the authorities for help will negate the defense. Defendants have raised the defense in cases involving kidnapping, treason, escape, possession with intent to distribute drugs, lying under oath, contempt, embezzlement, and fraud.

In *United States* v. *Solano*, 10 F.3d 682 (9th Cir. 1993), the defendant was charged with methamphetamine production. He claimed he committed the crime because of threats to his life and the lives of his family, but his defense failed when it was shown that he possessed the precursors to make the drug even after the individual threatening him had died. *In Dixon* v. *United States*, 126 S.Ct. 2437 (2006), the defendant lied when she filled out paperwork to purchase more than one handgun at different gun shows. The purchase of guns at gun shows is typically less regulated by federal law than the purchase of firearms from a licensed dealer. She was convicted under federal gun laws. At trial, Dixon said she committed the crime only because her boyfriend had threatened that if she did not, he would bring violence upon her and her children. The jury did not believe her. On appeal, the high Court said,

> The duress defense, like the defense of necessity that we considered in *United States* v. *Bailey*, 444 U. S. 394 (1980), may excuse conduct that would otherwise be punishable, but the existence of duress normally does not controvert any of the elements of the offense itself. As we explained in *Bailey*, "[c]riminal liability is normally based upon the concurrence of two factors, 'an evil-meaning mind [and] and evil-doing hand. . . .'" Like the defense of necessity, the defense of duress does not negate a defendant's criminal state of mind when the applicable offense requires a defendant to have acted knowingly or willfully; instead, it allows the defendant to "avoid liability . . . because coercive conditions or necessity negates a conclusion of guilt even though the necessary *mens rea* was present." Since she didn't prove it by a preponderance, her conviction is affirmed.

Applying the Rule of Law to the Facts: **When may a defendant make a successful duress defense?**

- A man entered a bank with a bomb collar around his neck. When police stopped him, he claimed that an unknown assailant had placed the bomb around his neck and was waiting nearby to detonate the bomb if he did not rob the bank. Is duress a reasonable defense?

Yes, the elements for a successful duress defense have been met. The offender was forced to commit a crime under the threat of physical harm or death. This example is drawn from the true story of an attempted robbery in Erie, Pennsylvania. While the man was waiting for the bomb squad, the bomb exploded, killing the would-be-robber.

6. Insanity

Rule of Law: **Insanity means that the defendant could not appreciate the nature of his conduct or did not think what he was doing was wrong.**

The issue of whether or not a defendant was "insane" at the time of the commission of his crime has been hotly debated in criminal law for decades. The defense of insanity is a legal question, not a medical or psychological one. That is, lawmakers decide on the definition of insanity. Some states, such as Kansas, Montana, Idaho, and Utah, have abolished the defense altogether but still allow evidence of a defendant's defective *mens rea* at the time of the commission of the crime. Meanwhile, the federal government has amended its definition and the burden of proof for such a claim on at

FIGURE 8.1 Handwritten legal brief in the "Unabomber" case.

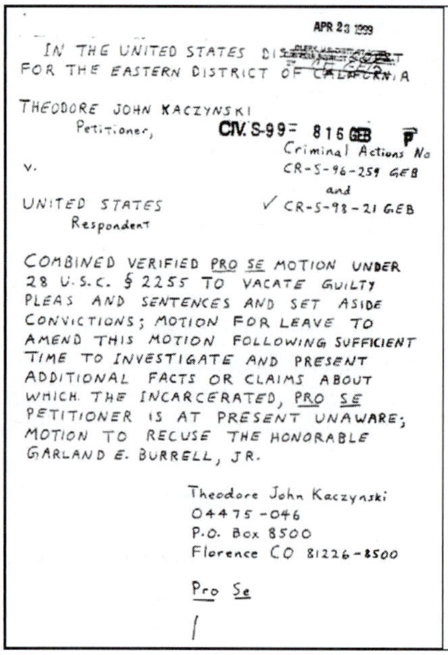

APR 23 1999

IN THE UNITED STATES DISTRICT COURT
FOR THE EASTERN DISTRICT OF CALIFORNIA

THEODORE JOHN KACZYNSKI
Petitioner,

CIV. S-99- 816 GEB P

Criminal Actions No
CR-S-96-259 GEB
and
CR-S-98-21 GEB

v.

UNITED STATES
Respondent

COMBINED VERIFIED PRO SE MOTION UNDER 28 U.S.C. § 2255 TO VACATE GUILTY PLEAS AND SENTENCES AND SET ASIDE CONVICTIONS; MOTION FOR LEAVE TO AMEND THIS MOTION FOLLOWING SUFFICIENT TIME TO INVESTIGATE AND PRESENT ADDITIONAL FACTS OR CLAIMS ABOUT WHICH THE INCARCERATED, PRO SE PETITIONER IS AT PRESENT UNAWARE; MOTION TO RECUSE THE HONORABLE GARLAND E. BURRELL, JR.

Theodore John Kaczynski
04475-046
P.O. Box 8500
Florence CO 81226-8500

Pro Se

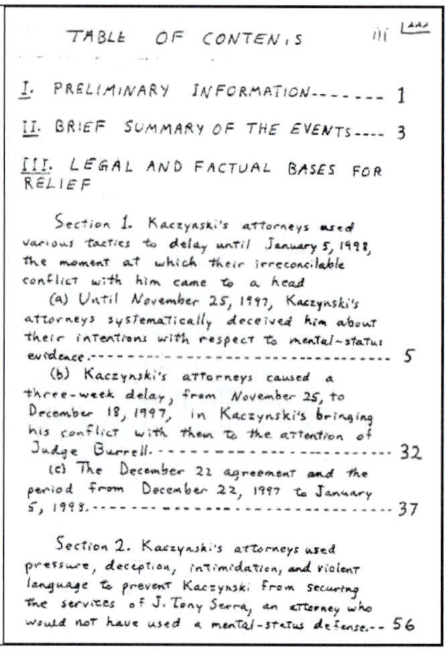

TABLE OF CONTENTS iii

least three occasions since the 1950s.[9] There are many permutations of the insanity defense and other defenses that are based on diminished or impaired *mens rea*. This section examines the most widely recognized of those defenses.

Some defendants go to great lengths to prevent their defense counsel from raising a defense of insanity or some other mental defect that would save the defendant from a harsher charge based on the ability to form *mens rea*. Theodore J. Kaczynski was a former professor at the University of California at Berkeley who was charged with a series of mail-bombings that killed 3 people and wounded 23. The federal government sought the death penalty for these crimes, even after promising his family, who helped the authorities catch Kaczynski, that it would not.[10] Rather than allow his attorneys to plead that he was insane, Kaczynski asked the court to let him represent himself, a motion the court denied. He eventually pleaded guilty and received a sentence of life without parole. The first pages of his handwritten appeal appear in Figure 8.1. In his appeal, he alleged that the trial judge's denial of his motion to represent himself left him no other choice than to plead guilty, since he did not wish his attorneys to portray him as mentally ill. His appeal on this issue was denied.[11]

a. M'Naghten Test for Insanity

The standard legal test for insanity was named after Daniel M'Naghten (some spellings include McNaughton), who came to believe that the British Prime Minister Robert Peel was part of a conspiracy to kill him. In 1843, M'Naghten waited outside Peel's residence at No. 10 Downing Street, intending to kill Peel, but he mistakenly killed Peel's secretary, Edward Drummond, instead. M'Naghten was held not responsible for Drummond's murder "by reason of insanity," a verdict that made Queen Victoria very unhappy. In

[9]*See* Edith Greene, Kirk Heilbrun, William H. Fortune, and Michael T. Nietzel. *Wrightsman's Psychology and the Legal System, Sixth Edition*. (Belmont, CA: Thomson Wadsworth, 2007).

[10]Personal communication, David Kaczynski, Summer 2005.

[11]"Unabomber's Appeal for a New Trial is Denied." *The New York Times*, February 13, 2001, p. A28

response, British Lords presented questions to high court judges who enunciated what is now known as the M'Naghten test for insanity that if "at the time of committing the act, the accused was laboring under such a defect of reason, from disease of the mind, as not to know the nature and quality of the act he was doing, or if he did know it, that he did not know what he was doing was wrong" then he could be excused from committing the crime and tendered to the proper mental facility.

The present-day definition of **insanity** applies if, at the time the accused committed the crime, he was suffering under such a defect of reason caused by a mental illness that he:

1. did not know that what he was doing was wrong and
2. did not know the nature and quality of his act.

It is important to note that a person could be suffering from an extreme mental illness and yet still know the difference between right or wrong, which would make the person legally sane. In June 2001, in Houston, Texas, housewife Andrea Yates said goodbye to her husband Rusty as he left for work at the nearby National Aeronautics and Space Administration ("NASA") facility. Then she proceeded to systematically drown her four sons and one daughter. She described chasing down her oldest son, Noah, as he ran for his life after seeing his four siblings laid out on the bed. As Noah lay lifeless in the tub, Andrea called the police and her husband to confess. At her first trial, her counsel entered a plea of not guilty by reason of insanity, as Andrea's motive for the drownings was to save the children because "they would burn in hell if she did not kill them while they were still innocents."

Despite Andrea's extensive psychiatric history that included inpatient hospital stays and treatment with powerful antipsychotic medication, the jury found her legally sane because her decision to wait for Rusty to leave for work before killing the children and her immediate call to authorities after the drownings indicated that she clearly knew right from wrong. Because Andrea could describe for police with chilling accuracy her actions in drowning her children one-by-one, one juror said "it seemed as if she was thinking pretty clearly."[12] Yates won a new trial because of nonexistent evidence introduced by prosecution expert Park Dietz, who testified about a crime-show episode in which a mother who had drowned her children was acquitted by reason of insanity. An author writing a book about Yates discovered that no such episode existed, and the appeals court reversed Yates's conviction, finding that "there is a reasonable likelihood that Dr. Dietz's false testimony could have affected the judgment of the jury."[13] At Yates's second trial in the summer of 2006, the jury found her not guilty by reason of insanity.

In our chapter opening scenario, Billy was suffering from **delusions**, which are persistent false fixed beliefs, and those delusions dictated his decisions to defend himself on the night in question even though, in reality, his life was never in danger.

b. The Durham Rule

In 1954 Chief Judge David Bazelon of the D.C. Court of Appeals wrote his famous decision in *Durham* v. *United States*, 214 F.2d 862 (D.C. Cir. 1954), which has since been overturned. What has been called the Durham Rule temporarily replaced M'Naghten in cases in which mental health experts could show that the defendant was not criminally responsible for his or her behavior because it was produced by a "mental disease

---

[12]"Who is Andrea Yates? A Short Story about Insanity." *Duke Journal of Gender Law & Policy*, Vol. 10 (2005), pp. 1–60.

[13]*Yates* v. *State*, 171 S.W.3d 215 (Tex. App. 2005); *see also* Skip Hollandsworth. "The Satanic Versus: At her Retrial This Summer, Andrea Yates Once Again Insisted that the Devil Made Her Do It. In a Way, the Devil Did." *Texas Monthly*, Vol. 34, No. 9 (September 2006).

or defect." The Durham Rule did not work, largely because it placed importance on the psychiatrists' ability to diagnose mental diseases or defects and did not place any importance on the jury's decision of whether or not the defendant had the requisite *mens rea* for the crime. In addition, alcoholics, compulsive gamblers, and other addicts used the defense with great success to escape from criminal responsibility.

c. The ALI Substantial Capacity Test

The American Legal Institute ("ALI"), authors of the Model Penal Code, introduced as part of the code the definition that a defendant was not responsible for his act if, at the time of the offense, as the result of mental disease or defect, he lacked "substantial capacity *either* to appreciate the criminality of his conduct *or* to conform his conduct to the requirements of the law." In these cases, defendants could be found not guilty by reason of insanity. Approximately half the state jurisdictions that allow a defendant to raise an insanity defense use the M'Naghten definition of insanity, while the other half employ the ALI definition. The typical evidentiary burden for proving insanity in most jurisdictions is on the defendant to prove insanity by clear and convincing evidence, a burden that is not as onerous as beyond a reasonable doubt.

The federal government amended the law allowing the use of an insanity plea in federal courts after the trial of John W. Hinckley, Jr. Hinckley claimed he was insane during his attempt to assassinate President Ronald Reagan in Washington, D.C., on March 31, 1981, when he shot not only the President, but three others as well. One victim, Reagan Press Secretary James Brady, was the inspiration for the gun-control effort dubbed the Brady Bill. The evidence presented at trial revealed that Hinckley, a failed college student from an upper-class family, had a history of mental disturbance. He had become fixated on the actress Jodie Foster, who, at age 13, had starred as a teenage prostitute in the movie "Taxi Driver." In this movie, Robert DeNiro plays cab driver Travis Bickel, who attempts to assassinate a political figure as a claim to fame. Hinckley stalked Foster while she was an undergraduate at Yale and tried to assassinate Reagan in an effort to impress Foster and win her affection.

The federal law at the time Hinckley went to trial used the ALI definition of insanity and placed the burden of proof on the prosecution. That is, once the defendant claimed he was not guilty by reason of insanity, the prosecution had to disprove his claim. After Hinckley's acquittal, the government changed the law and passed the Insanity Defense Reform Act of 1984, 18 U.S.C. §4241 et seq., which:

1. limited the definition of insanity to be applied by federal courts
2. shifted the burden of proof to the defendant to prove insanity by clear and convincing evidence
3. amended the federal rules of evidence to restrict expert testimony on whether or not the defendant was insane at the time of the crime, leaving that issue for the jury to decide
4. provided federal commitment procedures for persons with a mental disease or defect, and
5. amended the procedures to determine a defendant's competency to stand trial.

Now most all jurisdictions that retain the insanity defense place the affirmative burden on the defendant to prove his claim.

d. Guilty but Mentally Ill

Thirteen states allow a jury to conclude that a defendant remains criminally responsible, while acknowledging that the person's criminal behavior was most likely caused by mental illness, by finding the defendant guilty but mentally ill ("GBMI"). The GBMI verdict does not necessarily replace the verdict of guilty by reason of insanity, but does supplement it in the states that use it. Unlike the affirmative defense of insanity, GBMI is a verdict that jurors can return if they find that the evidence warrants it. The GBMI statute in Pennsylvania follows.

PENNSYLVANIA CONSOLIDATED STATUTES §314
GUILTY BUT MENTALLY ILL

    a. <u>General Rule</u> A person who timely offers a defense of insanity in accordance with the Rules of Criminal Procedure may be found "guilty but mentally ill" at trial if the trier of facts finds, beyond a reasonable doubt, that the person is guilty of an offense, was mentally ill at the time of the commission of the offense and was not legally insane at the time of the commission of the offense . . .

    c. <u>Definitions</u>

        1. "Mentally ill." One who as a result of mental disease or defect, lacks substantial capacity either to appreciate the wrongfulness of his conduct or to conform his conduct to the requirements of the law.

    d. <u>Common law M'Naghten's Rule preserved</u> Nothing in this section shall be deemed to repeal or otherwise abrogate the common law defense of insanity (M'Naghten's Rule) in effect in this Commonwealth on the effective date of this section.

If the defendant receives such a verdict, it is hoped that the defendant will be placed in a correctional facility that treats mentally ill convicts. Millionaire John E. DuPont of the DuPont chemical company was suffering from paranoid schizophrenia for years before he killed Olympic wrestler David Schultz as Schultz was coaching wrestlers at DuPont's state-of-the-art wrestling center. DuPont's jury returned a GBMI verdict, and he was transferred to the correctional facility in Camp Hill, Pennsylvania, specifically for the mental treatment he would receive.

e. Irresistible Impulse

Sometimes the defendant is cognizant of the wrongfulness of his conduct but due to a defect or disease of the mind he cannot control his actions. Such behavior allows for an irresistible impulse defense that he simply could not control his impulses to cause harm—that he had no emotional brakes between his irrational thoughts and the criminal conduct. In an 1868 case, a judge defined the defense to the jury when he said "if this impulse arises from a defect of reason, so that it cannot control the exercise of his mental powers, and the crime is committed in such a condition, he is in such a condition as excuses him from responsibility.[14] Another popular definition of the irresistible impulse states that an offender would commit the crime even if he had a "policeman at his elbow."[15]

f. Diminished Capacity

For those defendants for which a M'Naghten insanity plea is unavailable because they knew the difference between right and wrong and they might also have had the ability to appreciate the wrongfulness of the conduct, some states allow a plea of diminished capacity. Under this plea, the defendant can offer evidence that he was suffering from a mental disorder that negated his specific intent to commit the crime. Missouri jury instructions define mental disease or defect as "any mental abnormality regardless of its medical label, origin, or source." The definition includes "congenital and traumatic mental conditions as well as disease" but excludes certain conditions, such as criminal abnormal sexual conduct manifested by repeated criminal or otherwise antisocial conduct, and drug and alcohol abuse without psychosis.[16]

In the *Clark* case reprinted in part in Box 8.1, the defendant was suffering from paranoid schizophrenia when he shot and killed a police officer. Arizona uses a modified M'Naghten test for insanity and also limits and restricts expert testimony on insanity to

---

[14]*In re Cole's Trial*, 7 Abb. Pr. N.S. 321 (1868).

[15]*United States* v. *Kunak*, 5 U.S.C.M.A. 346 (1954).

[16]MAI-CR3d 306.02, 306.03 and RSMo §552.010.

BOX 8.1

Clark v. *Arizona*, 126 S.Ct. 2709 (2006)
Supreme Court of the United States

Justice Souter delivered the opinion of the Court.

FACTS

In the early hours of June 21, 2000, Officer Jeffrey Moritz of the Flagstaff Police responded in uniform to complaints that a pickup truck with loud music blaring was circling a residential block. When he located the truck, the officer turned on the emergency lights and siren of his marked patrol car, which prompted petitioner Eric Clark, the truck's driver (then 17), to pull over. Officer Moritz got out of the patrol car, and told Clark to stay where he was. Less than a minute later, Clark shot the officer, who died soon after but not before calling the police dispatcher for help. Clark ran away on foot but was arrested later that day with gunpowder residue on his hands; the gun that killed the officer was found nearby, stuffed into a knit cap.

At trial, Clark did not contest the shooting and death, but relied on his undisputed paranoid schizophrenia at the time of the incident in denying that he had the specific intent to shoot a law enforcement officer or knowledge that he was doing so, as required by the statute. Accordingly, the prosecutor offered circumstantial evidence that Clark knew Officer Moritz was a law enforcement officer. The evidence showed that the officer was in uniform at the time, that he caught up with Clark in a marked police car with emergency lights and siren going, and that Clark acknowledged symbols of police authority and stopped. The testimony for the prosecution indicated that Clark had intentionally lured an officer to the scene to kill him, having told some people a few weeks before the incident that he wanted to shoot police officers.

As to his insanity, then, Clark presented testimony from classmates, school officials, and his family describing his increasingly bizarre behavior over the year before the shooting. Witnesses testified, for example, that paranoid delusions led Clark to rig a fishing line with beads and wind chimes at home to alert him to intrusion by invaders, and to keep a bird in his automobile to warn of airborne poison. There was lay and expert testimony that Clark thought Flagstaff was populated with "aliens" (some impersonating government agents), [that] the "aliens" were trying to kill him, and [that] bullets were the only way to stop them. A psychiatrist testified that Clark was suffering from paranoid schizophrenia with delusions about "aliens" when he killed Officer Moritz, and he concluded that Clark was incapable of luring the officer or understanding right from wrong and that he was thus insane at the time of the killing. In rebuttal, a psychiatrist for the State gave his opinion that Clark's paranoid schizophrenia did not keep him from appreciating the wrongfulness of his conduct, as shown by his actions before and after the shooting (such as circling the residential block with music blaring as if to lure the police to intervene, evading the police after the shooting, and hiding the gun).

At the close of the defense . . . the judge noted that though Clark was indisputably afflicted with paranoid schizophrenia at the time of the shooting, the mental illness "did not . . . distort his perception of reality so severely that he did not know his actions were wrong." The sentence was life imprisonment without the possibility of release for 25 years.

ISSUE

The case presents two questions: whether due process prohibits Arizona's use of an insanity test stated solely in terms of the capacity to tell whether an act charged as a crime was right or wrong; and whether Arizona violates due process in restricting consideration of defense evidence of mental illness and incapacity to its bearing on a claim of insanity, thus eliminating its significance directly on the issue of the mental element of the crime charged (known in legal shorthand as the *mens rea*, or guilty mind)?

HOLDING

We hold that there is no violation of due process in either instance. [Arizona can use the right/wrong test for insanity *and* can dictate the limits of evidence introduced to establish or negate the *mens rea* element for murder].

RATIONALE

Clark first says that Arizona's definition of insanity, being only a fragment of the Victorian standard from which it derives, violates due process. The landmark English rule in M'Naghten's Case, 10 Cl. & Fin. 200, 8 Eng. Rep. 718 (1843), states that "the jurors ought to be told . . . that to establish a defence on the ground of insanity, it must be clearly proved that at the time of the committing of the act, the party accused was laboring under such a defect of reason, from disease of the mind, as not to know the nature and quality of the act he was doing; or, if he did know it, that he did not know he was doing what was wrong."

When the Arizona Legislature first codified [enacted a statute] an insanity rule, it adopted the full M'Naghten statement (subject to modifications in details that do not matter here). Under current Arizona law, a defendant will not be adjudged insane unless he demonstrates that "at the time of the commission of the criminal act [he] was afflicted with a mental disease or defect of such severity that [he] did not know the criminal act was wrong," Ariz. Rev. Stat. Ann. §13-502(A) (West 2001).

"If [Clark] did not know he was shooting at a police officer, or believed he had to shoot or be shot, even though his belief was not based in reality, this would establish that he did not know what he was doing was wrong." The trial court apparently agreed, for the judge admitted Clark's evidence of cognitive incapacity for consideration under the State's moral incapacity formulation. And Clark can point to no evidence bearing on insanity that was excluded. His psychiatric expert and a number of lay witnesses testified to his delusions, and this evidence tended to support a description of Clark as lacking the capacity to understand that the police officer was a human being. There is no doubt that the trial judge considered the evidence as going to an issue of cognitive capacity, for in finding insanity not proven he said that Clark's mental illness "did not . . . distort his perception of reality so severely that he did not know his actions were wrong." We are satisfied that neither in theory nor in practice did Arizona's 1993 abridgment of the insanity formulation deprive Clark of due process.

Clark's second claim of a due process violation challenges the rule adopted by the Supreme Court of Arizona in State v. Mott, 187 Ariz. 536 (1997). This case ruled on the admissibility of testimony from a psychologist [who] offered to show that the defendant suffered from battered woman syndrome and therefore lacked the capacity to form the *mens rea* of the crime charged against her. The state court held that testimony of a professional psychologist or psychiatrist about a defendant's mental incapacity owing to mental disease or defect was admissible, and could be considered, only for its bearing on an insanity defense; such evidence could not be considered on the element of *mens rea*, that is, what the State must show about a defendant's mental state (such as intent or understanding) when he performed the act charged against him.

Unlike observational evidence bearing on *mens rea*, capacity evidence consists of judgment, and judgment fraught with multiple perils: a defendant's state of mind at the crucial moment can be elusive no matter how conscientious the enquiry, and the law's categories that set the terms of the capacity judgment are not the categories of psychology that govern the expert's professional thinking. Although such capacity judgments may be given in the utmost good faith, their potentially tenuous character is indicated by the candor of the defense expert in this very case. Contrary to the State's expert, he testified that Clark lacked the capacity to appreciate the circumstances realistically and to understand the wrongfulness of what he was doing, but he said that "no one knows exactly what was on [his] mind" at the time of the shooting. And even when an expert is confident that his understanding of the mind is reliable, judgment addressing the basic categories of capacity requires a leap from the concepts of psychology, which are devised for thinking about treatment, to the concepts of legal sanity, which are devised for thinking about criminal responsibility.

This state of affairs does considerable injustice to psychiatry and, we believe, possibly to criminal defendants. These psychiatric disagreements . . . cause less than fully understanding juries or the public to conclude that psychiatrists cannot agree. In sum, these empirical and conceptual problems add up to a real risk that an expert's judgment in giving capacity evidence will come with an apparent authority that psychologists and psychiatrists do not claim to have. We think that this risk, like

(continued)

BOX 8.1

(continued)

the difficulty in assessing the significance of mental-disease evidence, supports the State's decision to channel such expert testimony to consideration on the insanity defense, on which the party seeking the benefit of this evidence has the burden of persuasion. Arizona's rule serves to preserve the State's chosen standard for recognizing insanity as a defense and to avoid confusion and misunderstanding on the part of jurors. For these reasons, there is no violation of due process, and no cause to

claim that channeling evidence on mental disease and capacity offends any "'principle of justice so rooted in the traditions and conscience of our people as to be ranked as fundamental.'"

CONCLUSION

The judgment of the Court of Appeals of Arizona [affirming Clark's conviction] is, accordingly affirmed.

---

the sole issue of insanity at the time the crime was committed, versus a general *mens rea* defense. For a good history of the *mens rea* diminished capacity defenses, students should read the opinion in its entirety.

Applying the Rule of Law to the Facts: When is a *mens rea* defense applicable?

- Tom was waiting at the underground subway station for the train to go uptown. As the train approached, Tom heard a voice inside his head urge him to push the man standing before him in front of the oncoming train (irresistible impulse), which he did. The man subsequently died from his injuries. But Tom wasn't there to see it, because he was convinced that a chip lodged in his stepfather's head had sent the mysterious message to Tom's brain. When police caught up with Tom, he was trying to saw his stepfather's head off at the neck to get at the offending chip (insanity). Tom told police that sawing off the head was the only logical way to stop the messages. What defenses may he use?

Irresistible impulse for pushing the man in front of the train and insanity for not being able to distinguish right from wrong.

g. What Happens to Those Found Not Guilty by Reason of Insanity?

Defendants who successfully raise an insanity defense and are found not guilty are often automatically committed to a secure mental hospital for an indefinite amount of time. In *Jones* v. *United States*, 463 U.S. 354 (1983), the U.S. Supreme Court held that a defendant who was acquitted of a criminal offense by reason of insanity could be confined to a mental institution until he has regained his sanity or is no longer a danger to himself or others, even if that commitment time turns out to be longer than any sentence he might have received had he been sentenced to the original crime. To determine whether the defendant is competent to be released, the mental institution holds a review hearing on the status of the offender, who may be conditionally released back into society. As with probation, if an offender fails to meet the conditions of his release, such as attending counseling sessions or refraining from taking illegal drugs, his conditional release may be revoked and he will be returned to the institution.

In 2005, federal district judge Paul L. Friedman allowed John Hinckley at least seven overnight visits, including three visits of three nights each and four visits of four nights each, to his parents' home in Williamsburg, Virginia. The overnight visits and travel were an extension of local outings and overnight visits with his parents within 50 miles of St. Elizabeth's hospital, where Hinckley has been treated since the assassination attempt.[17] Such liberal outings are allowed because of medical evidence which indicates that Mr. Hinckley no longer suffers from the psychotic delusions which persuaded him to try to kill President Reagan and that Hinckley "does not present a danger to himself or others." Federal prosecutors continue to object to Hinckley's visits, and in September 2006 they filed documents with the court indicating that the declining health of Hinckley's parents makes it difficult for them to supervise Hinckley during these visits.[18] The court has said that Hinckley shows no sign of psychosis and that he should be released.

Contrary to popular belief, most insanity pleas are not for murder or mayhem, but for lesser types of crime, such as theft.

7. Statute of Limitations

Rule of Law: There is no statute of limitations for the crime of murder.

Statutes of limitations place limits, defined by legislators, on the time during which an action can be brought in both civil and criminal cases. For example, if a man is injured after slipping and falling in a federal building, he has to bring a lawsuit against the federal government within two years of the injury, or he will be forever barred by the statute of limitations from bringing a claim. Many states have different statutes of limitations for various crimes, but there is no limitation for the crime of murder. Statutes of limitations can be tolled [stopped] by certain events, such as the suspect's leaving the jurisdiction and thwarting the process of justice from taking place. The constitutional limitation on statutes of limitations is that they cannot be retroactively applied in a manner that violates the ex post facto clause which prohibits criminalizing conduct that was not a crime when it was committed. In *Stogner* v. *California*, 539 U.S. 607 (2003), Stogner was indicted for sex-related abuse that occurred during the years 1955 and 1973. When the alleged abuse took place, the statute of limitations on the books for prosecuting such crimes was three years. California later amended its statute of limitations laws in child sex abuse cases because of the typically long delay between the occurrence of acts of molestation and the eventual disclosure of the abuse. The U.S. Supreme Court found in Stogner's favor and held that California's amended statute of limitations law violated the ex post facto clause of the Constitution.

IV. THE DEFENSES BASED ON JUSTIFICATION

Rule of Law: Necessity is a choice between two evils.

1. Necessity

Necessity as a defense means that the offender had to choose between committing the crime or suffering greater harm to himself. The development of the defense was first raised in the seminal case *Regina* v. *Dudley and Stephens*, 14 Q.B.D. 273 (1884), concerning three sailors and a cabin boy who were on a lifeboat after their ship sank. After 12 days adrift with no food or water, two of the older men, Thomas Dudley and Edward Stephens, killed 17-year-old cabin boy Richard Parker, ate his flesh, and drank his blood. After Dudley and Stephens were rescued, the Crown charged them with murder. They offered the defense of necessity, explaining that they had chosen the

---

[17]"Judge Allows Longer Travel by Hinckley." *The New York Times*, December 31, 2005, p. A13

[18]"Parents' Health Spurs Calls to Revisit John Hinckley's Trips." *Daily Press* (Newport News, VA), September 22, 2006.

lesser of two evils (eating the boy or dying themselves). The court recognized the dire circumstances of the men at sea but found them guilty of murder, saying

> To preserve one's life is generally speaking a duty, but it may be the plainest and the highest duty to sacrifice it. War is full of instances in which it is a man's duty not to live but to die. The duty in the case of a shipwreck, of a captain to his crew, of the crew to the passengers, of soldiers to women and children ... these duties impose on men the moral necessity, not of preservation, but of the sacrifice of their lives for others ... It is not correct, therefore, to say that there is any absolute or unqualified necessity to preserve one's life. In this case the weakest, the youngest, the most unresisting, was chosen. Was it more necessary to kill him than one of the grown men? The answer must be "No."

After the sailors were convicted, Queen Victoria later reduced their death sentences to six months' imprisonment.

The elements of necessity are as follows:

1. the offender was faced with two evils and chose the lesser of them
2. the offender acted to prevent imminent harm
3. there was a relationship between his conduct and the harm to be avoided
4. there were no legal alternatives.

A review of federal law has rejected the necessity defense in cases in which (1) a felon charged with possession of a firearm claimed necessity because he had to take the gun away from his girlfriend's son who was threatening suicide; (2) marijuana smokers were treating their glaucoma with the drug; (3) Americans smuggled Central American illegal aliens through a modern-day underground railroad because the Immigration and Naturalization Service and courts would not judiciously hear their cases; (4) antinuclear protesters destroyed infrastructure associated with nuclear energy; and (5) individuals brought the illegal drug laetrile into the United States to treat cancer patients.[19] The defense must introduce sufficient evidence that circumstances existed forcing the choice of the lesser evil and that there were no safer alternatives to choosing the lesser evil. The prosecution has the burden of proof that the defendant did not act out of necessity but instead, fulfilled the elements of the crime charged.

2. Self-Defense

Rule of Law: **One has a right to use reasonable force to repel an attack upon oneself or others.**

Self-defense is the right to defend oneself against force, injury, or death by meeting it with equal force. The law does not require an individual being attacked to accept the attack out of fear of being criminally responsible for harming his or her attacker. Self-defense is a complete defense. That is, if a victim of an attack maims or kills the attacker, the victim will spend no time in jail, because the attack was justified. But there are certain requirements that must be met to assert a valid self-defense claim. The successful self-defense claim has the following elements:

1. the victim was confronted
2. with an immediate physical threat
3. and had to use a reasonable amount of force
4. to repel the attack

---

[19]Citations correspond to the following numbers: (1) *United States* v. *Newcomb*, 6 F.3d 1129 (6th Cir. 1993); (2) *United States* v. *Burton*, 894 F.2d 188 (6th Cir. 1990); (3) *United States* v. *Aguilar*, 883 F.2d 662 (9th Cir. 1989); (4) *United States* v. *Montgomery*, 772 F.2d 733 (11th Cir. 1985); (5) *United States* v. *Richardson*, 588 F.2d 1235 (9th Cir. 1978).

When a person is confronted with a show of force sufficient to put his life in danger, it is justified to use force to repel such an attack. The prevailing view under the common law and in modern statutes is that, under an objective analysis, the force used by the victim must have been reasonable to repel the attack. The other qualifying factor for the victim to use force is that the threat of physical harm must be imminent, defined as "threatening to occur immediately; near at hand, impending." If a professional basketball player who stands over seven foot tall and weighs approximately 340 pounds approaches a man who is a little over five feet tall and weighs 115 pounds, can the smaller man stab the larger man as a defensive measure and claim that he felt that one slap from the larger man would send him through the door? No; using deadly force would be justified only if the smaller man reasonably believed that such force was necessary to prevent great bodily harm or death.

Applying the Law to the Facts: Is it self-defense?

- A man sitting quietly on a train in a subway was approached by four youths armed with a screwdriver and demanding money. The man had been robbed before and knew of recent muggings in the area. He took out his gun and shot the four boys. The man then approached one of the boys and said, "You don't look too bad," before shooting him again and paralyzing him.

Yes, it's self-defense. In 1984 Bernhard Goetz shot four African-American youths who had approached Goetz on the New York subway and asked him for five dollars. The charges of attempted murder were dismissed by the court, which found that Goetz reasonably feared for his life. Goetz was convicted of unlawfully carrying a concealed weapon.

a. Defense of Others

In certain situations, a person can claim self-defense on behalf of another who is being attacked as if the person were standing in the victim's shoes. If someone comes upon an old woman being attacked, the person could repel the attacker as if he were standing in the old woman's shoes. The amount of force used to repel the attack must still be reasonable given the situation. In *People* v. *Young*, 12 A.D.2d 262 (1st Dept. 1961), a messenger came upon two men beating a younger man. The messenger thought that the younger man needed assistance, so he entered the fray and broke one of the attackers' legs. The older men were plain clothes detectives making a lawful arrest, and the messenger was convicted of assault. In reversing his conviction, the appellate court said, "had the facts been as he thought them, he would have been a hero and not condemned as a criminal actor." The higher court then reversed the appeals court, and said,

"One who goes to the aid of a third person does so at his own peril. While the doctrine [of defense of others by standing in their shoes] adopted by the court below may have support in some states, we feel that such a policy would not be conducive to an orderly society . . . The right of a person to defend another ordinarily should not be greater than such person's right to defend himself." The New York legislature then amended their Penal Code to provide:

A person may use physical force upon another person when and to the extent he reasonably believes such to be necessary to defend himself or a third person from what he reasonably believes to be the use or imminent use of unlawful physical force by such other person.

b. Imperfect Self-Defense

In the law the term imperfect means incomplete or defective. In the context of self-defense, if the force used was disproportionate, the self-defense claim may fail. The basic rule of self-defense is that the victim can use no more force than necessary to repel the attack. **Imperfect self-defense** claims are raised typically in situations where the victim is claimed to have provoked the attack or is the initial aggressor, or the force used to repel an attack was unreasonable under the circumstances. In *United States* v. *Peterson*, 483 F.2d 1222 (1973), Peterson was inside his house when Keitt came to steal windshield wipers from an abandoned car on Peterson's property. Peterson approached Keitt with a gun, and Keitt approached Peterson with a raised wrench. Peterson warned Keitt not to take another step, then shot Keitt to death. On appeal for a conviction of manslaughter, Peterson claimed that the trial court was in error in not instructing the jury that he had a right to use deadly force to save himself from serious bodily harm or death, the threat posed by Keitt. The court upheld Peterson's conviction because, even though Keitt may have been the aggressor in coming to the property to steal, Peterson was not entitled to use more force than was necessary to repel the attack. "One cannot support a claim of self-defense by a self-generated necessity to kill. The right of homicidal self-defense is granted only to those free from fault in the difficulty; it is denied slayers who incite the fatal attack, encourage the fatal quarrel or otherwise promote the necessitous occasion for taking life." As for Peterson, a claim of self-defense that is imperfect will reduce what would normally be a murder charge to manslaughter because the perpetrator does not possess the requisite *mens rea* for an intentionally premeditated and deliberate murder.

c. Battered Woman Syndrome

Battered woman syndrome technically is not a defense, but a syndrome suffered by a woman or any person in a domestic relationship who has been repeatedly physically and emotionally battered by someone with whom they have an intimate connection. Anyone can be a battered person, not just a wife, and battering can take place in all types of relationships: parent–child, grandparent–grandchild, same-sex partners, and, most often, man–woman. The syndrome is often used in court to explain why a victim may kill his or her abuser when the abuser is not posing an immediate threat of harm: BWS is a type of self-defense whose focus is on the victim's inability to perceive threats of violence in the same reasonable frame of mind as someone who is not in a battering relationship. A noted scholar on violence in intimate relationships, Lenore Walker, states that most battering relationships revolve around a cycle of violence. The cycle of violence has three phases:

Phase 1: Tension-building phase
Phase 2: Acute battering incident
Phase 3: Honeymoon phase

When two people fall in love, they see each other through rose-colored glasses; everything about the other person seems wonderful. In a relationship in which violence is used as a means of control, the couple will eventually enter the first phase in a cycle of violence, the tension-building phase during which one partner begins to belittle and criticize the other about appearance, housekeeping or lovemaking skills, or ability to be a good parent. This phase is usually characterized by minor acts of violence such as pinches, slaps, or pulling of the hair. The second phase is an acute battering incident in which the victim is severely beaten, perhaps to the point where they may need medical care, as punishment for causing the batterer to lose control. The third phase is the honeymoon phase, during which the batterer may apologize, bring gifts home as a token of contrition, blame the beating on an intoxicated or drugged state, and make promises never to do it again. In time, the cycle of violence repeats again and again. The psychology of a battering relationship is unique, and popular culture holds many myths about battering victims that contribute to the victims' sense of isolation. The biggest myth is that a domestic violence victim can leave a relationship at any time. Actually, many

---

BOX 8.2

Pennsylvania v. *Stonehouse,* 555 A.2d 772 (1989)
Supreme Court of Pennsylvania

Justice Larsen delivered the opinion of the court.

FACTS

On the morning of March 17, 1983, Appellant[20] [Carol Stonehouse] shot and killed William Welsh. The events culminating in Welsh's death are so bizarre that one would be tempted to dismiss them as the stuff of pulp fiction were it not for the corroboration of disinterested witnesses and for the fact that the literature on the "battered woman syndrome" is replete with similar cases. The chronology of events leading to Welsh's death are as follows. In March of 1980, less than a month after Stonehouse completed her training as a police cadet and assumed her duties as a police officer in the City of Pittsburgh, Stonehouse met Welsh. Welsh was married at that time and had served as a Pittsburgh police officer for approximately twenty years. Stonehouse had been twice divorced. The two began dating shortly after they met. Within the first three months of their relationship, Welsh broke into Stonehouse's apartment once and, shortly thereafter, made such a nuisance of himself by banging on her door late at night, that she called the police. That incident was treated as a "domestic" by the officers, who knew Welsh, and no police report was filed. Stonehouse attributed Welsh's behavior to a drinking problem and continued dating him. Welsh was possessive and demanding with respect to his relationship with Stonehouse. By the fall of 1980, whenever Stonehouse did not do what he told her to do, Welsh would let the air out of the tires of her car. This occurred as often as two or three times a week. Welsh admitted doing this, but insisted that Stonehouse would never be able to prove he was doing it.

Arguments began to occur with some frequency, and, after one such argument, Welsh was able to enter Stonehouse's secured apartment building and place flowers outside her door. Welsh told Stonehouse the flowers were for her funeral. Welsh also put sugar in the gas tank of Stonehouse's car,

and on many occasions he would take Stonehouse's car and move it, or he would pull the ignition wires. It was also in the fall of 1980, that Welsh began to harass Stonehouse by telephoning her late at night. Welsh justified his acts of vandalism and harassment by stating to Stonehouse that she "deserved it." In the summer of 1981, Stonehouse's landlord did not renew Stonehouse's lease because of Welsh and the arguments that were disturbing the other tenants. When Stonehouse prepared to move from her apartment, Welsh came in, broke a box of dishes, and left without saying a word. Welsh left notes everywhere for Stonehouse—on her car, at work, at the spa, and he started to follow her everywhere she went. At trial, Stonehouse introduced three notes into evidence, which notes Welsh had evidently overlooked. One was blank; one stated: "Have a nice day, asshole," and the third stated: "41-year-old bifocal bitch."

Welsh continued to harass Stonehouse by filling her dresser drawers with water, soaking the clothes in her closet, and leaving beer bottles all over her apartment. One night, after Stonehouse's daughter and grandchild moved out at the end of 1981, Welsh turned on the gas in Stonehouse's apartment. Stonehouse became quite ill, but Welsh woke her in the morning with all the windows open, saying "I couldn't do it to you this time, you bitch. I'll do it the next time." Welsh continued to follow Stonehouse everywhere, and he continued to enter her apartment at night.

In September of 1982, Stonehouse filed harassment charges against Welsh with a magistrate. At the hearing, witnesses testified about Welsh breaking Stonehouse's doors and following her, and appearing uninvited at social events to which Stonehouse had been invited. Welsh admitted harassing Stonehouse and admitted breaking her nose. Welsh was ordered to stay away from Stonehouse for sixty days. At that time, Stonehouse dated another man briefly. Welsh gave the man's estranged wife Stonehouse's name, address and

(continued)

---

[20]For clarity, the word "Appellant" in the opinion has been replaced by "Stonehouse."

BOX 8.2

(continued)

phone number and warned the man not to see Stonehouse, saying "Remember, you got kids." Welsh also followed Stonehouse and that man on a date and threatened Stonehouse's companion with a gun. At the next hearing before the magistrate in November, 1982, the charges were dismissed because Welsh had not been harassing Stonehouse.

When Stonehouse returned to her residence she found that Welsh had again wrecked and defiled her apartment. There were seventeen knife slashes in Stonehouse's waterbed. The water damaged the apartment on the first floor occupied by another tenant, and ... flowed into the basement of the building. Drapes had been slashed or torn off the windows and stuffed into the toilet. Stonehouse's clothes were soaking in the bathtub with beet juice and hot water. Cleaning supplies, cold cream, lotion, food and potting soil were smeared all over the walls, windows, floors, mirrors and rugs. Curtain rods and racks were torn off the walls. The back door was off its hinges, and every closet was emptied, every piece of furniture upset. Stonehouse filed a police report, but did not pursue charges against Welsh with the magistrate because Welsh convinced her that his friends would say he had been elsewhere that night.

On March 16, 1983, the night before the shooting, Stonehouse drove to a friend's house. Welsh followed in his vehicle, tailgating Stonehouse and bumping into the rear of her car at traffic lights. Stonehouse and her woman friend went to a lounge and had a few drinks. Welsh appeared there, so Stonehouse and her friend left and went to an after hours club. Stonehouse spoke briefly with an old friend and neighbor, Steve Owens. Welsh, who had followed Stonehouse to the club and who also knew Owens, asked Stonehouse: "Are you going to take him home tonight, slut?" Stonehouse took her woman friend home shortly thereafter at about 4 or 5 in the morning, and returned to her apartment to prepare for bed.

Steve Owens went, uninvited, to Stonehouse's apartment and, shortly thereafter, Welsh began kicking the front door. Stonehouse did not go to the door, but she became quite upset, realizing that Welsh was "going to do something." Welsh then went to the back door and started kicking and

banging on it. Knowing that Welsh would be able to break in the back door, Stonehouse went to the door holding a gun at her side and let Welsh in. There was a struggle for the gun. Welsh took the gun from Stonehouse, but Stonehouse and Owens were able to retrieve the gun from Welsh. Owens testified that Welsh appeared to be "wild-eyed" and was not "the person that I had known." Welsh immediately left, and within seconds, Welsh threw a brick through the window of Stonehouse's car, prompting a neighbor to remark to her son: "He really looks like he's mad today."

Stonehouse called the police, and Owens left to get cigarettes as they waited for the police to arrive.

Stonehouse knew Welsh would return because he always returned, so she stepped out onto the back porch to look for him, not wanting to be caught with her guard down. As she leaned over the railing, Stonehouse saw Welsh on the ground below aiming his gun at her. Believing that she heard a shot, Stonehouse fired her gun twice. One of the bullets entered Welsh at the top of his right shoulder and exited near his clavicle, severing a major artery. At the time of his death, Welsh's blood alcohol level was .14. Welsh was found dead beside his van with the fingers of his left hand wrapped around the grip and trigger of a .357 Magnum revolver that had not been fired.

On September 14, 1983, a jury convicted Stonehouse of murder of the third degree . . . and Stonehouse was sentenced to seven to fourteen years imprisonment on July 25, 1984.

ISSUE

[Was Stonehouse's] trial counsel . . . ineffective in failing to request a jury instruction that would require the jury to consider the cumulative effects of psychological and physical abuse when assessing the reasonableness of a battered person's fear of imminent danger of death or serious bodily harm with respect to a claim of self-defense?

HOLDING

[Yes.] The trial court did not instruct the jury as to the legal relevance of the history of abuse presented at trial on behalf of Stonehouse. The failure of counsel to request this instruction was clearly erroneous under the law of this Commonwealth.

REASONING

When evidence of self-defense arises from any source, the Commonwealth must disprove self-defense beyond a reasonable doubt. To sustain that burden, the Commonwealth must prove that 1) the defendant did not reasonably believe that he or she was in danger of death or serious bodily injury; 2) the defendant provoked the use of force; or 3) the defendant had a duty to retreat and retreat was possible with complete safety. The trial court herein properly determined that Stonehouse had no duty to retreat. Nor was there any serious contention that Stonehouse provoked the attack on her by Welsh on the morning of March 17. [n.5 The prosecutor attempted to show that Stonehouse deliberately provoked Welsh's attacks by talking with and dating other men]. The only issue remaining, therefore, was whether Stonehouse had a reasonable belief that she was in imminent danger.

In *Commonwealth* v. *Watson*, 431 A.2d 949 (1981) this Court stated that "[where] there has been physical abuse over a long period of time, the circumstances which assist the court in determining the reasonableness of a defendant's fear of death or serious injury at the time of a killing include the defendant's familiarity with the victim's behavior in the past." Thus, the jury should have been apprised of the fact that the abuse Stonehouse suffered for three years was to be considered by the jury with respect to the reasonableness of Stonehouse's fear of imminent danger of death or serious bodily injury. Stonehouse's trial counsel had no reasonable basis for failing to request such a charge to the jury, and the absence of the charge was prejudicial to Stonehouse in that the jury

likely would have found Stonehouse not guilty of murder of the third degree if such an instruction had been given.

In addition, Stonehouse asserts that her trial counsel was ineffective in failing to present expert testimony regarding the characteristics of the victims of psychological and physical abuse, where uncontradicted testimony revealed that Stonehouse was the victim of such abuse, and the jury, without the aid of expert testimony, rendered a verdict based upon erroneous myths concerning the victims of such abuse. This is the issue that *amici* [plural of *amicus*, meaning friend (of the court)] framed in terms of the "battered woman syndrome."

It has long been the law of this Commonwealth that "[e]xpert testimony is admissible in all cases, civil and criminal alike, when it involves explanations and inferences not within the range of ordinary training, knowledge, intelligence and experience." Because the battered woman syndrome is not within the ordinary training, knowledge, intelligence, and experience of jurors, we believe that expert testimony regarding battered women is admissible as the basis for proving justification in the use of deadly force where the defendant has been shown to be a victim of psychological and physical abuse. "A battered woman is a woman who is repeatedly subjected to any forceful physical or psychological behavior by a man in order to coerce her to do something he wants her to do without any concern for her rights." Walker, *The Battered Woman* at xv (1979). Battered women have been compared to hostages, prisoners of war, and concentration camp victims,[21] and the battered woman syndrome is recognized as a post-traumatic stress disorder.

It is widely acknowledged that commonly held beliefs about battered women are subject to myths

(continued)

---

[21] The court's footnote reads: *See State* v. *Hundley*, 236 Kan. 461 (1985), where the court stated: The abuse is so severe, for so long a time, and the threat of great bodily harm so constant, it creates a standard mental attitude in its victims. Battered women are terror-stricken people whose mental state is distorted and bears a marked resemblance to that of a hostage or a prisoner of war. The horrible beatings they are subjected to brainwash them into believing there is nothing they can do. They live in constant fear of another eruption of violence. They become disturbed persons from the torture. See also Crocker, "The Meaning of Equality for Battered Women Who Kill Men in Self-Defense," *Harvard Women's Law Journal*, Vol, 8, No, 30 (1985), pp. 121, 128. Researchers have suggested that the psychological effects of the battered woman syndrome can be compared to classic brainwashing. Comment, "The Battered Spouse Syndrome as a Defense to a Homicide Charge Under the Pennsylvania Crimes Code," *Villanova Law Review*, Vol. 26 (1980), pp. 105, 111–12. These effects include fear, hyper-suggestibility, isolation, guilt, and emotional dependency, which culminate in a woman's belief that "she should not and can not escape."

BOX 8.2

(continued)

that ultimately place the blame for battering on the battered victim. For example, battered women are generally considered to be masochists who derive pleasure from being abused. This myth was exploited by the prosecutor in the instant case when he asked Stonehouse if she was "a willing participant in the activities that went on between [her] and William Welsh," and when he stressed to the jury in his closing argument that if Stonehouse had truly been an innocent victim she could have put an end to the relationship. Similarly, this myth was given credence by the Superior Court which determined that Stonehouse's assertion of self-defense was unreasonable because of "[t]he continued relationship between Stonehouse and the victim." These "blame the victim" myths enable juries to remain oblivious to the fact that battering is not acceptable behavior, and such myths do not begin to address why battered women remain in battering relationships.

Other myths commonly believed about battered women are that battered women are uneducated and have few job skills and that the police can protect the battered woman. These myths were also exploited by the prosecutor, who introduced testimony that detailed the police training Stonehouse had received, implying that her training made her incapable of being victimized by a batterer, and who argued to the jury that Stonehouse could have been rescued, if she had wanted to be rescued, by a law enforcement system ready, willing and able to protect women who are victims of domestic violence. [n.10 An additional myth advanced by the prosecutor was that Stonehouse used weapons to defend herself and having used weapons did not conform to the stereotype of battered women who suffer their beatings passively. Although there are battered women who do not defend themselves and die as a result of their injuries, the fact that a woman attempts to defend herself from a beating does not make her any less a battered woman when her attempts do not stop the repeated episodes of physical and emotional abuse.]

To the contrary, researchers have shown that many battered women are highly competent workers and successful career women, who include among their ranks doctors, lawyers, nurses, homemakers, politicians and psychologists. Moreover, statistics have shown that police departments do not make arrests as often in domestic assault cases as they do in nondomestic assault cases. *See Watson* v. *Kansas City, Kansas*, 857 F.2d 690 (10th Cir. 1988); *see also* testimony of Pittsburgh Police Lieutenant Michael Conroy, who was one of the first officers to arrive at Stonehouse's apartment on the morning of the shooting: "Any type of a domestic disturbance — very, very seldom is ever a police report made." A properly qualified expert would have been able to assail these myths and to inform the jury that battered women are nearly always subject to intense sexual jealousy which leads them to isolate themselves socially. Expert testimony would reveal that battered women view batterers "as omnipotent in terms of their ability to survey their women's activities," and that there are reasons for battered women's reluctance to seek help from others, such as fear, embarrassment, and the inability of police to respond in ways that are helpful to the battered women. Expert testimony would also have shown that among battered women who kill, the final incident that precipitates the killing is viewed by the battered woman as "more severe and more life-threatening than prior incidents."

On the basis of such expert testimony, the jury could have found that Stonehouse herein was a battered woman and that, like most battered women, Stonehouse was isolated and justifiably believed that no one could help her solve her predicament except herself. It was clear from the evidence presented at trial that Welsh's colleagues in the police department did little to protect Stonehouse from Welsh's surveillance, harassment, acts of vandalism, and assaults. Yet, the prosecutor argued to the jury that the lack of adequate police protection in this instance had less of a bearing on Stonehouse's sense of isolation than it did on the Commonwealth's theory that Stonehouse must not have really been a helpless victim of battering.

There was no reasonable basis for trial counsel not to call an expert witness to counter the erroneous battered woman myths upon which the Commonwealth built its case. Thus, trial counsel was ineffective, and the absence of such expert testimony was prejudicial to Stonehouse in that the jury was permitted, on the basis of unfounded myths, to assess Stonehouse's claim that she had a reasonable belief that she faced a life-threatening situation when she fired her gun at Welsh.

CONCLUSION

[We] reverse the order of Superior Court which affirmed the judgment of sentence, and we remand for a new trial consistent with this opinion.

victims have been threatened with death if they leave, and they are fully aware that it is only a matter of time before an acute battering incident occurs again. In the case reprinted in part in Box 8.2, the prosecutor insisted the victim could not be a battered woman because she was a police officer.

∂. Defense of Property

Under the **defense of property** doctrine, an individual may use force to protect his or her home, consistent with the philosophy that "a man's home is his castle." Generally, a person cannot use deadly force to defend property, such as setting up booby traps rigged to kill in the event that someone enters the door. The law frowns upon taking a life that cannot be replaced in defense of property, which can always be replaced. Also, rigging booby traps to protect property is generally unlawful because "to employ mechanical devices imperils the life of children, firemen, and policemen acting within the scope of their employment, and others" and may kill and maim others instead of the unwanted intruder.[22] When people are confronted within their own homes, the legal rules about the amount of force they may use to protect themselves and their property become different. In this scenario, the use of deadly force is defensible if it is reasonable to use force to repel the attack, if a reasonable amount of force was used, and if, in most, but not all, jurisdictions, the victim tried to resolve the situation by using a non-deadly alternative prior to using deadly force.

i. **Retreat Doctrine**   "A man's house is his castle—for where shall a man be safe if it be not in his house?"[23] The **retreat doctrine** declares that people who are confronted in their homes need not run away from their homes before using deadly force.[24] But justified self-defense is considered against the necessity to use force to protect oneself. One cannot rightly claim that an act of violence was necessary in self-defense if one had the option to retreat or run away from the threat. The Model Penal Code recognizes the retreat doctrine but many jurisdictions do not allow it because, the thinking goes, it is better for one to run away, where possible, than to kill someone. The issue of retreat usually arises only when deadly force is used.

3. Entrapment

Rule of Law: Entrapment is a defense which states that outrageous government conduct induced an individual to commit a crime who was not otherwise predisposed to commit the crime.

The defense of **entrapment** is based on outrageous government conduct that induces a defendant to commit a crime he was not otherwise criminally predisposed to commit. The entrapment defense most often arises in criminal cases in which undercover

---

[22]*People* v. *Ceballos*, 526 P.2d 241 (1974).

[23]Sir Edward Coke, Third Institute.

[24]*People* v. *Tomlins*, 107 N.E. 496 (N.Y. 1914) ("It is not now and never has been the law that a man assailed in his own dwelling is bound to retreat.")

officers pose as criminals and offer opportunities or otherwise induce defendants to commit crimes. In some cases, the undercover officers create fictitious crimes in order to ensnare the defendants into committing numerous small crimes, building up to more serious crimes over a period of time—a practice that serves two goals: (1) In the case of drugs, it eliminates the defense that the offender was not predisposed to commit the crime because he willingly did on numerous occasions, and (2) the larger the crime the undercover officers can encourage a defendant to commit, the longer the prison sentence is likely to be.

There are two tests to determine whether a defendant has been entrapped by the government, the objective and the subjective test. The U.S. Supreme Court discussed the subjective test in *Sorrells* v. *United States*, 287 U.S. 435 (1932), in which a government agent asked Sorrells to procure liquor during the Prohibition Era when it was illegal to do so. On the agent's third request, Sorrells did procure liquor and later was convicted for the offense. On appeal, Sorrells argued that the jury should have been given an entrapment instruction. The Supreme Court agreed with Sorrells and stated that if, under the defendant's personal *subjective* perception, "the criminal design originates with the officials of the government, and they implant in the mind of an innocent person the disposition to commit the alleged offense and induce its commission in order that they might prosecute," then the defendant may raise the entrapment defense. The *objective* test for entrapment does not examine the defendant's predisposition, but asks whether the government's interaction with citizens makes previously unpredisposed people willingly commit crimes. A majority of jurisdictions follow the *Sorrells* approach, which focuses on the subjective predisposition to commit the crime. For a look at the objective test at work, examine the reasoning used by the Pennsylvania Supreme Court *Pennsylvania* v. *Thompson*, reprinted in part in Box 8.3.

BOX 8.3

Pennsylvania v. *Thompson*, 484 A.2d 159 (1984)
Superior Court of Pennsylvania

Judge Montemuro delivered the opinion of the court.

FACTS

Beginning on May 1, 1980, state police Trooper Lucinda Hammond became involved in an undercover investigation of appellant[25] [Russell Thompson, a Carlisle policeman], a 46-year-old black male who was married and living with his wife and mentally retarded daughter in Carlisle. At the time this investigation began, he was a ten-year veteran of the Carlisle Borough Police Force. Trooper Hammond [the undercover officer] was a young, blonde, white female who apparently was very attractive.

Trooper Hammond's first "face-to-face" contact with Thompson was on July 10, 1980 at the square in Carlisle. He was on duty, and she approached him with a question about a false temporary driver's license which apparently was used as a pretext for starting a conversation. She testified that at the time her hair was long and straight and she wore mid-thigh cut-off shorts and a short-sleeved jersey. During the conversation which ensued, the two began talking about "partying"

---

[25]For clarity, the word "appellant" has been substituted with "Thompson."

and having a good time. Thompson discussed with Hammond his purported use of marijuana and she let him know that she "partied" and "got high." He then told her he would be able to get drugs for her.

The second encounter between Thompson and Hammond occurred on August 8, 1980 when she again walked up to him while he was on duty. She was again dressed in cut-offs and a jersey. There was a brief conversation, but no mention of drugs. Sometime after this meeting, Hammond began to telephone Thompson at his place of work, the Carlisle Police Station. These calls continued over the course of the investigation, totaling at least eight to ten in all. Thompson never contacted Hammond and she never provided him with a means of doing so.

The third direct contact between them occurred on September 3, 1980, when she again walked up to him while he was working. She wore a blouse that was open in the back and shoulders, as well as her by now standard cut-offs. Thompson recognized her immediately and started a friendly conversation, which included a discussion of drugs and getting high. He tried to get her to meet him after work at a tavern called the Oliver Plunkett, but she declined and instead arranged to meet him the next night at another tavern called Yancy's.

As had been arranged, they met and had drinks together at Yancy's on September 4. It was their fourth meeting and first date. Again the discussion turned to partying and getting high. Thompson stated to Hammond that he kept marijuana in his locker at work which he would seize during drug arrests and then use himself. This appears to have been mere braggadocio [there was no evidence that Thompson had ever made a drug arrest or had drugs in his police locker]. She asked if he was going to get some of this marijuana and he said no. He repeatedly, on that evening and throughout the investigation, indicated to her that he wanted her to trust him that [even though he was] a policeman, he liked fun too. He assured her that he was not trying to set her up.

The fifth direct contact occurred on September 29, after she had called him at the police station. They met again at Yancy's for a date, and she then asked him to obtain some marijuana for her personal use or "maybe make a little money on the side." He responded by again trying to get her to go to the Oliver Plunkett after hours with him, telling her she could get some marijuana if she would go

with him. She declined to do so and left Yancy's. The next and sixth personal contact did not occur until December 17, 1980. She had talked to him, however, on October 23 and 24, and, in another telephone conversation on November 25, had "point blank" asked him if he could make a deal for some drugs. On November 26 and December 3, she traveled to Carlisle looking for Thompson but could not find him. At the December 17 meeting, when he was on duty, she again asked him about getting drugs. As before, he wanted her to meet him after midnight and she would not do so.

It is clear from the testimony that on or about December 1980 or January 1981, they were kissing at the end of their dates or meetings, either at her car or while in his car. They were often seen together in public in Carlisle, and Thompson would put his arm around her and introduce her to his friends. She concluded from his conduct that he was possibly interested in a romantic or sexual relationship, although he always treated her respectfully.

Eventually, she arranged a meeting with him on the evening of March 23 at the Hamilton Lounge. She testified [about this meeting] on direct examination that: A. After he made these statements about being able to take care of me as far as drugs were concerned, seeing how this was something I had heard from him on several occasions before I just really didn't take it that seriously. And I just said to him, well, you know, you are all talk. I have heard this before. And that's all I ever hear is just talk. And he said, well, I am going to show you that I am on the level here. He said I am going to get a dime bag of grass this evening. And while I was talking with him another individual entered the bar . . . .

Q.   The codefendant in this case?

A.   That's correct.

Q.   Go ahead, what happened next?

A.   And shortly afterwards [Thompson] called over to Mr. Coleman. And he took a $10.00 bill out of his pocket and put it on the bar. And he said to Mr. Coleman, "I want you to get me a dime bag of grass."

Thompson thereafter obtained 4.5 grams of marijuana from his friend, a Mr. Coleman, and gave it to Hammond. Thompson and Hammond then left the bar and went to his car where he rolled some

(continued)

BOX 8.3

(continued)

marijuana cigarettes with papers supplied by Hammond. She offered to pay for the marijuana, but he refused to accept any money.

ISSUE

Did the [l]ower [c]ourt err in finding that under the facts in this case the police conduct in the investigation did not constitute entrapment as a matter of law?

HOLDING

[Yes, Thompson was entrapped by the Carlisle police.]

REASONING

We now turn our attention to the issue of entrapment. The present test for entrapment is set forth in section 313 of the Pennsylvania Crimes Code, 18 Pa.C.S. §313. That section states, in pertinent part,

§313. ENTRAPMENT

a. General rule.—A public law enforcement official or a person acting in cooperation with such an official perpetrates an entrapment if for the purpose of obtaining evidence of the commission of an offense, he induces or encourages another person to engage in conduct constituting such offense by either:
   1. making knowingly false representations designed to induce the belief that such conduct is not prohibited; or
   2. employing methods of persuasion or inducement which create a substantial risk that such an offense will be committed by persons other than those who are ready to commit it.

The test for entrapment in Pennsylvania under section 313 is an objective one which "focus[es] on the conduct of the police and will not be concerned with the defendant's prior criminal activity or other indicia of a predisposition to commit crime." This statute represented a significant shift in Pennsylvania law, in that it rejected the then-existing use of a subjective test in entrapment cases, *i.e.*, a test which focused on the defendant's predisposition to commit the crime. . . . A careful review of the record in this case reveals no

significant discrepancy in testimony of the Commonwealth's sole witness (Trooper Hammond) and of Thompson regarding the course of conduct between the two over a ten month period. Thompson was a middle-aged black male and the trooper was a young, blonde, attractive female. A series of meetings and telephone calls occurred over a ten-month period, all at the initiative of Trooper Hammond. Drugs were constantly discussed. Although it is not always clear who brought the subject up on each occasion; what is clear is that beginning on September 29, 1980, Hammond began requesting drugs from Thompson. By early 1981, and perhaps earlier, Hammond began to chide and criticize Thompson for his consistent failure to obtain or provide drugs. Beginning in late 1980 or early 1981, the two began kissing after each meeting. Hammond also permitted Thompson to put his arm around her, walked around in public with him, and socialized with his friends. The critical question, of course, is whether or not this uncontradicted testimonial evidence of police conduct establishes entrapment as a matter of law.

As [U.S. Supreme Court] Justice Frankfurter noted, this "crucial question [is] not easy of answer." *Sherman* v. *United States*, 356 U.S. at 382. . . . [T]he opinions of this court addressing the entrapment defense provide us with direction in deciding, even if not providing examples of, the existence of entrapment. In *Commonwealth* v. *Manley*, the appellant Manley acted as middle-man in four drug sales to an undercover officer which occurred over a period of a month and a half. The transactions had been set up by an informant who was a friend of Manley. Manley argued entrapment, contending that he was induced by the informant's repeated requests for drugs. In finding no entrapment existed as a matter of law, the *Manley* court noted that there was no evidence indicating the undercover agent was aware of the number or type of requests made by the informant, nor that the agent had "encouraged [the informant's] repeated requests in order to wear down Manley's resolve."

In *Commonwealth* v. *Stokes*, we found no entrapment existed in a case where the appellant Stokes sold heroin to an undercover agent. However, there the facts showed the officer had merely provided Stokes with a market for the drugs by letting Stokes know he was interested in buying some heroin, and had never importuned Stokes to make a sale. Hence, [the *Stokes* decision] reaffirmed the position, which was held in Pennsylvania prior to the enactment of section 313, that mere opportunity does not constitute entrapment. *See also Commonwealth* v. *Tami*, 455 A.2d 641 (1982). We have also stated that "artifice and stratagem are legitimate tactics that may be employed by law enforcement officials to detect and combat crime." *Commonwealth* v. *Lee*, 396 A.2d 724 (1978).

In light of all this, and under the facts of this case, we are convinced that the methods employed by the Commonwealth constitute entrapment as a matter of law. The Commonwealth, acting through Trooper Hammond, pursued a long-term, persistent course of persuasion and inducement aimed at luring Thompson into delivering marijuana to Hammond. The use of a young, blonde female to coax a middle-aged male, after months of kissing and socializing, into committing a minor crime is not police conduct that presents the "mere opportunity" to commit a crime. As this case clearly shows, opportunity and inducement are two separate consequences of police activity. The latter occurred here.

The law enforcement authorities clearly strayed beyond the limits of acceptable practice in this case. We cannot sanction methods of inducement such as this, which lure otherwise law-abiding citizens into crime. Here Thompson has conceded his guilt, as he must when the entrapment defense is invoked under the objective test. However, it is the Commonwealth that is guilty of the greater evil of playing an ignoble part.

CONCLUSION

Judgment of sentence is reversed.

V. Key Terms and Phrases

- alibi
- ALI substantial capacity test
- battered woman syndrome
- burden of persuasion
- burden of production
- consent
- defense of others
- defense of property
- delusions
- diminished capacity
- duress
- entrapment
- forensic assessment
- guilty but mentally ill
- imperfect self-defense
- infancy
- insanity
- intoxication
- irresistible impulse
- justification
- mental defect
- mental disease
- mistake of fact
- mistake of law
- M'Naghten test
- necessity
- not guilty by reason of insanity
- psychosis
- retreat doctrine
- self-defense
- statute of limitations

VI. Summary

1. **The public policy reasons for recognizing defenses to crime:** In American society, we want to punish criminal offenders on the basis of their legal and moral blameworthiness for their criminal conduct. Recognizing that there are certain defenses to criminal conduct allows fairness and equity to be interjected within the criminal justice system, as it reflects the fact that some people are not completely responsible for their actions or the crimes that they commit. Defenses are generally **affirmative defenses** and must be raised by the defendant, who has the **burden of production** (producing enough evidence to allow the issue to go to the jury) and the **burden of persuasion** (convincing the jury that it is more likely than not that the defense is valid).

2. **The different variations of the *mens rea*–based defenses such as infancy, intoxication, insanity:** There are different *mens rea* defenses that recognize a defendant's mental capacity and faculties may have been impaired at the time he or she committed the crime. One *mens rea* defense is the **insanity defense**, first recognized when Daniel M'Naghten killed the British Prime Minister's secretary under the delusion that the Prime Minister was trying to kill him. The **M'Naghten test** for insanity that is recognized in those jurisdictions which recognize an insanity defense provides that if the defendant could not distinguish right from wrong or did not know that his actions were wrong because he was laboring under a defect of the mind, then he is legally insane. There are

many variations of the insanity defense that allow defendants to ameliorate criminal conduct that was caused by their mental malfunctions even though they could be legally sane. These include the **irresistible impulse** defense, which recognizes that the defendant may have no emotional brakes to resist the impulse to commit a crime; the **ALI substantial capacity test**, which declares that if the defendant was unable to conform his conduct to the requirements of the law, then he has a defense; and the **guilty but mentally ill** verdict that gives juries an alternative to finding the defendant insane while still recognizing that the defendant's mental defect may have been the genesis of his criminal conduct.

3. **The various defenses based on justification and excuse, such as self-defense, necessity, duress and justification:** Sometimes people feel compelled to act out of **necessity** and choose the lesser of two evils, such as breaking into a cabin in the middle of a storm for life-saving shelter. Other times they commit crimes under **duress**, when they are compelled to commit a crime by another person who poses a serious immediate threat to the victim's own life. A third justification for criminal acts is **self-defense**, when someone is threatening bodily harm or death and the victim has the legal right to use the same amount of force to repel the attack. A victim may act in the **defense of others** as well, or defend property with less than deadly force, provided that the victim complies with the retreat laws applicable in his state jurisdiction.

4. **The consequences of making a mistake of law or a mistake of fact:** The **mistake of law** and **mistake of fact** are generally unavailable to defendants. When they are available for certain crimes, it is the jury's responsibility to resolve the issue whether such mistakes negate the *mens rea* required to find the defendant guilty of the crime charged.

5. **Battered woman syndrome, the defense of entrapment, and the statute of limitations: Battered woman syndrome** is not necessarily a defense, but rather a compilation of events and psychological reactions formed as a result of suffering repeated cycles of emotional and physical abuse that make the victim, usually a woman, kill or cause serious bodily harm to her partner, usually a male, based on her perception that her life is in danger, even though at the moment she maims or kills, there may be no overt threat to her life. Such evidence is usually introduced through expert testimony at the woman's trial. **Entrapment** is a defense which alleges that the government's conduct induced someone who is not otherwise predisposed to crime to commit a criminal act. The defendant has to show that the government's inducements to commit the crime were so attractive that, without them, the defendant would have remained law-abiding. The **statute of limitations** prevents the state from prosecuting some crimes because too much time has passed since the time the act occurred. There is no statute of limitations for the crime of murder.

VII. Discussion Questions

1. Do you think the insanity defense should be abolished? Why or why not?

2. Is the concept of diminished mental capacity a legal question or a medical one? Which professional discipline should be entrusted with defining the rules and regulations for mentally ill defendants in the criminal justice system?

3. Many compulsive disorders, such as pedophilia—sexual attraction to children—or substance abuse disorders—alcohol and drug addiction—are recognized as diseases or matters beyond the offender's control. Do you believe that punishment in prison is excessive for a disordered offender? If you think treatment is the solution, how should the offender repay society for the crimes caused by his or her disorder?

4. Describe the history of the development of the insanity defense.

5. Explain the difference between necessity and duress.

6. Why does the public not believe the so-called 'abuse excuses' that because offenders were mistreated as children or adults, their *mens rea* states may be diminished when they commit crimes?

VIII. Problem-Solving Exercises

1. In 2008, 11-year-old Patrick Boykin was accused of killing his 13-year-old sister. Boykin sobbed to investigators that the devil's voice kept telling him to kill her. Is he guilty of any crime, and if so, does he have any defenses?

2. Terry and Lynn were male lovers. Every Friday after work for three years, Terry would come home, drink some beer, and start to belittle Lynn. He would slap, kick, and punch Lynn, then apologize on Saturday morning and promise to stop drinking and never to do it again. After the California Supreme Court held on May 15, 2008, that same-sex couples have a constitutional right to marry Terry and Lynn planned to move to the Golden State to get legally married. In all of the

excitement and anticipation, Terry started to drink on Wednesday, Thursday, and Friday nights. His drinking episodes always culminated in slapping, kicking, and punching Lynn, and he always gave a remorseful apology. As they were loading the car for La Jolla, Terry said to Lynn, "What's taking you so long? I'm going to give it to you good," and Lynn responded by shooting him. Does Lynn have any defenses?

3. One night in a honky-tonk bar called the Hi-Ho Club, Mary was feeling good after drinking eight straight shots of Tequila. She was flirting with Bob when Bob's wife Nancy approached. Everyone in town knew Nancy had a reputation for having a short fuse and a violent temper. When Nancy approached Mary to tell her to get away from Bob, Mary, fearing the worst from Nancy, took out a pocket knife and stabbed Nancy in the leg. Nancy became enraged, lunged after Mary, and started to beat Mary's head into the hard concrete floor. Bob, fearing for Mary's life, pulled Nancy by the hair to get her off Mary. Nancy turned and slapped Bob just as Mary pulled out a revolver and shot Nancy in the back, paralyzing her from the waist down. Mary is being tried for attempted murder, and Bob is being tried with aggravated assault for pulling Nancy by the hair. Mary claims self-defense, and Bob claims defense of another when he was trying to defend Mary from Nancy. Discuss whether either defense will be successful.

4. John was a small-time drug dealer. One of his customers, Owen, was caught by federal drug agents. To negotiate for a less severe charge and, consequently, a less severe sentence, Owen decided to cooperate with the government and continue to make controlled purchases of drugs from John. The agents set up audio and video surveillance of John, and Owen continued to purchase small quantities of cocaine, but began to insist that John procure at least one kilogram of cocaine for Owen to buy. It took repeated requests and many months, but John finally secured the kilogram for Owen to buy. On the day of the proposed purchase, Owen told John he would get the money, and the agents discovered John in the car with the kilogram on his lap. At John's drug trial, he raised the defense of entrapment. Will he be successful?

IX. World Wide Web Resources

National Alliance for the Mentally Ill

http://www.nami.org/

U.S. Department of Justice Office on Violence Against Women

http://www.usdoj.gov/ovw/

Colorado's "Make My Day" Legislation

http://www.freecolorado.com/2003/04/makemyday.html

X. Additional Readings and Notes

Self-Defense

Kevin Heller. "Beyond the Reasonable Man? A Sympathetic but Critical Assessment of the Use of Subjective Standards of Reasonableness in Self-Defense and Provocation Cases." *American Journal of Criminal Law,* Vol. 26 (1998), pp. 1–120.

Imperfect Self-Defense

Geneva Brown. "When the Bough Breaks: Traumatic Paralysis—An Affirmative Defense for Battered Mothers." *William Mitchell Law Review,* Vol. 32 (2005), pp. 190–242.

Battered Woman Syndrome

Sarah Gibbs Leivick. "Use of Battered Woman Syndrome to Defend the Abused and Prosecute the Abuser." *Georgetown Journal of Gender and the Law,* Vol. 6 (2005), pp. 391-404.

Consent, Duress, and Necessity

Leo Katz. "Choice, Consent, and Cycling: The Hidden Limitations of Consent." *Michigan Law Review,* Vol. 104 (2006), pp. 628–670.

Luke Shulman-Ryan. "The Motion *in limine* and the Marketplace of Ideas: Advocating for the Availability of the Necessity Defense for some of the Bay State's Civilly Disobedient." *Western New England Law Review,* Vol. 27 (2005), pp. 299–364.

Insanity

Jennifer S. Bard. "Re-Aarranging Deck Chairs on the Titanic: Why the Incarceration of Individuals with Serious Mental Illness Violates Public Health, Ethical, and Constitutional Principles and Therefore Cannot Be Made Right by Piecemeal Changes to the Insanity Defense." *Houston Journal of Health Law and Policy,* Vol. 5 (2005), pp. 2–73.

Michael L. Perlin. "For the Misdemeanor Outlaw: The Impact of the ADA on the Institutionalization of Criminal Defendants with Mental Disabilities." *Alabama Law Review,* Vol. 52 (2000), pp. 193–238.

CHAPTER

9

Pretrial Identification, *Terry* Stops, and Arrests

"There is no force so democratic as the force of an ideal."

PRESIDENT CALVIN COOLIDGE

CHAPTER OBJECTIVES

Primary Concepts Discussed in This Chapter:

1. The methods of identifying suspects before trial
2. The legal standard for investigatory detentions (*Terry* stops)
3. The legal analysis guiding arrests
4. The legal remedy when the government uses excessive force

CHAPTER OUTLINE

Feature: *Chapter-Opening Case Study: Identification, Terry Stops, and Arrests*

Alice suspected Julie of trying to steal her boyfriend, Ed, and during a confrontation with her, she shot Julie and then went into hiding. Police interviewed known associates of Alice and began to tail Ed and watch his movements. One night after midnight, officers watched as Ed met two suspicious individuals, Elaine and Jimmy, in front of an electronics store. The three friends walked up and down the street in an obvious agitated manner, constantly looking around and pacing back and forth in front of the store. Thinking the trio was about to commit a crime, the officers approached the friends and began to ask routine questions about what the three were doing in the area [investigatory detentions or *Terry* stops are permissible on the basis of reasonable suspicion that criminal activity is afoot]. Officer Johns saw a weapon protruding from Elaine's pocket, immediately put his hands on Elaine, and took the gun out of her pocket [if, during a *Terry* stop, an officer has a reasonable belief that the suspect is armed, the officer can legally disarm the suspect]. Because Elaine did not have a permit to carry a concealed weapon, she was placed under arrest. Police then asked Jimmy for his name and asked him to produce identification, legal actions under the state's "Stop and Identify" statute. Jimmy refused, and he was placed under arrest [legal under a *Terry* stop to ask a suspect his name and require him to produce identification]. Ed showed his identification and was free to go.

Police continued following Ed until he led them to an apartment. Police watched as Alice came out and walked away. One officer bolted from his car and shouted to Alice, "Stop, you're under arrest!" As Alice began to run from the officer, he took out his revolver and shot her in the back [excessive force to shoot an unarmed fleeing felon to effectuate an arrest]. Alice was placed under arrest and taken to the hospital. When she recovered, officers took Alice down to the station to place her in a holding cell. A woman looking at mug shot books whispered to a nearby detective, "I think that's the woman who robbed me at gunpoint last year." Detectives then took Alice in handcuffs and walked her past the robbery victim, who again identified Alice as the robber [the one person show-up is the most suggestive technique of pretrial identification]. At their respective trials, Elaine moved to suppress the gun as the product of an unlawful search, Jimmy challenged the stop and identify statute as a violation of the Fourth Amendment, and Alice moved to suppress the pretrial show-up identification as unduly suggestive. Alice also brought a civil case of excessive force against the officer who shot and injured her. How should these cases be resolved?

INTRODUCTION

This chapter introduces the circumstances under which criminal justice professionals have legal authority to stop, question, detain, and arrest people in society, as well as the various law enforcement methods used to help victims and witnesses identify offenders before trial. The chapter explains the legal concepts of reasonable suspicion, probable cause, and unduly suggestive pretrial identification, and the standard to pursue a civil action against government officials who transcend their authority under the "color of law."

I. PRETRIAL IDENTIFICATION PROCEDURES

Identifying suspects is a three-step process: perceiving, remembering, and reporting.[1] There are many ways a defendant may be identified as the perpetrator of a crime before trial. Because some methods of **pretrial identification** are unduly suggestive and may impermissibly convince a witness that the suspect is the one who committed the crime even though he may be innocent, there are legal protections and technical considerations that protect a suspect from being misidentified as the perpetrator.

1. Eyewitness Identification

Rule of Law: There is a five-part test to determine eyewitness reliability. If a witness is not reliable or if the pretrial identification procedure is too suggestive, the identification may not be introduced against the defendant at trial.

An eyewitness is a person who saw a crime being committed. **Eyewitness identification** is the process by which the eyewitness identifies the suspect or the defendant as the actual perpetrator of the crime. Eyewitness identification is very potent evidence in court; when an eyewitness takes the witness stand, points to the defendant, and says, "That's the man who did it!" it has a strong impact on the jury. In recent years, though, many experts and psychological studies have indicated that eyewitness testimony is inherently unreliable. Out of the first 100 people exonerated and found not guilty due to DNA analysis, 98 had been convicted after being identified by an eyewitness as the one who committed the crime. Since the early 1980s, the study of eyewitness testimony has been conducted in a number of areas related to criminal justice, such as its influence on juror decision-making, the ability of the criminal justice system to protect those identified as guilty in case the witness was mistaken, the manner in which eyewitnesses to crime process information and retrieve memories to identify perpetrators, and interviewing techniques that officials can use with eyewitnesses to reduce or eliminate mistaken identifications. Research shows that, at trial, the confidence an eyewitness expresses in making the identification is the single most important factor of whether or not the jury believes the eyewitness's identification of the defendant. The primary criticism of eyewitness confidence at trial is that "accuracy of description is a rather poor predictor of accuracy of identification. Even more problematic is that biased line-up procedures can actually lead eyewitnesses to overestimate how good of a view they had of the perpetrator as well as lead them to develop false confidence."

The evolution of the legal standard relating to the admissibility of an eyewitness' identification of a suspect was clarified by two important decisions that remain the legal standard today, *Neil* v. *Biggers,* 409 U.S. 188 (1972) and *Manson* v. *Brathwaite,* 432 U.S. 98 (1977). In *Biggers,* the victim testified that she was grabbed from behind in the doorway to her kitchen and raped. When the victim screamed, her 12-year-old daughter came out of her bedroom and also began screaming. The rapist told the victim "tell her [the daughter] to shut up, or I'll kill you both." Over the next seven months, the victim could not identify the rapist from photographs, lineups, or even those who showed up for identification purposes. One day the police called the victim and asked her to come down to the station to identify Biggers, who was detained at the police station on another charge. The police instructed Biggers to say "shut up or I'll kill you" to the victim. The victim then identified Biggers as her rapist. Biggers was convicted of rape and, on appeal, argued that the victim's identification of him was unduly suggestive and

---

[1]Felice J. Levine and June Lovin Tapp. "The Psychology of Criminal Identification: The Gap from *Wade* to *Kirby*." *University of Pennsylvania Law Review,* Vol. 121 (1973), pp. 1079–1131.

therefore violated his due process rights to a fair trial. The U.S. Supreme Court held that even though the identification of Biggers in the one-man show-up in a police station was unduly suggestive that he was the rapist, under the totality of the circumstances test the victim's identification of Biggers was reliable and admissible in court. The totality of the circumstances test looks at all the unique facts and the inferences, or conclusions, that can be drawn from those facts in making a legal determination. The Court found that the length of time the victim looked at her rapist during the attack, the fact that she had not identified anyone over a seven-month period, and her certainty when she testified she had "no doubt" that Biggers raped her indicated that her identification was reliable. Biggers' conviction was affirmed.

Courts use a five-part test called the "Biggers test" to determine whether the eyewitness identification is reliable and, therefore, admissible against the defendant in court:

1. The opportunity of the eyewitness to view the offender at the time of the crime
2. The witness's degree of attention [during the crime]
3. The accuracy of the witness's prior description of the offender
4. The level of certainty displayed by the witness at the identification procedure, and
5. The length of time between the crime and the identification procedure.

In *Brathwaite,* the U.S. Supreme Court established an additional test in eyewitness identification cases to determine whether the eyewitness identification was reliable. The "Brathwaite test" has two prongs. First, the Court looked at whether the identification procedure itself was unduly suggestive. If the identification was unduly suggestive, the Court moved to the second prong which evaluated the circumstances under which the eyewitness made the initial identification. The facts of *Brathwaite* are illustrative. Officer Glover working undercover purchased heroin through the open door of an apartment. Within minutes of the purchase, Glover gave a description of the seller to fellow officer D'Onofrio. Officer D'Onofrio suspected Brathwaite might be the seller and obtained a mug shot and left it on Glover's desk. Two days later, Glover saw the photograph and identified Brathwaite as the heroin dealer. He was convicted and later appealed on the grounds that the pretrial identification procedure was unduly suggestive. The prosecution admitted that the identification procedure had been corrupted because there were no other photographs or suspects in a lineup to force Officer Glover to identify Brathwaite from many different people. The one photo array essentially transmitted "here's the guy" to Officer Glover. Despite the lack of objectivity in identifying Brathwaite, the U.S. Supreme Court used the *Biggers* five-part test and determined that, under the totality of the circumstances test, Officer Glover's identification was reliable. The *Brathwaite* decision reaffirmed the *Biggers* holding and reaffirmed that "reliability is the linchpin in determining the admissibility of identification testimony."

Applying the Rule of Law to the Facts: When is identification too suggestive?

- An eyewitness testified in front of a grand jury, at a preliminary hearing, and at trial that the man who had robbed her was wearing short sleeves and had no memorable features. The first trial ended in a hung jury when the defendant revealed that he had tattoos up and down his arms. In the defendant's second trial, the witness, who had learned about the tattoos, testified that she suddenly remembered that the robber wore a long-sleeved jacket to hide his gun. Must her identification of him be excluded as too suggestive?

No, the outside information that influenced the witness was not too suggestive to taint her identification of the defendant.[2]

---

[2]*Commonwealth* v. *Francis,* 453 N.E.2d 1204 (Mass. 1983).

2. Photospreads, Line-Ups, and Show-Ups

The **photospread,** also called the photo array, is a collection of at least six photographs of similar-looking people that is shown to the eyewitness in an effort to identify the offender. If the witness does identify the suspect from the photospread, the officer is to keep the entire spread and initial, date, and tag it as evidence for use at a later possible trial. In a **line-up,** at least six similar-looking people are brought into a room where the witness can view those in the line up but those in the line up cannot see the witness. In a **show-up,** the suspect is the only person brought before the eyewitness to answer the question "Is this the guy who did it or not?" Most people believe that only guilty people are arrested and, therefore, that if a suspect is in handcuffs, he must be the one who committed the crime. If an identification procedure suggests to the eyewitness that the suspect is the actual perpetrator, the identification will not be allowed at trial.

How does a court determine whether the police essentially delivered the suspect to the witness in an effort to get the witness to identify the suspect or whether the witness did, indeed, identify the suspect as the perpetrator without any influence from the police? The U.S. Supreme Court addressed the issue in *Stovall* v. *Denno,* 388 U.S. 293 (1967), in which the defendant was convicted and sentenced to death for the fatal stabbing of a doctor after the doctor's wife identified him as the perpetrator. At issue on appeal was the manner in which the doctor's wife identified Stovall before trial. The wife, Mrs. Behrendt, had been brutally attacked in the mauling that took her husband's life. She was in recovery in the hospital, and it was questionable whether or not she would live. Police brought Stovall to Mrs. Behrendt's bedside at the hospital. He was the only African-American in the room and he was in handcuffs. Mrs. Behrendt identified Stovall as her attacker and her husband's killer. The Supreme Court held that the show-up of Stovall was suggestive—that is, that the procedure did suggest to Mrs. Behrendt that Stovall was "the man"—but the identification was legally permissible because it did not create a substantial likelihood of mistaken identification. The Court did go on to state that the "practice of showing suspects singly to persons for the purpose of identification . . . has been widely condemned."[3] A case in which the high Court did find that the pretrial identification procedure was unduly suggestive, because the witnesses were essentially spoon-fed the suspect as the perpetrator of the crime, was *Foster* v. *California,* 394 U.S. 440 (1969). An eyewitness to a murder identified Foster after the following pretrial identification procedures took place:

1. the witness identified Foster in a line-up in which Foster was six inches taller than everyone else in the line-up
2. in the line-up, Foster was wearing clothes that the witness said the killer had worn
3. after the eyewitness spoke to Foster one-on-one, he remained uncertain whether Foster was actually the culprit until, finally,
4. the eyewitness viewed another line-up in which Foster was the only suspect presented from the first line-up the witness had viewed.

Reviewing these circumstances, the high Court said "it was all but inevitable" that the witness would identify Foster whether or not Foster "was in fact 'the man,'" and overturned Foster's conviction.

In the early 1990s, under the direction of President Clinton, the U.S. Department of Justice's research arm, the National Institute of Justice ("NIJ"), reviewed cases of people who had been wrongfully convicted. The NIJ found that in 80% of the cases eyewitness misidentification played a major role. At the same time, the Executive Committee of the American Psychology/Law Society appointed a subcommittee to draft guidelines for how law enforcement should conduct line-ups and photospreads to minimize the

---

[3]*Stovall,* 388 U.S. at 302.

danger of misidentification. U.S. Attorney General Janet Reno charged a working group with the task of coming up with solutions to the widespread problem of the prominent role faulty identification plays in securing faulty convictions, which brought together the researchers with the practitioners.[4]

In 1999, the Department of Justice published "Eyewitness Evidence: A Guide for Law Enforcement," developed and approved by the Technical Working Group for Eyewitness Evidence.[5] In 2001, after the wrongful conviction of an African-American man for the rape of a white female college student solely on the basis of her identification of him almost eight months after the attack occurred, New Jersey became the first state to mandate that all law enforcement agencies use the guidelines for adopting line-up and photospread procedures. In the case *New Jersey* v. *Cromedy,* 727 A.2d 457 (N.J. 1999), eight months after she had been raped, the victim saw Cromedy across the street and thought he was the man who had raped her. She ran home and telephoned police, giving them a description of the man she had just seen. Cromedy was picked up by police and, within 15 minutes of the victim's identification of him on the street, was placed by himself behind a one-way mirror, where the victim again identified him as the rapist. The victim had actually seen Cromedy before, two days after her attack, when police had showed her a photoarray of suspects that had included Cromedy, but the victim had failed to identify him as her attacker. Cromedy was convicted at trial, but his conviction was overturned because the judge refused to give the jury any instruction on the fallibility of cross-racial eyewitness identification and because there was no other evidence with which to support his conviction. Before retrial, Cromedy was exonerated by DNA evidence.

One of the main problems with false identifications, according to research, is that eyewitnesses identify people in a line-up or a photospread who look most like the offender relative to the other members of the line-up. For example, if a photospread contains six white men with long moustaches, and the real perpetrator was a white male with a long mustache, the eyewitness is going to pick out from the photospread the one who looks most like the offender, relative to the other five men. This process of making a relative judgment of which person in the photo array looks most like the offender means that the victim may feel confident about his or her choice even if the person being picked is not the real culprit. As Gary Wells and his fellow researchers have found, "[T]he relative judgment process will nevertheless yield a positive identification because there will always be someone who looks more like the culprit than do the remaining line-up members. The problem with the relative judgment process, therefore, is that it includes no mechanism for deciding that the culprit is none of the people in the line-up."[6] The primary antidote to the problems inherent in the relative judgment process is the sequential photoarray. An eyewitness only views one photo at a time and makes a clear decision that the photo is or is not the offender before viewing another person's photo. The sequential showing of photographs is a very inexpensive and relatively easy way to, according to research, reduce mistaken identification by fifty percent.[7]

[4]Gary L. Wells. "From the Lab to the Police Station: A Successful Application of Eyewitness Research." *American Psychologist,* Vol. 55 (2000), pp. 581–598.

[5]Technical Working Group for Eyewitness Evidence. *Eyewitness evidence: A guide for law enforcement* (Washington, DC: United States Department of Justice, National Institute of Justice, Document No. NCJ178240, 1999). http://www.ojp.usdoj.gov

[6]Gary L. Wells, Mark Small, Steven Penrod, Roy S. Malpass, Solomon M. Fulero, and C. A. Elizabeth Brimacombe. "Eyewitness Identification Procedures: Recommendations for Line-ups and Photospreads." *Law and Human Behavior,* Vol. 22 (1998), pp. 603–647.

[7]Nancy M. Steblay, Jennifer E. Dysart, Solomon Fulero, and Roderick C. L. Lindsay. "Eyewitness Accuracy Rates in Sequential and Simultaneous Line-Up Presentations: A Meta-Analytic Comparison." *Law & Human Behavior,* Vol. 25 (2001), pp. 459–473.

The DOJ's Eyewitness Evidence guidelines included four recommended changes for conducting line-ups and photospreads to reduce the incidence of faulty identification of innocent people:

1. The person who conducts the line-up or photospread should not be aware of which member of the line-up or photospread is the suspect. This is designed to prevent the officer from transmitting subtle cues to the witness indicating whether her choice is correct or not.

2. Eyewitnesses should be told that the suspect may not be in the line-up or photospread. According to the research, eyewitnesses are less likely to misidentify innocent people if they are told the offender may not actually be present in the identification process.

3. The suspect should not stand out as being different from the others on the basis of the description the witness gave police earlier. If the witness said the offender wore jeans and a tee shirt, and the suspect is the only one in the line-up wearing jeans and a tee shirt, then obviously the line-up is overtly suggestive.

4. Officers should get the witness to make a clear statement of identification prior to any feedback that confirms or denies her identification. Research shows that if, after a witness makes an identification,[8] the witness learns that another witness has identified the same suspect, the first witness's confidence in her identification is inflated. Also, any information the witness learns after making the first identification may alter her identification in a way that is not related to her own memory.

The legal remedy when an identification made pretrial is too suggestive is the exclusion of that identification from trial. The eyewitness can still identify the defendant in court as the man who committed the crime, but only if this identification has an independent source other than the suggestive identification procedure. In *Wisconsin* v. *Dubose,* reprinted in part in Box 9.1, the Wisconsin state court adopted more stringent pretrial identification procedures based on the interpretation of the state constitution and gave suspects in the jurisdiction more due process protection than allowed by U.S. Supreme Court precedent.

BOX 9.1

Wisconsin v. *Dubose,* 699 N.W.2d 582 (2005)
Supreme Court of Wisconsin

Judge Wood delivered the opinion of the Court.

FACTS

Timothy Hiltsley (Hiltsley) and Ryan Boyd (Boyd) left the Camelot Bar in Green Bay, Wisconsin, at approximately 1:00 a.m. on January 9, 2002. Hiltsley had been drinking at the bar and admitted to being "buzzed" when he left. In the parking lot, Hiltsley and Boyd encountered a group of men, some of whom Hiltsley recognized as regular customers of a liquor store where he worked. Dubose, an African-American, was one of the men he allegedly recognized. After a brief conversation, Hiltsley invited two of the men, along with Boyd, to his residence to smoke marijuana. When they arrived at Hiltsley's apartment, Hiltsley sat down on the couch to pack a bowl of marijuana. At that time, Dubose allegedly held a gun to Hiltsley's right temple and demanded money. After Hiltsley emptied his wallet and gave the men his money, the two men, both African-Americans, left his apartment. Within minutes after the incident, at approximately 1:21 a.m., one of Hiltsley's neighbors called the police to report a

---

[8]*See* Brian L. Cutler. "Juror Sensitivity to Eyewitness Identification Evidence." *Law & Human Behavior,* Vol. 14 (1990), pp. 185–191 (jurors give disproportionate weight to witness confidence in identifying the defendant).

possible burglary. She described two African-American men fleeing from the area, one of whom was wearing a large hooded flannel shirt. At the same time, Hiltsley and Boyd attempted to chase the men. They searched for the men in Boyd's car and hoped to cut them off. After driving nearly two blocks, Hiltsley got out of the car and searched for the men on foot.

During his search, Hiltsley flagged down a police officer that was responding to the burglary call. Hiltsley told the officer that he had just been robbed at gunpoint. He described the suspects as African-American, one standing about 5 feet 6 inches, and the other man standing a little taller. Another police officer also responded to the burglary call. As he neared the scene, he observed two men walking about one-half block from Hiltsley's apartment. This officer, Jeffrey Engelbrecht, was unable to determine the race of the individuals, but noted that one of the men was wearing a large hooded flannel shirt. The officer subsequently requested headquarters to dispatch a canine unit to help search for the men. While he waited at the perimeter for the canine unit, police headquarters reported another call in regard to an armed robbery at Hiltsley's apartment. The report indicated that the two suspects were African-American males, that one was possibly armed, and that the two calls were probably related.

. . . . The male who came out from behind the fence was Dubose, who was subsequently arrested. Dubose, who was not wearing a flannel shirt, told the police that he had been in an argument with his girlfriend and that he had just left her house. He thought she might have called the police on him, which is why he ran when he saw the squad car. After his arrest, he was searched. The search did not uncover any weapons, money, or contraband. Dubose was then placed in the back of a squad car and driven to an area near Hiltsley's residence.

At this location, the officers conducted a show-up procedure, giving Hiltsley the opportunity to identify one of the alleged suspects. The officers placed Hiltsley in the backseat of a second squad car, which was parked so that its rear window was three feet apart from the rear window of the squad car containing Dubose. The dome light was turned on in the car containing Dubose. The officers told Hiltsley

that Dubose was possibly one of the men who had robbed him at gunpoint, and asked Hiltsley if he could identify the man in the other squad car. Hiltsley told the police that he was 98 percent certain that Dubose, who sat alone in the back seat of the other squad car, was the man who held him at gunpoint. Hiltsley also told the police that he recognized him due to his small, slender build and hairstyle.

The squad cars separated and took both Hiltsley and Dubose to the police station. Approximately 10 to 15 minutes after the first show-up, the police conducted a second show-up. There, Hiltsley identified Dubose, alone in a room, through a two-way mirror. Hiltsley told police that Dubose was the same man he observed at the previous show-up, and that he believed Dubose was the man who robbed him. A short time after the second show-up, the police showed Hiltsley a mug shot of Dubose, and he identified him for a third time.

At trial, Hiltsley testified about the events and subsequent show-ups that occurred on January 9, 2002. He also identified Dubose in the courtroom as the man who held him at gunpoint on the night in question. The jury convicted Dubose of armed robbery on September 5, 2002.

ISSUE

[Were the show-ups unduly suggestive to require exclusion of the subsequent in-court identification?]

HOLDING

[Yes, in light of U.S. Supreme Court precedent, the show-ups were clearly prejudicial and the court of appeals decision upholding Dubose's conviction must be reversed]. We hold that evidence obtained from such a show-up will not be admissible unless, based on the totality of the circumstances, the show-up was necessary. A show-up will not be necessary, however, unless the police lacked probable cause to make an arrest or, as a result of other exigent [emergency] circumstances, could not have conducted a line-up or photo array.

REASONING

Over the last decade, there have been extensive studies on the issue of identification evidence,

(continued)

BOX 9.1

(continued)

research that is now impossible for us to ignore.[9] These studies confirm that eyewitness testimony is often "hopelessly unreliable." *Commonwealth* v. *Johnson,* 650 N.E.2d 1257 (Mass. 1995). The research strongly supports the conclusion that eyewitness misidentification is now the single greatest source of wrongful convictions in the United States, and responsible for more wrongful convictions than all other causes combined. In a study of 28 wrongful convictions conducted by the U.S. Department of Justice ("DOJ") determined that 24 (85 percent) of the erroneous convictions were based primarily on the misidentification of the defendant by a witness. In a similar study conducted by the Innocence Project at the Benjamin Cardozo School of Law, mistaken identifications played a major part in the wrongful conviction of over two-thirds of the first 138 postconviction DNA exonerations.[10] These statistics certainly substantiate Justice William J. Brennan, Jr.'s concerns in *Wade* that "the annals of criminal law are rife with instances of mistaken identification." *Wade,* 388 U.S. at 228.

. . . . [I]t is clear that the show-ups conducted were unnecessarily suggestive, and that the admission of identification evidence denied Dubose a right to due process under Article I, Section 8 of the Wisconsin Constitution. First, there existed sufficient facts at the time of Dubose's arrest to establish probable cause for his arrest. It was not necessary for the police to conduct the show-ups, since they had sufficient evidence against Dubose to arrest him without such show-ups. Next, the officers handcuffed Dubose and placed him in the back seat of a squad car. By placing a suspect in a squad car, the police implicitly suggest that they believe the suspect is the offender. This is similar to the situation in *Stovall,* where the United States Supreme Court held that the show-up procedure was suggestive when the defendant was brought into the hospital room in handcuffs and accompanied by police officers and prosecutors. Third, the police officers told the witness, Hiltsley, that they may have caught "one of the guys" who had

robbed him. Such a comment is suggestive and, as studies have shown, greatly increases the chance of misidentification. Although the court of appeals stated that it found "nothing wrong with a police procedure where officers indicate an individual is a possible suspect," we consider such a comment unnecessarily suggestive. Finally, after the first show-up was conducted and Dubose was positively identified, the police still conducted two more identification procedures, another show-up and a photo of Dubose, at the police station shortly after Dubose's arrival. These subsequent identification procedures were unnecessarily suggestive. Dubose had already been arrested and positively identified by Hiltsley. The record does not show that any exigent circumstances existed making the out-of-court identification procedures used here necessary.

Therefore . . . based on the totality of the circumstances, "[t]he suggestive elements in this identification procedure made it all but inevitable that [the witness] would identify [the defendant] whether or not he was in fact 'the man.' In effect, the police repeatedly said to the witness 'This is the man.'" *Foster* v. *California,* 394 U.S. 440 (1969). For similar reasons, as discussed above, we reverse the court of appeals and remand this case to the circuit court for further proceedings, consistent with the standards adopted herein.

CONCLUSION

We find strong support for the adoption of these standards in the Due Process Clause of the Wisconsin Constitution, Article I, Section 8. It reads in relevant part: "No person may be held to answer for a criminal offense without due process of law. . . ." Based on our reading of that clause, and keeping in mind the principles discussed herein, the approach outlined in *Biggers* and *Brathwaite* does not satisfy this requirement. We conclude instead that Article I, Section 8 necessitates the application of the approach we are now adopting . . . .

---

[9]The Court's internal quotations cite many leading studies on the fallibility of eyewitness identification.

[10]http://www.innocenceproject.org/understand/Eyewitness-Misidentification.php

3. Pretrial Identification and the Right to Counsel

Rule of Law: Once the right to counsel attaches at the initiation of adversary proceedings, by an arrest or other formal procedure, the suspect has a right to counsel at the pretrial identification procedure; there is no such right if formal adversary proceedings have not begun.

Under the Sixth Amendment's confrontation clause, discussed more fully in chapter 13, a defendant has a right to face his accuser at trial, and that right extends to having counsel present at certain pretrial identification procedures. The right to counsel does not attach or become viable for the defendant until the initiation of adversary proceedings, such as arrest, the initiation of charges by way of information or indictment, or a preliminary hearing. If the right to counsel attaches to have a lawyer present during the pretrial identification process and one is not provided, the subsequent identification of the defendant cannot be used at trial. *United States* v. *Wade,* 388 U.S. 218 (1967). Students must be careful to note where in the criminal trial process the pretrial identification occurs to determine whether the right to a lawyer attaches. Most pretrial identification procedures are conducted before charges are lodged against a suspect—that is, before a suspect has a right to a lawyer (specifically excluding situations where *Miranda* rights are given). Part of the pretrial process is the investigation of crime. One widely used and effective police tactic is the brief investigatory detention, also known as the *Terry* stop.

II. INVESTIGATORY DETENTIONS (*TERRY* STOPS)

The genesis of the Fourth Amendment was the Crown of England's abuse of criminal and civil process. Early American colonists witnessed the king abuse writs of assistance, which were papers authorizing the seizure of property to help pay the king's debtors, who would in turn pay dues to the king, and general warrants that were issued to seize and arrest authors, publishers, and printers of "seditious libels" advocating government reform. The Fourth Amendment is the legal mechanism by which the government can search people's personal property and belongings and seize it.[11] The late Honorable Charles E. Moylan, Jr., offered the following schematic device to conceptualize the language of the Fourth Amendment. The Fourth Amendment provides that:

The right of the people to be secure in their
1. persons,
2. houses,
3. papers, and
4. effects

against unreasonable searches and seizures, shall not be violated, and no warrants shall issue, [except]

1. upon probable cause,
2. supported by oath or affirmation, and
3. particularly describing
   a. the place to be searched, and
   b. the persons or things to be seized.[12]

The two prongs of the Fourth Amendment are generally known as the "reasonableness clause" and the "warrant clause." The Fourth Amendment does not prevent all

---

[11]Nelson B. Lasson. *The History and Development of the Fourth Amendment to the United States Constitution* (Baltimore: Johns Hopkins University, 1937).

[12]William W. Greenhalgh. *The Fourth Amendment Handbook: A Chronological Survey of Supreme Court Decisions,* 2nd ed. (Chicago, IL: American Bar Association, 2003), p. 8.

searches and seizures, only unreasonable ones. Searches and seizures are two distinct actions. A **search** is looking for evidence to use against a suspect in a criminal prosecution. A **seizure** denotes taking the evidence found, or taking/arresting a suspect. A seizure of a person does not depend on a formal arrest. The legal test for whether a person has been seized is whether "in view of all of the circumstances surrounding" the police encounter with the citizen a person reasonably believes he is not "free to leave."[13]

Rule of Law: The Fourth Amendment protects a reasonable expectation of privacy.

To understand the Fourth Amendment's protections, it is essential to understand how the U.S. Supreme Court defines privacy.

In *Katz* v. *United States,* reprinted in part in Box 9.2, Katz had been convicted for wagering illegal bets across state lines using the telephone, a federal crime. The evidence against him was obtained when federal agents put listening devices on the exterior panels of the public telephone booth where Katz conducted his gambling business. On appeal and in his defense, Katz's lawyers raised privacy interests that had been recently vindicated in the Supreme Court's fundamental liberty and substantive due process decisions regarding the freedom to purchase birth control. Katz's argument was that if the government could not intrude on the privacy of a couple's choice about when to conceive a child, surely the government could not intrude on conversations in a telephone booth that were intended to be private, even if the substance of those conversations was criminal. The Supreme Court found 8-1 in favor of Katz. As you read the case, note how the Court formulated the legal definition for an expectation of privacy that the Fourth Amendment would protect.

BOX 9.2

Katz v. *United States,* 389 U.S. 347 (1967)
Supreme Court of the United States

Justice Stewart delivered the opinion of the Court.

FACTS

The petitioner was convicted in the District Court for the Southern District of California under an eight-count indictment charging him with transmitting wagering information by telephone from Los Angeles to Miami and Boston, in violation of a federal statute.[14] At trial the Government was permitted, over the petitioner's objection, to introduce evidence of the petitioner's end of telephone conversations, overheard by FBI [Federal Bureau of Investigation] agents who had attached an electronic listening and recording device to the outside of the public telephone booth from which he had placed his calls. In affirming his conviction, the Court of Appeals rejected the contention that the recordings had been obtained in violation of the Fourth Amendment, because "[t]here was no physical entrance into the area occupied by [the petitioner]." We granted *certiorari* in order to consider the constitutional questions thus presented.

---

[13]*Michigan* v. *Chesternut,* 486 U.S. 567 (1988).

[14]18 U.S.C. §1084. That statute provides in pertinent part: "(a) Whoever being engaged in the business of betting or wagering knowingly uses a wire communication facility for the transmission in interstate or foreign commerce of bets or wagers of information assisting in the placing of bets or wagers on any sporting event or contest, or for the transmission of a wire communication which entitles the recipient to receive money or credit as a result of bets or wagers, or for information assisting in the placing of bets or wagers, shall be fined not more than $10,000, or imprisoned not more than two years, or both."

ISSUE

The petitioner has phrased those questions as follows:

A. Whether a public telephone booth is a constitutionally protected area so that evidence obtained by attaching an electronic listening and recording device to the top of such booth is obtained in violation of the right to privacy of the user of the booth.

B. Whether physical penetration of a constitutionally protected area is necessary before a search and seizure can be said to be violative of the Fourth Amendment to the United States Constitution.

We decline to adopt this formulation of the issues. In the first place, the correct solution of Fourth Amendment problems is not necessarily promoted by incantation of the phrase "constitutionally protected area." Secondly, the Fourth Amendment cannot be translated into a general constitutional "right to privacy." That Amendment protects individual privacy against certain kinds of governmental intrusion, but its protections go further, and often have nothing to do with privacy at all . . .

HOLDING

The Government's activities in electronically listening to and recording the petitioner's words violated the privacy upon which he justifiably relied while using the telephone booth and thus constituted a "search and seizure" within the meaning of the Fourth Amendment. The fact that the electronic device employed to achieve that end did not happen to penetrate the wall of the booth can have no constitutional significance.

REASONING

Because of the misleading way the issues have been formulated, the parties have attached great significance to the characterization of the telephone booth from which petitioner placed his calls. The petitioner has strenuously argued that the booth was a "constitutionally protected area." The Government has maintained with equal vigor that it was not. But this effort to decide whether or not a given "area," viewed in the abstract, is "constitutionally protected" deflects attention from the problem presented in this case.[15] For the Fourth Amendment protects people, not places. . . .

The Government urges that, because its agents relied upon [prior case law and] did no more here than they might properly have done with prior judicial sanction, we should retroactively validate their conduct. That we cannot do. It is apparent that the agents in this case acted with restraint. Yet the inescapable fact is that this restraint was imposed by the agents themselves, not by a judicial officer. They were not required, before commencing the search, to present their estimate of probable cause for detached scrutiny by a neutral magistrate. They were not compelled, during the conduct of the search itself, to observe precise limits established in advance by a specific court order. Nor were they directed, after the search had been completed, to notify the authorizing magistrate in detail of all that had been seized. In the absence of such safeguards, this Court has never sustained a search upon the sole ground that officers reasonably expected to find evidence of a particular crime and voluntarily confined their activities to the least intrusive means consistent with that end. "Over and again this Court has emphasized that the mandate of the [Fourth] Amendment requires adherence to judicial processes," and that searches conducted outside the judicial process, without prior approval by a judge or magistrate, are *per se* [without more] unreasonable under the Fourth Amendment—subject only to a few specifically established and well-delineated exceptions. And bypassing a neutral predetermination of the scope of a search leaves individuals secure from Fourth Amendment violations "only in the discretion of the police."

These considerations do not vanish when the search in question is transferred from the setting of a home, an office, or a hotel room to that of a telephone booth. Wherever a man may be, he is entitled to know that he will remain free from unreasonable searches and seizures. The government agents here ignored "the procedure of antecedent

---

[15]"It is true that this Court has occasionally described its conclusions in terms of "constitutionally protected areas," (citations omitted) but we have never suggested that this concept can serve as a talismanic solution to every Fourth Amendment problem."

[prior] justification—that is central to the Fourth Amendment," a procedure that we hold to be a constitutional precondition [a legal requirement that must be met in order to satisfy the Constitution] [to] the kind of electronic surveillance involved in this case. Because the surveillance here failed to meet that condition, and because it led to the petitioner's conviction, the judgment must be reversed. It is so ordered...

Justice Harlan, **concurring**

I join the opinion of the Court, which I read to hold only (a) that an enclosed telephone booth is an area where, like a home, and unlike a field, a person has a constitutionally protected reasonable expectation of privacy; (b) that electronic as well as physical intrusion into a place that is in this sense private may constitute a violation of the Fourth Amendment; and (c) that the invasion of a constitutionally protected area by federal authorities is, as the Court has long held, presumptively unreasonable in the absence of a search warrant...

Justice Black, **dissenting**

My objection is twofold: (1) I do not believe that the words of the Amendment will bear the meaning given them by today's decision, and (2) I do not believe that it is the proper role of this Court to rewrite the Amendment in order "to bring it into harmony with the times" and thus reach a result that many people believe to be desirable. . . .

Applying the Rule of Law to the Facts: **Should guests who package drugs have a legal expectation of privacy?**

- A police officer went to an apartment on the basis of a tip from a confidential informant that the occupants of the apartment were involved in drug-dealing. The officer looked through a gap in a closed blind and watched people putting a white powder into bags. He notified his superiors, who began preparing affidavits for a search warrant. A short time later, defendants Carter and Johns left the apartment and were arrested; they were in possession of a gun, cocaine, pagers, and a scale. The men claimed that the officer's initial observation through the window was an unreasonable search in violation of the Fourth Amendment and that all evidence seized should be suppressed. Did the defendants have an expectation of privacy that the law was bound to recognize?

No, the search was legal. The U.S. Supreme Court held that although the *Katz* holding protects "people, not places," drug dealers in a friends's place merely to conduct business can claim no expectation of privacy the Fourth Amendment would recognize or protect. The Court said, "Property used for commercial purposes is treated differently for Fourth Amendment purposes than residential property." *Minnesota* v. *Carter*, 119 S.Ct. 469 (1998).

- A robbery-murder suspect was staying at the home of two women friends. When police telephoned the home and told the women to tell the suspect to come out, they heard a male voice in the background. Without a warrant, police forcibly entered the home and arrested the suspect. He claimed that his Fourth Amendment expectation of privacy in his friends' home was violated and, therefore, that his arrest was illegal. Did he have an expectation of privacy?

Yes, the murder suspect did have an expectation of privacy in his friends' house because he was an overnight guest. In explaining this rationale the U.S. Supreme Court said in *Minnesota* v. *Olson*, 495 U.S. 91 (1990), that

Staying overnight in another's home is a longstanding social custom that serves functions recognized as valuable by society. We stay in others' homes when we travel to a strange city for business or pleasure, when we visit our parents, children, or more distant relatives out of town, when we are in between jobs or homes, or when we house sit for a friend. We will all be hosts and we will all be guests many times in our lives. From either perspective, we think that society recognizes that a houseguest has a legitimate expectation of privacy in his host's home.

The Court went on in *Olson* to explain that the analysis of whether a guest has an expectation of privacy does not turn on whether the owner can let people in and out of the property. Adults living temporarily in their parents' homes have a right to privacy even though the parents can control who comes into the home. "If the untrammeled power to admit and exclude were essential to Fourth Amendment protection, an adult daughter temporarily living in the home of her parents would have no legitimate expectation of privacy because her right to admit or exclude would be subject to her parents' veto." Thus, the expectation of privacy must be both objective [everyone would agree that there is an expectation of privacy in the thing or place to be searched] and subjective [individual to the person who has an expectation of privacy in the thing or place to be searched] for the law to recognize it as valid against unreasonable government intrusion.

1 The *Terry* Stop

Rule of Law: The *Terry* stop is a brief encounter between police and citizens to confirm or dispel the reasonable suspicion that criminal activity is afoot.

The **investigatory detention,** also called the *Terry* stop, is a temporary restraint of a citizen based on reasonable suspicion that criminal activity is afoot. The detention is brief and is designed to allow officers the freedom to ask questions to confirm or dispel their suspicion that a crime has been or will be committed. The detention is not an arrest; an arrest is a full seizure of the person and must follow from probable cause as discussed later in this chapter. How can a regular citizen distinguish between a detention and an arrest? By the level of law enforcement's intrusion on the citizen's personal integrity and freedom. Investigatory detentions are commonly known as *Terry* stops after the seminal case *Terry* v. *Ohio,* 392 U.S. 1 (1968), in which the U.S. Supreme Court defined the distinction between arrests and detentions:

> An arrest is a wholly different kind of intrusion upon individual freedom from [an investigatory detention] and the interests each is designed to serve are likewise quite different. An arrest is the initial stage of a criminal prosecution. It is intended to vindicate society's interest in having its laws obeyed, and it is inevitably accompanied by future interference with the individual's freedom of movement, whether or not trial or conviction ultimately follows. The [investigatory detention and] protective search for weapons, on the other hand, constitutes a brief, though far from inconsiderable, intrusion upon the sanctity of the person.

In the *Terry* case, Detective Martin McFadden was on duty one night when he noticed three men behaving suspiciously. Two of them were walking up and down the same street to look into a store window. They made 24 trips back and forth, while a third man stood watch. McFadden approached the two men, Terry and Chilton, and asked their names. When they mumbled a response, McFadden turned them to face one another, patted Terry down, and removed a gun from his coat pocket. Terry was convicted for carrying a concealed weapon. On appeal, the Supreme Court found that the officer's pat-down without probable cause was legal. The Court stated,

> . . . where a police officer observes unusual conduct which leads him reasonably to conclude in light of his experience that criminal activity may be afoot and that the persons with whom he is dealing may be armed and presently dangerous . . . and nothing . . . serves to dispel his reasonable fear for his own or others' safety, he is entitled for the

protection of himself and others in the area to conduct a carefully limited search of the outer clothing of such persons in an attempt to discover weapons which might be used to assault him.

The **reasonable suspicion** standard states that if police had specific and articulable facts that a crime was about to happen or did just happen—that criminal activity was afoot—then the police could briefly detain the suspect and ask questions. Furthermore, if the officers had a reasonable belief that the person they suspected of committing a crime was armed, police could lawfully conduct a **pat-down** for weapons to ensure the safety of both the officers and the public. The legal justification for a pat-down for weapons during a *Terry* stop is to disarm the suspect. A pat-down for weapons is not a full-blown search; probable cause is required in order to do such a search. **Specific and articulable facts** means that at the time of the seizure of the person, the officer "must be able to articulate something more than an 'inchoate and unparticularized suspicion or hunch.' . . . The Fourth Amendment requires 'some minimal level of objective justification' for making the stop."[16] If the investigatory detention lasts longer than is necessary to confirm or dispel the officer's reasonable suspicion that criminal activity is afoot, the detention may be transformed into an unlawful arrest because it was made without probable cause.

Claims that the scope of a *Terry* stop and frisk was exceeded and that the stop was transformed into an illegal arrest are difficult to sustain. In 2000 in Boston, Massachusetts, the author made such a claim on behalf of a client, Andres Campa, who had been charged in federal court with making false identification documents for illegal immigrants. While the defense was ultimately unsuccessful in getting the fruits of the unlawful search suppressed, the First Circuit Court of Appeals did acknowledge and agree with the defendant's argument that emptying Campa's pockets within seconds of seeing him enter an apartment, without more justification, exceeded the scope of a *Terry* pat-down and was a search for which there was no probable cause. The case is reprinted in part in Box 9.3.

BOX 9.3

United States v. Campa, 234 F.3d 733 (1st Cir. 2000)[17]
United States Court of Appeals for the First Circuit

Judge Coffin delivered the opinion of the court.

PROCEDURAL HISTORY

Andres Campa was arrested when he went to retrieve a package of counterfeit alien work permits ("green cards") at an apartment targeted by law enforcement authorities because a series of suspicious packages had been delivered there. He entered a conditional plea of guilty to charges relating to the counterfeiting and fraudulent use of various identification documents, reserving his right to appeal the district court's denial of his motion to suppress all evidence and statements obtained by authorities after his arrest . . . . Campa now brings that appeal, claiming that the district court erred in failing to find that he was unlawfully detained and searched upon entering the apartment.

---

[16]*United States* v. *Sokolow,* 490 U.S. 1 (1989) (internal citations omitted).

[17]Owen S. Walker, Federal Public Defender, with whom Stephanie A. Jirard, Federal Defender's Office, was on brief for [Campa]. Nadine Pellegrini, Assistant U.S. Attorney, with whom Donald K. Stern, United States Attorney, was on brief for appellee.

FACTS

For nearly a year before March 1999, the United States Postal Inspection Service had been investigating suspicious Express Mail packages addressed to 74 Thornton Street in Revere, Massachusetts. On March 19, Inspector Michael McCarran posed as a mailman and delivered the latest such package. Three other law enforcement officers accompanied him, but initially remained in the postal truck. A man later identified as Jose Bullon came to the door, stated that he was the addressee, "Francisco Valencia," and signed the name "Francis Palencia" on the delivery mail receipt. McCarran then summoned the other officers. Bullon agreed to speak with them and consented to the package being opened. Inside were forty blank green cards. Bullon admitted that Valencia was a fictitious name and that he was accepting the package for a man he knew as "Gorrito." He described Gorrito as a Hispanic male in his early twenties who usually wore a baseball cap. Bullon reported that Gorrito paid him $50 per package and that he previously had accepted about ten packages. Bullon stated that Gorrito manufactured the fraudulent documents in a nearby apartment on Highland Street. Expressing fear of retaliation if Gorrito learned of his cooperation, Bullon nonetheless disclosed that Gorrito was due at the Thornton Street apartment at about 2 P.M. that day, and he agreed to go with one of the officers to point out the Highland Street apartment.

At about 2:30 P.M., shortly after Bullon returned to the Thornton Street location, Bullon and McCarran saw two Hispanic males walking down the street toward the apartment. Bullon identified one of the men, who was wearing a baseball cap, as Gorrito. He later was identified as appellant Campa. [Campa] and the other man, Enrique Lara-Valirde, entered the apartment without knocking and were confronted just inside the door by three officers, who identified themselves, ordered the men to face the hallway wall, and then conducted a pat-down search. During the frisk of [Campa], Trooper Marron took keys, a beeper and a wallet from his pockets, dropping the items to the floor as they were removed. [Campa] and Lara-Valirde then were

escorted to the kitchen, where they sat down at a table. McCarran gathered the items removed during the frisk and placed them on the table.

At this point, the officers asked for identification. Lara-Valirde admitted that he had no identification and was in the United States illegally. [Trooper] Marron, a non-Spanish speaker, attempted to communicate with [Campa] by saying the word "identificacion" two or three times. In response, Campa took a New Jersey driver's license from his wallet and handed it to the officer. Marron recognized the license as a counterfeit and placed Campa under arrest. [Campa] subsequently moved to suppress the counterfeiting materials found in the Highland Street apartment and his statements to authorities admitting culpability. He argued that the officers did not have the requisite level of suspicion to justify the stop and pat-down search, that his arrest was unlawful, and that his confessions and all physical evidence seized should be suppressed as "fruit of the poisonous tree," *Wong Sun* v. *United States,* 371 U.S. 471, 487–88 (1963).

After a two-day evidentiary hearing, the district court concluded that the officers had a sufficient basis to detain Campa briefly for the purpose of exploring his relationship to the counterfeit green cards, but that the accompanying frisk was excessive in scope because the officers removed all items from his pockets without regard to whether they might be weapons. The court nonetheless refused to suppress any of the challenged evidence on the theory that its discovery was inevitable given the authority of the police to determine Campa's identity. The court believed that, even with a more limited frisk, Campa either would have provided the New Jersey license voluntarily, or the officers could and would have searched him to obtain it. On appeal, [Campa] renews his claim that the officers lacked even the reasonable suspicion necessary to conduct an investigatory stop authorized by *Terry* v. *Ohio,* 392 U.S. 1 (1968), and he maintains that the actions they took constituted a *de facto* [in reality] arrest that needed to be supported by the higher standard of probable cause.

(continued)

BOX 9.3

(continued)

ISSUE

[Campa] asserts that neither the record nor case law supports the district court's inevitable discovery theory [and that the evidence introduced against him should have been suppressed].

HOLDING

Our review of the record and relevant case law persuades us that the only Fourth Amendment violation that occurred—an improper frisk—was unrelated to [Campa]'s arrest and did not give the government access to the incriminating evidence. We therefore affirm the denial of [Campa]'s suppression motion.

RATIONALE

A. The *Terry* Stop-and-Frisk Standards

A warrantless search violates the Fourth Amendment unless it falls within one of the few carefully limited exceptions to that important constitutional protection. *Minnesota* v. *Dickerson,* 508 U.S. 366, 372 (1993). A consensual search is one such exception. *Schneckloth* v. *Bustamonte,* 412 U.S. 218, 219 (1973). Another was recognized in *Terry,* which held that a police officer with reasonable suspicion of criminal activity may detain a suspect briefly for questioning aimed at confirming or dispelling his suspicions . . . . The officer making the stop must possess "specific and articulable facts which, taken together with rational inferences from those facts, reasonably warrant that intrusion." In addition to the stop for questioning, *Terry* permits a pat-down search for weapons on the basis of an objectively reasonable belief that the suspicious individual is armed and presently dangerous. Such a protective search, designed to allow the officer to conduct his investigation without fear of violence, must be "strictly 'limited to that which is necessary for the discovery of weapons.'" Typically, this will be "a limited patting of the outer clothing of the suspect for concealed objects which might be used as instruments of assault." *Sibron* v. *New York,* 392 U.S. 40 (1968). If the frisk goes beyond what is necessary to determine if the suspect is armed, its fruits will be suppressed. *Dickerson,* 508 U.S. at 373; *see also United States* v. *Schiavo,* 29 F.3d 6 (1st Cir. 1994) (affirming suppression where officer's continued exploration of a bulging paper bag in suspect's pocket "'after having concluded that it contained no weapon was unrelated to the sole justification of the search under *Terry*'") (*quoting Dickerson,* 508 U.S. at 378).

2. The Detention. We reject the contention that the hallway encounter evolved into a *de facto* arrest. The detention was brief—a few minutes from the time the men arrived in the apartment until they were moved to the kitchen—and the circumstances were nearly the least intrusive possible for a stop and frisk.[18] Although [Campa] emphasizes that the two men raised their hands when asked to face the wall for the frisk, this form of compliance with the officers' instructions does not make the interaction tantamount to an arrest. The officers did not display weapons, use handcuffs or exert any physical force on the two men. Directing them to move the few steps from the hallway to the kitchen, presumably a larger space and thus a more natural setting for conversation, in all likelihood defused some of the tension surrounding the hallway frisk; it certainly was not a dramatic change in the officer-suspect relationship that converted a *Terry* stop into an arrest.

3. The Pat-Down Search. We agree with [Campa] and the district court, however, that the pat-down search conducted by the officers exceeded the permissible scope of a *Terry* detention. We are satisfied with the officers' judgment that a pat-down was justified, in light of Bullon's expression of concern for his safety if he betrayed Gorrito and the uncertainties of confronting the two men in an apartment where at least three other individuals of unknown allegiance were present.

---

[18]"*See, for example. United States* v. *Sowers,* 136 F.3d 24 (1st Cir. 1998) (courts must examine the totality of the circumstances "to locate a particular sequence of events along the continuum of detentions"); *see generally United States* v. *Acosta-Colon,* 157 F.3d 9 (1st Cir. 1998) (describing distinctions between investigatory stops and more coercive detentions); *United States* v. *Zapata,* 18 F.3d 971 (1st Cir. 1994) (same).

The officer who frisked [Campa], Trooper Marron, acknowledged, however, that he made no attempt to distinguish between bulging items that could be weapons and other types of concealed objects, reaching into [Campa]'s pockets whenever he felt a protrusion and emptying all items onto the floor. If this indiscriminate removal of items embraced objects that were readily identifiable by touch as nonweapons, then the further invasion of [Campa]'s privacy occasioned by removing them from his pockets was unnecessary and thus unlawful. *See Terry,* 392 U.S. at 29 (protective search for weapons "must . . . be confined in scope to an intrusion reasonably designed to discover guns, knives, clubs, or other hidden instruments for the assault of the police officer"); 4 Wayne R. LaFave, Search and Seizure §9.5(c) (3d ed. 1996) (discussing "what tactile sensations produced by the pat-down will justify a further intrusion into the clothing of the suspect"); *cf. Dickerson,* 508 U.S. at 375–76 ("plain feel" doctrine allows seizure of contraband detected during weapons frisk when "a police officer lawfully pats down a suspect's outer clothing and feels an object whose contour or mass makes its identity immediately apparent").

Although we recognize that searching by means of a pat-down is not an exact science, the government does not even argue that Trooper Marron thought [Campa]'s wallet—the item particularly at issue here—could be a weapon. He simply removed every bulging object as he searched, undoubtedly a convenient method for detecting weapons, but one that goes beyond the limited invasion of privacy authorized by *Terry* and its progeny. That the items were not actually "seized" and retained by the officers—and, indeed, might have been returned to [Campa] had he asked—minimizes the violation but does not erase it. We therefore conclude that [Campa] was subjected to an unlawful frisk.

Faced with an officer pressing him for "identificacion," we think it unsurprising that [Campa] responded with his driver's license, just as Lara-Valirde answered with the incriminating information that he was an illegal alien and had no identification. Indeed, there is no basis for concluding that [Campa] knew that the license was facially identifiable as a fake, and he may well have thought he could avoid greater difficulty by presenting it. But whatever his precise motivation, we conclude that disclosure of the license was not tainted by the earlier unlawful frisk. ("[O]ur cases make clear that evidence will not be excluded as 'fruit' unless the illegality is at least the 'but for' cause of the discovery of the evidence. Suppression is not justified unless 'the challenged evidence is in some sense the product of illegal governmental activity.'").

CONCLUSION

We therefore affirm the district court's denial of [Campa]'s motion to suppress the evidence of counterfeit document production that was obtained following his arrest.[19]

The following situations have been considered sufficiently suspicious to support an officer's authority to perform a pat-down and frisk for weapons on a person: running away when seeing officers in an area known for high levels of drug trafficking, double-parking a car close to an area of drug activity, averting the eyes when talking to police and driving a car with out-of-state plates, and walking out of an apartment where

---

[19]In the second footnote in the *Campa* case, the appellate court noted that the trial judge found Campa's testimony during the suppression hearing "not credible" concerning the turning over of his driver's license. In suppression hearings, defendants can testify without waiving their right against self-incrimination at trial. If Campa were to go to trial his suppression hearing testimony concerning the false documents could not be used to prove his guilt, but if he were to testify at trial, his suppression testimony could be used to impeach [discredit] his claims. The appellate court said that it was not going to disturb the trial judge's finding that Campa was not telling the truth, absent the trial judge making a big mistake in his ruling. The rationale behind giving deference to the trial judge is that he was present in court and observed Campa's demeanor while he was testifying. The appellate court can read the cold transcript only to glean what actually transpired at the suppression hearing. Because the fruits of the search, the illegal green cards, were not suppressed, Campa entered a conditional guilty plea allowing him to preserve the suppression motion ruling on appeal. He was sentenced to 24 months in prison under the Federal Sentencing Guidelines.

police were listening at the door and heard suspicious activity. The *Terry* reasonable suspicion legal standard does not provide officers with authority to take a suspect to the police station to take mug-shots or fingerprints or to put the suspect in a line-up without his or her consent or a warrant authorizing such behavior. In *Hayes* v. *Florida*, 470 U.S. 811 (1985), a rape suspect was taken to the police station for fingerprinting in an attempt to match his prints to those left at the various crime scenes. In analyzing the level of intrusiveness on a person's right to privacy in an investigatory detention allowed under *Terry,* the U.S. Supreme Court explained that "the line is crossed when the police, without probable cause or a warrant, forcibly remove a person from his home or other place in which he is entitled to be and transport him to the police station, where he is detained, although briefly, for investigative purposes. Such seizures, at least where not under judicial supervision, are sufficiently like arrests to invoke the traditional rule that arrests may constitutionally be made only on probable cause."

If a *Terry* stop lasts too long, it is transformed into an arrest not supported by probable cause, which is an illegal arrest. Any evidence retrieved from the suspect in an unlawful arrest will be suppressed by operation of the exclusionary rule discussed more fully in chapter 12. There is no concrete defining moment when a *Terry* stop becomes an arrest unsupported by probable cause. The Supreme Court declared, "Much as a 'bright line' rule would be desirable, in evaluating whether an investigative detention is unreasonable, common sense and ordinary human experience must govern over rigid criteria."[20] Therefore, courts will examine the totality of the circumstances in making the determination whether the *Terry* stop was proper, whether officers exceeded the scope of a lawful *Terry* search, and whether the detention lasted too long, and the stop was transformed into an arrest unsupported by probable cause.

The Fourth Amendment does not categorically prohibit police officers from conducting multiple frisks of a suspect during an investigative detention, even absent evidence that a suspect had an opportunity to arm himself in the interim. One judge commented to a defendant who challenged the multiple frisks by police, "I don't think there's a limitation on the number of people who pat-frisk you." The reasonableness of multiple frisks is determined by the totality of the circumstances.

a. Terry Stops of Automobiles

Rule of Law: The same legal standard that guides *Terry* stops of people applies with equal force to automobiles.

What happens when, during a roadside encounter, officers have a reasonable suspicion that criminal activity is afoot on the basis of the actions and statements of a driver and passengers in a vehicle? What does the law allow the officer to do? In *Delaware* v. *Prouse,* 440 U.S. 648 (1979), if officers have reasonable suspicion that the motorists are engaged in criminal activity, then the officers can detain motorists in their vehicles. To balance the safety concerns of the officer with the need to minimize intrusion on the privacy of the motorists, the officers not only can detain the motorists, but also order both the driver, *Pennsylvania* v. *Mimms,* 434 U.S. 106 (1977), and the passengers, *Maryland* v. *Wilson,* 519 U.S. 408 (1997), out of the car until the officer completes the traffic stop. It has been a topic in dispute whether passengers in vehicles that are stopped have standing, or the legal authority, to challenge the legality of the stop. In 2007, the U.S. Supreme Court answered yes to the question. In *Brendlin* v. *California,* 127 S.Ct. 2400 (2007), officers stopped a car to check its registration without reason to believe it was being operated unlawfully. One officer recognized passenger Brendlin, who was a parole violator. The officers formally arrested and searched him, the driver, and the car, finding, among other things, methamphetamine paraphernalia. Charged

---

[20]*United States* v. *Sharpe,* 470 U.S. 675 (1985).

with drug possession and manufacture, Brendlin moved to suppress the evidence obtained in searching his person and the car, arguing that the officers lacked probable cause or reasonable suspicion to make the traffic stop. The state argued in return that Brendlin, as a passenger, could not challenge the police authority for the stop because Brendlin was not driving nor did he own the car. But the high Court found in Brendlin's favor, holding that when the driver of the car is seized, the passenger is seized and can contest the constitutionality of the stop.

Courts are split [they have arrived at different conclusions for similar issues] on whether or not authority to search on the basis of reasonable suspicion extends to the trunk of a car, but *Terry* stops are legal if the stop is reasonable. If the detention is limited to the officer requesting a driver's license, vehicle registration, and personal identification from passengers; examining the outside of the car; and running a computer check on the driver's license or the license plates, then the stop is reasonable.[21] But if, during the stop, the driver and passengers make the officer fear for his safety, and if he believes that the motorists may be armed or that the passenger compartment contains weapons, the officer may order everyone out of the car and search for and remove those weapons. In *Michigan* v. *Long,* 463 U.S. 1032 (1983), police watched a car drive into a ditch and, upon investigation, found the driver intoxicated and a large knife lying on the floorboards. The officers frisked the driver and searched the passenger compartment. Long was convicted and claimed on appeal that the search was unlawful, but the U.S. Supreme Court disagreed, holding the officers' conduct reasonable when it "weighed the interest of the individual against the legitimate interest in crime prevention and detection and the need for law enforcement officers to protect themselves and other prospective victims of violence in situations where they lack probable cause for arrest."

Authority to search for weapons under *Terry* does not extend to the trunk of the car or to closed containers inside the car such as briefcases or luggage. The legal justification for a weapons frisk under *Terry* is officer safety, and presumably the motorists cannot get to the trunk to retrieve weapons to harm the officer.[22] But if the officer has probable cause that the occupants or vehicle is connected to a crime, then the search may extend to the trunk of the vehicle and any and all closed containers because there is legal authority to search for evidence of a crime and contraband.

Applying the Rule of Law to the Facts: When is lawful detention transformed into an arrest?

- A man named Gallardo was driving on the highway when he saw a sign that read, "Please be prepared to stop for the upcoming drug interdiction checkpoint." Unknown to Gallardo, the sign was a fake designed to induce potentially guilty parties carrying drugs to avoid stopping. Gallardo turned around before the checkpoint and was pulled over for investigatory questioning. His paperwork checked out, and the officer learned that at Gallardo's residence two years earlier, a big methamphetamine bust had occurred. As there was no cause to hold Gallardo, Gallardo prepared to leave the police presence when an officer said, "Do you have a minute?" The officer, who spoke very poor Spanish, explained to Gallardo that he was investigating drug crimes and then said to Gallardo, "I, I police, I police search car?" To which Gallardo replied, "No problem." Police found 78 pounds of cocaine in a hidden compartment in the trunk. Was the *Terry* stop illegally transformed into an arrest without probable cause?

No, Gallardo's actions indicated that he had consented to the search of his vehicle. The officer, who had 17 years of experience, had a legal basis to detain Gallardo past the requisite brief

[21]*See United States* v. *Childs,* 277 F.3d 947 (7th Cir. 2002).
[22]*See United States* v. *Valadez,* 267 F.3d 395 (5th Cir. 2001).

detention on the basis of the following information gleaned during his talk with Gallardo: starting in California, Gallardo put 3,000 miles on his truck in an effort to look for an apartment in Sioux City, Iowa, unlikely behavior for one who was consciously trying to be frugal; Gallardo had no criminal record but had a temporal association with a residence busted for drugs; and California is a known source of drugs that are later transported to the middle of the country. *United States* v. *Gallardo*, 495 F.3d 982 (8th Cir. 2007).

b. Requests for Identification

Rule of Law: Outside an airport or other government administrative search function, law enforcement requests for personal identification can be made only in the context of a *Terry* stop.

Are individuals legally required to identify themselves to police officers or run the risk of being arrested? In Nevada, police received a report of an assault and came upon Larry Hiibel and a woman parked by a side of the road. Officers asked Hiibel for his name and for identification. Hiibel, who appeared to be intoxicated, refused 11 times to identify himself and was arrested under Nevada's "stop and identify" statute. Hiibel challenged his arrest under the Fourth Amendment as an unreasonable seizure. The Supreme Court found in favor of the officers in *Hiibel* v. *Nevada*, 124 S.Ct. 2451 (2004), holding that the statute requiring identification serves the "purpose, rationale, and practical demands of a *Terry* stop" and was a limited intrusion when weighed against the government's interest in identifying a suspect's criminal record or mental disorder, or in clearing the suspect as the object of the investigation. The Court limited its holding to asking for identification within the context of the *Terry* stop only; authority to demand identification did not extend to anyone on the street for any reason.

III. THE ARREST

Rule of Law: An arrest is a seizure; a person who has been arrested does not feel free to leave or terminate the police encounter.

A person is seized and entitled to Fourth Amendment protection when officers physically restrain him by force or a show of authority such as yelling at a suspect "Stop police!" An **arrest** is a formal seizure. If an officer wishes to ask questions of someone on the street, the person may or may not consent to answer. **Consent** to abide by police wishes must be voluntary and must not be the product of unlawful coercion, such as by the threat or show of force or authority. "If a reasonable person would feel free to terminate the encounter, then he or she has not been seized."[23] As the U.S. Supreme Court has said, officers "do not violate the Fourth Amendment by merely approaching an individual on the street or other public place, by asking him if he is willing to answer some questions, by putting questions to him if the person is willing to listen, or by offering in evidence in a criminal prosecution his voluntary answers to such questions."[24] For Fourth Amendment purposes a seizure of a person occurs when a person's freedom of movement is restrained. A person may be seized even though not formally under arrest. After such an incident, courts will examine the totality of the circumstances surrounding the restraint to determine whether a reasonable person would have believed he was not free to leave.[25] To determine whether the Fourth Amendment applies to a police–citizen encounter, courts consider the following factors: the amount, if any, of pressure, force, or coercion police place upon the citizen to cooperate; the number of police officers and whether they are armed during the encounter with the

---

[23] *United States* v. *Drayton*, 536 U.S. 194 (2002).

[24] *Florida* v. *Royer*, 460 U.S. 491 (1983).

[25] *United States* v. *Mendenhall*, 446 U.S. 544 (1980).

citizen; whether police make any physical contact with the citizen, including preventing him from leaving the area; and how far, if at all, the police removed the citizen from the original point of encounter.[26]

The question to ask under all of the circumstances is whether "a reasonable person would feel free to decline the officers' requests or otherwise terminate the encounter."[27] The suspect must actually submit to police authority for a seizure/arrest to have occurred. The U.S. Supreme Court held in *California* v. *Hodari D., 499* U.S. 621 (1991), that a suspect who was throwing away his drugs while running away was not under arrest until he actually submitted to the officer's authority, not when the officer merely yelled out for the suspect to stop running. The issue was important because if Hodari D. was "under arrest" when he was throwing away his drugs, he might have had a sufficient legal challenge to the police seizure of the drugs, but the high Court concluded Hodari D. was not under arrest merely because the police were calling after him to stop. Thus, when Hodari D. threw his drugs away, his drugs became "abandoned property" that could be seized without violating the Fourth Amendment. Consequently, any property the suspect discards while fleeing is abandoned property, and the suspect is not entitled to any expectation of privacy afforded by the Fourth Amendment.

Applying the Rule of Law to the Facts: When is a suspect under arrest?

- Police picked up Judy at her neighbor's house and took her downtown to the police station for questioning in a robbery and homicide investigation. The police had no specific and articulable facts that linked Judy directly to the robbery, but Judy implicated herself during the course of the interview when she drew sketches of the crime scene. She was arrested, tried, and convicted of robbery. On appeal, Judy argued that she was really "under arrest" when she was taken from her neighbor's house and, at that time, the police had no probable cause to arrest her. Probable cause is the minimum amount of information linking a specific person to a specific crime giving the police legal authority to arrest the person. The police responded that Judy was not under arrest during the interview and, therefore, probable cause justifying the police action was unnecessary. How should the court rule?

Judy was under arrest from the time that the police picked her up, because if she had tried to leave the police station during questioning, the police would have stopped her. Therefore, the arrest was unsupported by probable cause and was illegal.[28]

If officers make a probable cause determination that leads them to arrest a suspect, and the arrest is made in public, then the officers do not need a warrant. In *United States* v. *Santana,* 427 U.S. 38 (1976), the U.S. Supreme Court extended this rule to **curtilage,** which is the immediate area surrounding a home. Undercover police officers purchased heroin from a drug dealer who had been inside Santana's house. When police approached Santana's house and identified themselves, Santana, who was standing in front of the open door retreated inside. Officers followed and arrested her. The high Court upheld Santana'a arrest as legal because when police first spotted her, she was standing in the doorway, where no right of privacy existed. To allow Santana to shut the door to evade arrest would thwart the legitimate law enforcement function of crime detection and prevention. Had Santana never stepped outside, police would have needed a warrant to cross the threshold of her home. The warrant protects the sanctity

---

[26]See Larry E. Holtz. *Contemporary Criminal Procedure: Court Decisions for Law Enforcement* (Longwood, FL: Gould Publications, 2004).

[27]*Florida* v. *Bostick,* 501 U.S. 429 (1991).

[28]*Dunaway* v. *New York,* 442 U.S. 200 (1979).

of the suspect's home or of a third party's home where the suspect may be staying; police must have an arrest warrant in order to enter and arrest someone inside.

A warrant is not required to arrest someone for a minor traffic violation, such as not wearing a seatbelt. In *Atwater* v. *City of Lago Vista,* 532 U.S. 318 (2001), Gail Atwater was driving with her three-year-old and five-year-old in the front seat of her pickup truck and no one was wearing a seatbelt. Atwater had failed to show any driving credentials or insurance papers. She was arrested for failing to wear a seatbelt or have her children wear seatbelts, not having proof of insurance, and driving without a license. The officer then threatened to take Atwater's children into custody, but a neighbor came by and took the children. She was then handcuffed, placed in the squad car, booked at the police station, and forced to remove her shoes, jewelry, and glasses and empty her pockets. Officers took a mug shot and placed her alone in a cell for one hour. She ultimately pleaded no contest to the seatbelt violation, paid a $50 fine, and appealed her conviction. The high Court upheld her conviction on the grounds that the Fourth Amendment should not be interpreted to limit an officer's authority to arrest without a warrant to minor offenses. The Court looked at the common-law history of arrests and determined that the Constitution authorized arrests for misdemeanor-level offenses. The Court noted that Atwater's arrest was the result of poor judgment by the police officer, who imposed "gratuitous humiliations" upon her, for she was a well-known resident of Lago Vista "with no place to hide and no incentive to flee." However unnecessarily punitive the officer's actions were towards Atwater, the arrest was legal.

In its ruling on *Michigan* v. *Summers,* 452 U.S. 692 (1981), the U.S. Supreme Court held that a search warrant provides authority to temporarily detain all persons on the premises where the search is conducted. According to the reasoning in *Summers,* the judge's finding of probable cause justifying the warrant supports a reasonable belief that people on the premises may be involved in criminal activity justifying the detention. The Court said, "Of prime importance in assessing the intrusion is the fact that the police had obtained a warrant to search respondent's house for contraband. A neutral and detached magistrate had found probable cause to believe that the law was being violated in that house, and had authorized a substantial invasion of the privacy of the persons who resided there. The detention of one of the residents while the premises were searched, although admittedly a significant restraint on his liberty, was surely less intrusive than the search itself."

1. Reasonable Force

Rule of Law: The amount of force used to effectuate an arrest is subject to the Fourth Amendment's reasonableness clause.

Since an arrest involves the restraint of a person and, sometimes, using force on the person, the Fourth Amendment's reasonableness requirement attempts to control the amount of force used during an arrest. The first case to apply the concept of Fourth Amendment reasonableness in the context of a police attempt to seize [arrest] a fleeing suspect was *Tennessee* v. *Garner,* 471 U.S. 1 (1985). Garner was a 15-year-old boy who was 5'4" and weighed 100–110 pounds. Police responded to a call about a prowler, saw Garner run away, and ordered him to stop. When Garner kept running away, the officer shot him once in the back of the head, killing him. Garner's family sued the officer for violating Garner's rights, but the law in Tennessee was on the side of the officer, allowing the police to use "all the necessary means to effect the arrest" of a fleeing suspect. The high Court made the Tennessee law invalid when it decided that "[t]he use of deadly force to prevent the escape of all felony suspects, whatever the circumstances, is constitutionally unreasonable. It is not better that all felony suspects die than that they escape. Where the suspect poses no immediate threat to the officer and no threat to others, the harm resulting from failing to apprehend him does not justify the use of deadly force to do so." Thus, if police use excessive force in effectuating arrests they have violated the Fourth Amendment's reasonableness clause.

In a similar case, *Graham* v. *Connor,* 490 U.S. 386 (1989), Graham was a diabetic who felt the onset of an insulin reaction and asked a friend to drive him to a nearby store to buy orange juice to stabilize his blood sugar. There was a long line at the store, so Graham left the store quickly without purchasing the juice, and he and his friend drove away. An officer who suspected Graham of criminal activity in the store followed, stopped the car, and ordered both men out. Graham ran around the car twice and passed out. The officer handcuffed Graham, shoved his face against the hood of the car, and then threw him headfirst into the police car. He suffered a broken foot, cuts on his wrists, a bruised forehead, and an injured shoulder. The friend explained Graham's medical condition to the officer and pleaded for sugar. After learning that Graham had done nothing wrong at the store, the officer released him. Graham then sued the police for using excessive force. On appeal from a lower court ruling in favor of the officer, the Supreme Court empathized with beat officers on foot patrols who often have to make split-second decisions about the amount of force necessary to effectuate an arrest. The Court stated, "The 'reasonableness' of a particular use of force must be judged from the perspective of a reasonable officer on the scene, rather than with the 20/20 vision of hindsight. . . . The calculus of reasonableness must embody allowance for the fact that police officers are often forced to make split-second judgments—in circumstances that are tense, uncertain, and rapidly evolving—about the amount of force that is necessary in a particular situation." Nonetheless, the Court found that the lower court did not properly examine the arresting officer's actions under the Fourth Amendment. The Court then remanded the case back for the correct application of the law.

Applying the Rule of Law to the Facts: What amount of force is reasonable during high-speed chases?

- Police placed an 18-wheel tractor trailer across two lanes of highway behind a curve in the road to block the path of a fleeing suspect and then placed a police car with its lights on facing oncoming traffic so that the fleeing suspect would be "blinded." He did not see the tractor-trailer before he smashed into it and was killed. Was the roadblock an "unlawful seizure"?

The suspect was "seized" by the 18 wheeler because the roadblock was designed to stop him. The case was sent back to lower court to determine if the roadblock was set up in a way to kill the suspect. If so, his seizure would be considered excessive and unreasonable under the Fourth Amendment. *Brower* v. *County of Inyo,* 489 U.S. 593 (1989).

- Deputy Timothy Scott terminated a high-speed pursuit of Harris's car by applying his push bumper to the rear of the vehicle, causing it to leave the road and crash. Harris was rendered quadriplegic. Was the crash an "unlawful seizure"?

No, the police officer's attempt to save innocent bystanders from injury by trying to stop a high-speed chase is not unreasonable under the Fourth Amendment—even if the suspect is placed at risk of injury or death by the officer's actions. *Scott* v. *Harris,* 127 S.Ct. 1769 (2007).

2. Government Actions Performed Under the "Color of Law"

Rule of Law: Citizens may sue the government when its agents use excessive force or otherwise violate the Fourth Amendment's reasonableness clause.

a. The §1983 Claim

Under the Civil Rights Act of 1871 as amended, a person may seek redress when a person acting under color of state law deprives a citizen of constitutional or federal rights pursuant to Title 42 U.S.C. §1983—the so-called **1983 claim.**[29] The statute under section 1983 is not a creation of federal rights, but a vindication of rights established elsewhere: It allows people to sue in civil court persons "who act under color of any [state] statute, ordinance, regulation, custom, or usage" in depriving another of "rights, privileges, or immunities secured by the Constitution and laws" of the United States. A §1983 claim is a federal cause of action allowable for state actors who deprive people of the federal civil rights under the "color of law." To establish a typical §1983 claim alleging use of excessive force by a government agent, the civilian must establish that:

1. the officer was acting under the color of state law, and
2. the officer's actions deprived the victim of rights protected by the laws or Constitution of the United States.

Courts must first determine whether the person was acting in a private or professional capacity when the harm occurred, as "under color of state law" means the "misuse of power, possessed by virtue of state law and made possible only because the wrongdoer is clothed with the authority of state law"—in other words, acting in an official capacity.[30]

b. The §1983 Claim and Police Misconduct

Some successful civil lawsuits brought pursuant to §1983 have found the police liable for acts of omission; that is, the police were guilty of not doing their jobs. For example, police arrested a driver on a Chicago expressway and left three children in the car to fend for themselves. In search of a telephone to call for help, the kids navigated eight lanes of a busy highway at night. The court found the officers liable for creating the danger to the children. The proper course of action would have been to take the children to social services.[31] Another successful §1983 claim arose in a case when a sheriff's deputy stopped a rescue effort for a drowning 12-year-old boy because of a dispute between rescue agencies over who had jurisdiction on the lake. The boy died when the deputy threatened to shoot divers who attempted to go into the lake in an effort to save the child.[32] One case in which a citizen's §1983 claim was unsuccessful involved serial killer Jeffrey Dahmer. On May 27, 1991, two Milwaukee, Wisconsin police officers, John Balcerzak and Joseph Gabrish, responded to a 9-1-1 call about an injured, bleeding "butt naked young boy."[33] The boy was 14-year-old Konerak Sinthasomphone.[34] Because Konerak was not a native English speaker, he was disoriented, and could not communicate

---

[29]42 U.S.C. §1983 (2000). This statute provides:

Every person who, under color of any statute, ordinance, regulation, custom, or usage, of any State or Territory or the District of Columbia, subjects, or causes to be subjected, any citizen of the United States or other person within the jurisdiction thereof to the deprivation of any rights, privileges, or immunities secured by the Constitution and laws, shall be liable to the party injured in an action at law, suit in equity, or other proper proceeding for redress, except that in any action brought against a judicial officer for an act or omission taken in such officer's judicial capacity, injunctive relief shall not be granted unless a declaratory decree was violated or declaratory relief was unavailable. For the purposes of this section, and Act of Congress applicable exclusively to the District of Columbia shall be considered to be a statute of the District of Columbia.

[30]*Monroe* v. *Pope,* 365 U.S. 167 (1961), *overruled in part, Monell* v. *Department of Social Services,* 436 U.S. 658 (1978).

[31]*White* v. *Rochford,* 592 F.2d 381 (7th Cir. 1979).

[32]*Ross* v. *United States,* 910 F.2d 1422 (7th Cir. 1990).

[33]Peter Kwan. "Jeffrey Dahmer and the Cosynthesis of Categories." *Hastings Law Journal,* Vol. 48 (1997), pp. 1257–1292. Citing approximately 38 newspaper articles reporting on the incidents described herein.

[34]Officers Balcerzak and Gabrish were later found to have violated their duty to protect Sinthasomphone and were fired in September 1991. In 1994, the officers were reinstated and honored by the police union as officers of the year for fighting for their jobs. Balcerzak was later elected president of the police union, and Gabrish became a police lieutenant in an adjacent town.

clearly with police. Dahmer greeted police in the alley and told them that the injured boy was "John Hmong." He said that the boy was his 19-year-old boyfriend who had wandered naked in the street while Dahmer went to get more beer. Two teenage African-American cousins who were on the street and had called emergency services tried to convince police that Dahmer was lying. The police escorted Dahmer and the boy up to Dahmer's apartment. Up in the apartment, Dahmer showed police photographs of the boy and articles of the boy's clothing to convince the officers that Dahmer and the boy were a couple. Because of his disorientation, Sinthasomphone was speaking only Laotian. Officer Gabrish later recounted that Dahmer "appeared to be a normal individual" and the officers were convinced that "all was well." The mother of one of the girls on the street, Glenda Cleveland, later called the police. The transcript of the telephone conversation between Cleveland and Officer Balcerzak follows:

CLEVELAND: Well how old was this child?

BALCERZAK: It wasn't a child it was an adult.

CLEVELAND: Are you sure?

BALCERZAK: Yep.

CLEVELAND: Are you positive? Because this child doesn't even speak English, my daughter had, you know uh, dealt with him before, seen him on the street . . .

BALCERZAK: Hm-hmm

CLEVELAND: . . . you know, catching earthworms.

BALCERZAK: Hm-mmm, hm-hmmm, no, no, he's, that's all taken care of ma'am.

CLEVELAND: Are you sure?

BALCERZAK: Ma'am, I can't make it any more clear, it's all taken care of. It's, you know, he's with his boyfriend in his boyfriend's apartment where he's got his belongings also, there's where it's released.

CLEVELAND: But I mean isn't this, I mean, what if he's a child and not an adult? I mean, are you positive this is an adult?

BALCERZAK: Ma'am. Ma'am.

CLEVELAND: Hm-hmm?

BALCERZAK: Like I explained to you. It's all taken care, it's as positive as I can be.

CLEVELAND: Oh I . . .

BALCERZAK: Okay, there's . . . I . . . I can't do anything about somebody's sexual preferences in life . . . you know.

CLEVELAND: Well no, I'm not saying anything about that, but it appeared to have been a child, this is my concern.

BALCERZAK: No.

CLEVELAND: No.

BALCERZAK: No, he's not.

CLEVELAND: He's not a child.

BALCERZAK: No he's not, okay?

CLEVELAND: (sigh)

BALCERZAK: And that's a, boyfriend/boyfriend thing and he's got belongings at the house where a. . . .

CLEVELAND: Hm-hmm.

When the officers returned Sinthasomphone to Dahmer's care, Dahmer drilled a hole in the boy's head and then strangled him to death. Dahmer was eventually caught and found guilty of killing over 30 men and boys. Sinthasomphone's estate brought a §1983 claim against the officers and the city of Milwaukee for depriving the boy's recognizable and cognizable federal civil rights to substantive due process and equal protection.[35] The federal court dismissed the Sinthasomphone family's claim because the police officers who encountered the boy had no legal duty to protect him from Dahmer.

Applying the Rule of Law to the Facts: When is it a duty to act, and when is it a cognizable §1983 claim?

- Juvenile case workers knew that five-year-old Joshua was being severely physically abused by his teenage brother Charlie. They removed Charlie from the home and placed him in a temporary detention center. Later they released Charlie and sent him back home, where he beat Joshua so badly that it left him profoundly retarded. The boys' mother sued the juvenile workers. How should the court rule?

The Court should find in favor of the state workers. In a similar case, the U.S. Supreme Court dismissed the §1983 claim and said that the Constitution "was to protect the people from the State, not to ensure that the State protected [the people] from each other."[36]

c. Qualified Immunity for Criminal Justice Professionals Acting Under the "Color of Law"

All criminal justice professionals—law enforcement, corrections, juvenile officers, and probation and parole officers—are entitled to **qualified immunity** [limited protection from civil lawsuits] in the performance of their duties. Certain actors in the criminal justice system, including legislators, judges, and prosecutors, enjoy absolute [complete] immunity and cannot be sued for any harm flowing from their acts and decisions made in the performance of their professional duties.[37] Police officers enjoy absolute immunity in certain limited situations. In order for an officer to receive immunity for professional acts, certain conditions must be met:

1. the officer must have acted reasonably
2. at the time the officer acted, the constitutional right in question must not have been clearly established.

The test for whether a right was "**clearly established**" at the time of the officer's alleged violation of another's rights is whether:

1. according to the current state of the law, the officer should have known the right existed, and
2. whether the officer's actions were reasonable under the circumstances.

Only if there is a question of law regarding the rights of the people will an officer be entitled to qualified immunity. Under the first prong of whether the officer should have known the right existed, take for example the right to be free from unreasonable searches and seizures. But officers should also know, for example, that the U.S. Supreme Court has held that the use of thermal imaging devices outside a home to search for heat lamps on the inside of the home (used for growing marijuana) is an unconstitutional search. *Kyllo* v. *United States,* 533 U.S. 27 (2001). The second prong of the analysis is whether the officer's actions were reasonable in complying with the legal standards as he understood them to

---

[35]*The Estate of Konerak Sinthasomphone* v. *City of Milwaukee,* 785 F.Supp. 1343 (E. D. Wis. 1992).

[36]*DeShaney* v. *Winnebago County Department of Social Services,* 489 U.S. 189 (1989).

[37]Information for this section derived from Alan K. Chen. "The Facts About Qualified Immunity." *Emory Law Review,* Vol. 55 (2006), pp. 229–277.

exist. If an officer executed a search warrant believing that probable cause existed and discovered later that it did not, the officer would be protected by qualified immunity. But in the case *Groh* v. *Ramirez,* 540 U.S. 551 (2004), reprinted in chapter 10, the high Court denied immunity to Groh, a federal agent who served a plainly defective search warrant. The Court explained that any reasonable officer in Groh's shoes would have known the warrant was bad, and since Groh had executed the warrant anyway, he could be sued personally for violating the Ramirez family's rights.[38]

In *Wilson* v. *Layne,* 526 U.S. 603 (1999), officers were executing an arrest warrant for a dangerous fugitive, the Wilsons' son. As officers executed the warrant at the Wilson home, they brought along a reporter and photographer. Officers, some in plain clothes, entered in the early morning with guns drawn. They arrested the fugitive's father, the elder Wilson, who then brought a §1983 claim against the police. In response, the officers sought qualified immunity. The U.S. Supreme Court found that, although the officers violated the Wilsons' Fourth Amendment rights by bringing journalists into the home, that aspect of the law—bringing media along during the execution of warrants—was not clearly established at the time of the officers' actions. Therefore, the officers were entitled to qualified immunity.

Applying the Rule of Law to the Facts: Is the right "clearly established?

- To punish a prisoner, Alabama prison guards handcuffed him to a hitching post on two occasions, one lasting seven hours, and denied him water and bathroom breaks. Are the guards eligible for qualified immunity?

No, even if the officers were unaware of the precise law they were violating, they should have known that torturing the prisoner violated the Eighth Amendment's ban against cruel and unusual punishment.[39]

IV. Key Terms and Phrases

- arrest
- §1983 claim
- criminal activity is afoot
- expectation of privacy
- Fourth Amendment
- investigatory detention

- line-up
- photospread
- prior identification
- probable cause
- qualified immunity
- search

- seizure
- specific and articulable facts
- show-up
- *Terry* stop
- totality of the circumstances

V. Summary

1. **The methods of identifying suspects before trial: Pretrial identification** procedures include the **line-up,** in which several people are placed behind a two-way mirror and the "fillers" are chosen for their similarity in appearance to the suspect; the **photospread,** in which one suspect is shown with at least five other fillers who are not suspects but may look similar to the suspect; and the most suggestive pretrial identification procedure, the **show-up,** in which the suspect, alone, is paraded past or in front of the eyewitness. In each instance, the eyewitness attempts to identify the offender whom he or she saw committing the crime in question. The U.S. Department of Justice guidelines recommends certain procedures to diminish the risk of erroneous eyewitness identifications, such as showing the witness **sequential photographs** to force him or her to make an absolute decision in identifying the suspect. Another procedure is to ensure that the officer conducting the photospread viewing does not know who the suspect is, so that the officer will avoid sending cues or signals to the eyewitness that they have or have not identified the suspect. The pretrial identification procedure must not be too suggestive, or it will be excluded at trial.

---

[38]For federal officers, their immunity claim is analyzed through the U.S. Supreme Court case, *Bivens* v. *Six Unknown Named Agents of Fed. Bureau of Narcotics,* 403 U.S. 388 (1971).

[39]*Hope* v. *Pelzer,* 536 U.S. 730 (2002).

2. **The legal standard for investigatory detentions/***Terry*** stops:** An **investigatory detention** is also known as a *Terry* stop because of the case *Terry* v. *Ohio* (1968). The *Terry* stop allows officers to briefly detain people on the streets and ask questions on the basis of reasonable suspicion that criminal activity is afoot—that a crime has been, is being, or will be committed. If, during a *Terry* stop, the officer has a reasonable belief that a person is armed, the officer can pat down the person's outer clothing for weapons only, but cannot conduct a full-blown search. *Terry* stops and frisks are allowed on the basis of the state's general police power to prevent crime and to disarm people for the safety of the officers involved and the general public. A *Terry* stop can last only as long the officer needs to confirm or dispel her reasonable suspicion that criminal activity is afoot. If it lasts longer, the stop is transformed into an arrest unsupported by probable cause and it is illegal.

3. **The legal analysis guiding arrests:** An **arrest** is a seizure of a person and requires an arrest warrant, unless it is conducted in a public place. To meet the constitutional requirements of the Fourth Amendment, the amount of force used to effectuate all arrests and seizures must be **reasonable force.** Officers may not shoot at unarmed fleeing felons. In the context of **high-speed chases,** in which the police chase suspects in vehicles—chases that may end up harming or killing others or the suspects—the same analysis of reasonable force under the Fourth Amendment is employed by the courts.

4. **The legal remedy when criminal justice actors cause harm:** A **§1983 claim** is an avenue to recover damages (money) from criminal justice professionals if they act in their official capacity—called acting under the "color of law"—to deprive citizens of a federally protected right. A lawsuit may be brought against officers under 42 U.S.C. §1983 if, for example, they use excessive force in effectuating an arrest or if they fail to protect those entrusted in their care. Justice professionals may avail themselves of **qualified immunity** in the execution of their official duties if the officer acted reasonably on the basis of a questionable constitutional right.

VI. Discussion Questions

1. What pretrial identification procedure makes a crime victim most comfortable? Do you believe that once an eyewitness identifies a suspect, the witness becomes gradually more secure in that identification even in the face of evidence that he or she may have misidentified the suspect? What factors do you think may contribute to this phenomenon, and what can law enforcement do to prevent it?

2. What is the danger in giving police on the street the authority to empty a suspect's pockets in the name of officer safety?

3. Describe in your own words the difference between an officer's "hunch" that criminal activity is happening and "specific articulable facts" that criminal activity is afoot.

4. Do you agree with the concept of giving criminal justice professionals immunity for performing their professional duties, even if in the performance of those duties they harm members of the public? Why or why not?

VII. Problem-Solving Exercises

1. Randy was arrested and charged with armed robbery. Police took him to the station, where they took a digital photograph of him and placed it in a photo array with five other photographs of men of similar height and weight. Unfortunately, Randy was the only man of color in the photo array. Police then assembled four robbery victims in a room, placed the photo array in front of them, and asked each victim to identify the robber. After looking at the photographs and talking amongst themselves, they all agreed that Randy was the robber. Does Randy have any valid objection(s) to the pretrial identification at his trial?

2. In Indianapolis, police suspected that a man inside a motel room was making methamphetamine in the bathroom. They decided to conduct a "knock and talk" whereby they get the suspect to open the door and see if he will reveal any incriminating information or see if they can see in plain view any obvious contraband. The suspect opened the motel door in response to the officers' knock. There were six uniformed and armed officers present. They asked if the suspect would be willing to step outside the door and talk to them. When he refused and tried to close the door, one officer placed his foot inside the door preventing the suspect from closing it. As the suspect stood inside the open doorway, police asked to come in, sit down, and talk, but the suspect refused. They told the suspect, "hey, if you have nothing to hide,

you'll let us in, because only guilty people don't want the police around." Reluctantly, the man let the police in, whereupon, in order to sit on the bed, one officer moved a jacket, revealing a firearm on the bed. Was the investigatory detention and subsequent search legal?

3. Steve was cramming for his criminal law final when he realized that his black backpack had been stolen from his seat at the library. He went to campus police and described the last person he had seen in the vicinity of his seat as a "slight, white male with a scruffy beard and wearing a grey sweatshirt with a prominent sport logo on the front." Officer Blue was on patrol when he received the report, and approximately two miles from campus, he noticed a white male with a grey sweatshirt getting into a parked car. When Blue approached and looked into the car, he saw a black backpack on the back seat. The man in the car said he was named Kent and claimed that the backpack was his. Blue called back at the station to bring Steve by Kent's car to see if he could identify him. When Steve arrived, Kent was handcuffed and sitting in back of Officer Blue's squad car, and Steve identified him as the man he had seen earlier. The backpack in Kent's car belonged to Steve. At his trial for larceny, Kent sought to suppress Steve's pretrial identification on the grounds that the show-up was unduly suggestive and should be excluded. You are the judge. Taking into consideration the applicable legal principles, how would you rule and why?

VIII. World Wide Web Resources

Homepage of professor Gary Wells, eyewitness memory expert

http://www.psychology.iastate.edu/faculty/gwells/
  homepage.htm

Department of Justice, *Eyewitness Evidence: A Guide for Law Enforcement*

http://www.ojp.usdoj.gov

Innocence Project documenting wrongful convictions based on erroneous eyewitness identification

http://www.innocenceproject.org

IX. Additional Readings and Notes

Arrests

Irving J. Klein. *Principles of the Law of Arrest, Search, Seizure, and Liability Issues* (Miami: Coral Gables, 1994).

Eyewitness Identification

Brian L. Cutler and Steven D. Penrod. *Mistaken Identification: The Eyewitness, Psychology, and the Law* (New York: Cambridge University, 1995).

Ronald P. Fisher. "Interviewing Victims and Witnesses of Crime." *Psychology, Public Policy, & Law,* Vol. 1 (1995), pp. 732–764.

Gary Wells and Eric P. Seelau. "Eyewitness Identification: Psychological Research and Legal Policy on Line-Ups." *Psychology, Public Policy, & Law,* Vol. 1 (1995), pp. 765–791.

CHAPTER 10
The Warrant Requirement

"Where law ends, tyranny begins."

—Margaret Thatcher, British Prime Minister

CHAPTER OBJECTIVES

Primary Concepts Discussed in This Chapter:

1. How to analyze Fourth Amendment problems
2. Some of the many sources used to establish probable cause
3. The five requirements for an arrest or search warrant
4. The special problem of electronic surveillance and bodily intrusions

CHAPTER OUTLINE

Feature: *Chapter-Opening Case Study: The Right of Privacy and the Government Power to Search and Seize*

Marsha and Amy were in room 231 at the Motel Easy, mixing baking soda as an additive to pure cocaine before weighing it and placing it in plastic bags for eventual sale. Anne was on the couch watching television and smoking marijuana. The motel security guard walked past the room, smelled the marijuana, and called the local drug interdiction squad [no expectation of privacy in smells escaping from the room into a public hallway]. As the officers walked by the open window with no shades, they saw Amy carrying what appeared to be a bag of cocaine [if the women expected privacy, they should have closed the window and drawn the blinds]. As other officers set up surveillance and called in to the local magistrate for a warrant to search the motel room and seize "any and all drug paraphernalia," they mistakenly told the clerk the room number was 321. Anne left the motel room to get a six-pack of beer from the car in the parking lot. After Anne retrieved the beer from the trunk, she saw the police and ran. Officers observed Anne throw a glassine baggie to the ground as she was running and yelled after her to "Stop!" [when suspects throw property away, they abandon it and have no expectation of privacy regarding it]. Police caught Anne and placed her in handcuffs. When the warrant arrived, in the place labeled "items to be seized," the prosecutor typed in "see attached sheet." On the attached sheet was the phrase "any and all household items that may be associated with the drug trade" [search terms that may encompass a wide variety of items do not satisfy the Fourth Amendment's particularity requirement].

When Trooper Smith gave the warrant to Trooper Jones and Trooper King to execute, they went to the motel room and knocked on the door. Marsha answered the door, and police restrained her and Amy while they conducted the search. As they were searching the room, police noticed a laptop computer. One officer asked, "Hey, how about searching this?" and another officer replied, "Sure, we got a warrant and the hard drive might contain evidence of drug dealing" [warrant is to search for only those items listed; if additional items are to be seized, they must be obviously illegal and in plain view]. When the officer clicked on the file folder labeled "private" he found digital images of homemade child pornography. Have the officers conducted lawful searches and seizures?

This chapter introduces the protection of the Fourth Amendment, the limits of the government's ability to invade people's privacy, and the legality of search and seizure.

1. How to Analyze Fourth Amendment Problems

Rule of Law: Each Fourth Amendment problem should be analyzed using five steps to ensure that the government officials involved complied with the law.

A method of analysis represented in Figure 10.1, determines whether the Fourth Amendment's protections apply, whether the government has violated those protections, and, if it has, what the appropriate legal remedy should be.

FIGURE 10.1 Schematic diagram for analyzing Fourth Amendment problems.

HOW TO ANALYZE FOURTH AMENDMENT PROBLEMS

1. Is there government action including acts of government informants?
2. Is there both an objective and subjective expectation of privacy in the thing or place to be
3. Was the search conducted in a reasonable manner?
4. Was a warrant required?

YES
If so, were the warrant requirements met?

1. Probable cause connecting specific person/place to crime
2. Described with particularity
3. Neutral and detached magistrate
4. Oath and affirmation

NO
Does a recognized exception apply?

1. Consent (voluntary)
2. Search incident to an arrest
3. Exigent circumstances
4. Plain view/Open fields
5. Plain feel
6. Special needs
7. Border searches
8. Inventory

IF REQUIREMENTS NOT MET

IF EXCEPTION DID NOT APPLY

Exclusionary Rule forms trunk of tree which derivative evidence ("fruit") becomes excludable at trial

Poisons all evidence (fruit) derived from initial bad search or seizure

Exclusionary rule poisons tree trunk

Initial search or seizure that violates the Constitution is **excluded** at trial and poisons the tree trunk which then poisons everything else (the fruit) derived (obtained) from the initial illegality

The **first step in analyzing** whether the Fourth Amendment protects a person's right against unreasonable search and seizure is to determine whether or not a government actor is involved. If a neighbor trespassed into her drug-dealing neighbor's house and took a kilogram of cocaine to turn over to the police, there is no search and seizure issue because the government was not involved in invading the drug dealer's privacy. The analysis changes if the neighbor was working at the behest of the police. Courts examine the contours of the relationship between private citizens and the police to indicate whether the neighbor was working at police direction. This might be the case if the police encouraged the search, if the police knew your neighbor was going to search and did nothing to stop it, or if there had been a relationship of joint investigative action between the neighbor and the police. If the court finds that the private citizen was working as the government's agent, then the Fourth Amendment protection applies to searches and seizures conducted by those agents.

The **second step** in the constitutional analysis is to determine whether there exists an expectation of privacy in the place to be searched or the thing to be seized. The **expectation of privacy** must be subjectively and objectively reasonable. If the person has both a **subjective** [personal to that individual] and **objective** [obvious to everyone else] expectation of privacy that society recognizes as reasonable, such privacy interest is protected against unwarranted government intrusion. As an illustration of a reasonable expectation of privacy, consider a student named Hillary who carries a backpack to class. Hillary has a subjective personal expectation of privacy regarding what is inside the backpack. Everyone else in the class shares Hillary's belief that Hillary had a right of privacy in her backpack. (Thus, the objective standard is met.) But if Hillary placed a kilogram of cocaine in a transparent cellophane wrapper on the backseat of her car in the parking lot, she might have a subjective expectation of privacy in her car, but most people walking by who could look right into the window and see the cocaine would not objectively expect Hillary to have a reasonable expectation of privacy in the car. Since Hillary's expectation of privacy in hiding the cocaine in the car is not both subjective and objective, the Fourth Amendment would not protect it. If Hillary had hidden her cocaine in the trunk of her car, the analysis of her expectation of privacy would change—would officers need a warrant to search the trunk?

In *Katz* v. *United States,* discussed in chapter 9, Katz had been convicted for placing illegal bets across state lines using the telephone, a federal crime. The evidence against him was obtained when federal agents put listening devices on the exterior panels of the public telephone booth where Katz conducted his gambling business. On appeal the U.S. Supreme Court held that the Fourth Amendment protects "people, not places."

The **third step** in analyzing Fourth Amendment problems is to determine whether or not the police action in conducting the search and seizure was "reasonable." In our opening scenario, the motel security guard smelled marijuana coming from Marsha, Amy, and Anne's motel room. People have no privacy rights in smells emanating from their rooms into a public area. Police then witnessed through an open window activity believed to be drug activity. At that point, the officers had two options: They could establish surveillance of the motel room while they called for a search warrant, or they could have knocked on the door and asked for consent to search. Discussed in chapter 11, for a citizen's consent to search to be legal, it must be voluntary. As part of a routine investigation, officers may conduct a "knock and talk," wherein the officers knock on a door and talk to the people inside. If, during the knock and talk, the officers coerce or threaten the inhabitants in an effort to gain consent to search the premises, such a search would be unreasonable because the officers pressured the occupants to let them inside. The linchpin of legal analysis on search and seizures is whether the officers' actions were reasonable in light of the circumstances and the level of intrusion on the citizen's privacy interests.

The **fourth step** in analyzing search and seizure problems is to determine whether or not sufficient probable cause exists to support the issuance of a warrant or, in the alternative, whether an exception to the warrant requirement applies. In the case described, is witnessing suspected criminal activity through an open window enough to justify a search inside the premises?

The **fifth step** in the analysis is to determine whether, in the case of a Fourth Amendment violation, the evidence seized will be excluded from the defendant's trial by operation of the exclusionary rule and fruit of the poisonous tree doctrines discussed more fully in chapter 12. The exclusionary rule prohibits the introduction at trial of illegally seized evidence and any derivative evidence found as a result of the initial illegality (fruit tainted by the poisoned tree).

2. The Warrant Requirement

Rule of Law: Any search or arrest in a private home without a warrant is *per se* [without more] illegal unless a well-established exception applies.

The **warrant** is the legal document that notifies the person whose property is to be searched of the legal authority for, and the limits of, the proposed search. Searches conducted without a warrant are *per se* [on its face] unreasonable, "subject only to a few specifically established and well-delineated exceptions."[1] A search warrant must indicate that there is probable cause that particular evidence of a crime, instrumentalities, fruits [money], or contraband will be found at a definite place. To fulfill the warrant requirement a neutral and detached magistrate [judge, judicial officer] must determine whether police have probable cause to conduct a search, seize evidence, or make an

---

[1] *Katz* v. *United States,* 389 U.S. 347 (1967).

arrest. Probable cause indicates that there exists objective proof on which everyone would agree, versus the subjective belief of one police officer, that a place to be searched contains contraband or that a specific person has committed a crime.

Sometimes there is no time to go to the courthouse and secure a written warrant. In those cases where time is of the essence, federal law allows officers to secure a warrant by telephone. The officer must prepare a "proposed duplicate original warrant" and read verbatim the contents of the warrant, such as the facts indicating criminal activity that forms the probable cause—the legal basis justifying the search—to the judge. The judge enters what the officer tells him onto an original warrant. If the judge finds probable cause, he will sign the original warrant and direct the officer to sign the judge's name on the duplicate warrant in the officer's possession. The judge must make a verbatim record of the telephone call by court reporter or some other device.[2]

A federal warrant is depicted in Figure 10.2.

a. Arrest Warrants

No warrant is required to arrest a suspect in a public place, because a person walking around in public has no expectation of privacy. Under the common law, no arrest warrant was required if a suspect was about to commit or had committed a felony in the presence of a police officer.[3] The warrant requirement is specifically designed to protect the sanctity of privacy in an individual's home. Prior to the 1980s, state laws allowed police to enter private homes without a warrant to arrest citizens suspected of committing felonies. In most cases, there was sufficient time to obtain a warrant, but sometimes officers entered homes without warrants, and sometimes they entered homes without the consent of anyone inside. The U.S. Supreme Court in *Payton* v. *New York*, 445 U.S. 573 (1980), found the entry of officers into private homes without consent of the residents and without a warrant to be unconstitutional under the Fourth Amendment and said,

> In terms that apply equally to seizures of property and to seizures of persons, the Fourth Amendment has drawn a firm line at the entrance to the house. Absent exigent [emergency] circumstances, that threshold may not reasonably be crossed without a warrant.

The Court went on to say that police with arrest warrants supported by probable cause have the "implicit authority to enter the suspect's house to make the arrest," but not necessarily to enter the home of a third party. What does an officer have to show to prove that he believes the target of the arrest warrant is actually on the premises of a third party to justify entry? The Eleventh Circuit Court of Appeals answered that issue in *United States* v. *Bervaldi*, 226 F.3d 1256 (11th Cir. 2000). In *Bervaldi*, officers went to Bervaldi's house to execute a search warrant for Deridder. Officers knocked repeatedly on Bervaldi's door. When a man matching Deridder's description answered the door and saw the officers, he immediately slammed the door shut. Officers then kicked the door down, entered the house, and caught Deridder within 20 feet of the front door. A cocked but unloaded 9 millimeter pistol was found nearby. Upon conducting a protective sweep, police smelled marijuana, and when Deridder gave consent to search, officers discovered 60 pounds of marijuana hidden in a kitchen cupboard. At trial, Deridder successfully moved to suppress the evidence, claiming that officers did not have a reasonable belief that Deridder, the subject of the warrant, lived at Bervaldi's house. The appellate court overturned the trial court's decision and allowed the evidence to be introduced against Deridder, holding that the presence of Deridder's car parked in the vicinity of Bervaldi's house and the

---

[2]F. R. Crim. P. 41(f).

[3]*See* Fed. R. Crim. P. 4(a). If a criminal complaint or an officer's affidavit filed with the complaint establishes probable cause that a crime had been committed and that the suspect committed it, the judge must issue an arrest warrant to an officer authorized to execute it.

FIGURE 10.2 Search Warrant.

U.S. District Court Search Warrant (2 pages)

Search Warrant

AO 93 (Rev. 5/95)   Search Warrant   •

United States District Court

_____ DISTRICT OF _____

In the Matter of the Search of
(Name, address or brief description of person or property to be searched)

SEARCH WARRANT

CASE NUMBER:

TO: _____ and any Authorized Officer of the United States

Affidavit(s) having been made before me by _____ who has reason to
Affiant
believe that ☐ on the person of or ☐ on the premises known as (name, description and/or location)

In the _____ District of _____ there is now
concealed a certain person or property, namely (describe the person or property)

I am satisfied that the affidavit(s) and any recorded testimony establish probable cause to believe that the person
or property so described is now concealed on the person or premises above-described and establish grounds for
the issuance of this warrant.

YOU ARE HEREBY COMMANDED to search on or before _____
Date
(not to exceed 10 days) the person or place named above for the person or property specified, serving this warrant
and making the search (in the daytime—6:00 A.M. to 10:00 P.M.) (at any time in the day or night as I find
reasonable cause has been established) and if the person or property be found there to seize same, leaving a copy
of this warrant and receipt for the person or property taken, and prepare a written inventory of the person or property
seized and promptly return this warrant to _____
U.S. Judge or Magistrate
as required by law.

_____   at   _____
Date and Time Issued   City and State

_____   _____
Name and Title of Judicial Officer   Signature of Judicial Officer

FIGURE 10.2 *(continued)*

Search Warrant

AO 93 (Rev. 5/85)   Search Warrant

	RETURN	
DATE WARRANT RECEIVED	DATE AND TIME WARRANT EXECUTED	COPY OF WARRANT AND RECEIPT FOR ITEMS LEFT WITH
INVENTORY MADE IN THE PRESENCE OF		

INVENTORY OF PERSON OR PROPERTY TAKEN PURSUANT TO THE WARRANT

CERTIFICATION

I swear that this inventory is a true and detailed account of the person or property taken by me on the warrant.

_____

Subscribed, sworn to, and returned before me this date.

_____ _____

U.S. Judge of Megistrate   Date

observation of him leaving the house while officers had the house under surveillance were sufficient to establish the reasonable belief that Deridder was inside; thus, the search was lawful.

What can officers do with the people who are found on the premises when they are executing the warrant? In *Michigan* v. *Summers*, 452 U.S. 692 (1981), Summers was on the front steps of his house when police arrived to execute a search warrant for drugs. While the search was going on, police detained Summers, who was eventually arrested, and drugs were found in his pocket when he was searched. The question arose on appeal whether the officers had legal authority to detain people at the scene when they were executing a search warrant, and the answer is yes. The Court held that "a warrant to search for contraband founded upon probable cause implicitly carries with it the limited authority to detain the occupants of the premises while a proper search is conducted," and holding Summers at the scene was lawful.

Applying the Rule of Law to the Facts: Is the search legal?

- Police had an arrest warrant for a suspect who was in an innocent individual's house. The police entered the innocent party's home to effectuate the warrant. The homeowner claimed that his Fourth Amendment rights were violated.

The high Court held that the police did violate the innocent individual's rights. The Court distinguished between the protections against unreasonable search afforded by the search warrant and "an individual's interest in the privacy of his home and possessions against the unjustified intrusion of the police." *Steagald* v. *United States,* 451 U.S. 204 (1981).

- Unknown to officers, the named African-American suspects in the arrest warrant had moved. When they arrived to execute the arrest warrant, officers ordered two white individuals out of bed. They were naked, and police waited for minutes before allowing them to dress. The individuals sued the police, claiming that their Fourth Amendment rights were violated.

The U.S. Supreme Court found in favor of the police and held that even if the police know the people in the house are not the named suspects in the warrant, they can detain them if necessary for officer safety. *Los Angeles* v. *Rettele,* 127 S.Ct. 1989 (2007).

Whether the warrant is to search a home or arrest someone inside a home, officers must supply the magistrate who will issue the warrant with enough information to determine whether the dictates of probable cause are satisfied.

3. Probable Cause

Rule of Law: Probable cause means the facts establish that it is more likely than not that a specific person committed a crime or a place to be searched contains contraband.

There are three different types of police citizen encounters, and different legal standards guide each one. The first type of encounter is consensual; the citizen consents to answering questions and allows law enforcement officers to search his or her personal belongings. The legal standard that guides the consensual encounter is that the citizen's consent must be given voluntarily. The police cannot threaten the citizen to get consent, saying, for example, "give us your consent or we will put you in jail." The second type of encounter, discussed in chapter 9, is the temporary detention, otherwise known as the *Terry* stop. The legal standard is based on reasonable suspicion that criminal activity is afoot. Police can stop and question an individual and, if the officer believes the person is armed, can pat down and frisk for weapons only. The third type of encounter is the full-blown arrest, in which the officers can handcuff and search the person fully and detain the person in jail. The legal standard for this most invasive and intrusive type of government action with an individual is probable cause. The police need probable cause that the citizen has committed or will commit a crime in order to arrest the citizen or to obtain a search warrant to search a specific place for evidence of illegal activity. **Probable cause** holds if

> . . . [under] the totality of the circumstances, as viewed by a reasonable and prudent police officer in light of his training and experience, would lead that police officer to believe that a criminal offense has been or is being committed.[4]

As discussed previously, the totality of the circumstances test takes all factors into account to determine whether there is sufficient probable cause to convince a judge that a warrant is justified to arrest a suspect or to search a particular place for specific items.[5] What may suffice as probable cause in one case may not in a similar case because the circumstances under which criminals commit crimes change all the time. The probable cause standard allows officers to be flexible in making the call that probable cause exists, but it must be based on more than a "hunch" that someone is engaged in criminal activity. The reasonable suspicion standard necessary for a *Terry* stop is based on the reasonable officer's perspective that criminal activity is afoot. The probable cause standard is based on the reasonable person standard that a crime has been or will be committed. An officer is required to base the probable cause determination upon **specific and articulable facts** that support the probable cause determination. Those facts should convince any person looking at the facts as presented by the officer that a crime has been or will be committed by the person named or that contraband will be found in a place to be searched. The officer should be aware that if an arrest or seizure is made and the suspect challenges the probable cause determination during a suppression hearing, the officer will have to testify (articulate) under oath to the (specific) facts that led to the conclusion that probable cause existed.

a. Sources of Probable Cause

i. Officer's Perceptions The law does not expect police officers to shut their eyes, cover their ears, and perform their jobs in a sensory vacuum. All law enforcement officers have been trained at professional academies and typically gain some experience early in their careers investigating crimes and interviewing witnesses, victims, and suspects. They can rely on the training and experience they have gained to determine whether there is probable cause to search and seize. Note that acts cannot merely suggest probable cause that a crime is being committed; they must specifically indicate criminal activity. A suspect running away from an approaching officer, without more, does not support a finding of probable cause. People can be afraid of the police for many reasons, and they have every constitutional right to run when they see police. But flight from the police in addition to other suspicious activity, such as presence in a high-crime area known for drug activity, will support a finding of probable cause.

For example, a drug suspect landed in Utah's airport from Hawaii via Los Angeles carrying a shoulder bag and retrieved no other luggage—somewhat suspicious given that Hawaii is a major tourist destination where people generally stay for a few days. The man was looking around and was visibly nervous—not necessarily criminal behavior. But when the officer approached to ask questions, the suspect dropped his bag and ran away—definitely suspicious behavior. His bag contained drugs, and the suspect was convicted on drug charges. On appeal, he argued that there was insufficient probable cause for his arrest, but the court disagreed, finding that, under all of the circumstances together, there was sufficient probable cause to believe that the suspect was engaged in activity he wanted to hide from police (drug possession) to justify his arrest.[6]

---

[4]*Beck* v. *Ohio*, 379 U.S. 89 (1964).

[5]*Illinois* v. *Gates*, 462 U.S. 213 (1983).

[6]*United States* v. *Bell*, 892 F.2d 959 (10th Cir. 1989).

ii. Collective Knowledge   A common source establishing probable cause is the **collective knowledge** of all of the information gathered by law enforcement agents during their investigations. One police officer trying to establish probable cause to arrest or search can rely on what other officers tell him and on information learned from other investigations, including those in different jurisdictions. Such secondhand hearsay ["Bill told me that Suzy said Mary sold drugs"] is considered reliable because of the nature of police work. An officer in Indiana who has received an All Points Bulletin describing a car that was last seen near the vicinity of a murder has probable cause to arrest a suspect driving that car on the basis of the collective knowledge of all of the officers investigating the crime.

iii. Presence in a "High-crime" Area   Just because people live in a densely packed urban area known for illegal drug activity does not give rise to probable cause that its residents are criminals. But if someone is closely associated with known criminals in the area, that fact can be used to establish probable cause. The courts use certain criteria to decide whether probable cause exists to search and arrest specifically for drug-related crimes:

1. The suspect is present in an area notorious for its drug trade
2. The suspect is engaging in a sequence of events typical of drug transactions—for example, many brief hand-to-hand transactions conducted late at night
3. The suspect attempts to escape after being confronted by police
4. The suspect attempts to conceal the subject of his business.[7]

All of the above factors taken in conjunction with other information known to law enforcement and personal observations may be used to establish probable cause.[8]

iv. Informants   **Informants** are people who give information to law enforcement about crime and criminals in exchange for a government benefit. A typical informant is a criminal who has been arrested and enters into a plea bargain with the government, either for reduced charges or for a lighter sentence that enables the person to stay on the streets and gather more information about criminal activity to help the police. Informants are also paid for the information they provide or for the actions they perform on behalf of law enforcement. For example, police set up controlled buys using informants to purchase drugs from suspected drug dealers. The purchases are controlled by the police who usually sit outside the drug house in an unmarked car monitoring the transaction from afar. Officers give the informant marked money from the police department's budget to buy drugs from a suspected dealer. When the drug purchase from the suspect is complete, the informant brings the drugs directly to his police handler waiting outside, who records and secures the evidence. Police must search the informant immediately prior and after the drug purchase to ensure that the only place the informant could have obtained the drugs is from the suspect. In federal drug prosecutions, it is common to outfit the informant with a recording device to catch on tape the suspect conducting the drug transaction and to videotape the transaction either from a surveillance position, or sometimes from cameras hidden in false radios in cars used by drug agents to make controlled buys. These tapes are preserved for later use against the defendant at trial, but often their existence convinces defendants to plead guilty or to enter a plea-bargain where the defendant can become an informant to catch his drug supplier. If the drug dealer is arrested at the conclusion of the controlled buy, the marked money found in his pocket or on the premises links the money to the informant's drugs in the handler's possession.

---

[7]*United States* v. *Green*, 670 F.2d 1148 (D.C. Cir. 1981).

[8]*United States* v. *Lima*, 819 F.2d 687 (7th Cir. 1987).

Because of their willingness to trade information for their own freedom, informants are inherently unreliable; they have an incentive to lie in exchange for a get-out-of-jail-free-card from the prosecutor. When information is used to establish probable cause for a warrant, the officer must show in the affidavit of probable cause supporting the warrant that the informant is reliable. The U.S. Supreme Court stated that the officer must show:

1. The informant's basis of knowledge (how, when, and where informant obtained information)
2. The basis for believing that the informant is telling the truth
   i. If the informant is an ordinary citizen, he or she is considered inherently credible; if the informant is a criminal, the government must show that the informant has given accurate information in the past that has led to more investigations, arrests or convictions.
   ii. The informant is giving information that is against his own penal interest (subjecting him to prison time); and
3. Independent corroboration of the informant's information. If the informant provided information that he witnessed the suspect cook and sell crack cocaine, the officer must state that he corroborated the information by surveillance which established the fact that the suspect was engaged in drug manufacture and trade.[9]

v. The Difference Between Informants and Anonymous Tips   Anonymous tips typically are insufficient to establish probable cause. Imagine if a vindictive husband called the police department to report, anonymously, that his wife was a child molester. If the wife was not a child molester and her husband simply wanted to use the police to harass the wife, precious resources would be wasted investigating spurious claims. If anonymous tips can be verified before the police take action, courts may deem such tips reliable. The high Court has defined the reliability of anonymous tips on the basis of the detail provided in the tip and whether or not the information given can be corroborated by independent verification. In *Alabama* v. *White*, 496 U.S. 325 (1990), the anonymous caller specifically said that Vanessa White would be leaving Lynwood Apartments driving a brown Plymouth station wagon with a broken taillight traveling to Dorsey's motel and would have an ounce of cocaine in a brown attaché case, all of which turned out to be true when White was arrested and consented to a search of her belongings. White was convicted and challenged the legal authority of the police in stopping her on the basis of the anonymous tip alone. The U.S. Supreme Court held that an anonymous tip may give rise to reasonable suspicion that criminal activity is afoot when the tip is sufficiently corroborated. In White's case, the tipster gave such detailed information about her activities and predictions of her movements that, once police confirmed the information, indicated an intimate knowledge of White for the tips to be sufficiently reliable. But in the case *Florida* v. *J.L.*, 529 U.S. 266 (2000), the high Court found that an anonymous tip alone was insufficient to establish reasonable suspicion that the juvenile J.L. was armed so that police could conduct a pat down and frisk. Police received an anonymous tip that a black man would be standing at a bus stop in a plaid shirt and would be carrying a weapon. Police went to the bus stop, saw a young man who fit the description, frisked him, and recovered the gun. J.L. was convicted, but the high Court overturned his conviction, finding that the frisk was unreasonable because the officers had nothing more than the tip to believe that the young man was engaged in criminal activity. Unlike the tip in the *White* case, which gave specific details that turned out to be true, the anonymous tip in the *J.L.* case was nothing more than "a man with a gun"; therefore, there was no legal justification for the stop.

---

[9]*See United States* v. *Rankin*, 261 F.3d 735 (8th Cir. 2001).

The same analysis about the reliability of anonymous tips applies to satisfying the probable cause requirement for a search warrant. On April 3, 2008, Texas authorities raided a ranch in Eldorado, Texas, and removed over 400 children believed to have been sexually abused or at risk for sexual abuse because of the early-marriage religious beliefs of the Fundamentalist Church of Jesus Christ of Latter Day Saints. The investigation was initiated upon an anonymous tip to a child abuse center allegedly made by a 16-year-old girl who said she was inside the compound, had been abused, and was fearful of suffering more abuse. The girl's information was shared with Child Protective Services, which contacted the Sheriff's Department and the Texas Rangers. Once inside the compound, officials could not locate the girl, and they still have not done so. On April 20, 2008, Rozita Swinton, a 33-year-old woman from Colorado Springs, Colorado, was arrested in connection with making the initial telephone calls from her home to the abuse hot line in Texas. The lawyers for the church members challenging the authority of Texas to search the religious compound will no doubt focus on the anonymous tip alone to establish sufficient probable cause to legally justify the initial entry into the compound.

If an informer has not been proven reliable and police do not independently corroborate the informer's information prior to making an investigatory stop, the stop may be deemed illegal, as held the Montana Supreme Court in *State* v. *Martinez*, 67 P.3d 207 (Mont. 2003). In the *Martinez* case, a woman met with a Billings, Montana, police detective and informed him that within three days a man named "Ricky" would be driving a load of marijuana to a Billings motel from Oregon in a particular vehicle. Police confirmed that the vehicle described by the informer was registered in Oregon to one of the defendants, Jesus Martinez, and that Martinez had registered at the motel several times in previous weeks. The informer was the girlfriend of defendant Daniel Olson. A few weeks later, the informer–girlfriend called police and said that "Ricky" had checked into the motel. Police put Martinez under surveillance, but did not see him engage in any activity associated with drug dealing. The next day, the informer–girlfriend notified police that Martinez and Olson were going to leave Montana to sell the marijuana. When Martinez and Olson were driving away from town, police stopped them and discovered the marijuana, which was subsequently used to convict the defendants of felony drug possession. The defendants appealed on the basis that the police lacked reasonable suspicion justifying the stop of their vehicle, and the Montana Supreme Court agreed. Finding that police relied on the informant–girlfriend, who had no proven track record of providing police with accurate information, to investigate and prosecute others, and that police never asked how the informant came by her incriminating information, she was, therefore, unreliable and her tip was legally insufficient to justify the vehicle stop. Martinez and Olson's convictions were overturned.

In sum, when criminal investigations gather information to stop, frisk or arrest members of the public, courts generally find anonymous tips insufficient to justify a stop. Anonymous tips which predict that a suspect will engage in certain criminal behavior that can be corroborated by police may be sufficient to justify a stop. The use of an informant as a basis for a stop must be predicated on the informant's track record of providing accurate information in the past that the police have relied upon in the successful investigation or prosecution of others.

vi. Other Lawful Evidence   As discussed more fully in chapter 11 on warrant exceptions, other evidence discovered as a result of consensual searches and interviews, found in plain view or discovered as a result of a *Terry* stop, may be sufficient to establish probable cause.

Applying the Rule of Law to the Facts: When does probable cause exist?

- The suspects were traveling north on interstate 95, a known drug route from Miami to New York. During a consensual search, officers found a large amount of money in small bundles, and one passenger volunteered that they had won the money gambling in New Jersey. Officers noted that the direction in which the car was traveling and the packaging of the money were inconsistent with this story. Also, the car was registered to someone else, a common tactic for drug dealers to avoid having their cars seized. Probable cause for drug activity?

Yes, there was probable cause to believe that the defendants were engaged in drug activity and that the money was drug related.[10]

4. Supported by Oath or Affirmation

Typically, when a search warrant is prepared, a state or federal prosecutor works in conjunction with the investigating officer to produce an **affidavit,** a statement of facts legally sufficient to establish probable cause sworn under the pains and penalties of perjury in front of a judge. As depicted in Figure 10.2, the format of a federal search warrant does not allow much room to type in the pages of facts that might support a probable cause determination. Therefore affidavits are started on the face of the warrant and usually finished on separate pages which are then "**incorporated by reference**" on the face of the warrant. Sometimes, too, the description of the things to be seized can be more than a page long. To satisfy the "particularity requirement" of the Fourth Amendment this list must also be "incorporated by reference" into the information included on the actual face of the warrant.

Before the search or seizure, the officer takes the warrant and her affidavit in front of the judge, raises her right hand, and swears or affirms that the information contained in the warrant and affidavit is true to the best of her knowledge and belief. In our chapter-opening scenario, the warrant for the search of Marsha, Amy, and Anne's motel room stated on its face, "see attached sheet," allegedly identifying items to be seized, but there was no indication that the accompanying list of items to be seized had been incorporated by reference into the warrant. This could be a fatal flaw that would render the drugs seized from the motel room inadmissible at trial. On the face of the warrant are blocks of space to enter specific information—for example, the address and description of place to be searched, the officer's name and title, the citation of the specific law being violated, the officer's signature, and the judge's signature indicating the officer has taken an oath that the information included in the warrant is true. Because there is not enough space to list all of the facts that may give rise to probable cause in each case, there is a box on the warrant which indicates that additional information is attached. The officer usually writes an affidavit containing detailed information used to establish probable cause and staples it to the warrant. Once the affidavit is attached to the warrant, it is "incorporated" into the physical warrant "by reference" to it on the warrant's face. Box 10.1 shows parts of the affidavit used in the steroids prosecution of the Balco laboratory.

Requiring the officer to swear to the truth of the facts establishing probable cause contained in the affidavit that is attached to the warrant not only impresses upon the officer the respect the courts give to the Fourth Amendment and to search and seizure issues, but also makes the officer personally responsible if the facts supporting the issuance of the warrant turn out to be false. In addition, the oath requirement protects the judge against charges that he or she issued an illegal warrant, because the

---

[10]*United States* v. *Anderson*, 676 F.Supp. 604 (E.D. Pa. 1987).

officer came before the judge and swore that the information contained in the probable cause affidavit was true.

5. The Neutral and Detached Magistrate

The Fourth Amendment requires an impartial judge—one with no prior knowledge of the case and no personal stake in the outcome of the case—issue the warrant, ensuring that there is a sufficient legal basis to justify the search or arrest. Judges must be fair and impartial in making decisions on the admissibility of evidence and in controlling the presentation of facts at trial. Court decisions have held that if the judge participates in the search, or has conducted an investigation into the crime, or serves as a part-time prosecutor, the judge's objectivity is compromised and the warrant issued is defective.[11] Courts require an impartial magistrate issue a warrant because police "may lack sufficient objectivity to weigh correctly the strength of the evidence supporting the contemplated action against the individual's interest in protecting his own liberty."[12] In short, society must not allow the fox (the police) to guard the chicken coop (to make the determination that the target of the investigation has committed a crime or stored contraband in a particular place).

Who is a neutral and detached magistrate in a small town where judicial officers may also have part-time jobs in law enforcement? In *Coolidge* v. *New Hampshire*, 403 U.S. 443 (1971), a 14-year-old girl was found murdered and Coolidge was a suspect. While he was at the police station taking a lie detector test, police went to his home, where Coolidge's wife turned over guns and clothing he was wearing on the night of the murder. Two weeks later, the attorney general of New Hampshire, who had a dual role as a justice of the police, issued a search warrant for Coolidge's car, where officers found incriminating evidence linking Coolidge to the murder in his trunk. Coolidge was convicted. During his appeal to the U.S. Supreme Court, the issue was whether the warrant was invalid because the attorney general was part of the executive branch of New Hampshire's government and was not neutral in the prosecution and enforcement of state criminal laws. The Court said that yes, members of the executive branch do not meet the Fourth Amendment's requirement that "inferences be drawn by a neutral and detached magistrate instead of being judged by the officer engaged in the often competitive enterprise of ferreting out crime." Because the issuance of the warrant violated the Fourth Amendment and thus violated Coolidge's rights, the case was overturned.

In *Lo-Ji Sales, Inc.* v. *New York*, 442 U.S. 319 (1979), an investigator for the New York State Police applied to the Town Justice for a warrant to search the defendant's "adult" bookstore. The investigator's affidavit asserted that at the store, the defendant offered for sale films that violated the state obscenity laws. The affidavit also requested that the judge accompany the investigator to the defendant's store to supervise execution of the warrant to "determine independently if any other items at the store were possessed in violation of the law and subject to seizure. The Town Justice agreed." At the time the justice signed the warrant, the warrant failed to list or describe specifically the items to be seized. Thereafter, the town justice, four state police, several detectives, and three members of the local prosecutor's office—11 in all—entered the bookstore and engaged in a search that lasted almost six hours. During the search, the judge viewed 23 films, determined that there was probable cause to believe that they were obscene, and then ordered the officers to seize the film, projectors, and 327 magazines. On appeal, the U.S. Supreme Court said, "This search warrant and what followed the entry of

---

[11]*See generally Iowa* v. *Fremont*, 06/06-1443 (May 2, 2008) (judge not neutral and detached by signing warrant when he once represented an occupant in his capacity as a private attorney).

[12]*Steagald* v. *United States*, 451 U.S. 204 (1981).

the premises are reminiscent of the general warrant or writ of assistance of the 18th century against which the Fourth Amendment was intended to protect." Not only was the particularity requirement not met, but the judge "did not manifest the neutrality and detachment of a judicial officer when presented with a warrant application for a search and seizure." He was acting as an adjunct law enforcement officer, which is improper under the Fourth Amendment.

6. The Particularity Requirement

The Fourth Amendment commands that the warrant must "particularly describe[e] the place to be searched and the persons or things to be seized." As interpreted by the Supreme Court in *Andresen* v. *Maryland*, 427 U.S. 463 (1976), the **particularity requirement** protects against general, exploratory searches and leaves "nothing . . . to the discretion of the officer executing the warrant." Courts take an inflexible position on the particularity requirement and have invalidated warrants that insufficiently explained what officers were to seize, such as documents and "any other material reflecting identity, and anything reflecting potential fraud," and warrants that were for "any and all evidence of a crime." Such a description, similar to the warrant in the chapter's opening scenario for "any and all household items that may be associated with the drug trade," is too broad and vague to withstand judicial scrutiny. A more complete definition of "drug paraphernalia" may be "any equipment, product, or material of any kind, which is primarily intended or designed for use in manufacturing, compounding, converting, concealing, producing, processing, preparing, injecting, ingesting, inhaling, or otherwise introducing into the human body a controlled substance."[13] Likewise, the place to be searched must be described fully. Warrants have been invalidated when the place to be searched was described as a single-family residence and in reality was an apartment building or when the location to search was identified by two subdivided lots with no reference to the buildings on the property to be searched.

If the warrant incorrectly states the number in the address of the place to be searched, as in our introductory scenario in which Amy, Marsha, and Anne's room number was "231" and the officer put the number "321" on the warrant, courts have found the warrant to be valid despite the minor error if the officer who observed the suspected criminal activity at an address was also a member of the team executing the search warrant.[14]

The probable cause determination ensures that if the same set of facts were presented to a room full of people, they would all find that it was more likely than not that the suspect committed the crime justifying her arrest or that contraband would be found in a specific place justifying the search. Box 10.1 shows parts of an affidavit from a Treasury Department Special Agent establishing probable cause to search businesses, homes, mailboxes, computers, and financial records of Balco Laboratories, a company linked to supplying steroids to enhance the performance of world-class and professional athletes. Note the specificity and detail the agent relates in his affidavit establishing probable cause to search, particularly in describing the places to be searched and the things to be seized.

In Special Agent Novitzky's affidavit, also notice how the following items were used to establish probable cause: his training and experience as a federal agent; information obtained through various methods of investigation, such as trash runs that retrieved letters; and information from an informant. Examine closely the information in

---

[13]21 U.S.C. §863

[14]*See United States* v. *Vega-Figueroa*, 234 F.3d 744 (1st Cir. 2000).

BOX 10.1

Affidavit of Special Agent Jeff Novitzky in Support of Request for Search Warrants[15]

I, Jeff Novitzky, being duly sworn, hereby depose and state as follows:

I. INTRODUCTION

1. This affidavit is submitted in support of a request for the issuance of five search warrants for locations under the authority and control of Victor Conte, Jr. The five locations to be searched are. . . . [Conte's business, residence, and private mailboxes].

2. This request for authorization to conduct searches at the above-referenced locations is based upon the development of facts which provide probable cause to believe that Victor Conte, Jr. and others are involved in a nationwide scheme to knowingly distribute athletic performance-enhancing drugs, including anabolic steroids, a federally controlled substance, to numerous elite professional athletes at a local, national and international level [in violation of federal law].

II. AFFIANT'S BACKGROUND

3. I am a Special Agent with the Internal Revenue Service, Criminal Investigation ("IRS-CI"), and have been so employed since 1993. During my 10 years with IRS-CI, I have conducted and/or participated in hundreds of criminal investigations involving income tax violations, money laundering violations, currency violations and other federal financial crimes. . . .

III. FACTS IN SUPPORT OF PROBABLE CAUSE

[Paragraphs 4–9 omitted].

A. Balco Laboratories, Inc. Background

10. On January 29, 2003, I spoke with Jaime Nazario, an employee of the Drug Enforcement Administration (DEA) in San Jose, California. Nazario ran the names of Victor Conte Jr. and Dr. Brian Halevie-Goldman [medical director of Balco Laboratories] through indices of authorized and registered controlled substance distributors that the DEA maintains. Nazario informed me that neither Conte nor Dr. Halevie-Goldman are currently authorized or registered

through the DEA to distribute or prescribe controlled substances. Nazario further informed me that it is illegal for a doctor or anyone else to distribute or prescribe a controlled substance without authorization and registration with the DEA.

[Paragraphs 11–16 omitted].

E. Examination of Discarded Trash

17. Since September 3, 2002, I have performed, on approximately a weekly basis, an examination of the discarded garbage of Balco Laboratories Inc., located at 1520 Gilbreth Road in Burlingame, California. I have regularly retrieved the discarded garbage from a public-access parking lot where it is placed for pickup. . . . Following is a partial listing of items retrieved from the discarded trash of Balco Laboratories . . . along with the date the evidence was retrieved.

- A torn, empty box [that had contained] multiple vials of Serostin, a human growth hormone (9/3/02);
- A torn, empty box of 200 mg vial of testosterone (9/10/02); [Testosterone is an anabolic steroid and classified as a Schedule III controlled substance as listed in Title 21, U.S.C. §802]. . . .
- At least eighty-four (84) empty, one-use syringe wrappers in various sizes (9/3/02 through 8/10/03); . . . .
- A November/December 2002 issue of "Anabolic Insider", an underground steroid publication (12/16/02);
- Various small envelopes and letters from an elite track and field athlete, who is currently the United States champion in his event, including the following:

Vic, here is a check for the next cycl (sic). I need it by the end of the week. [FN: A cycle is a common phrase used for the administration of anabolic steroids because the users typically cycle their use on an on-and-off basis so that their bodies will not shut down the natural production of testosterone].

Vic, here is $350, $300 for next + $50 for what I owed for last. Thanx

[Paragraphs 18–39 omitted].

(continued)

[15]http://www.findlaw.com (accessed on February 28, 2006).

BOX 10.1

(continued)

K. Emeric Delczeg

40. In the aforementioned interview of Conte in the November 13, 1998 article of "Testosterone" magazine, detailed earlier in this affidavit, Conte states: "A few of the older athletes feel that GH (growth hormone) supplementation has helped them extend their competitive career. I know a pro bodybuilder named Emeric Delczeg who's 47 years of age who supplements with GH . . . and he maintains a level of around 400 ng/ml. This is the level of a man twenty years younger."

41. On October 10, 2002, I received information from San Mateo County Narcotics Task Force (NTF) agent Ed Barberini that NTF had received information from a confidential informant that Emeric Delczeg was a steroid supplier to Balco Laboratories. Agent Barberini has informed me that the confidential informant who provided this information had pled guilty to felony steroid distribution charges a few years ago. Since the guilty plea, the informant has been providing information to the NTF on other individuals associated with steroids in an attempt to earn a reduced sentence in his criminal case. Agent Barberini has informed me that due to the cooperation provided by the informant, he has not done any jail time for his steroid conviction. The informant has never been paid by NTF. Agent Barberini has informed me that the informant has been deemed a reliable informant.

42. The informant told NTF that Delczeg, who is Bulgarian, obtains steroids and other performance enhancing drugs from Europe and provides them to Balco in exchange for permission to sell a supplement on which Balco or its subsidiary, SNAC System Inc., owns licensing rights. In October 2002, the informant told NTF that Delczeg was in Europe to purchase steroids for Balco.

[Paragraphs 43–68 omitted]

E. Probable Cause to Search Computers

69. As detailed extensively in this affidavit, evidence has been collected showing that Conte and others use computers in furtherance of their criminal activities. In summary, Conte makes postings to an Internet message board regarding athletes and steroids, sends e-mails to athletes and coaches regarding performance-enhancing drugs and drug testing and has received e-mails from suspected athletic performance-enhancing drug suppliers of which a hard copy of such an e-mail was thrown out in Conte's discarded garbage. Because of these facts, I believe that probable cause exists to search any computers found on the physical locations of Conte's business and residence.

70. Based on my training and experience (which includes the execution of search warrants involving personal computers), as well as from consultation with Special Agent Michael Farley, Computer Investigative Specialist, I am aware that searching and seizing information from computers often requires agents to seize most or all electronic storage devices and the related peripherals to be searched later by a qualified computer expert in a laboratory or other controlled environment. This is true because of the following:

(A) Computer storage devices can store the equivalent of millions of pages of information. Additionally, a suspect may try to conceal criminal evidence by, for example, storing it in random order with deceptive file names. This may require searching authorities to examine all of the stored data to determine which particular files are evidence or instrumentalities of crime. This sorting process can take weeks or months, depending on the volume of the data stored, and it would be impractical to attempt this kind of data search on site. . . . .

V. CONCLUSION

72. I believe that the forgoing facts presented in this affidavit present probable cause to believe that Victor Conte and others have committed violations of Title 21 U.S.C. §841, the possession with intent to distribute, and distribution, of anabolic steroids, and Title 18 U.S.C. §1956, the money laundering of profits earned from the drug distribution and mail fraud activities. Specifically this affidavit has presented evidence of: illegal anabolic steroid and other athletic performance-enhancing drug distribution to professional athletes, including the distribution of new, untested substances; the use of the mail to purchase epitestosterone, a substance used in the fraudulent defeat of athletic performance enhancing drug tests; the withdrawal of over $480,000 over a period of less than two years from Conte's accounts while paying most business and personal expenses with bank checks from those accounts; and the depositing

of large checks from numerous professional athletes into Conte's personal account instead of his business accounts, specifically at the request of Conte, constituting illegal money laundering transactions.

[Paragraph 73 omitted].

74. I declare under the penalty of perjury that the foregoing is true and correct and that this affidavit was executed at San Jose, California, on September _____ , 2003.

———————————————

Jeff Novitzky
Special Agent
Internal Revenue Service
Criminal Investigation

Attachment A-1 Description of Location to be Searched

Balco Laboratories/SNAC System Inc.
1520 Gilbreth Road
Burlingame, CA

Balco Laboratories and Snac System Inc. are businesses operated out of the same location in a commercial area in Eastern Burlingame. A blue sign reading Balco Laboratories is clearly posted above the entrance to the business. The numbers "1520" appear on a window just left of the main entryway into the facility facing Gilbreth Road.

Attachment B Items to be Seized

1. All controlled substances and other athletic performance-enhancing drugs, substances and paraphernalia including: anabolic steroids, human growth hormone, erythropoetin (EPO), stimulants, other prescription drugs, drug, substance and syringe packaging and containers, mail packaging and receipts, syringes and syringe wrappers.

[Paragraphs 2–3 omitted].

4. All financial documents and business records referencing Victor Conte Jr., James Valente, Balco Laboratories Inc., SNAC System Inc., and other employees or agents of these businesses relating to the purchase and sale of anabolic steroids, syringes, epitestoerone, human growth hormone, erythropoietin, athletic performance-enhancing controlled substance and electronic mail, bank statements and records, wire transfer records, money order, official bank checks, ledgers, invoices, accounting and payroll documents, records detailing the purchase of assets, documents detailing business expenses and documents relating to cash sources and cash expenditures from 1/1/94 through the present.

[Paragraph 5 omitted].

6. Address books, phone books, personal calendar, daily planners, journals, itineraries, rolodex indices and contact lists associated with Victor Conte, James Valente and any other employees or agents of Balco Laboratories and SNAC System, Inc.

[Paragraphs 7–8 omitted].

9. The terms "records," "documents," and "materials" include all of the items described in this Attachment in whatever form and by whatever means they have been created and/or stored. This includes any handmade, photographic, mechanical, electrical, electronic, and/or magnetic forms. It also includes items in the form of computer hardware, software, documentation, passwords, and/or data security devices.

   a. Hardware—consisting of all equipment that can collect, analyze, create, display, convert, store, conceal, or transmit electronic, magnetic, optical, or similar computer impulses or data. . . .

paragraphs 41–42 concerning the confidential informant's information used to help establish probable cause. Agent Novitzky stated that even though the informant had pled guilty to charges, he had yet to be sentenced, a common prosecutorial practice with the use of informants. Prosecutors want informants to plead guilty to charges so the informant is obligated to the state, but will delay sentencing until the informant's work gathering information for the government is over. The delay in sentencing informants is an issue defense counsel can exploit at trial when the informant takes an oath to testify truthfully. The truth, according to an informant, is the truth the prosecution wants to hear in exchange for leniency in his sentencing. As long as the informant has not been sentenced, the threat of punishing the informant more harshly with a stiff sentence remains over his head until he is finished testifying favorably on behalf of the government.

If the prosecution did not hold sentencing over the informant's head until after the informant testified at the criminal target's trial, the government would have no power to control the informant's testimony. Consider the informant mentioned in paragraph 41 of Novitsky's affidavit who provided information that Emeric Delczeg bought steroids for Balco Laboratories—we'll call him George. Let us assume that George had already been sentenced to a lenient sentence, one year for illegal steroid distribution, before he was called as a prosecution witness at Victor Conte's criminal trial. The prosecution would have negotiated a lenient sentence in exchange for George's expected testimony at Conte's trial that Emeric Delczeg supplied steroids to Balco Laboratories. But because the U.S. Constitution prevents double jeopardy—George cannot be tried for the same crime twice by the same sovereign—George would be completely free to tell the "truth"—that he made up the story about Delczeg as a way to secure a "get-out-of-jail free card" as an informant. The prosecution does not want George to be in a position where he is unable to provide the government with the testimony it expects to hear at trial—that Delczeg supplied steroids to Conte and Conte is guilty. Therefore, prosecutors make sure that informants plead guilty but are not sentenced until they testify at a defendant's trial with the version of the truth that the state is buying: that the defendant is guilty.

Note in Novitzky's affidavit the specificity with which he describes the places to be searched and the things to be seized. Retrieving computer data requires special expertise, and Novitzky's affidavit details his consultation with electronic experts to establish probable cause to search the computers. Reliable hearsay provided by other officers helped Agent Novitzky establish probable cause that Conte was involved in criminal activity. As a result of the search and seizure at Balco on July 15, 2005, Victor Conte pleaded guilty to distributing steroids and to money laundering and was sentenced to four months in prison and four months on probation. Many of the athletes associated with Conte and Balco have never regained their former stature.

Rule of Law: If the warrant is defective so that a reasonable officer would not have served it, the officer who does serve the defective warrant may be personally liable.

What happens when officers are not specific about the information that they include both on the face of the warrant and in the supporting affidavit? In the 2004–2005 Supreme Court term, there were many cases decided in favor of the government in criminal procedure matters including search and seizure. One of the decisions in favor of the citizens over the police, *Groh* v. *Ramirez*, detailed in Box 10.2, found a federal agent personally liable [responsible] for damages [money] to the people whose house was the subject of the search. The warrant was so defective in describing the things to be seized (instead it gave a description of the property—the house and its surroundings) that the Court found that no reasonable officer who has a duty to know the Fourth Amendment would have executed such a facially deficient [on its face, just by looking at it] warrant. As you read the case, ask yourself whether you agree with the Court's findings or whether police should be forgiven for mistakes in minor details.

BOX 10.2

Groh v. *Ramirez*, 540 U.S. 551 (2004)
Supreme Court of the United States

Justice Stevens delivered the opinion of the Court.

FACTS

Respondents, Joseph Ramirez and members of his family, live on a large ranch in Butte-Silver Bow

County, Montana. Petitioner, Jeff Groh, has been a Special Agent for the Bureau of Alcohol, Tobacco and Firearms (ATF) since 1989. In February 1997, a concerned citizen informed petitioner that on a number of visits to respondents' ranch the visitor

BOX 10.2

had seen a large stock of weaponry, including an automatic rifle, grenades, a grenade launcher, and a rocket launcher. Based on that information, petitioner [Groh] prepared and signed an application for a warrant to search the ranch. The application stated that the search was for "any automatic firearms or parts to automatic weapons, destructive devices to include but not limited to grenades, grenade launchers, rocket launchers, and any and all receipts pertaining to the purchase or manufacture of automatic weapons or explosive devices or launchers." [Groh] supported the application with a detailed affidavit, which he also prepared and executed, that set forth the basis for his belief that the listed items were concealed on the ranch. [Groh] then presented these documents to a Magistrate, along with a warrant form that petitioner also had completed. The Magistrate signed the warrant form.

Although the application particularly described the place to be searched and the contraband petitioner expected to find, the warrant itself was less specific; it failed to identify any of the items that petitioner intended to seize. In the portion of the form that called for a description of the "person or property" to be seized, petitioner typed a description of respondents' two-story blue house rather than the alleged stockpile of firearms. The warrant did not incorporate by reference the itemized list contained in the application. It did, however, recite that the Magistrate was satisfied the affidavit established probable cause to believe that contraband was concealed on the premises, and that sufficient grounds existed for the warrant's issuance. The day after the Magistrate issued the warrant, petitioner led a team of law enforcement officers, including both federal agents and members of the local sheriff's department, in the search of [the Ramirezes'] premises. Although respondent Joseph Ramirez was not home, his wife and children were. [Groh] states that he orally described the objects of the search to Mrs. Ramirez in person and to Mr. Ramirez by telephone. According to Mrs. Ramirez, however, [Groh] explained only that he was searching for "an explosive device in a box." At any rate, the officers' search uncovered no illegal weapons or explosives . . . No charges were filed

against the Ramirezes . . . The [Ramirezes] sued [Groh] and the other officers raising eight claims, including violation of the Fourth Amendment.

ISSUE

Is a warrant that fails to particularly describe the things to be seized on its face inherently invalid and is an officer who executes that warrant in good faith entitled to qualified immunity in a lawsuit for damages arising out of the execution of the warrant?

HOLDING

[Yes, the warrant is inherently defective if the particularity requirement is not met. No, an officer who executes a facially deficient warrant is not protected by immunity from a personal lawsuit.]

REASONING

The warrant was plainly invalid. The Fourth Amendment states unambiguously that "no Warrants shall issue, but upon probable cause, supported by Oath or affirmation, and *particularly describing* the place to be searched, and *the persons or things to be seized.*" (emphasis added.) The warrant in this case complied with the first three of these requirements: It was based on probable cause and supported by a sworn affidavit, and it described particularly the place of the search. On the fourth requirement, however, the warrant failed altogether. Indeed, [Groh] concedes that "the warrant was deficient in particularity because it provided no description of the type of evidence sought." The fact that the application adequately described the "things to be seized" does not save the warrant from its facial invalidity. The Fourth Amendment by its terms requires particularity in the warrant, not in the supporting documents.

[Groh] argues that even though the warrant was invalid, the search nevertheless was "reasonable" within the meaning of the Fourth Amendment. He notes that a Magistrate authorized the search on the basis of adequate evidence of probable cause, that [Groh] orally described to [Ramirezes] the items to be seized, and that the search did not exceed the limits intended by the Magistrate and described by petitioner. Thus, [Groh] maintains, his search of [the

(continued)

BOX 10.2

(continued)

Ramirezes'] ranch was functionally equivalent to a search authorized by a valid warrant.

We disagree. This warrant did not simply omit a few items from a list of many to be seized, or misdescribe a few of several items. Nor did it make what fairly could be characterized as a mere technical mistake or typographical error. Rather, in the space set aside for a description of the items to be seized, the warrant stated that the items consisted of a "single dwelling residence blue in color." In other words, the warrant did not describe the items to be seized at all. In this respect the warrant was so obviously deficient that we must regard the search as "warrantless" within the meaning of our case law.

It is incumbent on the officer executing a search warrant to ensure the search is lawfully authorized and lawfully conducted. Because [Groh] did not have in his possession a warrant particularly describing the things he intended to seize, proceeding with the search was clearly "unreasonable" under the Fourth Amendment. The Court of Appeals correctly held that the search was unconstitutional. Having concluded that a constitutional violation occurred, we turn to the question whether [Groh] is entitled to qualified immunity despite that violation. The answer depends on whether the right that was transgressed was "'clearly established'"—that is, "whether it would be clear to a reasonable officer that his conduct was unlawful in the situation he confronted."

Given that the particularity requirement is set forth in the text of the Constitution, no reasonable officer could believe that a warrant that plainly did not comply with that requirement was valid. No reasonable officer could claim to be unaware of the basic rule, well established by our cases, that, absent consent or exigency, a warrantless search of the home is presumptively unconstitutional. Indeed, as we noted nearly 20 years ago in [*Massachusetts* v.] *Sheppard*: "The uniformly applied rule is that a search conducted pursuant to a warrant that fails to conform to the particularity requirement of the Fourth Amendment is unconstitutional." Because not a word in any of our cases would suggest to a reasonable officer that this case fits within any exception to that fundamental tenet [proposition], [Groh] is asking us, in effect, to craft a new exception. Absent any support for such an exception in our cases, he cannot reasonably have relied on an expectation that we would do so.

CONCLUSION

Accordingly, [Groh is personally liable for conducting the unconstitutional search at the Ramirez ranch].

Justice Kennedy, Chief Justice Rehnquist, Justice Thomas and Justice Scalia **dissent.**

The majority decision in *Groh* stressed a recurrent and persistent theme in Supreme Court search and seizure decisions—anytime the scope and legal authority for what to seize is left up to the choice of the police officers conducting the search, it is unreasonable. If government officials do not follow the Fourth Amendment's specific requirements, then the government alone is left to judge whether probable cause or search authority exists, without any independent check in the form of a neutral and detached magistrate. Leaving such discretion in the government's hands puts the public at risk from law enforcement officers acting as investigator, judge, and jury with an obvious bias toward proving the guilt of the accused, the risk the Fourth Amendment was designed to prevent.

7. The Return

After the search is over, the officer has inventoried on the back of the warrant all items seized, and a copy is left at the place searched, all warrants must be "returned" to the issuing magistrate or judge, indicated in Figure 10.2. The officer returns the warrant in front of a judge and swears or affirms that the inventory of items seized is true and accurate. Federal Rule of Criminal Procedure 41(f)(1) requires the officer executing the warrant to enter on its face "the exact date and time it is executed." Next, the officer must "give a copy of the warrant and a receipt for the property taken to the person from whom, or from whose premises, the property was taken." If no one is home, the officer should leave a copy of the warrant and receipt for any property seized in a conspicuous location within the premises. The inventory of the property seized formally ensures that all property taken is accounted for. The inventory must be completed in the presence of another officer who must verify its accuracy; ideally, if the property owner is on the premises, he or she should sign the inventory acknowledging the removal of the property. The officer executing the warrant must return the warrant with the inventory to the magistrate who issued the warrant. A return must occur even if no property is seized. The magistrate then files all papers associated with the warrant and the return with the court clerk in the jurisdiction where property was seized. The officers do not have to inform the property owner how to get his or her seized property back. The property owner may seek the return of the property by filing a motion in the district where the property was seized.

8. The Service of the Warrant

Rule of Law: Police action during the execution of the warrant must be reasonable.

a. Knock and Announce

In order to execute a warrant, officers must "knock and announce" their presence and use force to enter only if entry is refused. Federal law on the execution of warrants provides that[16]

> The officer may break open any outer or inner door or window of a house, or any part of a house, or anything therein, to execute a search warrant, if, after notice of his authority and purpose, he is refused admittance or when necessary to liberate himself or a person aiding him in the execution of the warrant.

The average time to wait before forcing entry into a dwelling is affected by the circumstances known to the officers executing the search warrant. In *United States* v. *Banks*, 124 S.Ct. 521 (2003), the Court determined it was reasonable to wait 15–20 seconds before kicking down a door to execute a warrant. In *Banks*, Las Vegas officers working with federal agents executed a search warrant for evidence of drug dealing at the apartment of Mr. Banks. After the officers knocked and announced their presence, they broke down the front door with a battering ram just as Mr. Banks emerged from the shower, dripping wet. Banks was eventually convicted for possession of the weapons and cocaine found during the search, and on appeal, Banks argued that the 15–20 seconds the police waited before forced entry violated the Fourth Amendment's reasonableness clause. The Supreme Court disagreed. Holding that the totality of the circumstances determined the appropriate waiting period before using force is properly judged by officers on the scene who can properly assess the exigent/emergency circumstances, such as how quickly Banks could have flushed cocaine down the toilet or jumped out the back window, the 15–20 second wait was reasonable.

If the facts known to law enforcement prior to the execution of the warrant indicate that the officers' safety may be compromised by the knock and announce rule — for example, because of the nature of the suspected offense or known information about a suspect's prior convictions — then the officers can ask the issuing magistrate to issue a "no knock" on the warrant's face. This type of warrant allows officers to enter without announcement and may allow them to execute the search in the evening. Some

---

[16]18 U.S.C. §3109 (2000).

state statutes provide for no knock warrants in drug cases, but executing such warrants is dangerous and can have tragic consequences. On November 22, 2006, three officers of the Atlanta narcotics division executed a no knock warrant in a high-crime area on the basis that a confidential informant had purchased cocaine at the home where the warrant allowed the search. The officers, who were in plain clothes, cut through the home's burglar bars, forced entry by kicking in the door, and then announced that they were police. All three were shot in the face, arms, and legs by Kathryn Johnston, an 88-year-old woman who reportedly lived alone. The officers responded with gunfire of their own, killing Ms. Johnston. The confidential informant later contacted the media to say that he had not purchased drugs at Ms. Johnston's house on the day in question and that officers had called him after the shooting to cajole him into lying about buying the drugs. All eight officers of the narcotics squad were suspended with pay pending an investigation. As a result of the botched raid, two officers pled guilty to manslaughter and civil rights violations and on May 22, 2008, one officer was sentenced to over four years in prison for lying to investigators about the validity of the initial search warrant.

The latest U.S. Supreme Court pronouncement on the knock and announce rule is in the case *Hudson* v. *Michigan*, reprinted in part in Box 10.3, in which the high Court found that even if the officers violated the rule, the evidence seized would be admissible.

BOX 10.3

Hudson v. *Michigan*, 126 S.-Ct. 2159 (2006)
Supreme Court of the United States

Justice Scalia delivered the opinion of the Court.

FACTS

Police obtained a warrant authorizing a search for drugs and firearms at the home of petitioner Booker Hudson. They discovered both. Large quantities of drugs were found, including cocaine rocks in Hudson's pocket. A loaded gun was lodged between the cushion and armrest of the chair in which he was sitting. Hudson was charged under Michigan law with unlawful drug and firearm possession. This case is before us only because of the method of entry into the house. When the police arrived to execute the warrant, they announced their presence, but waited only a short time—perhaps "three to five seconds," before turning the knob of the unlocked front door and entering Hudson's home. Hudson moved to suppress all the inculpatory [tending to prove guilt] evidence, arguing that the premature entry violated his Fourth Amendment rights.

ISSUE

We decide whether violation of the "knock-and-announce" rule requires the suppression of all evidence found in the search?

HOLDING

[No.]

REASONING

The common-law principle that law enforcement officers must announce their presence and provide residents an opportunity to open the door is an ancient one. *See Wilson* v. *Arkansas*, 514 U.S. 927 (1995). Since 1917, when Congress passed the Espionage Act, this traditional protection has been part of federal statutory law, see 40 Stat. 229, and is currently codified at 18 U.S.C. §3109. [I]n *Wilson*, we were asked whether the rule was also a command of the Fourth Amendment. Tracing its origins in our English legal heritage, we concluded that it was. We recognized that the new constitutional rule we had announced is not easily applied. *Wilson* and cases following it have noted the many situations in which it is not necessary to knock and announce [for example, it is] not necessary when "circumstances present a threat of physical violence," or if there is "reason to believe that evidence would likely be destroyed if advance notice were given," or if knocking and announcing would be "futile." We require only that police "have a reasonable suspicion . . . under the particular circumstances" that one of these grounds for failing to knock and announce exists, and we have acknowledged that "this showing is not high." When the knock-and-announce rule does apply, it is not easy to determine precisely what officers must do. How many seconds' wait are too few? Our "reasonable wait time" standard, *see United States* v. *Banks*, 540 U.S. 31 (2003), is necessarily vague. *Banks* (a drug case, like this one) held that the proper measure was not how long it would take the resident to reach the door, but how long it would take to dispose of the suspected drugs—but that such a time (15 to 20 seconds in that case) would necessarily be extended when, for instance, the suspected contraband was not easily concealed. If our *ex post* [after the fact] evaluation is subject to such calculations, it is unsurprising that, *ex ante*, [beforehand] police officers about to encounter someone who may try to harm them will be uncertain how long to wait.

Happily, these issues do not confront us here. From the trial level onward, Michigan has conceded that the entry was a knock-and-announce violation. The issue here is remedy. *Wilson* specifically declined to decide whether the exclusionary rule is appropriate for violation of the knock-and-announce requirement. That question is squarely before us now. In *Weeks* v. *United States*, 232 U.S. 383 (1914), we adopted the federal exclusionary rule for evidence that was unlawfully seized from a home without a warrant in violation of the Fourth Amendment. We began applying the same rule to the States, through the Fourteenth Amendment, in *Mapp* v. *Ohio*, 367 U.S. 643 (1961). Suppression of evidence, however, has always been our last resort, not our first impulse. The exclusionary rule generates "substantial social costs." *United States* v. *Leon*, 468 U.S. 897 (1984), which sometimes include setting the guilty free and the dangerous at large. We have therefore been "cautious against expanding" it, *Colorado* v. *Connelly*, 479 U.S. 157 (1986), and "have repeatedly emphasized that the rule's 'costly toll' upon truth-seeking and law enforcement objectives presents a high obstacle for those urging [its] application." We have rejected "indiscriminate application" of the rule [in] *Leon* and have held it to be applicable only "where its re-

medial objectives are thought most efficaciously served," *United States* v. *Calandra*, 414 U.S. 338 (1974)—that is, "where its deterrence benefits outweigh its 'substantial social costs.'" We did not always speak so guardedly.

Until a valid warrant has [been] issued, citizens are entitled to shield "their persons, houses, papers, and effects," U.S. Const., Amdt. 4, from the government's scrutiny. Exclusion of the evidence obtained by a warrantless search vindicates that entitlement. The interests protected by the knock-and-announce requirement are quite different—and do not include the shielding of potential evidence from the government's eyes. One of those interests is the protection of human life and limb, because an unannounced entry may provoke violence in supposed self-defense by the surprised resident. Another interest is the protection of property. Breaking a house (as the old cases typically put it) absent an announcement would penalize someone who "'did not know of the process, of which, if he had notice, it is to be presumed that he would obey it. . . .'" The knock-and-announce rule gives individuals "the opportunity to comply with the law and to avoid the destruction of property occasioned by a forcible entry." And thirdly, the knock-and-announce rule protects those elements of privacy and dignity that can be destroyed by a sudden entrance. It gives residents the "opportunity to prepare themselves for" the entry of the police. "The brief interlude between announcement and entry with a warrant may be the opportunity that an individual has to pull on clothes or get out of bed." In other words, it assures the opportunity to collect oneself before answering the door. What the knock-and-announce rule has never protected, however, is one's interest in preventing the government from seeing or taking evidence described in a warrant. Since the interests that were violated in this case have nothing to do with the seizure of the evidence, the exclusionary rule is inapplicable.

CONCLUSION

For the foregoing reasons we affirm the judgment of the Michigan Court of Appeals [upholding Hudson's conviction for drug possession].

Applying the Rule of Law to the Facts: Must officers announce their presence before forcibly entering a residence?

- Officers preparing to execute a search warrant at Jill's house made no special provisions for a "no-knock" warrant. As they arrived at the house, officers saw two big pit bulls snarling inside at the window, and one officer remarked that he once heard Jill declare "I won't go back to prison ever again." On the basis of these facts, the officers decided not to knock and announce. Was their action legal?[17]

Yes, the dogs and expressed willingness of the suspect to avoid capture created circumstances of peril that made the unannounced entry justified.

II. SCOPE OF THE SEARCH

Rule of Law: The limits of the search are defined by the terms of the warrant itself.

Generally, police can search pursuant to the warrant only those areas specified in the warrant. "If the place to be searched is identified by street number, the search is not limited to the dwelling house, but may also extend to the garage and other structures deemed to be within" the surrounding area of the house and yard.[18] If the warrant is specific about the place to be searched, the officers are limited to search in that area only. If the warrant is for contraband that can be easily hidden, such as drugs or illegal weapons, officers can search drawers, closets, and closed containers where the contraband may be found. But a warrant to search a house does not extend to vehicles on the property, nor does a warrant to search a vehicle on the property extend to the buildings and homes on the property.

Is a warrant required to search a crime scene where a murder has occurred? The U.S. Supreme Court held in *Mincey* v. *Arizona*, 437 U.S. 385 (1978), that once a crime scene has been secured, no one is in need of aid, and no suspects are on the premises, a search warrant is required. Mincey was a drug dealer who had sold heroin to an undercover police officer. The officer came back later in the day with a bevy of other plain clothes police officers and an assistant prosecutor. Officer Headricks, who had purchased the heroin from Mincey, went into a back bedroom where shots were fired. The officer and another occupant at Mincey's apartment died. When detectives arrived 10 minutes after the shooting, they conducted a search that lasted for four days and resulted in over 200 items being seized. Upon conviction, Mincey appealed claiming that the search was unreasonable because it was conducted without a warrant, and the high Court agreed. An exception to the warrant requirement is exigent, or emergency, circumstances. The Court held here that the seriousness of the offense (murder of a police officer) did not, by itself, create exigent circumstances where evidence was in danger of being destroyed or removed, and there was sufficient time and opportunity to secure a search warrant with the ample probable cause that an officer had been killed at the property.

In our chapter-opening scenario, the officers had secured a warrant for drug paraphernalia and not child pornography. When they saw what appeared to be illegal pornography, it was incumbent upon the officers to secure another warrant stating the probable cause to search the computer files. The direct clicking on the "private" file without a warrant would likely be declared unlawful unless the magistrate deemed the file in plain view, discussed more fully in chapter 11. This would be a contentious conclusion, since the officers had to open the file for the child pornography images to appear and the images were not in plain view until the officer opened the file.

---

[17]Facts adapted from *United States* v. *Buckley*, 4 F.3d 552 (7th Cir. 1993); *State ex rel. Juvenile Dept. of Multnomah City* v. *Qutub*, 706 P.2d 962 (Or. Ct. App. 1985).

[18]W. Lafave, 2 *Search and Seizure: A Treatise on the Fourth Amendment* §4.10(a), 3rd ed. (1996).

1. Bodily Intrusions

Rule of Law: Bodily intrusions by government officials are subject to the most protection under the Fourth Amendment, unless they occur at the country's borders or to inmates in prison.

There are many situations in which courts must examine the circumstances surrounding the seizure—or taking—of property, people, and even bodily fluids. Certain circumstances, such as drunk-driving cases, where officer delay in obtaining a search warrant will result in the dissipation of the critical evidence—the defendant's blood alcohol level—allow for the "seizure" of a blood sample without a warrant. But a warrant is required for there are other types of bodily intrusions. The first prominent case in which the Supreme Court addressed the issue was *Rochin* v. *California*. In this case, officers first tried to choke morphine tablets out of the suspect's mouth. Then, when he successfully swallowed the pills, they took him to the hospital to pump his stomach for the evidence that would later be introduced at trial to convict him. The case is reprinted in part in Box 10.4.

Rochin v. *California*, 342 U.S. 165 (1952)
Supreme Court of the United States

Justice Frankfurter delivered the opinion of the Court.

FACTS

Having "some information that [Rochin] was selling narcotics," three deputy sheriffs of the County of Los Angeles, on the morning of July 1, 1949, made for the two-story dwelling house in which Rochin lived with his mother, common-law wife, brothers, and sisters. Finding the outside door open, they entered and then forced open the door to Rochin's room on the second floor. Inside they found petitioner sitting partly dressed on the side of the bed, upon which his wife was lying. On a "night stand" beside the bed the deputies spied two capsules. When asked "Whose stuff is this?" Rochin seized the capsules and put them in his mouth. A struggle ensued, in the course of which the three officers "jumped upon him" and attempted to extract the capsules. The force they applied proved unavailing against Rochin's resistance. He was handcuffed and taken to a hospital. At the direction of one of the officers a doctor forced an emetic solution through a tube into Rochin's stomach against his will. This "stomach pumping" produced vomiting.

In the vomited matter were found two capsules which proved to contain morphine [used to convict him on drug possession charges].

ISSUE

[Did the officers' actions with respect to pumping Rochin's stomach for evidence to use against him at trial violate the notions of fundamental fairness embodied in the Due Process Clause?]

HOLDING

[Yes.]

REASONING

[W]e are compelled to conclude that the proceedings by which this conviction was obtained do more than offend some fastidious squeamishness or private sentimentalism about combating crime too energetically. This is conduct that shocks the conscience. Illegally breaking into the privacy of the petitioner, the struggle to open his mouth and remove what was there, the forcible extraction of his stomach's contents—this course of proceeding by agents of government to obtain evidence is

(continued)

BOX 10.4

(continued)

bound to offend even hardened sensibilities. They are methods too close to the rack and the screw to permit of constitutional differentiation.

It has long since ceased to be true that due process of law is heedless of the means by which otherwise relevant and credible evidence is obtained. This was not true even before the series of recent cases enforced the constitutional principle that the States may not base convictions upon confessions, however much verified, and obtained by coercion. These decisions are not arbitrary exceptions to the comprehensive right of States to fashion their own rules of evidence for criminal trials. They are not sports in our constitutional law but applications of a general principle. They are only instances of the general requirement that States in their prosecutions respect certain decencies of civilized conduct. Due process of law, as a historic and

generative principle, precludes defining, and thereby confining, these standards of conduct more precisely than to say that convictions cannot be brought about by methods that offend "a sense of justice." *See* Mr. Chief Justice Hughes, speaking for a unanimous Court in *Brown* v. *Mississippi*, 297 U.S. 278. It would be a stultification of the responsibility which the course of constitutional history has cast upon this Court to hold that in order to convict a man the police cannot extract by force what is in his mind but can extract what is in his stomach.

CONCLUSION

On the facts of this case the conviction of the petitioner has been obtained by methods that offend the Due Process Clause. The judgment below must be Reversed.

After the *Rochin* decision set the standard of what might be reasonable in the search of body parts, the high Court again addressed the issue in *Schmerber* v. *California*, 384 U.S. 757 (1966). Schmerber suffered injuries in a drunk-driving accident, and police asked the physician to take a blood sample without a warrant, the results of which were used to convict the defendant. The Court said a warrant was not necessary under the circumstances, in part because the evidence would disappear if officers waited and partly because the taking of blood, fingerprints, or photographs for mug shots does not implicate the Fifth Amendment's right to be free from self-incrimination. On a similar rationale, the U.S. Supreme Court held in *Cupp* v. *Murphy*, 412 U.S. 291 (1973), that taking physical evidence that could easily be washed away, such as blood or skin scrapings under the skin, can likewise be taken from a defendant without a search warrant, even with a reasonable amount of force, to prevent the destruction of such evidence. Defendant Cupp voluntarily came to the police station to discuss his wife's murder, and police noticed biological evidence on his hands and under his nails—evidence used to convict Cupp of murder, a conviction that withstood Cupp's challenge that such evidence was taken without a warrant.

2. Electronic Surveillance

Rule of Law: Electronic surveillance is a highly invasive investigatory technique that is allowed only when normal investigative tools have failed.

After the Supreme Court's decision in *Katz* v. *United States* (1967), recognizing that the Fourth Amendment protects "people, not places," Congress enacted a strict protocol for law enforcement agents to follow when intercepting conversations for an investigatory purpose. The protocol was included in the comprehensive federal crime statute, Title III of the Omnibus Crime Control and Safe Street Act of 1968[19] ("Title III"). Title III law allows electronic surveillance only of conversations discussing the crimes of murder, kidnapping, gambling, robbery, bribery, extortion, drug dealing, or "other crimes dangerous to life, limb, or property, and punishable by imprisonment for more than one year." "Interception" of conversations is defined as "the aural [voice] or other acquisition of the contents of any wire, electronic, or oral communication through the use of any electronic, mechanical, or other device." 18 U.S.C. §2510(4). Only federal or state investigative law enforcement officers authorized by law to arrest or prosecute the above-named offenses may apply to conduct electronic surveillance. Many state statutes are patterned on the federal law of Title III, and many states also make private electronic surveillance a criminal offense. To secure authorization to eavesdrop on a suspect's conversations with others, Title III imposes a high burden on law enforcement in meeting the requirements for such a "search warrant." Federal agents and state officers have to declare to the court the following required information:

1. A full and complete statement of the alleged offense
2. The facilities from which the communications are to be intercepted
3. A particular description of the communications sought to be intercepted
4. The identity of the persons committing the offense (if known) and of the persons whose communications are to be intercepted
5. A full and complete statement of whether other investigative procedures have been tried and have failed, why they appear unlikely to succeed, or why they are too dangerous; and
6. A full and complete statement of the period of time for which the interception is to be maintained.

Title III allows eavesdropping at 30-day intervals, and extensions can be granted if it is shown that the investigation continues to be necessary. Monitoring conversations is a time-consuming activity for law enforcement. If agents are monitoring a suspect's telephone pursuant to a 30-day court order, all conversations within those 30 days, 7 days a week, 24 hours a day have to be monitored. Once the court finds probable cause in the supporting affidavits that state the known information leading investigators to believe that the defendant is committing one of the specific crimes and that less intrusive investigative means are inadequate to conduct a full investigation, the court will sign an order describing the type of communication to be intercepted. When officers are preparing to plant a listening device to effectuate the eavesdropping order, implied in the court order is the authority to enter the premises and plant the listening device, or bug. Title III also requires that the officers intercepting the suspect's communications comply with the following obligations, and if they fail to do so, the intercepted conversations may be excluded as evidence:

1. Officers must minimize the interception of conversations outside the scope of the order. Under Title III, officers are allowed only to listen to the conversations relevant to the crime for which the suspect is being investigated. If, for example, it is clear from listening to a bribery suspect's telephone conversation that he has dialed a phone sex provider, the officers are to minimize [turn down] the recording device as the conversation is not relevant to the investigation.
2. The court must seal [keep secret] the application for the wiretap order, the actual court order, and the tapes made of the intercepted communications.
3. An inventory of the conversations intercepted must be prepared and delivered to those named in the surveillance order, and others if the court deems necessary.

---

[19]Pub. L. No. 90-351 (1968), 82 Stat. 212, codified at 18 U.S.C. §§2510-2521 (2000 & West Supp. 2005). Title III expressly criminalizes wire tapping by private parties, *see Smoot* v. *United Transp. Union*, 246 F.3d 633 (6th Cir. 2001) (where the corporation and union won a money award from an employee who secretly taped conversations between a corporate executive, a union representative, and an arbitrator).

4. Officers may disclose the contents of the conversations to other officers; unauthorized disclosure to sources other than law enforcement, attorneys, and judges involved in the case, however, is prohibited.

Violation of the requirements of Title III can lead to the defendant suppressing all evidence derived from the intercepted conversations. Title III also expressly excludes tone-only paging devices and electronic transmitting devices that trace locations, such as transponders and beepers. The Fourth Amendment still applies to these devices, but requires a careful analysis.

As advances in electronic communications and technology grow, so, too, do law enforcement efforts to keep abreast of the latest crime-prevention technology. In 1986, Congress amended Title III by passing the Electronic Communications Privacy Act, which gave the federal government broad authority to intercept electronic communications, including e-mail, faxes, and cellular phone conversations. In 1994, the Communications Assistance for Law Enforcement Act ("CALEA")[20] was enacted to force the telecommunications industry to assist law enforcement efforts by helping law enforcement agents intercept suspect communications and develop technology that would help thwart suspects from evading electronic surveillance. Federal law enforcement has also appealed to the federal agency that controls mass communication, the Federal Communications Commission ("FCC"), to make broadband providers subject to CALEA requirements.

Applying the Rule of Law to the Facts:　Is a search legal?

- Federal agents placed a beeper in a container of chloroform in a store without a warrant but with the consent of the store's owner. The container was later moved, and the police tracked it to a cabin. The officers then obtained a search warrant for the cabin. Is the search legal?

Yes, the U.S. Supreme Court upheld the officers' actions. They followed the beeper only *to* the cabin, not *into* the cabin, until they had secured the proper warrant. *United States* v. *Knotts*, 460 U.S. 276 (1983).

- Officers placed a beeper on a suspect and used it to track the individual's movements inside a house.

Maybe legal; the Fourth Amendment may be violated depending on the circumstances. *United States* v. *Karo*, 468 U.S. 705 (1984).

- Officers used thermal imaging devices to track heat off a roof to detect infrared radiation not visible to the naked eye. The surveillance was an attempt to locate the concentrated use of heat lamps commonly used to grow marijuana inside a dwelling.

Not a legal search—the high Court held in *Kyllo* v. *United States*, 533 U.S. 27 (2001) that using heat sensors to track inside a home is too invasive. When "the Government uses a device that is not in general public use, to explore details of the home that would previously have been unknowable without physical intrusion, the surveillance is a 'search' and is presumptively unreasonable without a warrant."

---

[20]47 U.S.C. §§1001-10.

III. Key Terms and Phrases

- affidavit
- anonymous tip
- collective knowledge
- facially valid
- electronic surveillance

- exclusionary rule
- incorporated by reference
- informant
- no-knock warrant
- particularity requirement

- *per se*
- search
- seizure
- specific and articulable facts
- warrant

IV. Summary

1. **How to analyze Fourth Amendment problems:** The **first step** is to determine whether a government actor is involved. The **second step** is to determine whether an objective and subjective expectation of privacy exists. The **third step** is to determine whether the government's search or seizure was "reasonable." The **fourth step** is to determine whether a warrant was required for the search and seizure or, if not, whether a well-recognized exception to the warrant requirement applies. The **fifth step** is to determine the remedy for the violation if the government has failed to comply with the Fourth Amendment.

2. **Some of the many sources used to establish probable cause: Probable cause** may be established by officers' collective knowledge on the basis of reliable hearsay, corroborated anonymous tips, witness statements, a dog-sniff for narcotics, and the officer's observations based on his or her training and experience.

3. **The five requirements for an arrest or search warrant:** Searches conducted without a warrant are presumed to be unreasonable unless a well-recognized exception to the warrant requirement applies, discussed in chapter 11. The elements of the **warrant requirement** include **probable cause** connecting the person to be seized or the placed to be searched to criminal activity and a description that lays out with **particularity** the place to be searched and the things to be seized. In addition, the warrant must be issued under **oath**; that is,

the officer must swear or affirm in front of the magistrate (judge) that the facts contained in the warrant establishing probable cause are true to the best of the officer's knowledge and belief. Also, the warrant must be issued by a **neutral and detached magistrate**—a judge who has no prior extensive knowledge of the case and no personal stake in the outcome of the case. To execute a warrant, officers must **knock and announce** their presence and wait the amount of time the exigencies of the situation demand, in some cases as few as 15–20 seconds, before they conduct a forcible entry. Upon request, or by law in some states in drug cases, officers can obtain a **no-knock warrant** in which officers do not have to announce who they are before they forcibly enter the premises on the basis that, if the officers do announce their presence before entry, the occupants may destroy evidence or compromise the safety of the officers.

4. **The special problem of electronic surveillance and bodily intrusions: Electronic surveillance** by the government listening in on private telephone, oral communications, or e-mail communications is regulated by federal and state laws. Officers must show that less intrusive investigative methods will not work, have been tried and have been unsuccessful, or are too dangerous to attempt. Searches for bodily fluids and of body cavities must be reasonable under the Fourth Amendment.

V. Discussion Questions

1. Given that many ordinary citizens fear retaliation from criminal suspects if they were known to be informants to the police, why does the law require more than an anonymous tip to establish probable cause?

2. What do you think should be the appropriate legal standard when police want to enter the home of a person who is not a suspect or party to any criminal activity, but police have no other way to effectuate an arrest?

3. Do you think the Court would have decided the *Groh* v. *Ramirez* case differently if the police had found the evidence they were looking for or if the officers had relied on more than information from a concerned citizen to establish probable cause? ATF Agent Groh

and the dissenting justices in Groh's case argued that if "an officer has obtained a [defective] warrant and abided by its terms," he acted in good faith and Groh should be immune from the Ramirezes' civil suit. Do you agree?

4. Do you think that as long as officers have a warrant, they should be able to execute it wherever and whenever the suspect can be found? Explain your reasoning.

5. How do you feel about the expansion of federal power to force telecommunication providers to assist law enforcement in eavesdropping during investigations? Does the federal government have the power to force private companies and industries to do their bidding?

VI. Problem-Solving Exercises

1. Two police officers were on patrol in an apartment complex when they heard loud voices coming from a first-floor open window. As officers approached and looked through the window, they saw two men

screaming, shouting, and poking at one another. Both officers rushed through the front door and arrested both men for disorderly conduct. The men were convicted at a bench trial (without a jury) and seek to have their convictions vacated on the basis that the police did not have a warrant to enter the home. How should the appeals court rule? Explain your answer fully.

2. While a bus was at a rest area and the passengers had all disembarked, drug interdiction officers boarded and examined the luggage in the rack above the passenger seats. Officers took one of the bags to another area of the bus station and called the owner's name over the intercom system. When the passenger arrived at the back area, he consented to a search of the bag, in which officers then found cocaine. The defendant argued in a motion to suppress the cocaine that officers had illegally "seized" the bag when they removed it from the bus. Is the defendant correct, and why or why not?

3. A senior government official had befriended a young White House intern. When the intern began to confide in the official about her illicit affair with the president of the United States, the senior official began to tape-record the conversations without the knowledge or consent of the intern. When the affair was exposed, the official turned the tapes over to government investigators. Can the official be prosecuted under state wiretapping laws that prohibit wiretapping by private individuals?

4. Are the following descriptions particularly sufficient to meet the warrant requirement?
   a. An unknown make .38 caliber, blue, steel with wood grips revolver
   b. videotape and equipment used in a copyright infringement
   c. all doctor's files concerning an accident victim
   d. plaques, mirrors, and other items
   e. items related to the smuggling, packing, distribution, and use of controlled substances
   f. business papers that are evidence and instrumentalities of a violation of a general tax fraud statute.

VII. World Wide Web Resources

Survey of state electronic surveillance laws

http://www.ncsl.org/programs/lis/CIP/surveillance.htm

Electronic Privacy Information Center

http://www.epic.org/privacy/wiretap/

VIII. Additional Readings and Notes

Search and Seizure

Jeffrey A. Bekiares. "Constitutional Law: Ratifying Suspicionless Canine Sniffs: Dog Days on the Highways." *Florida Law Review,* Vol. 57 (2005), pp. 963–974.

Orin S. Kerr. "Searches and Seizures in a Digital World." *Harvard Law Review,* Vol. 119 (2005), pp. 532–585.

Irving J. Klein. *Principles of the Law of Arrest, Search, Seizure, and Liability Issues* (Miami: Coral Gables, 1994).

Nina Paul and Will Trachman. "Fidos and Fi-don'ts: Why the Supreme Court Should Have Found a Search in *Illinois* v. *Caballes.*" *Boalt Journal of Criminal Law,* Vol. 9 (2005), pp. 1–22.

Kathryn R. Urbonya. "Fourth Amendment Federalism?: The Court's Vacillating Mistrust and Trust of State Search and Seizure Laws." *Seton Hall Law Review,* Vol. 35 (2005), pp. 911–970.

Electronic Surveillance

Walter M. Brasch. "Fool's Gold in the Nation's Data-Mining Program." *Social Science Computer Review,* Vol. 23, No. 4 (2005), pp. 401–428.

Note. "Keeping Secrets in Cyberspace: Establishing Fourth Amendment Protection for Internet Communication." *Harvard Law Review,* Vol. 110 (1997), pp. 1591–1608.

Ric Simmons. "The Powers and Pitfalls of Technology: Technology-Enhanced Surveillance by Law Enforcement Officials." *New York University Annual Survey of American Law,* Vol. 60 (2005), pp. 711–733.

Civil Liberties

Paul G. Kauper. *Civil Liberties and the Constitution* (Westport, CT: Greenwood, 1962).

William H. Rehnquist. *All the Laws but One: Civil Liberties in Wartime* (New York: Knopf, 1998).

Lara Weibgen, ed.. *U.S. National Debate Topic, 2005–2006: U.S. Civil Liberties* (Bronx, NY: H. W. Wilson, 2005).

CHAPTER
11
Exceptions to the Warrant Requirement

"The principle that government officials cannot coerce entry into people's houses without a search warrant or applicability of an established exception to the warrant requirement of a search warrant is so well established that any reasonable officer would know it."

—CALABRETTA V. FLOYD, NO. 97-15385 (9TH CIR. 1999)

CHAPTER OBJECTIVES

Primary Concepts Discussed in This Chapter:

1. The legal basis for exceptions to the warrant requirement
2. How far officers can go during a search to protect their safety
3. Special searches, such as driving checkpoints, airports, borders, and special needs

CHAPTER OUTLINE

Feature: The Warrant Exceptions

I. WARRANTLESS SEARCHES AND SEIZURES

1. Consent
2. Search Incident to an Arrest
   Box 11.1 *Chimel* v. *California,* 395 U.S. 752 (1969)
3. Automobile Searches
   a. Search Incident to an Arrest in an Automobile
   b. Dog Sniffs
   c. Common Enterprise
   Box 11.2 *Maryland* v. *Pringle,* 540 U.S. 366 (2003)
   d. Driving Checkpoints
4. Protective Sweep
   Box 11.3 *Maryland* v. *Buie,* 494 U.S. 325 (1990)
5. Plain View/Open Fields
6. Plain Feel
   Box 11.4 *Minnesota* v. *Dickerson,* 508 U.S. 366 (1993)
7. Exigent Circumstances
8. Hot Pursuit
9. Good Faith
   Box 11.5 *Commonwealth* v. *Edmunds,* 526 Pa. 374 (1991)
10. Inventory Searches
11. Special Needs Searches
    a. Drug Testing in Schools
    b. Drug Testing of Government Employees
    c. DNA Collection

Feature: *Chapter-Opening Case Study: The Warrant Exceptions*

While police were executing the warrant in the motel room belonging to Marsha, Amy, and Anne from chapter 10, they heard suspicious activity coming from the adjoining room 232. The noises included frequent flushing of the toilet, blaring television sounds, and much shuffling and moving of heavy furniture. The officers decided to investigate and knocked on the door. Jodie answered the door; the officers identified themselves and asked what was going on. Jodie opened the door only partially, and when she tried to close it again, one officer stuck his foot in the door and said, "Listen, why don't you make it easy on yourself. We have a warrant on the way and we're going to be able to search this room when it gets here, so just let us in" [consent to enter may not be obtained by forcing submission to official authority]. Jodie opened the door and the officers entered. When the officers asked for permission to search the room, Jodie said "No." The officers noticed a bag of marijuana placed on the end table [if officers are legally in a place to be searched, contraband in plain view may be seized]. The officers seized the marijuana, searched the room, and found Nick with a large amount of cocaine in the bathroom. Officer Thomas placed Jodie and Nick under arrest and then emptied and searched all of their pockets, shoes, and bags [lawful search incident to an arrest].

After the search in the motel, police towed Nick's car and impounded it back at the police station. Officers began to inventory the contents of Nick's car when they found a closed briefcase in the trunk. They opened the briefcase and found a notebook with obvious drug notations and the names and addresses of buyers, along with the amount that each buyer owed to Anne, Amy, and Marsha, the women who had been previously arrested [inventory search is lawful pursuant to administrative regulations]. Officers Thomas and Everett recorded the information to use as a basis for future arrest warrants for the drug customers.

Jimmy, who was approaching the Motel Easy to buy drugs, witnessed the police in the vicinity and began to run away. As Officer Jones chased him, Jimmy ran inside a nearby apartment and slammed the door closed. Officer Jones kicked the door down and arrested Jimmy inside his apartment [lawful hot pursuit]. Officer Jones drew his service revolver and went through each room in Jimmy's apartment, opening closet doors, desk drawers, and even the refrigerator, looking for drugs [need specific and articulable facts that armed persons on premises to lawfully conduct protective sweep]. When the officers met back in front of the Motel Easy, they saw the manager get into his car and drive away. When the manager ran a stop sign, the officers pulled him over. The manager immediately got out of his vehicle and approached the police car. The officers arrested him under suspicion of running a drug ring and immediately searched his car, took his keys, unlocked the trunk, and found a pound of marijuana [when suspect under arrest, probable cause exists to search entire car as a lawful search incident to an arrest].

Did the officers act lawfully during the searches and seizures noted above?

INTRODUCTION

The U.S. Supreme Court has crafted a number of judicially [judge-made] recognized exceptions to the legal requirement to obtain a warrant based on balancing a citizen's right to privacy against the state's legitimate goal to prevent crime and enforce the law. The exceptions to the warrant requirement are called "warrantless" searches and seizures. Some warrant exceptions even dispense with the probable cause or reasonable suspicion requirements, such as drug interdiction sweeps on public conveyances such as buses, trains, and airport luggage storage areas, or roadblocks to catch drivers who are intoxicated. This chapter explores the many exceptions to the warrant requirement and the legal basis that justifies such intrusions upon personal privacy interests.

I. WARRANTLESS SEARCHES AND SEIZURES

1. Consent

Rule of Law: Legally valid consent is voluntary and free from coercion.

If an officer wishes to ask questions of someone on the street, the person has a choice whether or not to answer. **Consent** is a legal terms whereby one party requests another to comply with his wishes. The significance of giving consent is that police may then search and seize, and any evidence of illegal activity found during the search can and will be used against the suspect. To be legal, the consent to search a particular place or seize a specific item must be voluntary and not the product of coercion, threat or force. If a reasonable person in the citizen's shoes would not feel free to terminate the police encounter or to leave the police presence, then, under the law, he has been "seized."[1] As the U.S. Supreme Court has said, officers "do not violate the Fourth Amendment by merely approaching an individual on the street or other public place, by asking him if he is willing to answer some questions, by putting questions to him if the person is willing to listen, or by offering in evidence in a criminal prosecution his voluntary answers to such questions."[2] For Fourth Amendment purposes a seizure of a person occurs when a person's freedom of movement is restrained. A person may be seized even though not technically under arrest. As discussed in chapter 9, to determine whether the suspect merely submitted to government authority, courts look at the totality of the circumstances surrounding the police/citizen encounter in obtaining consent. To determine whether the suspect has given officers consent to search, courts consider the following factors:

1. Knowledge of the right to refuse—officers need not tell citizen of this right[3]
2. Level of intelligence, age, and language skills[4]
3. Level of cooperation with authorities

---

[1]*See United States* v. *Drayton,* 536 U.S. 194 (2002).

[2]*Florida* v. *Royer,* 460 U.S. 491 (1983).

[3]*Schneckloth* v. *Bustamonte,* 412 U.S. 218 (1973).

[4]Although one might expect that a person with a low level of intellectual functioning, a person under the influence of alcohol or drugs, or a person suffering extreme emotional distress would not be capable of giving voluntary consent, this is not true. *See* cases cited in footnote 20 in chapter 12.

4. Length of detention and nature of questioning by officers

5. Physical contact between the citizen and police

6. Any coercive tactics used by police.

Under the totality test, the above factors all play a role in the court's determination of whether consent to search/seize was voluntary. But if the court determines that the person consented to submit to a show of police authority, then the court will deem the consent was involuntarily given and the evidence discovered as a result of the consent search may be inadmissible. For instance, in the chapter's opening scenario, Jodie's consent to enter the motel room was involuntary because she was simply submitting to police authority when officers told her not to refuse them permission to search because they had a warrant on the way. As the U.S. Supreme Court has said, "[w]hen a law enforcement officer claims authority to search a home under a warrant, he announces in effect that the occupant has no right to resist the search. The situation is indistinct [the same] with coercion [and where] there is coercion there cannot be consent."[5] Remember to apply the totality of the circumstances test to determine if consent was voluntary.

Applying the Rule of Law to the Facts: Is it voluntary consent or mere submission to authority?

- Investigation into sexually explicit photographs of juveniles led to Charlie Johnson's home. Police informed Johnson of the nature of the investigation, read him his so-called *Miranda* rights and asked for consent to search Johnson's bedroom and computer. Johnson refused. Agents left to secure a search warrant via telephone. When the police returned to the home to await the warrant, they informed Johnson that the residence would have to be locked down while they waited for the warrant and again asked Johnson for his consent to search, adding that such consent "could possibly save time for us." If Johnson consented this time, was his consent voluntary?

Yes, consent is voluntary. In *United States v. Johnson,* the Seventh Circuit Court of Appeals held that Johnson gave his consent willingly and voluntarily based on a number of factors. He was 48 years old and technically savvy with computers. His reluctance to inconvenience his employers—he was a live-in nanny for their children—by having their movements restricted while police waited for the search warrant was not a response to coercive conduct on the part of the police. Johnson was given his rights pursuant to *Miranda* twice and twice waived them in an atmosphere that Johnson admitted was not threatening; the evidence found against Johnson was admitted.[6]

The next question courts ask in deciding whether a person's consent was voluntary is the person's authority to give consent. If a person shares an apartment with two other people, the person has the authority to give consent to search the common areas of the apartment that everyone shares, such as the living room, kitchen, and bathroom, but not the roommates' private bedrooms. As defined by the U.S. Supreme Court in *Katz* v. *United States,* 389 U.S. 347 (1967), the expectation of privacy that is protected against government intrusion must be both subjective [personal to the person] and objective [everyone would expect and recognize the same expectation of privacy]. Someone who shares an apartment has no authority to consent to search others' private areas, nor does a landlord have the authority to grant consent to search his tenants' rooms simply because he owns the property.[7]

---

[5]*Bumper* v. *North Carolina,* 391 U.S. 543 (1967).

[6]*United States* v. *Johnson,* 495 F.3d 536 (7th Cir. 2007).

[7]*United States* v. *Warner,* 843 F.2d 401 (9th Cir. 1988).

Recent Supreme Court case law allows joint tenants in common to refuse the authority to search where one tenant would grant such authority. In *Georgia* v. *Randolph*, 126 S.Ct. 1515 (2006), a married couple was going through a messy divorce, and the wife, Janet Randolph, gave police consent to search the house over her husband's objection, which at the time was legally sufficient consent for police to have authority to search. Officers discovered cocaine and used it to convict the husband, Scott Randolph, of illegal possession. On appeal, Randolph argued that his refusal to consent to search the common household should have trumped his wife's consent and the U.S. Supreme Court agreed with him. Justice Souter wrote for the majority that "in the circumstances here at issue, a physically present co-occupant's stated refusal to permit entry prevails, rendering the warrantless search unreasonable and invalid as to him." The *Randolph* decision changed long-standing precedent across the country allowing such consent searches over the objection of one tenant.

Sometimes officers will conduct a "knock and talk" to get the suspect to give consent. In *State* v. *Smith*, 488 S.E.2d 210 (N. C. 1997), the North Carolina Supreme Court described the **knock and talk** procedure as follows:

> The knock and talk procedure is a tactic used by law enforcement ... when they get information that a certain person has drugs in a residence but the officers don't have probable cause for a search warrant. The officers then proceed to the residence, knock on the door, and ask to be admitted inside. Thereafter gaining entry, the officers inform the person that they're investigating information that drugs are in the house. The officers then ask for permission to search and apparently are successful in many cases getting the occupant's "apparent consent."

The last item courts look at in the consent arena is the scope of the consent to search. If consent to search is given voluntarily, it ordinarily means that police have the authority to search everything within a specific area, for example the contents of a refrigerator if given consent to search a kitchen. Even though consent may be retracted at any time, it's logical that if police discover evidence of a crime or contraband during a consent search, then such discovery may give them probable cause to search further; rescinding consent to search at that point would be futile.

But if a motorist gives consent to search his car, does that consent extend to the locked briefcases within the car? The Supreme Court said yes in the case *Florida* v. *Jimeno*, 500 U.S. 248 (1991). Jimeno was stopped for a minor traffic violation and a police officer requested consent to search Jimeno's car based on the belief that Jimeno was carrying drugs. Jimeno consented and said he "had nothing to hide." When the officer found a kilogram of cocaine in a brown paper bag on the floor, Jimeno argued on appeal of his drug conviction that the officer had no authority to open the paper bag. The high Court disagreed with Jimeno and said that the proper inquiry about the scope of Jimeno's consent was, first, what a typical reasonable person would have understood by the exchange between the officer and suspect and, second, whether it was "reasonable for an officer to consider a suspect's general consent to a search of his car to include consent to examine a paper bag lying on the floor of the car." Finding such actions reasonable in light of the Fourth Amendment because illegal drugs are rarely strewn about the floor of the passenger compartment, the Court held that looking into the bag as part of the consent search was proper.

2. Search Incident to an Arrest

Rule of Law: Once a suspect is arrested, his person and the area within his immediate control are subject to lawful search.

Once a suspect has been arrested on the basis of probable cause, police do not need a warrant to conduct a **search incident to an arrest,** which is a full search of the suspect's person and clothing and the area immediately within his control. Dispensing with the warrant requirement to search a recent arrestee guarantees officer safety and prevents the potential destruction of evidence that the suspect could grab and dispose of quickly. The search incident to an arrest presumes that the initial arrest was lawful. If there was no probable cause for the arrest, any contraband discovered in the subsequent search may be suppressed as fruit of the poisonous tree. In the eyes of the U.S. Supreme Court, it does not matter whether the arrest or the search came first, as long as such arrest was based on probable cause before the search took place. "Where the formal arrest followed quickly on the heels of the challenged search . . . we do not believe it particularly important that the search preceded the arrest rather than vice versa" so long as what the search disclosed was "not necessary to support probable cause to arrest."[8]

The legal limitations on officers are emphasized in *Vale* v. *Louisiana,* 399 U.S. 30 (1970), where the Court stated that the search incident to an arrest is valid "only if it is substantially contemporaneous with the arrest and is confined to the immediate vicinity of the arrest." Incident to Vale's arrest, a search was conducted inside his home and drugs were found in the rear bedroom. Finding the search unlawful, the Court declared: "If a search of a house is to be upheld as incident to an arrest, that arrest must take place inside the house . . . not somewhere outside—whether two blocks away, . . . twenty feet away, . . . or on the sidewalk near the front steps." Thus, even if the arrest does take place inside the house, the search incident to the arrest must be confined to the area within the arrestee's "immediate control."

The case that set the legal standard for searches incident to an arrest is *Chimel* v. *California.* Chimel was a suspected burglar who was arrested pursuant to an arrest warrant. The police arrested Chimel inside his home and then searched the entire house for the next hour. In deciding that the search was unreasonable, the Supreme Court held that the police had gone too far. Read the *Chimel* case and see if you agree.

BOX 11.1

Chimel v. *California,* 395 U.S. 752 (1969)
United States Supreme Court

Justice Stewart delivered the opinion of the Court.

FACTS

Late in the afternoon of September 13, 1965, three police officers arrived at the Santa Ana, California, home of the petitioner [Chimel] with a warrant authorizing his arrest for the burglary of a coin shop. The officers knocked on the door, identified themselves to the petitioner's wife, and asked if they might come inside. She ushered them into the house, where they waited 10 or 15 minutes until the petitioner returned home from work. When the petitioner entered the house, one of the officers handed him the arrest warrant and asked for permission to "look around." The petitioner objected, but was advised that "on the basis of the lawful arrest," the officers would nonetheless conduct a search. No search warrant had been issued.

Accompanied by the petitioner's wife, the officers then looked through the entire three-bedroom house, including the attic, the garage, and a small workshop. In some rooms the search was relatively cursory. In the master bedroom and sewing room, however, the officers directed the petitioner's wife to open drawers and "to physically move contents of the drawers from side to side so that [they] might view any items that would have come from [the] burglary." After completing the search, they seized

---

[8]*Rawlings* v. *Kentucky,* 448 U.S. 98 (1980).

numerous items—primarily coins, but also several medals, tokens, and a few other objects. The entire search took between 45 minutes and an hour.

At the petitioner's subsequent state trial on two charges of burglary, the items taken from his house were admitted into evidence against him, over his objection that they had been unconstitutionally seized. He was convicted, and the judgments of conviction were affirmed by both the California Court of Appeal and the California Supreme Court. Both courts accepted the petitioner's contention that the arrest warrant was invalid because the supporting affidavit was set out in conclusory terms, but held that since the arresting officers had procured the warrant "in good faith," and since in any event they had had sufficient information to constitute probable cause for the petitioner's arrest, that arrest had been lawful. From this conclusion the appellate courts went on to hold that the search of the petitioner's home had been justified, despite the absence of a search warrant, on the ground that it had been incident to a valid arrest. We granted *certiorari* in order to consider the petitioner's substantial constitutional claims.

ISSUE

This brings us directly to the question whether the warrantless search of the petitioner's entire house can be constitutionally justified as incident to that arrest?

HOLDING

[No, the search of the house was overbroad as a search incident to Chimel's arrest.]

REASONING

Only last Term in *Terry* v. *Ohio,* we emphasized that "the police must, whenever practicable, obtain advance judicial approval of searches and seizures through the warrant procedure," and that "the scope of [a] search must be 'strictly tied to and justified by' the circumstances which rendered its initiation permissible." The search undertaken by the officer in that "stop and frisk" case was sustained under that test, because it was no more than a "protective . . . search for weapons." But in a companion case, *Sibron* v. *New York,* [392 U.S. 40 (1968)] we applied the same

standard to another set of facts and reached a contrary result, holding that a policeman's action in thrusting his hand into a suspect's pocket had been neither motivated by nor limited to the objective of protection. Rather, the search had been made in order to find narcotics, which were in fact found.

A similar analysis underlies the "search incident to arrest" principle, and marks its proper extent. When an arrest is made, it is reasonable for the arresting officer to search the person arrested in order to remove any weapons that the latter might seek to use in order to resist arrest or effect his escape. Otherwise, the officer's safety might well be endangered, and the arrest itself frustrated. In addition, it is entirely reasonable for the arresting officer to search for and seize any evidence on the arrestee's person in order to prevent its concealment or destruction. And the area into which an arrestee might reach in order to grab a weapon or evidentiary items must, of course, be governed by a like rule. A gun on a table or in a drawer in front of one who is arrested can be as dangerous to the arresting officer as one concealed in the clothing of the person arrested. There is ample justification, therefore, for a search of the arrestee's person and the area "within his immediate control"—construing that phrase to mean the area from within which he might gain possession of a weapon or destructible evidence. There is no comparable justification, however, for routinely searching any room other than that in which an arrest occurs—or, for that matter, for searching through all the desk drawers or other closed or concealed areas in that room itself. Such searches, in the absence of well-recognized exceptions, may be made only under the authority of a search warrant. The "adherence to judicial processes" mandated by the Fourth Amendment requires no less.

It is argued in the present case that it is "reasonable" to search a man's house when he is arrested in it. But that argument is founded on little more than a subjective view regarding the acceptability of certain sorts of police conduct, and not on considerations relevant to Fourth Amendment interests. Under such an unconfined analysis, Fourth Amendment protection in this area would approach the evaporation point. It is not easy to explain why, for instance, it is less subjectively "reasonable" to search a man's house when he is arrested on his front lawn—or just

(continued)

BOX 11.1

(continued)

down the street—than it is when he happens to be in the house at the time of arrest. As Mr. Justice Frankfurter put it:

> To say that the search must be reasonable is to require some criterion of reason. It is no guide at all either for a jury or for district judges or the police to say that an 'unreasonable search' is forbidden—that the search must be reasonable. What is the test of reason which makes a search reasonable? The test is the reason underlying and expressed by the Fourth Amendment: the history and the experience which it embodies and the safeguards afforded by it against the evils to which it was a response.

Thus, although "the recurring questions of the reasonableness of searches" depend upon "the facts and circumstances—the total atmosphere of the case," those facts and circumstances must be viewed in the light of established Fourth Amendment principles.

CONCLUSION

Application of sound Fourth Amendment principles to the facts of this case produces a clear result. The search here went far beyond the petitioner's person and the area from within which he might have obtained either a weapon or something that could have been used as evidence against him. There was no constitutional justification, in the absence of a search warrant, for extending the search beyond that area. The scope of the search was, therefore, "unreasonable" under the Fourth and Fourteenth Amendments, and the petitioner's conviction cannot stand.

Sometimes after officers arrest and handcuff the suspect in his home, they transport him from room to room, which allows them to "search the area within the suspect's immediate control"—this is referred to as "portable *Chimel.*" The fact that the defendant is handcuffed and cannot ostensibly reach a weapon to harm officers or destroy evidence makes no difference; the same conclusion holds true when a suspect is handcuffed and placed in the back of a locked police squad car, such as in *Thorton* v. *United States* (2004).

3. Automobile Searches

Rule of Law: Since automobiles are subject to licensing and inspection requirements, individuals have a lesser expectation of privacy in an auto than in their homes.

One well-recognized search warrant exception is the **automobile exception.** If police have probable cause that the car contains evidence of a crime or contraband and that "it is not practicable to secure a warrant because the vehicle can be quickly moved out of the locality or jurisdiction in which the warrant must be sought," then the police can search the vehicle without a warrant. *Carroll* v. *United States,* 267 U.S. 132 (1925). The warrantless search is justified by the car's mobility and by the myriad of state regulations that control cars, such as licensing and inspection requirements that diminish an owner's expectation of privacy in the vehicle. The Supreme Court observed in *South Dakota* v. *Opperman,* 428 U.S. 364 (1976):

> Automobiles, unlike homes, are subject to pervasive and continuing governmental regulation and controls, including periodic inspection and licensing requirements. As an everyday occurrence, police stop and examine vehicles when license plates or inspection stickers have expired, or if other violations, such as exhaust fumes or excessive noise, are noted, or if headlights or other safety equipment are not in proper working order.

What is the scope of police authority under state laws that regulate driving when balanced against the U.S. Constitution and the Fourth Amendment? The U.S. Supreme Court answered this question on April 23, 2008, when it decided *Virginia* v. *Moore,* 128

S.Ct. 1598 (2008). David Moore committed a state misdemeanor by driving without a license. Under Virginia law, when a police officer stops a person for a misdemeanor, the officer may not arrest the person, but only issue a summons and let him go. Moore was arrested and, pursuant to a warrantless search incident to arrest, was searched. Officers found crack cocaine and cash on Moore. He was convicted, and he appealed with the following argument: Because police violated state law in making the initial arrest (they were only allowed to issue a summons), the search incident to the arrest was unlawful, and all evidence discovered should have been suppressed and not used against him. The U.S. Supreme Court disagreed with Moore's argument and held that "when officers have probable cause to believe that a person has committed a crime in their presence, the Fourth Amendment permits them to make an arrest, and to search the suspect in order to safeguard evidence and ensure their own safety." In sum, the Fourth Amendment did not prevent Moore's arrest, and once the officers arrested Moore, regardless of state law that may or may not have supported the arrest, the officers had a right to search him and seize the illegal contraband.

Although vehicles are heavily regulated, drivers and passengers do not surrender their privacy rights simply by driving. The government's interest in conducting investigatory detentions or searches of vehicles must be balanced against the public's interest to be free from government intrusion. Automobile searches depend, like most other searches, on the facts of the case. If a car is sitting in a driveway under surveillance and officers have time to obtain a warrant to search it, police do not have automatic authority to search the car simply because it can be driven away.

a. Search Incident to an Arrest in an Automobile

When the driver or one of the passengers inside a car has been arrested on the basis of probable cause, the Supreme Court has held that officers may search, without a warrant, the passenger compartment of the car. In *New York* v. *Belton,* 453 U.S. 454 (1981), officers pulled over a car, ordered all of the occupants to get out, and lawfully arrested them. One officer searched the car and found a jacket on the floor with drugs inside one of the pockets. The jacket belonged to Belton, who was convicted of drug possession charges. The Supreme Court found that, on the basis of its decision in *Chimel* v. *California,* a search of the area "within the immediate control of the arrestee" was lawful, and stated that, in a car, this area encompassed the passenger compartment and any **closed containers** such as luggage, purses, briefcases, consoles, gloveboxes, and similar items designed to hold and conceal items. After the Court's decision in *Belton,* lower courts hearing appeals remained divided on the reach and scope of authority under the *Belton* decision to search passenger compartments.[9] Courts generally allowed a *Belton* search of a car incident to an arrest of the driver or occupant—even when the person arrested was in handcuffs and sitting in the backseat of a squad car unable to grab for weapons or destroy evidence as justified by the search incident to an arrest. But the question remained whether police could conduct a *Belton* search if the driver had pulled over, parked, and moved out of his car before police initiated contact.[10]

If officers had probable cause to arrest the suspect and put him in the squad car, did police then have the authority to search the suspect's car as an incident to that arrest, even though the suspect was nowhere near the vehicle? In 2004, the Supreme Court answered that question in the affirmative in *Thorton* v. *United States,* 541 U.S. 615 (2004). Thorton was driving when Officer Nichols ran a license plate check and

---

[9]*See generally* L. A. Lunney. "The Inevitably Arbitrary Placement of Bright Lines: *Belton* and its Progeny." *Tulane Law Review,* Vol. 79 (2004), pp. 365–400.

[10]*See United States* v. *Milton,* 52 F.3d 78 (4th Cir. 1995).

discovered the plates did not match Thorton's car. Nichols pulled him over, and Thorton parked his car, got out, and stood outside his car as Nichols approached. Thorton consented to a *Terry* frisk for weapons and admitted that he possessed crack and marijuana. Thorton was arrested and placed in the back of Nichols' unmarked police vehicle. Under the authority of *Belton,* Officer Nichols conducted a search incident to an arrest inside Thorton's car and found a weapon under the front seat. When Thorton challenged his conviction on drug and weapon charges, the Supreme Court found that Nichols had authority to conduct the search. The Court concluded that such a search is legal regardless of who initiates the contact: the police or the citizen. The import of the cases that establish the legality of warrantless automobile searches is the following: whether police initiate contact with a driver, or the driver gets out of the car and initiates contact with police, once an arrest based on probable cause has been made, even if the person arrested is in handcuffs and removed a distance from his own vehicle, a warrantless search incident to an arrest of the passenger compartment and all containers therein is lawful. The search can lawfully extend to the trunk because it is based on probable cause that a crime has been committed and is not limited to a *Terry* pat down and frisk for weapons. When the manager of the Motel Easy in our opening scenario was arrested and placed in the police car, the probable cause arrest provided the legal authority for the ensuing search of the closed trunk and containers for contraband under *Thorton.*

b. Dog Sniffs

Dog sniffs are nonintrusive and noninvasive on a citizen's privacy interests and therefore are not searches under the Fourth Amendment, but dog sniffs can provide the basis for probable cause to acquire the authority to search. If, during an investigative detention of a vehicle, a drug detection dog sniffs and alerts its handler to the presence of contraband, does the sniff constitute probable cause to search? In *Illinois* v. *Caballes,* 125 S.Ct. 834 (2005), a canine unit officer overheard a call about a motorist speeding and responded to the scene. The officer stopped the motorist, removed him from his car, and placed him in the officer's car. Later, a second canine unit officer arrived, and his dog went around Caballes's car and alerted to the presence of drugs in the trunk. The police searched the trunk and discovered drugs. Caballes was convicted and complained that there was no reasonable suspicion that a speeding motorist possessed drugs justifying the dog sniff. On appeal, the U.S. Supreme Court held that reasonable suspicion was not required to justify a dog sniff during a routine traffic stop and that the dog sniff established probable cause to search further, because a dog is only sniffing what is in public and his sniff is nonintrusive.

Applying the Rule of Law to the Facts: When is a search permissible?

- During a routine traffic stop, officers brought a drug-detection dog around the suspect's car and the dog alerted for a smell of marijuana. The officers then took the dog to the suspect's house, where, walking up the driveway, the dog alerted the officers to the presence of drugs again. The officers secured a search warrant and seized 64 marijuana plants. Were the dog sniffs sufficient probable cause for the warrant?

No, a home is different from a car and more than a dog alert is required to establish probable cause to search. *State* v. *Rabb,* 920 So.2d 1175 (Fla.App. 4 Dist. 2006)

c. Common Enterprise

What happens to passengers in a car that is stopped and searched where contraband is found? Can each passenger be held responsible for that contraband if no one speaks up and claims ownership? Under the law as explained in *Ybarra* v. *Illinois,* 444 U.S. 85

(1979), guilt by association is illegal but not in the small confines of a vehicle. As you read the *Maryland* v. *Pringle* case, ask yourself whether it is fair that if contraband is discovered in a car, officers have probable cause to arrest all occupants, even the occupants who claim ignorance about the presence of contraband. Under the doctrine of **common enterprise,** everyone in a car where guns or drugs are found is legally responsible for all of the contraband.

BOX 11.2

Maryland v. *Pringle,* 540 U.S. 366 (2003)
United States Supreme Court

Chief Justice Rehnquist delivered the opinion of the Court.

FACTS

At 3:16 a.m. on August 7, 1999, a Baltimore County Police officer stopped a Nissan Maxima for speeding. There were three occupants in the car: Donte Partlow, the driver and owner, respondent Pringle, the front-seat passenger, and Otis Smith, the back-seat passenger. The officer asked Partlow for his license and registration. When Partlow opened the glove compartment to retrieve the vehicle registration, the officer observed a large amount of rolled-up money in the glove compartment. The officer returned to his patrol car with Partlow's license and registration to check the computer system for outstanding violations. The computer check did not reveal any violations. Partlow then consented to a search of the vehicle. The search yielded $763 from the glove compartment and five plastic glassine baggies containing cocaine from behind the back-seat armrest. The officer questioned all three men about the ownership of the drugs and money, and told them that if no one admitted to ownership of the drugs he was going to arrest them all. The men offered no information regarding the ownership of the drugs or money. All three were placed under arrest and transported to the police station. Later that morning, Pringle waived his rights under *Miranda* v. *Arizona,* 384 U.S. 436 (1966) and gave an oral and written confession in which he acknowledged that the cocaine belonged to him, that he and his friends were going to a party, and that he intended to sell the cocaine or "[u]se it for sex."

PROCEDURAL HISTORY

The trial court denied Pringle's motion to suppress his confession as the fruit of an illegal arrest, holding that the officer had probable cause to arrest Pringle. A jury convicted Pringle of possession with intent to distribute cocaine and possession of cocaine. He was sentenced to 10 years' incarceration without the possibility of parole. The Court of Special Appeals of Maryland affirmed. The Court of Appeals of Maryland, by a divided vote reversed, holding that, absent specific facts tending to show Pringle's knowledge and dominion or control over the drugs, "the mere finding of cocaine in the back armrest when [Pringle] was a front seat passenger in a car being driven by its owner is insufficient to establish probable cause for an arrest for possession." We granted *certiorari* and now reverse.

ISSUE

[Did the police officer have probable cause to arrest Pringle making Pringle's arrest legal?]

HOLDING

[Yes.]

REASONING

We think it an entirely reasonable inference from these facts that any or all three of the occupants had knowledge of, and exercised dominion and control over, the cocaine. Thus a reasonable officer could conclude that there was probable cause to believe Pringle committed the crime of possession of cocaine, either solely or jointly. Pringle's attempt

(continued)

BOX 11.2

(continued)

to characterize this case as a guilt-by-association case in unavailing. His reliance on *Ybarra* v. *Illinois,* 444 U.S. 85 (1979) is misplaced ... We held [in *Ybarra*] that the search warrant did not permit body searches of all of the tavern's patrons and that the police could not pat down the patrons for weapons, absent individualized suspicion.

This case is quite different from *Ybarra.* Pringle and his two companions were in a relatively small automobile, not a public tavern ... a car passenger—unlike the unwitting tavern patron in *Ybarra*—will often be engaged in a common enterprise with the driver, and have the same interest in concealing the fruits or the evidence of their

wrongdoing. Here we think it was reasonable for the officer to infer a common enterprise among the three men. The quantity of drugs and cash indicated the likelihood of drug dealing, an enterprise to which a dealer would be unlikely to admit an innocent person with the potential to furnish evidence against him.

CONCLUSION

Accordingly, the judgment of the Court of Appeals of Maryland is reversed, and the case is remanded for further proceedings not inconsistent with this opinion.

Applying the Rule of Law to the Facts: **When does the law consider people to be engaged in a common enterprise?**

- Students at a fraternity party were stuffed into one big room dancing and having fun. Some students were drinking alcohol. Some were over 21 years of age and others were underage. Police arrived and arrested everyone in the room for supplying alcohol if they were of age and for underage drinking if they were not. Some underage students caught in the sweep are challenging the arrest as unsupported by probable cause. The police responded with the doctrine of common enterprise. Who is correct?

The students are correct. Even though a crowded party may be akin to the tight confines of a car under common enterprise, a big room in a house indicates that not all students share the common goal and purpose of underage drinking, and *Ybarra* would require individualized suspicion to support an arrest.

∂. Driving Checkpoints

It is constitutional for law enforcement to establish roadblocks and driving checkpoints that are tactics to investigate crime, detect drunk drivers and even check for illegal immigrants. *Michigan Dept. of State Police* v. *Sitz,* 496 U.S. 444 (1990); *United States* v. *Martinez-Fuerte,* 428 U.S. 543 (1976). In *Illinois* v. *Lidster* 124 S.Ct. 885 (2004), officers conducted random vehicle stops near the scene of a fatal hit-and-run to learn information from possible witnesses. Lidster was a drunk driver caught by the roadblock who challenged his conviction on the grounds that the investigatory checkpoint violated the Fourth Amendment's prohibition against unreasonable search and seizure. The high Court disagreed and said that such stops are "brief information-seeking" exchanges limited to discovering information. Because the intrusion on the drivers was minimal, the stops were legal.

However, if the objective of the roadblock is to check for illegal drugs, then such stops are illegal because the nature of the search is more intrusive. The law requires a reasonable suspicion that the driver or occupants are engaged in unlawful activity before a search of a car for drugs will be allowed. In *City of Indianapolis* v. *Edmond,* 531 U.S. 32 (2000), the city set up vehicle checkpoints to intercept illegal drugs. They conducted six checkpoints over a four-month period, stopping 1,161 vehicles and arresting 104 motorists. Fifty-five arrests were for drug-related crimes, while 49 were for offenses unrelated to drugs. The overall hit rate for drug arrests was approximately nine percent. At each checkpoint approximately 30 officers stopped a predetermined number of vehicles. Motorists challenged the roadblocks on Fourth Amendment grounds. The U.S. Supreme Court agreed with the motorists that such checkpoints violated the Constitution, stating

> We have never approved a checkpoint program whose primary purpose was to detect evidence of ordinary criminal wrongdoing . . . There is no doubt that traffic in illegal narcotics creates social harms of the first magnitude . . . But the gravity of the threat alone cannot be dispositive of questions concerning what means law enforcement officers may employ to pursue a given purpose. . . . We are particularly reluctant to recognize exceptions to the general rule of individualized suspicion where governmental authorities primarily pursue their general crime control ends.

In your analysis of the legality of checkpoints and roadblocks, always ask what the government's ultimate objective is in conducting the stop.

4. Protective Sweep

Rule of Law: To conduct a protective sweep, officers must have specific and articulable facts that armed persons are on the premises.

In an effort to ensure officer safety, when police arrest someone in a home or approach a crime scene, can officers make a protective sweep by drawing their weapons and searching for other armed people who may pose a safety threat? The short answer is no. Only when officers have a reasonable belief based on specific and articulable facts that armed and dangerous people are present may the officers legally make a cursory sweep looking for them. In *Maryland* v. *Buie,* police received a report of two armed robbers. After finding one and arresting him inside a house, they conducted a protective sweep for the other, during which they discovered a red running suit reportedly worn by one of the robbers. The red running suit was introduced at trial and was part of the evidence used to convict Buie. In an unsuccessful motion to overturn his conviction, Buie claimed that the officers had no legal authority to conduct the protective sweep and, therefore, that the seizure of the running suit was unlawful, but the Supreme Court disagreed.

BOX 11.3

Maryland v. *Buie,* 494 U.S. 325 (1990)
Supreme Court of the United States

Justice White delivered the opinion of the Court.

FACTS

On February 3, 1986, two men committed an armed robbery of a Godfather's Pizza restaurant in Prince George's County, Maryland. One of the robbers was wearing a red running suit. That same day, Prince George's County police obtained arrest warrants for respondent Jerome Edward Buie and his suspected accomplice in the robbery, Lloyd Allen. Buie's house was placed under police surveillance. On February 5, the police executed the arrest warrant for Buie. They first had a police department secretary telephone Buie's house to verify that he was home. The secretary spoke to a female first, then to Buie himself. Six or seven officers proceeded to Buie's house. Once inside, the officers fanned out through the first and

(continued)

BOX 11.3

(continued)

second floors. Corporal James Rozar announced that he would "freeze" the basement so that no one could come up and surprise the officers. With his service revolver drawn, Rozar twice shouted into the basement, ordering anyone down there to come out. When a voice asked who was calling, Rozar announced three times: "this is the police, show me your hands."

Eventually, a pair of hands appeared around the bottom of the stairwell and Buie emerged from the basement. He was arrested, searched, and hand-cuffed by Rozar. Thereafter, Detective Joseph Frolich entered the basement "in case there was someone else" down there. He noticed a red running suit lying in plain view on a stack of clothing and seized it. The trial court denied Buie's motion to suppress the running suit, stating in part: "The man comes out from a basement, the police don't know how many other people are down there. He is charged with a serious offense." The State introduced the running suit into evidence at Buie's trial. A jury convicted Buie of robbery with a deadly weapon and using a handgun in the commission of a felony. The Court of Special Appeals of Maryland affirmed the trial court's denial of the suppression motion. The court stated that Detective Frolich did not go into the basement to search for evidence, but to look for the suspected accomplice or anyone else who might pose a threat to the officers on the scene.

ISSUE

[Was the search of Buie's home justified without a warrant?]

HOLDING

[Yes.] The Fourth Amendment permits a properly limited protective sweep in conjunction with an in-home arrest when the searching officer possesses a reasonable belief based on specific and articulable facts that the area to be swept harbors an individual posing a danger to those on the arrest scene.

REASONING

It goes without saying that the Fourth Amendment bars only unreasonable searches and seizures,

Skinner v. *Railway Labor Executives' Assn.,* 489 U.S. 602 (1989). Our cases show that in determining reasonableness, we have balanced the intrusion on the individual's Fourth Amendment interests against its promotion of legitimate governmental interests. *United States* v. *Villamonte-Marquez,* 462 U.S. 579 (1983); *Delaware* v. *Prouse,* 440 U.S. 648 (1979). Under this test, a search of the house or office is generally not reasonable without a warrant issued on probable cause. There are other contexts, however, where the public interest is such that neither a warrant nor probable cause is required.

That Buie had an expectation of privacy in those remaining areas of his house, however, does not mean such rooms were immune from entry. In *Terry* [v. *Ohio,* 392 U.S. 1 (1968)] and *Long* [*Michigan* v. *Long,* 463 U.S. 1032 (1983), vehicle search for weapons] we were concerned with the immediate interest of the police officers in taking steps to assure themselves that the persons with whom they were dealing were not armed with, or able to gain immediate control of, a weapon that could unexpectedly and fatally be used against them. In the instant case, there is an analogous interest of the officers in taking steps to assure themselves that the house in which a suspect is being, or has just been, arrested is not harboring other persons who are dangerous and who could unexpectedly launch an attack. The risk of danger in the context of an arrest in the home is as great as, if not greater than, it is in an on-the-street or roadside investigatory encounter. A *Terry* and *Long* frisk occurs before a police–citizen confrontation has escalated to the point of arrest. A protective sweep, in contrast, occurs as an adjunct to the serious step of taking a person into custody for the purpose of prosecuting him for a crime. Moreover, unlike an encounter on the street or along a highway, an in-home arrest puts the officer at the disadvantage of being on his adversary's "turf." An ambush in a confined setting of unknown configuration is more to be feared than it is in open, more familiar surroundings.

We agree with the State, as did the court below, that a warrant was not required [to search the house where Buie was found]. We also hold that as an incident to the arrest the officers could, as a precautionary matter and without probable cause or reasonable suspicion, look in closets and other spaces immediately adjoining the place of arrest from which an attack could be immediately launched. Beyond that, however, we hold that there must be articulable facts which, taken together with the rational inferences from those facts, would warrant a reasonably prudent officer in believing that the area to be swept harbors an individual posing a danger to those on the arrest scene.

CONCLUSION

The Fourth Amendment permits a properly limited protective sweep in conjunction with an in-home arrest when the searching officer possesses a reasonable belief based on specific and articulable facts that the area to be swept harbors an individual posing a danger to those on the arrest scene. We therefore vacate the judgment below [holding the search an impermissible extension of the *Chimel* doctrine] and remand this case to the Court of Appeals of Maryland for further proceedings not inconsistent with this opinion.

The holding in *Buie* identified two situations in which protective sweeps would be authorized. A protective sweep of spaces/closets "immediately adjoining the place of arrest from which an attack could be immediately launched" is justified without probable cause or reasonable suspicion. The second type of sweep requires reasonable suspicion that "the area to be swept harbors an individual posing a danger to those on the arrest scene" and is not a full search, but is limited to those "spaces where a person may be found." If police go to Johnny's house and arrest him in his bedroom, and the officers know that Johnny is part of an armed and dangerous drug-dealing ring, officers may conduct a protective sweep by looking under his bed or in his bedroom closets without probable cause or reasonable suspicion that armed people are hiding in ambush. But if after arresting Johnny in the bedroom police seek to conduct a protective sweep of the kitchen, bathroom, and garage, officers have to point to specific and articulable facts that armed people are in the house. Their search would be limited to places where people could reasonably hide, such as in the hall closet, not inside the electric dishwasher. In our opening-chapter scenario, when Officer Jones arrested Jimmy inside his apartment, he could lawfully draw his weapon and search the apartment only on the basis of specific and articulable facts that other armed and dangerous people were in the apartment. Since most courts recognize that drugs and guns go hand in hand, Officer Jones may have been justified in searching the rooms and closets for other armed people, but he had no authority to search for drug evidence in desk drawers or the refrigerator.

In another Maryland case, *Dashiell* v. *State,* 792 A.2d 1185 (2002), the Maryland Court of Appeals held that inclusion in a search warrant application of an allegation that a residence used for drug trafficking contains firearms justifies frisking everyone on the premises when the warrant is executed. However, the court did not approve a blanket authority to frisk in all cases involving drug warrants. Members of a narcotics task force obtained a no-knock warrant to search a house suspected of being used by a male drug trafficking suspect to store drugs. The application in support of the warrant stated that informers had reported seeing guns in the apartment and on the suspect's person. When the officers arrived to execute the warrant, the only people present were the defendant, who was female; her children; and another woman. Pursuant to task force policy of frisking everyone present on the premises when a no-knock warrant is executed, the officers frisked the defendant and detected a plastic bag of cocaine used to convict her of a drug offense. The court concluded that the reasonable suspicion requirement of *Terry* v. *Ohio* controlled the analysis of the legality of the pat-down in this case. In finding the frisk legal on the basis of reliable information (weapons were believed to be located in the house and/or on the persons named in the warrant), the court cited *Maryland* v. *Buie,* where the U.S. Supreme Court recognized that police officers have additional reasons to be concerned about their safety when they are executing a warrant in a suspect's home.

5. Plain View/Open Fields

Rule of Law: The language of the Fourth Amendment protects only "persons, houses, papers and effects."

If obvious contraband is in **plain view**—that is, if anyone can see it without having to move or open anything and if the officers are at the location legally with a warrant or under a legally recognized warrant exception—they may seize the items. **Open fields** are typically patches of land over which one could fly in an airplane and see the contraband below—usually marijuana crops or methamphetamine laboratories in national forests. There are three legal requirements in order for items to be seized pursuant to the plain view exception:

1. The officer must have legal authority to be on the premises
2. The officer must have a legal basis to seize the evidence
3. The seized evidence must have a nexus/connection to a crime or be obvious contraband.

In our chapter-opening scenario, officers seized marijuana that was sitting in plain view on the end table in Jodie and Nick's motel room. But because the officers unlawfully coerced Jodie's consent in allowing them to enter the room, they were not in the motel room legally; therefore, the seizure of the marijuana on the basis of plain view was legally deficient.

Growing marijuana in an open field or finding other contraband in the open is also subject to seizure without a warrant, because "open fields do not provide the setting for those intimate activities that the [Fourth] Amendment is intended to shelter from government interference or surveillance." *Oliver* v. *United States,* 466 U.S. 170 (1984). The Fourth Amendment is specifically limited to a person's "papers, effects, and houses," so it does not protect contraband left in the open for the public to see. Certain actions are not considered a search for plain-view purposes, such as using a flashlight to get a better view of an item or trying to identify whether an item is contraband.[11]

The area immediately surrounding a dwelling is called **curtilage,** and people retain Fourth Amendment privacy rights in items contained within curtilage, but not beyond. People often wonder how far around the house curtilage extends. There is no set distance; it is simply a reasonable distance over which someone may expect to maintain privacy. Curtilage is also not defined by signs, fences, or "No Trespassing" warnings. The privacy interest in curtilage depends on the proximity to the structure. Four factors help define curtilage:[12]

1. The proximity of the home to the area claimed to be curtilage
2. Whether the area claimed to be curtilage is within an enclosure surrounding the home
3. The nature of the uses to which the curtilage is put, and
4. The steps taken to conceal the curtilage as a private area.

Property located outside of the curtilage may be treated as abandoned property. For example, if you place trash in a bin located next to your house, it is located within the curtilage and you retain a privacy interest in it. But once the garbage is placed out on

---

[11]*United States* v. *Desir,* 257 F.3d 1233 (11th Cir. 2001).

[12]*United States* v. *Dunn,* 480 U.S. 294 (1987).

the curb, it is outside the curtilage and considered abandoned. Law enforcement agents sometimes pose as garbage men, lawfully seize garbage and search it for incriminating evidence, as investigators did in the Balco Laboratories investigation reported in the affidavit in chapter 10.[13]

6. Plain Feel

Rule of Law: If, during a *Terry* pat down, an officer feels obvious contraband, the officer may seize it.

Occasionally, while patting down suspects during a *Terry* stop, officers may feel what they believe to be contraband. May they reach into the person's pocket and remove the item, under the logic that a person has no privacy right in things that are inherently illegal and a crime to possess? To permit officers to go into people's pockets unlawfully expands a *Terry* pat down into a full-blown search, but the plain feel exception to the warrant requirement is closely aligned with plain view and allows the officer to seize obvious contraband that he or she feels on a suspect. Three conditions for the **plain feel** exception to the warrant requirement must be met before contraband can be seized legally without a warrant:

1. The officer must lawfully be touching the person
2. The officer must have some independent constitutional justification for touching the person
3. Through the process of touching, the officer must have probable cause to believe that the object felt constitutes evidence of a crime or is obvious contraband.

Courts have construed the plain feel as a corollary to the plain view doctrine, along with plain smell and plain hearing, where smelling opium or marijuana may establish probable cause or where statements overheard by officers without the benefit of enhanced listening devices may establish probable cause.[14] In *Minnesota v. Dickerson*, the Supreme Court found that manipulating a suspect's pocket for what the officer believed to be obvious crack cocaine in a drug-infested area was a search unsupported by probable cause. As you read the case, ask yourself what the officers could have done to conduct a lawful search.

BOX 11.4

Minnesota v. Dickerson, 508 U.S. 366 (1993)
Supreme Court of the United States

Justice White delivered the opinion of the Court.

FACTS

On the evening of November 9, 1989, two Minneapolis police officers were patrolling an area on the city's north side in a marked squad car. At about 8:15 P.M., one of the officers observed respondent [Dickerson] leaving a 12-unit apartment building on Morgan Avenue North. The officer, having previously responded to complaints of drug sales in the building's hallways and having executed several search warrants on the premises, considered the building to be a notorious "crack house." According to testimony credited by the trial court, respondent began walking toward the police but, upon spotting the squad car and making

(continued)

---

[13]*California* v. *Greenwood*, 486 U.S. 35 (1988).

[14]*See Johnson* v. *United States*, 333 U.S. 10 (1948) (plain smell); *United States* v. *Jackson*, 588 F.2d 1046 (5th Cir. 1979) (plain hearing).

BOX 11.4

(continued)

eye contact with one of the officers, abruptly halted and began walking in the opposite direction. His suspicion aroused, this officer watched as respondent turned and entered an alley on the other side of the apartment building. Based upon respondent's seemingly evasive actions and the fact that he had just left a building known for cocaine traffic, the officers decided to stop respondent and investigate further. The officers pulled their squad car into the alley and ordered respondent to stop and submit to a pat-down search. The search revealed no weapons, but the officer conducting the search did take an interest in a small lump in respondent's nylon jacket. The officer later testified: "As I pat-searched the front of his body, I felt a lump, a small lump, in the front pocket. I examined it with my fingers and it slid and it felt to be a lump of crack cocaine in cellophane."

ISSUE

Thus, the dispositive question before this Court is whether the officer who conducted the search was acting within the lawful bounds marked by *Terry* at the time he gained probable cause to believe that the lump in respondent's jacket was contraband?

HOLDING

[No, the search went beyond a *Terry* stop and was unlawful.]

REASONING

We have already held that police officers, at least under certain circumstances, may seize contraband detected during the lawful execution of a *Terry* search. In *Michigan* v. *Long*, 463 U.S. 1032 (1983), for example, police approached a man who had driven his car into a ditch and who appeared to be under the influence of some intoxicant. As the man moved to reenter the car from the roadside, police spotted a knife on the floor-board. The officers stopped the man, subjected him to a pat-down search, and then inspected the interior of the vehicle for other weapons. During the search of the passenger compartment, the police discovered an open pouch containing marijuana and seized it. This Court up-

held the validity of the search and seizure under *Terry*. The Court held first that, in the context of a roadside encounter, where police have reasonable suspicion based on specific and articulable facts to believe that a driver may be armed and dangerous, they may conduct a protective search for weapons not only of the driver's person but also of the passenger compartment of the automobile. Of course, the protective search of the vehicle, being justified solely by the danger that weapons stored there could be used against the officers or bystanders, must be "limited to those areas in which a weapon may be placed or hidden." The Court then held: "If, while conducting a legitimate *Terry* search of the interior of the automobile, the officer should, as here, discover contraband other than weapons, he clearly cannot be required to ignore the contraband, and the Fourth Amendment does not require its suppression in such circumstances."

We also note that this Court's opinion in *Ybarra* v. *Illinois*, 444 U.S. 85 (1979), appeared to contemplate the possibility that police officers could obtain probable cause justifying a seizure of contraband through the sense of touch. In that case, police officers had entered a tavern and subjected its patrons to pat-down searches. While patting down the petitioner Ybarra, an "officer felt what he described as 'a cigarette pack with objects in it,'" seized it, and discovered heroin inside. The State argued that the seizure was constitutional on the grounds that the officer obtained probable cause to believe that Ybarra was carrying contraband during the course of a lawful *Terry* frisk. This Court rejected that argument on the grounds that "the initial frisk of Ybarra was simply not supported by a reasonable belief that he was armed and presently dangerous," as required by *Terry*. The Court added: "since we conclude that the initial pat down of Ybarra was not justified under the Fourth and Fourteenth Amendments, we need not decide whether or not the presence on Ybarra's person of 'a cigarette pack with objects in it' yielded probable cause to believe that Ybarra was carrying any illegal substance." The Court's analysis does not suggest, and indeed seems inconsistent with, the existence of a categorical bar against seizures of contraband detected manually during a *Terry* pat-down search.

It remains to apply these principles to the facts of this case. Respondent has not challenged the finding made by the trial court and affirmed by both the Court of Appeals and the State Supreme Court that the police were justified under *Terry* in stopping him and frisking him for weapons. . . . The State District Court did not make precise findings on this point, instead finding simply that the officer, after feeling "a small, hard object wrapped in plastic" in respondent's pocket, "formed the opinion that the object . . . was crack . . . cocaine." [The] District Court also noted that the officer made "no claim that he suspected this object to be a weapon," a finding affirmed on appeal (the officer "never thought the lump was a weapon"). The Minnesota Supreme Court, after "a close examination of the record," held that the officer's own testimony "belies any notion that he 'immediately'" recognized the lump as crack cocaine. Rather, the court concluded, the officer determined that the lump was contraband only after "squeezing, sliding and otherwise manipulating the contents of the defendant's pocket"—a pocket which the officer already knew contained no weapon.

Under the State Supreme Court's interpretation of the record before it, it is clear that the court was correct in holding that the police officer in this case overstepped the bounds of the "strictly circumscribed" search for weapons allowed under *Terry*. Where, as here, "an officer who is executing a valid search for one item seizes a different item," this Court rightly "has been sensitive to the danger . . . that officers will enlarge a specific authorization, furnished by a warrant or an exigency, into the equivalent of a general warrant to rummage and seize at will." Here, the officer's continued exploration of respondent's pocket after having concluded that it contained no weapon was unrelated to "the sole justification of the search [under *Terry*] . . . the protection of the police officer and others nearby." It therefore amounted to the sort of evidentiary search that *Terry* expressly refused to authorize, and that we have condemned in subsequent cases.

CONCLUSION

Because this further search of respondent's pocket was constitutionally invalid, the seizure of the cocaine that followed is likewise unconstitutional.

If, during a *Terry* pat down, an officer feel obvious contraband, such as brass knuckles, numchucks, or a syringe used for illegal drugs, the officer has the authority under *Dickerson* to reach into the suspect's pocket to remove the items. If the officer has to manipulate the item to identify it, then such manipulation is considered a search that can only be supported by probable cause.

7. Exigent Circumstances

Rule of Law: Exigent circumstances are emergency circumstances that justify a warrantless entry.

There is no general crime scene exception to the warrant requirement. If police respond to a scene of a multiple murder and have gone through the house to ensure that survivors are found and medical treatment provided, they must then secure a warrant to search the house further based on the probable cause that there were dead bodies at the scene. Police must have probable cause that a search of a residence will produce evidence of a crime and exigent/emergency circumstances may justify a warrantless entry into a dwelling. The following factors are well recognized in evaluating the existence of **exigent circumstances:**

1. The time required to secure a warrant
2. The reasonable belief that evidence will be destroyed if officers delay
3. The safety of officers or the public if police delay taking action, and
4. The suspect's awareness of police presence and likelihood of flight.[15]

---

[15]*People* v. *Yazum,* 196 N.E.2d 263 (N.Y. 1963).

A common example of exigent circumstances is cases involving drunk drivers. The alcohol content of the bloodstream gradually dissipates after alcohol is consumed. If police suspect someone has been drinking and driving, especially late at night when the courts are closed and the burdens of securing a warrant are high, officers are allowed to take the suspect to a medical facility to draw blood to preserve the blood alcohol content ("BAC") for possible later use at trial. In the case *Schmerber* v. *California,* 384 U.S. 757 (1966), Schmerber was being treated at a hospital for injuries sustained in an accident when police directed the doctor to take a vial of Schmerber's blood as evidence. He was later convicted of driving under the influence and, on appeal, complained that the warrantless extraction of his blood violated the Fourth Amendment. The Supreme Court disagreed. The body works quickly to eliminate alcohol and due to the imminent destruction of the evidence, the alcohol in Schmerber's blood, officers did not have time to obtain a warrant. The Court went on to state that only limited medical procedures were allowed and that although "the Constitution does not forbid the States minor intrusions into an individual's body under stringently limited conditions, [this] in no way indicates that it permits more substantial intrusions, or intrusions under other conditions."

In *Winston* v. *Lee,* 470 U.S. 753 (1985), the Court allowed a robbery suspect to refuse surgery to remove a bullet in his shoulder, a bullet the police wanted to use as evidence against him. The Court's analysis, represented in Figure 11.1, reasoned that although there were no apparent grave health risks of undergoing surgery, in balancing an individual's right to bodily integrity when weighed against the state's need for

FIGURE 11.1   Fourth Amendment bodily intrusion analysis.

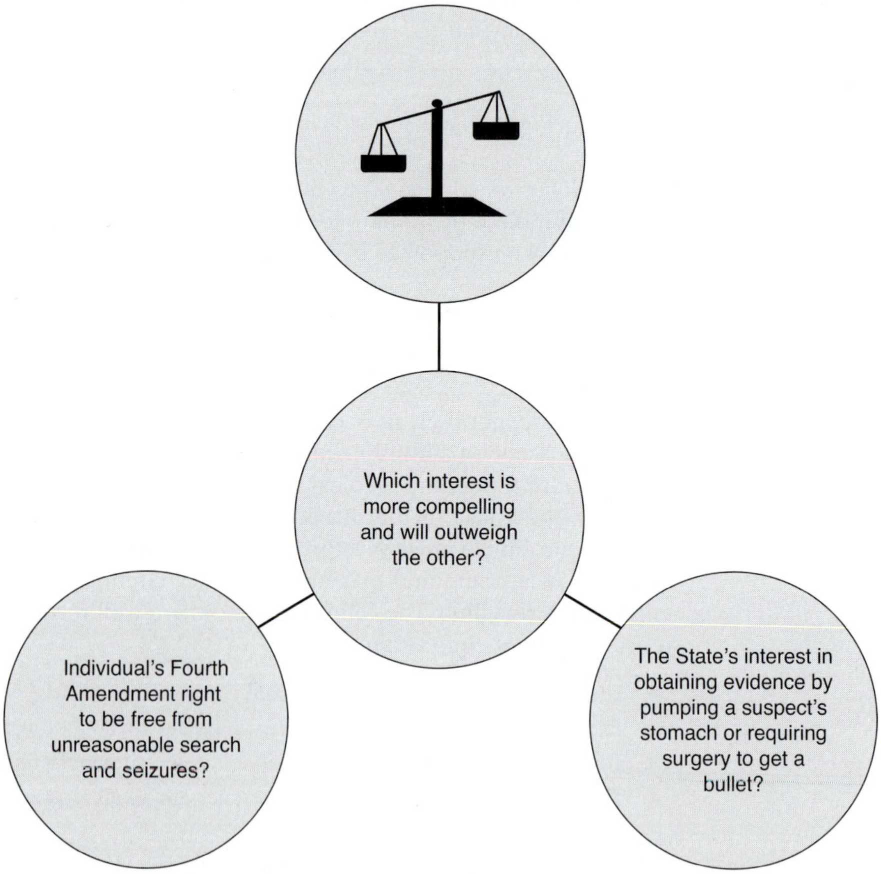

Which interest is more compelling and will outweigh the other?

Individual's Fourth Amendment right to be free from unreasonable search and seizures?

The State's interest in obtaining evidence by pumping a suspect's stomach or requiring surgery to get a bullet?

evidence, the state "failed to demonstrate that it would be 'reasonable' under the terms of the Fourth Amendment to search for evidence of this crime by means of the contemplated surgery."

8. Hot Pursuit

Rule of Law: The police need not stop a chase when they are in "hot pursuit" because the suspect enters a building, dwelling, or other structure.

A sister to exigent circumstances is the hot pursuit warrant exception. **Hot pursuit** allows officers to seize/arrest a suspect without a warrant when the suspect may escape or pose a danger to the public if left on the street. A suspect cannot run from the police who have probable cause to arrest her and then thumb her nose at them from the doorway and shout, "You can't come in without a warrant!" before she dashes inside. The U.S. Supreme Court recognized police authority to arrest someone in hot pursuit without the need for a warrant in *Warden* v. *Hayden,* 387 U.S. 294 (1967). In this case, police had probable cause to believe that a robber was inside a house he had entered a few minutes before, and they justified their warrantless entry of the home to arrest him on the basis of the exigent circumstances that he might flee or pose a danger to the public. Even if a suspect was first seen in the doorway of her home and ran inside to escape arrest, officers could follow her inside in some jurisdictions under the basis of hot pursuit.

Courts impose some limits on the hot pursuit exception to the warrant requirement:[16]

1. Officers must have probable cause to believe that the person they are chasing has committed a crime and is on the premises they are entering
2. Officers must believe that the suspect will escape or harm others if he or she is not immediately arrested
3. The initial power to arrest must be lawful, as in the plain view exception, and the officers must be on the premises legally for the ensuing search to be lawful
4. Hot pursuit only applies to serious felonies and misdemeanors, not minor traffic offenses
5. After the suspect has been arrested, the scope of the ensuing search may only be incident to that arrest and may not be expanded to areas where a warrant would be required.

In the chapter-opening scenario, Officer Jones could follow Jimmy into his apartment without a warrant following the chase of Jimmy that began on the street. The officer had probable cause to believe that Jimmy had committed or was about to commit a drug crime that would justify an arrest. Had there been only reasonable suspicion and not probable cause, the hot pursuit that extended inside the house would have been unlawful.

9. Good Faith

What happens when a police officer executes a legally deficient warrant while simply doing his job? In the Supreme Court case *United States* v. *Leon,* 468 U.S. 897 (1984), the Court held that evidence would be admissible even if seized pursuant to a deficient but "**facially valid**" warrant that appeared correct and legally sufficient. If the officers executed such a warrant in **good faith,** meaning that they had no unscrupulous motive in executing the warrant, and if the officers had no reason to believe that the warrant was defective, the evidence they seized, though illegally seized, would be admissible. The exclusionary rule is to prevent police from profiting from their own misconduct. If the officers are acting in good faith there is no sense punishing them by operation of the exclusionary rule. If the police seize evidence by virtue of a mistake in the warrant,

---

[16]Information derived from J. L. Worrall. *Criminal Procedure: From First Contact to Appeal* (Upper Saddle River, NJ: Pearson Education, 2004).

they are not acting in bad faith, searching illegally to obtain a prosecutorial advantage over a suspect. But if it was clear by the warrant's face that probable cause was lacking, or if the warrant failed to "particularize the place to be searched or the things to be seized," then the good-faith exception would not apply.

Jones v. *Wilhelm,* 425 F.3d 455 (7th Cir. 2005), was a case that was similar to *Groh* v. *Ramirez,* 540 U.S. 551 (2004), discussed in chapter 10, in which the federal agent was personally liable for serving a defective warrant that did not particularly describe the things to be seized. *Jones* concerned a police officer who was sued for entering the wrong apartment because he relied on a search warrant that did not sufficiently differentiate between two apartments on the same floor. The officer assumed, due to his own surveillance and observations, that he was entering the correct apartment and he believed his observations cured the warrant's defect. Finding the officer had no immunity from a lawsuit brought by the apartment's residents, the federal Court of Appeals held that a reasonable officer would have known his actions were unlawful. The court said the *Leon* good-faith exception did not apply because the officer knew that the warrant was defective and executed it anyway. The fact that the officer quickly realized he had the wrong apartment and called off the search did not make the search legal.

The precedent established by the *Leon* and *Groh* cases to apply to future cases is that any time a defective warrant is issued and executed in states recognizing the good-faith exception to the warrant requirement, the officer executing the warrant must ensure that the warrant is not so facially defective. Otherwise, he or she may be personally responsible for money damage to the people whose possessions were wrongfully searched and seized with the bad warrant.

As discussed in chapter 1, the Constitution's Supremacy Clause provides that the U.S. Supreme Court's decision in *Leon* would authorize in every jurisdiction the admission at a defendant's trial of improperly seized evidence. But the Tenth Amendment provides that all powers not specifically delegated to the federal government are left to the states. All states have their own constitutions, which may or may not mirror the federal Constitution. States and their respective legislators and court systems can make and interpret laws that benefit their citizens more than the federal government. For example, a state may decide not to have a death penalty. Even though the federal government allows this penalty, 14 states have rejected it, giving their citizens more protection from government power.[17] Many states do not recognize the good-faith exception to the exclusionary rule because their constitutions place a higher value on their citizens' expectations of privacy.[18] Pennsylvania does not recognize the good-faith exception. In states that do not recognize the good-faith exception, if officers make a mistake in drafting the warrant, the evidence seized pursuant to that warrant is inadmissible at the defendant's trial even though the officers acted in good faith in executing the warrant. Read the brief excerpt from the case *Commonwealth* v. *Edmunds,* taking particular care to follow the Pennsylvania Supreme Court's reasoning as to why the state constitution affords Pennsylvanians more protection of their right to privacy.

---

[17]*See* footnote 18 in chapter 14 for a list of states without the death penalty.

[18]States that refuse to recognize a good faith exception pursuant to the *Leon* holding are: Connecticut, Idaho, Michigan, New Jersey, New Mexico, New York, Pennsylvania, and Vermont. The following states recognize the *Leon* good faith exception to the search warrant requirement: Arkansas, California, Indiana, Kansas, Kentucky, Louisiana, Missouri, Ohio, South Dakota, Texas, Utah, Virginia, and Wyoming. States that have not explicitly rejected *Leon*, but nevertheless have refused to recognize its applicability, are Arizona, Florida, Georgia, Illinois, Minnesota, Mississippi, North Carolina, Washington, and Wisconsin. Even though the *Leon* holding is federal law and, by operation of the Supremacy Clause, federal law trumps state law, states can grant their citizens more rights under their respective state constitutions. *See* B. Latzer *State Constitutional Criminal Law,* §2.11–14.

BOX 11.5

Commonwealth v. *Edmunds*, 526 Pa. 374 (1991)

FACTS

[T]he search warrant failed to establish probable cause that the marijuana would be at the location to be searched on the date it was issued and . . . [the] warrant failed to set forth with specificity the date upon which the anonymous informants observed the marijuana [at the place to be searched]. [The marijuana was introduced at defendant's trial on the basis that, although the warrant was defective, the officers acted in good faith so the evidence seized should still be admissible against the defendant at his trial].

ISSUE

[W]hether Pennsylvania should adopt the "good-faith" exception to the exclusionary rule as articulated by the United States Supreme Court in the case *United States* v. *Leon*.

HOLDING

We conclude that a "good-faith" exception to the exclusionary rule would frustrate the guarantees embodied in Article I, Section 8, of the Pennsylvania Constitution.

RATIONALE

The linch-pin that has been developed to determine whether it is appropriate to issue a search warrant is the test of probable cause. . . . It is designed to protect us from unwarranted and even vindictive incursions upon our privacy. It insulates from dictatorial and tyrannical rule by the state, and preserves the concept of democracy that assures the freedom of citizens. This concept is second to none in its importance in delineating the dignity of the individual living in a free society. . . . Citizens in this Commonwealth possess such rights, even where a police officer in "good faith" carrying out his or her duties inadvertently invades the privacy or circumvents the strictures of probable cause.

CONCLUSION

To adopt a "good faith" exception to the exclusionary rule, we believe, would virtually emasculate those clear safeguards which have been carefully developed under the Pennsylvania Constitution over the past 200 years.

10. Inventory Searches

Rule of Law: **For inventory searches to be valid, they should be conducted pursuant to department regulations.**

Probable cause is not necessary for police to conduct an inventory search of a suspect's property once it enters police custody. An **inventory search** is a warrantless official cataloguing of items seized, most often from automobiles impounded at police stations. Once a car has been impounded at the police station, the police must safeguard individual property from theft or destruction. The legal requirements for an inventory search are that police departments have established unwritten rules and regulations for searching and cataloguing items found pursuant to such a search and that they follow those rules and regulations. In *South Dakota* v. *Opperman*, 428 U.S. 364 (1976), an illegally parked car was towed to a police lot and impounded. As officers conducted an inventory search of the vehicle's contents, they discovered marijuana in an unlocked glove compartment; the defendant was convicted of unlawful possession of drugs. The defendant appealed on the basis that the officers needed a warrant to look in the glove compartment during the search, but the U.S. Supreme Court held that no warrant was required for inventory searches because such actions fell under the police "community caretaking" function to protect property. The public policy for warrantless inventory searches is that they protect both a suspect's property and the police from baseless allegations of theft. Inventory searches also protect the police by allowing them to discover potentially dangerous items that can harm them or others. The legal requirements for an inventory search of an automobile are as follows:

1. The search follows a lawful impoundment of the vehicle
2. The search is of a routine nature, and
3. The search may not be a pretext for evidence gathering.

The police department policy for conducting inventory searches should be specific about the scope or limits of police authority to search.[19] The nature of the impound facilities matter little, as the high Court said "the police may still wish to protect themselves of the owners of the lot against false claims of theft or dangerous instrumentalities." In *Colorado* v. *Bertine,* 479 U.S. 367 (1987), the high Court held that closed containers such as briefcases, glove compartments, and trunks could be searched pursuant to an inventory search. Police cannot and should not use inventory searches to conduct further investigation for which a warrant would be typically required. Nevertheless, if the inventory search is conducted pursuant to lawful regulations, the officers' subjective motives for conducting the search are irrelevant and any contraband found will be lawfully seized and admissible at trial.

If contraband is discovered during an inventory search, then a more extensive search is permissible, but it still has to be based on the impracticality of securing a warrant. In *Florida* v. *Meyers,* 466 U.S. 380 (1984), the U.S. Supreme Court held that a second subsequent search was lawful because the constitutional authority to conduct the first inventory search was based on the administrative regulatory routine of the search. But the Court allows such warrantless inventory searches only when they follow clear guidelines adopted by the police department, which need not follow any set rules, but must be clear, followed, and understood by the officers conducting the search.

11. Special Needs Searches

The special needs exception to the warrant requirement allows for suspicionless searches when designed to serve "special needs, beyond the normal need for law enforcement."

a. Drug Testing in Schools

Students have a lesser expectation of privacy in a school setting than in general public areas, but they do not leave their constitutional rights at the steps of the schoolhouse door.[20] But when schoolteachers and administrators in Vernonia, Oregon, noticed increased drug use and disciplinary problems among students, the school board initiated a policy requiring student athletes, who were believed to be the leaders of the drug subculture, to undergo drug testing performed both at the beginning of their sport season and at least 10% of the time thereafter. The policy was implemented with the advice and consent of the parents. One student and his parents filed suit on Fourth Amendment grounds, and the U.S. Supreme Court decided in favor of the school district in *Vernonia School District 47J* v. *Acton,* 515 U.S. 646 (1995). The decision was made on the basis that the special needs for school discipline and the public safety needs in a public setting such as a school lead to a decreased expectation of privacy for students. Further legal justification for allowing the student search was that such a search was minimally invasive on the students'

---

[19]*Florida* v. *Wells,* 495 U.S. 1 (1990).

[20]*Tinker et al.* v. *Des Moines Independent Community School District et al.,* 393 U.S. 503 (1969).

expectation of privacy. Associate Justice Sandra Day O'Connor disagreed with the majority's holding to abandon the requirement of individualized suspicion of wrongdoing to conduct a search of someone—here, student athletes who were under no suspicion that they used drugs—and wrote in her dissent that "mass suspicionless searches are *per se* unreasonable within the meaning of the Fourth Amendment."

b. Drug Testing of Government Employees

In general, government employees have a lesser expectation of privacy in the terms of their employment and the tools of their work, their desks, their offices, and their computer files than do employees of private institutions. Since government employees do not "own" the equipment they use, which was bought and paid for with tax dollars collected from the public, public employees cannot claim an absolute privacy right in work-related items as they would in their own personal computers and files. In order to work for, or be promoted within, some government agencies, employees must undergo drug testing. When Customs Service employees challenged the Treasury Department's drug-testing program as a precondition to promotion eligibility, they lost their challenge. The Court held that the drug testing was legal because the drug results were not going to be used in criminal prosecutions, because it was necessary to promote drug-free people to positions of power, and because the nature of the intrusion into personal privacy (providing a urine sample in a cup) was minimal. *National Treasury Employees Union et al.* v. *Von Raab,* 489 U.S. 656 (1989).

c. DNA Collection

What about the collection and storage of genetic information of convicted offenders for inclusion in a national database for use in catching and convicting perpetrators? Is it a violation of the Fourth Amendment to collect blood for DNA typing where no exigency exists? Each individual's genetic make-up was determined at birth and will remain relatively unchanged until death. What legal justification can the government use to collect blood samples in the absence of probable cause that a particular person committed a specific crime but belongs, instead, to a general class of convicted offenders? The Supreme Court has deemed the involuntary taking of a biological sample a "search" under the Fourth Amendment. But the lower federal circuits are split on whether such a search falls under the "special needs" doctrine or whether it is legal under the "totality of the circumstances" approach.

The U.S. Supreme Court adopted a totality of the circumstances approach to determining the legality of warrantless searches of convicted offenders on probation. In *Samson* v. *California,* 126 S. Ct. 2193 (2006), the U.S. Supreme Court upheld a methamphetamine possession conviction based on a warrantless search of a parolee. The reasoning was that under state law, every prisoner on parole, as a condition of parole, may be subject to search with or without a warrant or just cause. The Court noted that probation is still punishment and those on probation "do not enjoy 'the absolute liberty'" of other citizens. It also found probation searches necessary to promote the legitimate governmental interests of public safety. Applying the *Samson* precedent to a case in which Leo Weikert was on supervised release and was ordered to give a blood sample to contribute to a DNA profile database, the First Circuit Court of Appeals held that such demand for a sample was legal under the totality approach, even though a minority of jurisdictions use the special needs approach to justify their demands. *United States* v. *Weikert,* 504 F. 3d 1 (1st Cir. 2007). The justification advanced by the government for DNA collection is, first, that DNA collection is a special need for law enforcement to maintain retrievable information in databases that can identify or eliminate suspects on the basis of their DNA, which "increase[s] the accuracy of the criminal justice system." Second, DNA collection serves a compelling state interest in assuring that guilty individuals are convicted and deters them from recidivism since they know that they will be caught if crime scene samples match their DNA. Third, incarcerated criminals and those on probation have diminished privacy rights; collection of a DNA sample constitutes a minimal intrusion of the privacy interest that they have in their genetic code.

12. Airports/Subways

Rule of Law: There is a diminished expectation of privacy for those who travel in public.

On July 22, 2005, in response to coordinated bombings on London's railway system, New York City implemented a random search procedure on its subways. Petitioners who rode the trains in New York challenged the mass suspicionless searches. The Court of Appeals for the Second Circuit confirmed the trial court's decision that "[t]he need to prevent a terrorist bombing of the New York City subway system is a governmental interest of the very highest order" that outweighed the minimal intrusion to passengers who used the 468 subway stations.[21] A similar rationale supports the heightened security in airports, and airport screening searches are legal administrative searches. The courts are clear that individuals who feel burdened by the brief intrusion on their liberty from using public trains and planes may travel by private means. But the changing nature of mass attacks using public conveyances justifies the suspicionless searches when weighed against minimal government intrusion on a person's privacy interests.

In *United States* v. *Aukai,* 497 F.3d 955 (9th Cir. 2007), the federal court of appeals held that an airline passenger who successfully walks through the x-ray machine and is subjected to a "secondary screening" by a Transportation Security Administration officer cannot choose to forego the screening and abandon his flight. Airport security was about to discover the contents of the pants pocket of defendant Aukai when he tried to leave the airport. When security found a methamphetamine pipe and Aukai was convicted of drug possession, he challenged the legality of the search. But the court found in favor of the government, stating "The constitutionality of an airport screening search, however, does not depend on consent . . . and requiring that a potential passenger be allowed to revoke consent to an ongoing airport security search makes little sense in a post–9/11 world." Courts today are more lenient in granting law enforcement the authority to protect public transportation venues and avenues.

13. Border Searches

Even before the foreign terrorist attacks on American soil on September 11, 2001, America has always had a vested interest in protecting the integrity of its borders.

In *United States* v. *Montoya de Hernandez,* 473 U.S. 531 (1985), the U.S. Supreme Court stated: "Routine searches of the persons and effects of entrants [at the border] are not subject to any requirement of reasonable suspicion, probable cause, or a warrant . . [O]ne's expectation of privacy [is] less at the border." Such a reduced expectation of privacy extends to the navigable waterways of the United States, highway checkpoints at the borders, and international airports, on the basic assumption that people entering the country enjoy a lesser expectation of privacy. By willfully and lawfully entering the country, people consent to be searched and no reasonable suspicion is required. The waiving of these individual rights allows the government to protect national security and to combat international drug smuggling.

After 9/11, the Supreme Court was willing to allow greater latitude to officers at inspection stations at border crossings. In *United States* v. *Cortez-Rocha,* 394 F.3d

---

[21]*MacWade* v. *Kelly,* 460 F.3d 260 (2d Cir. 2006).

1115 (9th Cir. 2005), the Ninth Circuit Court of Appeals held that removing and cutting open a truck's spare tire at the border was a reasonable search. Inspectors discovered over 42 kilograms of marijuana in a tire, and the defendant argued that since the customs officials had no individualized suspicion that he was engaged in criminal activity, the evidence should be suppressed. The Court rejected the defendant's claims and focused on whether cutting the tire destroyed the vehicle. Finding that it did not, it deemed the search constitutional. Referring to earlier U.S. Supreme Court precedent in which the Court found the removal and dismantling of a vehicle's gas tank constitutional in *United States* v. *Flores-Montano,* 541 U.S. 149 (2004), the federal appeals court analogized the spare tire to a closed container which the inspectors, who the Court said were intelligent and respectful, should be free to inspect in furtherance of their duties. Justice Clarence Thomas criticized such approach in *Flores-Montano* for giving "the government *carte blanche* to search and destroy all personal property at the border that does not affect vehicular operation." He concluded that, although safeguarding the border was of paramount concern, protection of Fourth Amendment rights remained a priority, especially in times "of great national distress."

No particularized suspicion of criminal activity is required to search at the border including the contents of a traveler's laptop computer. In July 2005, Michael Arnold arrived in Los Angeles on a flight from the Philippines and was asked by a U.S. Customs and Border Patrol agent to turn on his laptop. The officer noted two files labeled "Kodak pictures" and "Kodak memories" that, when clicked on, revealed one photo of two naked adult women. This discovery prompted agents to interrogate Arnold and further search the laptop's contents, which led to the discovery of child pornography. Arnold was charged for the child pornography and moved to suppress the evidence on the grounds that the search of the laptop was unreasonable in violation of the Fourth Amendment. The judge agreed with Arnold and granted his motion, stating, "[A]n invasive border search must be limited in scope and the scope must meet the reasonableness standard of the Fourth Amendment." *United States* v. *Arnold,* 454 F.Supp.2d 999 (C.D. Cal. 2006). The government appealed and after oral argument columnist Adam Liptak of *The New York Times* wrote that the appellate judges "seemed persuaded that a computer is just a container and deserves no special protection from searches at the border. The same information in hard-copy form [the judge's questions suggested] would doubtless be subject to search."[22] Indeed, on April 21, 2008, the appellate court did hold the evidence of child pornography could be introduced and used against Arnold at his trial finding reasonable suspicion is not required for customs officials to search laptops or other electronic storage devices at the border (2008 U.S. App. LEXIS 8590).

The USA PATRIOT Act[23] has special provisions that relate to entry into the country through its borders, but surely have an impact on who may be detained without probable cause. Section 412 permits federal law enforcement to take into custody any "alien" (noncitizen) who the officer has "reasonable grounds to believe" is "engaged in any other activity that endangers the national security of the United States."[24] The alien can be held for seven days, after which he must be released, charged criminally, or deported. If the alien is held on immigration rather than criminal charges, he may be held indefinitely.

---

[22]Adam Liptak. "If Your Hard Drive Could Testify . . ." *The New York Times*, January 7, 2008, p. A12.

[23]Uniting and Strengthening America by Providing Appropriate Tools Required to Intercept and Obstruct Terrorism Act of 2001, ("USA PATRIOT Act"), Public Law 107-56, 2001.

[24]USA PATRIOT Act.

FIGURE 11.2 Exceptions under the Fourth Amendment.

Exceptions to Probable Cause requirement	CASE LAW	Exception to Warrant Requirement
Search incident to arrest	*Chimel* v. *California,* (1969)	Search incident to arrest
Border searches	*U.S.* v. *Flores-Montano* (2004)	Border searches
Investigative detention	*Terry* v. *Ohio,* (1968)	Investigative detention
Consent	*Schneckloth* v. *Bustamonte,* (1973)	Consent
Airports	*U.S.* v. *Davis,* (1973)	Airports
Subways	*MacWade* v. *Kelley,* (2006)	Subways
Drug testing in school	*Vernonia Sch. Dist. 47J* v. *Acton,* (1995)	Drug testing in school
Plain view	*Texas* v. *Brown,* (1983)	Plain view
Open Fields	*Oliver* v. *United States,* (1984)	Open Fields
Sobriety Checkpoints	*Michigan* v. *Long,* (1983)	Sobriety Checkpoints
Information Checkpoints	*Illinois* v. *Lidster,* (2004)	Information checkpoints
Stop and Identify	*Hiibel* v. *Nevada,* (2004)	Stop and Identify
Inventory Searches	*Colorado* v. *Bertine,* (1987)	Inventory Searches
Special Needs	*Ferguson* v. *City of Charleston,* (2001)	Special Needs
	Cupp v. *Murphy,* (1973)	Exigent Circumstances
	Carroll v. *U.S.,* (1925)	Automobile searches
	U.S. v. *Raymond,* (1998)	Plain Touch
	Maryland v. *Buie,* (1990)	Protective Sweep

A list summarizing the most notable exceptions to the warrant requirement and the probable cause requirement is found in Figure 11.2.

14. Racial and Drug Courier Profiling

Rule of Law: As long as a traffic stop is legitimate (for example, for a broken taillight or a speeding violation), the officer's subjective or personal motives for making the stop do not matter.

Racial profiling occurs when the police use race or ethnicity as a factor in determining whether they will stop someone for a brief investigatory detention to determine whether criminal activity is afoot. With respect to the stopping and searching of cars, an officer's motives for the vehicle stop are irrelevant. If officers pull a car over for a traffic stop as a pretext to conduct a search for drugs for which they have no probable cause, their original motives do not matter if, indeed, they discover evidence that creates probable cause justifying the search. In *Whren* v. *United States,* 517 U.S. 806 (1996), vice-squad officers stopped a car for a traffic violation and discovered drugs. After being convicted for possession of crack cocaine, the defendants claimed on appeal that the police used the traffic violation as a "pretext" [a false reason] to pull the car over to search for drugs. The Supreme Court held that the officers' motives for the traffic stop were irrelevant, as long as the stop was lawful (lawful reasons are, for example, because the driver failed to stop at a stop sign long enough, failed to use her turn signal, or crossed over the yellow line while driving). The Court noted that "the constitutional reasonableness of traffic stops" does not depend "on the actual motivations of the individual officers involved." The officers' good or bad faith remains relevant to the warrant exception analysis, but not for traffic stops. In our opening-chapter scenario, the officers who were following the manager's car that ran a stop sign had legal authority to stop the car even if they were just following him to develop evidence of illegal drug activity.

Since the officers' motives in stopping vehicles are irrelevant as long as the person stopped has violated the law, how can one prove racial profiling? In New Jersey, the Attorney General—who is one of the few Attorneys General in the country responsible for all law enforcement officers in the state—conducted a study which found that, of all the consensual searches of cars on the New Jersey Turnpike, 77.2% were searches of people of color.[25] But the New Jersey statistics offer no benchmark as to whether traffic stops correlated with race correlate with finding illegal drugs. In *State* v. *Carty,* 170 N.J. 632 (2002), a New Jersey court imposed strict limits on consensual automobile searches, requiring that police have "reasonable and articulable suspicion" of criminal activity before the stop. The court said, "In the context of motor vehicle stops, where the individual is at the side of the road and confronted by a uniformed officer seeking to search his or her vehicle, it is not a stretch of the imagination to assume that the individual feels compelled to consent."

Ed Lemmon, head of the New Jersey Troopers Union, has said that drug possession is colorblind. "I've stopped white guys in pickup trucks with a camper compartment on top. Their chest is pounding; they're sweating, though it's the dead of winter. They won't look at you"—all signs of concealing drugs. Other indications that the driver's car has been outfitted to transport narcotics are windows that won't go all the way down (possibly indicating drugs in the doors), only one key in the ignition and no key ring, passengers not knowing each other's names, and passengers giving officers different stories about their supposed destination. One sergeant said about drug-dealing criminals, "Thank God they're stupid, or we'd be out of a job."[26]

The **drug courier profile** is an abstract of characteristics found to be typical of persons transporting illegal drugs. In *Florida* v. *Royer,* 460 U.S. 491 (1983), the detective was attracted by the following facts, which were considered to match the profile:

1. Royer was carrying American Tourister luggage that appeared to be heavy
2. He was between the ages of 25–35
3. He was casually dressed
4. He appeared pale and nervous and continually scanned his surroundings
5. He paid for his plane ticket in cash with a large number of bills
6. On the luggage identification card, he placed only his name and destination, not a full address and telephone number.

On the basis of these factors that comprised a profile of a typical drug courier—one paid to transport and deliver drugs—detectives detained Royer and discovered the drugs. He appealed and the U.S. Supreme Court upheld his conviction on the basis that the initial investigatory detention of him was lawful to give the officers time to either confirm or dispel their suspicions that he was carrying drugs. One federal court noted, "drug courier profile characteristics are often useful in focusing the attention of a law enforcement official on a particular individual and may be relied upon, in conjunction with other individualized factors, to support a finding of reasonable suspicion." *United States* v. *Gonzales,* 842 F.2d 748 (5th Cir. 1988.)

---

[25]Attorney General of New Jersey, *Interim Report of the State Police Review Team Regarding Allegations of Racial Profiling.* http://www.state.nj.us/lps/intm_419.pdf.

[26]Heather MacDonald. *Are Cops Racist?* (Chicago: Ivan R. Dee, 2003).

Applying the Rule of Law to the Facts: Is it permissible to stop someone who matches a courier profile?

- A woman arrived in Detroit from a drug source city, Los Angeles. She was the last person to disembark from the plane, she looked furtively around her at all times indicating her nervousness, and she did not claim any luggage. Is it legal to stop her on the basis of these factors?

Yes, the U.S. Supreme Court found that the combination of factors was sufficient to justify a brief investigatory detention and agents did not violate the Fourth Amendment in stopping her. *United States* v. *Mendenhall,* 446 U.S. 544 (1980).

II. Key Terms and Phrases

- automobile searches
- border searches
- closed containers
- common enterprise
- consent
- curtilage
- drug courier profiling

- drug testing
- exceptions to the warrant requirement
- exigent circumstances
- hot pursuit
- inventory search
- investigatory detention

- open fields
- plain feel
- plain view
- protective sweep
- racial profiling
- search incident to arrest
- special needs searches

III. Summary

1. **The legal basis for exceptions to the warrant requirement:** There are many exceptions to the warrant requirement. **Consent** of the suspect to a search must be voluntary and must not be the product of a submission to lawful authority. A **search incident to an arrest** may be conducted without a warrant and covers the person arrested and the area within his immediate control. The same standard applies to a person arrested in or near his car, even if he is handcuffed and sitting in the back of a patrol car.

2. **How far officers can go during a search to protect their safety:** As a general rule, if the officers have time to secure a warrant, then they should do so unless **exigent [emergency] circumstances** are present—for instance, when there is a likelihood that evidence will be destroyed or evaporate or when the safety of the officers or the public is in issue. Additionally, officers who are in **hot pursuit** have a right to chase a fleeing suspect indoors without needing to obtain a warrant. If the place to be searched has a lower expectation of privacy than a home (for example, a car) or if the person's status allows the government to intrude on that person's privacy more freely (for example, if the person is a student, convict, or probationer), a warrant to search may not be required. Because the language of the Fourth Amendment protects "papers, effects, houses," officers do not need a warrant to seize things in **plain view,** or on the basis of **plain touch,** or items that are in **open fields,** provided that the officers are on the premises legally and the evidence to be seized is obvious con-

traband. Officers may conduct a **protective sweep** in a home on the basis of specific and articulable facts that an armed and dangerous person is on the premises, as long as the area of the sweep is limited to the immediate area of the arrest and places within the premises where an armed person could be hiding.

3. **Automobile searches:** Because **automobiles** are mobile and heavily regulated, officers need not secure a warrant to conduct searches if probable cause exists. Due to the minimal intrusion on privacy interests and the government's need to stop drunk drivers or ask questions about recent crime, a warrant is not required at **driving checkpoints,** but random drug interdiction efforts require individualized suspicion and probable cause to search. **Inventory searches** must be conducted pursuant to a specific police protocol (although it need not be written) to be lawful.

4. **The legal justification for special searches: Special needs** searches involve the unique needs of law enforcement balanced against a lesser expectation of privacy in bodily fluids based on someone's status as a student, a government employee, or a prisoner/probationer. Searches at **airports** and on **subways** and at the country's **borders** are an extension of the special needs doctrine to prevent random attacks on public conveyances. **Racial and drug courier profiling** is used as an investigative tool to stop and ask questions of people on the basis of the belief that people of certain racial backgrounds are more likely to commit crimes or that people with certain behaviors

evidenced at public transportation sites may be engaged in criminal activity. The practice of using such profiles as a law enforcement tool has been generally condemned, but officers are allowed to stop people briefly in the context of an investigatory definition.

IV. Discussion Questions

1. How can law enforcement officers on the street determine, at a moment's notice, whether something in a pocket, especially in an oversize winter jacket or oversized pair of pants, is a weapon that will harm the officer and needs to be removed for officer safety or illegal contraband that the officer needs probable cause to remove from a suspect's pockets? Should the suspect's pockets be emptied as a matter of course for officer safety? What is the danger to the public if we allow officers the right to empty pockets without probable cause?

2. Do you believe that people consent when police ask whether they can search their homes or cars because they are afraid their refusal might be interpreted as guilt? Should citizens feel guilty for exercising the constitutional rights to be free from unreasonable searches and seizures? What social forces have contributed to the belief that if someone refuses a police request, the officers will get him anyway? Be specific in your answer.

3. How do officers differentiate between items that can be found in open spaces or with the aid of a flashlight and items that can be found only with a device for enhanced surveillance, such as night vision goggles and an extremely sensitive eavesdropping device? What well-defined legal principles can officers reference in making their decisions about the legality of their searches?

4. What are your thoughts on the good-faith exception to the warrant requirement? Does the exception exonerate officers who might be acting in bad faith, but simply claim that they were not? If a warrant lacked probable cause and the officers were aware of the defect, does the ability to claim that they were acting in good faith save the search anyway? What mechanism would prevent government abuses in jurisdictions that recognize the exception?

5. Why is racial or drug courier profiling so harmful if it works? If law enforcement officers stop someone on the basis of a profile and do find drugs, does that fact confirm and celebrate the need for such profiles, rather than detract from the reasons of using them?

V. Problem-Solving Exercises

1. Assume that a roadblock is set up not to obtain evidence of a recent crime but to actually find the perpetrator of a recent spate of robberies. Officers expect to identify the offender due to his nervousness, answers to police questions, or otherwise suspicious behavior. Is such a roadblock legal?

2. A husband and wife owned a home in rural Kentucky. The wife was a homemaker and did all the housekeeping and laundry. She often placed clean clothes in her husband's drawers and they both shared one closet. One day, police knocked on the door and asked for consent to search the home for marijuana. The wife, secure in the fact that she had nothing to hide, said yes. Her husband was in the bedroom and unequivocally refused consent to search. The police conducted the search based on the wife's consent and discovered a cache of automatic weapons that had obviously been altered to increase their shooting range in violation of federal law. The husband was charged with federal gun offenses and moved to suppress the guns on the basis that his wife's consent did not override his refusal. If you were the judge, how would you decide the case? Be sure to discuss all applicable legal issues necessary to properly decide the case.

3. On the basis of information received that a disgruntled high school student was "planning something big" at school in retaliation for being treated poorly by a fellow group of students, school administrators brought in bomb-sniffing dogs and had the dogs sniff all of the lockers. A dog alerted on the locker of student Patty Smith and the principal opened her locker and found an ounce of marijuana. Smith has moved to suppress the marijuana on the basis that the school conducted an unlawful search. You are the judge. Should you grant or deny Smith's motion? Explain your answer fully.

4. Officers came to Bob's motel room and arrested him for having a firearm within the city limits, a crime. Then they proceeded to search his room and found evidence of drug manufacturing in the bathroom. One officer said, "Where there's drugs and guns, there must be other people around. Let's conduct a protective sweep." They drew their revolvers and opened all the drawers and closets. Inside the closet, they found

Pedro hiding. Inside one dresser drawer, they found packets of heroin. Bob and Pedro were arrested and charged with drug possession and conspiracy to manufacture drugs. Bob claims that his consent to search was coerced, so the gun and drug evidence should be suppressed, while the officers claim that Bob's consent was valid and they discovered the evidence in plain view, so it should be admissible. Pedro claims that the protective sweep was conducted illegally and, therefore, that his arrest was unlawful. Which side is correct, the defense or the state?

5. Four African-American and Hispanic men were driving a beat-up Toyota Corolla on the interstate leading from New York to Florida when they were stopped for speeding. Police stopped this particular car because when they passed the men going in the opposite direction, the men all craned their necks to see whether the officers had noticed them. The driver could not verify his address nor did he have a registration for the car. The officer noticed that the roof of the car looked like it had been raised four inches and then welded back on. The officer ordered all of the men out of the car, frisked them, and then proceeded to search the interior of the car for weapons and drugs. He found a locked briefcase and asked the driver for the key. The driver gave the officer the key, and when the officer opened the briefcase, he discovered cocaine inside. All four men denied ownership of the drugs and all four have been charged with possession of the drugs. Was the stop and search lawful? Can the four defendants escape liability for drug possession by denying ownership of the contraband?

VI. World Wide Web Resources

American Civil Liberties Union

http://aclu.org/police/searchseizure/index.html/

VII. Additional Readings and Notes

Warrantless Arrests

Jack E. Call. "The Constitutionality of Warrantless Doorway Arrests." *Mississippi College Law Review,* Vol. 19 (1999), pp. 333–343.

Bryan Murray. "After *United States* v. *Vaneaton,* Does *Payton* v. *New York* Prevent Police from Making Routine Arrests Inside the Home?" *Golden State University Law Review,* Vol. 26 (1996), pp. 135–152.

CHAPTER

Interrogation and Confessions

12

"I didn't even know what those words [psychological coercion] meant, until I looked them up in the dictionary after I was accused of using it ... Shucks, I was just being a good old-fashioned cop, the only kind I know how to be ... I have never seen a prisoner physically abused, though I heard about those things in the early days ... That type of questioning just doesn't work. They'll just resist harder. You have to butter 'em up, sweet talk 'em, use that—what's the word?—psychological coercion."

—CAPTAIN LEAMING, A DETECTIVE WHOSE "CHRISTIAN BURIAL SPEECH" INDUCED A SUSPECT TO DIVULGE THE LOCATION OF HIS VICTIM'S BODY IN NIX V. WILLIAMS, 467 U.S. 431 (1984)

CHAPTER OBJECTIVES

Primary Concepts Discussed in This Chapter:

1. The genesis of the so-called *Miranda* warnings
2. The interrogation process
3. When *Miranda* warnings are required and when they are not
4. The legal consequences of violating the *Miranda* requirement
5. *Miranda* exceptions

CHAPTER OUTLINE

Feature: The Interrogation Process

I. THE EVOLUTION OF *MIRANDA* WARNINGS

1. Interrogation Techniques
Box 12.1 *Brown* v. *Mississippi*, 297 U.S. 278 (1936)
   a. Right to Consult with Counsel
   b. The Inbau & Reid Nine Steps of Interrogation
2. The *Miranda* Decision
Box 12.2 *Miranda* v. *Arizona*, 384 U.S. 436 (1966)
3. The *Miranda* Warnings and When to Advise
   a. Custody
   b. Interrogation
4. Trickery in Interrogations
   a. Voluntariness
Box 12.3 *Hardaway* v. *Young*, 302 F.3d 757 (7th Cir. 2002)
5. Invoking *Miranda*
   a. Right to Remain Silent
   b. Waiving *Miranda*
Box 12.4 *Missouri* v. *Seibert*, 542 U.S. 600 (2004)
   c. Exceptions to the Giving of *Miranda* Warnings
      i. *Miranda* at Investigatory Detentions and Traffic Stops

Feature: *Chapter-Opening Case Study: The Interrogation Process*

Al and Mike had been friends who had worked in the accounting office of a big shipping company.[1] In 1968, Al disappeared, along with a large sum of cash from the accounting office safe. Many years later, the cold case squad reopened the case and decided to focus their attention on Mike as they investigated the crime and Al's disappearance. Mike agreed to come to the police station for an interview [even if police encounter voluntary, once suspect feels he is not free to leave police presence he is in "custody" even if not formally under arrest]. The interviewers constructed a "scenario" in which Mike killed Al in a spontaneous fashion, and then they lied to Mike when they told him that the statute of limitations [the time allowed to initiate a court proceeding] had expired for Mike to be prosecuted for murder [in fact, there is no statute of limitations for murder]. Investigators also lied to Mike in telling him that he was their number one suspect and that they had a great deal of evidence such as fingerprints and an eyewitness linking him to Al's murder and disappearance [deception and lies are permissible interrogation techniques]. Police also told Mike that if he went to trial, it would take so long that all of Mike's savings would be depleted and his family's reputation would be ruined. After 30 minutes of questioning, Mike confessed to killing Al. Mike disclosed that he had killed Al after Al had discovered Mike stealing money. The investigator then gave Mike his rights pursuant to the Supreme Court's decision in *Miranda* v. *Arizona* (1964), and told Mike, "Okay, Mike, now I just want you to repeat what you just told us and I'm going to take notes this time," whereupon Mike restated his entire confession [double interviewing, taking two confessions while "cleansing" the second one with the giving of *Miranda* violates the Constitution's Fifth Amendment].

During a later interrogation session about the robbery, Mike indicated that he was tired of talking, refused to talk any further, and said he wanted a lawyer. Police asked Mike whether he had any children. When Mike said he had a son who would turn two years old next Saturday, the detective said, "Well, the time you're looking at means you're not going to see him until he's 17, and by then he'll have a new daddy. You have one minute to tell us about the robbery and this will be your last chance" [police must "scrupu-

---

[1]Facts modified from *United States* v. *LeBran*, 363 F.3d 715 (8th Cir. 2004).

lously honor" a suspect's request to stop talking, and police may not reinitiate interrogation without warning suspect again of *Miranda* warnings; if a request for counsel is made, police may only resume the interview if a lawyer is present]. Mike then confessed to the robbery [since Mike had requested a lawyer during the interrogation for the murder, his right to counsel attached only to that offense and not to the robbery, even if the robbery was closely related to the murder]. At the suppression hearing to exclude his confessions, Mike claimed that his confession was involuntary because the investigators wore him down and that the double interviewing was unconstitutional. How should the court rule?

This chapter examines the police/citizen encounter and the law protecting citizens during custodial interrogations. A brief history of the evolution of the *Miranda* rights is provided to give the student a perspective on the protections of the Fifth and Sixth Amendments as well as interrogation techniques that may lead to false confessions.

I. THE EVOLUTION OF *MIRANDA* WARNINGS

The Fifth and Sixth Amendments trace their origin to British common law. The Fifth Amendment was specifically enacted as a direct result of the colonists' experience under the British Crown when officials used torture to extract confessions. The Amendment's mandate in part that "No person . . . shall be compelled in any criminal case to be a witness against himself" is commonly known as the privilege against self-incrimination. The Fifth Amendment forces the government to prove guilt with evidence other than what comes from the defendant's tongue.[2] At a criminal trial, the power of the defendant's own words introduced against him is unmistakable. Research on jury trials indicates that juries believe a defendant's confessions are tantamount to guilt for the crime and "A confession is a conviction."[3] Popular myth assumes that innocent people do not confess to something they did not do. Furthermore, once a suspect has confessed, the weight of guilt is not easily overcome by new evidence of innocence, and some players in the criminal justice system actively resist such evidence. In one Pennsylvania case, Bruce Godschalk was wrongfully convicted of rape, and after 15 years in jail, new DNA tests conclusively proved that he was not the source of semen found in the case. Godschalk's original prosecutor, Montgomery County district attorney Bruce L. Castor, Jr., refused to initiate court proceedings leading to his release. When asked about the legal justification for keeping an innocent man behind bars, Castor replied, "I have no scientific basis. I know because I trust my detective and his [Godschalk's] tape-recorded confession. Therefore the [DNA] results must be flawed until someone proves to me otherwise."[4] When further DNA testing confirmed that Godschalk was not the source of the semen, he was released from prison, despite Castor's lament, "I am not convinced that Bruce Godschalk is innocent" and that he had "no reason to doubt the validity of his confession."[5] Thus, once a suspect confesses, it is very hard to change people's minds about that person's guilt, even in the face of scientific evidence. The Fifth Amendment protects against compelled self-incrimination, but people are certainly free to confess to crimes that they commit. There are many police training manuals and conferences on the science of inducing confessions through interrogation.

---

[2]The privilege against self incrimination was deemed applicable to the states via the Fourteenth Amendment's due process clause. *Malloy* v. *Hogan*, 378 U.S. 1 (1964).

[3]Lawrence S. Wrightsman and Saul M. Kassin. *Confessions in the Courtroom* (Newbury Park, CA: Sage Publications, 1993).

[4]Sara Rimer. "Convict's DNA Sways Labs, Not a Determined Prosecutor." *The New York Times*, February 6, 2002, p. A14.

[5]Sara Rimer. "DNA Testing in Rape Case Frees Prisoner after 15 Years." *The New York Times*, February 15, 2002. http://www.truthinjustice.org/PA-DNA.htm.

A confession alone is not enough evidence to support a conviction. At trial, the prosecution has the burden of proving the ***corpus delicti***—the body—of a criminal offense. The *corpus delicti* may not be established by a confession alone. The requirement of additional evidence other than a confession proving that the defendant committed a crime relies on our "long history of judicial experience with confessions and the realization that sound law enforcement requires police investigations which extend beyond the words of the accused."[6] In a child abuse case, the defendant had her conviction overturned because the state offered no corroboration for her confession that she had put her mouth on the genitalia of a toddler for whom she was babysitting. *State* v. *Torwirt,* 9 Neb. App. 52 (2000). Without *corpus delicti,* there can be no successful prosecution.

1. Interrogation Techniques

Rule of Law: Interrogations of suspects are inherently coercive.

Early court decisions often excluded confessions from trial because of their limited reliability and the known use of tricks, promises, threats, and physical violence to elicit the confession. When police forces became organized in the early nineteenth century, their interrogation techniques were crude and brutal. From the 1860s onward, documented interrogation techniques called the "third degree" included

> Rubbing lighted cigars against a suspect's arm or neck; lifting, kicking, squeezing a suspect's testicles; dragging, pulling, or lifting a woman by her hair; enlisting a dentist to grind down and drill into the nerves of a suspect's molars . . . giving someone the taps: at thirty-second intervals, the suspect was struck with a rubber hose on the side of the head [which caused] considerable pain; administering tear gas; and tightening a necktie to choking point.[7]

From the 1930s to the 1960s, the Supreme Court overturned convictions that resulted from confessions coerced from the defendants by police brutality, on the grounds that such confessions violated the right to a fair trial. In the following case, *Brown* v. *Mississippi,* the Supreme Court decided that confessions obtained after physical torture were inconsistent with the Fourteenth Amendment's due process clause, not the Fifth Amendment self-incrimination clause. It was not until the 1960s that the protection afforded suspects by the Fifth Amendment applied not just to the federal government's actions, but to actions taken by the states.

BOX 12.1

Brown v. *Mississippi,* 297 U.S. 278 (1936)
Supreme Court of the United States

Chief Justice Hughes delivered the opinion of the Court.

FACTS

The crime with which these defendants, all ignorant negroes, are charged, was discovered about one o'clock P.M. on Friday, March 30, 1934. On that night one Dial, a deputy sheriff, accompanied by others, came to the home of Ellington, one of the defendants, and requested him to accompany them to the house of the deceased, and there a number of white men were gathered, who began to accuse the defendant of the crime. Upon his denial they seized him, and with the participation

---

[6]*Smith* v. *United States,* 348 U.S. 147 (1954).

[7]Richard A. Leo. "From Coercion to Deception: The Changing Nature of Police Interrogation in America." *Crime, Law & Social Change,* Vol. 18 (1992), pp. 35–59.

of the deputy they hanged him by a rope to the limb of a tree, and having let him down, they hung him again, and when he was let down the second time, and he still protested his innocence, he was tied to a tree and whipped, and still declining to accede to the demands that he confess, he was finally released and he returned with some difficulty to his home, suffering intense pain and agony. The record of the testimony shows that the signs of the rope on his neck were plainly visible during the so-called trial. A day or two thereafter the said deputy . . . returned to the home of the said defendant and arrested him . . . and again severely whipped the defendant, declaring that he would continue the whipping until he confessed, and the defendant then agreed to confess to such a statement as the deputy would dictate, and he did so, after which he was delivered to jail.

All this having been accomplished . . . when the defendants had been given time to recuperate somewhat from the tortures to which they had been subjected . . . [the deputies came] to hear the free and voluntary confession of these miserable and abject defendants. The court thereupon appointed counsel, and set the case for trial for the following morning at nine o'clock, and the defendants were returned to the jail in the adjoining county about thirty miles away. The defendants were brought to the courthouse of the county on . . . April 5th, and the so-called trial was opened, and was concluded on the next day, April 6, 1934, and resulted in a pretended conviction with death sentences.

ISSUE

The question in this case is whether convictions, which rest solely upon confessions shown to have been extorted by officers of the State by brutality and violence, are consistent with the due process of law required by the Fourteenth Amendment of the Constitution of the United States?

HOLDING

[No. Confessions may not be obtained by torture]. In the instant case, the trial court was fully advised by the undisputed evidence of the way in which the confessions had been procured. The trial court knew that there was no other evidence upon which conviction and sentence could be based. Yet it proceeded to permit conviction and to pronounce sentence . . . The court thus denied a federal right fully established and specially set up and claimed. . . .

REASONING

The State stresses the statement in *Twining* v. *New Jersey*, 211 U.S. 78 (1908), that "exemption from compulsory self-incrimination in the courts of the States is not secured by any part of the Federal Constitution.". . . Compulsion by torture to extort a confession is a different matter. The State may not permit an accused to be hurried to conviction under mob domination—where the whole proceeding is but a mask—without supplying corrective process. [T]he trial equally is a mere pretense where the state authorities have contrived a conviction resting solely upon confessions obtained by violence. The due process clause requires "that state action, whether through one agency or another, shall be consistent with the fundamental principles of liberty and justice which lie at the base of all our civil and political institutions." It would be difficult to conceive of methods more revolting to the sense of justice than those taken to procure the confessions of these petitioners, and the use of the confessions thus obtained as the basis for conviction and sentence was a clear denial of due process. [T]he court [has] said: "Coercing the supposed state's criminals into confessions and using such confessions so coerced from them against them in trials has been the curse of all countries. It was the chief inequity, the crowning infamy of the Star Chamber, and the Inquisition, and other similar institutions. The constitution recognized the evils that lay behind these practices and prohibited them in this country . . . The duty of maintaining constitutional rights of a person on trial for his life rises above mere rules of procedure and wherever the court is clearly satisfied that such violations exist, it will refuse to sanction such violations and will apply the corrective."

CONCLUSION

[T]he judgment must be Reversed.

At the time of the *Brown* decision, the protections afforded citizens by the Bill of Rights applied only to actions taken by the federal government. Requiring the states to extend the same protections to the public took years and happened in a piecemeal manner. Since courts do not make law—only interpret it—the Court was left to continually use the Fourteenth Amendment's due process clause to invalidate convictions based on confessions extracted by brutality. The Court overturned convictions based on confessions obtained after the defendants were kept naked for hours,[8] promised psychiatric care to gain their trust and extract incriminating statements,[9] told they would be lynched,[10] told that welfare agencies would take their children if they did not cooperate,[11] or moved to a secret location so family and friends could not intervene.[12]

The practice of incorporating the protections of the Bill of Rights to state defendants began with *Gideon* v. *Wainwright*, 372 U.S. 335 (1963), in which the Court incorporated the Sixth Amendment right to counsel [access to a lawyer] at trial. In 1964, the Court decided in *Malloy* v. *Hogan*, 378 U.S. 1, that the Fifth Amendment right against self-incrimination specifically prohibited the states from using compelled confessions against a defendant at trial. *Malloy* inched the Court forward from *Gideon* and from *Mapp* v. *Ohio*, 367 U.S. 643 (1961), which required the states to exclude illegally obtained evidence in criminal trials.

The next step for due process protections via the Fourteenth Amendment came in the Court's decision in *Escobedo* v. *Illinois*, 378 U.S. 478 (1964), which established for the first time the right to have counsel present during an interrogation if counsel had already been hired. Mr. Escobedo had been arrested and interrogated about his involvement in a murder. His attorney secured his release, but police rearrested him and kept him away from his friends, family, and attorney despite his repeated requests that he be allowed to see his attorney. During questioning, police made Escobedo stand with his hands handcuffed behind his back while a Spanish-speaking officer told Escobedo that he could go home if he implicated another suspect. When Escobedo admitted some involvement in the murder, officers persisted in their questioning until Escobedo implicated himself further. By holding that Escobedo's confession was obtained illegally in violation of his Fifth and Sixth Amendment rights not to incriminate himself and to have an attorney present during questioning, the U.S. Supreme Court thus extended the *Mapp* exclusionary rule from the Fourth Amendment to evidence obtained as a result of police interrogations.

Applying the Rule of Law to the Facts: When is self-incrimination compelled?

- David was in the country illegally and was suspected of a rash of robberies. Police came to his place of employment and kept him long past the time he was

---

[8] *Malinski* v. *New York*, 324 U.S. 401 (1945). (A confession was coerced from a defendant who upon arrest was taken to a hotel, stripped, and kept naked, whereupon, after being held from 8 A.M. to 6 P.M., he confessed).

[9] *Leyra* v. *Denno*, 347 U.S. 556 (1954). (A confession was coerced from a murder suspect who had been subjected to many hours of day-and-night questioning; a state psychiatrist was then introduced to him as a "doctor" who questioned defendant).

[10] *Payne* v. *Arkansas*, 356 U.S. 560 (1958). (A confession was coerced from a "mentally dull 19-year-old Negro" when the police chief threatened him with mob violence).

[11] *Lynumn* v. *Illinois*, 372 U.S. 528 (1963). (A confession was coerced from a defendant who was told by police that welfare aid to her children would be cut off and that she would lose custody if she did not "cooperate").

[12] *Chambers* v. *Florida*, 309 U.S. 227 (1940). ("Confessions of the commission of a robbery and murder must be deemed involuntary, so as to render their use in obtaining convictions a violation of the due process clause of the Fourteenth Amendment, where obtained from young negroes arrested without warrant, held in jail without formal charges, and without being permitted to see or confer with counsel or friends, believing that they were in danger of mob violence, made at the end of an all-night session following five days of fruitless questioning, each by himself, by state officers and other white citizens, in the presence of from four to ten white men, and after a previous confession had been pronounced "unsatisfactory" by the prosecuting attorney").

to go home. They taunted him about possible deportation, kept him separated from family and friends, and kept insisting that David tell them the "truth." He eventually confessed. On appeal, David claimed he was forced to incriminate himself. The police said David was never in custody. Who is correct?

David is correct. Psychological coercion is just as effective during the interrogation process as are physical restraints.[13]

a. Right to Consult with Counsel

Rule of Law: The right to an attorney attaches once the adversary process begins.

The Sixth Amendment states that "[i]n all criminal prosecutions, the accused shall enjoy the right . . . to have the Assistance of Counsel for his defence." The high Court has interpreted the Sixth Amendment to provide for counsel when a suspect is facing jail time. The right attaches for rich and poor alike, and the government will pay for a lawyer if the suspect cannot afford one. The "right" to a lawyer attaches at the beginning of adversarial proceedings between the government and suspect, "whether by way of formal charge, preliminary hearing, indictment, information, or arraignment." *Kirby* v. *Illinois*, 406 U.S. 682 (1972). The suspect need not request counsel at these proceedings, and failure of the government to provide one may be deemed "harmless error," a mistake that did not seriously damage the suspect or affect his eventual conviction. But if counsel was required at trial and one was not provided, then his conviction must be overturned. The right to counsel attaches for the specific charge with which the suspect is accused. If the charge is murder, police may not "deliberately elicit" incriminating statements in the absence of counsel or its waiver. The deliberate elicitation prohibition even applies to paid or other informants hoping for lenient sentencing in exhange for helping law enforcement.

In *Massiah* v. *United States*, 377 U.S. 201 (1964), the defendant Massiah conspired with others to smuggle drugs into the country. Massiah and others were caught; he was indicted and retained counsel. Unbeknownst to Massiah, one of his codefendants began cooperating with the police and, on behalf of the government pursuant to a plea deal for leniency in sentencing, the codefendant began surreptitiously tape-recording Massiah's incriminating statements. At trial, the tape-recorded incriminating statements were introduced over Massiah's objection. The question before the U.S. Supreme Court was whether the government had violated Massiah's right to counsel because he already had an attorney when the informant's tape-recording of Massiah occurred. The high Court overturned Massiah's conviction and held that if a suspect has already been indicted for a crime, incriminating information cannot be elicited without his attorney being present. If a third party merely overhears the suspect make incriminating statements and informs the police, there is no Sixth Amendment violation. It is important to remember that the constitutional restrictions concerning search, seizure, and confessions apply only to the government and its agents, including informants and others working on the government's behalf; the restrictions do not apply to private citizens.[14]

The right to counsel is "offense-specific," which means that if the suspect is arraigned or indicted for murder and has an attorney, the police cannot elicit information about the murder. But officers may try to ask questions about other offenses that they believe the suspect has committed. *Texas* v. *Cobb*, 532 U.S. 162 (2001). If police violate a suspect's right to counsel because adversary proceedings have begun,

---

[13]*See United States* v. *Beraun-Panez*, 812 F.2d 578 (9th Cir. 1987).

[14]*See Kuhlmann* v. *Wilson*, 477 U.S. 436 (1986).

the prosecution cannot use the defendant's incriminating statements to prove his guilt, but can use it against him if he testifies at his own trial and contradicts his prior admissions. *United States* v. *Ortega*, 203 F.3d 675 (9th Cir. 2000). If the right to counsel attaches only by virtue of reading the *Miranda* warnings, a different analysis applies. As discussed later, and as a result of the U.S. Supreme Court's holding in *Miranda* v. *Arizona* (1964), suspects who are in custody and are about to be interrogated must first be informed of their right to remain silent and their right to have an attorney present during questioning before the interrogation can begin. The Court created the *Miranda* warnings to prevent police misconduct in pressuring suspects to confess. Typically, a suspect receives warnings per *Miranda* when he is under suspicion of committing a crime and before any charges have been brought or court proceedings begun. The right to counsel under *Miranda* is different from the Sixth Amendment right that attaches after the initiation of adversary proceedings. Legal Scholar James Tomkovicz explains the difference between the Sixth Amendment's constitutional basis for the exclusionary rule under *Massiah* versus the prophylactic measures of the exclusionary rule under *Miranda*:

> *Massiah* exclusion is akin to the suppression of statements under the Due Process and Self-Incrimination Clauses. Like those two guarantees, the Sixth Amendment safeguards an interest in not being convicted as a result of government methods deemed unfair by our Constitution. All three provisions [Fourth, Fifth and Sixth Amendments] are violated—and trials are unfair—when the evidentiary products of those methods are used to convict. When the state's pretrial conduct is of a sort that would be forbidden at trial, all three guarantees are enforced by constitutional rights to exclusion, not judicially developed exclusionary rules or remedies designed to prevent future wrongs or to guard against risks of present wrongs.[15]

In sum, Tomkovicz is saying that the exclusion of evidence obtained in violation of a Sixth Amendment right to counsel is based on the constitutional guarantees of due process and a right to a fair trial, while excluding evidence obtained in violation of the judge-made *Miranda* rule to give warnings is done so that judges can punish police misconduct and try to prevent future misconduct.

b. The Inbau & Reid Nine Steps of Interrogation

Rule of Law: An interrogation method designed to induce confessions may be used on suspects who are believed to be guilty.

The *Escobedo* v. *Illinois* decision opened the floodgates of appeals based on interrogation violations to the U.S. Supreme Court. Typically, a suspect has a legal right to counsel once formal charges have been brought. Interrogations that invite confessions are usually elicited before charges are brought. To resolve this discrepancy, the Court consolidated four cases into one, *Miranda* v. *Arizona*, and held that the Fifth and Sixth Amendments apply to state criminal proceedings. The Court also stated that given the inherently coercive nature of the interrogation process, officers would have to inform suspects of their constitutional rights and the suspects would have to give up those rights before an interrogation could legally begin.

An oft-cited and criticized instructional tool is the interrogation manual now in its fourth edition by Inbau, Reid, Buckley, and Jayne (2004)[16] (hereinafter "Inbau & Reid"). Inbau & Reid suggest using a nine-step approach to interrogate suspects be-

---

[15]James J. Tomkovicz. "Saving *Massiah* from *Elstad*: The Admissibility of Successive Confessions Following a Deprivation of Counsel." *William & Mary Bill of Rights Journal,* Vol. 15 (2007), pp. 711–764.

[16]Fred E. Inbau, John E. Reid, Joseph P. Buckley, and Brian C. Jayne. *Criminal Interrogation and Confessions*, 4th ed. (Sudbury, MA: Jones & Bartlett, 2004).

lieved to be guilty. The authors are adamant that an interrogation is accusatory in tone, is not a mere interview, and is not to be used on people believed innocent. The nine steps are as follows.

Step 1: Direct Positive Confrontation

"At the outset of the interrogation the guilty suspect is closely evaluating the investigator's confidence in his guilt. If the suspect perceives that the investigator is not certain of his guilt, he is unlikely to confess." Therefore the first step is to confront the suspect with the interrogator's certainty that the suspect committed the crime. The interrogator must watch the suspect closely to see if the suspect looks away or avoids eye contact, actions that may indicate guilt. An innocent person may aggressively deny the false accusation, while the guilty party may react passively. The interrogator may focus on a suspect's 'redeeming qualities,' which may justify his commission of the crime or exaggerate his suspected involvement in the crime to obtain a reaction from the suspect minimizing his involvement.

Step 2: Theme Development

In Step 2, the interrogator attempts to gain the suspect's trust by creating a theme while also offering reasons for committing the crime that are morally reasonable or justifiable, allowing the suspect to place himself at the crime scene while minimizing his acts, culpability, and blame for the crime. The following is an excerpt from an officer's deposition [sworn testimony before trial to preserve testimony] showing how and why the officer created a certain theme during the interrogation of a murder suspect. The officer used the ploy of giving the suspect a reasonable scenario or theme that the victim died accidentally after rough sex, knowing that, legally, once the defendant confessed to murder, the "theme" he has bought into to minimize his blameworthiness is not enough to save him from conviction and possibly the death penalty. In this sworn testimony, the detective is being asked about his practice of reviewing crime scene photos and of coming up with a "scenario" with which to confront the suspect with during the interrogation. The detective is being deposed [asked questions] by the lawyer for Salazar, the defendant; the prosecutor is present as well.

Florida v. *Martin Salazar,* 96-2169CF A02[17]
Deposition of Detective, June 3, 1996
Q. Now, you talk about a creative theme. What does that mean?
A. After looking at the crime scene photographs I decided that a possibility could be to speak to Mr. Salazar in relationship to a scenario that recreated the scene, which I thought after looking at the photographs might seem somewhat plausible to him, and this was created by me so I could use it as a tool to get him to tell the truth in relationship to what he did concerning the particular case.
Q. I'm not asking what always works, but is that the idea, you immediately hit them with the creative scenario?
A. No. With me looking at the photos it was obvious to me that those [police interviewers] that proceeded (sic) me were unsuccessful in getting Mr. Salazar to tell the truth. Looking at the crime scene photo book I created this scenario that looked plausible to me. And somebody that wasn't very skilled in knowing the ins and outs of the creative scenario, and these are words that I am using, what I did, I independently of anybody created this after looking at the crime scene photos.

---

[17]Salazar's case was eventually dismissed because of the state improperly withholding evidence, but when the state found a DNA expert who confirmed Salazar could not be excluded as a suspect, he was reindicted. Grand Jury Indictment of Martin Salazar for First Degree (Palm Beach County Ct., Oct. 7, 1997) (No. 97-11428CFA02).

I made up this scene of this bondage and autoerotic and all this other stuff and, if I presented that to Mr. Salazar, it may seem too plausible and only he could tell me if it was an accident or whether it was intentional. And Mr. Salazar, fortunately I think, bought into that scene, changed his negative way and said, yes, he had tied an electrical cord around her neck, et. cetera, et. cetera.

Q. Where did you learn about this creative scenario, creative theme?

A. I just made it up one day.

Q. I don't mean the particular one, the theory of a creative theme or a—

A. I've been a policeman a long time, it's just something that you go to school and you just learn. I think the basic thing you do in an interview, you try to work whatever is plausible to get somebody to tell you the truth, just work within the confines of what the law allows you to do. I was just walking around after looking at the crime scene photo book and it just flashed in my mind that I would try that. . . .

I remember a case where I got a guy to confess to murder where he killed a Guatemalan guy. And I convinced him that was okay because nobody cared about that Guatemalan guy and that makes people feel guilty, and you utilize that guilt and anxiety, and they'll feel better when they tell you they did. [I told him] nobody cares about that Guatemalan, people care about you, you're an American and he bought right into that, yeah, I really didn't mean to kill the guy in the robbery anyway. . . . Sure the consequences of them doing that is real significant if you know that they really want to tell you the truth and if you hit that right button.

Q. Detective, is there any danger when you use a creative theme or scenario that an individual who is innocent but recognizes the severity of the potential punishment they could be facing or its consequences of being charged with a crime and their family members, that they might buy into your scenario for reasons other than guilt?

A. Is it possible?

Q. Yeah.

A. It is possible, but not on this level case.

Q. Why not on this level of a case?

A. Because you can't buy into a scenario like that on a murder case. I mean you have to understand that the person that you're presenting the scenario to knows that they committed the offense, that they're buying into the creative version of it and it's just not plausible to me. If you're talking about retail theft, petty theft, burglary, trespassers, something minor like that, most of those cases you wouldn't bother with a scenario. But [is it] possible somebody admitted to wrapping an electrical cord around somebody's neck in a voluntary sexual scenario, I don't think so. . . . It's just after you deal with murder and you raise the anxiety and you give them an out and most of the time they'll take it.

The detective's deposition reveals that giving Salazar an escape hatch from the moral responsibility of murdering the woman was a powerful enough catalyst to produce a confession.

Step 3: Handling Denials

Inbau & Reid assert that criminals can commit crimes because they distort their motives for committing the crime. For example in a child molestation case, the offender may describe his actions as showing love and affection for the child, or simply teaching the child about sex, a subject about which everyone needs to learn. The authors advocate suggesting "a less revolting and more morally acceptable motivation or reason for the offense than that which is known or presumed." As the detective in the Salazar case shows, if an offender is presented with the scenario that the voluntary rough sex got out of control through no fault of his own, he can buy into that scenario because, in his mind, it diminishes his criminal responsibility.

Step 4: Overcoming Objections

A suspect's excuses are considered "objections" to the interrogator's unfailing belief in the suspect's guilt and to any proposed scenario into which the suspect may have not completely bought. To overcome these objections, officers should be aware that the suspect generates much less emotional anxiety for himself if he offers excuses as an alternative to outright denials. For instance, in Martha Stewart's perjury case her attorney in closing argument offered, "Here's a woman worth five billion dollars, why would she have to lie to save $58,000 dollars?" Suspects offer excuses as well, asking for example, "Why would I buy my wife a diamond ring if I wanted to kill her?" Suspects hope to deflect attention from their guilt by engaging in conversation designed to deflect suspicion, but when a suspect voices an objection, he is clearly trying to conceal the truth. The investigator should let the suspect voice the objection and then turn the objection around to incorporate it back into the interrogation theme.

Let's take, for example, the defendant Salazar mentioned in Step 2, theme development. Imagine that during Salazar's interrogation he had raised the objection to Detective Murphy's creative scenario of rough sex and said, "I wouldn't do a thing like that. I'm not a sex maniac." According to Inbau & Reid, Detective Murphy should first agree with Salazar and then turn it around, as follows:

"Yes, I believe you are not a pervert, Salazar, and I know you are not the type of guy who would hurt women. That's why I know that you and the girl were having consensual intercourse when you both decided to try some rough stuff and it got out of hand" (return to the theme that the strangulation happened by accident during rough sex).

Step 5: Procurement and Retention of a Suspect's Attention

After verbally engaging with officers, suspects may become emotionally withdrawn. At the signs of withdrawal, the investigator should move in close physical proximity as if in a sympathetic gesture, but the overall goal is to reestablish a connection with the suspect and become psychologically closer.

Step 6: Handling the Suspect's Passive Mood

The guilty suspect will become quiet after realizing that his tactics and tricks of evasion and deflection are not working on the interrogator. The officer should reestablish his theme and be alert for signs that the suspect is resigning himself to the fate that he has been caught.

Step 7: Presenting an Alternative Question

"Which shall it be, the pie or the cake?" Inbau & Reid suggest that framing the question as a choice to diners may produce more dessert orders. The same technique applies to guilty suspects who, after becoming resigned to their fate that they cannot escape, can now buy into the alternative question, "Did you plan on doing this since the day you got married, or did it pretty much happen on the spur of the moment because of the fight that you had?" The alternative question is the end result of developing the guilt-minimizing theme the suspect can buy into.

Step 8: Bringing the Suspect into the Conversation

Once a suspect adopts an alternative explanation of the crime it is imperative to immediately commit him to the details of and motive for the crime, which should then develop into a full confession. During this time, the interrogator should be alone with the suspect because the presence of others may inhibit him from speaking freely.

FIGURE 12.1 The Inbau & Reid Nine Steps of Interrogation.

Elimination of Innocent

| Crime or reason for interviewing or interrogation | Investigation and clinical fact analysis | Interview of suspects |

| **Step 1** The Direct, Positive Confrontation "Our investigation shows that you are the one who ..." | **Step 2** Theme Development "Joe, I can understand how this happened ..." | **Step 3** Handling Denials "Joe, listen to what I have to say ..." |

Ascending (more direct)   Descending (less direct)

Alternate Procedure

| **Step 4** Overcoming Objections "Joe, I'm sure that's true, but ..." | **Step 5** Keeping the Suspect's Attention "Joe, I'm sure that you care about this ..." | **Step 6** Handling the Suspect's Passive Mood "Joe, I'm sure this wasn't planned out ..." | **Step 7** Presenting the Alternative Question "Did you plan this out, or was it a spontaneous thing?" | **Step 8** Bringing the Suspect into the Conversation "I was sure that's what happened ..." | **Step 9** The Written Confession |

Criminal Interrogations and Confessions (Sudbury, MA: Jones and Bartlett, 2004) wwwjbpub.com. Reprinted with permission.

Step 9: The Written Confession

Once an oral confession has been obtained, it should be put in writing and signed and witnessed as soon as possible. In order to prove that the confession was voluntary, officers must prove that the suspect knowingly, intelligently, and voluntarily waived his rights per *Miranda* and spoke freely. A summary of the nine steps of interrogation appears in Figure 12.1.

2. The *Miranda* Decision

Rule of Law: *Miranda* **warnings are judge-made interpretations of the Fifth and Sixth Amendments.**

In March 1963, a young woman who worked at a refreshment stand in a movie theater in Phoenix, Arizona, was abducted by a man in a car and raped alongside the desert highway. Police arrested Ernesto Miranda, a 23-year-old laborer with a criminal past involving sex crimes, indecent exposure, attempted rape, and peeping into windows. The woman said that Miranda possibly looked like her attacker, but she wanted to hear him speak before she made a positive identification. But Miranda had confessed before any further investigation. Miranda described the interrogation later as one in which he was kept awake for hours, threatened with a long prison term if he did not confess, and promised medical care to get him treatment for his problems. The police, on the other hand, testified at Miranda's trial that he confessed willingly and without any threats or promises. The decision was 5–4 in favor of Miranda and stood as a rejection of the practice of making suspects psychologically vulnerable to the point at which they confess simply to make the torture stop.

BOX 12.2

Miranda v. *Arizona,* 384 U.S. 436 (1966)
Supreme Court of the United States

Chief Justice Warren delivered the opinion of the Court.

FACTS

In each [of the four cases consolidated to be heard on appeal], the defendant was questioned by police officers, detectives, or a prosecuting attorney in a room in which he was cut off from the outside world. In none of these cases was the defendant given a full and effective warning of his rights at the outset of the interrogation process. In all the cases, the questioning elicited oral admissions, and in three of them, signed statements as well which were admitted at their trials. They all thus share salient features—incommunicado interrogation of individuals in a police-dominated atmosphere, resulting in self-incriminating statements without full warnings of constitutional rights.

ISSUE

The constitutional issue we decide in each of these cases is the admissibility of statements obtained from a defendant questioned while in custody or otherwise deprived of his freedom of action in any significant way. We start here, as we did in *Escobedo* [v. *Illinois*, 378 U.S. 478 (1964)], with the premise that our holding is not an innovation in our jurisprudence, but is an application of principles long recognized and applied in other settings. We have undertaken a thorough re-examination of the *Escobedo* decision and the principles it announced, and we reaffirm it. That case was but an explication of basic rights that are enshrined in our Constitution—that "no person . . . shall be compelled in any criminal case to be a witness against himself," and that "the accused shall . . . have the Assistance of Counsel"—rights which were put in jeopardy in that case through official overbearing. These precious rights were fixed in our Constitution only after centuries of persecution and struggle. And in the words of Chief Justice Marshall, they were secured "for ages to come, and . . .

designed to approach immortality as nearly as human institutions can approach it," *Cohens* v. *Virginia*, 6 Wheat. 264 (1821).

HOLDING

Our holding briefly stated is this: the prosecution may not use statements, whether exculpatory or inculpatory, stemming from custodial interrogation of the defendant unless it demonstrates the use of procedural safeguards effective to secure the privilege against self-incrimination. By custodial interrogation, we mean questioning initiated by law enforcement officers after a person has been taken into custody or otherwise deprived of his freedom of action in any significant way. As for the procedural safeguards to be employed, unless other fully effective means are devised to inform accused persons of their right of silence and to assure a continuous opportunity to exercise it, the following measures are required.

Prior to any questioning, the person must be warned that he has a right to remain silent, that any statement he does make may be used as evidence against him, and that he has a right to the presence of an attorney, either retained or appointed. The defendant may waive effectuation of these rights, provided the waiver is made voluntarily, knowingly and intelligently. If, however, he indicates in any manner and at any stage of the process that he wishes to consult with an attorney before speaking there can be no questioning. Likewise, if the individual is alone and indicates in any manner that he does not wish to be interrogated, the police may not question him. The mere fact that he may have answered some questions or volunteered some statements on his own does not deprive him of the right to refrain from answering any further inquiries until he has consulted with an attorney and thereafter consents to be questioned.

REASONING

An understanding of the nature and setting of this in-custody interrogation is essential to our decisions

(continued)

BOX 12.2

(continued)

today. The difficulty in depicting what transpires at such interrogations stems from the fact that in this country they have largely taken place incommunicado. From extensive factual studies undertaken in the early 1930's, including the famous Wickersham Report to Congress by a Presidential Commission, it is clear that police violence and the "third degree" flourished at that time.

In a series of cases decided by this Court long after these studies, the police resorted to physical brutality—beating, hanging, whipping—and to sustained and protracted questioning incommunicado in order to extort confessions. The Commission on Civil Rights in 1961 found much evidence to indicate that "some policemen still resort to physical force to obtain confessions." The use of physical brutality and violence is not, unfortunately, relegated to the past or to any part of the country. Only recently in Kings County, New York, the police brutally beat, kicked and placed lighted cigarette butts on the back of a potential witness under interrogation for the purpose of securing a statement incriminating a third party. *People* v. *Portelli*, 205 N. E. 2d 857 (1965).

Again we stress that the modern practice of in-custody interrogation is psychologically rather than physically oriented. As we have stated before, "Since *Chambers* v. *Florida*, 309 U.S. 227, this Court has recognized that coercion can be mental as well as physical, and that the blood of the accused is not the only hallmark of an unconstitutional inquisition." *Blackburn* v. *Alabama*, 361 U.S. 199 (1960). [The Court recites a number of police interrogation tactics deemed inherently coercive, including the Inbau & Reid manual]. The potentiality for compulsion is forcefully apparent, for example, in [lower court decision] *Miranda*, where the indigent Mexican defendant was a seriously disturbed individual with pronounced sexual fantasies, and in *Stewart*, in which the defendant was an indigent Los Angeles Negro who had dropped out of school in the sixth grade. To be sure, the records do not evince overt physical coercion or patent psychological ploys. The fact remains that in none of these cases did the officers undertake to afford appropriate safeguards at the outset of the interrogation to insure that the statements were truly the product of free choice. It is obvious that such an interrogation environment is created for no purpose other than to subjugate the individual to the will of his examiner. This atmosphere carries its own badge of intimidation. To be sure, this is not physical intimidation, but it is equally destructive of human dignity.

The current practice of incommunicado interrogation is at odds with one of our Nation's most cherished principles—that the individual may not be compelled to incriminate himself. Unless adequate protective devices are employed to dispel the compulsion inherent in custodial surroundings, no statement obtained from the defendant can truly be the product of his free choice.

CONCLUSION

We have concluded that without proper safeguards the process of in-custody interrogation of persons suspected or accused of crime contains inherently compelling pressures which work to undermine the individual's will to resist and to compel him to speak where he would not otherwise do so freely. In order to combat these pressures and to permit a full opportunity to exercise the privilege against self-incrimination, the accused must be adequately and effectively apprised of his rights and the exercise of those rights must be fully honored.

The Court's reasoning in *Miranda* is deductive:

1. The self-incrimination clause protects against compelled self-incrimination
2. Common police interrogation techniques are inherently coercive and designed to compel self-incrimination, and
3. Procedural safeguards in the form of warnings about the right to remain silent and to have the assistance of counsel during questioning are necessary to ameliorate the compulsory aspects of police interrogation.

Two years after the *Miranda* decision was issued, Congress, unhappy with the new restrictions on police interrogations, tried to abolish *Miranda* via enactment of a federal law, 18 U.S.C. §3501. The statute provided that a confession was admissible if it was voluntary, even if the suspect had not received the *Miranda* warnings. Thirty-two years later, Charles Dickerson tried to suppress his statements made to federal investigators in a bank robbery investigation on the basis that he was not warned per *Miranda*. The Court of Appeals for the Fourth Circuit cited 18 U.S.C. §3501 and declared that the statute "rather than *Miranda*, governs the admissibility of [a] confession in federal court." When the debate was eventually decided by the U.S. Supreme Court in *Dickerson* v. *United States*, 530 U.S. 428 (2000), they decided "that *Miranda*, being a constitutional decision of this Court, may not be in effect overruled by an Act of Congress. . . ." As discussed in chapter 1, once the U.S. Supreme Court has interpreted the Constitution, here that the Fifth and Sixth Amendments require a suspect to be notified of his constitutional protections, it becomes the final word of the land by operation of the Constitution's Supremacy Clause.

3. The *Miranda* Warnings and When to Advise

Rule of Law: *Miranda* **warnings are required during custodial interrogations.**

There are no magic words that are required when advising a suspect of his rights pursuant to the *Miranda* holding. The warnings need not be read from a card, nor does a suspect have to sign a piece of paper indicating that he or she received and understood the warnings. As long as the warnings have "touched all of the bases required by *Miranda*" the warnings will be adequate.[18] The so-called warnings are

1. You have the right to remain silent
2. Anything you say can and will be used against you in a court of law
3. You have a right to have an attorney present during questioning
4. If you cannot afford an attorney, one will be appointed to represent you.

a. Custody

Rule of Law: If a suspect feels trapped by police presence, he or she is in custody.

The *Miranda* warnings need only be given to a suspect before a custodial interrogation. In short, **custody** is when a suspect perceives she is not free to leave, even if not formally under arrest, and **interrogation** is questioning by the police or other government agents that is designed to elicit incriminating information. The totality of the circumstances test guides the analysis of whether the suspect does not feel free to leave the police presence and is, therefore, in custody. To make the custody determination, courts will examine the following factors.

1. The duration of the detention
2. The nature and degree of the pressure applied to detain the suspect
3. The physical surroundings and location of the questioning, and
4. The language and posture of the officer(s) doing the questioning.[19]

The legal standard for whether or not a suspect is in custody is similar to the test for whether or not a "seizure" of the person has occurred under the Fourth Amendment, as discussed in chapter 9. "First, what were the circumstances surrounding the interrogation; and, second, given those circumstances, would a reasonable person have

---

[18]*Duckworth* v. *Eagan*, 492 U.S. 195 (1989).

[19]*See United States* v. *Booth*, 669 F.2d 1231 (9th Cir. 1981); *California* v. *Beheler*, 463 U.S. 1121 (1983).

felt that he or she was not at liberty to terminate the interrogation and leave." *Thompson* v. *Keohane*, 516 U.S. 99 (1995). Even if the police tell the suspect that she is free to go, but she believes she has no power to terminate the police encounter, she is in custody.

Applying the Rule of Law to the Facts: **Is the suspect in custody?**

- Police first questioned a suspect as a possible witness to the rape and murder of a 10-year-old girl. He soon transformed into a suspect when he admitted that he drove a car similar to one seen where the victim was found. During the interview, he disclosed his previous convictions for rape, kidnapping, and child molestation, after which officers advised him of his rights pursuant to *Miranda*. The suspect tried to suppress his statements given before *Miranda* warnings because he was in custody. The officers said they believed that suspect was not in custody until *Miranda* was given.

Yes, the suspect was in custody before *Miranda* warnings were given. The high Court held in *Stansbury* v. *California*, 511 U.S. 318 (1994), that whether or not the officer believes the suspect is in custody is irrelevant. The focal points in a custody analysis are the objective (what everyone can see) circumstances surrounding the interrogation. The important perspective for a custody analysis is the perception of the suspect, not of the police officer. If officers were allowed to determine when a suspect was in custody for *Miranda* purposes, they might never do so short of formal arrest.

- A 17-year-old suspect helped a friend steal a truck, and when the friend shot the truck owner, the suspect hid the gun. His parents took the suspect to the police station, where the interview lasted two hours and was recorded, but no *Miranda* warnings were given. He declined an offer for a break during questioning and made some incriminating statements. Months later, he was charged with murder and stated that his incriminating statements should be suppressed because he was in custody. The police said he was free to leave at any time. He was convicted and appealed. Was he in custody?

No, in *Yarborough* v. *Alvarado*, 541 U.S. 652 (2004), the high Court held that Alvarado was not in custody during police questioning by looking at the circumstances surrounding the interrogation and, therefore, *Miranda* warnings were not required, Alvarado's conviction was affirmed.

b. Interrogation

Rule of Law: **Interrogation is questioning by law enforcement agents designed to elicit incriminating responses.**

Interrogation encompasses a wide variety of police–citizen encounters in which officers try to elicit incriminating information from people. It may be difficult to distinguish between police banter and psychological ploys designed to get the suspect to talk. Where is the legal line drawn in using lies and tricks to induce a suspect to confess? If the psychological aspects of the interrogation process alone induce innocent people to confess, how can the criminal justice system prevent such miscarriages of justice?

4. Trickery in Interrogations

Rule of Law: **Confessions must be voluntary in order for them to be admissible as evidence against the defendant.**

a. Voluntariness

A confession will be admissible against the defendant at trial only if, under the totality of the circumstances, the confession was given voluntarily. Some of the circumstances courts investigate in a totality analysis to determine voluntariness of the confession are:[20]

1. Whether the suspect initiated contact with officers
2. Suspect's age and history of drug and alcohol problems
3. Suspect's physical problems, if any
4. Suspect's previous experience with the criminal justice system.

A confession is not considered legally voluntary if officers created pressure for the suspect to confess and if that pressure overbore the suspect's resistance to confessing. A suspect must prove police coercion before a confession will be found involuntary. Mental illness alone is insufficient to render a confession involuntary. A floridly psychotic man confessed to murder even though his mental impairment prevented him from understanding the import of the *Miranda* warnings. The high Court held that absent police coercion, the confession was voluntary. *Colorado* v. *Connelly*, 479 U.S. 157 (1986).

In the following case, *Hardaway* v. *Young*, Derrick Hardaway, a 14-year-old juvenile, was convicted of second-degree murder in the killing of 11-year-old Robert Sandifer. Hardaway filed a *writ of habeas corpus*, asking to be released because his imprisonment was illegal, claiming his confession was involuntary, but the appellate court disagreed. As you will learn in chapter 14, which discusses appeals, federal *habeas* relief can only be granted if the state court clearly misinterprets or misapplies federal law. Since that did not happen in Hardaway's case when the state court admitted his confession as voluntary, Hardaway lost his appeal. As you read the case, see if you agree that his confession was free from police coercion.

BOX 12.3

Hardaway v. *Young*, 302 F.3d 757 (2002) United States Court of Appeals for the Seventh Circuit

Judge Wood delivered the opinion of the court.

FACTS

On August 28, 1994, 11-year-old Robert "Yummy" Sandifer, a member of the Black Disciples street gang in Chicago's Roseland neighborhood, shot and killed 14-year-old Shavon Dean and wounded two other children. Sandifer himself then disappeared. An intensive police search for Sandifer ensued until Sandifer's body was found under a viaduct at 108th Street and Dauphin Avenue shortly after midnight on September 1. He had been shot twice in the back of the head. In the early morning hours of September 1, Cassandra Cooper telephoned the police and told them that Sandifer had been at her home around 11:30 P.M. the night before and that her daughter Jimesia saw Sandifer leave their porch with Hardaway and his older brother Cragg. At around 8 A.M., the police went to the Hardaway home. Hardaway was roused from sleep, told of the investigation, and, after conferring with his father,

(continued)

---

[20]*See generally Johnson* v. *Trigg*, 28 F.3d 639 (7th Cir. 1994). (The confession was ruled voluntary, although the 14-year-old defendant of below-average intelligence saw police arrest his terminally ill mother before confessing); *Cooks* v. *Ward*, 165 F.3d 1283 (10th Cir. 1998). (The confession was ruled voluntary despite the police threat that the defendant would "get the needle" unless he talked, because defendant later requested to speak to police); *Thompson* v. *Haley*, 255 F.3d 1292 (11th Cir. 2001). (The confession was ruled voluntary, although police told defendant his girlfriend might go to the electric chair if he did not confess because police had probable cause to arrest his girlfriend for murder).

BOX 12.3

(continued)

agreed to accompany the officers to the police station to help with the investigation. Hardaway's father was offered a ride to the station but declined, choosing instead to wait for his son Cragg to return home. Hardaway dressed and was transported to the police station unhandcuffed and placed in an unlocked interview room at about 8:30 A.M.

Two detectives, Robert Lane and Romas Arbataitis, questioned Hardaway at that time. Hardaway admitted to knowing Sandifer but stated that he had last seen him three days earlier. At about 10:30 A.M., the detectives interviewed Hardaway for a second time. This time they read him his *Miranda* rights . . . Hardaway then changed his story and confessed to being present when Cragg shot Sandifer. The detectives' conversation with Hardaway lasted about 15 minutes and he was then left alone in the interview room [for the next six hours, with brief interruptions]. At 4:30 P.M., two new detectives, John McCann and James Oliver, reiterated the *Miranda* warnings and then interviewed Hardaway, who repeated his story.

Questioning then ceased while an Assistant State's Attorney, Theresa Harney, and a youth officer, James Geraci, were contacted. At approximately 7:00 P.M., McCann, Harney, and Geraci met with Hardaway. Harney told Hardaway that Geraci was a youth officer and that he was present as an observer and to assist Hardaway if he had any questions or problems. Geraci then asked Hardaway if there was anything he could assist him with, to which Hardaway responded no. From that point onward, Geraci did absolutely nothing to assist Hardaway. Harney read Hardaway his *Miranda* rights yet again and informed him again that he could be tried as an adult. Hardaway then explained his rights back to Harney in his own words, stating that he did not have to speak with Harney if he didn't want to, that anything he told Harney she could tell a judge in a trial against him, that he could have an attorney there when he was questioned about the case, even if he or his family couldn't pay for one, and that his case could be moved out of juvenile court to adult court if the judge decided. Hardaway gave a statement to Harney in which he again confessed to the crime and then agreed to repeat the statement to a court reporter.

ISSUE

[Was Hardaway's confession involuntary?]

HOLDING

[No. Under the totality of the circumstances, Hardaway's confession was voluntary.]

REASONING

The Illinois state courts knew that they were supposed to apply a totality of the circumstances approach when evaluating Hardaway's claims, and they claimed to have done so. Age is clearly a relevant factor in this case, as it is in many areas of the law. Children under the age of 16 are treated differently from adults under Illinois law in a host of different ways. They may not marry, vote, serve on a jury, or make a will. Restrictions are placed on their ability to work, smoke, operate a motor vehicle, withdraw from compulsory education, and travel outdoors between midnight and 6:00 A.M. They cannot purchase airline tickets, consent to medical care, attend a raffle, or pierce their bodies, without parental permission. It is thus somewhat incongruous that the state of Illinois believes that children, in whose decisions the state has so little confidence in other areas, should be subjected to questioning for major crimes they are suspected of having committed without the continuous presence and assistance of a friendly adult.

Keeping Hardaway's extreme youth in mind, we turn to the second factor in our analysis: the fact that there was no friendly adult presence to guard against undue police influence. Hardaway's parents chose not to come to the station with him, and he never requested an attorney. The state courts did note that Youth Officer Geraci was present at the 7:00 and 10:45 P.M. statements, but we agree with the district court that this fact is meaningless. As far as the record shows, Geraci provided about as much assistance to Hardaway as a potted plant . . . We wish to make it clear that a state-provided youth officer who functions as nothing more than an observer will not be considered a friendly adult presence for purposes of the totality of the circumstances test.

We therefore must operate under the following procedural framework: the mere fact that Hardaway was 14 and questioned without an adult present does not by itself render his confession involuntary, but it does require that a court conduct a searching review of the facts to ascertain whether any undue intimidation or other forms of pressure caused him to confess involuntarily. The district court identified only one such factor, the duration of the interrogation. Hardaway was initially brought to the police station at 8:30 A.M. and briefly interviewed. By 10:30 A.M. he was considered a suspect, had received his *Miranda* warnings, and had been questioned again for another 15 minutes, at which time he changed his story slightly. At that point he was left more or less alone for over five hours. The statements made by Hardaway at 4:30, 7:00, and 10:45 P.M. were in all material respects identical.

If we were a state appellate court, we might well find that on balance the psychological tension caused by leaving a boy of 14 alone in an interview room, hungry, scared, and tired, was enough to exclude the confession. But we may set aside the contrary findings of the Illinois trial and appellate courts only if their determination was unreasonable. Hardaway was not psychologically tricked into confessing by officers but only confronted with truthful contradictory evidence. Second, Hardaway had extensive prior history with parts of the criminal justice system. Prior to the Sandifer murder Hardaway had been arrested 19 times between 1992 and 1994 . . . [t]hree of the complaints were adjusted in complaint screening, and seven were station adjustments. Hardaway had been placed on juvenile supervision, but had violated that supervision. Seven times Hardaway had appeared in juvenile court with appointed counsel. As the state courts recognized, past brushes with the law weigh against the normal presumption that youths are specially sensitive to coercion.

There is no doubt that Hardaway's youth, the lack of a friendly adult, and the duration of his interrogation are strong factors militating against the voluntariness of his confession; indeed, it seems to us that on balance the confession of a 14-year-old obtained in those circumstances may be inherently involuntary. Nevertheless, the weighing of factors under the totality of circumstances test is a subject on which reasonable minds could differ. Here the trial court stated that it weighed all relevant factors, and after doing so it concluded that the lack of any apparent coercion by the police, Hardaway's recitation of his rights, his mental capacity, and his past experience with the criminal justice system on balance rendered his confession voluntary and admissible. Even assuming that the weighing of factors by the Illinois state courts in this case was incorrect, the balance is close enough that, in the final analysis, it is not unreasonable. Keeping in mind our deferential standards of review . . . we are compelled to defer to the findings and the conclusion of the state courts.

CONCLUSION

Because the determination of the Illinois courts that Hardaway's confession was voluntary under the totality of the circumstances was not an unreasonable application of clearly established federal law, the district court should not have granted the *writ of habeas corpus*.

5. Invoking *Miranda*

Rule of Law: When a suspect exercises his rights under *Miranda*, it is always best for him to ask for an attorney to be present during questioning.

a. Right to Remain Silent

If upon hearing the *Miranda* warnings, a suspect indicates he wants to stop talking, officers must "**scrupulously honor**" the suspect's right and stop the interrogation immediately. The officers cannot continue questioning the suspect in an effort to change his mind and convince him to continue talking, or frighten him that this is his 'last chance' to help himself and cut a deal. Officers cannot try to cajole a suspect into talking by saying that he would talk if he had nothing to hide.[21] But if the suspect's request for counsel is ambiguous or if the suspect seems unsure whether he wishes to remain silent, police questioning may continue.

---
[21]*See Kyger* v. *Carlton,* 146 F.3d 374 (6th Cir. 1998).

b. Waiving Miranda

Rule of Law: *Miranda* **is a two-step process: the giving of the rights and a waiver of those rights.**

Before the prosecutor can introduce a statement made by the defendant incriminating him, the government must prove that:

1. Its agents gave the suspect *Miranda* warnings, and
2. The suspect waived those right "voluntarily, knowingly and intelligently."

The test for a legal waiver of *Miranda* rights is also two-pronged:

1. Understanding the rights given up by the waiver, and
2. Voluntarily waiving those rights.

As the high Court said of waiving *Miranda* protections in *Moran* v. *Burbine*, 475 U.S. 412 (1986):

> First the relinquishment of the right must have been voluntary . . . the product of free and deliberate choice rather than intimidation, coercion or deception. Second, the waiver must have been made with a full awareness both of the nature of the right being abandoned and the consequences of the decision to abandon it.

The prosecution bears the burden of proving at least by a preponderance of the evidence the *Miranda* waiver and the voluntariness of the confession.[22] A **preponderance of the evidence** standard is typically used in civil cases and is approximately a 51% quantum of proof. The preponderance standard is less than beyond a reasonable doubt, although some states require the state to prove waiver beyond a reasonable doubt in order to give their citizens more protection from government overbearing.[23]

A defendant's silence on the issue of waiver will not suffice. A prosecutor may not come to court with a signed confession to prove that the defendant waived his or her rights; *Miranda* requires more. "The record must show . . . that an accused was offered counsel but intelligently and understandingly rejected the offer. Anything less is not a waiver."[24] But if a suspect takes certain actions indicating a willingness to speak to police, his or her waiver may be inferred from the circumstances. Researchers who study confessions assert that, in order for a person to knowingly, intelligently, and voluntarily waive *Miranda* rights, the person must possess three abilities:

1. "An understanding of the words and phrases contained within the warnings" (for example, a mentally retarded suspect may interpret the word "waive" as "wave" to a friend, or a "wave" on a beach);
2. "An accurate perception of the intended functions of the *Miranda* rights (<u>for example</u>, that interrogation is adversarial, that an attorney is an advocate, that these rights trump police powers);
3. An appreciation of the consequences of giving up *Miranda* protections (<u>for example</u>, that anything the suspect says can be used against him in a court of law).[25]

To determine the validity of the waiver of *Miranda*, courts look at the totality of the circumstances of the interrogation.[26] Common sense dictates that factors unique

---

[22]*Colorado* v. *Connelly*, 479 U.S. 157 (1986); *Lego* v. *Twomey*, 404 U.S. 477 (1972).

[23]*See, for example, State* v. *Galloway*, 133 N.J. 631 (1993). (The prosecution must prove *Miranda* waiver beyond a reasonable doubt).

[24]*Carnley* v. *Cochran*, 369 U.S. 506 (1962).

[25]S. M. Kassin and G. H. Gudjonsson, quoting T. Grisso. *Juveniles' Waiver of Rights: Legal and Psychological Competence.* (New York: Plenum, 1981).

[26]*United States* v. *Curtis*, 344 F.3d 1057 (10th Cir. 2003).

FIGURE 12.2   Prototype Miranda Waiver Form.

Notification and Waiver of Rights

Before we ask you questions, you must **understand your rights.**
They are:

You have the right to remain silent.
Anything you say can and will be used against you in a court of law.
You have the right to talk to an attorney for advice before we ask you any questions and to have an attorney present during questioning.
If you decide to answer questions now without an attorney present, you have the right to stop talking at any time.
You also have the right to stop talking at any time until you confer with counsel.

Waiver of Rights

I have read this statement of my rights and understand my rights. I am willing to make a statement and answer questions. I do not want an attorney at this time. No promises or threats have been made to me to cooperate and no pressure or coercion of any kind has been used against me. I am _____ years of age and have completed the _____ grade. _____ is my first language.

_____
Signature

_____
Witness

Place:
Date:
Time:

to the suspect affect her understanding of the waiver, such as her mental state, level of intelligence, age, former involvement with the criminal justice system, use of illegal narcotics or other intoxicants, knowledge of English as a native or foreign tongue, and amount of time that elapsed between the giving of *Miranda* and the actual questioning. But actually, these factors make little or no difference in evaluating whether or not the suspect knew and understood both the rights and the consequences of giving them up. In *Campaneria* v. *Reid*,[27] the federal court of appeals found that despite the defendant's recent surgery, his pain, his dizziness, and ingestion of pain medication, his waiver of *Miranda* warnings was valid because the doctor's notes showed that he was awake and alert during questioning. In *Shakleford* v. *Hubbard*, 234 F.3d 1072 (9th Cir. 2000), the court found that the defendant had given a valid waiver of *Miranda* despite the fact that he had used cocaine, was excessively tired, and was mentally deficient.[28] The import of these cases is that a drunk, mentally retarded defendant recovering from painful surgery may be found to have voluntarily, knowingly, and willingly waived his rights if he is aware of the nature of the proceedings and the consequences of his actions in speaking to police. An example of a waiver form is provided in Figure 12.2.

---

[27]891 F.2d 1014 (2d Cir. 1989).

[28](Not ineffective assistance of counsel to withhold such evidence at suppression hearing).

The defendant does not have to sign a waiver in order for it to be effective. If the defendant thinks that he has not confessed unless he has signed something, his confession is still valid. In *Connecticut* v. *Barrett*, 479 U.S. 523 (1987), the Supreme Court held that an oral confession need not be suppressed when, after *Miranda* warnings, the suspect agreed to speak to the police, but indicated that he would not make a written statement without his lawyer present. The Court reasoned that the police should decline to take advantage of a suspect's willingness to speak. "The fact that officials took the opportunity provided by Barrett to obtain an oral confession is quite consistent with the Fifth Amendment. *Miranda* gives the defendant a right to choose between speech and silence, and Barrett chose to speak."

There is an additional issue of "double interviewing" suspects, a technique common in many jurisdictions prior to 2004. The practice and policy of investigators was to get friendly with the suspect before giving *Miranda* warnings in the hope that the suspect confessed. If the suspect confessed, then a "cleansing" or "sanitizing" interview was conducted after the suspect was informed of his or her rights under *Miranda*. In the suspect's mind, there was no difference between the "friendly" interrogation and subsequent confession, on the one hand, and the "sanitized" one that could be used in court against the suspect. In 2004, the high Court declared in *Missouri* v. *Seibert,* reprinted in part in Box 12.4, that the double-interviewing technique was unconstitutional. The law now requires investigators to give *Miranda* warnings immediately to all those in custodial interrogation settings.

BOX 12.4

Missouri v. *Seibert*, 542 U.S. 600 (2004)
Supreme Court of the United States

Justice Souter delivered the opinion of the Court.

FACTS

Patrice Seibert's 12-year-old son Jonathan had cerebral palsy, and when he died in his sleep she feared charges of neglect because of bedsores on his body. In her presence, two of her teenage sons and two of their friends devised a plan to conceal the facts surrounding Jonathan's death by incinerating his body in the course of burning the family's mobile home, in which they planned to leave Donald Rector, a mentally ill teenager living with the family, to avoid any appearance that Jonathan had been unattended. Seibert's son Darian and a friend set the fire, and Donald died. Five days later, the police awakened Seibert at 3 A.M. at a hospital where Darian was being treated for burns.

In arresting [Seibert], officer Kevin Clinton followed instructions . . . that he refrain from giving *Miranda* warnings. After Seibert had been taken to the police station and left alone in an interview room for 15 to 20 minutes, [Rolla, Missouri, officer Richard Hanrahan] questioned her without *Miranda* warnings for 30 to 40 minutes, squeezing her arm and repeating "Donald was also to die in his sleep." After Seibert finally admitted she knew Donald was meant to die in the fire, she was given a 20-minute coffee and cigarette break. Officer Hanrahan then turned on a tape recorder, gave Seibert the *Miranda* warnings, and obtained a signed waiver of rights from her. He resumed the questioning with "Ok, 'trice [Patrice], we've been talking for a little while about what happened on Wednesday the twelfth, haven't we?" and confronted her with her prewarning statements.

After being charged with first-degree murder for her role in Donald's death, Seibert sought to exclude both her prewarning and postwarning statements. At the suppression hearing, Officer Hanrahan testified that he made a "conscious decision" to withhold *Miranda* warnings, thus resorting to an interrogation technique he had been taught: question first, then give the warnings, and then repeat the question "until I get the answer that she's already provided once." He acknowledged that Seibert's ultimate statement was "largely a repeat of information . . . obtained" prior to the warning.

ISSUE

[Was Seibert's confession improperly admitted as evidence at her trial when her rights per *Miranda* were violated by the double interviewing technique?]

HOLDING

[Yes, Seibert's conviction was overturned.]

REASONING

Seibert argues that her second confession should be excluded from evidence under the doctrine known by the metaphor of the "fruit of the poisonous tree," developed in the Fourth Amendment context in *Wong Sun* v. *United States*, 371 U.S. 471 (1963): evidence otherwise admissible but discovered as a result of an earlier violation is excluded as tainted, lest the law encourage future violations. But the Court in [*Oregon* v. *Elstad*, 470 U.S. 298 (1985)] rejected the *Wong Sun* fruits doctrine for analyzing the admissibility of a subsequent warned confession following "an initial failure . . . to administer the warnings required by *Miranda*." In *Elstad*, "a simple failure to administer the warnings, unaccompanied by any actual coercion or other circumstances calculated to undermine the suspect's ability to exercise his free will" did not "so tain[t] the investigatory process that a subsequent voluntary and informed waiver is ineffective for some indeterminate period. Though *Miranda* requires that the unwarned admission must be suppressed, the admissibility of any subsequent statement should turn in these circumstances solely on whether it is knowingly and voluntarily made." . . .

After all, the reason that question-first [without reading the suspect *Miranda* warnings] is catching on is as obvious as its manifest purpose, which is to get a confession the suspect would not make if he understood his rights at the outset; the sensible underlying assumption is that with one confession in hand before the warnings, the interrogator can count on getting its duplicate, with trifling additional trouble. Upon hearing warnings only in the aftermath of interrogation and just after making a confession, a suspect would hardly think he had a genuine right to remain silent, let alone persist in so believing once the police began to lead him over the same ground again.

A more likely reaction on a suspect's part would be perplexity about the reason for discussing rights at that point, bewilderment being an unpromising frame of mind for knowledgeable decision. What is worse, telling a suspect that "anything you say can and will be used against you," without expressly excepting the statement just given, could lead to an entirely reasonable inference that what he has just said will be used, with subsequent silence being of no avail. Thus, when *Miranda* warnings are inserted in the midst of coordinated and continuing interrogation, they are likely to mislead and "depriv[e] a defendant of knowledge essential to his ability to understand the nature of his rights and the consequences of abandoning them." *Moran* v. *Burbine*, 475 U.S. 412 (1986). By the same token, it would ordinarily be unrealistic to treat two spates of integrated and proximately conducted questioning as independent interrogations subject to independent evaluation simply because *Miranda* warnings formally punctuate them in the middle. . . .

CONCLUSION

The judgment of the Supreme Court of Missouri [suppressing the confession] is affirmed.

c. Exceptions to the Giving of Miranda Warnings

Miranda warnings are required only in custodial interrogations, so if the suspect is either not in custody or not being asked questions designed to elicit incriminating information, *Miranda* does not apply. The goal of *Miranda* is prophylactic [preventive] in nature to prevent police coercion in overbearing a suspect's will to confess. There is no Fifth Amendment protection against giving blood samples, fingerprints, and photographs for identification purposes, giving handwriting samples, being forced to read a statement so a witness may hear a suspect's voice, or the filming of a videotape showing the defendant's drunken and slurred speech and stumbling steps at time of arrest. In certain situations, such protection from coercion to self-incriminate oneself is not required:

- *Volunteered statements.*   These are statements given spontaneously and not as a result of any police questioning, for example admitting the location of contraband even though no one asked. In *Colorado* v. *Connelly*, 479 U.S. 157 (1986), Connelly walked up to a Denver police officer and confessed to murder, a confession he reiterated at the police station. He suffered from psychotic delusions and his attorney tried to suppress his confession. The U.S. Supreme Court held that the police should not be prevented from using voluntary confessions as evidence when the officers did nothing to induce such a confession, even if a suspect is obviously mentally ill.

- *Public safety questions.*   As an example, consider "Where's the gun?" The answer may be incriminating, but the officer's goal to protect the public safety outweighs the individual's privilege not to self-incriminate. In *New York* v. *Quarles*, 467 U.S. 649 (1984), a female rape victim gave officers a description of her armed assailant. When Quarles was found nearby, officers asked him the location of the gun to which he replied, "over there." On appeal, Quarles argued that since he was cornered and essentially in custody and being "interrogated" when asked about the gun, he should have received *Miranda* warnings. The U.S. Supreme Court disagreed, holding that concern for public safety in retrieving the gun outweighed an inflexible application of *Miranda*.

- *Questioning by ordinary citizens.*   These are questions asked by shop clerks or journalists, who may ask some of the same questions that police do, but who are not government agents. The protections of the Bill of Rights are only against government actors.

- *Routine booking questions.*   Questions that ask name, age, date of birth, height, and weight do not constitute custodial interrogation. In *Pennsylvania* v. *Muniz*, 496 U.S. 582 (1990), Muniz was videotaped at the police station being booked on drunk-driving charges. At trial, the state introduced the videotape to show that Muniz could not answer a question correctly about the date of his sixth birthday. Muniz objected on the grounds that the videotape incriminated him and, therefore, that he was entitled to *Miranda* warnings. The U.S. Supreme Court disagreed and held that *Miranda* is not required during routine booking procedures.

- *Crime scene investigation questions.*   Questions designed to learn facts to aid in the investigation do not need to be preceded by *Miranda*.

- *Investigative detentions and routine traffic stops.*

- *Undercover officers.*   An undercover agent need not disclose her identity and risk her safety by giving *Miranda* warnings to a suspect. Any statements made by the suspect to a person he does not know is an undercover agent will not be excluded because of a failure to give *Miranda* warnings.

- *Informants.*   Civilian informants working for the government need not warn suspects of *Miranda* warnings because police coercion is usually not present in such situations.

- *Probation/parole individuals.*   Offenders on probation or parole may be ordered to give information as a condition of their conditional release status.

i. *Miranda* at Investigatory Detentions and Traffic Stops   Courts have held that temporary investigative detentions [*Terry* pat-downs and frisks], as well as routine traffic stops, are not custodial interrogations requiring *Miranda* warnings. The focus of analysis is the brevity of the police–citizen encounter, the noncoercive nature of the brief detention, and the fact that the questioning is detailed and limited in scope to the justification for the stop itself. In *Berkemer v. McCarty*, 468 U.S. 420 (1984), a state trooper in Ohio suspected Berkemer of drunk driving. Even though the officer "apparently decided as soon as [Berkemer] stepped out of his car that [Berkemer] would be taken into custody and charged with a traffic offense," Berkemer was not in custody for *Miranda* purposes. The U.S. Supreme Court reasoned that lawful roadside stops for traffic violations were noncustodial. Typically, police questioning in public places, at the suspect's workplace, in a hospital where the patient is not under arrest, or in stores, restaurants, and bars are generally considered noncustodial because public places do not have a "police-dominated atmosphere."[29] Similarly, interviews initiated by suspects who come to the police station after learning that officers wish to speak to them are noncustodial and voluntary on behalf of the suspect.[30] However, if the detention goes on too long and the person being questioned believes that he or she is not free to leave, the detention turns into an arrest, which naturally implies a custodial situation.

II. PENALTIES FOR VIOLATING MIRANDA

1. Exclusionary Rule

Rule of Law: The Exclusionary Rule is not a constitutional right but a judicial remedy to deter police misconduct in obtaining evidence in violation of the protections afforded a suspect under the Fourth, Fifth, and Sixth Amendments.

As discussed briefly in chapters 9–11 on search, seizure, and warrants, evidence taken in violation of a defendant's Fourth Amendment right to be free from unreasonable searches and seizures, Fifth Amendment right not to be compelled to incriminate himself, and Sixth Amendment right to have the assistance of counsel may not be used against a defendant at trial by operation of the exclusionary rule. The **exclusionary rule** is a judge-made rule designed to deter police misconduct in the way they conduct investigations. If police ignore the legal constraints of the Constitution that protect people from government abuse of power, then the police will be punished by the court, which will suppress [keep out] the illegally obtained evidence. Students must be fully aware of the difference between constitutional violations of the Fourth, Fifth, and Sixth Amendment rights and violations in the giving of the warnings per *Miranda*. The high Court declared that the warnings were prophylactic in nature and left to the states the mechanisms whereby police would give them. That is, there is no standard or set way a suspect must be warned of his right to remain silent or have counsel present during questioning—as long as he received the warnings.

Under a *Miranda* totality analysis, the warnings are only one factor in determining whether the confession was voluntary. If *Miranda* warnings were not given, but the confession was otherwise voluntary and did not run afoul of the Fifth Amendment "compelled" clause, the confession would be admissible. So, too, would any fruits of an unwarned confession. In *Oregon* v. *Elstad*, 470 U.S. 298 (1985), officers arrested the defendant in his home pursuant to a burglary warrant and Elstad admitted that he was at the crime scene. Officers then took Elstad to the police station and gave him *Miranda* warnings, and he signed a written confession. The lower court admitted the written confession, but not the first statement that was given without the benefit of *Miranda*.

On appeal, the high Court held that the first unwarned and voluntary confession did not automatically taint the second confession before which *Miranda* warnings were given. *Elstad* is still good law in light of the *Seibert* (2004) decision, because Elstad's first confession was spontaneous and not induced by police interrogation, unlike Seibert's initial confession that was the direct product of police interrogation. To be clear, if Elstad's

---

[29]*See, generally, United States* v. *Masse*, 816 F.2d 805 (1st Cir. 1987).

[30]*United States* v. *Jonas*, 786 F.2d 1019 (11th Cir. 1986).

confession had been compelled in violation of the Fifth Amendment, his first confession would have been excluded, and his second confession would have been tainted fruit and would have been suppressed.

2. Fruit of the Poisonous Tree and Attenuation

Rule of Law: The original illegality taints the tree trunk which then poisons the fruit; poisoned fruit must be suppressed unless there is time and distance between the initial taint and the eventual poison.

The fruit of the poisonous tree doctrine is an extension of the exclusionary rule. If the trunk of a tree is poison, so too is its fruit. If an initial illegal action by the police means that evidence is suppressed [poisoned trunk], any statements or physical evidence derived from the initial illegal action will be tainted [poisoned] as well. The seminal case in the area is *Wong Sun* v. *United States*, 371 U.S. 471 (1963). In *Wong Sun*, the arrest warrant for Mr. Toy was defective because of insufficient probable cause. The illegal arrest is the tree's poisoned trunk. Because of his arrest, Toy made incriminating statements. Those statements were tainted fruit and had to be suppressed as well. But if there is a gap between the initial illegality and the ultimate discovery of the evidence—a doctrine called **attenuation**—the evidence will be allowed and admissible.

To establish attenuation, the high Court said that the proper question to ask is "whether, granting the establishment of the primary illegality, the evidence to which instant objection is made has been come at by exploitation of that illegality or instead by means sufficiently distinguished to be purged of the primary taint." In the same course of conduct that led to the arrest of Mr. Toy, Mr. Wong Sun was arrested, again, as determined later, without sufficient probable cause, making the arrest illegal. Days later, on his own, Wong Sun went voluntarily to the police station and confessed to drug crimes. The high Court held Wong Sun's confession was not tainted fruit of the poisoned trunk because it was "sufficiently attenuated" from his illegal arrest.

Another example of attenuation is in the case *Brown* v. *Illinois*, 422 U.S. 590 (1975). Without probable cause police forcibly entered Brown's apartment and arrested him. Brown was given *Miranda* warnings and he made two incriminating statements. The state court held that the *Miranda* warnings broke the poisoned fruit chain between the illegal arrest and the later incriminating statements. The U.S. Supreme Court disagreed and held that the action of the police in giving *Miranda* warnings, alone, was insufficient to "dissipate the taint of [Brown's] illegal arrest." The Court said that courts should look at three factors to determine whether there has been sufficient attenuation between the initial illegality and the subsequent production of tainted evidence to hold the tainted evidence admissible.

1. The time elapsed between the illegality and the acquisition of the tainted evidence
2. The presence of intervening circumstances between the initial illegality and the taint
3. The purpose and flagrancy of the official misconduct that resulted in the initial illegal conduct on behalf of law enforcement.

An examination of the three factors in Brown's case showed that his confession was not sufficiently attenuated from the officer's initial illegality; therefore, his statements had to be suppressed.

The following case, *United States* v. *Patane*, illustrates these distinctions between the constitutional protections and the protections of the judge-made remedies of the exclusionary rule and *Miranda* warnings. In this case, the U.S. Supreme Court held that police failure to give *Miranda* warnings did not warrant the exclusion of the evidence about a gun, because it was not poisoned fruit. Physical evidence does not implicate the Fifth Amendment protections.

BOX 12.5

United States v. *Patane*, 542 U.S. 630 (2004)
Supreme Court of the United States

Justice Thomas delivered the opinion of the Court.

FACTS

In June 2001, Samuel Francis Patane was arrested for harassing his ex-girlfriend, Linda O'Donnell. He was released on bond, subject to a temporary restraining order that prohibited him from contacting O'Donnell. [Patane] apparently violated the restraining order by attempting to telephone O'Donnell. On June 6, 2001, Officer Tracy Fox of the Colorado Springs Police Department began to investigate the matter. On the same day, a county probation officer informed an agent of the Bureau of Alcohol, Tobacco, and Firearms (ATF), that [Patane], a convicted felon, illegally possessed a .40 Glock pistol. The ATF relayed this information to Detective Josh Benner, who worked closely with the ATF. Together, Detective Benner and Officer Fox proceeded to [Patane]'s residence.

After reaching the residence and inquiring into [Patane]'s attempts to contact O'Donnell, Officer Fox arrested [Patane] for violating the restraining order. Detective Benner attempted to advise [Patane] of his *Miranda* rights but got no further than the right to remain silent. At that point, [Patane] interrupted, asserting that he knew his rights, and neither officer attempted to complete the warning. Detective Benner then asked [Patane] about the Glock. [Patane] was initially reluctant to discuss the matter, stating: "I am not sure I should tell you anything about the Glock because I don't want you to take it away from me." Detective Benner persisted, and [Patane] told him that the pistol was in his bedroom. [Patane] then gave Detective Benner permission to retrieve the pistol. Detective Benner found the pistol and seized it.

ISSUE

[W]hether a failure to give a suspect the warnings prescribed by *Miranda* v. *Arizona*, 384 U.S. 436 (1966), requires suppression of the physical fruits of the suspect's unwarned but voluntary statements?

HOLDING

[No, physical evidence derived from unwarned statements is admissible.]

REASONING

Our cases also make clear the related point that a mere failure to give *Miranda* warnings does not, by itself, violate a suspect's constitutional rights or even the *Miranda* rule. So much was evident in many of our pre-*Dickerson* cases, and we have adhered to this view since *Dickerson*. *See Chavez* (plurality opinion) (holding that a failure to read *Miranda* warnings did not violate [Patane]'s constitutional rights); 538 U.S., at 789, (Kennedy, J., agreeing "that failure to give a *Miranda* warning does not, without more, establish a completed violation when the unwarned interrogation ensues"). This, of course, follows from the nature of the right protected by the Self-Incrimination Clause, which the *Miranda* rule, in turn, protects. It is 'a fundamental trial right.' It follows that police do not violate a suspect's constitutional rights (or the *Miranda* rule) by negligent or even deliberate failures to provide the suspect with the full panoply of warnings prescribed by *Miranda*. Potential violations occur, if at all, only upon the admission of unwarned statements into evidence at trial. And, at that point, "[t]he exclusion of unwarned statements . . . is a complete and sufficient remedy" for any perceived *Miranda* violation.

Similarly, because police cannot violate the Self-Incrimination Clause by taking unwarned though voluntary statements, an exclusionary rule cannot be justified by reference to a deterrent effect on law enforcement. . . . Our decision not to apply *Wong Sun* to mere failures to give *Miranda* warnings was sound at the time *Tucker* and *Elstad* were decided, and we decline to apply *Wong Sun* to such failures now.

(continued)

BOX 12.5

(continued)

The Court of Appeals ascribed significance to the fact that, in this case, there might be "little [practical] difference between [Patane]'s confessional statement" and the actual physical evidence. The distinction, the court said, "appears to make little sense as a matter of policy." But, putting policy aside, we have held that "[t]he word 'witness' in the constitutional text limits the" scope of the Self-Incrimination Clause to testimonial evidence. The Constitution itself makes the distinction. And although it is true that the Court requires the exclusion of the physical fruit of actually coerced statements, it must be remembered that statements taken without sufficient *Miranda* warnings are presumed to have been coerced only for certain purposes and then only when necessary to protect the privilege against self-incrimination. For the reasons discussed above, we decline to extend that presumption further.

CONCLUSION

[W]e reverse the judgment of the Court of Appeals [suppressing the gun] and remand the case for further proceedings consistent with this opinion.

---

3. Inevitable Discovery

Rule of Law: If the tainted evidence would have been found inevitably despite the initial illegality that poisoned the tree, it is admissible.

The exclusionary rule has two primary exceptions, the inevitable discovery and independent source doctrines. Under the **inevitable discovery** rule, a court may admit illegally obtained evidence if it would have been inevitably discovered by investigative means. The rule had a tortured history in the case *Nix* v. *Williams*, 467 U.S. 431 (1984).[31] In that case, mentally ill offender Williams had kidnapped and killed a ten-year-old girl. Police were informed by Williams's lawyer not to talk to him without the lawyer's presence. As officers transported Williams from a county jail, the officer gave Williams what is known as the "Christian burial speech" with Williams sitting in the back of the cruiser. Officers knew Williams to be a religious man. Detective Leaming said to Williams:

> "I want to give you something to think about while we're traveling down the road . . . They are predicting several inches of snow for tonight, and I feel that you yourself are the only person that knows where this little girl's body is . . . and if you get a snow on top of it you yourself may be unable to find it. And since we will be going right past the area [where the body is] on the way to Des Moines, I feel that we could stop and locate the body, that the parents of this little girl should be entitled to a Christian burial for the little girl who was snatched away from them on Christmas [E]ve and murdered. . . . [A]fter a snow storm [we may not be] able to find it at all."

Leaming told Williams he knew that the girl's body was in the area of Mitchellville—a town they would be passing on the way to Des Moines. Leaming concluded his speech by saying, "I do not want you to answer me . . . Just think about it . . . " Williams then directed the officers to the location of the victim's body, which was in the general vicinity where a search party had been looking. On appeal from his death sentence, the court found Leaming's speech to be a Sixth Amendment violation of Williams's right to counsel. Since Leaming committed a constitutional violation under the Sixth Amendment right to counsel rather than a failure to give *Miranda* warnings, the girl's body was excluded as evidence by operation of the fruit of the poisonous tree doctrine. That is, since the "confession" of the location of the girl's body was poisoned, the fruit (the

---

[31]Originally reported as *Brewer* v. *Williams*, 430 U.S. 387 (1977).

body) was tainted as well and was excluded. After retrial and more appeals, the U.S. Supreme Court heard the case and held that since the search party already in progress would have "inevitably discovered" the girl's body, the body should be admitted into evidence as an exception to the exclusionary rule.

4. Independent Source

Rule of Law: If evidence was found through an independent source to be unrelated to the initial illegality that poisoned the tree, it is admissible.

Independent source is an exception to the exclusionary rule that permits illegally obtained evidence to be introduced at trial if it was discovered through a source not connected with the initial illegality.[32] For example, during an investigation into drug dealing police entered a warehouse unlawfully without a warrant and discovered bales of marijuana. Some officers kept the warehouse under surveillance while others went to secure the warrant to search the warehouse. In the officer's affidavit establishing probable cause to search the warehouse, he did not mention that the police had already entered the warehouse illegally. The warrant was issued and the drug dealers were caught. At trial, they challenged the initial illegality that formed the basis of probable cause. The U.S. Supreme Court found that the officer's knowledge came from an "independent source" regardless of the unlawful search because the illegal search was not used as the basis for the warrant.[33] In another case in which stolen goods were illegally seized and suppressed by operation of the exclusionary rule, testimony about the goods was admissible because the witnesses' knowledge about the crime was an "independent source" and therefore fit the exception to the exclusionary rule.[34] The rationale of the independent source exception was explained by the high Court:

> [T]he interest of society in deterring unlawful police conduct and the public interest in having juries receive all probative evidence of a crime are properly balanced by putting the police in the same, not a worse, position that they would have been in if no police error or misconduct had occurred.... When the challenged evidence has an independent source, exclusion of such evidence would put the police in a worse position than they would have been in absent any error or violation. *Nix* v. *Williams*, 467 U.S. 431 (1984).

5. Collateral Uses of Excluded Evidence

Use of evidence that was obtained in violation of a suspect's Fifth Amendment rights may still be used in certain circumstances. The high Court held in *Mincey* v. *Arizona*, 437 U.S. 385 (1978), that it is a violation of due process to use a coerced confession not only to prove guilt, but for any purpose at trial, including impeaching the defendant with his own perjury in the witness stand. But such tainted evidence may still be introduced against a defendant in federal civil tax proceedings, *habeas corpus* proceedings, grand jury proceedings, deportation proceedings, parole revocation and sentencing hearings. The illegally obtained evidence may also be used to discredit the defendant if he or she testifies at trial. Even though a confession may be excluded from trial because of a failure to read *Miranda* warnings to the suspect, the confession may still be used against the defendant if he or she takes the stand and specifically contradicts his or her previous confession. To allow a defendant to benefit at the expense of the state's mistake by changing her story and committing perjury is untenable. *Harris* v. *New York*, 401 U.S. 222 (1971). But keep in mind that if the confession was taken in violation of a *Massiah* right to counsel, the confession must be suppressed for all purposes.[35]

---

[32]*Silverthorne Lumber Company* v. *United States*, 251 U.S. 385 (1920).

[33]*Murray* v. *United States*, 487 U.S. 533 (1988).

[34]*United States* v. *Ruhe*, 191 F.3d 376 (4th Cir. 1999).

[35]*See United States* v. *Kimball*, 884 F.2d 1274 (9th Cir. 1989).

III. Key Terms and Phrases

- admission
- confession
- *corpus delicti*
- custodial interrogation
- custody
- exclusionary rule
- Fifth Amendment

- fruit of the poisonous tree
- independent source
- inevitable discovery
- interrogation
- invoking *Miranda*
- knowing, intelligent, voluntary waiver

- privilege against self-incrimination
- public-safety exception
- scrupulously honor
- totality of the circumstances
- trickery in confessions

IV. Summary

1. **The genesis of the so-called *Miranda* warnings:** The history of police interrogations includes **third degree** interrogations, brutal practices to extract confessions. A **confession** is a complete admission of guilt for the charged crime. Because the Bill of Rights applied only to the actions of the federal government, until the 1960s the U.S. Supreme Court could only invalidate convictions based on federal actors. In 1964, Court held all incriminating **statements** taken in absence of counsel inadmissible. *Escobedo* v. *Illinois* (1964) extended the principle of inadmissibility of statements to include pre-arraignment states of interrogation.

2. **The interrogation process:** There are many interrogation techniques, but Inbau & Reid's training manual recommends **nine steps of interrogation** to induce the obviously guilty suspects to confess. **Trickery** in interrogations can lead to false confessions. In *Malloy* v. *Hogan* (1964) the Court held the Fourteenth Amendment's due process clause made the right to be free from self-incrimination applicable to the states.

3. **The situations in which *Miranda* warnings are required:** *Miranda* v. *Arizona* (1964) held that for a suspect to properly exercise his constitutional right not to incriminate himself and to have counsel present during questioning, he had to be apprised of his rights before any **custodial interrogation.** During custodial interrogation, the suspect believes he is not free to leave and law enforcement agents ask questions intended to elicit incriminating information.

4. **The legal consequences of violating the *Miranda* requirement:** If a suspect invokes the **right to remain silent,** all questioning must cease, but police may reinitiate interrogation after rewarning the suspect with *Miranda*. If a suspect invokes the right to have an **attorney present,** all questioning must stop until the suspect has had an opportunity to consult with counsel. A *Miranda* **waiver** may be invoked only by a person who is **knowing, intelligent, and acting voluntarily.** The burden is on the state to prove that the waiver was voluntary. Silence will not suffice as a waiver. To be admitted, a confession must have been given **voluntarily;** if it was produced through police coercion, it will be suppressed. The law as recognized by *Seibert* v. *Missouri* (2004) prohibits double interviewing, which is the practice of extracting a confession, then providing *Miranda* warnings, and then asking the suspect to repeat the confession. Statements taken in violation of *Miranda* must be suppressed by operation of the **exclusionary rule. Fruit of the poisonous tree** indicates that evidence which is derivative from an illegal act by law enforcement personnel must be suppressed. **Right to counsel** attaches at the beginning of the adversary process, that is, once formal charges are brought.

5. ***Miranda* exceptions: Exceptions** in which *Miranda* does not apply include situations involving public safety, volunteered and spontaneous confessions, routine booking statements, crime scene investigation questions, lawful traffic stops, and investigatory detentions.

V. Discussion Questions

1. What is the harm to the criminal justice system of allowing officers to present suspects with fabricated evidence during interrogations in order to induce confessions? Do you believe that the best way to catch a criminal is to act like one and to lie as a means to an end—here obtaining a confession from a guilty suspect? How do police know whether a suspect is really guilty before trial? Research the law in your jurisdiction for the limits to police deception in conducting interrogations. Does allowing police to be deceptive undermine the public's confidence in the criminal justice system?

2. A suspect in custody indicates that he wants to make a statement and wants to talk to a lawyer, but officers wait for three days before notifying counsel. In the meantime, the suspect has confessed. How would you rule on the admissibility of that confession?

VI. Problem-Solving Exercises

1. Officer Kay was responding to a call about shots fired when she came upon a car crash. Stopping to help, the officer noticed the driver, Fred, bleeding and saw a weapon nearby. Drawing her service revolver, the officer pointed it at him and asked, "Are there other weapons?" Fred indicated that there were five shotguns in the trunk. As Officer Kay was placing the suspect in handcuffs, he asked, "Do you see my friend Robby?" Officer Kay looked around and said, "No, but where does he live?" Fred said that Robby often dealt drugs from an apartment at 512 Main Street and stated that the two of them were involved in a shooting over a drug deal that had gone bad. Officers went to the apartment on Main Street, arrested Robby, and seized a significant quantity of cocaine. Robby sought to suppress the cocaine as tainted fruit from Fred's unlawful arrest. Will he be successful? Explain your answer fully.

2. After an eight-year-old boy was brutally raped and murdered, police identified his neighbor, Ray, as a suspect and took him to the police station for an interrogation. Using police practices from the past, officers used telephone books to hit Ray in the ribs without leaving marks, held him face up under an open faucet and let his throat fill with water before turning him over, and attached electrodes to his genitals which they threatened to turn on if Ray did not confess to the murder. Ray did confess. When police asked where the body was, Ray initially refused to tell them. While Ray was at the police station, a search party was searching near a local elementary school for the boy's body. Ray's sister came to the police station to report that Ray had indicated he had killed the boy and dumped his body "near a school yard." Ray eventually told police that the boy's body was under the swing set at the nearby school. At his murder trial, Ray claimed that his confession was coerced and should be excluded and that his telling the location of the boy's body was fruit of the poisonous tree. The state replied that under the inevitable discovery and independent source doctrines, the body should be admissible. How should the court rule and why?

VII. World Wide Web Resources

U.S. International Interrogation Policy

http://www.gwu.edu/~nsarchiv/NSAEBB/NSAEBB127/

Interrogations, Confessions and Videotape article

http://www.helvidius.org/files/2003/2003_Mahony.pdf

VIII. Additional Readings and Notes

Court History and the Fifth Amendment

Michael J. Ashraf. "*United States* v. *Patane: Miranda's* Excesses." *St. John's Journal of Legal Commentary*, Vol. 20 (2005), pp. 85–127.

Liva Baker. *Miranda: Crime, Law and Politics* (Boston: Atheneum, 1983).

Confessions

Saul M. Kassin. "The Psychology of Confession Evidence." *American Psychologist*, Vol. 52 (1997), pp. 221–233.

Richard A. Leo. "Inside the Interrogation Room." *Journal of Criminal Law & Criminology,* Vol. 86. No. 2 (1996), pp. 266–303.

Joseph T. McCann. "A Conceptual Framework for Identifying Various Types of Confessions." *Behavioral Sciences and the Law,* Vol. 16 (1998), pp. 441–453.

Richard J. Ofshe and Richard A. Leo. "The Social Psychology of Police Interrogation: The Theory and Classification of True and False Confessions." *Studies in Law, Politics & Society,* Vol. 16 (1997), pp. 189–251.

Roger W. Shuy. *The Language of Confession, Interrogation, and Deception* (Thousand Oaks, CA: Sage, 1998).

Deborah Young. "Unnecessary Evil: Police Lying in Interrogations." *Connecticut Law Review*, Vol. 28 (1996), pp. 425–477.

CHAPTER 13

The Constitution at Trial

"The Constitution does not provide for first and second class citizens."
— WENDELL WILLKIE (1944), REPUBLICAN PARTY NOMINEE
FOR PRESIDENT OF THE UNITED STATES, 1940

CHAPTER OBJECTIVES

Primary Concepts Discussed in This Chapter:

1. The protection for defendants during the discovery process
2. The protection for defendants from their lawyers
3. The protection for defendants in venue selection and jury selection
4. The rights of victims at a defendant's sentencing hearing

CHAPTER OUTLINE

Feature: The Constitution at Work at Trial

I. THE DEFENDANT'S RIGHTS AT TRIAL

1. Discovery
   Box 13.1 *Brady* v. *Maryland*, 373 U.S. 83 (1963)
2. Lawyers' Legal Obligations
   Box 13.2 *New York* v. *Francis R. Belge*, 372 N.Y.S.2d 798 (1975)
   a. Ineffective Assistance of Counsel
3. Trial
   a. Venue Selection
   Box 13.3 *Missouri* v. Baumruk, 85 S.W.3d 644 (Mo. banc 2002)
   b. The Sixth Amendment's Confrontation Clause
      i. Child Witnesses in Sex-Abuse Cases
      ii. The Right to Represent Oneself in Court
4. Jury Selection
   a. Challenges Based on Race or Gender
5. Closing Arguments
   Box 13.4 *Carruthers* v. *State*, 528 S.E.2d 217 (Ga. 2000)
6. Victims' Rights at Sentencing
   Box 13.5 *Payne* v. *Tennessee*, 501 U.S. 808 (1991)

II. Key Terms and Phrases

Feature: *Chapter-Opening Case Study: The Constitution at Work at Trial*

John, a native of Argentina, was an international drug dealer who was visiting his sister in Atlanta. Police had his sister's house under surveillance, and when they executed a search warrant for the house, they discovered a kilogram of heroin hidden behind the tiles in the basement ceiling. The heroin had been carefully wrapped in coffee beans and dryer sheets to camouflage the smell of the drugs and throw off the drug-detection dogs. John was arrested; when he met with his lawyer, he confessed to owning the drugs, but pleaded with his lawyer to help get him off the charges [law mandates zealous representation of defense clients even if defendant admits guilt]. Before his case came to trial, it was discovered that John had been molesting his four-year-old niece while staying at his sister's house and that on one prior occasion when he sold heroin, a customer named Joe overdosed and died. The state consolidated the drug and sexual abuse charges together for trial and decided to seek the death penalty for the drug-related death [allowable under federal law even if defendant did not personally cause the death]. The case received a lot of publicity, and public opinion polls in the local newspaper concluded that if John was guilty, he should be executed for his crime [defendant entitled to change venue if evidence indicates he cannot receive a fair trial].

When John's jury was being selected, the prosecutor struck all African-American and Hispanic men from the pool of potential jurors because the prosecutor thought men of color might identify with John and be sympathetic to his defense, and the state wanted to ensure a conviction [illegal under *Batson* v. *Kentucky*]. At trial, John grew disillusioned with his lawyer and insisted on representing himself [defendants have a constitutional right to defend themselves]. When the judge granted John's request, his lawyer felt free to become a witness for the state and testified in court about John's confession that the drugs found in his sister's house belonged to him. When the state called John's niece to the witness stand, she was so visibly afraid of John when she saw him at counsel table that she could not testify in court. The judge allowed her to testify via live feed video camera, but John objected on the grounds that he could not adequately cross-examine the child if she was not in front of him [video in lieu of live testimony implicates the Sixth Amendment's confrontation clause]. The judge overruled John's objection. The jury found John guilty of the drug-related death, but became deadlocked on the molestation charge.

At his death-penalty sentencing hearing, the family of the overdose victim made an impact statement about how John's actions has caused them a lifetime of pain. Then the victim's mother turned to address the jury directly and said, "Please sentence this vermin to death to avenge my son's death" [victims can make an impact statement at defendant's sentencing but may not advocate for a specific sentence]. How does constitutional law affect John's case?

INTRODUCTION

The government's goal in a criminal trial is to hold an offender accountable for crimes and, perhaps, to deprive him of liberty by securing a conviction for a prison sentence, or even for the death sentence, in a death-penalty trial. The defendant's goal at trial is, at a minimum, to vindicate his innocence or secure his liberty by avoiding an excessive sentence. Criminal law defines criminal behavior while criminal procedure defines the rules that guide the criminal process. Each state has the power to define its own criminal laws—for example, whether to recognize the M'Naghten test for insanity—but criminal procedure rules are fairly uniform throughout the nation: All defendants must be notified of the charges against them, all defendants have a right to counsel at trial, and all defendants charged with serious crimes have a right to have a jury decide their fate, for instance. Most criminal procedure rules are derived from the Bill of Rights, the first ten amendments to the Constitution. This chapter presents an overview of the constitutional rights and ideals that guide criminal procedure before and at trial to meet the ideal that everyone is treated equally at trial under the Constitution. The nuts and bolts of the actual trial process, including the introduction of evidence at trial, are covered in depth in chapter 2, but the constitutional mandates that guide the trial process are illuminated here.

I. THE DEFENDANT'S RIGHTS AT TRIAL

1. Discovery

Rule of Law: The rules of discovery mandate that both sides share information prior to trial, but the government has an affirmative duty to disclose exculpatory information that tends to prove innocence to the defense.

The prosecutor must follow certain rules of law to ensure due process for criminal defendants. Courts place certain obligations on the state in a criminal trial because the government has all the power to detain people during interrogation, search and seize evidence, enter into plea bargains with cooperating witnesses, pay informants, and have evidence tested at laboratories regardless of cost. Because the prosecutor has an advantage in controlling the information that will be used against the defendant at trial, his first duty to the defendant is to turn over discovery. **Discovery** is the process by which the state turns over all the evidence it has or intends to introduce at trial to the defense and the defense does the same for the prosecutor. This evidence may include results of scientific tests and witness statements. Both parties have to furnish a witness list with address and contact information so that each side may try to interview the witnesses before trial. If the defendant plans to raise the defenses of alibi and insanity, he must provide notice of such intent during discovery.

Neither the government nor the defense is required to turn over internal memoranda or reports done pursuant to investigating their cases and preparing the case for trial, often called "work product" or confidential information. How does the government decide what evidence it must, by law, turn over to the defense before trial? **Exculpatory evidence** is information tending to indicate that the defendant is innocent of the charges; the prosecutor alone decides what information is exculpatory and must turn over all such evidence in its possession to the defense.

To understand how exculpatory information works, let's assume the following hypothetical scenario: A man is on trial for the murder of his wife. The police discover that there were a few marauding thieves in the neighborhood seen around the time of the wife's disappearance. The defense asserts that these men may have been the real killers, who caught the wife unaware as she walked her dog through the park. Let's say that the police did arrest three men in the neighborhood on the day after the wife vanished and that one of the men confessed to killing her. Let's also assume that after a week in jail, the police concluded that these men were only garden-variety vagrants and that the man who had confessed was actually suffering from delusions and falsely confessed to the murder. During the time that the men were in police custody, police took statements from the men and wrote six police reports not only detailing the arrests and apparent connection to the wife's disappearance, but also describing the "confession." As a final piece to our hypothetical, let's assume that before the trial the prosecutor never disclosed to the existence of the police reports or the confession to the defense lawyer, because the prosecutor thought it was irrelevant to the question of who killed the wife. In this hypothetical, has the prosecutor broken the law? Who decides whether or not something is relevant to the defense? Who would you want to decide if you were on trial and evidence pertained to your case: the prosecutor, the judge, or your defense lawyer? In our hypothetical, the prosecutor has an obligation to turn the information over to the defense when they request it because the existence of other suspects could tend to prove the husband's innocence.

In *Brady* v. *Maryland*, the Supreme Court for the first time imposed on prosecutors broad disclosure obligations under applicable discovery rules. Brady was found guilty of murder and sentenced to death. At trial, Brady admitted to participating in the murder but claimed that his partner, Boblit, who was tried separately, did the actual shooting. Before trial, Brady's lawyer specifically asked to see the statements made by Boblit to the police. The prosecutor gave Brady's lawyer copies of many statements Boblit made, but he withheld the one statement in which Boblit actually admitted to the killing for which Brady was on trial. The Court held that withholding such **exculpatory evidence**—that which tends to prove the defendant innocent—violated Brady's due process rights. The reasoning from the *Brady* decision discussing why the government should be forced to disclose exculpatory information is reprinted in part in Box 13.1.

BOX 13.1

Brady v. *Maryland*, 373 U.S. 83 (1963)
United States Supreme Court

Justice Douglas delivered the opinion of the Court.

We now hold that the suppression by the prosecution of evidence favorable to an accused upon request violates due process where the evidence is material either to guilt or to punishment, irrespective of the good faith or bad faith of the prosecution.

[This principle] is not punishment of society for misdeeds of a prosecutor but avoidance of an unfair trial to the accused. Society wins not only when the guilty are convicted but when criminal trials are fair; our system of the administration of justice suffers when any accused is treated unfairly.

An inscription on the walls of the Department of Justice states the proposition candidly for the federal domain: "The United States wins its point whenever justice is done its citizens in the courts." A prosecution that withholds evidence on demand of an accused which, if made available, would tend to exculpate him or reduce the penalty helps shape a trial that bears heavily on the defendant. That casts the prosecutor in the role of an architect of a proceeding that does not comport with standards of justice.

In the spirit of *Brady*, the Supreme Court articulated the standard to test whether a prosecutor's nondisclosure of evidence violated a defendant's due process right to a fair trial in *United States* v. *Bagley*, 473 U.S. 667 (1985). Evidence is material and thus needed to be disclosed to the defense, the Court said, only if there is a "reasonable probability that, had the evidence been disclosed to the defense, the result of the proceeding would have been different." The burden is on the defendant to show that the outcome of his trial would have been different if the prosecution had given him the evidence it withheld. As the Supreme Court explained in *Kyles* v. *Whitley*, 514 U.S. 419 (1995), "The question is not whether the defendant would more likely than not have received a different verdict with the evidence, but whether in its absence he received a fair trial, understood as a trial resulting in a verdict worthy of confidence." The test for determining whether untimely disclosure of *Brady* information deprived the defendant of a fair trial is whether the disclosure was made so late as to prevent the defense from using the material effectively in preparing or presenting for trial. The materiality of evidence is determined by weighing several factors, including the importance of the witness, the significance of the evidence, and the strength of the prosecution's case. Several courts have urged prosecutors to disclose *Brady* material [exculpatory evidence tending to exonerate the accused] as soon as possible, preferably before trial, in order to secure a fair trial for the defendant. Sanctions on the prosecution for late disclosure of *Brady* material are rare. If trial is underway, a mistrial may be declared in favor of the defense. If the defendant had been convicted before the *Brady* violation was discovered, his conviction could be overturned. In extreme cases where prosecutors engaged in deliberate misconduct in withholding *Brady* information, a court could recommend disciplinary charges against the prosecutor.[1]

The rule of law announced in *Brady* was reiterated in the U.S. Supreme Court cases *Giglio* v. *United States*, 405 U.S. 150 (1972), and *United States* v. *Bagley*, 473 U.S. 667 (1985). *Giglio* requires that the prosecutor turn over any and all inducements (plea deals that reduce jail time for the witness), and benefits given to a witness in exchange for his or her testimony. But who decides whether evidence in the prosecutor's files is exculpatory to the accused and must, therefore, be turned over to the defense? The answer— only the prosecutor. There is no judicial oversight over exculpatory information in the prosecutor's possession unless a defense counsel asks a judge to examine the prosecutor's files *in camera* [in the judge's chambers]. Such requests are not likely to be granted, given both the volume of evidence that would need to be reviewed and the judge's lack of knowledge about the asserted defense—and thus the judge's inability to appreciate whether or not certain evidence exonerates the defendant.

Not only does the prosecutor decide what potentially exculpatory evidence in its file material to disclose to the defense, the prosecutor also decides when to disclose the material. The law requires only that *Brady* material be disclosed to the defense soon enough to make "effective" use of it, not necessarily soon enough to use it for proper preparation for trial. The federal appellate decision in *United States* v. *Rogers*, 960 F.2d 1501 (10th Cir. 1992), is illustrative of this doctrine:

> Rogers argues that he filed a specific request for certain documents five years before trial; that they were not produced until the last day of trial; and that he was given only three hours to review the documents. Rogers further argues that had he been given the documents in a timely manner, he could have reviewed, investigated, and properly developed his defense, and that it is probable that the jury would have reached a different

---

[1] *See ABA Standards for Criminal Justice* §§11-2.l(c), 11-2.2(a) (2d ed. 1982) (requiring prosecutor to disclose to defense "as soon as practicable" "any material or information within his possession or control which tends to negate the guilt of the accused or would tend to reduce his punishment therefore"); *ABA Standards for Criminal Justice* §3-3.11(a) (3d ed. 1993) (it is unprofessional conduct for prosecutor to fail to disclose to defense exculpatory information "at the earliest feasible opportunity").

result. We have held that, "the relevant standard of materiality does not focus on the trial preparation, but instead on whether earlier disclosure would have created a reasonable doubt of guilt that did not otherwise exist."

Thus, according to the decision in *Rogers* and similar cases, the prosecutor is required to disclose *Brady* and *Giglio* material, but does not necessarily have to turn it over in a manner in which the defendant can make any good use of it.

Applying the Rule of Law to the Facts: What is a *Brady* doctrine violation?

- John was charged with abducting three young women and forcing one at gunpoint to perform a sexual act upon him. After he was convicted, John discovered that before the case went to trial, someone had produced a note allegedly written by two of the women stating that John had been "played" for a fool. The state investigator to whom the note was shown did not take the note and urged the person who produced it to destroy it. Did the state violate the law?

Yes, the U.S. Supreme Court held in *Youngblood* v. *West Virginia*, 547 U.S. 867 (2006) that under *Brady* v. *Maryland* the state had a duty to take possession and turn over the exculpatory information to John to use in his defense.

2. Lawyers' Legal Obligations

Rule of Law: A defense lawyer does not have to report to authorities his clients' past crimes.

For defense attorneys to perform their job of defending clients properly, communication between the attorney and client must remain confidential. The attorney–client privilege allows the justice system to function at its best when a client has no fear that what he says to his lawyer will be used against him. In addition, client confidentiality ensures that the attorney is truly the client's advocate and not just a tool of the court system. Criminal defense attorneys need not disclose information that will subject their clients to further prosecution. As the Rules and the Code that guide an attorney's conduct in the zealous representation of his clients provide,[2] even if a client informs his attorney of past crimes or indicates a willingness to commit crime in the future, the attorney does not have to disclose that information to authorities (though he may if he wishes). The integrity of the adversary system would break down if an attorney became an arm of the prosecution in providing evidence against her client.

Where does society draw the line between zealous advocacy and criminal activity on the part of a lawyer? As Harvard Law Professor Alan Dershowitz once said, "All sides in a trial want to hide at least some of the truth." As you read the *Belge* case below, ask whether the lawyer's duty is stronger to the client or to the public. (Keep in mind that an attorney is, ultimately, an officer of the court who answers to the people.)

---

[2]Model Code of Professional Conduct Rule 1.6 (2003).

The Rule states as follows:

(a) A lawyer **shall** not reveal information relating to representation of a client unless the client gives informed consent, the disclosure is impliedly authorized in order to carry out the representation, or the disclosure is permitted by paragraph (b).

(b) A lawyer **may** reveal information relating to the representation of a client to the extent the lawyer reasonably believes necessary:
   (1) to prevent reasonably certain death or substantial bodily harm;
   (2) to secure legal advice about the lawyer's compliance with these Rules;
   (3) to establish a claim or defense on behalf of the lawyer in a controversy between the lawyer and the client, to establish a defense to a criminal charge or civil claim against the lawyer based upon conduct in which the client was involved, or to respond to allegations in any proceeding concerning the lawyer's representation of the client; or
   (4) to comply with other law or a court order.

BOX 13.2

New York v. Francis R. Belge, 372 N.Y.S.2d 798 (1975)
County Court of New York, Onondaga County

Judge Gale delivered the opinion of the court.

FACTS

In the summer of 1973 Robert F. Garrow, Jr., stood charged in Hamilton County with the crime of murder. The defendant was assigned two attorneys, Frank H. Armani and Francis R. Belge. A defense of insanity had been interposed by counsel for Mr. Garrow. During the course of the discussions between Garrow and his two counsel, three other murders were admitted by Garrow, one being in Onondaga County. On or about September of 1973 Mr. Belge conducted his own investigation based upon what his client had told him and with the assistance of a friend the location of the body of Alicia Hauck was found in Oakwood Cemetery in Syracuse. Mr. Belge personally inspected the body and was satisfied, presumably, that this was the Alicia Hauck that his client had told him that he murdered. This discovery was not disclosed to the authorities, but became public during the trial of Mr. Garrow in June of 1974, when to affirmatively establish the defense of insanity, these three other murders were brought before the jury by the defense in the Hamilton County trial.

ISSUE

[Did] Francis R. Belge, Esq., [violate] subdivision 1 of section 4200 of the Public Health Law, which requires that a decent burial be accorded the dead, and section 4143 of the Public Health Law, which requires anyone knowing of the death of a person without medical attendance, to report the same to the proper authorities?

HOLDING

[No.] . . . [A] confidential, privileged communication existed between [Belge] and Mr. Garrow, which should excuse the attorney from making full disclosure to the authorities. It is the decision of this court that Francis R. Belge conducted himself as an officer of the court with all the zeal at his command to protect the constitutional rights of his client.

REASONING

The National Association of Criminal Defense Lawyers, as *amicus curiae* [friends of the court who file briefs in support of one side in a case pending before the court] succinctly state the issue in the following language: If this indictment stands, "The attorney–client privilege will be effectively destroyed. No defendant will be able to freely discuss the facts of his case with his attorney. No attorney will be able to listen to those facts without being faced with the Hobson's choice of violating the law or violating his professional code of Ethics."

Initially in England the practice of law was not recognized as a profession, and certainly some people are skeptics today. However, the practice of learned and capable men appearing before the court on behalf of a friend or an acquaintance became more and more demanding. Consequently, the King granted a privilege to certain of these men to engage in such practice. There had to be rules governing their duties. These came to be known as "Canons." The King has, in this country, been substituted by a democracy, but the "Canons" are with us today, having been honed and refined over the years to meet the changes of time. Among those is the following, cited in *United States* v. *Funk*, 84 F Supp 967: "Confidential communications between an attorney and his client are privileged from disclosure . . . as a rule of necessity in the administration of justice."

Our system of criminal justice is an adversary system and the interests of the State are not absolute, or even paramount. "The dignity of the individual is respected to the point that even when the citizen is known by the state to have committed a heinous offense, the individual is nevertheless accorded such rights as counsel, trial by jury, due process, and the privilege against self incrimination." A trial is in part a search for truth, but it is only partly a search for truth. The mantle of innocence is flung over the defendant to such an extent that he is safeguarded by rules of evidence which frequently keep out absolute truth, much to the chagrin of juries. Nevertheless, this has been a part of our system since our laws were taken from the laws of England and over these many years has been found to best protect a balance between the rights of the individual and the rights of society.

The effectiveness of counsel is only as great as the confidentiality of its client–attorney relationship. If the lawyer cannot get all the facts about the case, he can only give his client half of a defense. This, of necessity, involves the client telling his attorney everything remotely connected with the crime. Apparently, in the instant case, after analyzing all the evidence, and after hearing of the bizarre episodes in the life of their client, they decided that the only possibility of salvation was in a defense of insanity. For the client to disclose not only everything about this particular crime but also everything about other crimes which might have a bearing upon his defense, requires the strictest confidence in, and on the part of, the attorney.

When the facts of the other homicides became public, as a result of the defendant's testimony to substantiate his claim of insanity, "Members of the public were shocked at the apparent callousness of these lawyers, whose conduct was seen as typifying the unhealthy lack of concern of most lawyers with the public interest and with simple decency." A hue and cry went up from the press and other news media suggesting that the attorneys should be found guilty of such crimes as obstruction of justice or becoming an accomplice after the fact. From a layman's standpoint, this certainly was a logical conclusion. However, the Constitution of the United States of America attempts to preserve the dignity of the individual and to do that guarantees him the services of an attorney who will bring to the Bar and to the Bench every conceivable protection from the inroads of the State against such rights as are vested in the Constitution for one accused of crime. Among those substantial constitutional rights is that a defendant does not have to incriminate himself. His attorneys were bound to uphold that concept and maintain what has been called a sacred trust of confidentiality.

There must always be a conflict between the obstruction of the administration of criminal justice and the preservation of the right against self incrimination which permeates the mind of the attorney as the alter ego of his client. But that is not the situation before this court. We have the Fifth Amendment right, derived from the Constitution, on the one hand, as against the trivia of a pseudo-criminal statute on the other, which has seldom been brought into play. Clearly the latter is completely out of focus when placed alongside the client–attorney privilege. An examination of the Grand Jury testimony sheds little light on their reasoning. The testimony of Mr. Armani added nothing new to the facts as already presented to the Grand Jury. He and Mr. Belge were co-counsel. Both were answerable to the Canons of professional ethics. The Grand Jury chose to indict one and not the other. It appears as if that body were grasping at straws.

CONCLUSION

It is the decision of this court that Francis R. Belge conducted himself as an officer of the court with all the zeal at his command to protect the constitutional rights of his client. Both on the grounds of a privileged communication and in the interests of justice the indictment [against Belge] is dismissed.

Applying the Rule of Law to the Facts: Is disclosure ever mandatory?

- Bill was at his attorney's office discussing his upcoming trial on charges of domestic violence. Bill said to his lawyer, "I can't wait to get off on these charges. When I do so, I'm going to get my wife good for bringing me down." Must the attorney disclose the client's plan of violence?

No, the attorney rules of conduct embodied in the <u>Model Code of Professional</u> Responsibility DR 4-101 (1969) state:

(C) A lawyer **may** reveal . . .
(3) the intention of his client to commit a crime and the information necessary to prevent the crime.

Bill's lawyer may disclose Bill's plan to the authorities if he wishes, but such disclosure is not mandatory.

a. Ineffective Assistance of Counsel

Rule of Law: The defense counsel's performance must be that of a reasonable attorney

If the attorney's performance before and during trial falls below the standard of a minimally competent attorney, the defendant may have grounds for a successful appeal of his conviction on the basis of a claim of ineffective assistance of counsel. The legal standard that a defendant has to meet to prove that his counsel fell below the standard of a reasonable attorney was expressed by the U.S. Supreme Court in *Strickland* v. *Washington*, 466 U.S. 668 (1984):

> First, the defendant must show that counsel's performance was deficient. This requires showing that counsel made errors so serious that counsel was not functioning as the "counsel" guaranteed the defendant by the Sixth Amendment. Second, the defendant must show that the deficient performance prejudiced the defense. This requires showing that counsel's errors were so serious as to deprive the defendant of a fair trial, a trial whose result is reliable. Unless a defendant makes both showings, it cannot be said that the conviction or death sentence resulted from a breakdown in the adversary process that renders the result unreliable.

The recent trend in successful claims of ineffective counsel is in death-penalty cases. Courts are finding more frequently that the defense counsel's performance in preparing and presenting death cases fails the standard enunciated by the high Court in *Strickland*.

3. Trial

a. Venue Selection

Rule of Law: Venue mandates that the trial take place where the crime took place.

The United States Constitution and many state constitutions provide that a criminal trial shall be held in the state, district, or county where the crime occurred. The rationale for trying the case in the place where the crime was committed ensures that the people most affected in the community have a chance to see justice served and the defendant can have access to witnesses and evidence that are geographically close by. In the founding days of the Republic, when the colonies were still under British rule, Parliament revived a law that allowed a colonist accused of treason to be brought back to England for trial. Faced with the prospect of defending themselves away from the emotional and financial support of their families, the colonists protested. As one legal scholar noted about being tried in the motherland, "For any accused, trial at a distant location would be inconvenient and expensive. For an accused of limited means, trial at a distant location could, in effect, mean a complete inability to present a defense to a charge."[3] Author Andrew Leipold has stated that this turmoil "led to the vicinage [neighborhood, near dwelling] provision in the Sixth Amendment, mandating that the jury be drawn from the "State and district" where the crime occurred."

Often judges hold evidentiary hearings before a jury is selected to allow both sides to introduce evidence in the form of opinion polls or newspaper stories that indicate media saturation about the case has tainted the local jury pool. In this situation, potential jurors may already believe the defendant is guilty and ignore the presumption of innocence because of the "facts" of the case they have learned through the newspapers and television coverage. This happened in the Missouri case of Kenneth Baumruk who shot and killed his wife in a St. Louis County courthouse. He was later tried on capital murder charges for that killing in the very same courthouse where the shooting occurred. Finding that trying the defendant at the crime scene was unconscionable, the court awarded Baumruk a new trial, but the state allowed him to plead guilty to life without parole instead.

---

[3]Andrew D. Leipold. "How the Pretrial Process Contributes to Wrongful Convictions." *American Criminal Law Review,* Vol. 42 (2005), pp. 1123–1165.

BOX 13.3

Missouri v. *Baumruk*, 85 S.W.3d 644 (2002)
Supreme Court of Missouri

Justice Wolff delivered the opinion of the court.

FACTS

On May 5, 1992, Kenneth Baumruk and his wife, Mary, were scheduled for a hearing in the St. Louis County circuit court for dissolution of marriage. Baumruk carried two .38 caliber handguns in his brief case to court that day. Before the scheduled hearing, the attorney for Baumruk's wife, Scott Pollard, discovered that he had a conflict of interest because he had represented [Kenneth] Baumruk in a previous dissolution. Judge Hais decided to make a record in open court and determined that the case would proceed only if both Mary and Kenneth Baumruk waived the conflict.

After Judge Hais administered the oath to Mary and Kenneth Baumruk, Pollard examined Mary regarding the conflict, and she stated that she wanted Pollard to remain as her attorney. Baumruk then reached into his brief case and retrieved the two handguns, stood and shot Mary in the neck. Baumruk turned toward Pollard, shooting him in the chest. He then shot attorney Seltzer in the chest and, when Seltzer turned to run, Baumruk shot him in the back. Next, Baumruk walked around the counsel table, put the gun near his wife's head and shot her again, killing her. Judge Hais escaped through the door behind his bench as Baumruk shot at him and pursued him.

As Baumruk proceeded down the hall outside of the courtroom, bailiff Fred Nicolay pushed a clerk and two attorneys into another judge's chambers and closed and locked the door. Baumruk then shot Nicolay in the shoulder and ran out into the hall. Baumruk then shot at a police officer and then shot and wounded a security officer. Police officers in the courthouse fired weapons at Baumruk, hitting him nine times. Two of the wounds were to his head. St. Louis media provided extensive coverage of the incident, describing it as a "rampage," "shooting spree" and "mayhem" that "terrorized hundreds of people." In the media reports, several hundred citizens filled the streets around the courthouse, and more gazed down on the scene from their office windows. Quotes in the media compared the scene to a fire fight in Vietnam. Hundreds were reported to have watched paramedics wheel Baumruk and the victims from the courthouse to ambulances.

After the shooting, the St. Louis County courthouse, which previously had not had metal detectors and other extensive security, received immediate attention. The number of security guards was doubled and metal detectors were installed. Media coverage, which was massive, centered not only on the shootings, but also on domestic violence, concealed weapons, and the fears of domestic relations lawyers and clients. Several years after the incident, a poll indicated that approximately 70% of the county residents still remembered Baumruk's shootings at the courthouse. [In 1998, after much legal wrangling over Baumruk's competency to stand trial due to his brain injury] the St. Louis County prosecutor obtained an 18-count indictment that included murder in the first degree in the death of Mary Baumruk.

ISSUE

[Was it an abuse of discretion by the judge in St. Louis County not to grant Baumruk's change of venue motion?]

HOLDING

[Yes, Baumruk's motion to change venue should have been granted by the trial judge].

REASONING

Whether to grant or deny a change of venue is within the discretion of the trial court. *State* v. *Feltrop*, 803 S.W.2d 1 (Mo. banc 1991). That ruling will not be disturbed unless it was a clear abuse of discretion. *State* v. *Barton*, 998 S.W.2d 19 (Mo. banc 1999). This discretion is abused when the record shows that the inhabitants of the county are so prejudiced against the defendant that a fair trial cannot occur in that county. However, the question is not whether the community remembers the case but whether the actual jurors of the case have fixed opinions such that they could not judge impartially whether the defendant was guilty.

(continued)

BOX 13.3

(continued)

Patton v. *Yount*, 467 U.S. 1025 (1984). There must be a "pattern of deep and bitter prejudice" or a "wave of public passion" such that the seating of an impartial jury is impossible. A change of venue is required when it is necessary to assure the defendant a fair and impartial trial.

Six years after the shootings, in 1998, and three years before Baumruk's trial, a poll conducted by political scientist Dr. Kenneth Warren found that about 70% of St. Louis County residents remembered the shooting incident that occurred at the courthouse. Dr. Warren's 1998 poll found that, of those who had heard about the shootings, over 80 percent said that Baumruk was definitely guilty and about 18 percent indicated that he was "probably guilty." Although the poll was conducted three years before the 2001 trial, most of its findings are consistent with the examination of prospective jurors when the case was brought for trial. Sixty-three of the 99 people who appeared for jury service said they had heard about the case in the media. Eight of the 12 jurors who ultimately sat on Baumruk's jury remembered the incident. One of the jurors acknowledged that, as a result of the media reports, he believed Baumruk was guilty.[4]

This required sense or appearance of neutrality is illustrated by *Turner* v. *Louisiana*, where two key witnesses for the state also served as the bailiffs attending the jury during the three-day trial, 379 U.S. 466 (1965). Even though the bailiffs assured the judge that they had not communicated with the jurors about the case, the Court found such an association between the jurors and two key prosecution witnesses, especially when those witnesses were deputy sheriffs, was wrong and undermined the basic guarantees of trial by jury. Id. at 474. This is not just a pretrial publicity, improper venue case. At its core, this case raises a serious question as to the "impartiality of the adjudicator" because of the environment in which the trial was held. *See Gray* v. *Mississippi*, 481 U.S. 648 (1987).

The jurors were aware that the courtroom in which they sat was the same as the crime scene and that the building in which they entered every day of trial was the scene of the terrifying events. The prosecutor emphasized the point, appealing to "the citizens of this county" to punish Baumruk "for what he did in this courthouse."

Jurors cannot be asked to place themselves in the shoes of the victims. *See State* v. *Rhodes*, 988 S.W.2d 521 (Mo. banc 1999). Here, the jurors arrived at the courthouse and entered through metal detectors that had been installed as a direct result of Baumruk's shooting spree. Jurors walked the same halls and used the same elevators, stairwells, and escalators that were used by escaping victims. The trial was held in a courtroom nearly identical to the courtroom that was the scene of the crime. The jurors, in effect, sat at the murder scene while determining guilt or innocence and the penalty to be imposed. The right to jury trial guarantees a fair trial by a panel of impartial, "indifferent" jurors. *Irvin* v. *Dowd*, 366 U.S. 717 (1961). Failure to give the accused a fair hearing violates the minimal standards of due process. The verdict must be based on the evidence that is developed at trial regardless of the heinousness of the crime or the apparent guilt of the offender. This Court's constitutional duty, as set forth in decisions of the United States Supreme Court and this Court, is to assure that a defendant receives a fair and impartial trial. No such assurance is possible where the jurors were influenced by pretrial publicity and by the atmosphere of the trial setting. The jurors, for the entire duration of their service, were invited to relive Baumruk's reign of terror and to identify with his victims at the very place where the events took place.

CONCLUSION

The judgment is reversed, and the case is remanded with instruction to the trial court to grant the change of venue.

---

[4] Even when the defendant's guilt seems obvious to all, the law still requires that the defendant be presumed innocent until the state proves him guilty beyond a reasonable doubt. If jurors come to the trial with their minds made up about the defendant's innocence or guilt, they are legally ineligible to sit on the jury because they will not listen to the evidence. Usually in a death penalty case, defendants are forced to go to trial to convince a jury to sentence them to life without parole ("LWOP"). If the state removed the death penalty as a sentencing option, many more "obviously guilty" defendants would plead guilty in exchange for an LWOP sentence.

Applying the Rule of Law to the Facts: Should the venue be changed?

- Sam Sheppard was a physician charged with murdering his wife. Before trial, many damaging news stories were published confirming community suspicions that the doctor was guilty. Newspapers also printed the names of prospective jurors, who began to receive mail about the case. Three months before trial, a televised inquest was held in a school gymnasium in front of hundreds of people. Should the court have granted Sheppard's change of venue motion?

Yes, the appeals court granted Sheppard's *habeas corpus* petition on the grounds that his due process rights were violated by the extensive negative pretrial publicity.[5]

b. The Sixth Amendment's Confrontation Clause

Rule of Law: Defendants exercise their confrontation clause rights by cross-examining witnesses at trial.

The Sixth Amendment guarantees the defendant the right to confront witnesses against him or her through the confrontation clause. The **confrontation clause** requires the witness to come forward and face the defendant, and the defendant has a right to confront the witness through the mechanism of cross-examination. Over time, the Supreme Court held the confrontation clause was deemed satisfied if the defendant had an opportunity before trial, such as in a preliminary hearing, to cross-examine the witness and if that witness was later unavailable at trial. The law was enunciated in *Ohio* v. *Roberts*, 448 U.S. 56 (1980), in which a witness testified in a preliminary hearing and then could not be found to testify at trial despite the state's repeated efforts. Her preliminary hearing testimony was allowed at Roberts' trial because the Court found that the witness was unavailable, and it was reliable because Roberts' lawyer had an opportunity to cross-examine her, even though he did not. This interpretation disadvantaged most defendants because preliminary hearings or other pretrial opportunities to cross-examine witnesses typically occur before the defense knows of all the evidence through the process of discovery.

But in 2004, the law changed in interpreting the confrontation clause in the case of Michael Crawford. Crawford attacked a man who had allegedly tried to rape Crawford's wife. Crawford claimed self-defense, and police took a tape recording of Crawford's wife making a statement that threw into question Crawford's version of events. At trial, the wife refused to testify on the basis of marital privilege. The Washington state appellate court, applying the *Roberts* precedent, held that admitting Crawford's wife's tape-recorded statement into evidence satisfied Crawford's right to confront witnesses because the tape was reliable, and now his wife was unavailable to testify at trial. On appeal to the U.S. Supreme Court, the Court overturned both Crawford's conviction and its *Roberts* precedent. The new rule enunciated in *Crawford* is that testimonial hearsay is admissible against the defendant only when the witness is unavailable to testify and the defendant had an opportunity to cross-examine the witness before trial. *Crawford* v. *Washington*, 541 U.S. 36 (2004). Since Crawford did not have an opportunity to cross-examine his wife at the time she made the tape-recorded statement, and since she was unavailable at trial because she refused to testify, his conviction was overturned.

i. Child Witnesses in Sex-Abuse Cases   What happens when the witness is too traumatized to come into court and confront the defendant? Does the defendant's Sixth Amendment right to confront witnesses against him outweigh and trump the witness's discomfort in coming into court? The question most often arises in child sexual molestation cases in which the entire dynamic of the abuse is the ultimate

---

[5]*Sheppard* v. *Maxwell*, 384 U.S. 333 (1966).

control of the child, either by threatening the child if the child discloses the abuse or, in a strange twist, in making the child believe that whatever affection is supplied by the offender will stop, and that the family will dissolve, if the child discloses. To ask the child to come and testify as the defendant "stares down" the child may create problems for the child. In 1988, the United States Supreme Court held that a screen separating the defendant from the witness violated the defendant's right to confront the witness face-to-face. *Coy* v. *Iowa*, 487 U.S. 1012 (1988). But two years later in 1990, the Court allowed the use of closed-circuit television to deliver the testimony of a child because the protection of a vulnerable witness was an important government interest. The defendant's rights were protected because he could communicate with his attorney who could then cross-examine the witness. *Maryland* v. *Craig*, 497 U.S. 836 (1990).

The reasoning behind the confrontation clause is to allow the jury to judge the credibility of the witness. For example, the jury may feel that a chronic drug addict who has a hard time remembering details is less reliable than a witness who has never used drugs. The ability to conduct cross-examination is critical as well. But the state does not get to use alternative means of testimony in every child sex abuse case by saying the child would have a hard time testifying in court. The state has to make a showing to the judge, usually before the child testifies and out of the presence of the jury, that the child will suffer severe emotional harm by having to confront the defendant in person. Such evidence can be developed from personal and professional testimony of those who have had contact with the victim and presumably have helped the victim overcome some of the effects of the abuse. Federal law has codified when the court can order the closed-circuit testimony if the child is unable to testify in open court:

1. if the child is afraid of the defendant, specifically because of the threats used to keep sexual abuse secret
2. if expert testimony establishes that the child would suffer emotional harm from testifying in the presence of the defendant
3. if the child suffers from a possible mental infirmity
4. if the behavior of the defendant or defense counsel makes the child unable to continue testifying in open court.

In our chapter's opening scenario, John, acting as his own counsel, has a right to confront his niece as she testifies against him concerning the alleged abuse she suffered at his hands. This right would be negated only if the prosecution asks for a hearing to introduce evidence showing that it would cause the niece more harm to face John, especially since he, and not a lawyer, would be the one conducting the cross-examination.

ii. The Right to Represent Oneself in Court　The Sixth Amendment gives the right to counsel, but what if a defendant wants to represent himself—is that right guaranteed by the Constitution? The Supreme Court held in *Faretta* v. *California*, 422 U.S. 806 (1975), that the Sixth Amendment does confer such a right on the defendant. The law favors granting of the right, but the court must establish that the defendant is aware of what she is doing and aware of what she is giving up by representing herself. In our chapter-opening scenario, John has every right to defend himself if the court rules in his favor. The factors that the court examines before granting the defendant the right to self-representation are:

1. the timing of the request
2. whether the request was made to delay the case
3. whether the case is so complicated that assistance of a trained lawyer is required
4. whether the defendant is incompetent and therefore cannot intelligently, knowingly, and voluntarily relinquish the right to counsel.

In the sniper case that gripped the country in 2002, with random shootings and killings around Washington, D.C., Maryland, and Virginia, the mastermind of the plot, John Muhammed, wanted to represent himself at trial. The colloquy [question and answer session with the defendant on the record in open court] reprinted in part below shows that before the judge granted Muhammed's wish to forego counsel, the judge wanted to make sure that Muhammed knew what he was doing and knew what he was giving up. The judge allowed Muhammed's attorneys to remain at the counsel table and to act as standby counsel for consultation. Muhammed was found guilty and sentenced to death.[6]

COURT:　Mr. Muhammed, I understand you have a motion.

ACCUSED [MUHAMMED]:　Yes sir. Can I represent myself?

COURT:　That is a motion that I think I am not required to grant constitutionally . . . My first question to you is, why do you want to represent yourself?

MUHAMMED:　Because I feel like I can speak better on my behalf . . . Because I know me, and I know what happened, and I know what didn't happen.

COURT:　Do you understand that there are rules of evidence that you must follow?

MUHAMMED:　I understand.

[Discussion about the distinction between argument and questioning]

COURT:　Okay. Tell me about your background. What is it in your background that makes you think you can adequately represent yourself in the trial? These men [Muhammed's court-appointed attorneys] have been trained for years and years and years. You told me the other day you were not dissatisfied with their representation. Is all that correct?

MUHAMMED:　That's correct, sir.

COURT:　Okay. Tell me what is in your background that makes you think you can adequately represent yourself.

MUHAMMED:　Sir, I don't think I can adequately represent myself. I know I can.

COURT:　Tell me how you can.

MUHAMMED:　Because I know me.

COURT:　Okay. But what do you know about the legal system? Do you understand how to cross-examine witnesses? Do you understand how to prepare pleadings [motions]? You know that there are certain motions that we've talked about for months in this case. I don't think you could have followed any of those motions. Do you?

MUHAMMED:　No, sir.

COURT:　No. There are going to be motions as we go along at trial. What makes you think that you can adequately make the proper motions at the proper time?

MUHAMMED:　Sir, if I don't speak on my behalf, I know I can't.

COURT:　Well, representing yourself is not the same as speaking on your behalf, is it? You certainly can be a witness and take the stand if you want to do that.

---

[6]Transcript provided courtesy of Court Reporter Ronald Graham and Associates, Inc.

MUHAMMED: Yes, sir.

COURT: I'm sure you've talked to them [Muhammed's attorneys] about that.

MUHAMMED: Yes.

COURT: So speaking for yourself is a different thing than representing yourself, isn't it?

MUHAMMED: Depending on the context, sir.

COURT: Well, I don't know what you mean by that.

MUHAMMED: Well, it just depends. I mean it all depends on what you are speaking about. Right now I'm talking to you, and I am representing myself.

COURT: You are exactly right, but we're not asking you to prepare instructions for the jury. We're not asking you to select a jury. We're not asking you to examine witnesses or cross-examine witnesses. You don't have any scientific knowledge, I assume, or DNA experience, do you?

MUHAMMED: No. I mean that can be assumed, sir.

COURT: So how do you think you can adequately represent yourself without the training that these lawyers have had for—let's see. Mr. Greenspun, you've been practicing for how long?

GREENSPUN: Twenty-five years.

COURT: Twenty-five years. Mr. Shapiro?

SHAPIRO: Twenty-nine years.

COURT: That's forty-nine years of legal experience, and you have zero.

MUHAMMED: And these lawyers are representing who?

COURT: You.

MUHAMMED: And the experiences that I have about me is a lot more than what they have about me.

COURT: Absolutely. I understand that; but a trial is not the same thing as standing up and telling the jury about you, is it?

MUHAMMED: No sir. It's a lot of motions. I understand that.

[Discussion about Muhammed's experience in the legal system, including a court-martial he suffered in the early 1990s].

COURT: Okay. Tell me about your educational background.

MUHAMMED: What do you want to know?

COURT: Did you graduate from high school?

MUHAMMED: Yes, sir.

COURT: Did you have any college?

MUHAMMED: No, sir.

COURT: Have you done any special reading of the law or anything else to help you prepare for this trial?

MUHAMMED: Not yet. No, sir.

COURT: Okay. If I do let you represent yourself, you understand that you have to comply with the rules of evidence? Just because you are representing yourself doesn't mean that you get any special treatment.

MUHAMMED: Yes, sir.

COURT: And if you make an objection that's improper, that will be the end of it. If you can't properly control yourself, then I will not allow you to continue representing yourself.

MUHAMMED: That's understandable, sir.

COURT: I have to say that I think it's a mistake for you to do this, and I'll tell you the reason why. This is an extremely complicated case. You've already heard us talk about that time after time in court. It goes over vast geographical boundaries and time periods, and it's taken these attorneys months and months to acquire what information they have about the case, so I think it's a tremendous mistake if you try to represent yourself. You understand that?

MUHAMMED: That's the third time I've heard it today. Yes, sir.

COURT: Okay. Maybe I'll say it three or four more times.

MUHAMMED: I'm not talking about from you. I'm talking about from them [Muhammed's attorneys].

COURT: Okay.

[Discussion with counsel about the role, if any, they will play in Muhammed's defense with the Court granting the request that they be standby counsel available for consultation with Muhammed throughout trial].

COURT: Mr. Muhammed, do you think that you fully understand what I'm telling you? That you have the right to have the attorneys represent you? That I strongly recommend that, and you want to go against that recommendation?

MUHAMMED: I understand fully what you're saying, sir.

COURT: And that's what you want to do?

MUHAMMED: Yes, sir.

COURT: And you want to represent yourself?

MUHAMMED: Yes, sir.

COURT: And that means you will be the only person speaking in the courtroom. They [Muhammed's attorneys] can sit at the table with you, and you can perhaps upon occasion ask them questions, but I don't expect you to ask them every question that's being formulated. That would, I think, unduly hinder the trial process. I would expect you to represent yourself.

MUHAMMED: That's my intent, sir.

COURT: Okay. Despite the court's admonition, you think it is in your best interest to represent yourself?

MUHAMMED: Yes, sir.

COURT: And you take full responsibility for whatever happens during the trial?

MUHAMMED: Yes, sir.

COURT: Okay. Finally, let me tell you this. If I believe that you are using your self-representation as a soapbox opportunity to get in inadmissible information or ask inadmissible questions, I may stop it and prohibit you from continuing to represent yourself and have your attorneys represent you; or if your conduct in the courtroom in any way is inappropriate, then I may no longer allow you to represent yourself. Do you understand that?

MUHAMMED:　Yes, sir.

COURT:　Okay. I'm going to grant your motion and allow you to represent yourself. I am going to direct Mr. Greenspun and Mr. Shapiro be standby counsel, that they assist you in every aspect in the case; but they cannot represent you any longer. You are going to be the one representing yourself; and I am going to inform the jury that that is, in fact, the position of the case. You understand that?

MUHAMMED:　Yes, sir.

4. Jury Selection

a. Challenges Based on Race or Gender

Rule of Law: In criminal prosecutions, the government cannot eliminate potential jurors based solely on their race or gender.

Many issues must be discussed with the potential jury pool, the venire, during jury selection, the process called *voir dire* [French for "to speak the truth"] to ensure that the defendant is tried in front of a group of people who can fairly and impartially judge the facts and evidence. The Sixth Amendment guarantees the defendant a speedy and public trial in front of a fair and impartial jury. The requirement that a defendant be tried by a "jury of [his or her] peers" does not necessarily mean that the defendant must be tried before a panel of people who share his socioeconomic background. It does mean that the government cannot systematically exclude people on the basis of race or gender from the jury simply because the state thinks it has a better chance at convicting the defendant if it removes all people from the jury who might sympathize with him due to his race or gender.

There are two types of challenges to remove potential members from the venire/jury pool. **Challenges for cause** are when a potential juror/venireman cannot be fair and impartial; perhaps an African-American woman who was raped by a white man could not be fair and impartial in deciding a case in which a white defendant was accused of raping a woman of color. Each side has an unlimited number of challenges for cause. The second type of challenge, of which there is a limited number for each side, is a **peremptory challenge** and allows a lawyer for either side to remove potential jurors for no reason at all. The number of peremptory challenges allowed depends on the nature of the case and the jurisdiction of the court. The lawyer does not have to explain to the court why he is exercising a peremptory challenge. But the U.S. Supreme Court has imposed upon the government the obligation to explain peremptory challenges if the government exercises these challenges in what appears to be a racially discriminatory manner—that is, removing all eligible African-American jury members in a trial with an African-American defendant to ensure that he is tried by an all-white jury.

In *Batson* v. *Kentucky* 476 U.S. 79 (1986), James Batson was convicted of second-degree murder. Batson is African-American, and his jury was all white after the prosecutor used four out of six peremptory strikes to dismiss African-Americans from the pool of potential jurors. On appeal, the U.S. Supreme Court found that such acts by a government agent, the prosecutor, denied Batson his right to equal protection under the Fourteenth Amendment. This was a claim that white defendants could also make, because discrimination practiced by the state interferes with *any* defendant's right to be tried by a fair and impartial jury.[7] Before *Batson*, the controlling law on race and

---

[7] *Holland* v. *Illinois*, 493 U.S. 474 (1990).

jury selection was set forth in *Swain* v. *Alabama*, 380 U.S. 202 (1965), a case placing the burden of proving a "longstanding pattern of discrimination" on the defendant. The defendant and not the state had to prove the prosecutor had exercised peremptory challenges in a racially discriminatory manner.

A recent Supreme Court case examined whether the government used race as a basis for peremptory challenges to strike potential African-American jury members. In *Miller-El* v. *Dretke*, 545 U.S. 231 (2005), the high Court found that the state's "race-neutral" explanations for removing potential jurors of color were not credible. Miller-El was convicted and sentenced to death for a killing during a 1985 robbery of a Holiday Inn in Dallas, Texas. At his trial, the prosecutor used peremptory challenges to remove 10 qualified African-American venire members. For many years prior to Miller-El's trial, the Dallas prosecutor's office had a policy of eliminating people of color from venires. The office also had a training manual "which urged prosecutors not to select 'Jews, Negroes, Dagos, Mexicans or a member of any minority race on a jury, no matter how rich or how well educated.'"[8] The high Court confirmed that the manual existed and that prosecutors systematically excluded African-Americans from juries, including Miller-El's. The Court explained:

> A Dallas County district judge testified that, when he had served in the District Attorney's Office from the late 1950s to early 1960s, his superior warned him that he would be fired if he permitted any African-Americans to serve on a jury. Similarly, another Dallas County district judge and former assistant district attorney from 1976 to 1978 testified that he believed the office had a systematic policy of excluding African-Americans from juries. Of more importance, the defense presented evidence that the District Attorney's Office had adopted a formal policy to exclude minorities from jury service. A manual entitled 'Jury Selection in a Criminal Case' [sometimes known as the Sparling Manual] was distributed to prosecutors. It contained an article authored by a former prosecutor (and later a judge) under the direction of his superiors in the District Attorney's Office, outlining the reasoning for excluding minorities from jury service. Although the manual was written in 1968, it remained in circulation until 1976, if not later, and was available at least to one of the prosecutors in Miller-El's trial." *Miller-El* v. *Cockrell*, 537 U.S. 322 (2003).[9]

As proof of this policy, the Court found in Miller-El's case that 91 percent of the eligible African-American venire members were peremptorily struck by the prosecution with no satisfactory race-neutral explanation. On the basis of the prosecutor's behavior, the Supreme Court vacated Miller-El's death sentence for the third time. On two prior occasions the high Court had remanded Miller-El's case to the lower court to fix the jury selection process, and both times the lower appellate court merely resentenced Miller-El to death.

In a similar race/jury selection case, *Johnson* v. *California*, 125 S.Ct. 2410 (2005), the prosecutor used three of his twelve peremptory challenges to remove all African-Americans from the venire leaving an all-white jury to convict Jay Johnson, who objected throughout the process. But the trial judge found that Johnson, who is African-American, did not make a facial showing of discrimination even though the judge never asked the prosecutor for a race-neutral explanation for striking the people of color. In overturning Johnson's death sentence, the U.S. Supreme Court found that

---

[8]April Castro. "Dallas Jury Selection Under Scrutiny in Death Penalty Appeal." *The Associated Press*, February 17, 2002. http://www.texnews.com/1998/2002/texas/jury0217.html (accessed on November 19, 2006).

[9]Miller-El's case had been back and forth from state to federal appellate courts including two prior trips to the U.S. Supreme Court in *Miller-El* v. *Cockrell*, 534 U.S. 1122 (2002), and *Miller-El* v. *Cockrell*, 537 U.S. 322 (2003) before the decision in the case at hand, *Miller-El* v. *Dretke*, 545 U.S. 231 (2005). All the cases involved the same issue of impermissible race discrimination in the state's exercise of its peremptory challenges in Miller-El's original trial.

the state court did not follow the required three-step *Batson* analysis to determine whether the defendant could make a *prima facie* showing of racial discrimination. In our chapter-opening scenario, the prosecutor's strikes of all men of color will not withstand scrutiny unless he offers a race-neutral reason for removing the men; the reason that such potential jurors may be sympathetic to the defendant may not be legally sufficient.

Note that the principles of *Batson* apply to gender discrimination as well. In *J.E.B.* v. *Alabama Ex Rel. T.B.*, 511 U.S. 127 (1994), a man was on trial for paternity and child support when the state used peremptory challenges to remove all men from the venire. That left 10 women to decide whether the petitioner was the father of the child and should pay child support. On appeal, the U.S. Supreme Court held, relying on the rationale of the *Batson* decision, that the Equal Protection Clause of the Fourteenth Amendment also prohibited gender discrimination in jury selection.

Applying the Rule of Law to the Facts: When is it discrimination in jury selection?

- A man charged with the sexual assault of his stepdaughter was allowed to exercise 15 peremptory challenges, and the state had 13. There were more men than women in the jury pool, and the prosecutor exercised all 13 of her challenges against prospective male jurors. Does the defendant have a claim on the basis of gender discrimination in jury selection?

No, the fact that more men than women were in the initial jury pool indicated that more men would be subject to removal from the pool. The defendant failed to make a prima facie case of discrimination as required under applicable law, *Batson* and *J.E.B.* v. *Alabama*.[10]

5. Closing Arguments

Rule of Law: Closing arguments are not evidence, but counsel must follow the legal rules of evidence.

The **closing argument** is the opportunity for attorneys to summarize the evidence for the jury and advocate for the conclusions they wish the jury to draw from the evidence. For example, a famous quip by the late famed defense attorney Johnnie Cochran, who successfully defended football Hall of Fame running back O. J. Simpson on double homicide charges, was "if the gloves do not fit, you must acquit." The statement referred to the tight fit of gloves which the prosecutors claimed Simpson had worn on the night of the killings. In an ill-advised trial tactic, the prosecution allowed Simpson to try them on; Simpson struggled getting the gloves on. The other theme advanced during closing arguments was "garbage in, garbage out" to highlight negligent evidence collection techniques that allowed, or so the defense claimed, scientific DNA samples to become contaminated; thus, their results placing Simpson at the murder scene were untrustworthy. The jury agreed with the defense's interpretation of the evidence and returned a verdict of not guilty.

Prosecutorial ethics demand that government actors ensure that justice is served in each and every case, but also constrain prosecutorial activities during trial. Many prosecutors during their closing arguments invite the jury to "do their duty" and convict the defendant or "speak for the victim" and convict. In the following case, *Carruthers* v. *State*, reprinted in part in Box 13.4, examine closely the Supreme Court of Georgia's reasoning. The court found error when a prosecutor cited the Bible as justification for a jury to award a death sentence. In overturning the death sentence, the court held that any actions designed to improperly inflame the jury's passion and to invite the jurors to decide cases on the basis of emotions rather than facts and evidence violated the defendant's right to a fair trial.

---

[10]*Aspen v. Bissonnette*, 480 F.3d 571 (1st. Cir. 2007).

BOX 13.4

Carruthers v. *State,* 528 S.E.2d 217 (Ga. 2000)
Supreme Court of Georgia

Justice Fletcher delivered the opinion of the court.

PROCEDURAL HISTORY

Anthony Carruthers was convicted of the malice murder of Jannette Williams and sentenced to death. Carruthers contends that the assistant district attorney made several improper arguments that warrant reversal of the death sentence. Finding no reversible error in the guilt/innocence phase of Carruthers' trial, we affirm the jury's verdict of guilt on all charges. However, because we conclude that the trial court erred in allowing the state to urge the jury to follow the religious mandates of the Bible rather than Georgia law, we reverse the sentence of death and remand the case for another jury to consider the proper sentence for the murder.

FACTS

The evidence at trial showed that on December 12, 1995, Williams picked up Carruthers and Billy Edward Easter, Jr., at Carruthers' residence, drove the men to her residence, and invited them in. After some friendly conversation, she sat on Carruthers' lap. When Carruthers whispered something in her ear, Williams responded that she had a boyfriend. Carruthers then grabbed her arm. Easter went upstairs to use the bathroom. When he heard the sound of breaking glass, he returned downstairs and saw Carruthers choking Williams. She fell to the floor unconscious or semi-conscious. Carruthers cut her throat with one knife and then threw it across the room, commenting that it was dull. As Williams showed signs of life, Carruthers obtained a larger knife from the kitchen and cut her neck in a repetitive motion, cutting most of the way through her neck. He then rolled her over and stabbed her eleven times in the chest.

Shortly after the murder, Carruthers' girlfriend observed Williams' automobile parked outside Carruthers' residence, his bloody clothes in his washing machine, and scratches on his neck. Carruthers and Easter drove to Florida in Williams'

car where Carruthers sold it for illegal drugs, and, upon discovering that the drugs were fake, chased and possibly shot at a man involved in the transaction. After returning to Georgia, Carruthers confessed to his girlfriend that he had killed a woman who owed him money. On December 20, 1995, Williams' automobile was discovered in Florida. Blood with DNA consistent with Williams' blood was recovered from the automobile.

Viewed in the light most favorable to the verdict, we find that the evidence adduced at trial was sufficient to authorize the jury's finding Carruthers guilty beyond a reasonable doubt of the crimes of which he was convicted.

Closing Arguments in Sentencing Phase

The United States Constitution and the Georgia Constitution guarantee criminal defendants the right to due process at trial. In addition, [Georgia law] requires this Court to review the death sentence to determine whether it "was imposed under the influence of passion, prejudice, or any other arbitrary factor." Carruthers filed a motion *in limine* [a motion to prevent admission at trial] to exclude during closing argument any Bible passages that appealed to the passion of the jury and would encourage it to impose a death sentence based on religion. During a pre-argument hearing, the prosecutor said that he intended to cite passages from the books of Romans, Genesis, and Matthew. The defendant objected to the biblical references, but the trial court overruled the objection and allowed the three passages.

During closing argument, the state urged the jury to impose a death sentence because the Bible states that society must deter criminals by taking the life of persons who kill other people. The state argued as follows:

> Now, ladies and gentlemen, let me talk to you a moment about some biblical references that help us in this case. Deterrence is very important and the Bible suggests to us why deterrence is appropriate. Romans tells us that every person is subject to the governing

(continued)

BOX 13.4

(continued)

authority, every person is subject. And in Matthew it tells us, who sheddeth man's blood by man shall his blood be shed for in the image of God made [he] man.[11] For all they who take the sword shall die by the sword, and this is a message that is very clear, that society must deter criminals.

ISSUE

[Does reference to the Bible during argument violate a defendant's due process right to a fair trial?]

HOLDING

[Yes]. It is difficult to draw a precise line between religious arguments that are acceptable and those that are objectionable, but we conclude that the assistant district attorney in this case overstepped the line in directly quoting religious authority as mandating a death sentence. In citing specific passages, he invoked a higher moral authority and diverted the jury from the discretion provided to them under state law.

RATIONALE

This Court has noted its concern about the use of biblical authority during closing arguments in death penalty trials. In *Hill* v. *State*, 263 Ga. 37 (427 S.E.2d 770) (1993), we stated that "it would be improper to urge a death penalty based upon the defendant's religious beliefs, or to urge that the teachings of a particular religion command the imposition of a death penalty in the case at hand." The problem is that biblical references inject the often irrelevant and inflammatory issue of religion into the sentencing process and improperly appeal to the religious beliefs of jurors in their decision on whether a person should live or die. Moreover, many passages in the Bible, Talmud, and other religious texts prescribe or command a sentence of death for killing. By quoting these texts during closing arguments, prosecutors may "diminish the jury's sense of responsibility and imply that another, higher law should be applied in capital cases, displacing the

law in the court's instructions." As a result, at least one state supreme court has adopted a rule prohibiting prosecutors from relying on any religious writing to support the death penalty during closing argument.

Although we have long declined to disapprove of passing, oratorical references to religious texts in arguments by counsel, we have distinguished those fleeting references from more direct references that urge that the teachings of a particular religion command the imposition of a death penalty. In contrast to biblical law, Georgia law gives the jury the discretion to recommend life imprisonment or death, provides stringent procedures and safeguards that must be followed during the trial, and permits the jury to impose the death penalty only in limited circumstances.

In addition, we have specifically disapproved of a prosecutor quoting verses from the Bible to support the death penalty. In *Hammond* v. *State*, we concluded that it was improper for the assistant district attorney to argue that the defendant had violated the law of God that "whoever sheds the blood of man by man shall his blood be shed." Despite this disapproval and repeated admonitions, prosecutors have continued to quote the Bible and urge its teachings, and trial courts have continued to permit the arguments. *See State* v. *Middlebrooks*, 995 S.W.2d 550 (Tenn. 1999) ("We have condemned Biblical and scriptural references in a prosecutor's closing argument so frequently that it is difficult not to conclude that the remarks in this case were made either with blatant disregard for our decisions or a level of astonishing ignorance of the state of the law in this regard.").

Unlike previous cases, however, where the defendants failed to object to the state's religious arguments at trial, the defense in this case anticipated the argument and tried to prevent it by filing a motion *in limine*, but the trial court denied the motion. Because the defendant received an adverse ruling on his objection, the standard of

---

[11]This passage comes from the Book of Genesis. "Whoso sheddeth man's blood, by man shall his blood be shed: for in the image of God made he man." Genesis 9:6 (King James Version).

review in this case is not whether the improper argument in reasonable probability changed the result of the trial, but simply whether the argument was objectionable and prejudicial.

Language of command and obligation from a source other than Georgia law should not be presented to a jury. *See Jones* v. *Kemp*, 706 F. Supp. 1534 (N.D. Ga. 1989) (when "arguments come from a source, like the Bible, which 'would likely carry weight with laymen and influence their decision,' the effect may be highly prejudicial to the defendant, and the confidence in the reliability of the jury's decision which must guide imposition of the death penalty may be undermined"), *See also United States* v. *Giry*, 818 F.2d 120 (1st Cir. 1987)

(such arguments are an "inflammatory appeal to the jurors' private, religious beliefs").

CONCLUSION

Therefore, we find that Carruthers' right to due process as secured by [Georgia statute], the Georgia Constitution, and the Constitution of the United States was abridged when the trial court allowed the inappropriate arguments from the Bible over objection. Because we cannot conclude beyond a reasonable doubt that the violation of Carruthers' state and federal constitutional rights was harmless, we reverse the jury's death sentence and remand the case for resentencing.

Many features of the *Carruthers* case can assist in understanding other cases. First, the attorney preserved the record for appeal by objecting via a motion *in limine* [a motion to exclude certain things at trial] to prevent the prosecutor from mentioning the Bible during closing arguments. Second, the court relied heavily on precedence which consistently held that bringing religion into a trial to influence a jury's deliberations was an error—meaning that the conviction would be overturned and the defendant retried. Yet the court noted that prosecutors continually ignored the law and judges continually made the wrong decisions in allowing such argument. The court's message is clear: if you keep bringing religion in, the cases will be reversed to do again. Retrying a case is very expensive and a burden on lawyers, witnesses, judges, victims, and defendants. Carruthers did not get an entirely new trial, as the court agreed, "He's guilty." He did get a new penalty phase in which the jury would redecide his sentence. When Carruthers was resentenced, he was sentenced to life without parole.[12]

6. Victims' Rights at Sentencing

Rule of Law: Determining a sentence is within the province of a judge or jury; victims may make impact statements but may not advocate for a specific sentence for the convicted defendant.

As a result of the victims' rights movement, today at a defendant's sentencing victims may testify about the impact the defendant's conduct has had on their lives, called a **victim-impact statement.** Prior Supreme Court precedent in the late 1980s prohibited victim-impact testimony on the grounds that it violated the Eighth Amendment's ban on cruel and unusual punishment by improperly invading the province of the jury to decide on a proper sentence. *Booth* v. *Maryland*, 482 U.S. 496 (1987); *South Carolina* v. *Gathers*, 490 U.S. 805 (1989). The Court changed its mind, though, in *Payne* v. *Tennessee*, 501 U.S. 808 (1991), where Payne killed a young mother and her daughter and left her young son for dead. At trial, the boy's grandmother testified that her grandson missed and often asked for his mother and sister. As you read the *Payne* case, ask yourself if you can envision any case in which a jury would not be moved to impose the harshest sentence possible in cases where victim impact testimony is introduced.

---

[12]http://www.dcor.state.ga.us/GDC/OffenderQuery/jsp/OffQryRedirector.jsp URL directs user to Georgia Department of Corrections homepage; must enter Carruthers' name to find inmate.

BOX 13.5

Payne v. *Tennessee,* 501 U.S. 808 (1991)
Supreme Court of the United States

Chief Justice Rehnquist delivered the opinion of the Court.

FACTS

Petitioner, Pervis Tyrone Payne, was convicted by a jury on two counts of first-degree murder and one count of assault with intent to commit murder in the first degree. He was sentenced to death for each of the murders and to 30 years in prison for the assault. The victims of Payne's offenses were 28-year-old Charisse Christopher, her 2-year-old daughter Lacie, and her 3-year-old son Nicholas. The three lived together in an apartment in Millington, Tennessee, across the hall from Payne's girlfriend, Bobbie Thomas. On Saturday, June 27, 1987, Payne visited Thomas' apartment several times in expectation of her return from her mother's house in Arkansas, but found no one at home. On one visit, he left his overnight bag, containing clothes and other items for his weekend stay, in the hallway outside Thomas' apartment. With the bag were three cans of malt liquor. Payne passed the morning and early afternoon injecting cocaine and drinking beer. Later, he drove around the town with a friend in the friend's car, each of them taking turns reading a pornographic magazine. Sometime around 3 P.M., Payne returned to the apartment complex, entered the Christophers' apartment, and began making sexual advances towards Charisse. Charisse resisted and Payne became violent. A neighbor who resided in the apartment directly beneath the Christophers heard Charisse screaming, "'Get out, get out,' as if she were telling the children to leave." The noise briefly subsided and then began, "horribly loud." The neighbor called the police after she heard a "blood curdling scream" from the Christophers' apartment.

When the first police officer arrived at the scene, he immediately encountered Payne, who was leaving the apartment building, so covered with blood that he appeared to be "sweating blood." The officer confronted Payne, who responded, "I'm the complainant." When the officer asked, "What's going on up there?" Payne struck the officer with the overnight bag, dropped his tennis shoes, and fled. Inside the apartment, the police encountered a horrifying scene. Blood covered the walls and floor throughout the unit. Charisse and her children were lying on the floor in the kitchen. Nicholas, despite several wounds inflicted by a butcher knife that completely penetrated through his body from front to back, was still breathing. Miraculously, he survived . . . after undergoing seven hours of surgery and a transfusion of 1,700 cc's of blood—400 to 500 cc's more than his estimated normal blood volume. Charisse and Lacie were dead. Charisse's body was found on the kitchen floor on her back, her legs fully extended. She had sustained 42 direct knife wounds and 42 defensive wounds on her arms and hands. The wounds were caused by 41 separate thrusts of a butcher knife. None of the 84 wounds inflicted by Payne were individually fatal; rather, the cause of death was most likely bleeding from all of the wounds. Lacie's body was on the kitchen floor near her mother. She had suffered stab wounds to the chest, abdomen, back, and head. The murder weapon, a butcher knife, was found at her feet. Payne's baseball cap was snapped on her arm near her elbow. Three cans of malt liquor bearing Payne's fingerprints were found on a table near her body, and a fourth empty one was on the landing outside the apartment door.

Payne was apprehended later that day hiding in the attic of the home of a former girlfriend. As he descended the stairs of the attic, he stated to the arresting officers, "Man, I ain't killed no woman." According to one of the officers, Payne had "a wild look about him. His pupils were contracted. He was foaming at the mouth, saliva. He appeared to be very nervous. He was breathing real rapid." He had blood on his body and clothes and several scratches across his chest. It was later determined that the blood stains matched the victims' blood types. A search of his pockets revealed a packet containing cocaine residue, a hypodermic syringe wrapper, and a cap from a hypodermic syringe. His overnight bag, containing a bloody white shirt, was found in a nearby dumpster. At trial, Payne took the stand and, despite the overwhelming and relatively uncontroverted evidence against him, testified that he had not harmed any of the Christophers. Rather, he asserted that another man had raced by him as he was walking up the stairs to the floor where the Christophers lived. He stated that he had gotten blood on himself when, after hearing moans from the Christophers' apartment, he had tried to help the victims. According to his testimony, he panicked and fled when he heard police sirens and noticed the blood on his clothes. The jury returned guilty verdicts against Payne on all counts. During the sentencing phase of the trial . . . [t]he State presented the testimony of Charisse's mother, Mary Zvolanek. When asked how Nicholas had been affected by the murders of his mother and sister, she responded: "He cries for his mom. He doesn't seem to understand why she doesn't come home. And he cries for his sister Lacie. He comes to me many times during the week and asks me, Grandmama, do you miss my Lacie? And I tell him yes. He says, I'm worried about my Lacie." In arguing for the death penalty during closing argument, the prosecutor commented on the continuing effects of Nicholas' experience, stating: "But we do know that Nicholas was alive. And Nicholas was in the same room. Nicholas was still conscious. His eyes were open. He responded to the paramedics. He was able to follow their directions. He was able to hold his intestines in as he was carried to the ambulance. So he knew what happened to his mother and baby sister. There is nothing you can do to ease the pain of any of the families involved in this case. There is nothing you can do to ease the pain of Bernice or Carl Payne, and that's a tragedy. There is nothing you can do basically to ease the pain of Mr. and Mrs. Zvolanek, and that's a tragedy. They will have to live with it the rest of their lives. There is obviously nothing you can do for Charisse and Lacie Jo. But there is something that you can do for Nicholas. Somewhere down the road Nicholas is going to grow up, hopefully. He's going to want to know what happened. And he is going to know what happened to his baby sister and his mother. He is going to want to know what type of justice was done. He is going to want to know what hap-

pened. With your verdict, you will provide the answer." The jury sentenced Payne to death on each of the murder counts.

ISSUE

[Does the] Eighth Amendment prohibit a capital sentencing jury from considering "victim impact" evidence relating to the personal characteristics of the victim and the emotional impact of the crimes on the victim's family?

HOLDING

[No.] The Eighth Amendment erects no *per se* [absolute] bar prohibiting a capital sentencing jury from considering "victim impact" evidence. To the extent that this Court held to the contrary in *Booth* and *Gathers*, those cases are overruled.

REASONING

Within the constitutional limitations defined by our cases, the States enjoy their traditional latitude to prescribe the method by which those who commit murder shall be punished. *Blystone* v. *Pennsylvania*, 494 U.S. 299 (1990). The States remain free, in capital cases, as well as others, to devise new procedures and new remedies to meet felt needs. Victim impact evidence is simply another form or method of informing the sentencing authority about the specific harm caused by the crime in question, evidence of a general type long considered by sentencing authorities. We think [our precedent in] *Booth* was wrong in stating that this kind of evidence leads to the arbitrary imposition of the death penalty. In the majority of cases, and in this case, victim impact evidence serves entirely legitimate purposes. In the event that evidence is introduced that is so unduly prejudicial that it renders the trial fundamentally unfair, the Due Process Clause of the Fourteenth Amendment provides a mechanism for relief. *See Darden* v. *Wainwright*, 477 U.S. 168 (1986).

Courts have always taken into consideration the harm done by the defendant in imposing sentence, and the evidence adduced in this case was illustrative of the harm caused by Payne's double murder. We are now of the view that a State may properly conclude that for the jury to assess

(continued)

BOX 13.5

(continued)

meaningfully the defendant's moral culpability and blameworthiness, it should have before it at the sentencing phase evidence of the specific harm caused by the defendant. "The State has a legitimate interest in counteracting the mitigating evidence which the defendant is entitled to put in, by reminding the sentencer that just as the murderer should be considered as an individual, so too the victim is an individual whose death represents a unique loss to society and in particular to his family."

By turning the victim into a "faceless stranger at the penalty phase of a capital trial," *Booth* deprives the State of the full moral force of its evidence and may prevent the jury from having before it all the information necessary to determine the proper punishment for a first-degree murder. The present case is an example of the potential for such unfairness. The capital sentencing jury heard testimony from Payne's girlfriend that they met at church; that he was affectionate, caring, and kind to her children; that he was not an abuser of drugs or alcohol; and that it was inconsistent with his character to have committed the murders. Payne's parents testified that he was a good son, and a clinical psychologist testified that Payne was an extremely polite prisoner and suffered from a low IQ. None of this testimony was related to the circumstances of Payne's brutal crimes. In contrast, the only evidence of the impact of Payne's offenses during the sentencing phase was Nicholas' grandmother's description—in response to a single question—that the child misses his mother and baby sister. Payne argues that the Eighth Amendment commands that the jury's death sentence must be set aside because the jury heard this testimony. But the testimony illustrated quite poignantly some of the harm that Payne's killing had caused; there is nothing unfair about allowing the jury to bear in mind that harm at the same time as it considers the mitigating evidence introduced by the defendant. The Supreme Court of Tennessee in this case obviously felt the unfairness of the rule pronounced by *Booth* when it said: "It is an affront to the civilized members of the human race to say that at sentencing in a capital case, a parade of witnesses may praise the background, character and good deeds of Defendant (as was done in this case), without limitation as to relevancy, but nothing may be said that bears upon the character of, or the harm imposed, upon the victims."

CONCLUSION

Reconsidering these decisions [*Booth, Gathers*] now, we conclude, for the reasons heretofore stated, that they were wrongly decided and should be, and now are, overruled. We accordingly affirm the judgment of the Supreme Court of Tennessee [upholding Payne's death sentence].

Applying the Rule of Law to the Facts: When is a closing argument improper?

- In a death-penalty case in which the defendant was charged with suffocating an elderly woman to death before stealing her weed-whacker to sell for crack money, the prosecutor put a bag over his head and writhed on the ground during his closing argument to simulate for the jury how the victim must have suffered before she died. Was this an improper argument under the law?

Yes, the prosecutor cannot legally ask the jurors to put themselves in the victim's shoes because "arguments for the death penalty designed to cause the jury to abandon reason in favor of passion are improper."[13]

In our chapter-opening scenario, the victim's mother could not ask the jury for a specific sentence of death for John, because such a request would invade the province of the jury. The next frontier in victim-impact contributions to a defendant's trial may

---

[13]*Missouri* v. *Rhodes*, 988 S.W.2d 521 (1997).

be in family members wearing signs, photographs, or carrying on protests in court. In *Carey* v. *Musladin*, 127 S.Ct. 649 (2006), the U.S. Supreme Court was asked the technical question of whether a federal court could grant *habeas corpus* relief if a state court allowed courtroom spectators to wear buttons with photographs of the victim's face. The high Court said it was not an erroneous application of law to allow the button-wearing practice, despite defense claims that such a practice created an "unacceptable risk that impermissible factors have caused a jury's verdict to be based not solely on evidence introduced at trial." It remains to be seen whether trial courts deem the practice of bringing photos of the victim in court, either by button or on a tee-shirt, to be too prejudicial to the defendant's right to a fair trial regardless of the technical legality of the practice.

II. Key Terms and Phrases

- challenge for cause
- confrontation clause
- discovery

- effective assistance of counsel
- exculpatory evidence
- jury selection

- peremptory challenge
- venue
- victim-impact statement

III. Summary

1. **The protection for defendants during the discovery process:** The U.S. Supreme Court requires the government, under *Brady* v. *Maryland* (1963), to disclose to the defendant any exculpatory information learned during the investigation. Exculpatory evidence is evidence tending to prove that the defendant is innocent.

2. **The protection for defendants from their lawyers:** A defendant has a right to represent himself and, if he so chooses, to be represented by counsel who must give **effective assistance of counsel,** which means the attorney's behavior at trial must meet the standard that a reasonable attorney would provide under the circumstances.

3. **The protection for defendants in the confrontation clause, venue selection, and jury selection:** The Sixth Amendment's **confrontation clause** which guarantees the defendant's right to confront witnesses against him through the process of cross-examination has been expanded by recent U.S. Supreme Court case law. Prior to the high Court's decision in *Crawford* v. *Washington* (2004), if hearsay statements had some indicia of reliability and the witness was unavailable, the statement could be used against the defendant. Since the *Crawford* decision, hearsay is admissible only if the witness is unavailable and the defendant had an opportunity to cross-examine that witness before he or she became unavailable. In child abuse cases, certain concessions are made so that traumatized children will find it easier to testify in open court against their abusers without violating the confrontation clause, as long as the state has

shown through expert testimony or otherwise that the child will suffer great mental harm if forced to confront the defendant face to face and as long as the defense counsel has the opportunity to cross-examine the child. The U.S. Supreme Court has interpreted the Sixth Amendment's requirement of a fair trial to mean that a defendant can be tried by a jury of his peers taken from a representative cross-section of the community. The fair cross section of the community requirement does not mean that a defendant has a right to be tried in front of a panel of people who are similar to him in race, age or socioeconomic background, but it does mean that the government cannot use its peremptory challenges to eliminate potential jurors on the basis of their race [under *Batson* v. *Kentucky* (1985)] or gender [under *J.E.B.* v. *Alabama Ex Rel. T.B.* (1994)]. If prosecutors exercise their peremptory strikes to remove people of color or one gender, the state must offer a neutral reason for doing so, but the decision to believe the state's reason for exercising the strike rests with the judge.

4. **The rights of victims at a defendant's sentencing:** In the death-penalty context, the jury recommends the sentence, but it is still within the judge's province to impose the sentence. In *Payne* v. *Tennessee* (1991), the high Court allowed **victim-impact statements,** that is, victims informing the court how the defendant's behavior and/or crime has had a negative effect on their lives. Such victim statements do not violate the defendant's constitutional right to be free from undue interference with the judicial process.

IV. Discussion Questions

1. What does the expression mean, "a lawyer who represents himself has a fool for a client"? Do you think John Muhammed was foolish to have represented himself, or was he, as he put it, in the best position to represent himself because he knew himself and the facts of the case better than his attorneys ever could?

2. How difficult do you think it is for defendants to "prove" that a prosecutor was removing potential jury members on the basis of their race or gender, especially if the prosecutor expressed a neutral reason for removing the juror, such as the prosecutor thought the person was "soft on crime" or "just could not be fair"?

3. Why do we hold prosecutors and law enforcement officers to high ethical standards in treating defendants fairly? Do you think a prosecutor who withholds exculpatory information from the defense in order to ensure a conviction in the short-term risks letting a potentially guilty man ultimately go free when that conviction is overturned for prosecutorial misconduct? Which do you think is a better outcome—following the law and securing a conviction while giving the defendant every opportunity to defend himself fully, or ignoring some of the defendant's rights to secure a sure conviction regardless of what might happen on appeal?

4. In our chapter-opening scenario, could the victim's family request that the jury sentence John to death for the drug-related murder? Why would such an action violate the Eighth Amendment, but a victim-impact statement not violate the Constitution? What is the difference between a victim making an impact statement at a defendant's sentencing hearing and witnesses or spectators wearing photographs of the victim on buttons throughout the trial?

V. Problem-Solving Exercises

1. During a confidential discussion, the murder suspect confessed to her attorney that if she were let out on bail, she planned to kill the judge in the case. Is it ineffective assistance of counsel to disclose the substance of the threat to the court? The police? The prosecutor? What if the threat were to kill all the potential jurors in the case? Does the attorney have an ethical obligation to keep such confidences confidential? Does he represent his client zealously if he repeats what she told him? Why or why not?

2. The prosecutor knows that the primary eyewitness, Bill, identified the defendant, Tom, as the suspect in a lineup only after first identifying someone else, Henry. Does the prosecutor have to inform the defense counsel of this fact? What if the prosecutor concluded that Bill was merely nervous or made a minor error before picking out the right guy? Does the legal analysis about the prosecutor's duty to disclose the information change?

3. Ali was a white supremacist on trial for a hate crime. During *voir dire*, the prosecutor used her peremptory strikes to eliminate as potential jurors all African-American and Hispanic men. Does Ali have a constitutional challenge to the composition of the jury if it is composed of only white jurors?

4. After a school shooting, the defendant went on trial. Members of the community wanted to address the defendant and shout out "scumbag" and "dirtbag" to make him feel really small before he was sentenced. Under the holding of *Payne* v. *Tennessee*, may the community members make such victim-impact statements in an effort to influence the court's imposition of the defendant's sentence?

5. Randy and Vonny were coconspirators involved in a drug distribution conspiracy. Randy was caught by police officers and was eager to make a deal that would allow him to remain on the street and act as an informant. He planned to relay information about the drug conspiracy back to the police in exchange for the officers sharing with the prosecutor the extent of his cooperation, in a hope of leniency and a reduction of charges. Randy was kept out on the street and informed the police of drug deals that were happening, so the police kept Vonny under surveillance. Right before the investigation was about to end and Randy's role as an informant was about to be exposed, Randy gave a statement to police detailing his role in the conspiracy. Right after Randy was exposed as an informant, he was shot dead. At Vonny's trial, the state sought to introduce Randy's statement made to police before he died. On the basis of his Sixth Amendment Confrontation Clause right, what objections, if any, can Vonny make to the admission of Randy's statement?

VI. World Wide Web Resources

A history of the United States Constitution
http://supreme.lp.findlaw.com/documents/consthist.html

Federal Rules of Evidence
http://www.law.cornell.edu/rules/fre/

VII. Additional Readings and Notes

Constitutional Criminal Procedure

Akhil Reed Amar. *The Constitution and Criminal Procedure: First Principles* (New Haven, CT: Yale University, 1998).

Bonnie Pettifor and Charles E. Petit. *Weeks* v. *United States: Illegal Search and Seizure* (Lawrence, KS: University Press of Kansas, 2000).

Confrontation Clause

Thomas Y. Davies. "*Crawford* and Beyond: Exploring the Future of the Confrontation Clause in Light of its Past: What Did the Framers Know, and When Did They Know It? Fictional Originalism in *Crawford* v. *Washington.*" *Brooklyn Law Review,* Vol. 71 (2005), pp. 105–217.

Kjirstin Graham. "Accomplice Confessions and the Confrontation Clause: *Crawford* v. *Washington* Confronts Past Issues with a New Rule." *Pepperdine Law Review,* Vol. 32 (2005), pp. 315–372.

Laurie E. Martin. "Child Abuse Witness Protections Confront *Crawford* v. *Washington.*" *Indiana Law Review,* Vol. 39 (2005), pp. 113–144.

John M. Spires. "Testimonial or Nontestimonial? The Admissibility of Forensic Evidence after *Crawford* v. *Washington.*" *Kentucky Law Journal,* Vol. 94 (2006), pp. 187–209.

Susanne C. Walther. "Pipe-Dreams of Truth and Fairness: Is *Crawford* v. *Washington* a Breakthrough for Sixth Amendment Confrontation Rights?" *Buffalo Criminal Law Review,* Vol. 9 (2006), pp. 453–474.

The Jury

Diane E. Courselle. "Struggling with Deliberative Secrecy, Jury Independence, and Jury Reform." *South Carolina Law Review,* Vol. 57 (2005), pp. 203–254.

Bennett L. Gersham. "Contaminating the Verdict: The Problem of Juror Misconduct." *South Dakota Law Review,* Vol. 50 (2005), pp. 322–351.

CHAPTER
14
Sentencing and Appeals

"With all due apology to The Mikado—*'let the punishment fit the crime'—All crimes are not the same even if they are called the same."*

ANONYMOUS PENNSYLVANIA JUDGE SURVEY RESPONDENT (2006)

CHAPTER OBJECTIVES

Primary Concepts Discussed in This Chapter:

1. How society determines the appropriate punishment for each offender
2. The different types of sentences
3. The significance of mandatory minimums, "Three strikes you're out" legislation, sentencing guidelines, and Megan's Laws
4. The death-penalty process
5. The legal requirements for different types of appeals and *habeas corpus* review

CHAPTER OUTLINE

Chapter Feature: The Fraternity Brothers and the Appropriate Punishment

I. SENTENCING PROCESS

1. Philosophy of Punishment
   Box 14.1 *Harmelin* v. *Michigan,* 501 U.S. 957 (1991)
2. Presentence Investigation
3. The Sentencing Hearing
4. Types of Sentences
   a. Determinate and Indeterminate Sentences
   b. Mandatory Minimums
   c. Enhancing a Sentence
   d. The Federal Sentencing Guidelines
   e. Suspended Sentences
      i. Probation
      ii. Parole
   f. Three-Strikes Laws
   g. Megan's Laws
5. Expungement of Sentences, Pardons, and Executive Clemency

II. THE DEATH PENALTY

1. Death Qualification of the Jury
2. Bifurcated Sentencing Procedure
   a. Aggravating and Mitigating Circumstances
3. New Evidence of Innocence and Exonerations
4. Competency to be Executed
5. The Execution Process

Feature: *Chapter-Opening Case Study: The Fraternity Brothers and the Appropriate Punishment*

Smoot University was famous for its active and boisterous fraternity and sorority life, the life of the Greeks. The campus hosted 52 different Greek houses, including Tri-Delt, otherwise known as Delta Delta Delta. The highlight of a Greek's life, once a pledge successfully maneuvered the pledge period, was to host drinking parties in which the primary goal of the hosts and party-goers was to consume as much alcohol as possible. True, there were members who did not drink, but they were in the minority.

One night, to celebrate the football team's homecoming win, Tri-Delt members paid for two exotic dancers to perform for the brothers. When the dancers arrived close to midnight, the men were in different states of inebriation. After the dancers started their routine, one brother, Sam, went up and groped a dancer's breast. Another brother screamed at one of the dancers that if she did not hurry up and take off her clothes, he was going to kill her. The dancer became frightened and ran to an upstairs bathroom, where three brothers followed her. One brother, Newt, held her down as the other two, Milton and Redbone, raped her repeatedly. When the dancer escaped, she screamed that she was going to call the police. John heard the dancer's threats, chased her down, strangled her to death, and buried her body in the backyard of the fraternity house. All of the men were caught and charged with various crimes of assault, battery, rape, false imprisonment, and, in John's case, first-degree premeditated murder, for which the state is seeking the death penalty. None of the fraternity brothers had been in trouble before, except Newt, who was convicted as a juvenile of drug conspiracy and assault and battery charges, and all of the brothers have claimed some form of intoxication defense.

What should the appropriate punishments be for each brother, and what factors should the judge consider in determining the appropriate sentence for each man?

INTRODUCTION

Sentencing is society's retribution for an offender's crime, while punishment is intended to protect society from the offender. Upon conviction, a defendant no longer enjoys the presumption of innocence; all the evidence used to convict is believed true. The guilty judgment allows the government to take away the defendant's liberty by imposing a prison sentence, and to monitor her activity by the operation of probation conditions, including drug testing or electronic monitoring. An offender may be released from jail after having served only part of the sentence, with his or her liberty still restricted through the imposition of parole. If an offender on parole violates conditions set by the court, the court can order her back to prison to serve the remainder of her sentence. There are especially harsh punishments, such as mandatory minimums that require the convict to serve no less than a specified number of years in prison, "three-strikes" laws, life imprisonment, and even death.

I. SENTENCING PROCESS

Rule of Law: The Eighth Amendment's ban against cruel and unusual punishment controls sentencing decisions.

1. Philosophy of Punishment

The Eighth Amendment to the Constitution provides, "Excessive bail shall not be required, nor excessive fines imposed, nor cruel and unusual punishments inflicted." Within the realm of sanctions imposed by the state that are not cruel and unusual are a wide range of punishments. When this country was founded, punishment was the sanction that was deemed appropriate to make the offender pay society back for the harm caused. As legal scholar K. Greenawalt writes about the purpose of punishment:

> Why should wrongdoers be punished? Most people might respond simply that they deserve it or that they should suffer in return for the harm that have done. Such feelings are deeply ingrained, at least in many cultures, and are often supported by notions of divine punishment for those who disobey God's laws. A simple retributivist justification provides a philosophical account corresponding to these feelings; someone who has violated the rights of others should be penalized, and punishment restores the moral order that has been breached by the original wrongful act.[1]

What constitutes cruel and unusual punishment must be measured by a **proportionality review.** Once a sentence is imposed, on appeal a court will examine the sentence to ensure that it is equivalent to sentences awarded to similarly situated offenders. For example, if a bank robber with an extensive criminal history is sentenced to 25 years, the sentence is deemed proportionate and will stand. In the case *Harmelin* v. *Michigan,* 501 U.S. 957 (1991), reprinted in part in Box 14.1, a young student was sentenced to life imprisonment for possessing more than 650 grams of cocaine. The primary issue for the U.S. Supreme Court on appeal was whether or not a life sentence for a first-time drug offense constituted cruel and unusual punishment; the Court said it was not.

Rule of Law: Sentencing punishes the offender, not the crime.

In the federal jurisdiction and in the majority of state jurisdictions, after an offender has been convicted by a jury verdict or guilty plea, the judge imposes the sentence. In a minority of states, after conviction, the jury also imposes the sentence. In death-penalty trials, the

---

[1]Kent Greenawalt. "Moral Justifications and Legal Punishment." In Stanford H. Kadish, ed., *Encyclopedia of Crime and Justice* (New York: Miles River, 1983), pp. 1337–1342.

BOX 14.1

Harmelin v. *Michigan*, 501 U.S. 957 (1991)
United States Supreme Court

Justice Scalia announced the decision of the Court.

FACTS

[Harmelin] was convicted of possessing 672 grams of cocaine and sentenced to a mandatory term of life in prison without possibility of parole.

ISSUE

[Harmelin] claims that his sentence is unconstitutionally "cruel and unusual" for two reasons: first, because it is "significantly disproportionate" to the crime he committed; second, because the sentencing judge was statutorily required to impose it, without taking into account the particularized circumstances of the crime and of the criminal.

HOLDING

The sentence is affirmed.

REASONING

Most historians agree that the "cruel and unusual Punishments" provision of the English Declaration of Rights was prompted by the abuses attributed to the infamous Lord Chief Justice Jeffreys of the King's Bench during the Stuart reign of James II. They do not agree, however, on which abuses. Jeffreys is best known for presiding over the "Bloody Assizes" following the Duke of Monmouth's abortive rebellion in 1685; a special commission led by Jeffreys tried, convicted, and executed hundreds of suspected insurgents. Some have attributed the Declaration of Rights provision to popular outrage against those proceedings. But the vicious punishments for treason decreed in the Bloody Assizes (drawing and quartering, burning of women felons, beheading, disemboweling, etc.) were common in that period—indeed, they were specifically authorized by law and remained so for many years afterwards.

[Harmelin] claims that his sentence violates the Eighth Amendment for a reason in addition to its alleged disproportionality. He argues that it is "cruel and unusual" to impose a mandatory sentence of such severity, without any consideration of so-called mitigating factors such as, in his case, the fact that he had no prior felony convictions. He apparently contends that the Eighth Amendment requires Michigan to create a sentencing scheme whereby life in prison without possibility of parole is simply the most severe of a range of available penalties that the sentencer may impose after hearing evidence in mitigation and aggravation, this claim has no support in the text and history of the Eighth Amendment.

CONCLUSION

We have drawn the line of required individualized sentencing at capital cases, and see no basis for extending it further. The judgment of the Michigan Court of Appeals is affirmed.

Justice Stevens, with whom Justice Blackmun joins, **dissenting:**

[A] mandatory sentence of life imprisonment without the possibility of parole does share one important characteristic of a death sentence: The offender will never regain his freedom. Because such a sentence does not even purport to serve a rehabilitative function, the sentence must rest on a rational determination that the punished "criminal conduct is so atrocious that society's interest in deterrence and retribution wholly outweighs any considerations of reform or rehabilitation of the perpetrator." Serious as this defendant's crime was, I believe it is irrational to conclude that every similar offender is wholly incorrigible.

jury makes a recommendation of a life sentence, a sentence of life without parole (depending on the jurisdiction), or a death sentence. The judge formally imposes the sentence after trial at a sentencing hearing and rarely deviates from the jury's recommendation. The following steps are typical steps in the sentencing process, but students should research the procedures followed in their respective states.

2. Presentence Investigation

The criminal justice system seeks to punish the offender, not the crime. It would be cruel and unusual punishment to punish a 12-year-old with death even if the child committed willful, deliberate, and premeditated murder with aggravating circumstances. Moreover, it may be important to the sentencing determination that, for example, an offender suffered brain damage as a child, committed the crime under duress because of threats of bodily harm or death to him or his family, willfully and intentionally stole as much money as possible, or lied during the trial—all of those facts would be relevant for the court in determining an appropriate sentence for the offender.

To determine the appropriate sentence, the court requires the collection of all important information about the offender, called a **presentence investigation.** To accomplish this goal, an officer of the court interviews the offender preferably with counsel present, verifies supplemental information by calling relevant references such as employers and family members, reviews the nature of the charges and the circumstances surrounding the crime, and makes a recommendation about the appropriate sentence in the case. Usually such reports contain sensitive information and are not available to the public. The report contains the defendant's family history, educational background and achievements, economic status, employment history, medical history, and history of drug use. It is wise for defense counsel to attend the presentence interview because some of the statements made by the defendant may be used against her at sentencing. In determining the sentence, the judge will consider the seriousness of the offense, the threat that the defendant will commit more crimes, any history of past crimes committed, age, experience, ties to the community, employment history, sincere efforts at apology, and acceptance of responsibility.

The result of the presentence investigation is the **presentence report,** which incorporates all the information gathered by the court officer and is presented to the prosecutor, defense counsel, and judge. The judge is not necessarily limited to the information contained in the presentence report, as the U.S. Supreme Court said that before determining a sentence "a judge may appropriately conduct an inquiry broad in scope, largely unlimited either as to the kind of information he may consider, or the source from which it may come."[2] The judge may legally consider any and all testimony adduced at trial or by the guilty plea, including any statements or testimony by the accused, and if the judge believes that the defendant committed perjury, that is a legal factor for the court to consider as well. The relevant federal statute provides, "No limitation shall be placed on the information concerning the background, character, and conduct of a person convicted of an offense which a court of the United States may receive and consider for the purpose of imposing an appropriate sentence." 18 U.S.C. §3661

3. The Sentencing Hearing

Prior to actual imposition of sentence, the court holds a **sentencing hearing** during which the judge hears arguments from both the prosecution and the defense and may accept additional evidence in aggravation, making the crime more serious, or in mitigation, factors that militate in favor of the defendant. At this time, the judge also hears the **allocution,** the last statement of the defendant to the court before sentence is imposed. The defendant has every right to address the court before the judge imposes sentence. Before being sentenced for a triple murder, one defendant said, "You know, I ask God to forgive me for what I done, and I hope you can find the same and feel it in your hearts. But I can't change what happened. I share the same pain you share. So that's all I can say."[3] On the other hand, some defendants refuse to apologize for their crime. In the case

[2]*United States* v. *Tucker,* 404 U.S. 443 (1972).

[3]*Missouri* v. *Buchanan,* 00CR165704-01, Sentencing, 4/22/02

of the so-called shoe bomber, Richard C. Reid pled guilty to federal charges of terroristic activity for trying to light a bomb concealed in his shoe on a transcontinental flight from the United Kingdom to America. At his sentencing hearing, Reid addressed Chief Judge William G. Young of the District Court for the District of Massachusetts and said, "I think I ought not to apologize for my actions. I am at war with your country." Judge Young then admonished Reid before sentencing him to life in prison and said:

> You are not an enemy combatant. You are a terrorist. You are not a soldier in any war. You are a terrorist. Look around this courtroom. Mark it well. The world is not going to long remember what you or I say here. Day after tomorrow it will be forgotten. But this, however, will long endure. Here in this courtroom and courtrooms all across America, the American people will gather to see that justice, individual justice, justice, not war, individual justice is in fact being done. . . . See that flag Mr. Reid? That's the flag of the United States of America. That flag will fly there long after this is all forgotten. That flag stands for freedom. You know it always will. Custody, Mr. Officer. Stand him down.[4]

In some circumstances, courts allow the victims to make an impact statement reflecting how the offender's crime has irrevocably altered their lives. Once deemed unconstitutional in *Booth* v. *Maryland,* 482 U.S. 496 (1987), as having an impermissible influence on the sentence, this practice was allowed four years later in *Payne* v. *Tennessee,* 501 U.S. 808 (1991). In *Payne,* Chief Justice Rehnquist stated that not allowing crime victims to address the court about the enduring harm they suffer as a result of the defendant's conduct "deprives the State of the full moral force of its evidence and may prevent the jury from having before it all the information necessary to determine the proper punishment for a first-degree murder."[5]

After the defendant's allocution, the judge pronounces a sentence and imposes a penalty for the offense. If the defendant has been convicted of multiple charges such as robbery and kidnapping, a judge may impose concurrent sentences [both running together] or consecutive sentences [allowing the sentence for robbery to run and, when it has finished, implementing the sentence for the kidnapping].

4. Types of Sentences

a. Determinate and Indeterminate Sentences

Determinate sentencing involves the imposition of fixed or flat time. In contrast, in **indeterminate sentencing,** the judge imposes a sentencing range, and if the prisoner exhibits good behavior in prison, he may be released early by a parole board. Determinate sentences, much like the three-strikes legislation explained later in this chapter, increase the prison population and the attendant strain on resources within the prison, including security, medical care, and rehabilitation resources. Such sentences reflect the public's wariness of the presumed revolving door at the prison gate.

Indeterminate sentencing was largely responsible for the enactment of tough sentencing reforms in the 1980s. In *Mistretta* v. *United States,* 109 S.Ct. 647 (1989), the U.S. Supreme Court said that in enacting the Federal Guidelines as part of the Sentencing Reform Act of 1984, Congress concluded that rehabilitation was failed corrections philosophy and that indeterminate sentencing had untenable consequences. These consequences included "the great variation among sentences imposed by different judges upon similarly situated offenders [and the] uncertainty as to the time the offender would spend in prison. Each was a serious impediment to an evenhanded and effective operation of the criminal justice system." Guidelines were enacted in state jurisdictions and the federal government as a way to achieve uniformity in sentencing.

---

[4]Winds of Change.net, http://windsofchange.net/archives/003845.php

[5]505 U.S. at 825.

b. Mandatory Minimums

In response to society's growing dissatisfaction with the perception that the criminal justice system was ineffective in dealing appropriately with offenders came the enactment of many laws that were designed to impose stringent punishment for offenders who were traditionally treated less harshly, such as first-time drug offenders. Particularly in response to the "war on drugs," states began to enact **mandatory minimum sentences** for which the offender would have to serve a minimum term of incarceration, typically five years, before any other penological efforts or attempts on behalf of the offender would be made. Given that most of the offenders were low-level members of drug conspiracies who carried all the risk of transporting the drugs, and minimum sentences of five and ten years were now determined on the weight of the drugs that each offender possessed, the prison population swelled. One New York state judge observed that "[f]aced with what it found to be a high recidivism rate in drug-related crimes, an inadequate response to less severe punishment, and an insidiously growing drug abuse problem, the Legislature could reasonable shift the emphasis to other penological purposes, namely, isolation and deterrence."[6]

In a survey of Commonwealth of Pennsylvania Common Plea Judges on Mandatory Minimum Sentencing Statutes released on October 4, 2006, one state court judge reiterated what U.S. Supreme Court Associate Justice Kennedy had to say about mandatory minimum schemes. The judge criticized the transfer of sentencing decisions from an independent judiciary to a prosecutor who could simply notify the defendant, or put him on "notice" of his intent to seek a mandatory minimum, which might induce the defendant to plead guilty to a lesser charge. The judge wrote that such a transfer of power upset the balance of justice, and added in an anonymous statement:

> The most pungent issue, however, involves the odor that arises from the prosecutors' use of their legislatively created and judicially sanctioned thumb screw. As long as mandatory minimum sentencing statutes are dependent for their imposition upon 'notice' by the Commonwealth, the government is free to use the notice as the sword of Damocles, forcing the accused to relinquish the most sacred rights guaranteed by our Constitutions. Under the guise of 'evidentiary considerations,' district attorneys are free to use the threat of mandatory imprisonment to coerce defendants out of exercising rights to suppress evidence (bad searches) and even to extract a guilty plea from an otherwise innocent accused to avoid certain incarceration.

The primary complaint among the Pennsylvania judges was that mandatory minimum sentences did not allow them to fashion appropriate sentences for the specific and unique facts of each case presented before them, which resulted in real miscarriages of justice. While they noted that the will of the people through the legislature has the authority to define crimes, grade them as felonies, and define the degrees of felonies and misdemeanors, the one-size-fits-all approach of mandatory minimums robs the spirit of justice from her course. The majority of survey respondents felt that mandatory minimum sentences did not help the administration of justice, but a few judges did praise the seeming uniformity of the sentences.

On the federal level, Congress directed the U.S. Sentencing Commission to conduct a study of mandatory minimum sentencing in the federal criminal justice system. The Commission found, in its 1991 report, that sentencing under the federal guidelines "is essentially a system of finely calibrated sentences" and implementing mandatory minimums might skew the "smooth continuum" of the guidelines. The report concluded, "the most efficient way for Congress to exercise its powers to direct sentencing policy is through the established process of sentencing guidelines . . . rather than through mandatory minimums."[7] The future of mandatory minimums will rest on how

---

[6]*People* v. *Broadie,* 371 N.Y.S.2d 471 (1975).

[7]Special Report to Congress. "Mandatory Minimum Penalties in the Federal Criminal Justice System." United States Sentencing Commission, August 1991.

the criminal justice system can handle the swollen and prison population that grew as a direct result of such policies.

c. Enhancing a Sentence

In 1994, George and Martha Washington, an African-American couple, moved into Derry township in New Jersey. One neighbor, Mr. Apprendi, decided to welcome the Washingtons by shooting .38 caliber bullets through their living room window. In *Apprendi* v. *New Jersey,* 530 U.S. 466 (2000), the sentencing judge found that Apprendi's crime was triggered by his racial bias against the Washingtons, and under the "hate crime enhancement" two years were added to Apprendi's sentence, which was already the maximum for his offense. On appeal, the U.S. Supreme Court decided that the judge's action in increasing the sentence violated Apprendi's Sixth Amendment right to a jury trial.

The Court reasoned that when the judge, as in Apprendi's case, makes findings of fact—such as the fact that Apprendi was motivated by racial hatred—which lead to increased prison time, this action deprives the defendant of his right to a jury trial as guaranteed by the Sixth Amendment. As a result of the *Apprendi* ruling, many sentences across the country that had been enhanced solely by a judge making determinations as to the appropriate sentence were reduced. When a state court judge determined the aggravating circumstances that made Timothy Ring eligible to receive the death penalty the Supreme Court said that due to *Apprendi*'s implication for a defendant's Sixth Amendment right to a fair trial, Ring's eligibility for death could be legally determined only by a jury, not a judge. As a result of the Supreme Court's decision in *Ring* v. *Arizona,* 536 U.S. 584 (2002), applying the *Apprendi* ruling to death sentences that had been determined by a judge alone and not a jury, 150 death-row inmates across the country had their death sentences commuted to life without the possibility of parole.

d. The Federal Sentencing Guidelines

In 1984, Congress enacted The Comprehensive Crime Control Act and the Sentencing Reform Act.[8] This legislation set mandatory minimum sentences for drug crimes and also authorized the creation of the United States Sentencing Commission, which promulgated the first set of codified sentencing guidelines for federal trial courts. The Commission's mandate was stated in pertinent part:

> The Comprehensive Crime Control Act of 1984 foresees guidelines that will further the basic purpose of criminal punishment by deterring crime, incapacitating the offender, providing just punishment, and rehabilitating the offender. It delegates to the commission broad authority to review and rationalize the federal sentencing process.

The Commission drafted the Federal Sentencing Guidelines ("Guidelines"), which were then passed into law by Congress in 1987 in an effort to minimize sentencing disparities based on jurisdiction or offender characteristics. The Guidelines assigned numbers for each crime and each type of criminal history and, as critics contended, reduced federal sentencing to a mathematical calculation rather than an individual sentence. The Guidelines made all sentences determinate and eliminated the system of parole whereby prisoners, in exchange for good behavior, had their sentences reduced by 15% for any sentence over a year. An example of how to determine a sentence under the Guidelines is illustrated by Figure 14.1. The real life example is from 2006.

From the time of their enactment in 1987 until 2005, the Guidelines were mandatory and bound all defendants tried and convicted in federal court. On appeal, courts examined whether trial judges had sentenced within the guideline range for a particular crime. Recent Supreme Court decisions have made significant changes in Guidelines law following the precedent of *Apprendi* v. *New Jersey* (1999).

---

[8]The Comprehensive Crime Control Act of 1984, P.L. 98-473; The Sentencing Reform Act of 1984, 18 U.S.C. §§3551-3626 and 28 U.S.C. §§991-998.

FIGURE 14.1   Calculating a federal sentence.

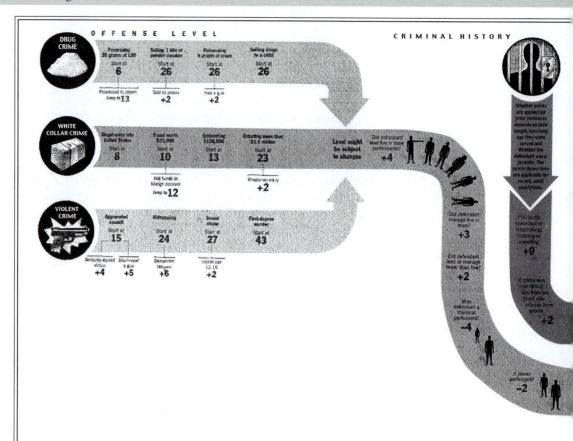

Reprinted with permission, The Washington Post.

A REAL-LIFE EXAMPLE

The case of **Martin Miller** of Bethesda illustrates how the grid works. Last September, U.S. District Judge Paul Friedman sentenced Miller for defrauding his business partners. An offense level of 14 and criminal history category of I put Miller in the range of 15 to 21 months. In the end, Friedman gave him 15 months in prison.

How Miller's criminal history level was determined:

No criminal record	Points: 0
	Category I

How Miller's offense level was determined:

Fraud	6
Loss between $173,017 and $200,000	+7
More than minimal planning	+2
Abused position of trust	+2
	17
Accepted responsibility	−3
	Level: 14

SOURCES: U.S. Sentencing Commission, Guidelines Manual, court records

NAL HISTORY

...ance ...ays	Each prior sentence from 60 days to 13 months +2	Each prior sentence more than 13 months +3	If crime committed while defendant on parole or probation +2	Two prior violent crime or drug convictions mark you "career offender" Start at 13 (Category VI)	Total the points to determine category

SE LEVEL

...me ...e?	Did defendant abuse a position of trust? +2	Did defendant use a special skill? +2	Did defendant obstruct justice? +2	Did defendant accept responsibility? −2 or −3 Depending on offense level	Total the points to determine offense level

FEDERAL SENTENCING GRID

Ranges specified in the grid are shown as months in prison.

CRIMINAL HISTORY CATEGORY

OFFENSE LEVEL	I (0–1 point)	II (2–3 points)	III (4–6 points)	IV (7–9 points)	V (10–12 points)	VI (13 or more)
1	0-6 mos	0-6	0-6	0-6	0-6	0-6
2	0-6	0-6	0-6	0-6	0-6	1-7
3	0-6	0-6	0-6	0-6	2-8	3-9
4	0-6	0-6	0-6	2-8	4-10	6-12
5	0-6	0-6	1-7	4-10	6-12	9-15
6	0-6	1-7	2-8	6-12	9-15	12-18
7	0-6	2-8	4-10	8-14	12-18	15-21
8	0-6	4-10	6-12	10-16	15-21	18-24
9	4-10	6-12	8-14	12-18	18-24	21-27
10	6-12	8-14	12-18	15-21	21-27	24-30
11	8-14	10-16	12-18	18-24	24-30	27-33
12	10-16	12-18	15-21	21-27	27-33	30-37
13	12-18	15-21	18-24	24-30	30-37	33-41
14	15-21	18-24	21-27	27-33	33-41	37-46
15	18-24	21-27	24-30	30-37	37-45	41-51
16	21-27	24-30	27-33	33-41	41-51	46-57
17	24-30	27-33	30-37	37-46	46-57	51-63
18	27-33	30-37	33-41	41-51	51-63	57-71
19	30-37	33-41	37-46	46-57	57-71	63-78
20	33-41	37-46	41-51	51-63	63-78	70-87
21	37-46	41-51	46-57	57-71	70-87	77-96
22	41-51	46-57	51-63	63-78	77-96	84-105
23	46-57	51-63	57-71	70-87	84-105	92-115
24	51-63	57-71	63-78	77-96	92-115	100-125
25	57-71	63-78	70-87	84-105	100-125	110-137
26	63-78	70-87	78-97	92-115	110-137	120-150
27	70-87	78-97	87-108	100-125	120-150	130-162
28	78-97	87-108	97-121	110-137	130-162	140-175
29	87-108	97-121	108-135	121-151	140-175	151-188
30	97-121	108-135	121-151	135-168	151-188	168-210
31	108-135	121-151	135-168	151-188	168-210	188-235
32	121-151	135-168	151-188	168-210	188-235	210-262
33	135-168	151-188	168-210	188-235	210-262	235-293
34	151-188	168-210	188-235	210-262	235-293	262-327
35	168-210	188-235	210-262	235-293	262-327	292-365
36	188-235	210-262	235-293	252-327	292-365	324-405
37	210-262	235-293	262-327	292-365	324-405	360-life
38	235-293	262-327	292-365	324-405	360-life	360-life
39	262-327	292-365	324-405	360-life	360-life	360-life
40	292-365	324-405	360-life	360-life	360-life	360-life
41	324-405	360-life	360-life	360-life	360-life	360-life
42	360-life	360-life	360-life	360-life	360-life	360-life
43	life	life	life	life	life	life

The *Apprendi* precedent established "other than the fact of a prior conviction, any fact that increases the penalty for a crime beyond the prescribed **statutory maximum** must be submitted to a jury, and proved beyond a reasonable doubt." (emphasis added) Criminal statutes define both the crime and its maximum sentence, called the "statutory maximum." The import of the *Apprendi* case for sentencing was if a defendant's sentence was going to be enhanced, either he had to admit to sufficient facts during his guilty plea colloquy or, if he went to trial, the jury would have to find those facts warranting the enhancement beyond a reasonable doubt. To minimize *Apprendi's* ruling on a judge's ability to enhance sentences under guideline sentencing schemes, judges interpreted the term "statutory maximum" narrowly. Judges continued to make factual findings and enhance sentences as long as the defendant's guideline sentencing range was within the "statutory maximum." Thus, the judge would run afoul of *Apprendi* only if the judge made independent factual findings that increased the defendant's sentence beyond the maximum sentence allowed by statute.

The high Court closed this loophole in *Blakely* v. *Washington,* 542 U.S. 296 (2004), where Blakely pled guilty to kidnapping with a statutory maximum sentence of 53 months in prison. The judge decided that Blakely's crime was heinous and added three more years to his sentence. When Blakely complained that he did not admit to the facts that supported the judge's enhancement decision, the judge found the enhanced sentence legal because the state "statutory maximum" for class B felonies was 10 years, and Blakely's sentence was within that range. On appeal, the U.S. Supreme Court found in Blakely's favor and held "the 'statutory maximum' for *Apprendi* purposes is the maximum sentence a judge may impose solely on the basis of the facts reflected in the jury verdict or admitted by the defendant. In other words, the relevant 'statutory maximum' is not the maximum sentence a judge may impose after finding additional facts, but the maximum he may impose without any additional findings." Because the *Blakely* decision only applied to Washington State's guideline scheme, the next question for the Court was whether all sentencing guidelines that allowed judges to make factual findings violated the Constitution's guarantee to a fair trial.

The high Court answered that question in *United States* v. *Booker,* 543 U.S. 220 (2005) (and a companion case, *United States* v. *Fanfan*). Booker, convicted by a jury on drug charges, was facing a guideline range of 210-262 months in prison (17 ½-22 years). The judge found additional relevant facts at sentencing, allowable findings under the Guidelines, and increased Booker's sentence to 30 years imprisonment. Because federal law made the Guidelines mandatory, the judge had to follow the law in imposing sentence. Applying its *Apprendi* and *Blakely* precedents to Booker's case, the high Court finally held the features of the Federal Sentencing Guidelines violated the Sixth Amendment's right to a jury trial. The Guidelines are no longer mandatory. Federal judges are still required to base their sentences on Guideline calculations, but the judges have discretion to award a sentence within a minimum and maximum range of punishment defined by applicable law.

Applying the Rule of Law to the Facts: Is it a legal sentence?

- Mr. Smith was convicted by a jury of sexual abuse of a minor. At sentencing, pursuant to state law that provided for a determinate sentencing scheme, the judge found an aggravating circumstance that increased the sentence from 12 to 16 years. Under recent U.S. Supreme Court rulings, did this increase of sentence by the judge violate Smith's Sixth Amendment right to have a jury find all factors that increased his sentence beyond a reasonable doubt?

Yes, in *Cunningham* v. *California,* 127 S.Ct. 856 (2007), the U.S. Supreme Court found that Cunningham's sentence violated the Sixth Amendment under *Blakely* and *Booker,* because the judge alone could find the aggravating circumstance. Also, the judge could do so at the lower evidentiary standard of a preponderance of evidence rather than the more stringent requirement of the burden of proof at trial—beyond a reasonable doubt.

Rule of Law: A suspended sentence can be reinstated if the defendant fails to live up to the conditions for release set by the court.

e. Suspended Sentences
In certain cases, judges have discretion to suspend or delay the imposition of a sentence of confinement to a penal institution. A **suspended sentence** is a sentence in which, if the convict fails to meet certain restrictions and conditions of the terms set out by the court—for example, avoiding known felons and undergoing regular drug testing by providing urine samples—the judge can order the offender to return to prison and serve the remainder of the original sentence. Two types of suspended sentences discussed below are probation and parole, which are adjudicated sentences that can be imposed when the offender violates a term or condition of the sentence.

i. Probation   **Probation** is a system whereby a convicted offender is released into the community subject to control and supervision by a probation agency before completing the full jail term, if any. When the defendant's sentence is divided between prison and probation, it is called a split sentence. Probation can be granted without serving any term of imprisonment. According to statistics compiled by the U.S. Department of Justice in 2004, 1 in every 32 adults is on probation, reaching a total of almost 6.9 million men and women. Research indicates that men are more likely to be on probation for crimes against the public, such as weapons offenses, drunk driving, and traffic offenses, while women are sentenced to probation for offenses relating to property, such as stealing. For certain serious crimes, such as murder or kidnapping, the granting of probation as a sentence without jail time is prohibited. Misdemeanor crimes, on the other hand, usually receive a sentence of straight probation. Once on a probationary status, an offender will go to prison only if he or she violates the terms of probation, such as using illegal drugs when a condition of remaining in the community is no drug use.

If the law allows a sentence of probation, the decision to grant probation rests with the judge. The probationer must abide by specific conditions of probation to remain in the community and out of prison. These include not associating with known felons, seeking and keeping a job, paying monthly visits to the probation office, submitting to random drug testing, and requesting permission before leaving the jurisdiction for short periods of time. Probationers are also subject to unannounced home visits and warrantless searches and seizures of their persons and homes. If the probationer violates the terms of probation, her probation officer usually presents to a judge a warrant detailing the violations and asking for a probation-revocation hearing. The probationer has a right to counsel at the hearing, and the result may be a warning, the imposition of more stringent conditions, or revocation of probation.

ii. Parole   **Parole** is different from probation because it is an early release from prison. Recommendations for release on parole are usually made by a parole board, typically composed of political appointees of the state governor or other elected official. The primary criticism of parole boards is that there are no formal requirements for the members who sit in judgment of prisoners and the board may be unduly influenced by public opinion about a particular convict. The goal of parole is for the government to keep a close and watchful eye on the offender as she makes her way back into society while retaining the ability to return her to prison if she fails to meet the parole conditions, which mirror the conditions for those on probation. The system of granting parole to prisoners was not immune to the changes within the criminal justice system as the punishment trend moved away from rehabilitation toward increased incarceration; some states abolished parole altogether while others, including the federal government, renamed parole "supervised release."[9]

Applying the Rule of Law to the Facts: **Should offenders be given more chances or be sent to jail?**

- A woman had originally been sentenced to a term of probation on misdemeanor assault charges stemming from an altercation at a manicurist shop over a dispute about how much money she owed. There were additional battery charges when she resisted arrest. The defendant had moved residences without securing permission, had briefly left the state without notifying her parole officer, had been rearrested for an altercation over a cell phone, and had withdrawn from court-ordered anger management. Should the judge put the defendant in jail?

Yes, on the basis of the defendant's numerous instances of noncompliance with the court-ordered conditions of probation, the judge revoked probation and imposed the original 12-month sentence of imprisonment on the original assault charge.[10]

f. Three-Strikes Laws

In the 1990s society became fatigued with the revolving door of prison for repeat offenders. As a play on the baseball term "three strikes, you're out," **three-strikes laws** were enacted to sentence a defendant more severely—for terms up to life in prison—upon conviction for his third serious crime. In the case *Lockyer* v. *Andrade,* 123 S.Ct. 1166 (2003), the defendant stole $150 worth of videotapes, which, under California law, was his "third strike"—meaning that the theft was his third conviction—calling for a mandatory sentence of two consecutive terms of 25-years-to-life in prison. On appeal, the U.S. Supreme Court rejected Andrade's argument that his sentence was excessive. Relying on its precedent in *Hamelin* v. *Michigan* reprinted in Box 14.1, the high Court held that states were allowed the freedom to administer their police function by enacting tough sentences upon conviction for certain crimes. According to author and sentencing expert Michael Tonry, mandatory life sentences for people who have not killed anyone "often keep offenders in prison long after it makes incapacitative sense—because crime, especially violent crime is a young man's game and older prisoners age out of their violent proclivities."[11] Many states, particularly California, have started to reevaluate three-strikes laws. California is the only state that allows a nonviolent crime to constitute a third strike. Offenders with nonviolent third strikes, such as Andrade the video thief, make up close to 60% of third-strike offenders in California. The result for California is a prison system bloated with aged and infirm prisoners who will spend the rest of their natural lives decaying at public expense.

g. Megan's Laws

Megan's Law is a federal law enacted in 1996 and named after Megan Kanka, a seven-year-old who was killed by a convicted sex offender living in her New Jersey neighborhood unbeknownst to the community. The public and legislative response to Megan's murder was to enact state and federal laws aimed at controlling "sexually violent predators" through a system of community registration and notification. All states now have some form of Megan's Law. The legal implications of Megan's Laws are twofold: the designation of a sexual predator and the procedures of community notification.

---

[9]States that have abolished parole are Arizona, Delaware, Illinois, Indiana, Kansas, Maine, Minnesota, Mississippi, New Mexico, North Carolina, Ohio, Oregon, Virginia, and Washington.

[10]Facts taken from the case of entertainer "Foxy Brown," whose real name is Inga Marchand, who was sentenced to jail on September 7, 2007, for violating conditions of probation. Retrieved from http://www.muchmusic.com/news/story.asp?id=19834.

[11]Michael Tonry. *Sentencing Matters* (New York: Oxford University, 1996).

A review of New Jersey's Megan's Law indicates how it works. First, sex offenders are notified by the court or by mail of their duty to register with local law enforcement.[12] Offenders fill out a sexual offender registration form listing their name, address, make of car, license plate number, and physical description, as well as the specifics of the sex offense, and include a photograph. They are then separated into three tiers based on their perceived risk of reoffending. Tier ranking dictates who in the community has to be notified that the offender lives in the neighborhood. The classifications and notification scheme are as follows:

1. Tier 1: low risk to reoffend: notify law enforcement only
2. Tier 2: moderate risk to reoffend: notify law enforcement, schools, and community organizations likely to encounter the offender
3. Tier 3: high risk to reoffend: notify law enforcement, schools, organizations, and members of the public.

Judges can alter an offender's tier classification number, and some offenders introduce expert testimony in an effort to have their tier number—and hence the level of community notification—lowered. Anyone convicted of a sex offense by trial or guilty verdict in New Jersey is subject to the above process. The law excludes community notification for some sex offenders, most notably incest offenders or those who commit sex acts with a child in their own households. The exemption follows from the erroneous argument that those who prey upon children in their own homes are not "predatory" and are unlikely to molest outside of the home. In the case *In the Matter of Registrant R.F.,* 317 N.J. Super. 379 (1998), the court refused to notify schools that an incest offender lived close by on the justification that:

> [The offender's] acts arose from a trusting relationship between him and his victims. They were not predatory in the sense of the Guidelines that he placed himself in a household which included these children in order to offend against them. Nothing in the evidence suggests that he is given to prowling schoolyards or other areas serving children.

The U.S. Supreme Court has upheld the constitutionality of registration, notification of community,[13] and the civil commitments of sexual offenders after they have served their prison punishment for their crimes. In *Kansas* v. *Hendricks,* 521 U.S. 346 (1997), the Court held that laws allowing for the civil commitment of sex offenders were "non-punitive, remedial legislation," not punishment.[14] If a dangerous sex offender is about to be released from prison, many laws allow for the involuntary civil commitment of the offender in a mental hospital. Because the high Court has held such commitment as treatment, not punishment, the offender may be held indefinitely pursuant to the assessment of the physicians.

The current trend in local communities is to make sex offenders move by declaring certain tracts of property "child safety zones" that offenders cannot enter. In Franklin Township, New Jersey, the public defender's office is suing the local government for forcing convicted sex offenders to leave the area, even if they own their own homes within the "child safety zone." The Franklin County ordinance, "adopted 13 months ago, applies only to those convicted of sex crimes against minors, and follows the state's three-tiered system. High-risk offenders cannot live within 3,000 feet of designated places, including schools, parks and campgrounds, churches, theaters, bowling alleys, libraries. and convenience stores. The zone extends 2,500 feet for the moderate-risk group and 1,000 feet for

---

[12]Specifics of Megan's Law derived from R. Corrigan. "Making Meaning of Megan's Law." *Law & Social Inquiry,* Vol. 31 (2006), pp. 267–308.

[13]*See Connecticut Department of Public Safety* v. *Doe* (2003); *Smith* v. *Doe* (2003).

[14](The state must reassess an offender's states every six months)

low-risk offenders. The ordinance also prohibits loitering in those areas."[15] Parole officers who are charged with tracking sex offenders complain about such restrictive residency laws making their jobs more difficult, because it is more challenging to place offenders in housing, ensure that the offender will live in a stable environment to continue treatment for sexual disorders, and deal with the inevitable upheaval of the offender's family when the offender returns home after prison and they all have to move.

Applying the Rule of Law to the Facts: Is it just to sentence someone to life in prison for homelessness?

- Georgia registry law for sex offenders provides that offenders who receive a second violation for not notifying the state of their residence will automatically serve a life sentence. Larry W. Moore, Jr., was homeless and failed to register his address with the state, his second violation. Is a life sentence for him cruel and unusual punishment?

The Georgia law, which is currently being challenged, forbids offenders from living within 1,000 feet of schools, churches, swimming pools, and school bus stops. As of the fall of 2007, at least 15 offenders had been arrested due to homelessness since the law took effect.[16]

5. Expungement of Sentences, Pardons, and Executive Clemency

Several states allow for certain offenses to be sealed or expunged from a defendant's record, which means sealed from public view or destroyed. Usually first-time offenders who successfully complete a rehabilitative effort are eligible for record expungement, as are people who were arrested but never convicted or those who successfully completed alternative diversion programs. In the U.S. Supreme Court decision *Dickerson* v. *New Banner Institute, Inc.,* 103 S.Ct. 986 (1983), the Court reviewed the wide variety of expungement statutes in the states by observing that

> ...some are applicable only to young offenders [Michigan] ...some [are] available only to persons convicted of certain offenses [New Jersey], others, however, permit expunction of a conviction for any crime including murder [Massachusetts]. Some are confined to first offenders [Oklahoma]; [s]ome are discretionary [Minnesota] while others provide for automatic expunction under certain circumstances [Arizona]. The statutes vary in the language to describe what they do. Some speak of expunging the conviction, others of "sealing" the file or of causing the dismissal of the charge. The statutes also differ in their actual effect. Some are absolute; others are limited. Only a minority address questions such as whether the expunged conviction may be considered in sentencing for a subsequent offense or in setting bail on a later charge, or whether the expunged conviction may be used for impeachment purposes, or whether the convict may deny the fact of his conviction.

Students should research the law in their respective jurisdictions to determine what type of statute applies to offenders in their home states.

Pardons and executive clemency are tools available to the Executive Branch, the President, or a state Governor to wipe the slate clean with expungement of conviction for persons who have no other available avenue for redress for their claims that they have been wrongfully convicted or they have served their debt to society. Article II of the U.S. Constitution gives the President the authority "to grant Reprieves and Pardons for Offenses against the United States, except in Cases of Impeachment," commonly called the Pardons Clause. Writer Samuel Morison noted that "The president may, and occasionally does, pardon individuals after the commission of an offense, but prior to their

---

[15]Laura Mansnerus. "Zoning Laws that Bar Pedophiles Raise Concerns for Law Enforcers." *The New York Times,* November 27, 2006, p. A1.

[16]Shaila Dewan. "Homelessness Could Mean Life in Prison for Offender." *The New York Times,* August 3, 2007, p. A13.

being convicted of any specific crime, in which event a pardon would not only preclude the imposition of punishment for the pardoned offense, but would obviously forestall the creation of any record of a conviction."[17] A pardon may also come after conviction.

On July 2, 2007, President George W. Bush commuted (waived) the 30-month prison sentence that his Vice President's Chief of Staff, I. Lewis "Scooter" Libby, received on March 6, 2007, upon conviction for four felony counts of lying to federal agents about his role in disclosing the name of a Central Intelligence Agency ("CIA") agent. Naming American CIA operatives puts their lives in jeopardy, and it is a crime to divulge such information. Since the President commuted Libby's sentence before he had served a day in jail, there were questions about the legality of the commutation, but Libby did have to pay a fine.

II. THE DEATH PENALTY

Since biblical times death as punishment has been deemed legally appropriate for certain crimes. The death penalty is capital punishment. Examples of capital punishment abound in the Bible. In Genesis, God annihilated all life except for those creatures on Noah's ark and destroyed Sodom and Gomorrah because of rampant sin. During the time of Moses, God carried out the plague of death for all first-born sons of Egypt. The death penalty was given for crimes regarded as trivial today, such as disrespecting one's parents or taking the animals out of the barn too soon. From religion we get the concept of *lex talionis* [a life for a life].

Modern death-penalty jurisprudence began with the case *Furman* v. *Georgia,* 408 U.S. 238 (1972), in which the U.S. Supreme Court declared the death penalty illegal and invalidated all death statutes nationwide. Finding that the lack of statutes guiding jury decision-making resulted in death sentences that were "wanton and freakishly imposed," the Court concluded that the death penalty violated the Eighth Amendment. In response to the *Furman* decision, state legislatures went to work giving more structure to death penalty laws—an example of which is California's in chapter 2, Box 2.1. When these newly constituted death laws came before the Supreme Court for review two years later in *Gregg* v. *Georgia,* 428 U.S. 153 (1976), the high Court reinstated death as legal punishment.[18] The major difference in the new laws was the bifurcated (two-stage) trial process with one innocence phase and then a sentencing phase.

Rule of Law: Potential jurors who are unwilling to impose a death sentence are legally ineligible to hear and decide death-penalty cases.

1. Death Qualification of the Jury

The process of picking a death-penalty jury is called "**death qualification.**" In order for potential jurors to be picked to hear a death-penalty case they must express willingness during *voir dire* to impose a death sentence upon the defendant. If moral or religious reasons prevent a venireperson from seriously considering imposing a death sentence, the person is legally unqualified to hear the case. The first U.S. Supreme Court cases that challenged the exclusion of jurors who were opposed to the death penalty from sitting

---

[17]Samuel T. Morison. "The Politics of Grace: On the Moral Justification of Executive Clemency." *Buffalo Criminal Law Review,* Vol. 9 (2005), pp. 1–37.

[18]The following states do not have the death penalty: Alaska, Hawaii, Iowa, Maine, Massachusetts, Michigan, Minnesota, New Jersey, North Dakota, Rhode Island, Vermont, West Virginia, and Wisconsin. The District of Columbia also does not have the death penalty, and New York, which reinstated the death penalty in 1995, had its law invalidated by the state's highest appellate court in 2004. Some states, such as New Hampshire and Connecticut, have the death penalty, but rarely use it, executing only one person between the two states in the past 40 years.

on death-penalty cases were *Witherspoon* v. *Illinois,* 391 U.S. 510 (1968), and *Wainwright* v. *Witt,* 469 U.S. 412 (1985). If a juror's views on the imposition of the death penalty "prevent or substantially impair the performance of his duties as a juror in accordance with his instructions and his oath," then he cannot sit in such a case. If a potential juror were asked during *voir dire* whether he could impose a death sentence, and he answered "no, not under any circumstances," then he would be excused from jury duty; such potential jurors are called "'*Witherspoon*' or '*Witt*' Excludables."

U.S. Supreme Court Associate Justices Brennan and Marshall disagreed that people morally opposed to the death penalty should be excluded from jury service on death cases. In their statement of dissent from the majority holdings, they said:

> Like the death-qualified juries that the prosecution can now mold to its will to enhance the chances of victory, this Court increasingly acts as the adjunct of the State and its prosecutors in facilitating efficient and expedient conviction and execution irrespective of the Constitution's fundamental guarantees. One can only hope that this day too will soon pass . . .

Studies show that death-qualified juries are more likely to convict defendants and more likely to believe the state's witnesses over the defendant's witnesses.[19] These findings make sense: If only jurors who are willing to sentence the defendant to death get on the jury, then evidence of guilt may be a foregone conclusion in their minds. Jurors may already be thinking of an appropriate sentence before they hear a single witness testify or see one piece of tangible evidence introduced. In 2007, the U.S. Supreme Court reaffirmed the *Witherspoon/Witt* Excludable analysis in *Uttecht* v. *Brown,* 127 S.Ct. 2218 (2007). Defendant Uttecht was sentenced to death in Washington state and appealed on the grounds that one potential juror was removed from the panel because he stated that he could not impose a death sentence if selected to serve at Uttecht's trial. In a 5–4 decision, the high Court declined Uttecht's appeal and held that the trial judge had the authority to determine the qualifications of potential death jurors and that appellate courts should defer to those judges. In the wake of the Court's opinion, legal scholars feared that a decreased standard of review of death qualification may lead to juries that are more likely to impose death sentences.

2. Bifurcated Sentencing Procedure

The high Court stated in *Furman* v. *Georgia* that the death penalty may be fairly imposed upon criminal defendants in a two-part trial, "a bifurcated proceeding at which the sentencing authority" receives information relevant to deciding the proper sentence and receives guidelines on how to use that information. The bifurcated, two-phase death-penalty trial upheld as constitutional in *Gregg* v. *Georgia* is used in every death-penalty jurisdiction today. The first stage of a death trial is the innocence phase, in which the prosecution has the burden of proving beyond a reasonable doubt the defendant guilty of first-degree murder. If the jury returns a guilty verdict on the murder charge, the trial proceeds to the second, sentencing phase in which the jury determines whether life in prison or death is the appropriate sentence.

The sentencing phase is a mini-trial in which the prosecutor has to prove beyond a reasonable doubt that there was at least one aggravating circumstance making the defendant eligible for the death penalty. The defendant often offers mitigating circumstances, such as his age or that the murder was committed under extreme emotional duress. These circumstances do not excuse the crime, but do explain the characteristics

---

[19]*See* Claudia L. Cowan, William C. Thompson, and Phoebe C. Ellsworth. *The Effects of Death Qualification on Jurors' Predisposition to Convict and on the Quality of Deliberation.* Vol. 8, Law and Human Behavior, pp. 53–80. (Study results provide strong support for the hypothesis that death-qualified jurors are more likely to convict than are jurors excludable under the *Witherspoon* criteria.).

of the defendant when he committed the crime and may sway the jury to award a sentence of life without parole. In the majority of death jurisdictions, a life sentence leaves no possibility of parole or early release. The U.S. Supreme Court has held that jurors must be informed that life without parole means the defendant will not leave prison until he dies of old age or other causes. *Shafer* v. *South Carolina,* 532 U.S. 36 (2001). The National Jury Project survey of capital sentencing jurors reveals that, among the jurisdictions where the life option is life without parole, jurors are more likely to vote for the death penalty, unless the term "without parole" is properly explained.

a. Aggravating and Mitigating Circumstances

Before the jury can impose a sentence of death, the jurors must find at least one **aggravating circumstance** that makes the defendant eligible for the death penalty, as listed in Box 2.1. All death-penalty statutes list **mitigating circumstances,** but nonstatutory mitigators must be considered by the jury in determining a proper sentence. Some states allow for the "weighing" of aggravating and mitigating circumstances against each other, as if on the scale of justice. Those states allow that if the jury finds that the aggravating circumstances—say, the killing of a peace officer—outweigh the mitigating circumstances of the defendant, such as the fact that he was acting under the dominion and control of someone else at the time of the murder, then a death sentence may or must be imposed. In some death-penalty–weighing jurisdictions where aggravating circumstances are weighed against the mitigating circumstances, a jury never has to award a death sentence even if it finds that the aggravators outweighed the mitigators, which is often the case. By contrast, in Pennsylvania, if the jury finds that the aggravators outweigh the mitigators, the jury has no choice under state law but to impose death.

In *Kansas* v. *Marsh,* 126 S.Ct. 2516 (2006), the U.S. Supreme Court held that where the aggravating and mitigating circumstances were of equal weight, a state could still make it mandatory for the jury to impose a death sentence. Michael Marsh killed a woman and her baby and was sentenced to death. In Kansas, if the aggravators are of equal weight to the mitigators, the jury has no discretion and is required under the law to award a death sentence. On appeal, Marsh's complaint was that the statutory scheme created an "unconstitutional presumption in favor of death." The U.S. Supreme Court said that even if Marsh's argument was true, it was within the police power of state legislatures to determine that state's sentencing procedures.

3. New Evidence of Innocence and Exonerations

The U.S. Supreme has recognized the right of inmates on death row to challenge their convictions on the basis of new evidence and recent decisions have exonerated previously convicted defendants. In its 5–3 decision, the Court held that new evidence, including DNA test results, raised sufficient doubt to merit a new hearing for Tennessee death-row inmate Paul House, sentenced to death for the rape and murder of his neighbor. Writing for the majority in his case, *House* v. *Bell,* 126 S.Ct. 2064 (2006), Justice Kennedy declared, "Although the issue is close, we conclude that this is the rare case where—had the jury heard all the conflicting testimony—it is more likely than not that no reasonable juror viewing the record as a whole would lack reasonable doubt." The Court identified three aspects of House's case that, when considered as a whole, qualified him to gain access to a *habeas corpus* hearing in federal court. The first piece of new evidence was recent DNA test results indicating that House was not the source of semen found in the murder victim; the source was instead the victim's husband. Second, new statements from three witnesses linked the victim's husband to the crime. Lastly, the reliability of blood evidence presented at House's trial was called into question.[20]

---

[20]Richard C. Dieter. *Blind Justice: Juries Deciding Life and Death with Only Half the Truth.* October 2005. http://www.deathpenaltyinfo.org/BlindJusticeReport.pdf (accessed November 2, 2006).

A similar case where the issue was how to treat new alibi evidence in death cases was that of Randy Lee Guzek, who was found guilty in Oregon of capital murder and sentenced to death. On three, successive appeals, the Oregon Supreme Court affirmed Guzek's conviction but vacated his sentence and ordered a new sentencing hearing each time. When the case came before the U.S. Supreme Court, the issue was whether Oregon could limit the admission of evidence exonerating Guzek if Guzek's jury refused to believe his alibi evidence at his original trial. The Court held in the state's favor and held that such limitation of introducing new alibi evidence did not violate a capital defendant's constitutional rights. *Oregon* v. *Guzek,* 126 S. Ct. 1226 (2206). As noted in the *Herrera* v. *Collins* case reprinted in Box 14.2, there is a high legal hurdle to overcome for death-row inmates who claim they are actually innocent of the crime.

4. Competency to be Executed

Rule of Law: The Eighth Amendment protects society's weak and young from the death penalty.

Societal standards on death as a just punishment for certain crimes has informed the U.S. Supreme Court's **evolving standards of decency** standard. If society viewed death as too harsh a sentence for the crime of rape, as shown by the fact that many death-penalty states were not executing rapists, then the high Court would remove rape from the list of crimes that could make an offender death-eligible. In the case *Coker* v. *Georgia,* 433 U.S. 584 (1977), the Supreme Court held, "the death penalty, which is unique in its severity and irrevocability, is an excessive penalty for the rapist who, as such, does not take human life." Since *Coker,* the death penalty has been reserved for murder convictions. On April 16, 2008, the U.S. Supreme Court heard the appeal of Patrick Kennedy, who was convicted and sentenced to death in Louisiana for the aggravated rape of his eight-year-old stepdaughter, who survived the attack. *Kennedy* v. *Louisiana,* No. 07-343. The state of Louisiana upheld Kennedy's death sentence and argued against Kennedy's appeal to the U.S. Supreme Court. The state has distinguished its law allowing the death penalty for the rape of a child under 12 by stating that the high Court's *Coker* precedent applies only to the rape of adult women. In a legal twist, Louisiana argued that the evolving standards of decency and the new trend toward the harsh punishment of sex offenders who rape children allows death as an appropriate punishment for such crimes. Other states with statutes allowing death as punishment for child rape are Georgia, Montana, Oklahoma, South Carolina, and Texas, but Louisiana is the only such state to allow death for a first-time sex offender.[21]

On the basis of the evolving decency standard, the high Court exempted mentally retarded offenders from the death penalty. In *Atkins* v. *Virginia,* 536 U.S. 304 (2002), Daryl Atkins had been convicted of abduction, armed robbery, and capital murder in the state of Virginia, but appealed his sentence on the grounds that he was mentally retarded—that his IQ (intelligence quotient) was 59 when the average IQ is 100.[22] In 1989, the Supreme Court had rejected challenges from retarded offenders that they should be exempt from the death penalty because of their disability. *Penry* v. *Lynaugh,* 492 U.S. 302 (1989). But by the time Atkins's case came before the Court, the Court cited that many of the death-penalty states had, over the years, exempted the retarded from state death statutes. Given the evolving standard of decency across the country with respect to death-penalty jurisprudence, the Supreme Court, too, held that executing the retarded violated the Eighth Amendment's prohibition on cruel and unusual punishment.

---

[21]Linda Greenhouse. "Justices to Decide If Rape of a Child Merits Death." *The New York Times,* January 5, 2008, p. A27.

[22]The American Association of Mental Retardation ("AAMR") defines the condition as suffering from "substantial limitations in present functioning, existing concurrently with related limitations in two or more of the following applicable adaptive skill areas: communication, self-care, home living, social skills, community use, self-direction, health and safety, functional academics, leisure, and work. Mental retardation manifests before age 18."

On the basis of the *Atkins* decision, Christopher Simmons, who had been sentenced to death for the rape and murder of Shirley Crook, appealed to the U.S. Supreme Court on the grounds that the evolving standards of decency, based on a "national consensus against the execution of juvenile offenders," required that the Court exempt from eligibility for the death sentence those who committed murder before they reached their 18th birthday. The Court agreed and reasoned that adulthood began at age 18, when people became eligible to vote, join the armed forces, serve on juries, enter into legally binding contracts, and marry without parental consent. So 18 should also be the demarcation age to receive a death sentence, and any juveniles who commit first-degree murder are ineligible to receive the death penalty, even if they were tried as adults in adult court. *Roper* v. *Simmons,* 543 U.S. 551 (2005).

In 1986, the U.S. Supreme Court ruled in *Ford* v. *Wainwright,* 477 U.S. 399 (1986), that it was cruel and unusual punishment to execute the insane. The Court did not spell out a specific standard to determine insanity, but Justice Powell's concurring opinion stated that the Constitution required that a condemned man about to be executed must be able to recognize what exactly he is being punished for: He must understand the relationship between his crime and the punishment. The Court revisited this standard in its 2007 decision in the case of *Panetti* v. *Quarterman,* 127 S.Ct. 2842 (2007). Scott Panetti murdered his in-laws in 1992 in front of his wife and three-year-old child. He was sentenced to death after he represented himself. He was schizophrenic and claimed "that his body had been taken over by an alter ego he called Sarge Ironhorse and that demons were bent on killing him for his Christian beliefs."[23] He showed up to court wearing western shirts and cowboy boots, alleged that President Kennedy had healed his wounds with coconut milk during World War II, tried to subpoena Jesus, refused to take his medication which kept his psychosis at bay, and insisted that he was being executed in retaliation for preaching the gospel. The high Court remanded the case, holding that the lower court had used too narrow a standard to determine Panetti's competency and eligibility for execution. On May 25, 2008, a federal judge in Texas found Panetti mentally competent to be executed initiating a new round of appeals.

Applying the Rule of Law to the Facts: Can the state force a defendant to become competent to be executed?

- A young man convicted and sentenced to death began to exhibit signs of schizophrenia during his appeals process, which lasted 24 years. At one point, he decided to stop taking his medication and was rendered incompetent. The state applied for a court order to forcibly medicate the prisoner. His lawyers argued that it was not in the prisoner's best interest to be forcibly medicated to restore him to competency so that the state could then execute him. Which side will win?

The state. If the medication of prisoners is necessary, even if it is to restore competency so that they may be executed, the state has a right to forcibly medicate the prisoner.[24]

5. The Execution Process

In June 2006, the U.S. Supreme Court unanimously ruled that death row inmates could raise challenges to lethal injection as cruel and unusual punishment. Even after they have exhausted their regular appeals, they can pursue their claim as a civil rights action. *Hill v.*

[23]Ralph Blumenthal. "Justices Block Execution of Delusional Texas Killer." *The New York Times,* June 29, 2007, p. A21.

[24]These facts are adapted from *Singelton* v. *Norris,* 319 F.3d 1018 (8th Cir. 2003). In 2003, the federal court of appeals held that forcing Singelton to take medication to treat his schizophrenia to make him "sane" enough to be executed was legal. The U.S. Supreme Court refused to hear his case. Toward the end of the legal battle, Singelton abandoned his appeals, willingly took his medication, was restored to competency, and was executed by the state of Arkansas on January 6, 2004.

McDonough, 126 S.Ct. 2096 (2006). Clarence Hill was strapped to the gurney in Florida's execution chamber with lines in his arms ready to deliver the lethal cocktail when the Supreme Court blocked his January 2006 execution. Mr. Hill's attorney charged that Florida had adopted its lethal injection procedure without medical research or expertise, that "unqualified" prison officials carried it out, and that the drugs used would "create a dangerous likelihood that Mr. Hill will be conscious throughout the execution process and, as a result, will experience an excruciatingly painful and protracted death."[25] Governor Jeb Bush rescheduled Hill's execution before the lower court could hear his case again, and Hill's final appeal to the U.S. Supreme Court to stop his September 20, 2006, execution was denied.

But legal challenges to lethal injection continued. Thirty-five out of the 36 death-penalty states use lethal injection of, first, sodium thiopental, which acts as anesthesia, then, pancuronium bromide, which causes suffocation by paralyzing the muscles, and, finally, potassium chloride, which stops the heart. On April 16, 2008, the U.S. Supreme Court decided *Baze* v. *Rees,* 553 U.S.__(2008), in which two Kentucky death-row inmates challenged the lethal injection process as a violation of the Eighth Amendment's ban on cruel and unusual punishment because the condemned prisoner could suffer acute pain through the process if the first sedative drug is administered improperly. The Court upheld the chemical cocktail execution method even if it resulted in pain, because it "does not establish the sort of 'objectively intolerable risk of harm' that qualifies as cruel and unusual" under the Eighth Amendment; the Constitution does not demand the elimination of all risk of pain "either by accident or as an inescapable consequence of death." When the Court issued its decision in *Baze,* many states announced new execution dates for their death-row prisoners. Some states allow inmates to choose their method of execution if it was legal when they were awarded their sentences of death. Thus, Tennessee permitted Daryl K. Holton to choose electrocution when he was executed on September 12, 2007, for killing his four children with an assault rifle in retaliation for losing visitation rights with the children.

III. THE APPELLATE PROCESS

1. Motion for a New Trial and Appeals

Appellate court rules for each state and the federal government dictate the appeals process for each sovereign. Typically, the first step a defendant takes after conviction is to file with the trial judge a **motion for a new trial** alleging mistakes the prosecutor and trial judge made at trial. Most motions for a new trial are denied as a matter of routine unless "the interests of justice so require."[26] A defendant has a period of time defined by statute in which to file a motion for a new trial based on newly discovered evidence—that is, evidence that the defendant could not, with due diligence and his utmost effort, have discovered before or during his trial. Otherwise, the time limitation on the filing of a motion for a new trial on grounds other than new evidence is approximately one week.

Typically, defense counsel must preserve an issue for an appeal by raising and making the appropriate objections at trial. For example, after a motion to suppress the defendant's confession is denied, once the prosecution seeks to introduce the defendant's confession, the defense counsel must object to preserve the issue of the confession's

---

[25]Abby Goodnough. "Inmate Awaits Final Ruling on Lethal Injection." *The New York Times,* September 19, 2006, p. A14.

[26]Fed. R. Crim. P. 33.

admissibility for appeal. If the defense counsel does not object to evidence at trial and other trial issues that operate to the detriment of the defendant's due process rights to a fair trial, then the issue has been lost for appeal purposes. There are some situations in which the defense lawyer's failure to object is such a gross deviation from the reasonable standard of care standard for defense counsel that an appellate court might find such deviance a "plain error" and grant the defendant appellate relief on that basis, as discussed below.

By law, a court must hear **mandatory appeals.** For example, the highest court in Maryland is mandated by law to hear appeals in death-penalty cases, appeals in legislative redistricting cases, cases concerning removal of certain public officers, and certifying certain questions of law. For all other types of appeals, the court has discretion whether or not to issue a *writ of certiorari* to entertain the appeal, called a **discretionary appeal.** If a court declines to hear a discretionary appeal, it need not give any reason for its refusal. The appointment of counsel for indigent convicts pursuing their appeals has been litigated frequently. The U.S. Supreme Court held in *Douglas* v. *California,* 372 U.S. 353 (1963), that if the appeal is a right established by law and the client is indigent, the state must appoint counsel. If the appeal is discretionary on the part of the defendant the state need not provide counsel. In *Barbour* v. *Allen,* No. 06-10605, six prisoners on Alabama's death row filed suit over the state's unwillingness to pay for lawyers to represent them in post-conviction review. Alabama is the only state in the country that does not provide counsel at this "state-court version of federal *habeas corpus*" review.[27] The federal appeals court ruled against the inmates and the U.S. Supreme Court declined to hear their case.

If the defendant is claiming that his federal constitutional rights have been violated, he must be heard by all applicable state courts and "**exhaust his remedies**" before becoming eligible for an audience in federal court. Even at the state level, courts do not want to be in the position of making a decision that may conflict with another court. The exhaustion of remedies requirement is formalized and highly structured for a reason. Defendants must squeeze all available review out of one court before being allowed access to a higher court. Such formal processing makes sense: The system wants cases resolved at the lowest level and with the least use of judicial resources. The same reasoning applies to appeals: If a lower court can answer the question and address the issue, there is no reason to go forward. This is one reason death-penalty appeals may take a long time to process through no fault of the defendant. If a lower appellate court makes a decision and sends the case back to the trial court again, the procedure starts all over with a new death verdict. All death cases are eligible for federal appellate review because of the constitutional issues involved in every death case, specifically the Eighth Amendment's ban on cruel and unusual punishment.

Before or during trial, very few issues can be appealed to a higher court. To prevent the delay that an appeal could cause in the midst of a trial on the federal level and in most state jurisdictions, the trial must be completed and the decision final before an appellate court will review a conviction. The "**final judgment rule**" requires that appeals be heard only on issues that had been completely decided, but there are exceptions. In *Cohen* v. *Beneficial Industrial Loan Corp.,* 337 U.S. 541 (1949), the U.S. Supreme Court declared that an exception to the final judgment rule could be made for decisions that "finally determine claims of right separable from and collateral to, rights asserted in the action [that are] too important to be denied review and too independent of the cause itself to require that appellate consideration be

---

[27]Linda Greenhouse. "Passengers Granted Same Right as Drivers." *The New York Times,* June 19, 2007, p. A12.

deferred until the whole case is adjudicated." The final judgment exception is known as the "**collateral order doctrine**" and allows appeal from a judgment that:

1. leaves no doubt on an issue in the case
2. is not related to whether or not the defendant is innocent or guilty, and
3. cannot be appealed once a final judgment has entered in the case.

For example, an order committing a defendant to a federal medical facility for an examination or requiring a defendant to be forcibly medicated is immediately appealable under the collateral order doctrine. In each of these cases, the decision is unrelated to the defendant's guilt, the defendant cannot appeal the order once the trial is over, and the order leaves no doubt about an issue in the case, here the mental status of the defendant.[28] Under the collateral order doctrine, motions relying on the Double Jeopardy protection of the Fifth Amendment and motions to reduce excessive bail are immediately appealable, but not motions to dismiss on the basis of speedy trial or violations in the grand jury, or motions to suppress evidence.[29]

An **interlocutory appeal** is made before the case has been finally decided. Courts are reluctant to entertain appeals in the middle of a trial because of the delay in the process. A common issue that defendants wish to appeal before the trial is over is the suppression of evidence. Such interlocutory appeals are not allowed until after trial. As said in *Carroll* v. *United States,* 354 U.S. 394 (1957), "Promptness in the dispatch of the criminal business of the courts is by all recognized as in the highest degree desirable. Greater expedition is demanded by a wholesome public opinion. Delays in the prosecution of criminal cases are numerous and lengthy enough without sanctioning appeals that are not plainly authorized by statute."

The rationale for the final judgment rule is that many evidence suppression issues cannot be properly decided without developing all of the evidence through a full trial, although federal law allows the prosecution to file an interlocutory appeal of a trial judge's denial of exclusion of evidence. The government filed such a motion contesting the ruling by federal district court Judge Harold Baer, Jr. This judge granted a defense motion to suppress and exclude 80 pounds of heroin and cocaine and a voluntary confession in a drug conspiracy case on the grounds of police misconduct and a search and seizure violation. The prosecution filed an interlocutory appeal, and then the judge changed his mind and allowed the evidence to be used against the defendants before the appellate court could rule on the government's motion. The judge stated that he had changed his mind on the basis of new evidence and not on the vociferous outcry from the government and the public from his initial ruling to exclude the evidence from trial. The judge then recused [removed] himself from the case.[30]

2. Writ of Habeas Corpus

Another avenue for a court to review the legality of a defendant's sentence is by filing a *habeas corpus* petition (which literally means "you have the body"). The *writ of habeas corpus* is provided for in the Constitution, Art. I, Sec. 9, which provides in part: "The Privilege of the Writ of Habeas Corpus shall not be suspended, unless when in Cases of Rebellion or Invasion the public Safety may require it." A **habeas corpus** petition asks either a state or federal court to review the legality of the defendant's detention and imprisonment. In the federal system, 28 U.S.C. §2254 allows a state prisoner to

---

[28]*See generally United States* v. *Filippi,* 211 F.3d 649 (1st Cir. 2000); *United States* v. *Gomes,* 289 F.3d 71 (2d Cir. 2002).

[29]"Annual Review of Criminal Procedure (Federal)." *Georgetown Law Journal* (2003).

[30]"U.S. District Judge Baer Removes Himself from Controversial Drug Case." (1996) http://www.ndsn.org/summer96/baer.html.

file a writ of *habeas corpus* in federal court "only on grounds that the prisoner's confinement violates the Constitution, laws or treaties of the United States." Since the writ is limited to constitutional claims, courts are careful not to usurp the balance of power between federal and state adjudication of claims and disposition of criminal cases, which is the province of the state police power.

State prisoners must exhaust all state appellate remedies before filing a *habeas* petition to federal courts. In *Anderson* v. *Harless,* 459 U.S. 4 (1982), the defendant was convicted at a trial court in Michigan and filed a direct appeal to the intermediate Michigan Court of Appeals on the basis that the judge erred in giving jury instructions. The appellate court confirmed Harless's conviction. Then he appealed to the highest appellate court in the state, the Michigan Supreme Court, which also affirmed his conviction. Harless filed a *habeas* petition with the federal district court, the trial court, which issued a writ finding in his favor, but the U.S. Supreme Court reversed the trial court's decision.

The high Court held that Harless had not exhausted his state appellate remedies because he changed the basis of his appeal. The Supreme Court stated that the new claim had not been properly addressed by the state court below and that failure rendered his *habeas* claim defective. The reasoning behind the Court's decision is that *habeas* is an extraordinary writ and federal courts want to give state courts a fair "opportunity to apply controlling legal principles to the facts bearing upon [her] constitutional claim."[31]

a. Standard for Granting Habeas Review

As stated, federal *habeas* law requires the defendant to first exhaust his state court appeals by presenting his claims to the state courts. 28 U.S.C.S. §2254 "Common *habeas corpus* claims include Sixth Amendment claims of ineffective assistance of counsel, Fifth Amendment claims concerning statements obtained in violation of *Miranda* v. *Arizona,* prosecutorial misconduct, significant judicial error, and claims of insufficient evidence."[32] Under a *habeas* standard of review, a court examines the legality of the defendant's confinement. The court does not review the defendant's conviction, but the lawfulness of his custody. Justice Frankfurter, in his separate opinion in *Brown* v. *Allen,* 344 U.S. 443 (1953), stated:

> Insofar as [federal *habeas*] jurisdiction enables federal district courts to entertain claims that State Supreme Courts have denied rights guaranteed by the United States Constitution, it is not a case of a lower court sitting in judgment on a higher court. It is merely one aspect of respecting the Supremacy Clause of the Constitution whereby federal law is higher than State law.

Habeas law was changed dramatically by the enactment under President Clinton of the **Antiterrorism and Effective Death Penalty Act of 1996,** Pub. L. No. 104-132 which limits the number of federal *habeas* petitions filed by convicts, limits the filing and granting of more than one successive *habeas* petition based on the same set of facts or circumstances, and severely circumscribes access to federal *habeas* review from death-row inmates. The U.S. Supreme Court has upheld the limits on second successive *habeas* writs on the basis that the convict has access to appellate relief, but not limitless access to the judicial system.

b. Habeas Corpus and Actual Innocence

Does the fact, as the defendant claims, that he is actually innocent raise a constitutional claim sufficient to grant *habeas corpus* review? According to the case *Herrera* v. *Collins,* 506 U.S. 390 (1993), the answer is no. Herrera was sentenced to death for

---

[31] *Picard* v. *Connor,* 404 U.S. 270 (1971).

[32] "Annual Review of Criminal Procedure (Federal)." *Georgetown Law Journal* (2003).

killing two Texas police officers. After numerous appeals, he raised in a *habeas corpus* petition the fact that affidavits [sworn statements] tended to prove that he was actually innocent of the crime. The U.S. Supreme Court declined to grant his *habeas* petition, reasoning that the petition could not be heard because no constitutional issue was raised. As you read the case excerpt in Box 14.2, determine whether you would have found Herrera "actually innocent" of capital murder on the basis of the "new" evidence he submitted to prove that others were the actual guilty parties.

BOX 14.2

Herrera v. *Collins*, 506 U.S. 390 (1993)
Supreme Court of the United States

Chief Justice Rehnquist delivered the opinion of the Court.

PROCEDURAL HISTORY

Petitioner Leonel Torres Herrera was convicted of capital murder and sentenced to death in January 1982. He unsuccessfully challenged the conviction on direct appeal and state collateral proceedings in the Texas state courts, and in a federal *habeas* petition. In February 1992—10 years after his conviction—he urged in a second federal *habeas* petition that he was "actually innocent" of the murder for which he was sentenced to death, and that the Eighth Amendment's prohibition against cruel and unusual punishment and the Fourteenth Amendment's guarantee of due process of law therefore forbid his execution. He supported this claim with affidavits tending to show that his now-dead brother, rather than he, had been the perpetrator of the crime.

FACTS

Shortly before 11 P.M. on an evening in late September 1981, the body of Texas Department of Public Safety Officer David Rucker was found by a passer-by on a stretch of highway about six miles east of Los Fresnos, Texas, a few miles north of Brownsville in the Rio Grande Valley. Rucker's body was lying beside his patrol car. He had been shot in the head. At about the same time, Los Fresnos Police Officer Enrique Carrisalez observed a speeding vehicle traveling west towards Los Fresnos, away from the place where Rucker's body had been found, along the same road. Carrisalez, who was accompanied in his patrol car by Enrique Hernandez, turned on his flashing red lights and pursued the speeding vehicle.

After the car had stopped briefly at a red light, it signaled that it would pull over and did so. The patrol car pulled up behind it. Carrisalez took a flashlight and walked toward the car of the speeder. The driver opened his door and exchanged a few words with Carrisalez before firing at least one shot at Carrisalez' chest. The officer died nine days later.

Petitioner Herrera was arrested a few days after the shootings and charged with the capital murder of both Carrisalez and Rucker. He was tried and found guilty of the capital murder of Carrisalez in January 1982, and sentenced to death.

In February 1992, petitioner lodged the instant *habeas* petition—his second—in federal court, alleging, among other things, that he is innocent of the murders of Rucker and Carrisalez, and that his execution would thus violate the Eighth and Fourteenth Amendments. In addition to proffering the above affidavits, petitioner presented the affidavits of Raul Herrera, Jr., Raul, Senior's son, and Jose Ybarra, Jr., a schoolmate of the Herrera brothers. Raul, Junior, averred that he had witnessed his father shoot Officers Rucker and Carrisalez and petitioner was not present. Raul, Junior, was nine years old at the time of the killings. Ybarra alleged that Raul, Senior, told him one summer night in 1983 that he had shot the two police officers. Petitioner alleged that law enforcement officials were aware of this evidence, and had withheld it in violation of *Brady* v. *Maryland*, 373 U.S. 83 (1963).

ISSUE

[Does Herrera's] showing of innocence entitles him to relief in this federal *habeas* proceeding?

HOLDING

We hold that it does not.

REASONING

Petitioner asserts that the Eighth and Fourteenth Amendments to the United States Constitution prohibit the execution of a person who is innocent of the crime for which he was convicted. This proposition has an elemental appeal, as would the similar proposition that the Constitution prohibits the imprisonment of one who is innocent of the crime for which he was convicted. After all, the central purpose of any system of criminal justice is to convict the guilty and free the innocent. But the evidence upon which petitioner's claim of innocence rests was not produced at his trial, but rather eight years later. In any system of criminal justice, "innocence" or "guilt" must be determined in some sort of a judicial proceeding. Petitioner's showing of innocence, and indeed his constitutional claim for relief based upon that showing, must be evaluated in the light of the previous proceedings in this case, which have stretched over a span of 10 years. A person when first charged with a crime is entitled to a presumption of innocence, and may insist that his guilt be established beyond a reasonable doubt. *In re Winship,* 397 U.S. 358 (1970). All of these constitutional safeguards, of course, make it more difficult for the State to rebut and finally overturn the presumption of innocence which attaches to every criminal defendant.

Once a defendant has been afforded a fair trial and convicted of the offense for which he was charged, the presumption of innocence disappears. *Cf. Ross* v. *Moffitt,* 417 U.S. 600 (1974). Here, it is not disputed that the State met its burden of proving at trial that petitioner was guilty of the capital murder of Officer Carrisalez beyond a reasonable doubt. Thus, in the eyes of the law, petitioner does not come before the Court as one who is "innocent," but, on the contrary, as one who has been convicted by due process of law of two brutal murders.

Claims of actual innocence based on newly discovered evidence have never been held to state a ground for federal *habeas* relief absent an independent constitutional violation occurring in the underlying state criminal proceeding. Chief Justice Warren made this clear in *Townsend* v. *Sain,* 372 U.S. 293 (1963):

> Where newly discovered evidence is alleged in a *habeas* application, evidence which could not reasonably have been presented to the state trier of facts, the federal court must grant an evidentiary hearing. Of course, such evidence must bear upon the constitutionality of the applicant's detention; the existence merely of newly discovered evidence relevant to the guilt of a state prisoner is not a ground for relief on federal *habeas corpus.*

This rule is grounded in the principle that federal *habeas* courts sit to ensure that individuals are not imprisoned in violation of the Constitution—not to correct errors of fact.[33]

. . . Finally, the affidavits must be considered in light of the proof of petitioner's guilt at trial—proof which included two eyewitness identifications, numerous pieces of circumstantial evidence, and a handwritten letter in which petitioner apologized for killing the officers and offered to turn himself in under certain conditions. That proof, even when considered alongside petitioner's belated affidavits, points strongly to petitioner's guilt. This is not to say that petitioner's affidavits are without probative value. Had this sort of testimony been offered at trial, it could have been weighed by the jury, along with the evidence offered by the State and petitioner, in deliberating upon its verdict. Since the statements in the affidavits contradict the evidence received at trial, the jury would have had to decide important issues of credibility. But coming 10 years after petitioner's trial, this showing of innocence falls far short of that which would have to be made in order to trigger the sort of constitutional claim which we have assumed, *arguendo,* to exist.

CONCLUSION

The judgment of the Court of Appeals [holding Herrera's claim of actual innocence was not sufficient alone to sustain a *habeas corpus* petition] is Affirmed.

---

[33]"*See, for example, Moore* v. *Dempsey,* 261 U.S. 86 (1923) (J. Holmes) ("What we have to deal with [on *habeas* review] is not the petitioners' innocence or guilt but solely the question whether their constitutional rights have been preserved"); *Hyde* v. *Shine,* 199 U.S. 62 (1905) ("It is well settled that upon *habeas corpus* the court will not weigh the evidence"); *Ex parte Terry,* 128 U.S. 289 (1888) ("As the *writ of habeas corpus* does not perform the office of a writ of error or an appeal, [the facts establishing guilt] cannot be reexamined or reviewed in this collateral proceeding").

In Herrera's *habeas* petition, he attached affidavits that claimed the actual murderer was his deceased brother. In rejecting his claim, the Supreme Court held that actual innocence claims never form the basis for federal relief "absent an independent constitutional violation occurring in the underlying state criminal proceeding." In other words, if the defendant had a constitutionally error-free trial, the fact that he may actually be innocent would not meet the threshold requirement for obtaining federal *habeas* review. Even if Herrera were factually innocent, he had no independent constitutional claim to satisfy the *habeas* standard of review. In 1992, Herrera was executed, still protesting his innocence.

Applying the Rule of Law to the Facts: **Should *habeas corpus* review be granted?**

- A defendant allegedly stabbed a fellow prison inmate to death. Three eyewitnesses testified at his death-penalty trial claiming to have seen the defendant stab the other inmate in the back. Over a 15-year period, all three witnesses recanted their testimony, claiming that they were forced or tricked into testifying. There was no other physical evidence connecting the defendant to the crime. Can the defendant get *habeas* review on his claim of "actual innocence?"

No, under the *Herrera* standard, the defendant cannot secure *habeas corpus* review on a "free standing" claim [unrelated to any constitutional violation at trial] of innocence. In the case of Joseph Amrine, his conviction had been upheld in both state and federal appeals. According to the Eighth Circuit Court of Appeals, Amrine had "not shown actual innocence entitling him to review of his procedurally barred claims [because of elapsed time] or that his constitutional rights were violated" despite recantations from the three eyewitnesses to the murder and the lack of physical evidence linking Amrine to the crime. After a release of the videotape "Unreasonable Doubt: The Joe Amrine Case" capturing the informants' recantations and the ensuing public outcry that Amrine had been wrongfully convicted, the Missouri Supreme Court heard oral argument to answer the question whether the state could, and should, grant Amrine *habeas* review on his actual innocence claims.

On February 4, 2003, the day of oral argument for Amrine's *habeas* petition in front of Missouri's highest court, his lawyer, Sean O'Brien, argued that it would be a violation of the Eighth Amendment's prohibition on cruel and unusual punishment to execute Amrine, an innocent man. As stated in *Herrera,* the law was on the government's side; by all accounts if one ignored the witness recantations, Amrine had received a constitutionally fair trial. Missouri Assistant Attorney General Frank Jung tried to persuade the Missouri high court that Amrine failed to meet the "gateway" for *habeas* relief because Amrine's presentation of evidence that the three witnesses had recanted their testimony, without more, was not enough for Amrine to get his foot in the courthouse door. When asked by the Missouri justices whether Missouri would have to execute Amrine if he had received a fair trial, but was still actually innocent of the murder, Jung responded in the following exchange:

MISSOURI SUPREME COURT JUSTICE:	Just to make sure we're clear on this, if we find in a particular case DNA evidence actually excludes somebody as the murderer, then we must execute them anyway if we can't find an underlying constitutional violation at the trial?
ASSISTANT ATTORNEY GENERAL JUNG:	That's the standard, your honor. . . .
COURT:	That's the state's position then, right?
JUNG:	Yes, your honor.

In the ensuing uproar that the State of Missouri's position was to execute an innocent man on the technicality that he could not prove that his trial was constitutionally defective, the Missouri Supreme Court ordered Amrine released, and on July 28, 2003, he walked out after 18 years on death row for a murder he did not commit.

IV. Key Terms and Phrases

- aggravating circumstances
- allocution
- capital punishment
- collateral order doctrine
- death qualification
- determinate sentencing
- discretionary appeal
- evolving standards of decency
- exhaustion of remedies

- expungement
- final judgement rule
- Federal Sentencing Guidelines
- *habeas corpus*
- indeterminate sentencing
- mandatory appeal
- mandatory minimums
- Megan's Laws
- mitigating circumstances

- final motion for a new trial
- pardon
- parole
- presentence investigation
- presentence report
- probation
- sentencing hearing
- suspended sentence
- "three-strikes" laws

V. Summary

1. **How society determines the appropriate punishment for each offender:** Before sentencing, the court orders a **presentence investigation** in which all relevant information about the offender is compiled in a **presentence report** for the judge to make an appropriate sentence. Later, at a **sentencing hearing,** the judge will hear sentencing recommendations from the prosecutor and the defense counsel and hear any victim-impact testimony if allowed.

2. **The different types of sentences:** The main types of sentences are **indeterminate,** which is a range of years, and **determinate,** which is a fixed number of years. One type of **suspended sentence** is **probation,** the release of the offender into the community under specific restrictions, often given to offenders for committing misdemeanors. Another type of suspended sentence is **parole,** in which an offender serving an indeterminate sentence can reduce the time he spends in prison through good behavior. As with probation, offenders on parole must meet certain conditions to remain in society, such as abstaining from drugs and alcohol, seeking and maintaining employment, and reporting to a court officer (probation or parole officer) to gauge progress. If an offender fails to meet the court-imposed conditions, the suspended sentence ends and the actual sentence is imposed; the offender is then likely to return to prison to serve the balance of the original sentence.

3. **The significance of mandatory minimums, "three-strikes" legislation, sentencing guidelines, and Megan's Laws:** As the "war on drugs" became a popular focus of law enforcement and crime control efforts in the late 1970s and early 1980s, so, too, did the legislative response to enact **mandatory minimums,** the minimum (least) amount of time an offender will serve for committing certain crimes, mainly moving a certain weight of drugs. Also part of the justice reform movement was the transfer of sentencing discretion away from judges by the enactment of sentencing guidelines, such as the **Federal Sentencing Guidelines,** a grid that formulates sentences in terms of months on the basis of the offender's criminal history (past crimes committed) and the conviction for the current crime. Recent U.S. Supreme Court decisions have made the federal guidelines advisory and not mandatory as they once were. At one point, judges could enhance a criminal sentence if the crime had certain aggravating circumstances. The high Court held that any fact that is used to increase (enhance) a defendant's must be found by a jury beyond a reasonable doubt. Similar to these punitive reforms, **"three-strikes"** legislation allows for offenders who commit three serious or violent felonies to be sentenced to life without parole, which the U.S. Supreme Court has said does not violate the Eighth Amendment's prohibition against cruel and unusual punishment. **Megan's Laws,** which require community notification and registration of sex offenders, are also constitutional, as is the civil commitment of holding sex offenders in mental hospitals after the termination of their sentence because, as the Supreme Court has said, such incarceration at a hospital is treatment and not "punishment."

4. **The death-penalty process:** **Capital punishment** (the death penalty) has been recognized as a legal punishment since the founding of the country. The process whereby a jury is selected for a death-penalty case is called **death qualification** and examines whether each potential juror is willing to impose the death penalty. Death-penalty cases are **bifurcated** into two mini-trials with one jury. The first part of the trial is to determine whether the defendant is guilty; if the jury finds the de-

fendant guilty, the second mini-trial is a sentencing hearing during which the same jury will determine whether the defendant lives or dies. At the sentencing phase of a capital trial, the state must introduce **aggravating circumstances** that make the defendant eligible for the death penaly—that is, death is appropriate punishment only for murder, but some murders are aggravated (the murder of a child or a police officer, for example), and these make death an available punishment for the defendant. In contrast, the defendant offers **mitigating circumstances,** which is anything that would tend to explain, not excuse, the defendant's conduct surrounding the murder. Recent case law allows states to force juries to return a death sentence if mitigating and aggravating circumstances are equally weighted and prevent the defendant from arguing that he is actually innocent during his sentencing phase. There has been much scrutiny surrounding capital punishment in America because of the number of men who have been wrongfully convicted, sentenced to death, and then **exonerated** and released (over 120 so far). New developments in the law question the **competency** of convicts to be executed.

5. **The legal requirements for different types of appeals and** *habeas corpus* **review:** The first step for a defendant upon being found guilty is to file a **motion for a new trial.** Appeal rules are set by state and federal appellate rules and most allow appeals only when cases are finished, called the **final judgment rule.** The final judgment rule prevents the system from being bogged down. An exception to the final judgment rule is the **collateral order doctrine** that gives a defendant the chance to appeal certain issues that will be moot when the trial is over. An **appeal** is generally a motion to a court higher than the trial court asking for review of the legality of the conviction on the basis of the sufficiency of the evidence or the incorrect application of law. There are two types of appeals. An **interlocutory appeal** is filed before or during trial and is granted under very limited circumstances on the grounds that to delay the judicial process while appeals of minor issues take place would grind the system to a halt. A **final appeal** is taken after the trial is over and can only be taken pursuant to the **final judgment rule** that the case is finally over. Every defendant convicted at trial gets one **appeal of right** as a matter of law, whereby the appellate court must hear the first appeal filed by the defendant; it is usually a direct appeal to the next highest court in the appellate structure. The next type of appeal is a **discretionary appeal,** discretionary not because the convict may or may not file the second appeal, but because the appellate court can choose—have discretion—to hear the appeal. The U.S. Supreme Court only hears discretionary appeals, those cases it chooses. Some cases, especially death sentences, have **mandatory appeal** provisions where the highest appellate court in the state must review the defendant's conviction, even if the defendant never files an appeal. The first **standard of review** an appellate court will use in deciding whether to affirm [uphold] or reverse [undo] the defendant's conviction is whether the error at trial was substantial and significant enough to violate the defendant's right to a fair trial—whether, had the error not occurred, the outcome of the trial would have been different. Also, before a higher court of appeal will take a case from a lower court of appeals, the defendant must have **exhausted all remedies** at the lower court. The **Antiterrorism and Effective Death Penalty Act of 1996** limits the number of appeals that can be filed by individuals convicted of capital murder and also limits successive *habeas* petitions based on the same set of facts or circumstances. **Actual innocence** is a claim brought by a convict that he has been wrongfully convicted and is "actually innocent" of the crime.

VI. Discussion Questions

1. If you were a state legislator charged with managing your state's entire budget and monetary resources, which philosophy of punishment would you adopt in your state and why? Which of the above punishments has the best chance for long-term success and, in the long run, will save your state money? Can you think of programs within your state that reflect each sentencing purpose?

2. What would the effect on the criminal justice system be if the high Court decided in favor of Herrera? Do you agree with the Court that a defendant's claim that is actually innocent is only available to him "where the prisoner supplements his constitutional claim with a colorable showing of factual innocence?" Would you grant *habeas corpus* review to "freestanding claims of actual innocence," that is, those claims which cannot show that the trial was marred by constitutional error? Why or why not?

3. Assign appropriate punishment for the Tri-Delt brothers from the chapter-opening scenario according to their respective level of culpability.

4. In the case *McCleskey* v. *Kemp,* 481 U.S. 279 (1987), the defendant introduced a study by University of Iowa Professor David Baldus that proved African-American defendants who killed white victims were significantly more likely to receive death sentences than any other

racial combination of defendant and victim. The U.S. Supreme Court refused to cite the Baldus study as fact, but the study has been cited many times in defendants' challenges to the imposition of the death penalty. On the basis of your experiences and your study of criminal justice issues to date, do you agree with defendant McCleskey that the Court should have recognized the "fact" of racial discrimination in death-penalty sentencing, or do you agree with the Court that race discrimination, while it sometimes matters in the criminal justice context, is not enough to overturn lawfully imposed death sentences? Explain your reasoning.

5. Explain the functions of an appellate court in the criminal justice system.

6. What is the history of the *writ of habeas corpus* in America?

VII. Problem-Solving Exercises

1. William Page was convicted by a federal jury of possessing 45 grams of cocaine and faced a prison term under the Federal Sentencing Guidelines of 21 years and 10 months. At the sentencing hearing, the judge determined that Page was responsible for the distribution of an additional 25 grams of cocaine, which would increase his sentence by an additional 24 months. After the hearing, the judge imposed an enhanced sentence of 23 years and 10 months. Page appealed on the basis of the U.S. Supreme Court rulings on judge-issued sentencing enhancements. If you were the appellate judge, how would you rule?

2. During jury selection in a capital case, the following exchange took place between defense counsel and the potential venire person, Mr. Smith:

   ATTORNEY: Would you be able to give serious consideration to a sentence of life without parole, instead of the death penalty?

   SMITH: Well, if there's no evidence otherwise, I probably—I mean, I believe in capital punishment, but that's not, I have to be really convinced. That's what I'm saying.

   ATTORNEY: Are you saying you really have to be convinced by the State, or you really have to be convinced by me?

   SMITH: I would have to be convinced that the person was not deserving of capital punishment.

   ATTORNEY: Would you require me to put on evidence to persuade you that life imprisonment would be appropriate in this case before you would give serious consideration to a life sentence?

   SMITH: I believe so.

   ATTORNEY: And you understand that the burden of proof is on the state?

   SMITH: Yes.

   ATTORNEY: But you would nonetheless require us to put on, to convince you otherwise?

   SMITH: Right.

   ATTORNEY: Against the death sentence.

   SMITH: Right.

   Mr. Smith was not struck for cause and remained on the jury, and the defendant was sentenced to death. Does the defendant have a basis for appeal that Smith was on the jury and wanted the defendant to prove he should live?[34]

3. California has changed its sex offender law. According to the old law, after a sex offender finished his sentence, he could be committed to a mental hospital with a hearing held every 24 months to determine whether he could be released on the grounds that he no longer posed a danger to himself or others. According to the new law, civil commitment is indefinite unless the offender can prove that something has changed—for example, that he has successfully completed treatment. In order to successfully complete treatment, an offender must admit that he's guilty. Tom, who maintains that he is innocent, entered a plea in which he did not admit guilt, but admitted that the state had enough evidence to convict him should he go to trial. Tom wanted to avoid a trial to spare his daughter from being forced to testify against him. The prison will not allow his daughter to visit because Tom is an untreated sex offender. Because Tom says he's innocent, he is not a suitable candidate for treatment and, therefore, he can be held indefinitely under a civil commitment order. Tom brings suit, claiming that his First Amendment right to freedom of association with his daughter is being deprived and his Due Process rights are being violated because he's being punished for asserting his innocence. If Tom's case makes its way up to the U.S. Supreme Court, which side will win—the prison or Tom?

4. Florida's three-strikes law allows anyone convicted three times for certain felonies, including aggravated stalking, child abuse, and murder, to be sentenced to life without parole. Billy, who has two prior convictions, one for aggravated stalking and one for child

---

[34]Facts taken from *Anderson v. Missouri*, 196 S.W.3d 28 (2006).

abuse, now faces a driving under the influence accident in which a victim was killed. The prosecutor could charge Billy with murder, making him eligible for three strikes sentencing, but the prosecutor likes Billy and agrees to a plea bargain whereby Billy will plead guilty to reckless driving and serve a sentence of two years. When the victim's family members learn of the plea deal, they are furious and appeal to a judge for help invalidating the prosecutor's decision. Can the prosecutor willingly and knowingly lower charges to avoid three-strikes sentencing? Does your answer change if it is mandatory minimum sentencing? Explain your answer fully.

5. Tammy was on probation for robbery. One of her probation conditions was that she stay away from known felons. At Thanksgiving dinner, both Tammy and her cousin Denny, who had just been released from prison on a gun charge, showed up to dinner at her mother's house. Denny and Tammy smoked some marijuana together in her car outside her mother's house. Tammy's parole officer, who happened to be in the neighborhood for her own turkey celebration, saw Tammy behind the wheel. The probation officer ordered Tammy out of the car, conducted a search, and learned that Denny was a felon. The next business day, the probation officer filed a petition asking the court to find Tammy in violation of her probation conditions, revoke her suspended sentence, and send her to jail for two years. What, if any, defenses does Tammy have?

VIII. World Wide Web Resources

The Sentencing Project

http://www.sentencingproject.org

United States Sentencing Commission

http://www.ussc.gov

Government Manipulation of the Federal Sentencing Guidelines

http://www.uakron.edu/lawrev/witten.html

Death Penalty Information Center

http://www.deathpenaltyinfo.org/

IX. Notes and Additional Readings

Punishment

Michael Tonry. "The Functions of Sentencing and Sentencing Reform." *Stanford Law Review,* Vol. 58 (2005), pp. 37–66.

Franklin E. Zimring. "Penal Policy and Penal Legislation in Recent American Experience." *Stanford Law Review,* Vol. 58 (2005), pp. 323–338.

Three-Strikes Laws

Joy M. Donham. "Third Strike or Merely a Foul Tip?: The Gross Disproportionality of *Lockyer* v. *Andrade. Akron Law Review,* Vol. 38 (2005), pp. 369–411.

Robert G. Lawson. "Difficult Times in Kentucky Corrections—Aftershocks of a "Tough on Crime" Philosophy." *Kentucky Law Journal,* Vol. 93 (2005), pp. 305–376.

The Death Penalty

James R. Acker and Charles S. Lanier. "May God—or the Governor—Have Mercy: Executive Clemency and Executions in Modern Death-Penalty Systems." *Criminal Law Bulletin,* Vol. 36 (2000), pp. 200–237.

William C. Bailey. "Imprisonment v. the Death Penalty as a Deterrent to Murder." *Law & Human Behavior,* Vol. 1 (1977), pp. 239–260.

Margaret Vandiver. "The Impact of the Death Penalty on the Families of Homicide Victims and of Condemned Prisoners." In James R. Acker, Robert M. Bohm, and Charles S. Lanier, Eds. *America's Experiment with Capital Punishment: Reflections on the Past, Present and Future of the Ultimate Penal Sanction* (Durham, NC: Carolina Academic Press, 1998), pp. 477–505.

Federal Sentencing Guidelines

Rosemary T. Cakmis. "The Role of the Federal Sentencing Guidelines in the Wake of *United States* v. *Booker* and *United States* v. *Fanfan." Mercer Law Review,* Vol. 56 (2005), pp. 1131–1167.

Michael E. O'Neill and Linda D. Maxfield. "Judicial Perspectives on the Federal Sentencing Guidelines and the Goals of Sentencing: Debunking the Myths." *Alabama Law Review,* Vol. 56 (2005), pp. 85–119.

Probation

Howard Abadinsky. *Probation and Parole: Theory and Practice,* 8th ed. (Upper Saddle River, NJ: Prentice Hall, 2003).

Alfred B. Heilbrun, Jr., L. C. Heilbrun, and Kirk Heilbrun. "Impulsive and Premeditated Homicide: An Analysis of Subsequent Parole Risk of the Murderer." *Journal of Criminal Law & Criminology,* Vol. 69 (1978), pp. 108–114.

The Constitution of the United States of America

We the People of the United States, in Order to form a more perfect Union, establish Justice, insure domestic Tranquility, provide for the common defence, promote the general Welfare, and secure the Blessings of Liberty to ourselves and our Posterity, do ordain and establish this Constitution for the United States of America.

Article I

Section 1

All legislative Powers herein granted shall be vested in a Congress of the United States, which shall consist of a Senate and House of Representatives.

Section 2

1. The House of Representatives shall be composed of Members chosen every second Year by the People of the several States, and the Electors in each State shall have the Qualifications requisite for Electors of the most numerous Branch of the State Legislature.

2. No Person shall be a Representative who shall not have attained to the Age of twenty-five Years, and been seven Years a Citizen of the United States, and who shall not, when elected, be an Inhabitant of that State in which he shall be chosen.

3. Representatives and direct Taxes shall be apportioned among the several States which may be included within this Union, according to their respective Numbers, which shall be determined by adding to the whole Number of free Persons, including those bound to Service for a Term of Years, and excluding Indians not taxed, three fifths of all other Persons. The actual Enumeration shall be made within three Years after the first Meeting of the Congress of the United States, and within every subsequent Term of ten Years, in such Manner as they shall by Law direct. The Number of Representatives shall not exceed one for every thirty Thousand, but each State shall have at Least one Representative; and until such enumeration shall be made, the State of New Hampshire shall be entitled to chuse three, Massachusetts eight, Rhode Island and Providence Plantations one, Connecticut five, New York six, New Jersey four, Pennsylvania eight, Delaware one, Maryland six, Virginia ten, North Carolina five, South Carolina five, and Georgia three.

4. When vacancies happen in the Representation from any State, the Executive Authority thereof shall issue Writs of Election to fill such Vacancies.

5. The House of Representatives shall chuse their Speaker and other Officers; and shall have the sole Power of Impeachment.

Section 3

1. The Senate of the United States shall be composed of two Senators from each State, chosen by the Legislature thereof, for six Years; and each Senator shall have one Vote.

2. Immediately after they shall be assembled in Consequence of the first Election, they shall be divided as equally as may be into three Classes. The Seats of the Senators of the first Class shall be vacated at the Expiration of the Second Year, of the second Class at the Expiration of the fourth Year, and of the third class at the Expiration of the sixth Year, so that one third may be chosen every second Year; and if Vacancies happen by Resignation, or otherwise, during the Recess of the Legislature of any State, the Executive thereof may make temporary Appointments until the next Meeting of the Legislature, which shall then fill such Vacancies.

3. No Person shall be a Senator who shall not have attained to the Age of thirty Years, and been nine Years a Citizen of the United States, and who shall not, when elected, be an Inhabitant of that State for which he shall be chosen.

4. The Vice President of the United States shall be President of the Senate, but shall have no Vote, unless they be equally divided.

5. The Senate shall chuse their other Officers, and also a President pro tempore, in the absence of the Vice President, or when he shall exercise the Office of the President of the United States.

6. The Senate shall have the sole Power to try all Impeachments. When sitting for that Purpose, they shall be on Oath or Affirmation. When the President of the United States is tried, the Chief Justice shall preside: And no Person shall be convicted without the Concurrence of two thirds of the Members present.

7. Judgment in Cases of Impeachment shall not extend further than to removal from Office, and disqualification to hold and enjoy any Office of honor, Trust or

Profit under the United States: but the Party convicted shall nevertheless be liable and subject to Indictment, Trial, Judgment and Punishment, according to Law.

Section 4

1. The Times, Places and Manner of holding Elections for Senators and Representatives, shall be prescribed in each State by the Legislature thereof; but the Congress may at any time by Law make or alter such Regulations, except as to the Places of chusing Senators.

2. The Congress shall assemble at least once in every Year, and such Meeting shall be on the first Monday in December, unless they shall by Law appoint a different Day.

Section 5

1. Each House shall be the Judge of the Elections, Returns and Qualifications of its own Members, and a Majority of each shall constitute a Quorum to do Business; but a smaller Number may adjourn from day to day, and may be authorized to compel the Attendance of absent Members, in such Manner, and under such Penalties as each House may provide.

2. Each House may determine the Rules of its Proceedings, punish its members for disorderly Behaviour, and, with the Concurrence of two thirds, expel a Member.

3. Each House shall keep a Journal of its Proceedings, and from time to time publish the same, excepting such Parts as may in their Judgment require Secrecy; and the Yeas and Nays of the Members of either House on any question shall, at the Desire of one fifth of those Present, be entered on the Journal.

4. Neither House, during the Session of Congress, shall, without the Consent of the other, adjourn for more than three days, nor to any other Place than that in which the two Houses shall be sitting.

Section 6

1. The Senators and Representatives shall receive a Compensation for their Services, to be ascertained by Law, and paid out of the Treasury of the United States. They shall in all Cases, except Treason, Felony and Breach of the Peach, be privileged from Arrest during their Attendance at the Session of their respective Houses, and in going to and returning from the same; and for any Speech or Debate in either House, they shall not be questioned in any other Place.

2. No Senator or Representative shall, during the Time for which he was elected, be appointed to any civil Office under the Authority of the United States, which shall have been created, or the Emoluments whereof shall have been encreased during such time; and no Person holding any Office under the United

States, shall be a Member of either House during his Continuance in Office.

Section 7

1. All Bills for raising Revenue shall originate in the House of Representatives; but the Senate may propose or concur with Amendments as on other Bills.

2. Every Bill which shall have passed the House of Representatives and the Senate, shall, before it become a Law, be presented to the President of the United States; If he approve he shall sign it, but if not he shall return it, with his Objections to that House in which it shall have originated, who shall enter the Objections at large on their Journal, and proceed to reconsider it. If after such Reconsideration two thirds of that House shall agree to pass the Bill, it shall be sent, together with the Objections, to the other House, by which it shall likewise be reconsidered, and if approved by two thirds of that House, it shall become a law. But in all such Cases the Votes of both Houses shall be determined by Yeas and Nays, and the Names of the Persons voting for and against the Bill shall be entered on the Journal of each House respectively. If any Bill shall not be returned by the President within ten Days (Sundays excepted) after it shall have been presented to him, the Same shall be a Law, in like Manner as if he had signed it, unless the Congress by their Adjournment prevents its Return, in which Case it shall not be a Law.

3. Every Order, Resolution, or Vote to Which the Concurrence of the Senate and House of Representatives may be necessary (except on a question of Adjournment) shall be presented to the President of the United States; and before the Same shall take Effect, shall be approved by him, or being disapproved by him, shall be repassed by two thirds of the Senate and House of Representatives, according to the Rules and Limitations prescribed in the Case of a Bill.

Section 8

1. The Congress shall have Power To lay and collect Taxes, Duties, Imposts and Excises, to pay the Debts and provide for the common Defence and general Welfare of the United States; but all Duties, Imposts and Excises shall be uniform throughout the United States;

2. To borrow Money on the credit of the United States;

3. To regulate Commerce with foreign Nations, and among the several States, and with the Indian Tribes;

4. To establish a uniform Rule of Naturalization, and uniform Laws on the subject of Bankruptcies throughout the United States;

5. To coin Money, regulate the Value thereof, and of foreign Coin, and to fix the Standard of Weights and Measures;

6. To provide for the Punishment of counterfeiting the Securities and current Coin of the United States;

7. To establish Post Offices and post Roads;

8. To promote the Progress of Science and useful Arts, by securing for limited Times to Authors and Inventors the exclusive Right to their respective Writings and Discoveries;

9. To constitute Tribunals inferior to the supreme Court;

10. To define and punish Piracies and Felonies committed on the high Seas, and Offenses against the Law of Nations;

11. To declare War, grant Letters of Marque and Reprisal, and make Rules concerning Captures on Land and Water;

12. To raise and support Armies, but no Appropriation of Money to that Use shall be for a longer Term than two Years;

13. To provide and maintain a Navy;

14. To make Rules for the Government and Regulation of the land and naval Forces;

15. To provide for calling forth the Militia to execute the Laws of the Union, suppress Insurrections and repel Invasions;

16. To provide for organizing, arming, and disciplining, the Militia, and for governing such Part of them as may be employed in the Service of the United States, reserving to the States respectively, the Appointment of the Officers, and the Authority of training the Militia according to the discipline prescribed by Congress;

17. To exercise exclusive Legislation in all Cases whatsoever, over such District (not exceeding ten Miles square) as may, by Cession of particular States, and the Acceptance of Congress, become the Seat of the Government of the United States, and to exercise like Authority over all Places purchased by the Consent of the Legislature of the State in which the Same shall be, for the Erection of Forts, Magazines, Arsenals, dock-Yards, and other needful Buildings;—And

18. To make all Laws which shall be necessary and proper for carrying into Execution the foregoing Powers, and all other Powers vested by this Constitution in the Government of the United States, or in any Department or Officer thereof.

Section 9

1. The Migration or Importation of such Persons as any of the States now existing shall think proper to admit, shall not be prohibited by the Congress prior to the Year one thousand eight hundred and eight, but a Tax or Duty may be imposed on such Importation, not exceeding ten dollars for each Person.

2. The Privilege of the Writ of Habeas Corpus shall not be suspended unless when in Cases of Rebellion or Invasion the public Safety may require it.

3. No Bill of Attainder or ex post facto Law shall be passed.

4. No Capitation, or other direct, Tax shall be laid, unless in Proportion to the Census or Enumeration herein before directed to be taken.

5. No Tax or Duty shall be laid on Articles exported from any State.

6. No Preference shall be given by any Regulation of Commerce or Revenue to the Ports of one State over those of another; nor shall Vessels bound to, or from, one State, be obliged to enter, clear or pay Duties in another.

7. No Money shall be drawn from the Treasury, but in Consequence of Appropriations made by Law; and a regular Statement and Account of the Receipts and Expenditures of all public Money shall be published from time to time.

8. No Title of Nobility shall be granted by the United States: And no Person holding any Office of Profit or Trust under them, shall, without the Consent of the Congress, accept of any present, Emolument, Office, or Title, of any kind whatever, from any King, Prince or foreign State.

Section 10

1. No State shall enter into any Treaty, Alliance, or Confederation; grant Letters of Marque and Reprisal; coin Money; emit Bills of Credit; make any Thing but gold and silver Coin a Tender in Payment of Debts; pass any Bill of Attainder, ex post facto Law, or Law impairing the Obligation of Contracts, or grant any Title of Nobility.

2. No State shall, without the Consent of Congress, lay any Imposts or Duties on Imports or Exports, except what may be absolutely necessary for executing its inspection Laws: and the net Produce of all Duties and Imposts, laid by any State on Imports or Exports, shall be for the Use of the Treasury of the United States; and all such Laws shall be subject to the Revision and Controul of the Congress.

3. No state shall, without the Consent of Congress, lay any Duty of Tonnage, keep Troops, or Ships of War in time of Peace, enter into any Agreement or Compact with another State, or with a foreign Power, or engage in War, unless actually invaded, or in such imminent Danger as will not admit of Delay.

Article II

Section 1

1. The executive Power shall be vested in a President of the United States of America. He shall hold his Office

during the Term of four Years, and, together with the Vice President, chosen for the same Term, be elected, as follows:

2. Each state shall appoint, in such Manner as the Legislature thereof may direct, a Number of Electors, equal to the whole Number of Senators and Representatives to which the State may be entitled in the Congress: but no Senator or Representative, or Person holding an Office of Trust or Profit under the United States, shall be appointed an Elector.

   The Electors shall meet in their respective States, and vote by Ballot for two Persons, of whom one at least shall not be an Inhabitant of the same State with themselves. And they shall make a List of all the Persons voted for, and of the Number of Votes for each; which List they shall sign and certify, and transmit sealed to the Set of the Government of the United States, directed to the President of the Senate. The President of the Senate shall, in the presence of the Senate and House of Representatives, open all the Certificates, and the Votes shall then be counted. The Person having the greatest Number of Votes shall be the President, if such Number be a Majority of the whole Number of Electors appointed; and if there be more than one who have such Majority, and have an equal Number of Votes, then the House of Representatives shall immediately chuse by Ballot one of them for President; and if no Person have a Majority, then from the five highest on the List the said House shall in like Manner chuse the President. But in chusing the President, the Votes shall be taken by States, the Representation from each State having one Vote; a quorum for this Purpose shall consist of a Member or Members from two thirds of the States, and a Majority of all the States shall be necessary to a Choice. In every Case, after the Choice of the President, the Person having the greatest Number of Votes of the Electors shall be the Vice President. But if there should remain two or more who have equal Votes, the Senate shall chuse from them by Ballot the Vice President.

3. The Congress may determine the Time of chusing the Electors, and the Day on which they shall give their Votes; which Day shall be the same throughout the United States.

4. No Person except a natural born Citizen, or a Citizen of the United States, at the time of the Adoption of this Constitution, shall be eligible to the Office of President; neither shall any Person be eligible to that Office who shall not have attained to the Age of thirty five years, and been fourteen Years a Resident within the United States.

5. In Case of the removal of the President from Office, or of his Death, Resignation, or Inability to discharge the Powers and Duties of the said Office, the Same shall devolve on the Vice President, and the Congress may by Law provide for the Case of Removal, Death, Resignation or Inability, both of the President and Vice President, declaring what Officer shall then act as President, and such Officer shall act accordingly, until the Disability be removed, or a President shall be elected.

6. The President shall, at stated Times, receive for his Services, a Compensation, which shall neither be increased nor diminished during the Period for which he shall have been elected, and he shall not receive within that Period any other Emolument from the United States, or any of them.

7. Before he enter on the Execution of his Office, he shall take the following Oath or Affirmation:—"I do solemnly swear (or affirm) that I will faithfully execute the Office of President of the United States, and will to the best of my Ability, preserve, protect and defend the Constitution of the United States."

Section 2

1. The President shall be Commander in Chief of the Army and Navy of the United States, and of the Militia of the several States, when called into the actual Service of the United States; he may require the Opinion, in writing, of the principal Officer in each of the executive Departments, upon any Subject relating to the Duties of their respective Offices, and he shall have Power to grant Reprieves and Pardons for Offenses against the United States, except in Cases of Impeachment.

2. He shall have Power, by and with the Advice and Consent of the Senate, to make Treaties, provided two thirds of the Senators present concur; and he shall nominate, and by and with the Advice and Consent of the Senate, shall appoint Ambassadors, other public Ministers and Consuls, Judges of the supreme Court, and all other Officers of the United States, whose Appointments are not herein otherwise provided for, and which shall be established by Law: but the Congress may by Law vest the Appointment of such inferior Officers, as they think proper, in the President alone, in the Courts of Law, or in the Heads of Departments.

3. The President shall have Power to fill up all Vacancies that may happen during the Recess of the Senate, by granting Commissions which shall expire at the End of their next Session.

Section 3

He shall from time to time give to the Congress Information of the State of the Union, and recommend to their Consideration such Measures as he shall judge necessary and expedient; he may, on extraordinary Occasions, convene both Houses, or either of them, and in Case of Disagreement between them, with Respect to the Time of Adjournment, he may adjourn them to such Time as he shall think proper; he shall receive Ambassadors and other public Ministers; he shall take Care that the Laws be faithfully executed, and shall Commission all the Officers of the United States.

Section 4

The President, Vice President and all civil Officers of the United States, shall be removed from Office on Impeachment for, and Conviction of, Treason, Bribery, or other high Crimes and Misdemeanors.

Article III

Section 1

The judicial Power of the United States, shall be vested in one supreme Court, and in such inferior Courts as the Congress may from time to time ordain and establish. The Judges, both of the supreme and inferior Courts, shall hold their Offices during good Behaviour, and shall, at stated Times, receive for their Services, a Compensation, which shall not be diminished during their Continuance in Office.

Section 2

1. The judicial Power shall extend to all Cases, in Law and Equity, arising under this Constitution, the Laws of the United States, and Treaties made, or which shall be made, under their Authority;—to all Cases affecting Ambassadors, other public Ministers and Consuls;—to all Cases of admiralty and maritime Jurisdiction;—to Controversies to which the United States shall be a party;—to Controversies between two or more States;—between a State and Citizens of another States;—between Citizens of different States;—between Citizens of the same State claiming Lands under Grants of different States, and between a State, or the Citizens thereof, and foreign States, Citizens or Subjects.

2. In all cases affecting Ambassadors, other public Ministers and Consuls, and those in which a State shall be Party, the supreme Court shall have original Jurisdiction. In all the other Cases before mentioned, the supreme Court shall have appellate Jurisdiction, both as to Law and Fact, with such Exceptions, and under such Regulations as the Congress shall make.

3. The Trial of all Crimes, except in Cases of Impeachment, shall be by Jury; and such Trial shall be held in the State where the said Crimes shall have been committed; but when not committed within any State, the Trial shall be at such Place or Places as the Congress may by Law have directed.

Section 3

1. Treason against the United States, shall consist only in levying War against them, or in adhering to their Enemies, giving them Aid and Comfort. No Person shall be convicted of Treason unless on the Testimony of two Witnesses to the same overt Act, or on Confession in open Court.

2. The Congress shall have Power to declare the Punishment of Treason, but no Attainder of Treason shall work Corruption of Blood, or Forfeiture except during the Life of the Person attained.

Article IV

Section 1

Full Faith and Credit shall be given in each State to the public Acts, Records, and judicial Proceedings of every other State. And the Congress may by general Laws prescribe the Manner in which such Acts, Records and Proceedings shall be proved, and the Effect thereof.

Section 2

1. The Citizens of each State shall be entitled to all privileges and Immunities of Citizens in the several States.

2. A Person charged in any State with Treason, Felony, or other Crime, who shall flee from Justice, and be found in another State, shall on demand of the executive Authority of the State from which he fled, be delivered up, to be removed to the state having Jurisdiction of the Crime.

3. No Person held to Service of Labour in one State, under the Laws thereof, escaping into another, shall, in Consequence of any Law or Regulation therein, be discharged from such Service or Labour, but shall be delivered up on Claim of the Party to whom such Service or Labour may be due.

Section 3

1. New States may be admitted by the Congress into this Union; but no new State shall be formed or erected within the Jurisdiction of any other State; nor any State be formed by the Junction of two or more States, or Parts of States, without the Consent of the Legislatures of the States concerned as well as of the Congress.

2. The Congress shall have power to dispose of and make all needful Rules and Regulations respecting the Territory or other Property belonging to the United States; and nothing in this Constitution shall be so construed as to Prejudice any Claims of the United States, or of any particular State.

Section 4

The United States shall guarantee to every State in this Union a Republican Form of Government, and shall protect each of them against Invasion; and on Application of the Legislature, or of the Executive (when the Legislature cannot be convened) against domestic Violence.

Article V

The Congress, whenever two thirds of both Houses shall deem it necessary, shall propose Amendments to this Constitution, or, on the Application of the Legislatures of two thirds of the several States, shall call a Convention for proposing Amendments, which, in either Case, shall be valid to all Intents and Purposes, as part of this Constitution, when ratified by the Legislatures of three fourths of the several States, or by Conventions in three fourths thereof, as the one or the other Mode of Ratification may be proposed by the Congress; Provided that no Amendment which may be made prior to the Year One thousand eight hundred and eight shall in any Manner affect the first and fourth Clauses in the Ninth Section of the first Article; and that no State, without its Consent, shall be deprived of its equal Suffrage in the Senate.

Article VI

1. All Debts contracted and Engagements entered into, before the Adoption of this Constitution, shall be as valid against the United States under this Constitution, as under the Confederation.

2. This Constitution, and the Laws of the United States which shall be made in Pursuance thereof; and all Treaties made, or which shall be made, under the Authority of the United States, shall be the supreme Law of the Land; and the Judges in every State shall be bound thereby, any Thing in the Constitution or Laws of any State to the Contrary notwithstanding.

3. The Senators and Representatives before mentioned, and the Members of the several State Legislatures, and all executive and judicial Officers, both of the United States and of the several States, shall be bound by Oath or Affirmation, to support this Constitution; but no religious Test shall ever be required as a Qualification to any Office or public Trust under the United States.

Article VII

The Ratification of the Conventions of nine States, shall be sufficient for the Establishment of this Constitution between the States so ratifying the Same. Done in Convention by the Unanimous Consent of the States present the Seventeenth Day of September in the Year of our Lord one thousand seven hundred and Eighty seven and of the Independence of the United States of America the Twelfth.

ARTICLES IN ADDITION TO, AND AMENDMENT OF, THE CONSTITUTION OF THE UNITED STATES OF AMERICA, PROPOSED BY CONGRESS, AND RATIFIED BY THE SEVERAL STATES, PURSUANT TO THE FIFTH ARTICLE OF THE ORIGINAL CONSTITUTION.

Amendment I (1791)

Congress shall make no law respecting an establishment of religion, or prohibiting the free exercise thereof; or abridging the freedom of speech, or of the press; or the right of the people peaceably to assemble, and to petition the Government for a redress of grievances.

Amendment II (1791)

A well regulated Militia, being necessary to the security of a free state, the right of the people to keep and bear Arms, shall not be infringed.

Amendment III (1791)

No Soldier shall, in time of peace be quartered in any house, without the consent of the Owner, nor in time of war, but in a manner to be prescribed by law.

Amendment IV (1791)

The right of the people to be secure in their persons, houses, papers, and effects, against unreasonable searches and seizures, shall not be violated, and no Warrants shall issue, but upon probable cause, supported by Oath or affirmation, and particularly describing the place to be searched, and the persons or things to be seized.

Amendment V (1791)

No person shall be held to answer for a capital, or otherwise infamous crime, unless on a presentment or indictment of a Grand Jury, except in cases arising in the land or naval forces, or in the Militia, when in actual service in time of War or public danger; nor shall any person be subject for the same offence to be twice put in jeopardy of life or limb; nor shall be compelled in any criminal case to be a witness against himself, nor be deprived of life, liberty, or property, without due process of law; nor shall private property be taken for public use, without just compensation.

Amendment VI (1791)

In all criminal prosecutions, the accused shall enjoy the right to a speedy and public trial, by an impartial jury of the State and district wherein the crime shall have been committed, which district shall have been previously ascertained by law, and to be informed of the nature and cause of the accusation; to be confronted with the witnesses against him; to have compulsory process for obtaining witnesses in his favor, and to have the Assistance of Counsel for his defence.

Amendment VII (1791)

In Suits at common law, where the value in controversy shall exceed twenty dollars, the right of trial by jury shall be preserved, and no fact tried by a jury, shall be otherwise re-examined in any Court of the United States, than according to the rules of the common law.

Amendment VIII (1791)

Excessive bail shall not be required, nor excessive fines imposed, nor cruel and unusual punishments inflicted.

Amendment IX (1791)

The enumeration in the Constitution, of certain rights, shall not be construed to deny or disparage others retained by the people.

Amendment X (1791)

The powers not delegated to the United States by the Constitution, nor prohibited by it to the States, are reserved to the States respectively, or to the people.

Amendment XI (1798)

The Judicial power of the United States shall not be construed to extend to any suit in law or equity, commenced or prosecuted against one of the United States by Citizens of another State, or by Citizens or Subjects of any Foreign State.

Amendment XII (1804)

The Electors shall meet in their respective states and vote by ballot for President and Vice-President, one of whom, at least, shall not be an inhabitant of the same state with themselves; they shall name in their ballots the person voted for as President, and in distinct ballots the person voted for as Vice-President, and they shall make distinct lists of all persons voted for as President, and of all persons voted for as Vice-President, and of the number of votes for each, which lists they shall sign and certify, and transmit sealed to the seat of the government of the United States, directed to the President of the Senate;—The President of the Senate shall, in the presence of the Senate and House of Representa-

tives, open all the certificates and the votes shall then be counted;—The person having the greatest number of votes for President, shall be the President, if such number be a majority of the whole number of Electors appointed; and if no person have such majority, then from the persons having the highest numbers not exceeding three on the list of those voted for as President, the House of Representatives shall choose immediately, by ballot, the President. But in choosing the President, the votes shall be taken by states, the representation from each state having one vote; a quorum for this purpose shall consist of a member or members from two-thirds of the states, and a majority of all the states shall be necessary to a choice. And if the House of Representatives shall not choose a President whenever the right of choice shall devolve upon them, before the fourth day of March next following, then the Vice-President shall act as President, as in the case of the death or other constitutional disability of the President—The person having the greatest number of votes as Vice-President, shall be the Vice-President, if such number be a majority of the whole number of Electors appointed, and if no person have a majority, then from the two highest numbers on the list, the Senate shall choose the Vice-President; A quorum for the purpose shall consist of two-thirds of the whole number of Senators, and a majority of the whole number shall be necessary to a choice. But no person constitutionally ineligible to the office of President shall be eligible to that of Vice-President of the United States.

Amendment XIII (1865)

Section 1

Neither slavery nor involuntary servitude, except as a punishment for crime whereof the party shall have been duly convicted, shall exist within the United States, or any place subject to their jurisdiction.

Section 2

Congress shall have power to enforce this article by appropriate legislation.

Amendment XIV (1868)

Section 1

All persons born or naturalized in the United States and subject to the jurisdiction thereof, are citizens of the United States and of the State wherein they reside. No State shall make or enforce any law which shall abridge the privileges or immunities of citizens of the United States; nor shall any State deprive any person of life, liberty, or property, without due process of law; nor deny to any person within its jurisdiction the equal protection of the laws.

Section 2

Representatives shall be apportioned among the several States according to their respective numbers, counting the whole number of persons in each State, excluding Indians not taxed. But when the right to vote at any election for the choice of electors for President and Vice-President of the United States, Representatives in Congress, the Executive and Judicial officers of a State, or the members of the Legislature thereof, is denied to any of the male inhabitants of such State, being twenty-one years of age, and citizens of the United States, or in any way abridged, except for participation in rebellion, or other crime, the basis of representation therein shall be reduced in the proportion which the number of such male citizens shall bear to the whole number of male citizens twenty-one years of age in such State.

Section 3

No person shall be a Senator or Representative in Congress, or elector of President and Vice President, or hold any office, civil or military, under the United States, or under any State, who, having previously taken an oath, as a member of Congress, or as an officer of the United States, or as a member of any State legislature, or as an executive or judicial officer of any State, to support the Constitution of the United States, shall have engaged in insurrection or rebellion against the same, or given aid or comfort to the enemies thereof. But Congress may by a vote of two-thirds of each House, remove such disability.

Section 4

The validity of the public debt of the United States, authorized by law, including debts incurred for payment of pensions and bounties for services in suppressing insurrection or rebellion, shall not be questioned. But neither the United States nor any State shall assume or pay any debt or obligation incurred in aid of insurrection or rebellion against the United States, or any claim for the loss or emancipation of any slave; but all such debts, obligations and claims shall be held illegal and void.

Section 5

The Congress shall have power to enforce, by appropriate legislation, the provisions of this article.

Amendment XV (1870)

Section 1

The right of citizens of the United States to vote shall not be denied or abridged by the United States or by any State on account of race, color, or previous condition of servitude.

Section 2

The Congress shall have power to enforce this article by appropriate legislation.

Amendment XVI (1913)

The Congress shall have power to lay and collect taxes on incomes, from whatever source derived, without apportionment among the several States, and without regard to any census or enumeration.

Amendment XVII (1913)

The Senate of the United States shall be composed of two Senators from each State, elected by the people thereof, for six years; and each Senator shall have one vote. The electors in each State shall have the qualifications requisite for electors of the most numerous branch of the State legislatures.

When vacancies happen in the representation of any State in the Senate, the executive authority of such State shall issue writs of election to fill such vacancies: Provided, That the legislature of any State may empower the executive thereof to make temporary appointments until the people fill the vacancies by election as the legislature may direct.

This amendment shall not so be construed as to affect the election or term of any Senator chosen before it becomes valid as part of the Constitution.

Amendment XVIII (1919)

Section 1

After one year from the ratification of this article the manufacture, sale, or transportation of intoxicating liquors within, the importation thereof into, or the exportation thereof from the United States and all territory subject to the jurisdiction thereof for beverage purposes is hereby prohibited.

Section 2

The Congress and the several States shall have concurrent power to enforce this article by appropriate legislation.

Section 3

This article shall be inoperative unless it shall have been ratified as an amendment to the Constitution by the legislatures of the several States, as provided in the Constitution, within seven years from the date of the submission hereof to the States by the Congress.

Amendment XIX (1920)

The right of citizens of the United States to vote shall not be denied or abridged by the United States or by any State on account of sex.

Congress shall have power to enforce this article by appropriate legislation.

Amendment XX (1933)

Section 1

The terms of the President and Vice President shall end at noon on the 20th day of January, and the terms of Senators and Representatives at noon on the 3d day of January, of the years in which such terms would have ended if this article had not been ratified; and the terms of their successors shall then begin.

Section 2

The Congress shall assemble at least once in every year, and such meeting shall begin at noon on the 3d day of January, unless they shall by law appoint a different day.

Section 3

If, at any time fixed for the beginning of the term of the President, the President elect shall have died, the Vice President elect shall become President. If a President shall not have been chosen before the time fixed for the beginning of his term, or if the President elect shall have failed to qualify, then the Vice President elect shall act as President until a President shall have qualified; and the Congress may by law provide for the case wherein neither a President elect nor a Vice President elect shall have qualified, declaring who shall then act as President, or the manner in which one who is to act shall be selected; and such person shall act accordingly until a President or Vice President shall have qualified

Section 4

The Congress may by law provide for the case of the death of any of the persons from whom the House of Representatives may choose a President whenever the right of choice shall have devolved upon them, and for the case of the death of any of the persons from whom the Senate may choose a Vice President whenever the right of choice shall have devolved upon them.

Section 5

Sections 1 and 2 shall take effect on the 15th day of October following the ratification of this article.

Section 6

This article shall be inoperative unless it shall have been ratified as an amendment to the Constitution by the legislatures of three-fourths of the several States within seven years from the date of its submission.

Amendment XXI (1933)

Section 1

The eighteenth article of amendment to the Constitution of the United States is hereby repealed.

Section 2

The transportation or importation into any State, Territory or possession of the United States for delivery or use therein of intoxicating liquors, in violation of the laws thereof, is hereby prohibited.

Section 3

This article shall be inoperative unless it shall have been ratified as an amendment to the Constitution by conventions in the several States, as provided in the Constitution, within seven years from the date of the submission hereof to the States by the Congress.

Amendment XXII (1951)

Section 1

No person shall be elected to the office of the President more than twice, and no person who has held the office of President, or acted as President, for more than two years of a term to which some other person was elected President shall be elected to the office of President more than once. But this Article shall not apply to any person holding the office of President when this Article was proposed by Congress, and shall not prevent any person who may be holding the office of President, or acting as President, during the term within which this Article becomes operative from holding the office of President or acting as President during the remainder of such term.

Section 2

This article shall be inoperative unless it shall have been ratified as an amendment to the Constitution by the legislatures of three-fourths of the several States within seven years from the date of its submission to the States by the Congress.

Amendment XXIII (1961)

Section 1

The District constituting the seat of Government of the United States shall appoint in such manner as Congress may direct:

A number of electors of President and Vice President equal to the whole number of Senators and Representatives in Congress to which the District would be entitled if it were a State, but in no event more than the least populous State; they shall be in addition to those appointed by the States, but they shall be considered, for the purposes of the election of President and Vice President, to be electors appointed by a State; and they shall meet in the District and perform such duties as provided by the twelfth article of amendment.

Section 2

The Congress shall have power to enforce this article by appropriate legislation.

Amendment XXIV (1964)

Section 1

The right of citizens of the United States to vote in any primary or other election for President or Vice President, for electors for President or Vice President, or for Senator or Representative in Congress, shall not be denied or abridged by the United States or any State by reason of failure to pay poll tax or other tax.

Section 2

The Congress shall have power to enforce this article by appropriate legislation.

Amendment XXV (1967)

Section 1

In case of the removal of the President from office or of his death or resignation, the Vice President shall become President.

Section 2

Whenever there is a vacancy in the office of the Vice President, the President shall nominate a Vice President who shall take office upon confirmation by a majority vote of both Houses of Congress.

Section 3

Whenever the President transmits to the President pro tempore of the Senate and the Speaker of the House of Representatives his written declaration that he is unable to discharge the powers and duties of his office, and until he transmits to them a written declaration to the contrary, such powers and duties shall be discharged by the Vice President as Acting President.

Section 4

Whenever the Vice President and a majority of either the principal officers of the executive departments or of such other body as Congress may by law provide, transmit to the President pro tempore of the Senate and the Speaker of the House of Representatives their written declaration that the President is unable to discharge the powers and duties of his office, the Vice President shall immediately assume the powers and duties of the office as Acting President.

Thereafter, when the President transmits to the President pro tempore of the Senate and the Speaker of the House of Representatives his written declaration that no inability exists, he shall resume the powers and duties of his office unless the Vice President and a majority of either the principal officers of the executive department or of such other body as Congress may by law provide, transmit within four days to the President pro tempore of the Senate and the Speaker of the House of Representatives their written declaration that the President is unable to discharge the powers and duties of his office. Thereupon Congress shall decide the issue, assembling within forty-eight hours for that purpose if not in session. If the Congress, within twenty-one days after receipt of the latter written declaration, or, if Congress is not in session, within twenty-one days after Congress is required to assemble, determines by two-thirds vote of both Houses that the President is unable to discharge the powers and duties of his office, the Vice President shall continue to discharge the same as Acting President;

otherwise, the President shall resume the powers and duties of his office.

Amendment XXVI (1971)

Section 1

The right of citizens of the United States, who are eighteen years of age or older, to vote shall not be denied or abridged by the United States or by any State on account of age.

Section 2

The Congress shall have power to enforce this article by appropriate legislation.

Amendment XXVII (1992)

No law, varying the compensation for the services of the Senators and Representatives, shall take effect, until an election of Representatives shall have intervened.

Selected Excerpts from the Model Penal Code

PART 1: General Provisions

Article 1. Preliminary

§1.04. Classes of Crimes; Violations

1. An offense defined by this Code or by any other statute of this State, for which a sentence of [death or of] imprisonment is authorized, constitutes a crime. Crimes are classified as felonies, misdemeanors or petty misdemeanors.

2. A crime is a felony if it is so designated in this Code or if persons convicted thereof may be sentenced [to death or] to imprisonment for a term which, apart from an extended term, is in excess of one year.

3. A crime is a misdemeanor if it is so designated in this Code or in a statute other than this Code enacted subsequent thereto.

4. A crime is a petty misdemeanor if it is so designated in this Code or in a statute other than this Code enacted subsequent thereto or if it is defined by a statute other than this Code which now provides that persons convicted thereof may be sentenced to imprisonment for a term of which the maximum is less than one year.

5. An offense defined by this Code or by any other statute of this State constitutes a violation if it is so designated in this Code or in the law defining the offense or if no other sentence than a fine, or fine and forfeiture or other civil penalty is authorized upon conviction or if it is defined by a statute other than this Code which now provides that the offense shall not constitute a crime. A violation does not constitute a crime and conviction of a violation shall not give rise to any disability or legal disadvantage based on conviction of a criminal offense.

6. Any offense declared by law to constitute a crime, without specification of the grade thereof or of the sentence authorized upon conviction, is a misdemeanor.

7. An offense defined by any statute of this State other than this Code shall be classified as provided in this Section and the sentence that may be imposed upon conviction thereof shall hereafter be governed by this Code.

§1.05. All Offenses Defined by Statute; Application of General Provisions of the Code

1. No conduct constitutes an offense unless it is a crime or violation under this Code or another statute of this State.

2. The provisions of Part I of the Code are applicable to offenses defined by other statutes, unless the Code otherwise provides.

3. This Section does not affect the power of a court to punish for contempt or to employ any sanction authorized by law for the enforcement of an order or a civil judgment or decree.

§1.12. Proof Beyond a Reasonable Doubt; Affirmative Defenses; Burden of Proving Fact When Not an Element of an Offense; Presumptions

1. No person may be convicted of an offense unless each element of such offense is proved beyond a reasonable doubt. In the absence of such proof, the innocence of the defendant is assumed.

2. Subsection (1) of this Section does not:
   a. require the disproof of an affirmative defense unless and until there is evidence supporting such defense; or
   b. apply to any defense which the Code or another statute plainly requires the defendant to prove by a preponderance of evidence.

3. A ground of defense is affirmative, within the meaning of Subsection (2) (a) of this Section, when:
   a. it arises under a section of the Code which so provides; or
   b. it relates to an offense defined by a statute other than the Code and such statute so provides; or
   c. it involves a matter of excuse or justification peculiarly within the knowledge of the defendant on which he can fairly be required to adduce supporting evidence.

4. When the application of the Code depends upon the finding of a fact which is not an element of an offense, unless the Code otherwise provides:
   a. the burden of proving the fact is on the prosecution or defendant, depending on whose interest or contention will be furthered if the finding should be made; and
   b. the fact must be proved to the satisfaction of the Court or jury, as the case may be.

5. When the Code establishes a presumption with respect to any fact which is an element of an offense, it has the following consequences:

a. when there is evidence of the facts which give rise to the presumption, the issue of the existence of the presumed fact must be submitted to the jury, unless the Court is satisfied that the evidence as a whole clearly negatives the presumed fact; and

b. when the issue of the existence of the presumed fact is submitted to the jury, the Court shall charge that while the presumed fact must, on all the evidence, be proved beyond a reasonable doubt, the law declares that the jury may regard the facts giving rise to the presumption as sufficient evidence of the presumed fact.

6. A presumption not established by the Code or inconsistent with it has the consequences otherwise accorded it by law.

§1.13. General Definitions

In this Code, unless a different meaning plainly is required:

1. "statute" includes the Constitutional and a local law or ordinance of a political subdivision of the State;

2. "act" or "action" means a bodily movement whether voluntary or involuntary;

3. "voluntary" has the meaning specified in Section 2.01;

4. "omission" means a failure to act;

5. "conduct" means an action or omission and its accompanying state of mind, or, where relevant, a series of acts and omissions.

6. "actor" includes, where relevant, a person guilty of an omission;

7. "acted" includes, where relevant, "omitted to act";

8. "person," "he" and "actor" include any natural person and, where relevant, a corporation or an unincorporated association;

9. "element of an offense" means (i) such conduct or (ii) such attendant circumstances or (iii) such a result of conduct as
   a. is included in the description of the forbidden conduct in the definition of the offense; or
   b. establishes the required kind of culpability; or
   c. negatives an excuse or justification for such conduct; or
   d. negatives a defense under the statue of limitations; or
   e. establishes jurisdiction or venue;

10. "material element of an offense" means an element that does not relate exclusively to the statute of limitations, jurisdiction, venue or to any other matter similarly unconnected with (i) the harm or evil, incident to conduct, sought to be prevented by the law defining the of-

fense, or (ii) the existence of a justification or excuse for such conduct;

11. "purposely" has the meaning specified in Section 2.02 and equivalent terms such as "with purpose," "designed" or "with design" have the same meaning;

12. "intentionally" or "with intent" means purposely;

13. "knowingly" has the meaning specified in Section 2.02 and equivalent terms such as "knowing" or "with knowledge" have the same meaning;

14. "recklessly" has the meaning specified in Section 2.02 and equivalent terms such as "recklessness" or "with recklessness" have the same meaning;

15. "negligently" has the same meaning specified in Section 2.02 and equivalent terms such as "negligence" or "with negligence" have the same meaning;

16. "reasonably believes" or "reasonable belief" designates a belief which the actor is not reckless or negligent in holding.

Article 2. General Principles of Liability

§2.02. Requirement of Voluntary Act; Omission as Basis of Liability; Possession as an Act

1. A person is not guilty of an offense unless his liability is based on conduct which includes a voluntary act or the omission to perform an act of which he is physically capable.

2. The following are not voluntary acts within the meaning of this Section:
   a. a reflex or convulsion;
   b. a bodily movement during unconsciousness or sleep;
   c. conduct during hypnosis or resulting from hypnotic suggestion;
   d. a bodily movement that otherwise is not a product of the effort or determination of the actor, either conscious or habitual.

3. Liability for the commission of an offense may not be based on an omission unaccompanied by action unless:
   a. the omission is expressly made sufficient by the law defining the offense; or
   b. a duty to perform the omitted act is otherwise imposed by law.

4. Possession is an act, within the meaning of this Section, if the possessor knowingly procured or received the thing possessed or was aware of his control thereof for a sufficient period to have been able to terminate his possession.

§2.02. General Requirements of Culpability

1. *Minimum Requirements of Culpability.*   Except as provided in Section 2.05, a person is not guilty of an

offense unless he acted purposely, knowingly, recklessly or negligently, as the law may require, with respect to each material element of the offense.

2. *Kinds of Culpability Defined.*
   a. *Purposely.* A person acts purposely with respect to a material element of an offense when:
      i. if the element involves the nature of his conduct or a result thereof, it is his conscious object to engage in conduct of that nature or to cause such a result; and
      ii. if the element involves the attendant circumstances, he is aware of the existence of such circumstances or he believes or hopes that they exist.
   b. *Knowingly.* A person acts knowingly with respect to a material element of an offense when:
      i. if the element involves the nature of his conduct or the attendant circumstances, he is aware that his conduct is of that nature or that such circumstances exist; and
      ii. if the element involves a result of his conduct, he is aware that it is practically certain that his conduct will cause such a result.
   c. *Recklessly.* A person acts recklessly with respect to a material element of an offense when he consciously disregards a substantial and unjustifiable risk that the material element exists or will result from his conduct. The risk must be of such a nature and degree that, considering the nature and purpose of the actor's conduct and the circumstances known to him, its disregard involves a gross deviation from the standard of conduct that a law-abiding person would observe in the actor's situation.
   d. *Negligently.* A person acts negligently with respect to a material element of an offense when he should be aware of a substantial and unjustifiable risk that the material element exists or will result from his conduct. The risk must be of such a nature and degree that the actor's failure to perceive it, considering the nature and purpose of his conduct and the circumstances known to him, involves a gross deviation from the standard of care that a reasonable person would observe in the actor's situation.

3. *Culpability Required Unless Otherwise Provided.* When the culpability sufficient to establish a material element of an offense is not prescribed by law, such element is established if a person acts purposely, knowingly or recklessly with respect thereto.

4. *Prescribed Culpability Requirement Applies to All Material Elements.* When the law defining an offense prescribes the kind of culpability that is sufficient for the commission of an offense, without distinguishing among the material elements thereof, such provision shall apply to all the material elements of the offense, unless a contrary purpose plainly appears.

5. *Substitutes for Negligence, Recklessness and Knowledge.* When the law provides that negligence suffices to establish an element of an offense, such element also is established if a person acts purposely, knowingly or recklessly. When recklessness suffices to establish an element, such element also is established if a person acts purposely or knowingly. When acting knowingly suffices to establish an element, such element also is established if a person acts purposely.

6. *Requirement of Purpose Satisfied if Purpose Is Conditional.* When a particular purpose is an element of an offense, the element is established although such purpose is conditional, unless the condition negatives the harm or evil sought to be prevented by the law defining the offense.

7. *Requirement of Knowledge Satisfied by Knowledge of High Probability.* When knowledge of the existence of a particular fact is an element of an offense, such knowledge is established if a person is aware of a high probability of its existence, unless he actually believes that it does not exist.

8. *Requirement of Willfulness Satisfied by Acting Knowingly.* A requirement that an offense be committed willfully is satisfied if a person acts knowingly with respect to the material elements of the offense, unless a purpose to impose further requirements appears.

9. *Culpability as to Illegality of Conduct.* Neither knowledge nor recklessness or negligence as to whether conduct constitutes an offense or as to the existence, meaning or application of the law determining the elements of an offense is an element of such offense, unless the definition of the offense or the Code so provides.

10. *Culpability as Determinant of Grade of Offense.* When the grade or degree of an offense depends on whether the offense is committed purposely, knowingly, recklessly or negligently, its grade or degree shall be the lowest for which the determinative kind of culpability is established with respect to any material element of the offense.

§2.03. Causal Relationship Between Conduct and Result; Divergence Between Result Designed or Contemplated and Actual Result or Between Probable and Actual Result

1. Conduct is the cause of a result when:
   a. it is an antecedent but for which the result in question would not have occurred; and
   b. the relationship between the conduct and result satisfies any additional causal requirements

imposed by the Code or by the law defining the offense.

2. When purposely or knowingly causing a particular result is an element of an offense, the element is not established if the actual result is not within the purpose or the contemplation of the actor unless:
   a. the actual result differs from that designed or contemplated, as the case may be, only in the respect that a different person or different property is injured or affected or that the injury or harm designed or contemplated would have been more serious or more extensive than that caused; or
   b. the actual result involves the same kind of injury or harm as that designed or contemplated and is not too remote or accidental in its occurrence to have a [just] bearing on the actor's liability or on the gravity of his offense.

3. When recklessly or negligently causing a particular result is an element of an offense, the element is not established if the actual result is not within the risk of which the actor is aware or, in the case of negligence, of which he should be aware unless:
   a. the actual result differs from the probable result only in respect that a different person or different property is injured or affected or that the probable injury or harm would have been more serious or more extensive than that caused; or
   b. the actual result involves the same kind of injury or harm as the probable result and is not too remote or accidental in its occurrence to have a [just] bearing on the actor's liability or on the gravity of his offense.

4. When causing a particular result is a material element of an offense for which absolute liability is imposed by law, the element is not established unless the actual result is a probable consequence of the actor's conduct.

§2.02. *Ignorance or Mistake*

1. Ignorance or mistake as to a matter of fact or law is a defense if:
   a. the ignorance or mistake negatives the purpose, knowledge, belief, recklessness or negligence required to establish a material element of the offense; or
   b. the law provides that the state of mind established by such ignorance or mistake constitutes a defense.

2. Although ignorance or mistake would otherwise afford a defense to the offense charged, the defense is not available if the defendant would be guilty of another offense had the situation been as he supposed.

In such case, however, the ignorance or mistake of the defendant shall reduce the grade and degree of the offense of which he may be convicted to those of the offense of which he would be guilty had the situation been as he supposed.

3. A belief that conduct does not legally constitute an offense is a defense to a prosecution for that offense based upon such conduct when:
   a. the statute or other enactment defining the offense is not known to the actor and has not been published or otherwise reasonably made available prior to the conduct alleged; or
   b. he acts in reasonable reliance upon an official statement of the law, afterward determined to be invalid or erroneous, contained in (i) a statute or other enactment; (ii) a judicial decision, opinion or judgment; (iii) an administrative order or grant of permission; or (iv) an official interpretation of the public officer or body charged by law with responsibility for the interpretation, administration or enforcement of the law defining the offense.

4. The defendant must prove a defense arising under Subsection (3) of this Section by a preponderance of evidence.

§2.05. *When Culpability Requirements Are Inapplicable to Violations and to Offenses Defined by Other Statutes; Effect of Absolute Liability in Reducing Grade of Offense to Violation*

1. The requirements of culpability prescribed by Sections 2.01 and 2.02 do not apply to:
   a. offenses which constitute violations, unless the requirement involved is included in the definition of the offense or the Court determines that its application is consistent with effective enforcement of the law defining the offense; or
   b. offenses defined by statutes other than the Code, insofar as a legislative purpose to impose absolute liability for such offenses or with respect to any material element thereof plainly appears.

2. Notwithstanding any other provision of existing law and unless a subsequent statute otherwise provides:
   a. when absolute liability is imposed with respect to any material element of an offense defined by a statute other than the Code and a conviction is based upon such liability, the offense constitutes a violation; and
   b. although absolute liability is imposed by law with respect to one or more of the material elements of an offense defined by a statute other than the Code, the culpable commission of the offense may be charged and proved, in which event negligence

with respect to such elements constitutes sufficient culpability and the classification of the offense and the sentence that may be imposed therefore upon conviction are determined by Section 1.04 and Article 6 of the Code.

§2.06. Liability for Conduct of Another; Complicity

1. A person is guilty of an offense if it is committed by his own conduct or by the conduct of another person for which he is legally accountable, or both.

2. A person is legally accountable for the conduct of another person when:
   a. acting with the kind of culpability that is sufficient for the commission of the offense, he causes an innocent or irresponsible person to engage in such conduct; or
   b. he is made accountable for the conduct of such other person by the Code or by the lawdefining the offense; or
   c. he is an accomplice of such other person in the commission of the offense.

3. A person is an accomplice of another person in the commission of an offense if:
   a. with the purpose of promoting or facilitating the commission of the offense, he
      i. solicits such other person to commit it; or
      ii. aids or agrees or attempts to aid such other person in planning or committing it; or
      iii. having a legal duty to prevent the commission of the offense, fails to make proper effect so to do; or
   b. his conduct is expressly declared by law to establish his complicity.

4. When causing a particular result is an element of an offense, an accomplice in the conduct causing such result is an accomplice in the commission of that offense, if he acts with the kind of culpability, if any, with respect to that result that is sufficient for the commission of the offense.

5. A person who is legally incapable of committing a particular offense himself may be guilty thereof, if it is committed by the conduct of another person for which he is legally accountable, unless such liability is inconsistent with the purpose of the provision establishing his incapacity.

6. Unless otherwise provided by the Code or by the law defining the offense, a person is not an accomplice in an offense committed by another person if:
   a. he is a victim of that offense; or
   b. the offense is so defined that his conduct is inevitably incident to its commission; or

   c. he terminates his complicity prior to the commission of the offense and
      i. wholly deprives it of effectiveness in the commission of the offense; or
      ii. gives timely warning to the law enforcement authorities or otherwise makes proper effort to prevent the commission of the offense.

7. An accomplice may be convicted on proof of the commission of the offense and of his complicity therein, though the person claimed to have committed the offense has not been prosecuted or convicted or has been convicted of a different offense or degree of offense or has an immunity to prosecution or conviction or has been acquitted.

§2.07. Liability of Corporations, Unincorporated Associations and Persons Acting, or Under a Duty to Act, in Their Behalf

1. A corporation may be convicted of the commission of an offense if:
   a. the offense is a violation or the offense is defined by a statute other than the Code in which a legislative purpose to impose liability on corporations plainly appears and the conduct is performed by an agent of the corporation acting in behalf of the corporation within the scope of his office or employment, except that if the law defining the offense designates the agents for whose conduct the corporation is accountable or the circumstances under which it is accountable, such provisions shall apply; or
   b. the offense consists of an omission to discharge a specific duty of affirmative performance imposed on corporations by law; or
   c. the commission of the offense was authorized, requested, commanded, performed or recklessly tolerated by the board of directors or by a high managerial agent acting in behalf of the corporation within the scope of his office or employment.

2. When absolute liability is imposed for the commission of an offense, a legislative purpose to impose liability on a corporation shall be assumed, unless the contrary plainly appears.

3. An unincorporated association may be convicted of the commission of an offense if:
   a. the offense is defined by a statute other than the Code which expressly provides for the liability of such an association and the conduct is performed by an agent of the association acting in behalf of the association within the scope of his office or employment, except that if the law defining the offense designates the agents for whose conduct the

association is accountable or the circumstances under which it is accountable, such provisions shall apply; or

b. the offense consists of an omission to discharge a specific duty of affirmative performance imposed on associations by law.

4. As used in this Section:

a. "corporation" does not include an entity organized as or by a governmental agency for the execution of a governmental program;

b. "agent" means any director, officer, servant, employee or other person authorized to act in behalf of the corporation or association and, in the case of an unincorporated association, a member of such association;

c. "high managerial agent" means an officer of a corporation or an unincorporated association, or, in the case of a partnership, a partner, or any other agent of a corporation or association having duties of such responsibilities that his conduct may fairly be assumed to represent the policy of the corporation or association.

5. In any prosecution of a corporation or an unincorporated association for the commission of an offense included within the terms of Subsection (1)(a) or Subsection (3)(a) of this Section, other than an offense for which absolute liability has been imposed, it shall be a defense if the defendant proves by a preponderance of evidence that the high managerial agent having supervisory responsibility over the subject matter of the offense employed due diligence to prevent its commission. This paragraph shall not apply if it is plainly inconsistent with the legislative purpose in defining the particular offense.

6. a. A person is legally accountable for any conduct he performs or causes to be performed in the name of the corporation or an unincorporated association or in its behalf to the same extent as if it were performed in his own name or behalf.

b. Whenever a duty to act is imposed by law upon a corporation or an unincorporated association, any agent of the corporation or association having primary responsibility for the discharge of the duty is legally accountable for a reckless omission to perform the required act to the same extent as if the duty were imposed by law directly upon himself.

c. When a person is convicted of an offense by reason of his legal accountability for the conduct of a corporation or an unincorporated association, he is subject to the sentence authorized by law when a natural person is convicted of an offense of the grade and the degree involved.

§2.08. Intoxication

1. Except as provided in Subsection (4) of this Section, intoxication of the actor is not a defense unless it negatives an element of the offense.

2. When recklessness establishes an element of the offense, if the actor, due to self-induced intoxication, is unaware of a risk of which he would have been aware had he been sober, such unawareness is immaterial.

3. Intoxication does not, in itself, constitute mental disease within the meaning of Section 4.01.

4. Intoxication which (a) is not self-induced or (b) is pathological is an affirmative defense if by reason of such intoxication the actor at the time of his conduct lacks substantial capacity either to appreciate its criminality [wrongfulness] or to conform his conduct to the requirements of law.

5. *Definitions.* In this Section unless a different meaning plainly is required:

a. "intoxication" means a disturbance of mental or physical capacities resulting from the introduction of substances into the body;

b. "self-induced intoxication" means intoxication caused by substances which the actor knowingly introduces into his body, the tendency of which to cause intoxication he knows or ought to know, unless he introduces them pursuant to medical advice or under such circumstances as would afford a defense to a charge of crime;

c. "pathological intoxication" means intoxication grossly excessive in degree, given the amount of the intoxicant, to which the actor does not know he is susceptible.

§2.09. Duress

1. It is an affirmative defense that the actor engaged in the conduct charged to constitute an offense because he was coerced to do so by the use of, or a threat to use, unlawful force against his person or the person of another, which a person of reasonable firmness in his situation would have been unable to resist.

2. The defense provided by this Section is unavailable if the actor recklessly placed himself in a situation in which it was probable that he would be subjected to duress. The defense is also unavailable if he was negligent in placing himself in such a situation, whenever negligence suffices to establish culpability for the offense charged.

3. It is not a defense that a woman acted on the command of her husband, unless she acted under such coercion as would establish a defense under this Section. [The presumption that a woman, acting in the presence of her husband, is coerced is abolished.]

4. When the conduct of the actor would otherwise be justifiable under Section 3.02, this Section does not preclude such defense.

§2.10. Military Orders

It is an affirmative defense that the actor, in engaging in the conduct charged to constitute an offense, does no more than execute an order of his superior in the armed services which he does not know to be unlawful.

§2.11. Consent

1. *In General.* The consent of the victim to conduct charged to constitute an offense or to the result thereof is a defense if such consent negatives an element of the offense or precludes the infliction of the harm or evil sought to be prevented by the law defining the offense.

2. *Consent to Bodily Harm.* When conduct is charged to constitute an offense because it causes or threatens bodily harm, consent to such conduct or to the infliction of such harm is a defense if:
   a. the bodily harm consented to or threatened by the conduct consented to is not serious; or
   b. the conduct and the harm are reasonably foreseeable hazards of joint participation in a lawful athletic contest or competitive sport; or
   c. the consent establishes a justification for the conduct under Article 3 of the Code.

3. *Ineffective Consent.* Unless otherwise provided by the Code or by the law defining the offense, assent does not constitute consent if:
   a. it is given by a person who is legally incompetent to authorize the conduct charged to constitute the offense; or
   b. it is given by a person who by reason of youth, mental disease or defect or intoxication is manifestly unable or known by the actor to be unable to make a reasonable judgment as to the nature or harmfulness of the conduct charged to constitute the offense; or
   c. it is given by a person whose improvident consent is sought to be prevented by the law defining the offense; or
   d. it is induced by force, duress or deception of a kind sought to be prevented by the law defining the offense.

§2.13. Entrapment

1. A public law enforcement official or a person acting in cooperation with such an official perpetrates an entrapment if for the purpose of obtaining evidence of the commission of an offense, he induces or encourages another person to engage in conduct constituting such offense by either:
   a. making knowingly false representations designed to induce the belief that such conduct is not prohibited; or
   b. employing methods of persuasion or inducement which create a substantial risk that such an offense will be committed by persons other than those who are ready to commit it.

2. Except as provided in Subsection (3) of this Section, a person prosecuted for an offense shall be acquitted if he proves by a preponderance of evidence that his conduct occurred in response to an entrapment. The issue of entrapment shall be tried by the Court in the absence of the jury.

3. The defense afforded by this Section is unavailable when causing or threatening bodily injury is an element of the offense charged and the prosecution is based on conduct causing or threatening such injury to a person other than the person perpetrating the entrapment.

Article 3. General Principles of Justification

§3.01. Justification an Affirmative Defense; Civil Remedies Unaffected

1. In any prosecution based on conduct which is justifiable under this Article, justification is an affirmative defense.

2. The fact that conduct is justifiable under this Article does not abolish or impair any remedy for such conduct which is available in any civil action.

§3.02. Justification Generally: Choice of Evils

1. Conduct which the actor believes to be necessary to avoid harm or evil to himself or to another is justifiable, provided that:
   a. the harm or evil sought to be avoided by such conduct is greater than that sought to be prevented by the law defining the offense charged; and
   b. neither the Code nor other law defining the offense provides exceptions or defenses dealing with the specific situation involved; and
   c. a legislative purpose to exclude the justification claimed does not otherwise plainly appear.

2. When the actor was reckless or negligent in bringing about the situation requiring a choice of harms or evils or in appraising the necessity for his conduct, the justification afforded by this Section is unavailable in a prosecution for any offense for which recklessness or negligence, as the case may be, suffices to establish culpability.

§3.03. Execution of Public Duty

1. Except as provided in Subsection (2) of this Section, conduct is justifiable when it is required or authorized by:
   a. the law defining the duties or functions of a public officer or the assistance to be rendered to such officer in the performance of his duties; or
   b. the law governing the execution of legal process; or
   c. the judgment or order of a competent court or tribunal; or
   d. the law governing the armed services or the lawful conduct of war; or
   e. any other provision of law imposing a public duty.

2. The other sections of this Article apply to:
   a. the use of force upon or toward the person of another for any of the purposes dealt with in such sections; and
   b. the use of deadly force for any purpose, unless the use of such force is otherwise expressly authorized by law or occurs in the lawful conduct of war.

3. The justification afforded by Subsection (1) of this Section applies:
   a. when the actor believes his conduct to be required or authorized by the judgment or direction of a competent court or tribunal or in the lawful execution of legal process, notwithstanding lack of jurisdiction of the court or defect in the legal process; and
   b. when the actor believes his conduct to be required or authorized to assist a public officer in the performance of his duties, notwithstanding that the officer exceeded his legal authority.

§3.04. Use of Force in Self-Protection

1. *Use of Force Justifiable for Protection of the Person.*   Subject to the provisions of this Section and of Section 3.09, the use of force upon or toward another person is justifiable when the actor believes that such force is immediately necessary for the purpose of protecting himself against the use of unlawful force by such other person on the present occasion.

2. Limitations on Justifying Necessity for Use of Force.
   a. The use of force is not justifiable under this Section:
      i. to resist arrest which the actor knows is being made by a peace officer, although the arrest is unlawful; or
      ii. to resist force used by the occupier or possessor of property or by another person on his behalf, where the actor knows that the person using the force is doing so under a claim of right to protect the property, except that this limitation shall not apply if:
         1. the actor is a public officer acting in the performance of his duties or a person lawfully assisting him therein or a person making or assisting him therein or a person making or assisting in a lawful arrest; or
         2. the actor has been unlawfully dispossessed of the property and is making a re-entry or recaption justified by Section 3.06; or
         3. the actor believes that such force is necessary to protect himself against death or serious bodily harm.
   b. The use of deadly force is not justifiable under this Section unless the actor believes that such force is necessary to protect himself against death, serious bodily harm, kidnapping or sexual intercourse compelled by force or threat; nor is it justifiable if:
      i. the actor, with the purpose of causing death or serious bodily harm, provoked the use of force against himself in the same encounter; or
      ii. the actor knows that he can avoid the necessity of using such force with complete safety by retreating or by surrendering possession of a thing to a person asserting a claim of right thereto or by complying with a demand that he abstain from any action which he has no duty to take, except that:
         1. the actor is not obliged to retreat from his dwelling or place of work, unless he was the initial aggressor or is assailed in his place of work by another person whose place of work the actor knows it to be; and
         2. a public officer justified in using force in the performance of his duties or a person justified in using force in his assistance or a person justified in using force in making an arrest or preventing an escape is not obliged to desist from efforts to perform such duty, effect such arrest or prevent such escape because of resistance or threatened resistance by or on behalf of the person against whom such action is directed.
   c. Except as required by paragraphs (a) and (b) of this Subsection, a person employing protective force may estimate the necessity thereof under the circumstances as he believes them to be when the force is used, without retreating, surrendering possession, doing any other act which he has no legal duty to do or abstaining from any lawful action.

3. *Use of Confinement as Protective Force.*   The justification afforded by this Section extends to the use of confinement as protective force only if the actor takes all reasonable measures to terminate the confinement as soon as he knows that he safely can, unless the person confined has been arrested on a charge of crime.

§3.05. *Use of Force for the Protection of Other Persons*

1. Subject to the provisions of this Section and of Section 3.09, the use of force upon or toward the person of another is justifiable to protect a third person when:
   a. the actor would be justified under Section 3.04 in using such force to protect himself against the injury he believes to be threatened to the person whom he seeks to protect; and
   b. under the circumstances as the actor believes them to be, the person whom he seeks to protect would be justified in using such protective force; and
   c. the actor believes that his intervention is necessary for the protection of such other person.

2. Notwithstanding Subsection (1) of this Section:
   a. when the actor would be obliged under Section 3.04 to retreat, to surrender the possession of a thing or to comply with a demand before using force in self-protection, he is not obliged to do so before using force for the protection of another person, unless he knows that he can thereby secure the complete safety of such other person; and
   b. when the person whom the actor seeks to protect would be obliged under Section 3.04 to retreat, to surrender the possession of a thing or to comply with a demand if he knew that he could obtain complete safety by so doing, the actor is obliged to try to cause him to do so before using force in his protection if the actor knows that he can obtain complete safety in that way; and
   c. neither the actor nor the person whom he seeks to protect is obliged to retreat when in the other's dwelling or place of work to any greater extent than in his own.

§3.06. *Use of Force for the Protection of Property*

1. *Use of Force Justifiable for the Protection of Property.* Subject to the provisions of this Section and of Section 3.09, the use of force upon or toward the person of another is justifiable when the actor believes that such force is immediately necessary:
   a. to prevent or terminate an unlawful entry or other trespass upon land or a trespass against or the unlawful carrying away of tangible, movable property, provided that such land or movable property is, or is believed by the actor to be, in his possession or in the possession of another person for whose protection he acts; or
   b. to effect an entry or re-entry upon land or to retake tangible movable property, provided that the actor believes that he or the person by whose au-

thority he acts or a person from whom he or such other person derives title was unlawfully dispossessed of such land or movable property and is entitled to possession, and provided, further, that:
   i. the force is used immediately or on fresh pursuit after such dispossession; or
   ii. the actor believes that the person against whom he uses force has no claim of right to the possession of the property and, in the case of land, the circumstances, as the actor believes them to be, are of such urgency that it would be an exceptional hardship to postpone the entry or re-entry until a court order is obtained.

2. *Meaning of Possession.* For the purposes of Subsection (1) of this Section:
   a. a person who has parted with the custody of property to another who refuses to restore it to him is no longer in possession, unless the property is movable and was and still is located on land in his possession;
   b. a person who has been dispossessed of land does not regain possession thereof merely by setting foot thereon;
   c. a person who has a license to use or occupy real property is deemed to be in possession thereof except against the licensor acting under claim of right.

3. *Limitations on Justifiable Use of Force.*
   a. Request to Desist.
      The use of force is justifiable under this Section only if the actor first requests the person against whom such force is used to desist from his interference with the property, unless the actor believes that:
      i. such request would be useless; or
      ii. it would be dangerous to himself or another person to make the request; or
      iii. substantial harm will be done to the physical condition of the property which is sought to be protected before the request can effectively be made.
   b. *Exclusion of Trespasser.* The use of force to prevent or terminate a trespass is not justifiable under this Section if the actor knows that the exclusion of the trespasser will expose him to substantial danger of serious bodily harm.
   c. *Resistance of Lawful Re-entry or Recaption.* The use of force to prevent an entry or re-entry upon land or the recaption of moveable property is not justifiable under this Section, although the actor believes that such re-entry or recaption is unlawful, if:
      i. the re-entry or recaption is made by or on behalf of a person who was actually dispossessed of the property; and

ii. it is otherwise justifiable under paragraph (1)(b) of this Section.

d. *Use of Deadly Force.* The use of deadly force is not justifiable under this Section unless the actor believes that:

   i. the person against whom the force is used is attempting to dispossess him of his dwelling otherwise than under a claim of right to its possession; or

   ii. the person against whom the force is used is attempting to commit or consummate arson, burglary, robbery or other felonious theft or property destruction and either:

     1. has employed or threatened deadly force against or in the presence of the actor; or

     2. the use of force other than deadly force to prevent the commission or the consummation of the crime would expose the actor or another in his presence to substantial danger of serious bodily harm.

4. *Use of Confinement as Protective Force.* The justification afforded by this Section extends to the use of confinement as protective force only if the actor takes all reasonable measures to terminate the confinement as soon as he knows that he can do so with safety to the property, unless the person confined has been arrested on a charge of crime.

5. *Use of Device to Protect Property.* The justification afforded by this Section extends to the use of a device for the purpose of protecting property only if:

a. the device is not designed to cause or known to create a substantial risk of causing death or serious bodily harm; and

b. the use of the particular device to protect the property from entry or trespass is reasonable under the circumstances, as the actor believes them to be; and

c. the device is one customarily used for such a purpose or reasonable care is taken to make known to probable intruders the fact that it is used.

6. *Use of Force to Pass Wrongful Obstructor.* The use of force to pass a person whom the actor believes to be purposely or knowingly and unjustifiably obstructing the actor from going to a place to which he may lawfully go is justifiable, provided that:

a. the actor believes that the person against whom he uses force has no claim or right to obstruct the actor; and

b. the actor is not being obstructed from entry or movement on land which he knows to be in the possession or custody of the person obstructing him, or in the possession or custody of another person by whose authority the obstructor acts, unless the circumstances, as the actor believes

them to be, are of such urgency that it would not be reasonable to postpone the entry or movement on such land until a court order is obtained; and

c. the force used is not greater than would be justifiable if the person obstructing the actor were using force against him to prevent his passage.

§3.07. Use of Force in Law Enforcement

1. *Use of Force Justifiable to Effect an Arrest.* Subject to the provisions of this Section and of Section 3.09, the use of force upon or toward the person of another is justifiable when the actor is making or assisting in making an arrest and the actor believes that such force is immediately necessary to effect a lawful arrest.

2. *Limitations on the Use of Force.*

a. The use of force is not justifiable under this Section unless:

   i. the actor makes known the purpose of the arrest or believes that it is otherwise known by or cannot reasonably be made known to the person to be arrested; and

   ii. when the arrest is made under a warrant, the warrant is valid or believed by the actor to be valid.

b. The use of deadly force is not justifiable under this Section unless:

   i. the arrest is for a felony; and

   ii. the person effecting the arrest is authorized to act as a peace officer or is assisting a person whom he believes to be authorized to act as a peace officer; and

   iii. the actor believes that the force employed creates no substantial risk of injury to innocent persons; and

   iv. the actor believes that:

     1. the crime for which the arrest is made involved conduct including the use or threatened use of deadly force; or

     2. there is a substantial risk that the person to be arrested will cause death or serious bodily harm if his apprehension is delayed.

3. *Use of Force to Prevent Escape from Custody.* The use of force to prevent the escape of an arrested person from custody is justifiable when the force could justifiably have been employed to effect the arrest under which the person is in custody, except that a guard or other person authorized to act as a peace officer is justified in using any force, including deadly force, which he believes to be immediately necessary to prevent the escape of a person from a jail, prison, or other institution for the detention of persons charged with or convicted of a crime.

4. *Use of Force by Private Person Assisting an Unlawful Arrest.*

a. A private person who is summoned by a peace officer to assist in effecting an unlawful arrest, is justified in using any force which he would be justified in using if the arrest were lawful, provided that he does not believe the arrest is unlawful.

b. A private person who assists another private person in effecting an unlawful arrest, or who, not being summoned, assists a peace officer in effecting an unlawful arrest, is justified in using any force which he would be justified in using if the arrest were lawful, provided that
   i. he believes the arrest is lawful, and
   ii. the arrest would be lawful if the facts were as he believes them to be.

5. *Use of Force to Prevent Suicide or the Commission of a Crime.*

   a. The use of force upon or toward the person of another is justifiable when the actor believes that such force is immediately necessary to prevent such other person from committing suicide, inflicting serious bodily harm upon himself, committing or consummating the commission of a crime involving or threatening bodily harm, damage to or loss of property or a breach of the peace, except that:
      i. any limitations imposed by the other provisions of this Article on the justifiable use of force in self-protection, for the protection of others, the protection of property, the effectuation of an arrest or the prevention of an escape from custody shall apply notwithstanding the criminality of the conduct against which such force is used; and
      ii. the use of deadly force is not in any event justifiable under this Subsection unless:
         1. the actor believes that there is a substantial risk that the person whom he seeks to prevent from committing a crime will cause death or serious bodily harm to another unless the commission or the consummation of the crime is prevented and that the use of such force presents no substantial risk of injury to innocent persons; or
         2. the actor believes that the use of such force is necessary to suppress a riot or mutiny after the rioters or mutineers have been ordered to disperse and warned, in any particular manner that the law may require, that such force will be used if they do not obey.

   b. The justification afforded by this Subsection extends to the use of confinement as preventive force only if the actor takes all reasonable measure to terminate the confinement as soon as he knows that he safely can, unless the person confined has been arrested on a charge of crime.

Article 4. Responsibility

§4.01. Mental Disease or Defect Excluding Responsibility

1. A person is not responsible for criminal conduct if at the time of such conduct as a result of mental disease or defect he lacks substantial capacity either to appreciate the criminality [wrongfulness] of his conduct or to conform his conduct to the requirements of law.

2. As used in this Article, the terms "mental disease or defect" do not include an abnormality manifested only by repeated criminal or otherwise anti-social conduct.

§4.02. Evidence of Mental Disease or Defect Admissible When Relevant to Element of the Offense; [Mental Disease or Defect Impairing Capacity as Ground for Mitigation of Punishment in Capital Cases]

1. Evidence that the defendant suffered from a mental disease or defect is admissible whenever it is relevant to prove that the defendant did or did not have a state of mind which is an element of the offense.

2. Whenever the jury or the Court is authorized to determine or to recommend whether or not the defendant shall be sentenced to death or imprisonment upon conviction, evidence that the capacity of the defendant to appreciate the criminality [wrongfulness] of his conduct or to conform his conduct to the requirements of law was impaired as a result of mental disease or defect is admissible in favor of sentence of imprisonment.

§4.03. Mental Disease or Defect Excluding Responsibility Is Affirmative Defense; Requirement of Notice; Form of Verdict and Judgment When Finding of Irresponsibility Is Made

1. Mental disease or defect excluding responsibility is an affirmative defense.

2. Evidence of mental disease or defect excluding responsibility is not admissible unless the defendant, at the time of entering his plea of not guilty or within ten days thereafter or at such later time as the Court may for good cause permit, files a written notice of his purpose to rely on such defense.

3. When the defendant is acquitted on the ground of mental disease or defect excluding responsibility, the verdict and the judgment shall so state.

4.04. Mental Disease or Defect Excluding Fitness to Proceed

No person who as a result of mental disease or defect lacks capacity to understand the proceedings against him or to assist in his own defense shall be tried, convicted or sentenced for the commission of an offense so long as such incapacity endures.

§4.05. Psychiatric Examination of Defendant with Respect to Mental Disease or Defect

1. Whenever the defendant has filed a notice of intention to rely on the defense of mental disease or defect excluding responsibility, or there is reason to doubt his fitness to proceed, or reason to believe that mental disease or defect of the defendant will otherwise become an issue in the cause, the Court shall appoint at lease one qualified psychiatrist or shall request the Superintendent of the _____ Hospital to designate at least one qualified psychiatrist, which designation may be or include himself, to examine and report upon the mental condition of the defendant. The Court may order the defendant to be committed to a hospital or other suitable facility for the purpose of the examination for a period of not exceeding sixty days or such longer period as the Court determines to be necessary for the purpose and may direct that a qualified psychiatrist retained by the defendant be permitted to witness and participate in the examination.

2. In such examination any method may be employed which is accepted by the medical profession for the examination of those alleged to be suffering from mental disease or defect.

3. The report of the examination shall include the following:
   a. a description of the nature of the examination;
   b. a diagnosis of the mental condition of the defendant;
   c. if the defendant suffers from a mental disease or defect, an opinion as to his capacity to understand the proceedings against him and to assist in his own defense;
   d. when a notice of intention to rely on the defense of irresponsibility has been filed, an opinion as to the extent, if any, to which the capacity of the defendant to appreciate the [wrongfulness] of his conduct or to conform his conduct to the requirements of law was impaired at the time of the criminal conduct charged; and
   e. when directed by the Court, an opinion as to the capacity of the defendant to have aparticular state of mind which is an element of the offense charged. If the examination cannot be conducted by reason of the unwillingness of the defendant to participate therein, the report shall so state and shall include, if possible, an opinion as to whether such unwillingness of the defendant was the result of mental disease or defect.

The report of the examination shall be filed [in triplicate] with the clerk of the Court, who shall cause copies to be delivered to the district attorney and to counsel for the defendant.

§4.08. Legal Effect of Acquittal on the Ground of Mental Disease or Defect Excluding Responsibility; Commitment; Release or Discharge

1. When a defendant is acquitted on the ground of mental disease or defect excluding responsibility, the Court shall order him to be committed to the custody of the Commissioner of Mental Hygiene [Public Health] to be placed in an appropriate institution for custody, care and treatment.

2. If the Commissioner of Mental Hygiene [Public Health] is of the view that a person committed to his custody, pursuant to paragraph (1) of this Section, may be discharged or released on condition without danger to himself or to others, he shall make application for the discharge or release of such person in a report to the Court by which such person was committed and shall transmit a copy of such application and report to the prosecuting attorney of the county [parish] from which the defendant was committed. The Court shall thereupon appoint at least two qualified psychiatrists to examine such person and to report within sixty days, or such longer period as the Court determines to be necessary for the purpose, their opinion as to his mental condition. To facilitate such examination and the proceedings thereon, the Court may cause such person to be confined in any institution located near the place where the Court sits, which may hereafter be designated by the Commissioner of Mental Hygiene [Public Health] as suitable for the temporary detention of irresponsible persons.

3. If the Court is satisfied by the report filed pursuant to paragraph (2) of this Section and such testimony of the reporting psychiatrists as the Court deems necessary that the committed person may be discharged or released on condition without danger to himself or others, the Court shall order his discharge or his release on such conditions as the Court determines to be necessary. If the Court is not so satisfied, it shall promptly order a hearing to determine whether such person may safely be discharged or released. Any such hearing shall be deemed a civil proceeding and the burden shall be upon the committed person to prove that he may

safely be discharged or released. According to the determination of the Court upon the hearing, the committed person shall thereupon be discharged or released on such conditions as the Court determines to be necessary, or shall be recommitted to the custody of the Commissioner of Mental Hygiene [Public Health], subject to discharge or release only in accordance with the procedure prescribed above for a first hearing.

4. If, within [five] years after the conditional release of a committed person, the Court shall determine, after hearing evidence, that the conditions of release have not been fulfilled and that for the safety of such person or for the safety of others his conditional release should be revoked, the Court shall forthwith order him to be recommitted to the Commissioner of Mental Hygiene [Public Health], subject to discharge or release only in accordance with the procedure prescribed above for a first hearing.

5. A committed person may make application for his discharge or release to the Court by which he was committed, and the procedure to be followed upon such application shall be the same as that prescribed above in the case of an application by the Commissioner of Mental Hygiene [Public Health]. However, no such application by a committed person need be considered until he has been confined for a period of not less than [six months] from the date of the order of commitment, and if the determination of the Court be adverse to the application, such person shall not be permitted to file a further application until [one year] has elapsed from the date of any preceding hearing on an application for his release or discharge.

§4.09. Statements for Purposes of Examination or Treatment Inadmissible Except on Issue of Mental Condition

A statement made by a person subjected to psychiatric examination or treatment pursuant to Sections 05, 4.06 or 4.08 for purposes of such examination or treatment shall not be admissible in evidence against him in any criminal proceeding on any issue other than that of his mental condition but it shall be admissible upon that issue, whether or not it would otherwise be deemed a privileged communication [, unless such statement constitutes an admission of guilt of the crime charged].

§4.10. Immaturity Excluding Criminal Conviction; Transfer of Proceedings to Juvenile Court

1. A person shall not be tried for or convicted of an offense if:
   a. at the time of the conduct charged to constitute the offense he was less than sixteen years of age [, in which case the Juvenile Court shall have exclusive jurisdiction]; or
   b. at the time of the conduct charged to constitute the offense he was sixteen or seventeen years of age, unless:
      i. the Juvenile Court has no jurisdiction over him, or,
      ii. the Juvenile Court has entered an order waiving jurisdiction and consenting to the institution of criminal proceedings against him.

2. No court shall have jurisdiction to try or convict a person of an offense if criminal proceedings against him are barred by Subsection (1) of this Section. When it appears that a person charged with the commission of an offense may be of such an age that criminal proceedings may be barred under Subsection (1) of this Section, the Court shall hold a hearing thereon, and the burden shall be on the prosecution to establish to the satisfaction of the Court that the criminal proceeding is not barred upon such grounds. If the Court determines that the proceeding is barred, custody of the person charged shall be surrendered to the Juvenile Court, and the case, including all papers and processes relating thereto, shall be transferred.

Article 5. Inchoate Crimes

§5.01. Criminal Attempt

1. *Definition of Attempt.* A person is guilty of an attempt to commit a crime if, acting with the kind of culpability otherwise required for commission of the crime, he:
   a. purposely engages in conduct which would constitute the crime if the attendant circumstances were as he believes them to be; or
   b. when causing a particular result is an element of the crime, does or omits to do anything with the purpose of causing or with the belief that it will cause such result without further conduct on his part; or
   c. purposely does or omits to do anything which, under the circumstances as he believes them to be, is an act or omission constituting a substantial step in a course of conduct planned to culminate in his commission of the crime.

2. *Conduct Which May Be Held Substantial Step Under Subsection (1)(c).* Conduct shall not be held to constitute a substantial step under Subsection (1)(c) of this Section unless it is strongly corroborative of the actor's criminal purpose. Without negativing the sufficiency of other conduct, the following, if strongly corroborative of the actor's criminal purpose, shall not be held insufficient as a matter of law:

a. lying in wait, searching for or following the contemplated victim of the crime;

b. enticing or seeking to entice the contemplated victim of the crime to go to the place contemplated for its commission;

c. reconnoitering the place contemplated for the commission of the crime;

d. unlawful entry of a structure, vehicle or enclosure in which it is contemplated that the crime will be committed;

e. possession of materials to be employed in the commission of the crime, which are specially designed for such unlawful use or which can serve no lawful purpose of the actor under the circumstances;

f. possession, collection or fabrication of materials to be employed in the commission of the crime, at or near the place contemplated for its commission, where such possession, collection or fabrication serves no lawful purpose of the actor under the circumstances;

g. soliciting an innocent agent to engage in conduct constituting an element of the crime.

3. *Conduct Designed to Aid Another in Commission of a Crime.*   A person who engages in conduct designed to aid another to commit a crime which would establish his complicity under Section 2.06 if the crime were committed by such other person, is guilty of an attempt to commit the crime, although the crime is not committed or attempted by such other person.

4. *Renunciation of Criminal Purpose.*   When the actor's conduct would otherwise constitute an attempt under Subsection (1)(b) or (1)(c) of this Section, it is an affirmative defense that he abandoned his effort to commit the crime or otherwise prevented its commission, under circumstances manifesting a complete and voluntary renunciation of his criminal purpose. The establishment of such defense does not, however, affect the liability of an accomplice who did not join in such abandonment or prevention.

Within the meaning of this Article, renunciation of criminal purpose is not voluntary if it is motivated, in whole or in part, by circumstances, not present or apparent at the inception of the actor's course of conduct, which increase the probability of detection or apprehension or which make more difficult the accomplishment of the criminal purpose. Renunciation is not complete if it is motivated by a decision to postpone the criminal conduct until a more advantageous time or to transfer the criminal effort to another but similar objective or victim.

§5.02. Criminal Solicitation

1. *Definition of Solicitation.*   A person is guilty of solicitation to commit a crime if with the purpose of promoting or facilitating its commission he commands, encourages or requests another person to engage in specific conduct which would constitute such crime or an attempt to commit such crime or which would establish him complicity in its commission or attempted commission.

2. *Uncommunicated Solicitation.*   It is immaterial under Subsection (1) of this Section that the actor fails to communicate with the person he solicits to commit a crime if his conduct was designed to effect such communication.

3. *Renunciation of Criminal Purpose.*   It is an affirmative defense that the actor, after soliciting another person to commit a crime, persuaded him not to do so or otherwise prevented the commission of the crime, under circumstances manifesting a complete and voluntary renunciation of his criminal purpose.

§5.03. Criminal Conspiracy

1. *Definition of Conspiracy.*   A person is guilty of conspiracy with another person or persons to commit a crime if with the purpose of promoting or facilitating its commission he:

   a. agrees with such other person or persons that they or one of more of them will engage in conduct which constitutes such crime or an attempt or solicitation to commit such crime; or

   b. agrees to aid such other person or persons in the planning or commission of such crime or of an attempt or solicitation to commit such crime.

2. *Scope of Conspiratorial Relationship.*   If a person guilty of conspiracy, as defined by Subsection (1) of this Section, knows that a person with whom he conspires to commit a crime has conspired with another person or persons to commit the same crime, he is guilty of conspiring with such other person or persons, whether or not he knows their identity, to commit such crime.

3. *Conspiracy With Multiple Criminal Objectives.*   If a person conspires to commit a number of crimes, he is guilty of only one conspiracy so long as such multiple crimes are the object of the same agreement or continuous conspiratorial relationship.

4. *Joinder and Venue in Conspiracy Prosecutions.*

   a. Subject to the provisions of paragraph (b) of this Subsection, two or more persons charged with criminal conspiracy may be prosecuted jointly if:

      i. they are charged with conspiring with one another; or

      ii. the conspiracies alleged, whether they have the same or different parties, are so related that they constitute different aspects of a scheme or organized criminal conduct.

b. In any joint prosecution under paragraph (a) of this Subsection:

    i. no defendant shall be charged with a conspiracy in any county [parish or district] other than one in which he entered into such conspiracy or in which an overt act pursuant to such conspiracy was done by him or by a person with whom he conspired; and

    ii. neither the liability of any defendant nor the admissibility against him of evidence of acts or declarations of another shall be enlarged by such joinder; and

    iii. the Court shall order a severance or take a special verdict as to any defendant who so requests, if it deems it necessary or appropriate to promote the fair determination of his guilt or innocence, and shall take any other proper measures to protect the fairness of the trial.

5. *Overt Act.* No person may be convicted of conspiracy to commit a crime, other than a felony of the first or second degree, unless an overt act in pursuance of such conspiracy is alleged and proved to have been done by him or by a person with whom he conspired.

6. *Renunciation of Criminal Purpose.* It is an affirmative defense that the actor, after conspiring to commit a crime, thwarted the success of the conspiracy, under circumstances manifesting a complete and voluntary renunciation of his criminal purpose.

7. *Duration of Conspiracy.* For purposes of Section 1.06 (4):

a. conspiracy is a continuing course of conduct which terminates when the crime or crimes which are its object are committed or the agreement that they be committed is abandoned by the defendant and by those with whom he conspired; and

b. such abandonment is presumed if neither the defendant nor anyone with whom he conspired does any overt act in pursuance of the conspiracy during the applicable period of limitation; and

c. if an individual abandons the agreement, the conspiracy is terminated as to him only if and when he advises those with whom he conspired of his abandonment or he informs the law enforcement authorities of the existence of the conspiracy and of his participation therein.

§5.04. Incapacity, Irresponsibility or Immunity of Party to Solicitation or Conspiracy

1. Except as provided in Subsection (2) of this Section, it is immaterial to the liability of a person who solicits or conspires with another to commit a crime that:

a. he or the person whom he solicits or with whom he conspires does not occupy a particular position or have a particular characteristic which is an element of such crime, if he believes that one of them does; or

b. the person whom he solicits or with whom he conspires is irresponsible or has an immunity to prosecution or conviction for the commission of the crime.

2. It is a defense to a charge of solicitation or conspiracy to commit a crime that if the criminal object were achieved, the actor would not be guilty of a crime under the law defining the offense or as an accomplice under Section 2.06 (5) or 2.06 (6)(a) or (b).

§5.05. Grading of Criminal Attempt, Solicitation and Conspiracy; Mitigation in Cases of Lesser Danger; Multiple Convictions Barred

1. *Grading.* Except as otherwise provided in this Section, attempt, solicitation and conspiracy are crimes of the same grade and degree as the most serious offense which is attempted or solicited or is an object of the conspiracy. An attempt, solicitation or conspiracy to commit a [capital crime or a] felony of the first degree is a felony of the second degree.

2. *Mitigation.* If the particular conduct charged to constitute a criminal attempt, solicitation or conspiracy is so inherently unlikely to result or culminate in the commission of a crime that neither such conduct nor the actor presents a public danger warranting the grading of such offense under this Section, the Court shall exercise its power under Section 6.12 to enter judgment and impose sentence for a crime of lower grade or degree or, in extreme cases, may dismiss the prosecution.

3. *Multiple Convictions.* A person may not be convicted of more that one offense defined by this Article for conduct designed to commit or to culminate in the commission of the same crime.

§5.06. Possessing Instruments of Crime; Weapons

1. *Criminal Instruments Generally.* A person commits a misdemeanor if he possesses any instrument of crime with purpose to employ it criminally. "Instrument of crime" means:

a. anything specially made or specially adapted [sic] for criminal use; or

b. anything commonly used for criminal purposes and possessed by the actor under circumstances which do not negative unlawful purpose.

2. *Presumption of Criminal Purpose from Possession of Weapon.* If a person possesses a firearm or other weapon on or about his person, in a vehicle occupied by him, or otherwise readily available for use, it shall be presumed that he had the purpose to employ it criminally, unless:
   a. the weapon is possessed in the actor's home or place of business;
   b. the actor is licensed or otherwise authorized by law to possess such weapon; or
   c. the weapon is of type commonly used in lawful sport.

"Weapon" means anything readily capable of lethal use and possessed under circumstances not manifestly appropriate for lawful uses which it may have; the term included a firearm which is not loaded or lacks a clip or other component to render it immediately operable, and components which can readily be assembled into a weapon.

3. *Presumptions as to Possession of Criminal Instruments in Automobiles.* Where a weapon or other instrument of crime is found in an automobile, it is presumed to be in the possession of the occupant if there is but one. If there is more than one occupant, it shall be presumed to be in the possession of all, except under the following circumstances:
   a. where it is found upon the person of one of the occupants;
   b. where the automobile is not a stolen one and the weapon or instrument is found out of view in a glove compartment, car trunk, or other enclosed customary depository, in which case it shall be presumed to be in the possession of the occupant or occupants who own or have authority to operate the automobile;
   c. in the case of a taxicab, a weapon or instrument found in the passenger's portion of the vehicle shall be presumed to be in the possession of all the passengers, if there are any, and, if not, in the possession of the driver.

§5.07. *Prohibited Offensive Weapons*

A person commits a misdemeanor if, except as authorized by law, he makes, repairs, sells, or otherwise deals in, uses or possesses any offensive weapon. "Offensive weapon" means any bomb, machine gun, sawed-off shotgun, firearm specially made or specially adapted for concealment or silent discharge, any blackjack, sandbag, metal knuckles, dagger, or other implement for the infliction of serious bodily injury which serves no common lawful purpose. It is a defense under this Section for the defendant to prove by a preponderance of evidence that he possessed or dealt with the weapon solely as a curio or in a dramatic performance, or that he possessed it briefly in consequence of having found it or taken it from an aggressor, or under circumstances similarly negativing any purpose or likelihood that the weapon would be used unlawfully. The presumptions provided in Section 5.06(3) are applicable to prosecutions under this Section.

PART II: Definition of Specific Crimes Offenses Involving Danger to The Person

Article 210. Criminal Homicide

§210.0. *Definitions*

In Articles 210–213, unless a different meaning plainly is required:

1. "human being" means a person who has been born and is alive;
2. "bodily injury" means physical pain, illness or any impairment of physical condition;
3. "serious bodily injury" means bodily injury which creates a substantial risk of death or which causes serious, permanent disfigurement, or protracted loss or impairment of the function of any bodily member or organ;
4. "deadly weapon" means any firearm, or other weapon, device, instrument, material or substance, whether animate or inanimate, which in the manner it is used or is intended to be used is known to be capable of producing death or serious bodily injury.

§210.1. *Criminal Homicide*

1. A person is guilty of criminal homicide if he purposely, knowingly, recklessly or negligently causes the death of another human being.
2. Criminal homicide is murder, manslaughter, or negligent homicide.

§210.2. *Murder*

1. Except as provided in Section 210.3(1)(b), criminal homicide constitutes murder when:
   a. it is committed purposely or knowingly; or
   b. it is committed recklessly under circumstances manifesting extreme indifference to the value of human life. Such recklessness and indifference are presumed if the actor is engaged or is an accomplice in the commission of, or an attempt to commit, or flight after committing, or attempting to commit

robbery, rape or deviate sexual intercourse by force or threat of force, arson, burglary, kidnapping or felonious escape.

2. Murder is a felony of the first degree [but a person convicted of murder may be sentenced to death, as provided in Section 210.6].

§210.3. Manslaughter

1. Criminal homicide constitutes manslaughter when:
   a. it is committed recklessly; or
   b. a homicide which would otherwise be murder is committed under the influence of extreme mental or emotional disturbance for which there is a reasonable explanation or excuse. The reasonableness of such explanation or excuse shall be determined from the viewpoint of a person in the actor's situation under the circumstances as he believes them to be.

2. Manslaughter is a felony of the second degree.

§210.4. Negligent Homicide

1. Criminal homicide constitutes negligent homicide when it is committed negligently.

2. Negligent homicide is a felony of the third degree.

§210.5. Causing or Aiding Suicide

1. *Causing Suicide as a Criminal Homicide.* A person may be convicted of criminal homicide for causing another to commit suicide only if he purposely causes such suicide by force, duress or deception.

2. *Aiding or Soliciting Suicide as an Independent Offense.* A person who purposely aids or solicits another to commit suicides is guilty of a felony of the second degree if his conduct causes such suicide or an attempted suicide, and otherwise of a misdemeanor.

§210.6. Sentence of Death for Murder; Further Proceedings to Determine Sentence

1. *Death Sentence Excluded.* When a defendant is found guilty of murder, the Court shall impose sentence for a felony of the first degree if it is satisfied that:
   a. none of the aggravation circumstances enumerated in Subsection (3) of this Section was established by the evidence at the trial or will be established if further proceedings are initiated under Subsection (2) of this Section; or
   b. substantial mitigating circumstances, established by the evidence at the trial, call for leniency; or
   c. the defendant, with the consent of the prosecuting attorney and the approval of the Court, pleaded guilty to murder as a felony of the first degree; or

   d. the defendant was under 18 years of age at the time of the commission of the crime; or
   e. the defendant's physical or mental condition calls for leniency; or
   f. although the evidence suffices to sustain the verdict, it does not foreclose all doubt respecting the defendant's guilt.

2. *Determination by Court or by Court and Jury.* Unless the Court imposes sentence under Subsection (1) of this Section, it shall conduct a separate proceeding to determine whether the defendant should be sentenced for a felony of the first degree or sentenced to death. The proceeding shall be conducted before the Court alone if the defendant was convicted by a Court sitting without a jury or upon his plea of guilty or if the prosecuting attorney and the defendant waive a jury with respect to sentence. In other cases it shall be conducted before the Court sitting with the jury which determined the defendant's guilt or, if the Court for good cause shown discharges that jury, with a new jury empaneled for the purpose.

   In the proceeding, evidence may be presented as to any matter that the Court deems relevant to sentence, including but not limited to the nature and circumstances of the crime, the defendant's character, background, history, mental and physical condition and any of the aggravating or mitigating circumstances enumerated in Subsections (3) and (4) of this Section. Any such evidence not legally privileged, which the Court deems to have probative force, may be received, regardless of its admissibility under the exclusionary rules of evidence, provided that the defendant's counsel is accorded a fair opportunity to rebut any hearsay statements. The prosecuting attorney and the defendant or his counsel shall be permitted to present argument for or against sentence of death.

   The determination whether sentence of death shall be imposed shall be in the discretion of the Court, except that when the proceeding is conducted before the Court sitting with a jury, the Court shall not impose sentence of death unless it submits to the jury the issue whether the defendant should be sentenced to death or to imprisonment and the jury returns a verdict that the sentence should be death. If the jury is unable to reach a unanimous verdict, the Court shall dismiss the jury and impose sentence for a felony of the first degree.

   The Court, in exercising its discretion as to sentence, and the jury, in determining upon its verdict, shall take into account the aggravating and mitigating circumstances enumerated in Subsections (3) and (4) and any other facts that it deems relevant, but it shall not impose or recommend sentence of death unless it finds one of the aggravating circumstances enumerated in Subsection (3) and further finds that there are no mitigating circumstances sufficiently substantial to call for leniency. When the issue is submitted to the jury, the Court shall so instruct and also shall inform the jury of the nature of the sentence of imprisonment that may be imposed, including its implication with respect to possible release upon parole, if the jury verdict is against sentence of death.

Alternative formulation of Subsection (2)

1. *Determination by Court.* Unless the Court imposes sentence under Subsection (1) of this Section, it shall conduct a separate proceeding to determine whether the defendant should be sentenced for a felony of the first degree or sentenced to death. In the proceeding, the Court, in accordance with Section 7.07, shall consider the report of the presentence investigation and, if a psychiatric examination has been ordered, the report of such examination. In addition, evidence may be presented as to any matter that the Court deems relevant to sentence, including but not limited to the nature and circumstances of the crime, the defendant's character, background, history, mental and physical condition and any of the aggravating or mitigating circumstances enumerated in Subsections (3) and (4) of this Section. Any such evidence not legally privileged, which the Court deems to have probative force, may be received, regardless of its admissibility under the exclusionary rules of evidence, provided that the defendant's counsel is accorded a fair opportunity to rebut any hearsay statements. The prosecuting attorney and the defendant or his counsel shall be permitted to present argument for or against sentence of death.

   The determination whether sentence of death shall be imposed shall be in the discretion of the Court. In exercising such discretion, the Court shall take into account the aggravating and mitigating circumstances enumerated in Subsections (3) and (4) and any other facts that it deems relevant but shall not impose sentence of death unless it finds one of the aggravating circumstances enumerated in Subsection (3) and further finds that there are no mitigating circumstances sufficiently substantial to call for leniency.

2. *Aggravating Circumstances.*
   a. The murder was committed by a convict under sentence of imprisonment.
   b. The defendant was previously convicted of another murder or of a felony involving the use or threat of violence to the person.
   c. At the time the murder was committed the defendant also committed another murder.
   d. The defendant knowingly created a great risk of death to many persons.
   e. The murder was committed while the defendant was engaged or was an accomplice in the commission of, or an attempt to commit, or flight after committing or attempting to commit robbery, rape or deviate sexual intercourse by force or threat of force, arson, burglary or kidnapping.
   f. The murder was committed for the purpose of avoiding or preventing a lawful arrest or effecting an escape from lawful custody.
   g. The murder was committed for pecuniary gain.
   h. The murder was especially heinous, atrocious or cruel, manifesting exceptional depravity.

3. *Mitigating Circumstances.*
   a. The defendant has no significant history of prior criminal activity.
   b. The murder was committed while the defendant was under the influence of extreme mental or emotional disturbance.
   c. The victim was a participant in the defendant's homicidal conduct or consented to the homicidal act.
   d. The murder was committed under circumstances which the defendant believed to provide a moral justification or extenuation for his conduct.
   e. The defendant was an accomplice in a murder committed by another person and his participation in the homicidal act was relatively minor.
   f. The defendant acted under duress or under the domination of another person.
   g. At the time of the murder, the capacity of the defendant to appreciate the criminality [wrongfulness] of his conduct or to conform his conduct to the requirements of law was impaired as a result of mental disease or defect or intoxication.
   h. The youth of the defendant at the time of the crime.

Article 211. Assault; Reckless Endangering; Threats

§211.0. Definitions

In this Article, the definitions given in Section 210.0 apply unless a different meaning plainly is required.

§211.1. Assault

1. *Simple Assault.* A person is guilty of assault if he:
   a. attempts to cause or purposely, knowingly or recklessly causes bodily injury to another; or
   b. negligently causes bodily injury to another with a deadly weapon; or
   c. attempts by physical menace to put another in fear of imminent serious bodily injury.

   Simple assault is a misdemeanor unless committed in a fight or scuffle entered into by mutual consent, in which case it is a petty misdemeanor.

2. *Aggravated Assault.* A person is guilty of aggravated assault if he:
   a. attempts to cause serious bodily injury to another, or causes such injury purposely, knowingly or recklessly under circumstances manifesting extreme indifference to the value of human life; or
   b. attempts to cause or purposely or knowingly causes bodily injury to another with a deadly weapon.

   Aggravated assault under paragraph (a) is a felony of the second degree; aggravated assault under paragraph (b) is a felony of the third degree.

§211.2. Recklessly Endangering Another Person

A person commits a misdemeanor if he recklessly engages in conduct which places or may place another person in danger of death or serious bodily injury. Recklessness and danger shall be presumed where a person knowingly points a firearm at or in the direction of another, whether or not the actor believed the firearm to be loaded.

§211.3. Terroristic Threats

A person is guilty of a felony of the third degree if he threatens to commit any crime of violence with purpose to terrorize another or to cause evacuation of a building, place of assembly, or facility of public transportation, or otherwise to cause serious public inconvenience, or in reckless disregard of the risk of causing such terror or inconvenience.

Article 212. Kidnapping and Related Offenses; Coercion

§212.0. Definitions

In this Article, the definitions given in section 210.0 apply unless a different meaning plainly is required.

§ 212.1. Kidnapping

A person is guilty of kidnapping if he unlawfully removes another from his place of residence or business, or a substantial distance from the vicinity where he is found, or if he unlawfully confines another for a substantial period in a place of isolation, with any of the following purposes:

a. to hold for ransom or reward, or as a shield or hostage; or

b. to facilitate commission of any felony or flight thereafter; or

c. to inflict bodily injury on or to terrorize the victim or another; or

d. to interfere with the performance of any governmental or political function.

Kidnapping is a felony of the first degree unless the actor voluntarily releases the victim alive and in a safe place prior to trial, in which case it is a felony of the second degree. A removal or confinement is unlawful within the meaning of this Section if it is accomplished by force, threat or deception, or, in the case of a person who is under the age of 14 or incompetent, if it is accomplished without the consent of a parent, guardian or other person responsible for general supervision of his welfare.

§ 212.2 Felonious Restraint

A person commits a felony of the third degree if he knowingly:

a. restrains another unlawfully in circumstances exposing him to risk of serious bodily injury; or

b. holds another in a condition of involuntary servitude.

§ 212.3. False Imprisonment

A person commits a misdemeanor if he knowingly restrains another unlawfully so as to interfere substantially with his liberty.

§ 212.4. Interference with Custody

1. *Custody of Children.* A person commits an offense if he knowingly or recklessly takes or entices any child under the age of 18 from the custody of its parent, guardian or other lawful custodian, when he has no privilege to do so. It is an affirmative defense that:
   a. the actor believed that his action was necessary to preserve the child from danger to its welfare; or
   b. the child, being at the time not less than 14 years old, was taken away at its own instigation without enticement and without purpose to commit a criminal offense with or against the child.

   Proof that the child was below the critical age gives rise to a presumption that the actor knew the child's age or acted in reckless disregard thereof. The offense is a misdemeanor unless the actor, not being a parent or person in equivalent relation to the child, acted with knowledge that his conduct would cause serious alarm for the child's safety, or in reckless disregard of a likelihood of causing such alarm, in which case the offense is a felony of the third degree.

2. *Custody of Committed Persons.* A person is guilty of a misdemeanor if he knowingly or recklessly takes or entices any committed person away from lawful custody when he is not privileged to do so. "Committed person" means, in addition to anyone committed

under juvenile warrant, any orphan, neglected or delinquent child, mentally defective or insane person, or other dependent or incompetent person entrusted to another's custody by or through a recognized social agency or otherwise by authority of law.

§ 212.5. Criminal Coercion

1. *Offense Defined.*   A person is guilty of criminal coercion if, with purpose unlawfully to restrict another's freedom of action to his detriment, he threatens to:
   a. commit any criminal offense; or
   b. accuse anyone of a criminal offense; or
   c. expose any secret tending to subject any person to hatred, contempt or ridicule, or to impair his credit or business repute; or
   d. take or withhold action as an official, or cause an official to take or withhold action.

   It is an affirmative defense to prosecution based on paragraphs (b), (c) or (d) that the actor believed the accusation or secret to be true or the proposed official action justified and that his purpose was limited to compelling the other to behave in a way reasonably related to the circumstances which were the subject of the accusation, exposure or proposed official action, as by desisting from further misbehavior, making good a wrong done, refraining from taking any action or responsibility for which the actor believes the other disqualified.

2. *Grading.*   Criminal coercion is a misdemeanor unless the threat is to commit a felony or the actor's purpose is felonious, in which cases the offense is a felony of the third degree.

Article 213. Sexual Offenses

§213.0. Definitions

In this Article, unless a different meaning plainly is required:

1. the definitions given in Section 210.0 apply;
2. "sexual intercourse" includes intercourse per os or per anum, with some penetration however slight; emission is not required;
3. "deviate sexual intercourse" means sexual intercourse per os or per anum between human beings who are not husband and wife, and any form of sexual intercourse with an animal.

§213.1. Rape and Related Offenses

1. *Rape.*   A male who has sexual intercourse with a female not his wife is guilty of rape if:
   a. he compels her to submit by force or by threat of imminent death, serious bodily injury, extreme pain or kidnapping, to be inflicted on anyone; or

   b. he has substantially impaired her power to appraise or control her conduct by administering or employing without her knowledge drugs, intoxicants or other means for the purpose of preventing resistance; or
   c. the female is unconscious; or
   d. the female is less than 10 years old.

   Rape is a felony of the second degree unless
   i. in the course thereof the actor inflicts serious bodily injury upon anyone, or
   ii. the victim was not a voluntary social companion of the actor upon the occasion of the crime and had not previously permitted him sexual liberties, in which cases the offenses is a felony of the first degree.

2. *Gross Sexual Imposition.*   A male who has intercourse with a female not his wife commits a felony of the third degree if:
   a. he compels her to submit by any threat that would prevent resistance by a woman of ordinary resolution; or
   b. he knows that she suffers from a mental disease or defect which renders her incapable of appraising the nature of her conduct; or
   c. he knows that she is unaware that a sexual act is being committed upon her or that she submits because she mistakenly supposes that he is her husband.

§213.2. Deviate Sexual Intercourse by Force or Imposition

1. *By Force or Its Equivalent.*   A person who engages in deviate sexual intercourse with another person, or who causes another to engage in deviate sexual intercourse, commits a felony of the second degree if:
   a. he compels the other person to participate by force or by threat of imminent death, serious bodily injury, extreme pain or kidnapping, to be inflicted on anyone; or
   b. he has substantially impaired the other person's power to appraise or control his conduct, by administering or employing without the knowledge of the other person drugs, intoxicants or other means for the purpose of preventing resistance; or
   c. the other person is unconscious; or
   d. the other person is less than 10 years old.

2. *By Other Imposition.*   A person who engages in deviate sexual intercourse with another person, or who causes another to engage in deviate sexual intercourse, commits a felony of the third degree if:
   a. he compels the other person to participate by any threat that would prevent resistance by a person of ordinary resolution; or

b. he knows that the other person suffers from a mental disease or defect which renders him incapable of appraising the nature of his conduct; or

c. he knows that the other person submits because he is unaware that a sexual act is being committed upon him.

§213.3. Corruption of Minors and Seduction

1. *Offense Defined.* A male who has sexual intercourse with a female not his wife, or any person who engages in deviate sexual intercourse or causes another to engage in deviate sexual intercourse, is guilty of an offense if:

   a. the other person is less than [16] years old and the actor is at least [4] years older than the other person; or

   b. the other person is less than 21 years old and the actor is his guardian or otherwise responsible for general supervision of his welfare; or

   c. the other person is in custody of law or detained in a hospital or other institution and the actor has supervisory or disciplinary authority over him; or

   d. the other person is a female who is induced to participate by a promise of marriage which the actor does not mean to perform.

2. *Grading.* An offense under paragraph (a) of Subsection (1) is a felony of the third degree. Otherwise an offense under this section is a misdemeanor.

§213.4. Sexual Assault

A person who has sexual contact with another not his spouse, or causes such other to have sexual contact with him, is guilty of sexual assault, a misdemeanor, if:

1. he knows that the conduct is offensive to the other person; or

2. he knows that the other person suffers from a mental disease or defect which renders him or her incapable of appraising the nature of his or her conduct; or

3. he knows that the other person is unaware that a sexual act is being committed; or

4. the other person is less than 10 years old; or

5. he has substantially impaired the other person's power to appraise or control his or her conduct, by administering or employing without the other's knowledge drugs, intoxicants or other means for the purpose of preventing resistance; or

6. the other person is less than [16] years old and the actor is at least [4] years older than the other person; or

7. the other person is less than 21 years old and the actor is his guardian or otherwise responsible for general supervision of his welfare; or

8. the other person is in custody of law or detained in a hospital or other institution and the actor has supervisory or disciplinary authority over him.

   Sexual contact is any touching of the sexual or other intimate parts of the person for the purpose of arousal or gratifying sexual desire.

§213.5. Indecent Exposure

A person commits a misdemeanor if, for the purpose of arousing or gratifying sexual desire of himself or of any person other than his spouse, he exposes his genitals under circumstances in which he knows his conduct is likely to cause affront or alarm.

§213.6. Provisions Generally Applicable to Article 213

1. *Mistake as to Age.* Whenever in this Article the criminality of conduct depends on a child's begin below the age of 10, it is no defense that the actor did not know the child's age, or reasonably believed the child to be older than 10. When criminality depends on the child's being below a critical age other than 10, it is a defense for the actor to prove by a preponderance of the evidence that he reasonably believed the child to be above the critical age.

2. *Spouse Relationships.* Whenever in this Article the definition of an offense excludes conduct with a spouse, the exclusion shall be deemed to extend to persons living as man and wife, regardless of the legal status of their relationship. The exclusion shall be inoperative as respects spouses living apart under a decree of judicial separation. Where the definition of an offense excludes conduct with a spouse or conduct by a woman, this shall not preclude conviction of a spouse or woman as accomplice in a sexual act which he or she causes another person, not within the exclusion, to perform.

3. *Sexually Promiscuous Complainants.* It is a defense to prosecution under Section 213.3, and paragraphs (6), (7) and (8) of Section 213.4 for the actor to prove by a preponderance of the evidence that the alleged victim had, prior to the time of the offense charged, engaged promiscuously in sexual relations with others.

4. *Prompt Complaint.* No prosecution may be instituted or maintained under this Article unless the alleged offense was brought to the notice of public authority within [3] months of its occurrence or, where the alleged victim was less than [16] years old or otherwise incompetent to make complaint, within [3] months after a parent, guardian or other competent person specially interested in the victim learns of the offense.

5. *Testimony of Complainants.* No person shall be convicted of any felony under this Article upon the uncorroborated testimony of the alleged victim. Corroboration may be circumstantial. In any prosecution before a jury for an offense under this Article,

the jury shall be instructed to evaluate the testimony of a victim or complaining witness with special care in view of the emotional involvement of the witness and the difficulty of determining the truth with respect to alleged sexual activities carried out in private.

Offenses Against Property Article 220. Arson, Criminal Mischief, and Other Property Destruction

§220.1. Arson and Related Offenses

1. *Arson.*   A person is guilty of arson, a felony of the second degree, if he starts a fire or causes an explosion with the purpose of:
   a. destroying a building or occupied structure of another; or
   b. destroying or damaging any property, whether his own or another's to collect insurance for such loss. It shall be an affirmative defense to prosecution under this paragraph that the actor's conduct did not recklessly endanger any building or occupied structure of another or place any other person in danger of death or bodily injury.

2. *Reckless Burning or Exploding.*   A person commits a felony of the third degree if he purposely starts a fire or causes an explosion, whether on his own property or another's, and thereby recklessly:
   a. places another person in danger of death or bodily injury; or
   b. places a building or occupied structure of another in danger of damage or destruction.

3. *Failure to Control or Report Dangerous Fire.*   A person who knows that a fire is endangering life or a substantial amount of property of another and fails to take reasonable measures to put out or control the fire, when he can do so without substantial risk to himself, or to give a prompt fire alarm, commits a misdemeanor if:
   a. he knows that he is under an official, contractual, or other legal duty to prevent or combat the fire; or
   b. the fire was started, albeit lawfully, by him or with his assent, or on property in his custody or control.

4. *Definitions.*   "Occupied structure" means any structure, vehicle or place adapted for overnight accommodation or persons, or for carrying on business therein, whether or not a person is actually present. Property is that of another, for the purposes of this section, if anyone other than the actor has a possessory or proprietary interest therein. If a building or structure is divided into separately occupied units, any unit not occupied by the actor is an occupied structure of another.

§220.2. Causing or Risking Catastrophe

1. *Causing Catastrophe.*   A person who causes a catastrophe by explosion, fire, flood, avalanche, collapse of building, release of poison gas, radioactive material or other harmful or destructive force or substance, or by any other means of causing potentially widespread injury or damage, commits a felony of the second degree if he does so purposely or knowingly, or a felony of the third degree if he does so recklessly.

2. *Risking Catastrophe.*   A person is guilty of a misdemeanor if he recklessly creates a risk of catastrophe in the employment of fire, explosives or other dangerous means listed in Subsection (1).

3. *Failure to Prevent Catastrophe.*   A person who knowingly or recklessly fails to take reasonable measures to prevent or mitigate a catastrophe commits a misdemeanor if:
   a. he knows that he is under an official, contractual or other legal duty to take such measures; or
   b. he did or assented to the act causing or threatening the catastrophe.

§220.3. Criminal Mischief

1. *Offense Defined.*   A person is guilty of criminal mischief if he:
   a. damages tangible property of another purposely, recklessly, or by negligence in the employment of fire, explosives, or other dangerous means listed in Section 220.2(1); or
   b. purposely or recklessly tampers with tangible property of another so as to endanger person or property; or
   c. purposely or recklessly causes another to suffer pecuniary loss by deception or threat.

2. *Grading.*   Criminal mischief is a felony of the third degree if the actor purposely causes pecuniary loss in excess of $5,000 or a substantial interruption or impairment of public communication, transportation, supply of water, gas or power, or other public service. It is a misdemeanor if the actor purposely causes pecuniary loss in excess of $100, or a petty misdemeanor if he purposely or recklessly causes pecuniary loss in excess of $25. Otherwise criminal mischief is a violation.

Article 221. Burglary and Other Criminal Intrusion

§221.0. Definitions

In this Article, unless a different meaning plainly is required:

1. "occupied structure" means any structure, vehicle or place adapted for overnight accommodation of

persons, or for carrying on business therein, whether or not a person is actually present.

2. "night" means the period between thirty minutes past sunset and thirty minutes before sunrise.

§221.1. Burglary

1. *Burglary Defined.* A person is guilty of burglary if he enters a building or occupied structure, or separately secured or occupied portion thereof, with purpose to commit a crime therein, unless the premises are at the time open to the public or the actor is licensed or privileged to enter. It is an affirmative defense to prosecution for burglary that the building or structure was abandoned.

2. *Grading.* Burglary is a felony of the second degree if it is perpetrated in the dwelling of another at night, or if, in the course of committing the offense, the actor:
   a. purposely, knowingly or recklessly inflicts or attempts to inflict bodily injury on anyone; or
   b. is armed with explosives or a deadly weapon.
   An act shall be deemed "in the course of committing" an offense if it occurs in an attempt to commit the offense or in flight after the attempt or commission.

3. *Multiple Convictions.* A person may not be convicted both for burglary and for the offense which it was his purpose to commit after the burglarious entry or for an attempt to commit that offense, unless the additional offense constitutes a felony of the first or second degree.

§221.2. Criminal Trespass

1. *Buildings and Occupied Structures.* A person commits an offense if, knowing that he is not licensed or privileged to do so, he enters or surreptitiously remains in any building or occupied structure, or separately secured or occupied portion thereof. An offense under this Subsection is a misdemeanor if it is committed in a dwelling at night. Otherwise it is a petty misdemeanor.

2. *Defiant Trespasser.* A person commits an offense if, knowing that he is not licensed or privileged to do so, he enters or remains in any place as to which notice against trespass is given by:
   a. actual communication to the actor; or
   b. posting in a manner prescribed by law or reasonably likely to come to the attention of intruders; or
   c. fencing or other enclosure manifestly designed to exclude intruders. An offense under this Subsection constitutes a petty misdemeanor if the offender defies an order to leave personally communicated to him by the owner of the premises or other authorized person. Otherwise it is a violation.

3. *Defenses.* It is an affirmative defense to prosecution under this Section that:
   a. a building or occupied structure involved in an offense under Subsection (1) was abandoned; or
   b. the premises were at the time open to members of the public and the actor complied with all lawful conditions imposed on access to or remaining in the premises; or
   c. the actor reasonably believed that the owner of the premises, or other person empowered to license access thereto, would have licensed him to enter or remain.

Article 222. Robbery

§222.1. Robbery

1. *Robbery Defined.* A person is guilty of robbery if, in the course of committing a theft, he:
   a. inflicts serious bodily injury upon another; or
   b. threatens another with or purposely puts him in fear of immediate serious bodily injury; or
   c. commits or threatens immediately to commit any felony of the first or second degree.
   An act shall be deemed "in the course of committing a theft" if it occurs in an attempt to commit theft or in flight after the attempt or commission.

2. *Grading.* Robbery is a felony of the second degree, except that it is a felony of the first degree if in the course of committing the theft the actor attempts to kill anyone, or purposely inflicts or attempts to inflict serious bodily injury.

Article 223. Theft and Related Offenses

§223.0. Definitions

In this Article, unless a different meaning plainly is required:

1. "deprive" means:
   a. to withhold property of another permanently or for so extended a period as to appropriate a major portion of its economic value, or with intent to restore only upon payment of reward or other compensation; or
   b. to dispose of the property so as to make it unlikely that the owner will recover it.

2. "financial institution" means a bank, insurance company, credit union, building and loan association, investment trust or other organization held out to the public as a place of deposit of funds or medium savings or collective investment.

3. "government" means the United States, any State, county, municipality, or other political unit, or any de-

partment, agency or subdivision of any of the foregoing, or any corporation or other association carrying out the functions of government.

4. "movable property" means property the location of which can be changed, including things growing on, affixed to, or found in land, and documents although the rights represented thereby have no physical location. "Immovable property" is all other property.

5. "obtain" means:
   a. in relation to property, to bring about a transfer or purported transfer of a legal interest in the property, whether to the obtainer or another; or
   b. in relation to labor or service, to secure performance thereof.

6. "property" means anything of value, including real estate, tangible and intangible personal property, contract rights, choses-in-action and other interests in or claims to wealth, admission or transportation tickets, captured or domestic animals, food and drink, electric or other power.

7. "property of another" includes property in which any person other than the actor has an interest which the actor is not privileged to infringe, regardless of the fact that the actor also has an interest in the property and regardless of the fact that the other person might be precluded from civil recovery because the property was used in an unlawful transactions or was subject to forfeiture as contraband. Property in possession of the actor shall not be deemed property of another who has only a security interest therein, even if legal title is in the creditor pursuant to a conditional sales contract or other security agreement.

§223.1. Consolidation of Theft Offenses; Grading; Provisions Applicable to Theft Generally

1. *Consolidation of Theft Offenses.* Conduct denominated theft in this Article constitutes a single offense. An accusation of theft may be supported by evidence that it was committed in any manner that would be theft under this Article, notwithstanding the specification of a different manner in the indictment or information, subject only to the power of the Court to ensure fair trial by granting a continuance or other appropriate relief where the conduct of the defense would be prejudiced by lack of fair notice or by surprise.

2. *Grading of Theft Offenses.*
   a. Theft constitutes a felony of the third degree if the amount involved exceeds $500, or if the property stolen is a firearm, automobile, airplane, motorcycle, motorboat or other motor-propelled vehicle, or in the case of theft by receiving stolen property, if the receiver is in the business of buying or selling stolen property.

   b. Theft not within the preceding paragraph constitutes a misdemeanor, except that if the property was not taken from the person or by threat, or in breach of a fiduciary obligation, and the actor proves by a preponderance of the evidence that the amount involved was less than $50, the offense constitutes a petty misdemeanor.

   c. The amount involved in a theft shall be deemed to be the highest value, by any reasonable standard, of the property or services which the actor stole or attempted to steal. Amounts involved in thefts committed pursuant to one scheme or course of conduct, whether from the same person or several persons, may be aggregated in determining the grade or the offense.

3. *Claim of Right.* It is an affirmative defense to prosecution for theft that the actor:
   a. was unaware that the property or service was that of another; or
   b. acted under an honest claim of right to the property or service involved or that he had a right to acquire or dispose of it as he did; or
   c. took property exposed for sale, intending to purchase and pay for it promptly, or reasonably believing that the owner, if present, would have consented.

4. *Theft from Spouse.* It is no defense that theft was from the actor's spouse, except that misappropriation of household and personal effects, or other property normally accessible to both spouses, is theft only if it occurs after the parties have ceased living together.

§223.2. Theft by Unlawful Taking or Disposition

1. *Movable Property.* A person is guilty of theft if he unlawfully takes, or exercises unlawful control over, movable property of another with purpose to deprive him thereof.

2. *Immovable Property.* A person is guilty of theft if he unlawfully transfers immovable property of another or any interest therein with purpose to benefit himself or another not entitled thereto.

§223.3. Theft by Deception

A person is guilty of theft if he purposely obtains property of another by deception. A person deceives if he purposely:

1. creates or reinforces a false impression, including false impression as to law, value, intention or other state of mind; but deception as to a person's intentions to perform a promise shall not be inferred from the fact alone that he did not subsequently perform the promise; or

2. prevents another from acquiring information which would affect his judgment of a transaction; or

3. fails to correct a false impression which the deceiver previously created or reinforced, or which the deceiver knows to be influencing another to whom he stands in a fiduciary or confidential relationship; or

4. fails to disclose a known lien, adverse claim or other legal impediment to the enjoyment of property which he transfers or encumbers in consideration for the property obtained, whether such impediment is or is not valid, or is or is not a matter of official record.

The term "deceive" does not, however, include falsity as to matters having no pecuniary significance, or puffing by statements unlikely to deceive ordinary persons in the group addressed.

§223.4. Theft by Extortion

A person is guilty of theft if he obtains property of another by threatening to;

1. inflict bodily injury on anyone or commit any other criminal offense; or

2. accuse anyone of a criminal offense; or

3. expose any secret tending to subject any person to hatred, contempt or ridicule, or to impair his credit or business repute; or

4. take or withhold action as an official, or cause an official to take or withhold action; or

5. bring about or continue a strike, boycott or other collective unofficial action, if the property is not demanded or received for the benefits of the group in whose interest the actor purports to act; or

6. testify or provide information or withhold testimony or information with respect to another's legal claim or defense; or

7. inflict any other harm which would not benefit the actor.

It is an affirmative defense to prosecution based on paragraphs (2), (3) or (4) that the property obtained by threat of accusation, exposure, lawsuit or other invocation of official action was honestly claimed as restitution or indemnification for harm down in the circumstances to which such accusation, exposure, lawsuit or other official action relates, or as compensation for property or lawful services.

§223.5. Theft of Property Lost, Mislaid, or Delivered by Mistake

A person who comes into control of property of another that he knows to have been lost, mislaid, or delivered under a mistake as to the nature or amount of the property or the identity of the recipient is guilty of theft if, with purpose to deprive the owner thereof, he fails to take reasonable measures to restore the property to a person entitled to have it.

§223.6. Receiving Stolen Property

1. *Receiving.* A person is guilty of theft if he purposely receives, retains, or disposes of moveable property of another knowing that it has been stolen, or believing that it has probably been stolen, unless the property is received, retained, or disposed with purpose to restore it to the owner. "Receiving" means acquiring possession, control or title, or lending on the security of the property.

2. *Presumption of Knowledge.* The requisite knowledge or belief is presumed in the case of a dealer who:

   a. is found in possession or control of property stolen from two or more persons on separate occasions; or

   b. has received stolen property in another transaction within the year preceding the transaction charged; or

   c. being a dealer in property of the sort received, acquires it for a consideration which he knows is far below its reasonable value.

   "Dealer" means a person in the business of buying or selling goods including a pawnbroker.

§223.7. Theft of Services

1. A person is guilty of theft if he purposely obtains services which he knows are available only for compensation, by deception or threat, or by false token or other means to avoid payment for the service. "Services" include labor, professional service, transportation, telephone or other public service, accommodation in hotels, restaurants or elsewhere, admission to exhibitions, use of vehicles or other movable property. Where compensation for service is ordinarily paid immediately upon the rendering for such service, as is the case of hotels and restaurants, refusal to pay or absconding without payment or offer to pay gives rise to a presumption that the service was obtained by deception as to intention to pay.

2. A person commits theft if, having control over the disposition of service, of others, to which he is not entitled, he knowingly diverts such services to his own benefit or to the benefit of another not entitled thereto.

§223.8. Theft by Failure to Make Required Disposition of Funds Received

A person who purposely obtains property upon agreement, or subject to a known legal obligation, to make specified payment or other disposition, whether from such property or its proceeds or from his own property to be reserved in equivalent amount, is guilty of theft if he deals with the property obtained as his own and fails to make the required payment or disposition. The foregoing applies notwithstanding that it may be impossible to identify particular property as belonging to the victim at the time of the actor's failure to make the required payment or disposition. An officer or employee of the government or of a financial institution is presumed:

1. to know any legal obligation relevant to his criminal liability under this Section, and
2. to have dealt with the property as his own if he fails to pay or account upon lawful demand, or if an audit reveals a shortage or falsification of accounts.

Article 224. Forgery and Fraudulent Practices

§224.0. Definitions

In this Article, the definitions given in Section 223.0 apply unless a different meaning plainly is required.

§224.1. Forgery

1. *Definition.*   A person is guilty of forgery if, with purpose to defraud or injure anyone, or with knowledge that he is facilitating a fraud or injury to be perpetrated by anyone, the actor:
   a. alters any writing of another without his authority; or
   b. makes, completes, executes, authenticates, issues or transfers any writing so that it purports to be the act of another who did not authorize that act, or to have been executed at a time or place or in a numbered sequence other than was in fact the case, or to be a copy of an original when no such original existed; or
   c. utters any writing which he knows to be forged in a manner specified in paragraphs (a) or (b).
       "Writing" includes printing or any other method of recording information, money, coins, tokens, stamps, seals, credit cards, badges, trademarks, and other symbols of value, right, privilege, or identification.
2. *Grading.*   Forgery is a felony of the second degree if the writing is or purports to be part of an issue of money, securities, postage or revenue stamps, or other instruments issued by the government, or part of an issue of stock, bonds or other instruments representing interest in or claims against any property or enterprise. Forgery is a felony of the third degree if the writing is or purports to be a will, deed, contract, release, commercial instrument, or other document evi-

dencing, creating, transferring, altering, terminating, or otherwise affecting legal relations. Otherwise forgery is a misdemeanor.

§224.5. Bad Checks

A person who issues or passes a check or similar sight order for the payment of money, knowing that it will not be honored by the drawee, commits a misdemeanor. For the purposes of this Section as well as in any prosecution for theft committed by means of a bad check, an issuer is presumed to know that the check or order (other than a postdated check or order) would not be paid, if:

1. the issuer had no account with the drawee at the time the check or order was issued; or
2. payment was refused by the drawee for lack of funds, upon presentation within 30 days after issue, and the issuer failed to make good within 10 days after receiving notice of that refusal.

§224.8. Commercial Bribery and Breach of Duty to Act Disinterestedly

1. A person commits a misdemeanor if he solicits, accepts or agrees to accept any benefit as consideration for knowingly violating or agreeing to violate a duty of fidelity to which he is subject as:
   a. partner, agent or employee of another;
   b. trustee, guardian, or other fiduciary;
   c. lawyer, physician, accountant, appraiser, or other professional adviser or informant;
   d. officer, director, manager or other participant in the direction of the affairs of an incorporated or unincorporated association; or
   e. arbitrator or other purportedly disinterested adjudicator or referee.
2. A person who holds himself out to the public as being engaged in the business of making disinterested selection, appraisal, or criticism of commodities or services commits a misdemeanor if he solicits, accepts or agrees to accept any benefit to influence his selection, appraisal or criticism.
3. A person commits a misdemeanor if he confers, or offers or agrees to confer, any benefit the acceptance of which would be criminal under this Section.

Offenses Against the Family Article 230. Offenses Against the Family

§230.1. Bigamy and Polygamy

1. *Bigamy.*   A married person is guilty of bigamy, a misdemeanor, if he contracts or purports to contract

another marriage, unless at the time of the subsequent marriage:

  a. the actor believes that the prior spouse is dead; or
  b. the actor and the prior spouse have been living apart for five consecutive years throughout which the prior spouse was not known by the actor to be alive; or
  c. a Court has entered a judgment purporting to terminate or annul any prior disqualifying marriage, and the actor does not know that judgment to be invalid; or
  d. the actor reasonably believes that he is legally eligible to remarry.

2. *Polygamy.*   A person is guilty of polygamy, a felony of the third degree, if he marries or cohabits with more than one spouse at a time in purported exercise of the right of plural marriage. The offense is a continuing one until all cohabitation and claim of marriage with more than one spouse terminates. This Sections does not apply to parties to a polygamous marriage, lawful in the country of which they are residents or nationals, while they are in transit through or temporarily visiting this State.

3. *Other Party to Bigamous or Polygamous Marriage.*   A person is guilty of bigamy or polygamy, as the case may be, if he contracts or purports to contract marriage with another knowing that the other is thereby committing bigamy or polygamy.

§230.2. Incest

A person is guilty of incest, a felony of the third degree, if he knowingly marries or cohabits or has sexual intercourse with an ancestor or descendant, a brother or sister of whole or half blood [or an uncle, aunt, nephew or niece of whole blood]. "Cohabit" means to live together under the representation or appearance of being married. The relationships referred to herein include blood relationships without regard to legitimacy, and relationship of parent and child by adoption.

§230.4. Endangering Welfare of Children

A parent, guardian, or other person supervising the welfare of a child under 18 commits a misdemeanor if he knowingly endangers the child's welfare by violating a duty of care, protection or support.

§230.5. Persistent Non-Support

A person commits a misdemeanor if he persistently fails to provide support which he can provide and which he knows he is legally obliged to provide to a spouse, child or other dependent.

Offenses Against Public Administration
Article 240. Bribery and Corrupt Influence

§240.0. Definitions

In Articles 240–243, unless a different meaning plainly is required:

1. "benefit" means gain or advantage, or anything regarded by the beneficiary as gain or advantage, including benefit to any other person or entity in whose welfare he is interested, but not an advantage promised generally to a group or class of voters as a consequence of public measures which a candidate engages to support or oppose;

2. "government" includes any branch, subdivision or agency of the government of the State or any locality within it;

3. "harm" means loss, disadvantage or injury, or anything so regarded by the person affected, including loss, disadvantage or injury to any other person or entity in whose welfare he is interested;

4. "official proceeding" means a proceeding heard or which may be heard before any legislative, judicial, administrative or other governmental agency or official authorized to take evidence under oath, including any referee, hearing examiner, commissioner, notary or other person taking testimony or deposition in connection with any such proceeding;

5. "party official" means a person who holds an elective or appointive post in a political party in the United States by virtue of which he directs or conducts, or participates in directing or conducting party affairs at any level of responsibility;

6. "pecuniary benefit" is benefit in the form of money, property, commercial interests or anything else the primary significance of which is economic gain;

7. "public servant" means any officer or employee of government, including legislators and judges, and any person participating as juror, advisor, consultant or otherwise, in performing a governmental function; but the term does not include witnesses;

8. "administrative proceeding" means any proceeding, other than a judicial proceeding, the outcome of which is required to be based on a record or documentation prescribed by law, or in which law or regulation is particularized in application to individuals.

§240.1. Bribery in Official and Political Matters

A person is guilty of bribery, a felony of the third degree, if he offers, confers or agrees to confer upon another, or solicits, accepts or agrees to accept from another:

1. any pecuniary benefit as consideration for the recipient's decision, opinion, recommendation, vote or other exercise of discretion as a public servant, party official or voter; or

2. any benefit as consideration for the recipient's decision, vote, recommendation or other exercise of official discretion in a judicial or administrative proceeding; or

3. any benefit as consideration for a violation of a known legal duty as public servant or party official.
    It is no defense to prosecution under this section that a person whom the actor sought to influence was not qualified to act in the desired way whether because he had not yet assumed office, or lacked jurisdiction, or for any other reason.

§240.2. Threats and Other Improper Influence in Official and Political Matters

1. *Offenses Defined.*   A person commits an offense if he:
    a. threatens unlawful harm to any person with purpose to influence his decision, opinion, recommendation, vote or other exercise of discretion as a public servant, party official or voter; or
    b. threatens harm to any public servant with purpose to influence his decision, opinion, recommendation, vote or pecuniary benefit as consideration for exerting special influence upon a public servant or procuring another to do so. "Special influence" means power to influence through kinship, friendship or other relationship, apart from the merits of the transaction.

2. Paying for Endorsement or Special Influence. A person commits a misdemeanor if he offers, confers or agrees to confer any pecuniary benefit receipt of which is prohibited by this Section.

Article 241. Perjury and Other Falsification in Official Matters

§241.0. Definitions

In this Article, unless a different meaning plainly is required:

1. the definitions given in Section 240.0 apply; and

2. "statement" means any representation, but includes a representation of opinion, belief or other state of mind only if the representation clearly relates to state of mind apart from or in addition to any facts which are the subject of the representation.

§241.1. Perjury

1. *Offense Defined.*   A person is guilty of perjury, a felony of the third degree, if in any official proceeding he makes a false statement under oath or equivalent affirmation, or swears or affirms the truth of a statement previously made, when the statement is material and he does not believe it to be true.

2. *Materiality.*   Falsification is material, regardless of the admissibility of the statement under rules of evidence, if it could have affected the course or outcome of the proceeding. It is no defense that the declarant mistakenly believed the falsification to be immaterial. Whether a falsification is material in a given factual situation is a question of law.

3. *Irregularities No Defense.*   It is not a defense to prosecution under this Section that the oath or affirmation was administered or taken in an irregular manner or that the declarant was not competent to make the statement. A document purporting to be made upon oath or affirmation at any time when the actor presents it as being so verified shall be deemed to have been duly sworn or affirmed.

4. *Retraction.*   No person shall be guilty of an offense under this Section if he retracted the falsification in the course of the proceeding in which it was made before it became manifest that the falsification substantially affected the proceeding.

5. *Inconsistent Statements.*   Where the defendant made inconsistent statements under oath or equivalent affirmation, both having been made within the period of the statute of limitations, the prosecution may proceed by setting forth the inconsistent statements in a single count alleging in the alternative that one or the other was false and not believed by the defendant. In such case it shall not be necessary for the prosecution to prove which statement was false but only that one or the other was false and not believed by the defendant to be true.

6. *Corroboration.*   No person shall be convicted of an offense under the Section where proof of falsity rests solely upon contradiction by testimony of a single person other than the defendant.

§241.2. False Swearing

1. *False Swearing in Official Matters.*   A person who makes a false statement under oath or equivalent affirmation, or swears or affirms the truth of such a statement previously made, when he does not

believe the statement to be true, is guilty of a misdemeanor if:

a. the falsification occurs in an official proceeding; or

b. the falsification is intended to mislead a public servant in performing his official function.

Offenses Against Public Order and Decency Article 250. Riot, Disorderly Conduct, and Related Offenses

§250.1. Riot; Failure to Disperse

1. *Riot.* A person is guilty of riot, a felony of the third degree, if he participates with [two] or more others in a course of disorderly conduct:

   a. with purpose to commit or facilitate the commission of a felony or misdemeanor;

   b. with purpose to prevent or coerce official action; or

   c. when the actor or any other participant to the knowledge of the actor uses or plans to use a firearm or other deadly weapon.

2. *Failure of Disorderly Persons to Disperse Upon Official Order.* Where [three] or more persons are participating in a course of disorderly conduct likely to cause substantial harm or serious inconvenience, annoyance or alarm, a peace officer or other public servant engaged in executing or enforcing the law may order the participants and others in the immediate vicinity to disperse. A person who refuses or knowingly fails to obey such an order commits a misdemeanor.

§250.2. Disorderly Conduct

1. *Offense Defined.* A person is guilty of disorderly conduct if, with purpose to cause public inconvenience, annoyance or alarm, or recklessly creating a risk thereof, he:

   a. engages in fighting or threatening, or in violent or tumultuous behavior; or

   b. makes unreasonable noise or offensively coarse utterance, gesture or display, or addresses abusive language to any person present; or

   c. creates a hazardous or physically offensive condition by any act which serves no legitimate purpose of the actor.

   "Public" means affecting or likely to affect persons in a place to which the public or a substantial group has access; among the places included are highways, transport facilities, schools, prisons, apartment houses, places of business or amusement, or any neighborhood.

2. *Grading.* An offense under this section is a petty misdemeanor if the actor's purpose is to cause substantial harm or serious inconvenience, or if he persists in disorderly conduct after reasonable warning or request to desist. Otherwise disorderly conduct is a violation.

§250.4. Harassment

A person commits a petty misdemeanor if, with purpose to harass another, he:

1. makes a telephone call without purpose of legitimate communication; or

2. insults, taunts or challenges another in a manner likely to provoke violent or disorderly response; or

3. makes repeated communications anonymously or at extremely inconvenient hours, or in offensively coarse language; or

4. subjects another to an offensive touching; or

5. engages in any other course of alarming conduct serving no legitimate purpose of the actor.

§250.5. Public Drunkenness; Drug Incapacitation

A person is guilty of an offense if he appears in any public place manifestly under the influence of alcohol, narcotics or other drugs, not therapeutically administered, to the degree that he may endanger himself or other persons or property, or annoy persons in his vicinity. An offense under this Section constitutes a petty misdemeanor if the actor has been convicted hereunder twice before within a period of one year. Otherwise the offense constitutes a violation.

§250.6. Loitering or Prowling

A person commits a violation if he loiters or prowls in a place, at a time, or in a manner not usual for law-abiding individuals under circumstances that warrant alarm for the safety of persons or property in the vicinity. Among the circumstances which may be considered in determining whether such alarm is warranted is the fact that the actor takes flight upon appearance of a peace officer, refuses to identify himself, or manifestly endeavors to conceal himself or any object. Unless flight by the actor or other circumstances makes it impracticable, a peace officer shall prior to any arrest for an offense under this Section afford the actor an opportunity to dispel any alarm which would otherwise be warranted, by requesting him to identify himself and explain his presence and conduct. No person shall be convicted of an offense under this Section if the peace officer did not comply with the preceding sentence, or if it appears at trial that the explanation given by the actor was true and, if believed by the peace officer at the time, would have dispelled the alarm.

Article 251. Public Indecency

§251.1. Open Lewdness

A person commits a petty misdemeanor if he does any lewd act which he knows is likely to be observed by others who would be affronted or alarmed.

1. *Prostitution.* A person is guilty of prostitution, a petty misdemeanor, if he or she:
   a. is an inmate of a house of prostitution or otherwise engages in sexual activity as a business; or
   b. loiters in or within view of any public place for the purpose of being hired to engage in sexual activity.
   "Sexual activity" includes homosexual and other deviate sexual relations. A "house of prostitution" is any place where prostitution or promotion of prostitution is regularly carried on by one person under the control, management or supervision of another. An "inmate" is a person who engages in prostitution in or through the agency of a house of prostitution. "Public place" means any place to which the public or any substantial group thereof has access.
2. *Promoting Prostitution.* A person who knowingly promotes prostitution of another commits a misdemeanor or felony as provided in Subsection (3). The following acts shall, without limitation of the foregoing, constitute promoting prostitution:
   a. owning, controlling, managing, supervising or otherwise keeping, alone or in association with others, a house of prostitution or a prostitution business; or
   b. procuring an inmate for a house of prostitution or a place in a house of prostitution for one who would be an inmate; or
   c. encouraging, inducing, or otherwise purposely causing another to become or remain a prostitute; or
   d. soliciting a person to patronize a prostitute; or
   e. procuring a prostitute for a patron; or
   f. transporting a person into or within this state with purpose to promote that person's engaging in prostitution, or procuring or paying for transportation with that purpose; or
   g. leasing or otherwise permitting a place controlled by the actor, alone or in association with others, to be regularly used for prostitution or the promotion of prostitution, or failure to make reasonable effort to abate such use by ejecting the tenant, notifying law enforcement authorities, or other legally available means; or
   h. soliciting, receiving, or agreeing to receive any benefit for doing or agreeing to do anythingforbidden by this Subsection.

3. *Grading of Offenses Under Subsection (2).* An offense under Subsection (2) constitutes a felony of the third degree if:
   a. the offense falls within paragraph (a), (b) or (c) of Subsection (2); or
   b. the actor compels another to engage in or promote prostitution; or
   c. the actor promotes prostitution of a child under 16, whether or not he is aware of the child's age; or
   d. the actor promotes prostitution of his wife, child, ward or any person for whose care, protection or support he is responsible.
   Otherwise the offense is a misdemeanor.
4. *Presumption from Living off Prostitutes.* A person, other than the prostitute or the prostitute's minor child or other legal dependent incapable of self-support, who is supported in whole or substantial part by the proceeds of prostitution is presumed to be knowingly promoting prostitution in violation of Subsection (2).
5. *Patronizing Prostitutes.* A person commits a violation if he hires a prostitute to engage in sexual activity with him, or if he enters or remains in a house of prostitution for the purpose of engaging in sexual activity.
6. *Evidence.* On the issue whether a place is a house of prostitution the following shall be admissible evidence; its general repute; the repute of the persons who reside in or frequent the place; the frequency, timing and duration of visits by non-residents. Testimony of a person against his spouse shall be admissible to prove offenses under this Section.

§251.3. Loitering to Solicit Deviate Sexual Relations

A person is guilty of a petty misdemeanor if he loiters in or near any public place for the purpose of soliciting or being solicited to engage in deviate sexual relations.

§251.4. Obscenity

1. *Obscene Defined.* Material is obscene if, considered as a whole, its predominant appeal is to prurient interest, that is, a shameful or morbid interest, in nudity, sex or excretion, and if in addition it goes substantially beyond customary limits of candor in describing or representing such matters. Predominant appeal shall be judged with reference to ordinary adults unless it appears from the character of the material or the circumstances of its dissemination to be designed for children or other specially susceptible audience. Undeveloped photographs, molds, printing plates, and the like, shall be deemed obscene notwithstanding that processing or other acts may be required to make the obscenity patent or to disseminate it.

2. *Offenses.* Subject to the affirmative defense provided in Subsection (3), a person commits a misdemeanor if he knowingly or recklessly:

a. sells, delivers or provides, or offers or agrees to sell, deliver or provide, any obscene writing, picture, record or other representation or embodiment of the obscene; or

b. presents or directs an obscene play, dance or performance, or participates in that portion thereof which makes it obscene; or

c. publishes, exhibits or otherwise makes available any obscene material; or

d. possesses any obscene material for purposes of sale or other commercial dissemination;or

e. sells, advertises or otherwise commercially disseminates material, whether or not obscene, by representing or suggesting that it is obscene.

A person who disseminates or possesses obscene material in the course of his business is presumed to do so knowingly or recklessly.

3. *Justifiable and Non-Commercial Private Dissemination.* It is an affirmative defense to prosecution under this Section that dissemination was restricted to:

a. institutions or persons having scientific, educational, governmental or other similarjustification for possessing obscene material; or

b. non-commercial dissemination to personal associates of the actor.

4. *Evidence; Adjudication of Obscenity.* In any prosecution under this Section, evidence shall be admissible to show:

a. the character of the audience for which the material was designed or to which it was directed;

b. what the predominant appeal of the material would be for ordinary adults or any special audience to which it was directed, and what effect, if any, it would probably have on conduct of such people;

c. artistic, literary, scientific, educational or other merits or the material;

d. the degree of public acceptance of the material in the United States;

e. appeal to prurient interest, or absence thereof, in advertising or other promotion of the material; and

f. the good repute of the author, creator, publisher or other person from whom the material originated.

Expert testimony and testimony of the author, creator, publisher or other person from whom the material originated, relating to factors entering into the determination of the issue of obscenity, shall be admissible. The Court shall dismiss a prosecution for obscenity if it is satisfied that the material is not obscene.

Glossary

A

Accessory after the fact: One who helped a principal party escape or hide from justice

Accessory before the fact: One who helped a principal party plan to commit a crime, but who was not present during its commission

Acquit: On the part of a jury, to find the defendant not guilty at trial

Actual innocence: A defendant's claim that to be "actually innocent" of a crime for which he or she has been convicted

Actual possession: Exercising dominion and control over contraband

Actus reus: A wrongful act; criminal responsibility attaches when *actus reus* combines with a guilty mind (*mens rea*)

Administrative regulation: Rules and guidelines enacted to fulfill the legislature's broad grant of authority to fulfill the administrative agency's public mission

Admissible evidence: Evidence that the judge has decided may be told or shown to the jury

Admission: Acknowledgment by the suspect or defendant that he or she did commit one or more elements of the crime

Affidavit: Written and sworn document signed under the pains and penalties of perjury

Affirm: An appellate court's decision to uphold a lower court's decision

Affirmative defense: A defense raised that, if successfully presented, may lead to a reduction or complete negation of criminal liability, such as intoxication, insanity, or alibi

Aggravated assault and battery: Assault that an offender commits while in the commission of another crime or against a victim who is a member of a protected class, such as a child, a law enforcement officer, or a prison employee

Aggravating circumstances: Those factors making the crime unusually heinous and perhaps warranting a more severe punishment

Alibi: A defense which states that the defendant could not have committed the crime because he or she was at a location other than the scene of the crime when the crime was committed

***Alford* plea:** A plea in which the defendant does not admit that he or she is guilty of the crime charged, but admits that the government has sufficient evidence to sustain a conviction should the defendant elect to go to trial

Allocution: Formal dialogue between the court and the defendant at three specific times in the trial process: 1. when it is necessary to establish the legal sufficiency of a guilty plea; 2. when it is necessary to establish the defendant's competency and willingness to defend himself at trial; and 3. when the defendant exercises his right to address the court before sentence is imposed

AMBER alert system: Nationwide system using media outlets to alert the public that a child has been abducted

Anonymous tip: Information about a crime that has occurred or may soon occur, delivered to law enforcement by a person who does not reveal his or her identity. Standing alone, an anonymous tip is insufficient to establish probable cause; if the anonymous information is corroborated with independent evidence, the tip may be considered part of the probable cause determination

Antitrust action: A lawsuit brought against a company thought to be fixing prices for commodities and eliminating market competition

Appellate court: A higher court that reviews a lower court's proceedings

Arson: The malicious and unlawful burning of structures and/or property

Assault: In general, an aggressive action that places the victim in fear of an imminent battery; certain specific physical attacks are also defined as assaults

Assumption of the duty: Undertaking a course of action on behalf of someone else, such as a bystander helping an accident victim

Attempt: An intent to commit a crime, and an act taken to commit the crime, without the crime having been completed

Automobile search: A search by law enforcement officers of a private vehicle for contraband. There is a lesser expectation of privacy in automobiles than in homes, because automobiles run on public streets and are subject to registration and inspection requirements

B

Bail: Collateral (cash, property, assets) pledged before trial, usually by a suspect's family or friends, to secure the suspect's release and ensure his or her attendance at trial

Bailee: One who has a fiduciary (caretaking) responsibility by contract to care for the property belonging to another

Bailor: One who owns property and hires another to care for it

Battered woman syndrome: A subset of self-defense; a collection of symptoms caused by a repeated cycle of physical abuse that causes the victim to live in constant fear of being beaten, maimed, or killed

Battery: Intentional and unconsented touching that is harmful or offensive to the person being touched

Beyond a reasonable doubt: The legal standard at a criminal trial by which the prosecution has to prove each and every element of the crime to establish the defendant's guilt

Border searches: A type of warrantless search. People entering the country at the borders have a lesser expectation of privacy because no one has an absolute right to enter the country

Bribery: The offering, receiving, or soliciting of any thing of value to influence official action or the discharge of a legal or public duty

Burden of persuasion: The burden of convincing the trier of fact (judge or jury) that the legal claim or defense is valid

Burden of production: The burden of introducing a legally sufficient quantum of evidence to permit the trier of fact (judge or jury) to consider the issue or defense during their deliberations

Burden of proof: The prosecution's obligation to introduce enough evidence to overcome the presumption (belief) that the defendant is innocent

Burglary: Breaking and entering into a structure with the intent to commit a felony once inside. The breaking may be achieved though fraud and deceit, rather than by physical force

C

Capital punishment: Government-sanctioned homicide as a punishment for the crime of first-degree murder

Case brief: Process of organizing information from a case law

Causation: The action of causing or producing harm

Charge bargaining: The practice of dropping the more serious charges against a defendant in exchange for a defendant's guilty plea to a lesser charge

Charge conference: A meeting during which the lawyers for both sides submit proposed jury instructions to the judge on the basis of the evidence introduced at trial

Charging decision: The decision by the prosecutor about what charges, if any, to bring against a defendant

Chilling effect: The impact of vague or overbroad laws that repress free speech rights by making people fear criminal reprisal for the content of their speech

Circumstantial evidence: Indirect evidence from which the jury must infer (conclude) that the defendant is guilty as charged

Clean Air Act (CAA): Legislation that sets goals and standards for the quality and purity of U.S. air

Clean Water Act (CWA): Legislation that set goals and standards for the quality and purity of U.S. water

Clear and present danger: A risk posed to public safety by certain speech or conduct; the government has the legal authority to suppress such speech and conduct

Closed containers: Any bags, luggage, tupperware containers, purses, briefcases, or other items that are closed and may be searched for contraband and evidence under certain circumstances

Closing argument: The prosecutor and defense counsels' final arguments to the jury to persuade the jury to find in their favor; arguments by counsel are not evidence

Collateral order doctrine: An exception that allows appeals from a final judgment

Collective knowledge: At the time of a search or seizure, all information known to all law enforcement and shared with officers on the scene

Color of law: Government action that occurs under the cloak of legal authority. A "color of law" claim alleges that a government official misused his or her power while acting in an official capacity

Commerce Clause: Article I, section 8, clause 3 of the Constitution, conferring jurisdiction upon the federal government to prosecute crimes when the alleged criminal activity substantially affects interstate commerce

Common enterprise: The legal doctrine holding all occupants in a vehicle liable for all contraband found and seized inside

Common law: Judge-made law based on societal custom and tradition

Competency: The ability to understand the nature of the trial proceedings and to assist defense counsel in the preparation of the case for trial, required of defendants at all stages of the criminal proceeding

Comprehensive Environmental Response, Compensation, and Liability Act (CERCLA): Commonly known as "Superfund," a law that requires the cleanup of toxic waste sites and assigns costs for their cleanup

Concurrence: The simultaneous presence of two or more conditions. The concurrence of *mens rea* and *actus reus* generates criminal liability for an offense

Concurrent jurisdiction: Simultaneous federal and state power to hear a case, even though only one sovereign (government) typically prosecutes the case

Conditional plea: A guilty plea entered on the "condition" that the defendant preserves certain issues on appeal, such as the legality of the judge's ruling on the suppression of evidence

Confession: A statement by which the suspect or defendant accepts full responsibility for the crime charged

Confrontation Clause: The Sixth Amendment of the Constitution, which gives defendants the right to see, hear, and confront (cross-examine) all witnesses against them in open court

Consent: An individual's voluntary grant of authority for police to search an area over which that person has dominion and control; alternatively, a defense based on the victim's willing participation in the crime

Constructive possession: A set of circumstances from which a jury could infer that an offender had dominion and control over contraband, even if it was not in his or her physical possession

Conversion: Illegally making another person's property one's own without the initial intent to steal; for example, using another's lawn mower as one's own, keeping found property without any attempt to return it to its rightful owner, or holding out to the public another's property as one's own, such as taking care of another's dog but claiming ownership of the animal

Copyright: A right granted by statute to the creator of a literary or artistic work for a limited period to publish or copy the work

Corpus delicti: The body of the crime; in a murder, for example, the corpus delicti is the murdered person's body

Crimes against morality: Crimes that offend society's collective sense of morality, such as prostitution, gambling, and drug and alcohol offenses (not including drunk driving)

Criminal mischief: Defacing property, including damaging the integrity of the property

Curtilage: The area immediately surrounding a structure in which a resident retains an expectation of privacy

Custodial interrogation: A session during which a suspect is not free to leave the police presence and is subject to questioning designed to elicit incriminating information. Police are required to give *Miranda* warnings prior to beginning custodial interrogation

Custody: A situation in which a suspect perceives that he or she is not free to leave, even if not formally under arrest

D

Deadly-weapon doctrine: A standard which allows a jury to infer that the defendant had the specific intent to kill if he or she used a deadly weapon during the commission of a crime

Defense of others: A defense that a defendant may claim if he or she came to the aid of another in peril and if self-defense would be justified on the part of the person in peril

Deliberations: After all evidence has been presented and all arguments have been delivered by counsel, the decision-making process in which the jury engages to determine whether or not the accused is innocent

Delusion: A false fixed belief; commonly held by mentally ill offenders who are paranoid

Demonstrative evidence: Illustrative evidence, such as a map, diagram, photograph, or model used to help the jury understand the witness's testimony

Determinate sentencing: A sentence imposed for a fixed period of time that cannot be shortened by probation or parole

Deterrence: Punishing offenders, or passing laws that guarantee certain penalties for crimes, as a warning to would-be criminals that crime does not pay

Diminished capacity: A defense maintaining that the functioning of an offender's brain at the time he or she committed an offense was impaired

Direct evidence: Tangible items and witness testimony tending to prove a fact in the case

Discovery: The pretrial exchange of evidence between the prosecution and defense

Discretionary Function Exception (DFE): An exception allowing the government to escape liability in tort (injury) lawsuits on the basis of the official's decisions made in the best interest of the government

Disorderly conduct: Conduct that disturbs the public order

Disturbing the peace: Conduct that tends to annoy all citizens and that disrupts the community by its noise levels

Dog sniff: A procedure involving dogs trained to seek out drugs, bombs, or other contraband by smell and alert their handlers to the presence of these items. A dog sniff does not count as a search

Drug and alcohol offenses: Crimes related to the legal or illegal use or abuse of substances

Drug testing: Typically legal warrantless searches of people whose special status means that they have fewer rights to privacy than other people. Among the people with such special status are students, public employees, and people in pretrial release, probation, and parole programs

Duress: A defense claiming that a person was forced to commit a crime because of force or a threat of force. Duress is never a defense to murder

Duty by contract: A relationship created by contract that defines legal obligations between two or more parties, such as landlord/lessee or employer/employee

Duty by relationship: A legal obligation created by family relationships defined by marriage, birth, and adoption

E

Eighth Amendment: Amendment that states, "Excessive bail shall not be required, nor excessive fines imposed, nor cruel and unusual punishments inflicted"

Element: Each part of a crime—the prohibited act(s) and the required mental state—that must be proven to the jury for a finding of guilt

Embezzlement: The taking of property belonging to another person that is acquired lawfully and then is unlawfully converted for the offender's personal use

Entrapment: A defense based on government inducement to commit a crime that the defendant had no prior disposition to commit

Environmental crimes: Crimes that punish polluters for tainting the country's air and water supply and land resources

Environmental Protection Agency (EPA): Executive branch agency of the federal government responsible for enforcing environmental laws

Espionage: The surreptitious gathering and transmitting of U.S. national security information on behalf of a foreign power

Equal protection: A concept embodied by the Fourteenth Amendment that mandates equal treatment for all under the law

Evolving standards of decency: The legal standard by which the U.S. Supreme Court removes certain defendants—for example, juveniles who kill, and mentally retarded offenders—from eligibility for the death penalty

Exclusionary Rule: A judge-made rule that excludes from trial all evidence seized in violation of the Constitution (for example, evidence taken in violation of the Fourth Amendment ban on unreasonable search and seizure, the Fifth Amendment prohibition against compelled self-incrimination, or the Sixth Amendment right to counsel)

Exculpatory evidence: Evidence tending to exonerate (prove the innocence of) the accused

Exhaustion of remedies: The process a convicted defendant must go through in order to exhaust all available appellate remedies before a higher court entertains the appeal

Exigent circumstances: Emergencies that require fast action on the part of law enforcement to prevent the dissipation or disappearance of evidence, often cited as justification for undertaking a warrantless search

Expectation of privacy: A reasonable individual's confidence that certain places and things will not be examined by others. When the expectation of privacy exists, officers typically need a warrant in order to search and seize property

Expert witness: A witness, usually with particular expertise, who can testify about his or her opinion on an ultimate issue at trial on the basis of his or her knowledge, training, and experience. Different rules apply when insanity is raised as a defense

Expungement: The sealing or destroying of a defendant's criminal record

Eyewitness identification: Trial testimony during which an eyewitness identifies the defendant as the perpetrator. Such identifications hold great influence over juries, but research indicates that they may be unreliable

F

Facial review: The court's examination of the law "on its face"—by the plain meaning of the law's language

Facially valid: A law or warrant that appears legal "on its face"

Factual cause: The underlying reason for the ultimate harm; "but for" (if not for) this initial act, the harm would not have occurred

Factual impossibility: A defense based on the physical impossibility of completing the crime; for example, it is impossible to pick an empty pocket

False confession: A statement by an innocent individual that he or she committed the crime in question; sometimes elicited by brutality during interrogation

False imprisonment: Restraining someone's liberty or freedom of movement by force or threat of force

False pretenses: Lies intended to induce the owner of property to surrender title or possession of the property

False statements: Lies that a person knowingly makes to the government with the purpose to mislead or deceive

Federalism: Dual sovereignty of the federal and state governments

Federal Tort Crimes Act (FTCA): The primary law allowing people to bring civil tort (injury) lawsuits against the federal government

Felony murder: A crime in which a death results from the commission, or attempted commission, of a felony (rape, robbery, kidnapping, arson, mayhem, felonious escape, burglary). All co-felons are responsible for the death

Fifth Amendment: Amendment to the Constitution that provides for indictment by grand jury for a capital or "otherwise infamous crime"; prevents double jeopardy, or being tried for the same crime twice by the same sovereign; prevents compelled self-incrimination; contains a due process clause and provides just compensation when the government takes property by eminent domain

Fighting words: Statements that, by their very utterance, incite violence from the audience

Final judgment rule: A rule that allows appeals only from decisions that completely decide an issue, not earlier in the process

First Amendment: Amendment to the Constitution that protects five freedoms: to establish and practice religion, peaceably assemble, practice free speech (which includes expressive conduct, not just verbal speech), maintain a free press, and petition the government for redress of grievances

First-degree murder: Willful, deliberate, and premeditated murder, the highest form of specific-intent murder. The typical punishments are life imprisonment without parole, and the death penalty

Food, Drug, and Cosmetic Act: The primary federal law that regulates food purity, drug advertisements, and cosmetic and medical devices

Forensic assessment: A mental evaluation to determine the defendant's competency and/or his mental status at the time of the offense

Forfeiture: The taking and selling of criminally tainted private property for the benefit of the U.S. Treasury and local law enforcement agencies that participated in the seizure of the assets

Forgery: Alteration of signatures or documents for financial gain; also, the documents or signatures themselves

Fourteenth Amendment: Amendment to the Constitution that was enacted to make newly freed slaves citizens;

contains Equal Protection and Due Process Clauses that protect all citizens from government overreaching

Fourth Amendment: Amendment to the Constitution that has two clauses: a reasonableness clause that prevents the government from conducting unreasonable searches and seizures, and a warrants clause that requires a warrant to search or arrest someone, absent the well-defined judicial exceptions

Fruit of the poisonous tree: Doctrine that punishes police misconduct by excluding from trial all evidence derived from an initial illegal action when police seized said evidence in violation of the Constitution

Full faith and credit: Article 4, section 1, of the Constitution that provides for comity (mutual courtesy) between states. Each state should respect and treat the laws of other states as its own, unless the host state finds the sister state's laws immoral

G

Gambling: The dealing of, operating, and maintaining for pay any game of chance not controlled by the government; frequently, but not always, illegal

General intent: The taking of action, but not necessarily to bring about a specific result

Good faith: Government action with no nefarious motive

Good-faith exception: An exception to the warrant requirement. Officers who execute a defective warrant in good faith will not be penalized by the Exclusionary Rule by the federal government and in some states

Good Samaritan laws: Laws protecting medical workers from personal injury lawsuits when they assist an injured person; some jurisdictions protect nonmedical persons, but only in well-defined emergencies

Grand jury: An investigative body composed of ordinary citizens who determine whether to return an indictment if there exists sufficient evidence that a felony has been committed. Provided for in the Fifth Amendment

Guilty but mentally ill: A finding that the defendant is criminally responsible for his conduct, but that his conduct was caused by a mental disease or defect

Guilty plea: An admission of guilt by the defendant that negates the need for a trial

H

Habeas corpus: A writ (motion) that permits a prisoner to challenge the legality of his or her confinement

Hearsay: An out-of-court statement offered for its truth at trial

Heat of passion: An act of provocation so severe that it would induce a reasonable person to kill; raised successfully at trial, it may reduce murder charges to manslaughter

Holding: The court's decision on a case or its answer to the legal questions presented in the case

Homicide: The killing of one human being by another. Not all homicides are crimes; some are accidents, and some are justified

Hot pursuit: A legal form of warrantless seizure conducted by officers who continue to chase a retreating suspect from the street into a dwelling without first obtaining a warrant

I

Identity theft: Acquisition of personal information about another person to gain something of value

Imperfect self-defense: Legally defective claim of self-defense that involves the use of excessive force to repel an attack

Impossibility: The defense that one cannot be guilty of an attempt crime that was impossible to commit

Incarceration: Incapacitation of offenders by imprisonment

Incest: Sexual relations between nonspousal family members related by blood, marriage, or adoption

Incorporation by reference: The addition of more information composing an affidavit establishing probable cause; when these additional statements are too long to fit on the face of the warrant, they are instead attached to the warrant and "incorporated by reference" into it

Independent source: An exception to the Exclusionary Rule; illegally obtained evidence may be admissible if it is discovered from a source independent of the officers' initial illegal conduct

Indeterminate sentencing: A sentence of a range of years of imprisonment, such as 7 to 15 years, with the expectation that good behavior while in prison will result in an earlier release

Indictment: Formal felony charges brought by a grand jury

Individualized suspicion: The requirement under the Fourth Amendment that law enforcement believe an individual is involved in crime; prevents suspects from being stopped, arrested, or convicted solely by guilt by association

Inevitable discovery: The judgment that illegally obtained evidence would "inevitably" have been discovered anyway by police as they proceeded in their immediate investigation, so that the evidence in question will be admissible at trial

Infancy: Irrebutable presumption that children up to age 7 possess no *mens rea*. There is a rebuttable presumption that children aged 8–14 years possess no *mens rea*, but such presumption can be overcome by proof that the juvenile is able to appreciate the criminality of his or her conduct

Information: A charging document filed by a prosecutor in which the defendant waives the right to be charged by an indictment or the criminal charge does not rise to a felony

Injunction: A request to the court for an order that will take immediate effect preventing a party from taking action

Intelligible principle: A guiding precept that restrains and limits the power Congress delegates to the Executive or Judicial branches to carry out government functions

Intent: The mental desire to bring about a particular result; a conscious disregard of risks created by an offender's actions

Interlocutory appeal: An appeal filed before a final judgment is rendered in a particular case

Interrogation: Questioning by law enforcement officials designed to elicit incriminating information from a suspect

Intervening cause: An independent event that breaks the causal chain between the initial offender's actions and the ultimate harm suffered

Intoxication: An altered state produced by the ingestion of drugs or alcohol; the condition may be voluntary or involuntary and may negate specific *mens rea* for some crimes

Investigatory detention: A brief seizure of an individual conducted for the sole purpose of confirming or dispelling the officer's suspicion that "criminal activity is afoot"

Illegal gratuity: An object of value, usually money, voluntarily given to a person in a position of power in return for a favor

Irresistible impulse: A mental disease or defect that prevents an offender from being able to resist the impulse to commit a criminal act

J

Judge: An individual who presides over the courtroom and who is either appointed or elected, hears and decides pretrial motions, rules on the admissibility of evidence both before and during trial, and instructs the jury on the particular law to apply to the facts of the case

Judicial review: The power that the U.S. Supreme Court granted to itself to invalidate an act of the Executive and Legislative branches

Jury instructions: Rules and definitions of law that control the issues in the case; read to the jury by the judge before deliberations

Jury nullification: The situation in which the jury acquits the defendant even though there is evidence proving guilt

Justifiable homicide: A murder that is legally justified by the circumstances, for example, self-defense

Justification: A legal excuse that eliminates an individual's criminal responsibility for actions that would otherwise be crimes

K

Kidnapping: The unlawful taking away and confinement of another by force or threat of force

Knowing, intelligent, and voluntary waiver: A waiver that a suspect must give after hearing *Miranda* warnings. The suspect must appreciate the rights he or she is giving up (knowing), must understand the consequences of waiving those rights (intelligent), and must waive those rights of his or her own free will without external duress or coercion (voluntary)

Knowingly: *Mens rea* state in which the actor takes certain actions not necessarily to bring about the desired result, but with the substantial certainty that such a result will occur

L

Larceny: The taking away of the personal property of another without that person's consent and with the intent to permanently deprive the owner

Larceny by trick: Theft that results when a thief's lies convince the owner of some property to alter legal statements to allow the property or its title to pass into the thief's hands, under the mistaken belief that this would benefit the owner

Lay witness: An ordinary person who can testify to matters such as intoxication, speed, insanity, and distance within the normal range of adult experience

Least restrictive means: The way in which the government may achieve its legitimate objectives (by the least intrusive means possible) when weighed against an individual's privacy interests

Legal impossibility: Actions that do not constitute a crime

Legislative history: Transcripts of legislative debate in enacting statutes that are used by courts to gain a clear meaning of the words used in the statute

Lesser included offense: A less serious offense that is included in the charge of a more serious offense; for example, assault is subsumed under murder

Line-up: A technique in which a victim stands behind a two-way mirror and looks at five or six similar-looking people lined up by the police in an effort to identify the offender

M

Mail fraud: A scheme to defraud that uses the U.S. Postal Service or a private mail carrier in its execution

Mala in se: Crimes regarded as inherently evil, such as murder, rape, and kidnapping

Mala prohibita: Crimes that are punishable because the laws define such conduct as criminal; examples are speeding violations, food inspection violations, and licensing violations

Malice aforethought: The historical term for premeditation

Mandatory appeal: An obligatory appeal that an appellate court must hear and decide

Manslaughter: An unintentional killing, or an intentional killing done in the heat of the passion and without premeditation

Manual for Courts-Martial: A guide dictating the operation of courts-martial (military trials)

Mayhem: Permanent disfigurement of a victim

Megan's Laws: Laws that require sex offenders to register and possibly notify the communities in which they live of their criminal history

Mental defect: A mental disorder that impairs the way the brain processes information

Mental disease: A mental disorder recognized by the American Psychological Association and listed in the DSM-IV

Merger: The combination of lesser offenses into a more serious crime upon conviction for the more serious offense; for example, battery merges into attempted murder

Mistake of fact: The erroneous belief in certain facts that leads the person to act (or fail to act) accordingly

Mistake of law: An erroneous legal conclusion arrived at by a party who knows all the facts

Mitigating factors: Circumstances tending to explain, but not excuse, the offender's crime

M'Naghten test: The standard by which an accused person is deemed insane and not criminally responsible for a crime if, at the time of committing the act, the person suffered from a defect of reason from mental disease that rendered him or her unable to understand the nature and quality of the act or unable to realize that what he or she was doing was wrong

Model Penal Code (MPC): The model that defines uniform concepts of criminal liability, defenses, and sentencing; the MPC is not law, but is a model upon which many states have patterned their own criminal and penal codes

Money laundering: Interjecting illegally obtained money into a legal stream of commerce to disguise the money's illegal origins

Motion: An oral or written application for a court order

Motion for a new trial: Motion alleging errors committed during a trial and typically filed seven days after the verdict with the original trial judge. Defendants have up to three years to file a motion for a new trial on the basis of newly discovered evidence

Motion to suppress: A request for a judge to allow or exclude specific evidence at trial

N

Necessary and Proper Clause: Article I, section 18, of the Constitution, which gives Congress broad authority to make all laws that are "necessary and proper" for carrying out its government functions

Necessity: A defense created by having to choose the lesser of two evils

Negligently: Describes actions that deviate from the standard of care that a reasonable person would exercise

Neutral and detached: The attitude of the judge toward a case, expressing no vested interest in the outcome of the case and fairness to both sides in deciding the issue

Ninth Amendment: Amendment that states, "The enumeration in the Constitution, of certain rights, shall not be construed to deny or disparage others retained by the people"

Nondelegation doctrine: The statement in the Constitution that forbids the three branches of government to share power. The Supreme Court has held, however, that Congress may share what power it has with the Executive and Judicial branches, subject to an intelligible principle

Not guilty by reason of insanity: A plea entered by a defendant or a verdict decided by a jury that eliminates criminal responsibility because at the time the crime was committed, the defendant was suffering from a mental disease or defect that prevented him from forming the requisite *mens rea*

O

Objection: Preserving the record for appeal by formally protesting the trial court's decisions

Obscenity: Patently offensive sexual material that is defined by the *Miller* test as having no artistic, political, scientific, or literary value (for example, child pornography)

Obstruction of justice: Impeding or obstructing the judicial or legislative process

Occupational Safety and Health Act (OSHA): A federal law designed to protect workers from workplace safety hazards

Open fields: Areas that are clearly visible from a flyover in a plane. A warrantless search is permissible in open fields because the Fourth Amendment recognizes privacy interests only in "papers, effects, and houses"

Opening statement: The prosecutor and defense counsels' opening remarks to the jury informing them what evidence they intend to introduce at trial

Overblock: Filtering on public computers that may prevent library users from accessing legally permissible material

Overbreadth: A doctrine which invalidates laws that prohibit both protected and unprotected speech

P

Panhandling: The practice of asking strangers for money in public places such as the street

Parole: A prisoner's early release from jail, prison, or other confinement under supervision of a court officer after serving a sentence of confinement; may be revoked for failure to abide by court's conditions

Particularity requirement: The requirement on the face of a warrant that, according to the Fourth Amendment, the place to be searched and things to be seized be described specifically

Patent and Copyright Clause: Article I, section 8, clause 8, of the Constitution, which secures the exclusive right of authors and inventors to their respective works for a limited time

Perjury: A knowing and willful lie by a witness made under oath in a judicial or administrative or legislative proceeding

Personal property: Personal possessions that can be moved from one place to another

Phishing: A phony, but real-looking, Internet website that steals patrons' passwords, personal information, or money when they pay by credit card online

Photospread: A series of photographs of similar-looking people shown to a victim, who attempts to identify the perpetrator among them

Plain view: A warrantless seizure of contraband out in the open by officers lawfully on the premises

Plea bargaining: A process of negotiation between the prosecutor and the defendant to avoid trial; the defendant pleads guilty to certain charges in exchange for concessions from the government

Plea colloquy: A series of questions asked of the defendant by the judge in open court to ensure that the defendant is aware of the rights he or she is waiving by pleading guilty

Precedent: Prior cases that are close in facts or legal principles to the case now under consideration and that may form the basis for a ruling

Preliminary hearing: A hearing to determine whether there is sufficient evidence to hold the defendant for trial

Preponderance of the evidence: A legal standard that makes the existence of the disputed fact in question more likely than not; this standard does not go as far as "beyond a reasonable doubt"

Presentence investigation: An investigation by the court of the defendant's life and crime conducted to assist the judge in imposing an appropriate sentence

Presentence report: The written result of the presentence investigation

Presumption of innocence: The assumption that, under the law, a defendant is innocent until the prosecutor proves each and every element of the crime beyond a reasonable doubt

Pretrial identification: Before trial, the identification of the suspect by a witness

Pretrial motions: A series of motions brought to resolve issues before trial begins, for example, venue and admission or exclusion of specific evidence and testimony

Principal: The criminal actor who committed the crime

Principle of legality: Notice of what conduct is criminal

Prior restraint: Preventing the exercise of a free speech right before the speech or expression actually occurs, for example, not issuing a parade permit to the Ku Klux Klan

Probable cause: A determination made by examining all the facts and circumstances tending to establish that a crime has been, is being, or will be committed

Probation: A sentence releasing the defendant into the community under court supervision without the defendant having served any time in prison, often granted to young individuals for a minor crime or a first offense

Procedural due process: Notice from the government to citizens that there is a complaint against them and that the citizens will have the opportunity to in court to defend against the complaint

Proportionality review: Process by which a court compares sentences imposed on similarly situated defendants to ensure that they have been sentenced equally

Prosecutorial discretion: The sole decision-making authority of the prosecutor to decide the charges against a defendant

Prostitution: The performance of sex acts in exchange for money or other thing of value

Protective sweep: A cursory examination by police to eliminate a possible threat to officer safety, following specific information that armed people are on the premises

Proximate cause: The actor's initial act from which the harm suffered was a reasonably foreseeable consequence

Prurient interest: A lustful, morbid, or shameful interest in nudity, sex and/or excretion

Psychosis: A break from reality suffered by some mentally ill offenders

Public corruption: Unlawful acts that degrade the public trust in the body politic

Purposely: Having a specific intent or a desire to cause a specific result

R

Racketeer Influenced and Corrupt Organizations Act (RICO): Comprehensive law enacted in the 1970s to combat organized crime. Elements include a pattern of racketeering activity and investment in a business that affects interstate commerce

Rape: Sex against the victim's will and without his or her consent

Rape shield laws: Laws that prevent the defendant from introducing evidence about the victim's sexual reputation or previous sexual activity with people other than the defendant to discredit her report of rape, except where such exclusion would violate the Confrontation Clause

Rational relationship: The means used by the government to achieve the ends of legitimate government interest to protect public health, safety, and welfare

Real property: Land and its permanent structures, such as houses, barns, and other buildings

Reasonable suspicion: Legal standard based on specific and articulable facts (more than a hunch) that criminal activity is afoot, which means that a crime has been, is being, or will be committed

Recidivist: A habitual, incorrigible criminal

Recklessly: Manner whereby an actor consciously disregards a substantial and unjustifiable risk of harm that his or her behavior creates; the actor knows of the risk of harm and ignores it

Rehabilitation: Training an offender to successfully reintegrate into society

Reliable hearsay: Information generated by a law enforcement agency as part of its investigative duties, that is considered reliable and that may help establish probable cause. Other forms of hearsay are generally untrustworthy because they are secondhand information.

Resource Conservation and Recovery Act (RCRA): Legislation that sets standards for the management of hazardous waste sites

Restitution: An offender's repayment to society and the victim for the harm caused by his or her crime

Reverse and remand: Actions taken by an appellate court if it finds error in a lower court's proceedings; the appellate court will reverse (overturn) the lower court's decision and remand the case (send the case back to the lower court) for further proceedings

Riot: Public disturbance involving threats of violence or actual acts of violence

S

Scienter: Knowledge that an offender must possess in order for him or her to be held criminally responsible

Scrupulously honor: Do without fail. During interrogation, if a suspect expresses a desire to stop talking, officers must stop questioning immediately

Search: A government invasion of an area in which a person has a reasonable expectation of privacy

Search incident to an arrest: A warrantless search of an arrestee's person and the area within his or her immediate control

Second Amendment: Amendment to the Constitution that states, "A well regulated Militia, being necessary to the security of a free state, the right of the people to keep and bear Arms, shall not be infringed"

Second-degree murder: A death that results from an offender's intent to cause serious bodily harm, or a murder that lacks one element of first-degree murder (such as *premeditation*)

Sedition: Communication or agreement to commit treason or lesser similar offenses against the United States

Seizure: The government's acquisition of certain personal property, either contraband or potential evidence of a crime, or the deprivation of a person's liberty due to the person's arrest

Selective prosecution: The government's use of an impermissible motive to select certain defendants for prosecution

Self-defense: A complete defense based on the use of force to repel a physical attack

Sentencing hearing: After conviction, a hearing with evidence to help the judge determine an appropriate sentence

Seventh Amendment: Amendment to the Constitution that provides for jury trials in civil cases

Sex offenses: Crimes of violence that use sex as a weapon

Show-up: Type of pretrial identification in which the suspect, alone, is brought before the victim for identification; the most suggestive type of pretrial identification

Sixth Amendment: Amendment to the Constitution that provides the defendant with the following rights: to be notified of the charges against him, to confront witnesses against him at trial, to subpoena people for trial, to have a speedy and public trial tried in the venue where the crime occurred, and to have the assistance of counsel

Sodomy: Oral/genital contact or anal intercourse

Solicitation: The procurement of others to commit a crime. The crime of solicitation is complete when one person entices another to commit a crime, regardless of whether the crime is completed

Special circumstances: Aggravating circumstances that a prosecutor may file to convert a first-degree murder case into a death-penalty case

Specific and articulable facts: Facts that a police officer can cite that would support the legality of a stop and frisk

Specific intent: The intent to bring about a specific result

Stalking: Repeated acts of communication or physical harassment by a compulsive offender toward a victim— for example, physical surveillance, phone calls, e-mails, or other obsessive behavior

Standard of review: The legal standard by which courts review and decide appeals

Standing: The legal right to challenge the government's search or seizure

Stare decisis: Let the decision stand; a judgment that precedent should be followed

Statement: Any oral or written declaration made by a suspect or defendant

Statute of limitations: A defense alleging that the time in which to prosecute certain crimes has elapsed. There is no statute of limitations for the crime of murder

Statutory law: Laws written and passed by federal and state legislatures and then codified and compiled in code books for easy reference

Strict liability: No *mens rea* required to be punished; guilt attaches when the act is committed

Strict scrutiny: The level of review that courts use to examine government regulation of fundamental freedoms

Substantive due process: The protection that individuals enjoy from governmental interference with fundamental liberties such as contraception, procreation, and marriage

Suspended sentence: Imposition of a sentence in which the amount of time to be served is nullified. A suspended sentence can be reimposed if the offender violates the terms of probation or parole

T

Tenth Amendment: Amendment to the Constitution which states that all powers that the Constitution does not grant the federal government, if not prohibited by the Constitution, are left to the states

Terrorism: Using threats, murder, and mayhem to achieve illegitimate political goals

Terroristic threats: Threatening violence to cause public pandemonium, or threatening specific harm to a person

***Terry* stop:** The brief detainment and questioning of a person by police to either confirm or dispel their reasonable suspicion that criminal activity is afoot. If officers have a reasonable belief that the person is armed, officers can pat down the outer clothing for weapons only

The §1983 claim: Title 42 U.S.C. §1983, the legal gateway to sue the government for any official acting "under the color of law" to deprive a citizen of a federally protected right

Third Amendment: Amendment to the Constitution that prohibits the government in a time of peace from quartering soldiers in private homes without the owner's consent or during wartime without following the law

Third degree: Torturous interrogation tactics which induce the defendant to confess to the crime

"Three-strikes" legislation: Punitive laws imposing mandatory life sentence in prison upon conviction of a third felony

Totality of the circumstances: When judged as a whole, all the facts and circumstances used to determine the legality of police action

Trademark: A distinctive mark of authenticity that distinguishes one vendor's goods from another's

Transferred intent: The harm intended for one person that instead affects a different person. For example, when Sam means to hit Amy but hits Bill by mistake, Sam's specific intent to harm Amy transfers to Bill; Sam will be held responsible for Bill's injury

Treason: The offense of attempting by overt acts to overthrow the government, or of betraying the country for the benefit of a foreign power

U

Underblock: Filtering on public computers that misses material that the government wishes to restrict

Uniform Code of Military Justice: Federal law that provides the military branches—the Departments of the Army, Air Force, and Navy (Marines)—with a list of behaviors deemed criminal, together with the punishment for each such behavior

Unlawful assembly: The gathering of no fewer than five people for the purpose of engaging in disorderly conduct

Unprotected speech: Speech and expression not protected by the First Amendment, such as fighting words, statements posing a clear and present danger, and obscenities

USA PATRIOT Act: Post–9-11 legislation that consolidates law enforcement efforts to combat terrorism against America

Uttering: Passing fraudulent checks

V

Vagrancy: The crime of being a person who, with no visible means of support, travels from place to place and depends upon the kindness of strangers for food, clothing, and shelter

Vagueness: The quality of a statute that renders it difficult to interpret. A statute is void-for-vagueness and unconstitutional when people of ordinary intelligence must guess at the words' meaning as expressed in the law

Venue: The place where a trial is held, usually in the same district that the crime was committed

Verdict form: The form upon which the jury enters their verdict

Victim-impact statement: At the defendant's sentencing hearing, the statements by victims during which they inform the court of the irrevocable harm caused by the defendant's crime

W

Warrant: A legal order to seize specific property connected to crimes or to arrest a specific person suspected of criminal activity

Wharton's Rule: The guideline that one person cannot be held criminally responsible for conspiracy to commit a crime that, under the law, takes two to commit, such as gambling or prostitution

White-collar crimes: Financial crimes committed by people who hold financial positions of trust to corporations and shareholders

Wire fraud: A scheme to defraud and the use of wires (telephones, bank transfers, computers) to execute the scheme

Writ of certiorari: An order from the U.S. Supreme Court ordering a lower court to forward the case record

Writ of mandamus: An application to the court to order a public official to perform a duty imposed by law

Y

Year-and-a day-rule: Doctrine that if victim died within one year and one day of harm caused by offender, offender would be liable for the death; advances in medical science have rendered most such laws obsolete

Z

Zealous advocate: An attorney who speaks with enthusiasm on behalf of a client. A defense attorney must be a zealous advocate for his or her clients at all times

Table of Cases

Index